LEE KUAN YEW

Vol. 1

LEE KUAN YEW

Vol. 1

ALEX
JOSEY

TIMES BOOKS
International

© Alex Josey 1968
First published 1968 by
Donald Moore Press Ltd, Singapore
Reprinted 1969
Revised edition published 1971 by
Donald Moore for
Asia Pacific Press (Pte) Ltd, Singapore

1980 TIMES BOOKS INTERNATIONAL
TIMES CENTRE
No. 1, New Industrial Road
Singapore 1953

Printed by Chong Moh Offset Printing Pte. Ltd.

038008

FOR
ROSA LILIAN JANE JOSEY

"Political problems do not primarily concern truth or falsehood: they relate to good or evil. What in the result is likely to produce evil is politically false; that which is productive of good, politically true."

Burke

"We, the developing nations, are determined to bring happiness and prosperity to our people and to discard the age-old shackles that have tied us not only politically but economically—the shackles of colonialism and other shackles of our own making."

Nehru
at the Bandung Conference, 1955

"Lee Kuan Yew is one of the most outstanding dynamic minds in world statesmanship today..."

Fenner Brockway, M.P.
in the House of Commons, 1963

"Mr Lee Kuan Yew is too clever by half..."

Tunku Abdul Rahman
Prime Minister of Malaysia, 1966

Introduction

In the Introduction to the first edition I said that this was a book about Lee Kuan Yew, Prime Minister of Singapore, told in part by Lee himself. Most of the book consists of direct quotations from speeches he made since 1950.

The second edition contains most of the earlier speeches, as well as the major speeches Lee gave in 1968, 1969 and 1970, and his speeches at the 1971 Commonwealth Prime Ministers' Conference held in Singapore. There are also many more pages of illustrations in this edition.

More than a political biography, this is a book of value to politicians in other developing states. Most of their problems are the kind of problems that Lee Kuan Yew has had to contend with. His thinking on these matters has made Singapore unique as a rapidly progressing developing nation.

Alex Josey
Singapore, 1971

Contents

Introduction vii

PART ONE

1 Early Days 3

2 The People's Action Party 13

3 Lee's Basic Beliefs 20

4 Men in Gaol 34

5 Ambition 39

6 Vietnam and The United States 45

7 Asian Socialism 48

8 The English Language 54

9 Leadership and Religion 57

10 Can Democracy Survive? 65

11 The Malays and the Chinese 72

12 Was Multiracial Malaysia Ever Possible? 83

PART TWO

13 The Year of Power 1959 93

14   The Year of Power 1960   116

15   The Year of Power 1961   129

16   The Year of Power 1962   151

17   The Year of Power 1963   166

18   The Year of Power 1964   194

19   The Year of Power 1965   230

20   The Year of Power 1966   301

21   The Year of Power 1967   356

22   The Year of Power 1968   416

23   The Year of Power 1969   480

24   The Year of Power 1970   548
     and The First Commonwealth Heads of
     Government Conference in Asia, 1971

PART THREE

25   How Much of a Chinese is Lee Kuan Yew?   599

Index   623

Part One

Early Days

I

LEE Kuan Yew was born at 92, Kampong Java Road, Singapore, on 16 September, 1923. His family have lived in Singapore for more than a hundred years and come from the Hakkas, a northern Chinese tribe of tough wanderers.

Lee Kuan Yew is an intellectual. He looks like an intellectual. He speaks like a scholar. His command of English is unusual. He is a quick thinker. At Cambridge he took a double first in Law, and in the final examination was placed first in the honours list, winning a star for special distinction. A British diplomat once described Lee as "the most brilliant man around, albeit just a bit of a thug", a judgment considered fair enough in a political arena where an ability to meet opponents on their terms is an essential part of the successful politician's make-up. "We are playing for keeps," Lee Kuan Yew warned the militant communists. He defeated them in democratically held elections, and in a referendum. Today, most of Lee's political enemies have either retired from politics or are in goal. In the 1968 elections fifty-one of the fifty-eight PAP candidates for an enlarged Parliament were returned unopposed. Early in 1970 five members of parliament retired. In the subsequent by-elections, in April, the newly formed United National Front contested two seats, the PAP all five. Three of the PAP candidates were returned unopposed: the other two were returned with substantial majorities.

3

Five feet ten and a half inches tall, Lee Kuan Yew weighs 160 pounds. He watches his weight carefully. He rarely eats rice or bread, seldom drinks beer. He walks with a slight swagger, his shoulders thrown forward a little as each foot comes down. This may seem to indicate Lee Kuan Yew's confidence or natural aggressiveness. More likely it is due to the fact that he has rather tender feet.

In his personal habits, Lee is inclined to be finicky. His hands are always scrupulously clean, his nails neatly cut and filed. He is incapable of doing anything slovenly or carelessly, whether it is putting on a highly polished shoe, or reaching an important decision. There is no room on his large desk for anything other than the letter to be signed or the file to be read.

Like President Kennedy, whom Lee admired, Lee Kuan Yew seldom reads for distraction. Like Kennedy, he does not want to waste a single second. Every moment of his life he seeks to invest, not spend. Aloof in manner, he is slow to make friends. He is suspicious of the hail-fellow-well-met approach. Lee's sense of humour, developing with age, is not always kind. He suffers fools not at all, but he rarely prejudges anyone. Upon first encounter all are met on terms of equality. An exchange of a few sentences, however, is often sufficient for Lee's decion: either the person reacts intelligently or he does not, and this judgment will apply to prime minister and dock-worker, don or road-sweeper.

Lee is a combined Left-wing demagogue and emphatic realist. Some things are possible. Others are not. He believes deeply in democratic methods, and his philosophy is built around the sanctity of law and the free will of the people: but there are times when he is reluctantly forced to take strict, even non-democratic measures against a minority of thugs, secret-society gangsters and political opportunists—those who have placed themselves outside the rules—in order that he shall preserve the greatest good for the community as a whole. Lee never forgets that Singapore is in Asia, where Western concepts of democracy have yet to be understood by the masses and accepted as a way of life.

Lee is attractive to women. His face is rugged, and slightly pocked. His thick black hair, which has no parting, is streaked with grey. When he smiles and laughs his personality is changed completely. These are the moments of relaxation. His normal expression is a mixture of intense concentration and aggressiveness. Lee is not an ivory-tower intellectual and is inclined to be critical of them ("It is amazing the number of highly intelligent persons in the world who make no contribution at all to the well-being of their fellow countrymen"), for he is by nature and by reasoning an attacker of problems, not a student of the abstract.

Lee Kuan Yew is the eldest son of Lee Chin Koon, a retired employee of the Shell Company. Lee's father now works in a shop in the High Street, where he sells watches and jewellery. His mother, Chua Jim Neo, is famed in the state as an expert teacher of cooking in the Chinese and Malay styles. She was 16 when he was born. His father was 20.

4

Lee Kuan Yew married Kwa Geok Choo on 30 September, 1950. In his year, Lee Kuan Yew was the most brilliant of all scholars in Singapore. He won a prize which entitled him to a scholarship at Raffles College. The war had begun in Europe, and his plans to go to an English university had to be postponed, and so he accepted his prize and put in two years at Raffles College. "And there two things happened which have since stood me in very good stead. I met my future wife, and I got a grounding in economics."

Kwa Geok Choo, Lee Kuan Yew's wife, was the most brilliant girl scholar of her year. Educated at the Methodist Girls' School (she is not a Christian) she was first in the Senior Cambridge Examination for the whole of Malaya. At Raffles College, Miss Kwa graduated in 1947 and was awarded a Queen's Scholarship. Then she went to Cambridge where she became the first Malayan woman to be awarded first class honours, which she obtained after only two years of study.

The Lees have three children, two boys and a daughter. Lee Hsien Loong was born in 1952; Lee Wei Ling, the daughter, in 1955, and Lee Hsien Yang in 1957. Lee Kuan Yew is a very happily married man. With his wife, who is head of the legal firm of Lee and Lee, he is an active participant in the joys and troubles of his children's growing up. Hsien Loong showed early signs of following in the footsteps of his gifted parents: by the time he was fourteen he could read, write and speak Russian, English, Malay and Mandarin with ease and fluency, and his interests range from playing the clarinet to nuclear physics.

Lee Kuan Yew is a socialist. To Lee socialism means social justice, better living, freedom and peace. Lee argues that, holding these principles, socialists must work out the best way of bringing all this about in their own countries. He is essentially an idealist, yet a practical and ruthless idealist. "You start off with idealism, you should end up in maturity with a great deal of sophistication giving a gloss to that idealism," he told a youth gathering in Singapore in 1967. Lee is a hard worker and a disciplinarian. Most days, with a teacher, he polishes his Mandarin and his Malay, for it is of vital importance in a multi-racial nation that the leader should be able to communicate directly with as many of the people as possible, and more people in Singapore speak Malay and Chinese than English.

Lee Kuan Yew is also a firm believer in the importance of keeping fit. Every morning he does exercises, which include press-ups, skipping, and arm exercises with small weights. He has a very light breakfast, sips China tea throughout the day, and makes dinner, also never heavy, his main meal. He enjoys a glass or two of wine in the evening.

Lee Kuan Yew is probably the best golfing Prime Minister in the world. He took up the game while studying in Cambridge, where he discovered that golf could provide him with regular exercise all the year round whilst clad in sweater and gloves—essential clothing most of the

5

time in England for a man born in the tropics. He is Prime Minister of the independent sovereign Republic of Singapore, the newest and smallest state in Asia. He first became Prime Minister in 1959, when he was 35.

II

Strategically placed geographically, just north of the Equator, where the waters of the South China Sea meet the Indian Ocean, at the southern tip of the Malayan Peninsula, a stone's throw from Indonesia, about half way between China and Australia and New Zealand, a few jet hours from Japan and India, the Republic of Singapore is a flat tropical island of some 224 square miles, a third the size of Greater London. Here live in harmony a multiracial population of two million industrious people, most of them of Chinese descent. They enjoy one of the highest standards of living in the East. The Chinese have been in Singapore a long time. They were there hundreds of years before Raffles came. Singapore in the fourteenth century was known as Tumasik, and in a report written in 1349, Wang Ta-yuan, a Chinese merchant adventurer, gave the impression that a fairly large settlement of Chinese was already living on the island.

With an internationally famous free port, the fourth busiest in the world, and an equally renowned airport capable of accommodating and servicing the largest and fastest aircraft, Singapore, at least until the end of 1971, will continue to provide accommodation for Britain's military, air and naval presence East of Suez. In 1968, Mr Harold Wilson's Government unexpectedly decided to withdraw all British forces from Singapore by 1971, and, at the end of 1968, the naval base, which cost the British millions of pounds to build, was handed over as a gift to the Singapore Government for conversion into a commercial undertaking, "a practical illustration", as Singapore's Foreign Minister remarked at the handing-over ceremony, "of successful decolonization". Politically, Singapore is neutral, but the People's Action Party Government, led by Lee Kuan Yew, insists upon the right inherent in all independent sovereign states that Singapore shall make its own defence arrangements. Early in 1971 the British prepared to withdraw their bases. Talks were then proceeding for a five power defence arrangement between Singapore, Malaysia, Britian, New Zealand and Australia. Singapore has a well-trained police force and efficient armed forces, including patrol ships and fighter aircraft. National Service was introduced in 1967.

Just over a hundred and fifty years ago, when Sir Stamford Raffles of the East India Company was rowed up the muddy creek,

6

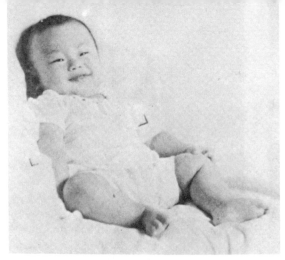

Lee when an infant

One-year-old Lee Kuan Yew in the arms of his father, then twenty

Undergraduates at Cambridge, 1946

Young Lee in Chinese dress on a festive occasion

Cutting the wedding cake in 1950

At Cambridge in June 1949. Mr and Mrs Lee Kuan Yew with Lee's Censor and friend, W. S. Thatcher

At Cambridge in 1949. Lee Kuan Yew with Trevor C. Thomas (now Vice-Chancellor of the University of Liverpool) and Kwa Geok Choo (Mrs Lee Kuan Yew)

The Lee family in 1967 in Cambodia, after the Prime Minister had received an honorary doctorate of law from the Royal University. (Back—Mrs Lee, Lee Hsien Loong. Front—Lee Hsien Yang and Miss Lee Wei Ling)

Proud father at Lee Wei Ling's "graduation"

Mrs Lee Kuan Yew and the boys Hsien Loong (left) and Hsien Yang

in search of a suitable place in which to establish a British trading post, he found Singapore an island of marshy swamps, scrub and thick forest. On the coastal fringe a few Malay fishermen lived in primitive huts, and inland were settled a handful of Chinese gambier growers.

Raffles was a young man of considerable knowledge, ability, energy and vision. He bought the island for a few silver dollars. In less than two centuries, man's sweat and talent changed this almost deserted island into a modern, bustling city state, with tall blocks of workers' flats, a national theatre, air-conditioned factories, up-to-date schools and universities, radio and television (including schools television), a multi-million dollar industrial complex (the largest in Southeast Asia), a network of fast highways, a parliament, and, among other features of modernity, a computered banking and commercial service without equal in the East.

Singapore has no natural resources apart from the collective ability of its population. The humidity is high and the temperature ranges between eighty-seven and seventy-five degrees fahrenheit. Copious rain falls throughout the year, the average rainfall being ninety-six inches, much of it flowing down the deep monsoon drains to the sea. Most of Singapore's drinking water has to be bought from Johore, in Malaysia, to which Singapore is connected by a mile-long causeway. Plans were made in 1966 to enable Singapore to provide the bulk of its own drinking water by the 1970s. Singapore undoubtedly owes much of its wealth and prosperity to its unrivalled focal position in Southeast Asia on the international sea route from the Indian Ocean to the China Sea, and on the air route west and north across Asia, and east across the Pacific and southeast to Australia. Its economically strategic position at the centre of one of the world's richest areas of natural wealth, and its deep-water harbour, have made it the natural outlet for the products of Malaysia and neighbouring countries. With its highly developed wholesale and retail commerce, banking system, insurance, shipping and storage facilities, and generations of inherited commercial skill and initiative, Singapore ranks among the greatest of the world's commercial centres and is virtually the commercial and financial heart of the whole of Southeast Asia.

By 1970, Singapore had additionally become a fast-developing manufacturing state with its own steel mills and shipbuilding yards. An appreciable number of American and East and West European industrialists had also decided to make Singapore their regional distributive centre.

Singapore remained under British control, to some extent, if not fully (except from 1942 to 1945 when the Japanese occupied the island), from 1819 until it achieved independence. This was brought about through merger with Malaya (the hinterland which European, Chinese and Indian pioneers and capital helped enormously to develop) and

7

with Sabah and Sarawak. Singapore, Malaya, Sabah and Sarawak became Malaysia on 16 September, 1963. The new state was acclaimed internationally as a unique experiment in multiracialism.

On 9 August, 1965, Singapore was separated from Malaysia, and became an independent and sovereign nation. A month later Singapore became the 116th member of the United Nations, and, in October, 1965, the twenty-second member of the British Commonwealth of Nations. The decision to separate Singapore from Malaysia was made by the Malaysian Government and was reluctantly accepted by the Singapore Government in order to forestall any likelihood of communal rioting which Tunku Abdul Rahman, the Malaysian Prime Minister, thought possible if they refused. The Separation Agreement provided for full co-operation between the two territories, especially in external defence and trade.

The constitutional head of the Republic, elected by Parliament in 1971, is Dr B.H. Sheares. Singapore has a parliamentary system of government based on full adult suffrage. Every citizen of twenty-one years of age and over has the right, indeed, by law, the obliga-tion, to vote once he is registered as a voter. Malay is the national language (though Singapore is multiracial in language, education and outlook), and there are special provisions to assist the Malays: for example, the Malays are entitled to free education up to university and professional level. Members of Parliament may deliver their speeches in Malay, Mandarin, Tamil or English. There is simultaneous translation. English is the basic language of government, law and trade.

The People's Action Party came into being in 1954 as a nationalist movement. Lee Kuan Yew, the Secretary-General, and two other mem-bers of the PAP, stood for election to the new Assembly in 1955, and won their seats easily. This Assembly of thirty-two had an elected majority of twenty-five. It was within the bounds of possibility that, had they wished, the PAP could have won most of them, but this would have meant that the party would have had to make the Constitution work, whereas they opposed the Constitution and Lee became an assemblyman in order to use the Assembly as a platform from which he could attack the Constitution and continue the struggle for com-plete self-government.

In 1959, largely through the efforts of Lee and his colleagues, Britain agreed to constitutional changes which did bring in a fully elected legislature and self-government. In these circumstances, the PAP was prepared to make a bid for power and the party won forty-three of the fifty-one seats. Lee Kuan Yew formed the government and became Singapore's first Prime Minister.

It was in 1961 that Tunku Abdul Rahman, Prime Minister of the Federation of Malaya, proposed the creation of Malaysia. Singapore at once declared its full support, and at rallies and in private discussions Lee Kuan Yew and other PAP leaders helped to persuade doubters in Sabah and Sarawak. Immediately, the underground Communist Party rallied its forces in political parties, in trade unions and in the high schools and other organizations, to resist Malaysia. They mounted a powerful campaign, based upon communism and Chinese chauvinism, calling for merger between Singapore and Malaysia, a proposition which they knew the Tunku would never accept because an amalgamation of the two territories without Sabah and Sarawak would mean that the Chinese would outnumber the Malays. Lee fought for Malaysia because it would mean multiracialism; because this was the only way then that Singapore could free itself entirely from the remnant shackles of colonialism; and because Malaysia offered all the territories a chance to develop a common market of some ten million people. It was a bitter fight and the outcome was uncertain almost until the end.

Lee Kuan Yew was determined that there should never be any doubt in anybody's mind as to exactly where the people of Singapore stood on this vital issue, and, ignoring a great deal of friendly advice which urged him not to risk his political career, Lee held a nationwide referendum. His faith was justified: seventy-one per cent of the electorate voted in favour of merger and Malaysia. In many ways it was a personal triumph for Lee. No man struggled harder for the creation of Malaysia.

Thus, on 16 September, 1963, Singapore became part of the Kingdom of Malaysia. Lee Kuan Yew remained Prime Minister of the State of Singapore, which continued to handle its own labour and education, but not the police or finance or communications. General elections were held five days later, and the people showed their appreciation of Lee's work by returning the PAP to office (as the local government), with thirty-seven of the fifty-one seats. Less than two years later Singapore separated from Malaysia.

Lee retained the confidence of the people, and, during the next four years and more, Singapore continued to gather strength. In 1968, the PAP were again re-elected, and Lee could speak with optimism of Singapore's future as a viable state in spite of Britain's announcement to withdraw its military presence, and all that this meant to the nation's economy.

But politically, Lee's very success created considerable difficulties for parliamentary democracy. The argument is simple. Lee has produced "good government by good men", a worthy objective in the eyes of most citizens of Chinese origin. Why, therefore, they ask, encourage an opposition which might upset that? Is not good government what the people and the nation yearn for?

This attitude, this satisfaction with things as they are, means that Lee Kuan Yew, much against his own desires, will have to face the possibility of being Prime Minister for perhaps another decade. Lee would

9

be the first to agree that no man anywhere is indispensable. He would also resent any implication that the Republic of Singapore is in any way his own creation, either as an accidental or a deliberate piece of handiwork. Only David Marshall, the first Chief Minister, ever tried deliberately to conceive an independent Singapore outside Malaya, or Malaysia. Singapore in its present form just happened. It fell out of Malaysia, which Lee had helped to create and in which he firmly believed, because Lee and his Cabinet insisted upon a multiracial Malaysia.

"We must live in the world as we find it," the pragmatic Lee Kuan Yew constantly reminds everyone, and he, and all those capable of thought and in possession of all the facts, know that a great deal of work still remains to be done before the survival of the Republic of Singapore, to which Lee has fully committed himself, can be assured. In these circumstances Lee will continue to serve "as a leader among other leaders", which is how Lee Kuan Yew looks upon himself, for as long as is needed to complete the task. He never sought the Prime Minister's job in the first place. He never schemed for power; there is no Lee Kuan Yew group in the party which keeps him in office. Since his return to Singapore in 1950, after his university days, he has been the natural nationalist leader. Not even the communists sought to displace him as leader when they tried twice to grab control of the People's Action Party. They wanted to use him, not replace him.

Even so, Lee Kuan Yew has no intention of spending the rest of his life in office. An admirer of Sir Robert Menzies' decision to quit as Prime Minister of Australia while at his zenith, he is determined to lay down his burden in ample time to prevent himself from becoming old and crusty with power, and to enjoy another more leisurely sort of life. He would like to write books, about Southeast Asia and about politics. It is unlikely that he will ever return to law.

Like other busy men, he finds the trappings of office convenient. There are cars, secretaries, officials, servants. They are essential if the work is to be done and appointments kept. They are part of the job. Lee has no interest in the trappings for their own sake. When he can, he dispenses with them. Like Harold Wilson, he cleans his own shoes when he has time, and happily does the odd jobs round the house which most ordinary citizens, husbands and fathers have to do.

Yet he is watchful of the dignity of his high office, of which, for the time being, he is the custodian. When he is on duty, which is most of the time except when he is with his family in his own home in Oxley Rise (he uses his official residence only for government entertainment), he is the Prime Minister, and he is conscious of his office and respects it, though power rests easily upon him. Lee never asserts himself; he has no need ever to remind anyone that he is the leader in Singapore. This is understood by every one, even by those who do not like him.

10

Lee no longer has to remind people that he is as good as Harold Macmillan, President Nixon, or anyone else. They are now prepared to accept his judgment that he is. Unfortunately, security is a problem in a state where militant communists and racialists are not unknown, and this restricts Lee's freedom a great deal. Armed men, trained to become part of the scenery, move with him along the golf course; the jeep which is never far away is in direct radio contact with all the other police vehicles at strategic positions on the roads near by. All this no longer bothers Lee. He shrugs his shoulders. "This," he says, "is the world we live in."

III

Sir John Nichol, then Governor of Singapore, opened the first session of the first Singapore Legislative Assembly on 22 April, 1955. He said it was an epoch in the constitutional history of Singapore. "In the period of 136 years since its establishment under the British flag as a trading centre, Singapore has been transformed from the small village which was located here, where this House of Assembly stands, to a centre of world trade with its port ranking as the tenth busiest in the world." Ten years later, Lee Kuan Yew was speaking of Singapore as the fifth busiest port in the world.

The first business day at that first session of the first Assembly was held on 25 April. Lee Kuan Yew was on his feet minutes after it opened to protest against thanking the British Secretary of State for his Message to the Assembly. "Far be it from the People's Action Party not to observe the civilities and courtesies of life," he said, "but I think it is important that we should take this occasion to remind ourselves what we have to be grateful for..." Lee went on to move an amendment which in effect, he said, would reaffirm that the Assembly still believed that "this Constitution is no good".

"The government of this cosmopolitan island has hitherto been in the hands of professional administrators," Sir John Nichol had said when opening the Assembly. "Today," he had continued, "Singapore is governed by a Council of Ministers answering to a Legislature which is predominantly popularly elected."

"We believe," declared Lee, "that this country is fit now for full self-government and, but for that useless, spineless lot that was supposed to represent the people of Singapore in that Constitution Commission, we would not today find ourselves with the Governor's triumvirate, the men whom the Government has referred to as professional administrators—and no doubt they are, capable and efficient... we say this Constitution is a sham. We say this Constitution is colonialism in

11

disguise ... no one knows how long this Assembly will last, but, so long as this Assembly lasts, let it never be forgotten that there are only twenty-five men here who can stand up and say, 'I speak for the people. I speak for the people of the constituency I represent'; that four men are here by leave and licence of His Excellency the Governor of Singapore; that they represent no one but themselves and their friends whom they are supposed to typify; and that the three professional administrators are in three pivotal positions. And we can only hope that there are men of stature on the front benches opposite, who will prove that this Constitution is not worth working and is unworkable..."

CHAPTER TWO

The People's Action Party

I

TUNKU Abdul Rahman, Malayan nationalist, leader of the Malays, was among those on the platform when Lee Kuan Yew, on 21 November, 1954, proposed the formation of the People's Action Party. The whole of the Malayan Peninsula was then under colonial rule, and few people at that meeting thought it possible that within three years the Tunku would be the elected Prime Minister of an independent Malaya. Lee's hand is revealed in the PAP Manifesto, which the inaugural meeting adopted, and which still guides the party in principle.

The basic aim of the PAP was to secure national freedom without the use of force. While an appeal was specifically addressed to workers —"We must reduce inequalities of wealth and ensure that workers by hand and brain get the full fruits of their industry and enterprise"— there is no reference in the Manifesto to socialism. This was deliberately omitted so that every citizen, rich and poor, employer and worker, could look upon the PAP as a nationalist movement. "We are also prepared to co-operate with other political parties genuinely interested in achieving real, not spurious, independence for our country," stated the Manifesto.

The PAP's inaugural meeting was the biggest political rally since 1948. *The Straits Times* reported that the theme of the meeting was independence immediately. "There could be no compromise on that," said Lee Kuan Yew. "We reject the Singapore and Federation constitutions because ultimate power and control still rest in the colonial power and not in the hands of the people. No constitution which curtails the sovereignty of the people can be acceptable to us." Lee complained that the arbitrary powers the Emergency Regulations gave to the Executive made it impossible for serious nationalist movements to exist. He gave the PAP's main objectives: to end colonialism and to establish an independent national State of Malaya comprising "the territories now known as the Federation of Malaya and the Colony of Singapore"; to create a democratic unitary government of Malaya based on universal adult suffrage of all those born in Malaya or who adopt Malayan nationality; to abolish the unjust inequalities of wealth and opportunity "inherent in the present system"; to establish an economic order which would give to all citizens the right to work "and the full economic returns for their labour and skill; to ensure a decent living and social security to all those who through sickness, infirmity or old age can no longer work; to infuse into the people of Malaya a spirit of national unity, self-respect and self-reliance and to inspire them with a sense of endeavour in the creation of a prosperous, stable and just society."

Tunku Abdul Rahman attended as president of the United Malays National Organization. He promised UMNO's full support. Sir Tan Cheng Lock, president of the Malayan Chinese Association, was also there. He said that the PAP could count upon the MCA.

II

Nobody has ever denied that communists then stood shoulder to shoulder with the nationalists within the PAP. Lee Kuan Yew was aware of this. But, from the start, he made his position clear. He was willing to form a united front with anyone prepared to fight with him, constitutionally, to rid Singapore and Malaya of British control. Lee will not listen to British protests that Britain never intended to challenge independence, and wished only to bring it about realistically and practically. Not believing this, Lee and his party adopted a fighting posture, and he still feels that the British would never have handed over complete government of the island to the local people had they not, in effect, forced the British to do so.

Lee Kuan Yew knew better than most that when he accepted communist support he was riding a tiger, and he was prepared for the insults and attacks which followed in the Western press. It was this decision, and his subsequent careful, not always head-on, tackling of other problems, successfully, it transpired, which annoyed the which-

14

side-are-you-on? type of politican, and caused *Time* magazine to refer to him as Shifty Lee.

Lee expected the communists within the party ranks to make attempts to capture the party and he will agree that once they nearly did. What might have happened to the PAP had not Lim Yew Hock, then Chief Minister, stepped in and arrested half the PAP Committee on the grounds that they were communists, will never be known. Lee was confident they would have been out-manoeuvred, and they were, when he refused to carry on as Secretary-General unless he was backed up by a committee in which he could have full confidence. Lee was never prepared to become the tool of the communists, as David Marshall, the unfortunate first Chief Minister, became until the communists discarded him as a useless instrument in the 1963 general elections. Forsaken by the communists, Marshall lost his deposit, faced with the sad truth that his own supporters totalled no more than 416 voters.

Probably the only non-communist ever to have sat astride the communist tiger in a nationalist movement and survived, and beaten the communists to their knees with a policy of open confrontation, Lee knew that in the end the communists were bound to clash with the non-communist nationalists. He feared this might happen after the formation of Malaysia, not before, when the communists pretending to be socialists might be firmly entrenched. To his amazement and relief, the communists challenged him while Singapore technically remained a British possession with self-government. They mistimed and misjudged, and one of the reasons was the expulsion from the party of the former treasurer, Australian-trained accountant, Ong Eng Guan.

After capturing the city council, the PAP made Ong Eng Guan mayor of the city. Ong was Chinese-educated, and at that stage the PAP had few Chinese-educated leaders. They deliberately built up Ong to serve the party, and they thought him capable of carrying out party instructions. Instead, they built a monster. Not to put too fine a point on it, Ong became crazed with power, daily issued a stream of orders which stunned everyone, except childish extremists, with whom he became popular, and in the process all but brought the city facilities to a complete standstill. Misguidedly, the PAP tried to capitalize on his popularity, and when, in 1959, they won the general elections and formed the government, Lee Kuan Yew made Ong Minister for National Development, gave him control of city installations, and entrusted him with the acute problem of providing the people with houses. This was a major blunder.

Ong was not fit for the task, and he failed to erect a single dwelling. In a public inquiry, a judge described him as a man capable of telling an untruth when it suited him, and evidence revealed that he had given jobs to his friends. In the end, Lee took over, and within a short while the Government achieved international fame for the speed with which thousands of low-cost housing units were erected. But the damage had been done.

Angry at his dismissal, Ong attacked Lee's leadership, taking an extreme Left line. Expelled from the party, Ong Eng Guan resigned his Assembly seat and, promising his Chinatown voters heaven on earth, soundly and triumphantly defeated the PAP candidate. It was at this point that the pro-communists in the PAP made their fatal mistake. They thought that Ong and his new party might snatch the extreme Left initiative from them. They threatened Lee, demanding that he should follow their line. Lee refused and, in another by-election, the pro-communists threw their weight at the last moment behind David Marshall, then chairman of the Workers' Party. Lee was to be taught a lesson.

By a narrow majority, Marshall was elected to the Assembly again and the pro-communists waited confidently for Lee Kuan Yew to give way. Lee stood fast. He declined to be intimidated. Instead he accepted the challenge in the Assembly, and called for a vote of confidence. Pro-communists, waverers and opportunists within the PAP abstained: the national united front was broken. Thirteen of the PAP's thirty-nine Assemblymen resigned or were expelled. Shortly afterwards, the deserters formed the Barisan Sosialis (Socialist Front), and the antagonists stood where the lines were drawn.

For two years the Right votes of Lim Yew Hock kept Lee Kuan Yew in power, but in the end it was Lee himself who decided the date of the general elections. Seldom in parliamentary history could there have been a more masterly performance. With supreme confidence, having helped to bring about merger and Malaysia as dreamed of more than a decade before, Lee Kuan Yew went to the people seeking approval to continue his work.

III

In the 1950s the PAP, believing firmly in the need for an anti-colonial united front with communist elements, was being severely criticized. Australian journalists and politicians, convinced that Lee was playing a dangerous game and suspicious of the man himself, joined in the criticism. Said one Australian: "Lee walks like a duck. He quacks like a duck. He is a duck." Lee does walk in a deliberate and distinctive manner: he puts his feet down carefully, and his body, like his whole personality, moves forward aggressively. But he is no duck. And neither does he deserve to be described as unfavour-

16

ably disposed towards Australia or Australians. He clashed with a couple of Australian journalists, with one as a result of persistent questioning in depth, and he did remark angrily and loudly that he thought that certain Australians were interfering in the formation of Malaysia. But to pretend that he is anti-Australian is not to understand a man fully aware of the political and military realities of life. Lee is pro-Asian, and he is politically inclined towards neutrality, co-existence and the need for smaller states to work together as much as possible to prevent themselves from being exploited by the larger powers. He gets along well, in consequence, with Prince Sihanouk of Cambodia. This does not make him unfriendly towards Australia, or any other country. If Lee considers British diplomats, merchants, and journalists to be smoother, more polished, more confident, and less brash than the pushful Australian, this may be because of his long association with the British. At Cambridge the kindness and learning of his tutors and lecturers left upon him an enduring impression of what is best in Britain.

No man is more conscious than Lee Kuan Yew of the impact of communism upon the largely Chinese population in Singapore. He studied communism carefully during his student days in London and he finally concluded, after deep thought, that this ruthless discipline was unnecessary for the development of Malaya. He was willing to listen to arguments that in one form or another communism might be suited to China or the Soviet Union. But not to Malaya. He thought that for many reasons it was the duty of the English-educated in Malaya to assist in bringing about real social cohesion and to lead the fight against colonialism. At the same time it was necessary for them to be on their guard against communism. He argued that, whatever the rights and wrongs of communism, no one could deny the tremendous appeal it made upon Asian masses. He told students in London in 1950 that they could not insulate themselves from the nationalist revolts that had swept the European powers from Asia. They had to participate. They had to provide a reasonable alternative to communism. Lee has always possessed this sense of history, of being able to look forward as well as to remember the past. His awareness of political developments and trends in the newly emergent Afro-Asian countries is based less upon doctrine than upon a study of events. If he has a fault in this direction, it is his anxiety constantly to "analyse the current situation". This is an absorbing but not always rewarding occupation. Yet, if criticized, he could with justification claim many brilliant perceptions, many instances when his forecast of likely developments has been proved correct.

Lee's deep interest in foreign affairs, therefore, is understandable. Once he had become Prime Minister and was firmly in the saddle, and work had begun on the more pressing domestic problems, Lee

17

went abroad, making contact with other Afro-Asian leaders, creating friendships, explaining Singapore and Malaysia, exchanging ideas, learning, gaining more knowledge. On these tours he had long and useful talks with Nehru, Ne Win, Sihanouk, Nasser, Tito, Ayub Khan, Sukarno, and a host of others.

IV

Lee Kuan Yew is Secretary-General of the People's Action Party, as Mao Tse-tung is Chairman of the Communist Party of China. Both give direction to their respective parties. Lee presents the annual report drawn up under his direction by the staff. By 1967 the PAP had become a cadre party, with a strong headquarters and a branch in all fifty-eight constituencies. Total membership of the party is in the region of 35,000 of whom an undisclosed number are cadres. Only cadres can vote, and take part in certain meetings. Cadres are obliged to serve an apprenticeship as ordinary members. At headquarters there is an organizing secretary with a full-time paid staff of twenty. Each PAP member of parliament must pay a percentage of his parliamentary salary of $1,000 per month into party funds. Cabinet ministers, including the Prime Minister, also contribute a part of their ministerial salaries.

In early 1971, the position was that the highly organized People's Action Party and the weak United National Front were the only two non-racial political parties in Singapore capable of making the parliamentary system, though it was thought possible that a third party might emerge before 1973, when the next general elections were expected to be held. In 1971 the UNF had no representation in Parliament. There was a Malay party and a Chinese party. Neither had any elected members of parliament. The Malay party concerned itself mostly with communal matters. Other parties existed in name only.

Following the Peking line, the Barisan Sosialis by then had totally abandoned any pretence of supporting democratic government. They refused to take part in the 1968 general election and their subsequent activity consisted of publishing communist propaganda, staging illegal demonstrations, and organizing sporadic attacks upon PAP branch premises and on traffic lights and community centres. For the time being, this lack of parliamentary opposition (and the anti-social behaviour of the Barisan Sosialis which is handled by the police) does not unduly worry Lee Kuan Yew. The Republic is new and there is a lot of work to be done. It could be argued that for a few years anyway, the Government could reasonably direct all its activities to essential tasks. Politics could wait a while. Besides, Lee Kuan Yew has no doubts that the real Opposition continues to be the Malayan Communist Party

18

(the force behind the Barisan Sosialis). If Lee fails before the parliamentary system is properly established, there is every likelihood that the Barisan Sosialis would fight elections again to achieve power and to destroy democratic government.

In the PAP, members' interest is maintained by regular organized meetings, sports, courses on political and other subjects, by events conceived to attract housewives and families. Every PAP member of parliament, or parliamentary candidate, is required by the party to hold a "meet the people" session each week. This applies to all cabinet ministers as well.

Shortly after its formation, the PAP made an appeal for money for a "Building Fund" and this, in addition to regular contributions from members of parliament, and occasional profits from special organized events, dramatic performances and musical variety shows, is the main source of the PAP's finances. After more than ten years in office the PAP has become respectable in the eyes of Singapore merchants and traders, and it is unlikely that they would fail to support the party with contributions if this should ever become necessary. No publicity has ever been given to any large donation to the party by anyone since its inception. Party officials are disinclined to discuss internal party affairs. This is not surprising in a region where every organization, political and otherwise, is alert against communist infiltration.

CHAPTER THREE

Lee's Basic Beliefs

MALAYSIA Day, 16 September, 1963, was Lee Kuan Yew's fortieth birthday, but any high hopes which might have been entertained that this happy coincidence would lead to a rapid, smooth and deeper understanding between Lee Kuan Yew and Tunku Abdul Rahman and between Singapore and Malaya (relations had never been harmonious since Lee Kuan Yew's arrival on the political scene) were shattered within the week. Malaysia, as we shall see, got off to a very bad start.

On 21 September, when Malaysia was five days old, Lee was swept back into office as Prime Minister of Singapore, in a snap general election. The minimum of legal notice had been given because for weeks Singapore had been politically agitated over the referendum to determine whether or not it should become part of Malaysia, and Lee Kuan Yew considered, not unreasonably, that the people were ready to vote again for their government without another prolonged political campaign. He reckoned the people knew which way they wanted to vote. It was also time to lower the temperature and for every one to get back to work.

On the eve of the Singapore poll, in a dramatic gesture, Tunku Abdul Rahman, Malaysia's Prime Minister, president of the United Malays National Organization, and leader of the ruling Alliance Party (comprising the United Malays National Organization, the Malayan Chinese Association and the Malayan Indian Congress), surprisingly persuaded by his Kuala Lumpur Chinese advisers, intervened in the general election. Lee was shocked. Earlier, he had made a public announcement that the People's Action Party would not contest the following year's Federal elections. He was also given to understand that the Tunku would not interfere in Singapore's elections. Yet, a few hours before 618,000 voters went to the polling booths, the Tunku appealed publicly to the Singapore electorate to vote for his Alliance Party. People thought that the weight of the Tunku's great prestige would seriously affect the PAP's chances, especially in those constituencies with large numbers of Malays.

Nothing of the sort happened. On the contrary, most Malays voted for the PAP, and non-racialism. In an emphatic manner the Malays in Singapore told the Tunku they preferred Lee Kuan Yew's leadership in Singapore to the Chinese leadership the Tunku was recommending, even though this meant voting against United Malays National Organization candidates.

Disappointed and angry that the Singapore Malays rejected all the UMNO candidates, the Tunku, famed for his sporting activities on the football field and the race track, failed to send Lee a word of congratulation on winning the elections, but instead issued a churlish statement saying how shocked he was. He blamed Malay traitors for UMNO's staggering defeat. He criticized the elections, as "hurriedly arranged", though he grudgingly admitted that the PAP was a well-organized political force capable of keeping the communists in their proper place.

Then Syed Jaafar Albar, a prominent official of UMNO, made some explosive and much less philosophical comments, charging Lee Kuan Yew with being a 100 per cent dictator. Albar promised to "fix him" when he showed up in the Malaysian parliament, and added, "We are prepared to use both fists and words to teach Lee a lesson in democracy."

Most observers could understand the Tunku's delicate position. As the leader of the Malays he could hardly refuse to associate himself with an outburst of Malay surprise and pain (illogical though the outburst might appear to him as a non-racist) if he wished to continue to be their fearless defender.

In such a mood, the Tunku hastened to Singapore, accompanied by Syed Jaafar Albar, and at a mass rally of UMNO supporters made the rather odd remark that Lee had profited by playing upon the people's fear of communism. At the same time he repeated that certain Malays had betrayed UMNO during the elections. He predicted they would not last long. In cold print, away from the emotionalism of a Malay political meeting, this severe criticism of sophisticated Malays, condemned because they voted for Lee Kuan Yew's non-communalism, appears strange coming from such a noted non-communalist as the Tunku. But it was mild compared to the vicious

21

outburst from Albar. The Tunku was forced to watch while Lee's pictures were burnt.

Lee did not remain silent. At a public meeting the following day he stressed the need for co-operation "on equal terms, not that of master and servant", and he called for an intelligent appraisal of realities. "In Malaysia," he pointed out, "there are forty-three per cent Malays and indigenous people, forty-one per cent Chinese, ten per cent Indians, and six per cent others." He warned the Malays, in other words, that they were in no position to throw their weight about. He asked UMNO not to look upon the PAP as a hostile force just because the PAP in the Singapore general elections defeated all the UMNO candidates, but as a political rival, like themselves pro-democratic and pro-Malaysia. He said that the PAP Government was anxious to co-operate fully with the Central Government. He acknowledged their final supremacy.

Within hours, the Tunku came out with a carefully worded statement, stoutly defending his Chinese advisers and the MCA against Lee's telling arguments. At the same time, he promised that the Central Government would work closely with the Government of Singapore. Lee Kuan Yew, preparing to leave for Kuala Lumpur, at once welcomed the Tunku's response and offer of co-operation, and added, "I accept his condition." Gestures having been made on both sides, Lee began discussions in the capital to "sort out difficulties and set the course for honourable co-operation for the next five years"

II

In a message to the Tunku on his sixtieth birthday earlier in the year, Lee described the Tunku as "the symbol of a tolerant, happy and prosperous country". Lee added: "Every time the Tunku appears, it is always the tolerant, cheerful personality—moving easily among all races and classes—a man completely at ease, relaxed, at peace with himself and with the world, practical, and, most important of all, successful."

Unlike the relaxed Tunku, Lee's attitude towards life is unsmilingly serious. He is a thoughtful man. When he was meeting the Malayan Communist Party head-on he found little to laugh about. From 1954, until the battle was won in 1963, he was tough, determined and unsmiling. Nowadays, anxious to soften his public image, he will hurriedly relax his expression in a smile when the occasion demands. But then, as the Malays say, the heart does not smile. Lee is intense. Life is too grim for him to chuckle over trivialities: chuckling will not solve problems, serious intellectual exercise may.

22

Malicious observers say that a political opponent's discomfort is certain to raise a laugh with Lee at any time, and this is probably true. It is not an abnormal characteristic. When told, for example, that Prime Minister Lee Kuan Yew had been pushed into a deep drain by a mob he was trying to reason with, the genial Tunku is reported to have laughed until tears came to his eyes.

Because he is unrelaxed, because he cannot suffer fools, because he believes there are so many wrongs and deficiencies and problems in the world that must be rectified and solved so that people can eat more and live better and more reasonable lives, and because he is preoccupied most of the time by these problems, Lee does not make friends easily. He is not willing to mingle socially. He derives no enjoyment from cocktail parties and refuses to attend unless protocol insists. He will rarely accept an invitation to a meal unless business is to be discussed over food. He seldom goes to the cinema, except with his children. But he can be tempted to play chess with them, or to talk with them in English, Mandarin, or Malay. He lives a full life, much of it dedicated to putting his world right, the rest being given over to his family and to physical and healthful exercise. His daily schedule leaves him little time to enlarge his circle of friends, even if he wished to, and he has no such inclination. Closest to him, after the immediate members of his family, are his political colleagues. They have gone through political fire together, they have been tested, and friendship has survived and been cemented.

What must be remembered when examining the relationship between Lee and the Tunku is the fact that Lee is a socialist and a hardworking citizen of Chinese origin, conscious of a culture that goes back 4,000 years, a culture with a profound literature and language, enriched by hosts of philosophers, painters, poets, writers, administrators and soldiers. Tunku Abdul Rahman is an educated prince of a people with no comparable culture. Both in their different ways wanted to better the lot of the people, Lee by planning and organization, the Tunku in other ways.

Lee Kuan Yew is of Hakka stock. The Hakkas are men from the north: tough invaders, the aggressors. Lee is kindly, sensitive, and sensible, and believes strongly in the need for a high standard of public and private morals. He was genuinely puzzled by the Profumo-Keeler scandal, and could not begin to understand how a Minister could involve himself in so sordid an affair. In short, Lee is an essentially decent man: impatient, perhaps, of man's weaknesses, intolerant of slipshod work, angered by dereliction of duty, abuse of trust, and misuse of the public's confidence.

This does not make Lee stuffy, so much as tough. Whatever he says or does, the fighting, suspicious Hakka peers through. Lee has not always been conscious of his tough exterior. He was, in fact, shocked to discover how aggressive, almost bellicose ("gangster-like",

23

to use his own words) he appeared, when he saw himself on television for the first time. He was silent for a few moments. Then he said "Good God!" He saw a fierce, menacing figure glowering at him, unsmiling, ready to give or take a blow. He did not like what he saw. This was not the figure the political Lee wanted to present to the electorate: and from that moment he set out, unwisely some thought, to soften the image.

But the screen did not lie, and in Asia, where politics and living call for tough leadership, friends wondered whether advantage was to be gained from hiding the truth—which is that Hakka Lee is an admixture of aggression and wary defence. In 1963, his public speeches, if not his television smiles, were punctuated with evidence of his true personality. "I am prepared to meet you, anywhere, anytime," he says. "I'll fix you," he threatens. To some, this fighting spirit, always apparent, is a symptom of latent inferiority, or basic insecurity. "What's the matter with Lee?" demanded his old political enemy, Lim Yew Hock. "The man keeps on saying he will fight, fight, fight. He's always wanting to fight." But to most people all this is a manifestation of Lee's intellectual and physical courage. "You have just got to face these things," he will say. "You can't run away."

Now, Lee Kuan Yew, more confident, the early battles over and won, the enemy routed, is less threatening, more philosophical, older and wiser.

III

Lee's aggressive personality is noticeable, and immediately felt, just as the Tunku's relaxed affability instantly charms and soothes. He possesses astonishing ability to focus his powerful intellect directly upon the problem under consideration, forcefully and rapidly, and this, combined with his readiness to judge the other person's motives highly suspicious and most likely damaging to his own interests, leaves him, with few endearing qualities. Not many men have been able, at one and the same time, to be tough, realistic, capable of working efficiently under great pressure and at high speed for long hours, and yet to remain relaxed, ready to accept men and matters at face value, and popular.

In the end, most ruthless seekers of high standards and efficiency must be content with men's grudging respect until they become old enough to be legends worthy of affection and love. Lee would not quarrel with that: he would rather be respected than loved.

Oddly enough, Lee's natural suspicion of motives and actions, and his experience of meeting many men in high positions, has not made

24

him a good judge of character, though he never fails to recognize a man's intelligence. He is capable of assessing outstanding merit, but on occasions his judgment of lesser men is faulty. He relentlessly drives the civil service as he drives himself, and there are times when he mistakes enthusiasm, eagerness or pushfulness, for talent. Praise or criticism, perhaps misplaced, can upset civil servants, although nobody doubts the honesty of purpose behind the Prime Minister's remarks.

Lee is a supremely confident person, whose confidence causes his enemies to brand him as arrogant, and the People's Action Party to look upon him as an anchor to sanity and resolve. If arrogance means conceit, Lee is not arrogant, but his confidence is realistically based upon his belief that he is cleverer than most, and this has been proved in scholastic examinations and political tussles, to which Lee, in his early political days, did not hesitate publicly to refer.

He once told a group of civil servants, in illustration of a point he was making: "I speak to Harold Macmillan and Duncan Sandys as equals. At Cambridge I got two firsts and a star for distinction. Harold Macmillan did not." In the political arena he asked: "Where are Lim Yew Hock and his party now? We have smashed them. We thought these things out better than they did." He was justified: the Singapore Alliance Party failed to win a single seat in the 1963 general elections.

Lee's confidence, essential to Asian leadership, his sureness, his highly developed critical faculty, his impatience with less than what he feels entitled to expect, tend to make him unfair. He refuses to listen to explanations, and this can be a fault. "I want no excuse," he will say. "Produce the goods, and on time." Lee believes, with sincerity, that he could make a good film, write a good book, produce a good newspaper, build a good house or road, as well as or better than most. And the exasperating truth is that, given the appropriate technical training, he probably could. Certain of this, Lee will not readily listen to explanation of failure or shortcomings. A snag is that, like many other leaders and commanders, Lee is not proficient at giving verbal instructions. What may be no more than the germ of an idea in his mind, he will toss out for action. What finally appears may be very different from what Lee himself would have produced. In the absence of clear-cut and precise instructions this is inevitable: minds work differently. What is dangerous is that in trying to probe his mind, and to please him and avoid unjust criticism, there is a tendency for assistants to play safe and create in consequence a climate of sycophancy, and this is a grave threat to efficiency which Lee tries desperately to avoid.

Because of this difficulty in giving precise verbal instructions in detail, Lee does not rank as an outstanding organizer. Probably his mind is too sharp, for frequently, no sooner is a decision made, than it is amended or improved upon. This may be one of the reasons why critics in Kuala Lumpur say he is far too agile. Yet there are probably few men in Asia capable of matching Lee in presenting an argument, forcefully, reasonably, lucidly. His skilful explanation to the United Nations Committee on Colonialism of the true meaning of Malaysia impressed seasoned statesmen from the West as well as from the East. They felt that there was a performance not often witnessed at the United Nations. Lee's skill as a debater began during his Cambridge days, and, although he is not above a descent into frivolity, appearing anxious to score childish points, his oratory, in the opinion of experienced British members of parliament who have listened to him, is equal to anything heard in the House of Commons.

Lee is best in debate. In English, if not in Malay, he is no great platform speaker. He is no rabble-rouser and could never arouse a mob as Sukarno could. This is because he directs his words to a man's common sense, not to his emotions. Sukarno shouted and ranted, whereas Lee must explain and argue, sometimes using words which send even the well-educated to their dictionaries. One of Lee's most pleasant attributes, for a man reputed to be arrogant, is his readiness to treat everybody, at first meeting, as his intellectual equal. His attitude changes only if he discovers that the person is not. Friends have been amazed that Lee should pay attention to arguments from persons obviously his intellectual inferiors, but Lee's natural instinct is to expect them to be as sensible as he is, until proved otherwise.

Keeping in touch with modern developments, Lee studies television techniques, and it is on the screen rather than the public platform that he now makes the better impression. His appeal continues to be to common sense, to what is reasonable and sensible. He has never made extravagant promises to the people. He believes the ordinary man is not a fool, and expects people to make the correct judgment if they are told the truth and given the facts. That is why he reasoned that the people of Singapore must reject communism. "Let us meet the communists in open argument": that was his policy. "Confront them: match their lies with truth: give facts when they distort." That is how Lee beat them at the polls in September, 1963, scoring thirty-seven seats to the thirteen captured by the pro-communist Barisan Sosialis, the fifty-first falling to Ong Eng Guan, the former Mayor. Ong was the only successful United People's Party candidate. The party, created by Ong in 1961 after his expulsion from the PAP, fielded forty-six candidates, as many as the Barisans. Only the PAP contested all fifty-one seats. In 1965, Ong suddenly and rather mysteriously resigned his seat, thus causing a by-election in a constituency at a time when the relationship between Singapore and Kuala Lumpur was under severe strain.

What made Lee Kuan Yew enter politics? "I did not enter politics," Lee insists. "The Japanese brought politics to me." In a speech he spoke about the Japanese invasion of Singapore in 1942. He was then a student at Raffles College, later to become the University of Singapore. Lee said his whole world suddenly collapsed. All the false values were smashed. Overnight the country that was Malaya and was theirs became strange. Road signs appeared in Japanese. The Japanese said: "Look, this is our country, yours and mine." Lee said that he and his friends asked themselves: Have the Japanese a right to do this? "Slowly enough we decided that they had none: that this was our country. We will govern it ourselves."

Lee said that the Japanese occupying forces were blind and brutal and made him, and a whole generation like him, in Singapore and Malaya, work for freedom—freedom from servitude and foreign domination. "We decided that from then on our lives should be ours to decide, that we should not be the pawn and playthings of foreign powers." In that hour a Malaysian nationalist leader was born. This solemn promise to free Singapore from foreign rule, from colonial domination, was made in Singapore's awful darkness, when thousands of British and Indian and Australian soldiers rotted in Changi Gaol, when the people of Singapore groaned under the oppressive rule of an alien dictatorship, and when the young, rather bewildered and hapless Lee Kuan Yew was nineteen years old.

During the Japanese occupation, Lee learned Japanese and became a translator for the official news agency. When the misery of those years finally ended, he hurried off to Cambridge to complete his education. He studied hard, paid court to the girl student at Girton later to become his wife, found time to play golf, make a few visits to the Continent, explore the south of England on his motorcycle, and prepare himself mentally for what he believed would be a stern struggle to free Malaya from the bonds of British colonialism. To this day Lee is not prepared to believe that all he had to do was to push an open door. Clement Attlee had already freed India and Burma. Britain wanted to liquidate colonial commitments as quickly as possible. In Malaya, the communists' revolt held up constitutional progress, but when the Tunku reorganized the United Malays National Organization and formed the Alliance, the British Government needed little persuasion to work with an independent Malaya. Lee believed the British intended to hold Singapore as a colony for as long as possible.

In January, 1950, while the Malayan communists, who were mostly Chinese, fought to set up liberated areas (and were forced instead still further into the jungle), Lee escaped briefly from his studies at

Cambridge to debate the future of Malaya in the Malayan Forum. This was a group of overseas Malayans, created by the Tunku, in which several of today's leaders of Singapore and Malaysia, including Dr Toh Chin Chye, Singapore's Minister of Science and Technology, Tun Razak, who became Prime Minister of Malaysia in 1970, and Dr Goh Keng Swee, Singapore's Defence Minister and Deputy Chairman of the PAP, tested their first serious political beliefs. Lee Kuan Yew spoke to the Malayan Forum on "The Returned Student". He was twenty-seven.

Foreign undergraduates in London have always received the closest attention from British communists. Some of the best African revolutionaries against colonialism have been produced in British universities. Lee Kuan Yew was, therefore, in an excellent position to study dispassionately, though eagerly, the best arguments which communism could advance. In London and Cambridge there were opportunities to examine these arguments critically. He came to the conclusion that communism was not suitable for Singapore or Malaya. In this talk, his first political address, Lee explained why. He also underlined the importance of the returned student to Malaya, believing that whether he was communist or a non-communist nationalist, the student's role in the post-war future could be vital. He said that the superior social and economic position of the returned student was an important fact in Malayan society. Whether this privileged position he enjoyed as a member of a social or monied class was justifiable was another matter. But it was the inevitable accompaniment of the supremacy of the British in the country. The English in Malaya formed the ruling caste. The Englishman had superimposed on the people his language, institutions and way of life. His was the model of perfection, and the closer an approximation to his standards the individual Asian attained, the better would be his social and economic position. That was beyond controversy. In the few years the Japanese were the ruling caste, there were already signs that the nearer one was to being a Japanese, the better off one was going to be in a Japanese-dominated Malaya. "Had they stayed long enough, I have no doubt that those of us who could speak Japanese, who behaved like the Japanese, and who had been educated in Japan, would have been the most favoured class of Malayan. For we would have been the most acceptable to the rulers, who because of their economic and military hold on the country could dispense such extra privileges. Many of us will remember the unhappy spectacle of English-speaking, Western-educated colleagues suddenly changing in their manner of speech, dress and behaviour, making blatant attempts at being good imitation Japs. Indeed, some were sent to Japan so as to be better educated to enlighten their ignorant countrymen in Malaya and doubtless also to become the privileged class, second only to the genuine Japanese himself. It is pertinent to note that the Malayan student returned from Britain ceased under Japanese domination to occupy that second-class status, except in so far as it was impracticable to dispense with his services for the time being.

"It is four years now since the British have returned. For them, nothing could be better than to revert to the pleasant orderly society of 1939. Once again the English-educated are given their old privileges: and, of this English-educated class, the returned students form the uppermost crust."

Lee said it was relevant to observe the part this class (the returned students) played in British-dominated India, Dutch-dominated Indonesia, and the American-dominated Philippines. "In the brief space of four years, we have seen the emergence of six Asiatic countries to national independence: India, Pakistan, Burma, Ceylon, Indonesia, the Philippines. Malaya now finds herself the only remnant of colonial imperialism left in Southeast Asia surrounded by these new Asiatic national states. The only other fragment of colonialism left in Asia is French Indo-China.

"In all these new Asiatic states it is the returned students who have led the fight for independence. The Indians, Pakistanis, Ceylonese, and Burmese returned from England, the Indonesians returned from Holland, the Filipinos returned from America: they have formed the spear-head of national movements.

"If this should conjure visions of future greatness in any of us, I hasten to add that the pattern of events never quite repeats itself, and there are cogent reasons for believing that this pattern will not do so in Malaya. Had there not been the difficult racial problem in Malaya, had there not been a Chinese community almost as large as the Malay, had the population been six million, all Malays, I venture to suggest that British imperialism in Malaya would be well on its way out. But the facts being what they are, we must accept British rule for some time, during which we can attain a sufficient degree of social cohesion, and arouse a sufficient degree of civic and political consciousness among the various races of Malaya. This time is vital if we are to avoid a political vacuum that may otherwise follow British withdrawal from Malaya.

"Returned students in any British colony fall broadly into two classes: (1) the rich man's son, and (2) the impecunious government scholar. The first on returning home finds himself better equipped to be a bigger and more efficient capitalist entrepreneur. The second finds himself linked up with the colonial administrative system, given positions second only to the Englishman who must, necessarily, in a colonial system always be at the top. But they will be better off than their fellow Asiatics who have not been to England. Hence both groups on returning to Malaya find themselves a part of the vested interests of the country, both somewhat reluctant to dislodge

29

the system under which they enjoy these advantages. . .

"Empires never last forever. Either the master and subject races finally merge into one unified society, as in Britain, where the Welsh and Scots, once English-dominated, now form part of one political society, enjoying equal rights with the English. Or the Empire ends with subject races violently resisting and finally emerging as a separate national and political entity, as in the case of the Irish Republic, India, Pakistan and Indonesia. The indefinite continuance of the subjugation of one race by another is only possible where the subject race is inherently, both mentally and physically, inferior.

"Anthropologists are unable to prove any innate superiority of one race over another. This scientific fact, and the historical fact that no empire has been able to last more than a thousand years is, I think, no mere coincidence. We in Malaya are now seeing British domination, after over a hundred years, enter its last phase. Colonial imperialism in Southeast Asia is dead except in Malaya, and our generation will see it out.

"No sane man, whether he be English, Malay, Indian, Eurasian, or Chinese, can honestly study the situation in that part of the world, and not come to the conclusion that, either with or without the opposition of the Western-educated intelligentsia in Malaya, British imperialism will end. The two things we the returned students can help to decide are: firstly, how soon and orderly the change will be, and secondly, whether we shall find a place at all in the new Malaya. At the moment it is clear that the only party organized to force the British to leave, and to run the country, is the communist party. They are not merely so many bandits, shooting and being shot at in the jungle, and creating terror for the sake of terror. Theirs is a tightly knit organization making their bid for power.

"It is this element of international communism which I fear will make the pattern of development that has unfolded in India, Burma, Ceylon, etc., unlikely in Malaya. In all these countries the leaders from the educated classes, the returned students, had time to organize and were already organized, like the Indian Congress Party, before communism became a force in the political life of these countries. But this does not mean that communism is not a force in these countries. It is, right now, the biggest threat to the newly established national governments of Asia. How far these governments can counter the appeal and force of communism will depend on how far they are bold enough to carry out social reforms in the teeth of their own vested interest. That is another feature in the political development of our neighbours: the active support of native capitalists in the national aspirations of their fellow countrymen. But it is abundantly clear to Malayan vested interests, and that would include Chinese and Indian commercial interests, the Malay royal families, and the professional classes, that with the disappearance of the British Raj must also dis-

30

appear the great inequality in wealth of the peoples of Malaya. For any independent Malayan government to exist, it must win popular support, and to gain any popular support it must promise, and do, social justice. Indeed, and this is a fact important enough to warrant repetition, the continued existence of the new Asiatic states depends upon whether they are able to carry out long overdue reforms; whether they can, without the communist religion, do all that a communist state can do for the masses.

"We, the returned students, would be the type of leaders that the British would find relatively the more acceptable. For if the choice lies, as in fact it does, between a communist republic of Malaya, and a Malaya within the British Commonwealth, led by people who despite their opposition to imperialism still share certain ideals in common with the Commonwealth, there is little doubt which alternative the British will find the lesser evil.

"Despite the general political apathy that exists in Malaya there are many who are awakening to the critical position Malaya is in, both internally and in relation to the rest of Southeast Asia. If we, who can become the most privileged part of the local population under British rule, openly declare that British imperialism must go, the effect will be immediate. But if we do not give leadership, it will come from the other ranks of society, and if these leaders attain power, as they will with the support of the masses, we shall find that we, as a class, have merely changed masters. The difference between the British, the Japanese and the new masters who will arise if we remain unorganized will be a difference only of degree and not of kind.

"The first problem we face is that of racial harmony between Chinese and Malays. The second is the development of a united political front that will be strong enough, without resorting to armed force, to demand a transfer of power. To both these problems we, the Malayan students in England, whatever our race and creed, can make a substantial contribution. If we who are thought of as the intelligentsia of Malaya cannot make a sincere start now towards a solution of these problems, the future is grim. No class in Malaya is better equipped to lead a Malayan nationalist movement. The common man in Malaya, rightly or wrongly, associates intelligence and ability with an education in England, perhaps for the reason that such an education makes possible a greater and more rapid acquisition of wealth in a British Malaya.

"We have already seen the birth of Malay nationalism, we are seeing the first movements of a Malayan Chinese nationalism. There is no doubt that the other racial groups will also organize themselves. This may be a prelude to a pan-Malayan movement, or it may be the beginning of serious dissensions and communalism that may end in another Palestine. The prerequisite of Malayan independence is the existence of a Malayan society, not Malay, not Malayan Chinese, not Malayan Indian, not Malayan Eurasian, but Malayan, one that embraces the various races already in the country. Were it possible to eliminate the non-Malay population by deporting them to their countries of origin, there would be no danger of another Palestine. But even the most extreme Malay nationalist will concede that the Chinese, Indian and Eurasian population already in the country cannot be excluded by this simple process. Irresponsible communal leadership will bring disaster. Since, therefore, the non-Malay communities must be accepted as part of the present and future Malaya, it follows that unity must be attained.

"We can study with profit the solution Switzerland has found for her racial problems. Here is a national state, with three large racial groups—French, German and Italian—and a fourth small group, the Romansh, able to maintain its unity and independence through all the strain and stress of two world wars, when French, Germans and Italians were fighting on different sides. Whether we have the Palestinian or Swiss pattern emerging in Malaya is still in the balance.

"The present political situation is rapidly changing. Colonialism, with its fantastic discrepancies in wealth and power, will end whether or not we do anything. It is not a question of our fighting for independence in the way the Indian Congress Party fought for theirs. It is whether we are to play any part at all in the political life of the country. There is still time for us to organize ourselves into a force in the country. But the final question is what each individual returned student will do when he goes back to Malaya, for, in the last eventuality, any party, any society, any body politic, consists of individuals.

"There can be no leaders without a body to lead. There can be no body to lead if there be no cohesion. As a single individual, any Malayan nationalist who attempted to propagate ideas that would lead to the end of British Malaya would be considered undesirable by the British authorities. Their main interest is to prolong British control of our country. For them Malaya means dollars. Losing Malaya would mean a big widening of the dollar gap, with consequent loss of essential imports to Britain and resulting unemployment. We must be prepared to see that, whatever the political label of the British Government in Britain, be it Conservative, Labour, or even Communist, British colonial policy in Malaya may remain unchanged in its fundamentals. A British Labour government may sincerely believe in socialist, egalitarian principles, but no British government can of its own free will give independence to Malaya, and face the British electorate unabashed when the British cost of living index has gone up by some twenty points.

"But our trump-card is that responsible British leaders realize that independence must and will come to Malaya and that therefore, it will be better to hand Malaya to leaders sympathetic to the British mode of life, willing for Malaya to be a member of the British Com-

32

monwealth, and, what is most important, willing to remain in the sterling area. For the alternative is military suppression, a policy which another imperialist power has found impossible in Indonesia. We may take heart in the knowledge that no one can concede more graciously an already untenable position than the English. Our duty is clear: to help to bring about social cohesion, and to bring home to even the most die-hard imperialist that his is an untenable position.

"What actual steps we take when we get back will depend on the political temper at that time. Whether we can openly advocate and propagate our views, or whether we should be more discreet and less vociferous, is something that can be answered only when the time comes. Only if a spirit of co-operation and political independence be infused among our fellow Malayans can pan-Malayan political parties really exist, and Malayan leadership emerge. We must break the soporific Malayan atmosphere and bring home the urgency of the problems facing us. We must break down the belief that we are inferior and will always remain inferior to the Europeans. If every returned student makes known his convictions to his own immediate circle, the cumulative effect will be tremendous. . .

"If," concluded Lee Kuan Yew, "we fail to fulfil our duty, the change that still will come must be a violent one, for, whatever the rights and wrongs of communism, no one can deny its tremendous appeal to the masses. Whatever our political complexion, from deep blue Tory to bright red Communist, we must all remember that we are not indispensable in this struggle for freedom. But we can affect the speed and orderliness of the change. What the individual returning home chooses to do is a question of personal inclination, economic circumstances, and political convictions. But if the majority of us choose to believe that Malaya can be insulated from the nationalist revolts that have swept the European powers from Asia, then we may find that there is no place for us in the Malaya that is to be after the British have departed."

Six months after making this speech, which contained in essence his basic political beliefs, Lee Kuan Yew was back in Singapore.

CHAPTER FOUR

Men in Gaol

I

TWELVE years in office taught Lee Kuan Yew many things: he has become less truculent, but he is still a ready fighter, willing to take on anyone. Life is a challenge to him. He is impatient for change but he wants to reform and hesitates to destroy in order to rebuild unless this is unavoidable: he hates poverty, and he considers it unnecessary. He does not believe that the best way to ensure that the poor have a better way of life is to provide charity. "Give a man a gold coin, and he will spend it and ask for more," he often argues. Lee's socialism consists mainly of a firm belief that the state must equip all with an education which will permit them to make the fullest use of their talents and abilities. Lee has never believed that all men are equal: but he insists that all men and women must be given an equal chance to make the fullest use of their own talents.

Lee is a good listener, provided the argument is an intelligent one. Journalists trying to be clever can discover a rude Lee. "Look, I'm sorry. You are talking nonsense. You have all your facts wrong. You don't know what you are talking about. I cannot waste time talking to you." Lee feels that time is racing ahead, and there is much to be done. He has no intention of swimming with the tide: he knows which way he wants to go and his arguments and his attitudes constantly reflect his determination to keep on that path. He does not put his faith in the abstract: he believes that God helps those who help themselves. Nothing to him is more important than attending to the present life. This makes him a realist, a materialist believing that destiny is for human beings to determine. By all means have faith, he would say, but place reliance also on hard work and deep study: most problems are man made, and man must un-make them. Lee is a perfectionist and, although he hates shoddy work, he is angered more by those who do not try. Trying is important to Lee Kuan Yew: not everyone can make the grade—that is life and nothing can change it—but everyone must be capable of making the effort.

Lee is a finicky fusser over detail, and also a political scientist who can produce visions of broad outline and wide horizons. In between expounding a theory embracing the whole of Southeast Asia, he can grumble about the fumes from diesel-driven buses, complain that his steak is not quite right, argue that the weight of a borrowed golf club caused him to hook his shot. But Lee never confuses his priorities.

Every leader manipulating power selects priorities, and in so doing concerns himself more with important decisions than with minor matters. Lee can make important decisions and stand by them. They are never made without considerable thought, reflection, consultation, and deeper thought. Once he has made a decision he stands firm, having weighed every possibility. On unimportant matters, such as arranging dates for social events, he can dither and change his mind. This can cause a great deal of inconvenience, especially if the changes are last-minute ones. Either he does not care, or, more likely, he is unaware of the detailed work involved in an altered schedule. Partly this lack of consideration for others is probably due to the fact that, ever since he has been old enough to think for himself, he has been in a position of authority. There was a brief interlude during the Japanese occupation when he, and practically everyone else in Singapore, were not in this position. Lee's face was slapped with the rest and he, too, obediently bowed as required to his Japanese overlord. But that was different. What Lee lacks is the knowledge of what a friendly order or instruction involves. For many years, in some capacity or other, he has been accustomed to giving orders. He was too young to have been a soldier. He would have profited from the experience, for then he would have discovered that unreasonable orders cannot be carried out, even with the best will in the world. Lee's skill and drive in achieving administrative wonders in his city state is accepted. These are problems he has carefully studied. But his impossible demands to loyal typists, for instance, to do something which nobody with twenty fingers operating a jet-driven typewriter could possibly accomplish, make people unnecessarily irritable and cause them to believe that Lee is testy and, worse, unfair.

These are small imperfections in a man suited to a more complex political situation than that afforded by a small island of less than 250 square miles, and a population of no more than two million.

35

Lee is not a brilliant organizer, in spite of his fascination with and interest in detail, and his genuine curiosity about a wide variety of subjects, ranging from the most suitable trees to grow in parks to the best bricks to use in state-erected flats. He is a good planning general, a good surveyor of the overall scene, and, when occasion calls, a good and efficient infighter. He is intelligent enough to know that no general can fight alone. He can congratulate himself upon his talent for attracting to his side the best brains in the island. Equally important, perhaps even more important, is his success in winning the confidence of the civil service. Politicians may make the plans and give the instructions, but, in a developing state especially, nothing will happen to the best of plans and the clearest of instructions, unless there is an efficient and loyal civil service.

Lee was a most capable lawyer when he turned politician. He has a legalistic attitude towards most problems: he is, therefore, a most conservative revolutionary, but revolutionary he undoubtedly is in that he knows that the Malay peasant, and the Chinese and Indian peasant, must be introduced to modernity, "to a better and fuller life", as he puts it. Today is the era of the transistor: most poor homes have one, and everybody knows what is happening in the outside world. Television screens, the central feature of most community centres, show what is going on. Radio and television are the great awakeners in developing countries. Lee is acutely aware of all these implications. In Singapore he controls state radio and television.

Lee is a man of considerable energy. On a long, arduous tour of Africa he was the only member of his mission not to suffer illness or complaint. This in spite of the fact that he is something of a hypochondriac, and swallows large and small pills, of many colours, every day. He catches chills easily, and carefully avoids draughts, and changes his vest and shirt whenever he feels that his body temperature is changing. He drinks a great deal of warm Chinese tea from flasks during the day, and never drinks anything chilled—not even beer.

Lee in person proves always to be as good as his remarkable reputation. This is because he makes no conscious effort to be Lee, the Asian intellectual: he behaves naturally, he never acts: he is Lee Kuan Yew all the time, in the privacy of his home and on the street corner enjoying himself haranguing the mob.

Lee Kuan Yew is a late sleeper. He normally has to be awakened about eight o'clock. He tries to get to bed before one in the morning. He surfaces slowly, but once he has bathed and had a very light breakfast, he is ready for the day's work. He is at his best in the forenoon and prefers to take decisions then. He believes that he should concentrate hard for about three hours, and then break off for a while, preferably for an hour or two of exercise on the golf

36

course, before going back to the evening's work. He holds that working ten or twelve hours at a stretch may be necessary for some workers engaged on routine matters, but that it is no way for a Prime Minister of even a tiny state to organize his life. The type of work he does would, he is sure, suffer from long hours at a desk. He will come in at, say, ten o'clock, and his three personal secretaries then find their lives hardly worth living for the next three hours. Their notebooks filled, Lee may spend the next two or three hours having a swift desk lunch and seeing callers. At about three o'clock, when those who have lunched well find themselves growing sleepy (heat and humidity seem to evade even the best air-conditioners after a heavy lunch) Lee makes for the golf course. Shortly after seven he is usually back at work again, going through papers from the despatch boxes which await him at home.

Lee is aggressive, or perhaps it would be true to say he is aggressively defensive, for he is by nature and education a polite man in the Western sense (he will stand aside and permit a woman to go first, which is not yet an Oriental custom). He is not sensitive or touchy about his personal status: he can enjoy himself as one in a crowd, providing he is not on duty. Lee considers polite people civilized, and impolite and uncouth ones uncivilized and uncultured. Lee understands the need for protocol. He will, for example, go forward and greet the President of the Republic and solemnly shake hands every night of the week if state occasions, banquets, etc. demand. "These are the rules of the game," he will say, "and they must be rigorously observed. There must be form, dignity, and no slovenliness." Lee is not the sort of man to slap anyone on the back.

He is loyal to his friends, but his first loyalties are to his principles and to the task ahead. When a former Minister was suspiciously involved in a matter which showed poor judgment, the Prime Minister stripped him of all offices, and henceforth knew him not. They had, in the old days, been comrades fighting together. Lee never forgot this, but, when the man failed to live up to the high standards which leadership in Singapore demanded, he dismissed him and let the law take its course. This is not common in Asia. A man ceases to be Lee Kuan Yew's friend the moment he strays from the narrow path of rectitude. In this Lee is ruthless, as he feels he must be, because of the special high position the leaders in developing states in Asia must occupy if they are to compete with the communists.

II

How is it that Lee Kuan Yew, a brilliant lawyer, a man professing profound regard for the rule of law, can lock up political opponents for years without a proper trial?

Lee spoke of some of the anxieties "which occasionally assail my colleagues and me about the continuance of the rule of law in newly emergent societies" at a dinner of the Singapore Advocates' and Solicitors' Society (18 March, 1967). Lee claimed that the fact that the rule of law was reasonably established in Singapore is cause for quiet congratulation. "It might easily have been otherwise. There were moments in 1964 and in 1965 when we felt that perhaps we were going the way of so many other places in the world." Lee admitted that a very heavy price had been paid in order that standards should be maintained, and that there should be a Bar and judges and police to produce witnesses. "We have departed in quite a number of material aspects, in very material fields, from the principles of justice, and the liberty of the individual," he confessed. That was the heavy price that had to be paid: "620 criminal detainees... 100 of whom are murderers, kidnappers and armed robbers". Lee said that some of these cases were self-confessed and had been acquitted at trial. "To let them out would be to run the very grave risk of undermining the whole social fabric." There were 620 criminal law supervisees, men "on whom the due processes of law were unable to place even an iota of evidence". Lee admitted that all this was true. "We have had to adjust, to temporarily deviate from ideas and norms. This is a heavy price. We have over a hundred political detainees, men against whom we are unable to prove anything in a court of law... Your life and this dinner would not be what they are if my colleagues and I had decided to play it according to the rules of the game. So let us always remember that the price we have had to pay in order to maintain normal standards in the relationship between man and man, man and authority, citizen and citizen, citizen and authority is the detention of these 620 men and women under the Criminal Law Temporary Provisions Ordinance. But it is an expression of an idea when we say Temporary Provisions."

Political prisoners are treated well in Singapore. Lim Chin Joo, younger brother of Lim Chin Siong, the communist open front leader, was arrested in 1957. Prison authorities encouraged him to study. He did, and renounced communism. When he was released in 1966 he came out a lawyer, having taken his law degree by correspondence. Today, he is the secretary of the Appeals Board under the Land Act.

Confused with the ideological struggle between the Soviet Union and China, Lim Chin Siong also renounced politics in 1969, and Lee Kuan Yew arranged for him to travel to England for medical treatment and studies.

After the 1955 general elections David Marshall, who was to become Chief Minister, and Lee congratulate each other on becoming assemblymen.

22 April 1955, Lee Kuan Yew attends the first Legislative Assembly. In front of him is Lim Chin Siong, later exposed by Lee as the communist-front leader.

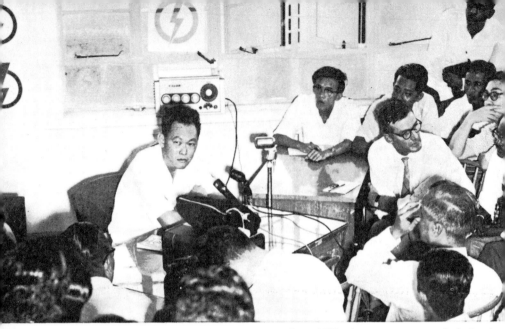

At a Press conference at the party headquarters on 1 June 1959, the secretary-general declared that "we will not form the Government unless the detainees are released".

An historic occasion, June 1959. Lee leaves the Istana after telling the Governor he will form a government providing his friends are released from prison

Electioning 1963

Addressing political rallies (above and right)

Lee, the party man, meets supporters

Welcomed at a Malay kampong

CHAPTER FIVE

Ambition

I

LEE'S family association with Singapore goes back more than a hundred years. There was an ancestor of Lee's in Singapore soon after Sir Stamford Raffles, with his red-jacketed soldiers, rowed up the muddy creek to where Singapore's Parliament House now stands, which Lee Kuan Yew's oratory dominates as Churchill's dominated the House of Commons. Lee's great-grandfather was Lee Bok Boon, and, in the manner of the Chinese of those days, Bok Boon, having crossed the China Sea to a foreign land in search of a fortune, returned to China to die. He left Lee's grandfather, Lee Hoon Leong, in Singapore. Lee Hoon Leong made a fortune and when his son, Lee Chin Koon, presented him with a grandson the old towkay declared that he should be educated to become the equal of any Englishman.

In 1955 Lee Kuan Yew said that he thought it would be possible by means of education to produce in fifteen to twenty years a generation which was completely Malayan, by which he meant multiracialist, owing loyalty to Singapore and Malaya, rather than separate groups of colonial subjects interested only in their own languages and cultures.

Lee himself at that time was already working hard, several hours a day, to fit himself to become a Malayan leader, capable of meeting and talking to most people in their own tongues. At school he had picked up Malay, was in fact a good Malay speaker, but his Chinese dialects had been neglected. With characteristic energy and application, Lee Kuan Yew became a student again. He perfected his Malay, he struggled with Chinese dialects, until, today, Lee's ability to make public speeches in English, Malay, and two Chinese dialects is taken for granted. A great deal of hard work went into the acquisition of these skills, as several teachers will testify, but to Lee to be able to converse with other Malayans direct was vital to racial harmony. It was something which just had to be learnt.

Records show that Lee Kuan Yew himself has always been more of a Malayan than a Chinese. This came about as a result of his early formative years at school, where he mingled with boys of other races, all Malayans, understanding and speaking, as youngsters can, several languages. Mixing early in this way with fellow Malayans, Lee escaped racialism. In his kindergarten days Lee attended a small Chinese school; he went to his first English school, the Telok Kurau English School, in 1931, when he was eight. He was then living with his maternal grandfather, Chua Kim Teng.

"He was a lively boy," Lim Lam San, one of his teachers, revealed. "He was rather mischievous. A good mixer. Not unduly studious, but he was bright, very bright, and good in English. That was his strong point." At the end of 1935 young Lee left to go to Raffles Institution, founded more than a hundred and forty years ago by the great imperialist "that Singapore may be an intellectual as well as the commercial entrepot of Southeast Asia", where Lee quickly established himself as a hard-working student. He was usually at the top of his class, but he did not ignore games, and even played cricket. There is still in existence Lee's school record in which Mr Campos, a teacher with commendable foresight, predicted that Lee Kuan Yew was destined to "do well, unusually well. He is likely to attain a high place in life."

Another of his teachers at Raffles Institution was Lim Tay Boh, later to become the Vice-Chancellor of the University of Singapore. Professor Lim taught Lee economics and it was obvious then that Lee was an outstanding scholar. He was especially strong in English language and English literature. At Raffles Institution Lee won scholarships and prizes, and practically the whole time he was there he dominated the school in mathematics, and with his fluent style in essay-writing.

Lee left Raffles Institution in 1939 hoping to go to an English university. But war clouds were gathering in Europe and Lee, instead, made use of a scholarship he had won to mark time in Raffles College. Lee read an interesting but difficult combination of subjects: economics, mathematics and English literature. He was proving himself an able student in all these subjects, and was also beginning to make a name for himself as an orator in Union debates, when the Japanese bombed Singapore, and he, with everyone else, was plunged into the turmoil of war. Lee became a mobile medical orderly in the local defence set-up, and, in common with his fellow-citizens, had a thoroughly unpleasant time during the Japanese occupation.

He recalled later how he narrowly escaped massacre in 1942. At a concentration centre the Japanese ordered him onto a lorry, "presumably to do some work for the Japanese. But somehow I felt that particular lorry was not going to carry people to work." He made excuses, and managed to escape. The people on the lorry never came back. The Japanese troops had a habit of collecting lorry-loads of youths from time to time and taking them away and shooting them.

"Such," remarked Lee Kuan Yew, "was their blindness and brutality. They never knew what they did to a whole generation like me. But they did make me, and a whole generation like me, determined to work for freedom—freedom from servitude and foreign domination. I did not enter politics: they brought politics upon me. I decided that our lives should be ours to decide... that we should not be the pawns and playthings of foreign powers."

During the occupation, Lee worked as a translator in the Japanese official news agency, and had access to world news. He therefore knew, though the Japanese tried to hide the truth, that the Allies were winning the war, and that another battle for Singapore was becoming more and more likely. Biding his time, Lee one day in 1945 moved out of Singapore. The Japanese were suspicious that he was quietly telling people the truth.

With the surrender of the Japanese forces in September, 1945, the wish of his grandfather still ringing in his ears, Lee Kuan Yew at once quickly organized what he called "an atmosphere of study" at his home, and invited his old tutor, Professor Lim Tay Boh, to give the first of many informal lectures there. This did not last long: the educational authorities were soon reorganizing the schools and the colleges, and Lee himself was impatient to get to England. University places were hard to get; even harder to come by was a passage on a ship. Eventually, Lee Kuan Yew was squeezed onto a troopship. He landed at Liverpool, where bomb-scarred buildings, half-empty shops, dull gray roof slates, battle-weary and drab-clothed Britons, and the English weather, combined to make a rather grim picture for a lonely young man of the tropics making his first journey away from the sun.

In London, where he studied for a term at the London School of Economics, conditions were worse. "I found life in London rather trying. Having come from a relatively small city, the idea of waking up in the morning, and rumbling down the tube from Swiss Cottage to Holborn, and dashing round from Holborn to Aldwych, and popping up at Aldwych and running across to go down to the London School of Economics, and getting out to catch I don't know what number bus to University College up King Street, and then back again to King's College, frightened me. I thought I was going absolutely crackers. This wasn't my idea of university life. I think it got me down a bit—buses, fumes, tubes—and I managed to persuade the

Censor at Cambridge to take me in as a student. I missed a term. I think I was extremely lucky."

Rooms were difficult to find in Cambridge, but Lee was already convinced that where there is a will there is a way, and he was taken into Fitzwilliam's early in 1947. His Censor was Mr W. S. Thatcher. Mr Thatcher had a great influence on him, and they remained good friends and corresponded frequently until Thatcher's death in 1966.

Lee was back in Singapore on 1 August, 1950. The port authorities looked hard at his passport and at him. In London, Lee had already been noted as a nationalist with Leftist leanings. He came back eager to enter the political arena, and he did this through the trade union movement. His eyes still focused on merger with Malaya, as it had been when the Japanese awakened his dormant Asian nationalism, Lee moved relentlessly towards his objective. By the time he was ready to form the People's Action Party in 1954, Lee was legal adviser to more than a hundred trade unions. He was suddenly thrust into public attention as the legal brains behind a successful postmen's strike which achieved its purpose through the sympathy of a letterless public.

II

In Lee, wrote Seymour Freidin in the *New York Herald Tribune*, "there is a combustible combination of pragmatism, democratic reform, evolutionary socialism and visionary scope. This 230 square-mile island, with a large majority Chinese population among its nearly two million people, is really too small for someone of such talents. It brought him grief in the recent past and may cause additional heartache in the foreseeable future." Freidin wrote that early in 1966. He is wrong if he believes that Lee is ambitious to move into other territories: Lee thinks he may be able to influence events in Southeast Asia through reason and argument, if the big powers who really determine events will listen. His own personal ambitions are to make a good job of the Republic of Singapore, and in the 1970s to retire from politics, still a youngish man, in his fifties, to become part of the establishment he is trying so hard now to create (to become the director of the People's Association, perhaps), in order to provide the continuity which Lee believes Europe has shown to be essential if a nation, no matter how tiny, is to have some sort of heritage, tradition, background, if the nation is to be bigger and more lasting than current personalities.

Tunku Abdul Rahman made the same mistake of believing that Lee Kuan Yew is ambitious in a personal sense. "Mr Lee is a highly ambitious man," the Tunku told Malay leaders in 1966, "he feels Singapore is too small for his aspirations... he wants a bigger stage for his dictatorial performances. Mr Lee has become prouder since the outside world proclaimed him as a wise and clever man. But he is living in a dream world..."

Freidin was right in saying that Lee Kuan Yew is something of a visionary, but he is a planner and calculator more than a dreamer. He wants to improve, to reform, to better, and he is prepared to take unpopular decisions in order to move in this direction: his motives may be sheer idealism, but he is also a realist. a practical man: he understands the use of power, and he knows what is possible. His colleagues are the same: they are selfless, and collectively dedicated to honest efficient government. They are the lowest paid Cabinet in the world, a state of affairs that Lee himself realizes is not intelligent if good men are to be attracted to politics. They all seriously believe they hold a sacred trust. Whether this remarkably high standard will obtain among the leadership of the second generation remains to be seen.

John Cantwell of the Associated Press once asked Lee Kuan Yew about his personal ambitions. Cantwell told Lee that in Hongkong (in 1965), while Singapore was still part of Malaysia, Tunku Abdul Rahman, Malaysia's Prime Minister, described Lee Kuan Yew as "a very clever person, but too ambitious". Cantwell asked Lee: "What really are your personal ambitions?" Lee Kuan Yew replied: "My personal ambition is to ensure that people like myself, and their children, and my children, have a future in this country. My roots are here. I have been here three generations, nearly a hundred years. I have no other loyalties, no other homeland. And I want to bring about a situation which will secure the future for those like me."

Cantwell said he thought that the Tunku was suggesting that perhaps one day Lee personally hoped for greater power in Malaysia. Was that so?

Lee replied that he had stated many times that for a long time it would be of advantage to Malaysia to have a Malay, or a person of indigenous stock, as prime minister. "Naturally I want to be able to have a greater say in the policies to build this Malaysia, not necessarily as prime minister." He went on to say that even if a multiracial party emerged in Malaysia (the PAP already dominated Singapore) and won the majority of seats, "I think we will go out of our way to ensure that the prime minister is a Malay." Internally, this would assure everybody, "particularly the Malays and the indigenous people, that we intend to do it the friendly way, respecting everybody's rights, and understanding our obligations to raise the level of the Malays and the level of the education of the Malays. Secondly our neighbours will be happier. People might think, if a Chinese took over, that this is the sign of things to come. In the next generation... once we have established that Malaysian society, it will make no difference whether it is a Chinese, or an Indian, a Pakistani, Eurasian, Ceylonese or Malay, or Dusun or Dayak who becomes the prime minister."

CHAPTER SIX

Vietnam and the United States

I

WHEN Robert Kennedy went to the Far East in 1964, Indonesia's confrontation of Malaysia was still in progress. Senator Kennedy saw Sukarno and later saw Lee. Kennedy, back in the United States, promoted the "let Asians solve Asian problems" solution, and this provoked Lee Kuan Yew into some scathing remarks. "He's not very bright," he said. When a *Time-Life* man asked Lee in 1965 what he thought of Kennedy's idea (first advocated by the aggressor, President Sukarno) Lee Kuan Yew questioned whether Indonesia's confrontation of Malaysia was, in fact, an Asian problem. Who gave the Indonesians the guns, the ships, the aircraft and submarines which created this Asian problem? Did Asians give them, or Russians? And what exactly does an Asian solution to an Asian problem mean? "It means the solution provided by bigger Asian powers to smaller Asian powers, because that is what it must mean. If an Asian solution to an Asian problem is applied in South Vietnam, where will Mr Kennedy be in the Senate? How does he defend what President Johnson is trying to do in South Vietnam? Assuming that everybody accepts this is really the American intention—to bring peace, not to conquer South Vietnam, not to colonize it, but just to prevent the erosion of non-communist communist states by the bigger communist powers, how does an Asian solution to an Asian problem there work? It means first, the Americans are out. All right. Are the North Vietnamese out? They are Asians, aren't they? All right. What about the Chinese and the

Indians? Are they in or are they out? They are in, I assume, because they are Asians. So the Indians are going to support South Vietnam, take the role of the Americans? I don't see them doing that. They are not that way inclined. So who is going to balance up this thing? Who has given the MiGs to the North Vietnamese anyway? Were they manufactured by the North Vietnamese? Is this an Asian problem? So, you see, I think we must be very careful before we start repeating these catchwords and catchphrases."

In April, 1965, Robert Morse of *Time-Life* asked Lee Kuan Yew: What should the United States be doing in Southeast Asia?

Lee replied: "Convince Asians that a non-communist group of nations could survive, and can flourish as well as, if not more than, the communist states in Asia. First of all, you've got to get Asians to believe that a non-communist Asia is possible, is viable and worth fighting for, for themselves. Asians are not interested in fighting for abstract things like democracy; the 'free societies of the West' mean nothing to them. It is when Asians opt out of the fight, as in South Vietnam, that you are in great difficulties because then you have to fight on Asian territory... If people are going to believe that non-communist Asia will lose to communist Asia, well then everybody makes their adjustments accordingly, and nobody fights for non-communist states in Asia and that's the end. That's the first thing: the will to resist must not be allowed to melt away.

"Secondly, that a positive contribution can be made by America and the more advanced countries, by Europe, by Britain, to help these non-communist countries advance economically...

"We don't want to be recipients of gifts because that's a waste of time. We want trade, not aid. This is the slogan that's being pushed forward by Afro-Asians at all U.N. gatherings—how to free trade between the developed and the underdeveloped countries. And I think the Americans and the Europeans and the British have just got to make up their minds whether they want to compete with the communist bloc for world support. In other words, not allow Asian and African countries slowly one by one to be drawn to the other camp by default..."

In April, 1967, Lee was questioned by *Time* magazine on his feelings about the American role in Vietnam, about the United States taking a stand there, and about the United States preserving security in other small states in Southeast Asia.

Lee Kuan Yew replied: "Well, first let me say that I think this was not the best place in Asia or Southeast Asia to have taken a stand. If you had consciously made a choice with the hindsight you now have, I doubt whether you would have drawn the line as you found it in South Vietnam. You have gone in and raised the stakes with every commitment, increasing the price that you will have to pay for failure to live up to your declared objectives. The worry is

46

whether your open society will allow you to conduct the kind of battle the South Vietnamese war is going to become—a protracted, bitter battle with no prospects of spectacular or decisive victory. The danger of popular pressures growing up around your institutions of power, your Presidency and your Congress, for swift and decisive victory, is the greatest danger in your Vietnamese situation. If you can just hold the situation and prevent the other side from winning, you will have made a valuable contribution to the long-term stability of the region. If you cannot resist pressures for more intense effort and quicker results, then I see grave trouble for the whole of Asia, for the whole world."

"What," Lee was asked "in the long run, do you think is the proper, permanent role the United States should play in Asia? Is it a permanent presence?"

"Nobody," replied Lee, "can really prophesy these things—what is to happen in the late 1970s, the mood of the second post-war generation leadership throughout the countries of South and Southeast Asia, and their relationship with other big powers in the world, not just in the region."

"You don't see the United States wanting to dominate Southeast Asia, do you?"

"I don't think, in the 70s, that the problem for Asia is whether you want to dominate Southeast Asia. Your problem is whether you can prevent it from being added on to somebody else's strength, and the natural desire to prevent it from being swung over to the other scale. The smaller countries in Southeast Asia would prefer the comfort of their own separate selves, which is only possible if there are countervailing forces to enable them not to fall into the orbit of the larger powers in the continent."

"Is Singapore actively considering membership in one of the regional associations or groupings?"

"Singapore," declared the Prime Minister, "has nothing to lose in joining any regional association or group, provided it is not based on ethnic or ideological exclusiveness. In fact, in the long term, this is the only way in which the smaller and not very viable countries in Southeast Asia can sustain their separate existence in a world dominated by two or three super powers."

47

CHAPTER SEVEN

Asian Socialism

I

LEE Kuan Yew is a patient revolutionary. At the tenth anniversary Congress of the People's Action Party, he stressed that one of the most important tasks of a democratic socialist party like the PAP is "to maintain basic faith and conviction in its ideals. It has to struggle to establish socialist values in a very capitalistic system." For six years Lee's Government had been confronted with a completely and, Lee could truthfully have added, a highly successful capitalist economy, "which we could not convert into a socialist economy without disastrous consequences to everyone". It was just not possible to change Singapore's entrepot economy into a socialist economy: that was why the PAP fought to obtain a broader and more viable base for socialism in Malaysia, while at the same time turning to industrialization to expand the basis of Singapore's economy.

In the meantime, rather than trying to revolutionize the state's economy, the PAP "retained the purity of its ultimate beliefs, and resisted the temptations of the moment" by endeavouring to redistribute the rewards of labour in a capitalist system through social welfare, educational opportunities, housing, and a raising of the standards of living. By "temptations of the moment" Lee meant corruption, which he considers to be inherent in the capitalist system, and which, in his view, "buys politicians", and enables "those in authority to establish a paradise for themselves". This, according to Lee, is what has happened in many of the newly independent countries. But not in Singapore. Here, he said, "democratic socialists could be proud of having worked the capitalist system efficiently".

Lee Kuan Yew claimed that "the idealistic drive to establish a more equal and just society, where man does not exploit man, where wealth and rank are not the arbiter of a man's family fortunes and the fate of his children, still burns". Democratic socialists must seek the ultimate "in a society where man does not exploit his fellow man, where differences of language, religion or culture are completely subdued by the identity of common interests, in an equal and just society where man is rewarded on the basis of merit and effort".

Lee Kuan Yew explained that his ideal society "is where all men are equal, if not in their ultimate performance, at least equal in the chance of seeking equal education, fulfilment, and rewards".

The PAP's direct interest in socialism followed their rout in the Malaysian elections of 1964. Lee realized then that UMNO could never be expected to collaborate with the progressive, socialist People's Action Party: UMNO leaders looked upon Lee's gesture as a threat to the basis upon which the Alliance functioned, which indeed it was, for Lee was in fact attacking racialism. The Malays would have none of it. It is difficult to understand why Lee felt that the effort of trying to work with a non-progressive, essentially traditionalist, Malay leadership was worthwhile. He believed that if the PAP preached socialism and multiracialism from the beginning, thus in effect attacking UMNO, its policy would be misinterpreted as an attempt by the Chinese to take over the country. In 1964, having tried and failed to work with UMNO, Lee Kuan Yew decided to make a direct approach to the Malay masses on a class basis. It was a long-term stratagem which should have ιeen adopted when the party was formed in 1955; now it was probably too late. Lee's attitude was that in the past the fight was against colonialism and communism, then for merger and Malaysia. Now the emphasis could be upon socialism. With Malaysia there was a foundation for socialism. But first, he warned, "we must preach the gospel of an independent democratic Malaysia. There could be no socialist society otherwise." He admitted it would probably be a slow process. Public opinion had to be mobilized.

The PAP leadership did not know it then but time was quickly running out. The decision to launch an ideological offensive, to attract the Malays to the People's Action Party and socialism, was ten years too late. In the party's Statement of Objectives and Policy, issued on its tenth anniversary (a statement which bore recognizable signs of Lee Kuan Yew's composition) the PAP asserted: "Our hope of order and sensible development is that more and more educated Malays. . . will emerge. . . in the Malay leadership. . . This process of Malay socialists emerging to take over the leadership of a democratic socialist movement in Malaysia may take years. We can only hope that it will not come too late. . . "

The party statement expressed the belief that "Malay poverty can be abolished only by democratic socialist economic planning. The system of free enterprise, which now prevails throughout all sectors of the Malaysian economy, cannot bring about a better life for Malay peasants, however suitable it may be as a means of development and progress in trade and industries in the cities.

"It is the role of the PAP in Malaysia," the statement continued, "to convince the moderate leadership of the Malays that there is a rational economic method to abolish rural poverty." The PAP warned that an "irrational political solution, as has been attempted in Indonesia through xenophobic nationalism, expropriation of property, and so on, could lead to the disintegration of Malaysia."

Lee Kuan Yew hoped that the "moderate Malay leadership" would accept his contention that there is an "identity of purpose" in abolishing rural poverty. The reasons the Malay leadership wished to improve the condition of the Malay peasantry were obvious. "The Malaysian urban democratic socialist has an equally compelling, if intellectual, reason also to desire this." In this way, Lee argued, the wide disparities in wealth between city and countryside could be diminished; unrestricted free enterprise would increase these disparities.

Whatever the merit of Lee's arguments, the Malay leadership in the Alliance Government moved further away from, not closer to, Singapore's Premier. Tan Siew Sin, leader of the Malayan Chinese Association, the Tunku's Finance Minister, joined in the attack upon him. Tan publicly accused Lee of running a fascist-type government ("Hitler's government was also efficient") and declared that Lee ruled Singapore by fear. Tan said there was no democracy in Singapore. Businessmen, he contended, spoke in whispers, fearful of government spies.

Tan Siew Sin had never been able to accept the judgment of an interviewer in the *Washington Post* (1965) that Lee is "considered by many to be the most brilliant politician in Southeast Asia today". Tan's dislike of Lee began long before Lee Kuan Yew contemptuously referred to "political eunuchs" in Kuala Lumpur. There are basic differences between the two men. Tan Siew Sin is the president of the Malayan Chinese Association, but does not speak Chinese. According to Dr R. K. Vasil (*Quest*, 1966), Tan contested both the 1959 and 1964 elections in a constituency where sixty-five per cent of the electorate is Malay, "not to prove the point that a Chinese could be returned by a predominantly Malay electorate, but because he could not have got elected from a constituency with a large Chinese vote". Dr Vasil said that Tan Siew Sin is one of the "right kind of leaders" acceptable to, and under the "control" of, the leadership of the Malays.

Lee Kuan Yew, on the other hand, has always been acknowledged to be the leader of the People's Action Party; his eminence has never been challenged, not even in the darkest days. Notwithstanding that, and admitting his talents, Lee Kuan Yew, in the final analysis, is no more than the collective leadership of the People's Action Party. This is the strength he represents. This collective leadership encompasses in Singapore the English-educated, the Chinese-educated, the Malay leadership, and the leadership of the non-Malays and non-Chinese. Whether or not the PAP could survive the sudden removal of Lee Kuan Yew from the scene is debatable. The succession is not automatic, and a struggle for power between the English-educated and the Chinese-educated cannot be ruled out in certain circumstances. It is remarkable that Lee and the other English-educated leaders were so readily accepted by the Chinese-educated masses as their leaders: this was partly because Lee and his colleagues made it their business to learn the Chinese language, which enabled them to make direct contact. It was also due in no small measure to Lee Kuan Yew's dynamic leadership and his political and personal integrity.

II

Early in 1967, at the Delegates' Conference of the Singapore National Trade Union Congress, Lee Kuan Yew explained the need for a new approach to the problem of worker-employer relationships in a developing state moving into industrialization, where most of the industry was in the hands of private enterprise. "Since complete independence," Lee said, "Singapore in a year and a half has experienced vast changes.

"This is a new situation. All slogans relevant under old circumstances are a waste of time now. Great victories scored in the past on behalf of the workers or on behalf of the people of Singapore over old enemies are no longer of any value, other than for the experience we have gained from them. For we face new challenges.

"Change is the very essence of life. The moment we cease to change, to be able to adapt, to adjust, to respond effectively to new situations, we have begun to die. I should be loath to believe that the NTUC is one of those organizations which is dying. It will be a pity, because a lot of work went into it. But I will add this: that what we stand for—not as represented in the NTUC alone but in other associations, bodies and groups—does not intend to die and will not die."

Lee claimed that the position in 1967 was vastly improved...
"We have identified problems—the new ones. We know all the old ones. We have redefined them in so many different ways that everybody is familiar with the new problems. We have not yet succeeded in getting the whole people to get a complete grasp of the problems. But they are with us, identifying, adjusting, thinking, searching for new solutions. And, despite all your shortcomings, the NTUC is also better for the tribulations it has had to go through recently. There is now, at least, an attempt to grasp the realities." (Lee was referring to the strong action taken by the Government against union leaders responsible for calling an illegal strike. They were arrested and convicted.) "Even if we do nothing, each one of us will change, and so will an organization managed by a dozen or so people and with some few hundred delegates. Each individual changes. Every experience we go through registers, alters our responses, our assessments of what we want to do the next time. Even if we do not change—which is impossible—the situation around us, the environment, the policies, the thinking, the ideas, the motivations of the people around us, change...

"Quite a number of the union leaders whom I knew of old could barely sign their names. They were the products of the old generation. They had qualities of leadership: extra amounts of adrenalin and all the other glandular activity that makes people do these things, and some guts to take some risks with their own personal fortunes.

"But the younger generation growing up, who will constitute two-thirds of your membership, are not going to trust their luck to people who cannot sign their names... The disparity will be even greater in their emotional responses, in their attitudes, their values...

"The capacity to anticipate change and, even more important, the determination and the ability to begin to make the changes and adjustments and adaptations now in anticipation of that change which is required, determines how successful we are, not just as individuals but as a group, as representatives of a movement, of a union, of society. This is the crux of life. We have moved from what was a quiet, trading-cum-garrison community into a centre of great intellectual ferment with a mass of two million people, who will never be able to find meaningful lives unless our industrialization programme succeeds, and unless we eventually cease to be dependent on the garrison for our living. There is a changed world. And Britain, seeing her role in the context not of today but of the late 1970s, begins the first steps now...

"Only two under-developed countries in Asia in recent times have made the technological age. The Japanese are one of them. The Chinese are not as advanced industrially as the Japanese... But, by the time people can split the atom and put rockets on the spot where they want them—albeit only a few hundred miles away—a lot of effort must have gone in; a lot of wealth must have gone in, wealth obtained

by hard work. Ask yourself: 'Would I do this for my country?'
"You can easily give up. There are any number of reasons why
we can all collapse. You have heard them. We have no large natural
resources. There are a number of people who can do us in and, in
fact, have an almost irresistible impulse to want to do us in, if for no
other reason than it seems that we are doing all right. This is a fact
of life. Nobody, not even the best computers that man has yet
designed, can draw for you a picture of the world at the end of this
century... But in the immediate future, so far as we are concerned
—never mind what the shape of Southeast Asia is going to be at the
end of this century... I can see two extremes: either a relatively
harmonious, co-operative effort in which constructive endeavour is
the order of the day and standards of life are going up in Southeast
Asia, an endeavour in which we can play a not insignificant part; or
there is a great deal of manipulation of this region by governments
or nations or people with larger economic resources than any of these
nations can ever hope to acquire, either for ideological or purely selfish
national ends. These are the two extremes...

"Whichever way it goes, our position in Southeast Asia will be
immeasurably strengthened if we have well-educated, well-trained, well-
organized trade unions, community associations, political groups to
act cohesively and effectively in pursuance of our collective interest."

III

In May, 1965, after his return from the Socialist Conference in
Bombay, Lee Kuan Yew was asked in a television interview by John
Cantwell of Associated Press what he thought about the future of
socialism in Asia. Lee said, "It depends upon whether the socialists
in the various countries in Asia are realistic...

"I think in all those countries the socialist has got to be realistic
and practical in his approach. If you are going to have a planned
economy, take over everything, plan your economy before you have
got your technicians and your technocrats, how do you do it unless
you have a really big power who says, 'Look, let me help you and
train these men for you'? Whereas, if you take a more pragmatic
approach and say, 'Well, all right, let's build up these skills and this
capacity for industrial production, half-socialist, half-capitalist, and
let the future be decided by the next generation,' I think you will
make better progress. We haven't driven out the capitalists in Singapore; we are doing fairly well. But we have redistributed the
benefits of industrial and economic activity in Singapore in a much
fairer way."

CHAPTER EIGHT

The English Language

IN 1956, Lee Kuan Yew was speaking strongly against the policy of the colonialist-dominated Singapore Government to encourage the use of the English language in education. In debate in the Assembly (on 12 April, 1956) Lee said he thought it fitting that someone who was English-educated should oppose this trend. He explained why. Every time he spoke the English language, he said, "there is a sense—I would not say of humiliation—but definitely of inadequacy, that I have not the same facility and control over my own language. That is something you must understand, or you will not understand what is happening in Asia."

He continued: "May I put it, without apologies, in a very personal way? We all like to live our lives again through our children. We know that we should do what is best for them. But unconsciously we do for them what we wish our parents had done for us. When I was born the British Navy ruled the waves. My grandfather, who was a chin-chew on a steamship between Indonesia and Singapore, had the greatest respect for the British Navy. He made a great deal of money because, he said, there was no piracy in Malayan waters. He lived until he saw the *Prince of Wales* sunk by Japanese aeroplanes. Imagine it, aeroplanes, made in Japan, sank the *Prince of Wales*! He died shortly afterwards. I am sure that the sinking of the *Prince of Wales* had nothing to do with his death, but I think an age had passed with him. I was sent to an English school to equip me for an English university in order that I could then be an educated man—the equal of any Englishman—the model of perfection! I do not know how far they have succeeded in that. I grew up, and finally graduated. At the end of it, I felt—and it was long before I entered politics, in fact it is one of the reasons why I am here—that the whole set of values was wrong, fundamentally and radically wrong. When I read Nehru—and I read a lot of Nehru—I understood him when he said: 'I cry when I think that I cannot speak my own mother tongue as well as I can speak the English language.' I am a less emotional man. I do not usually cry, or tear my hair, or tear paper, or tear my shirt off, but that does not mean that I feel any the less strongly about it. My son is not going to an English school. He will not be a model Englishman. I hope, of course, that he will know enough English to converse with his father on matters other than the weather. I hope also that in time to come I will know enough Malay to converse with him on the problems of humidity and heat control in the tropics. But whatever the difficulties in family relationships, he is going to be part of Asia, part of Malaya."

What Lee was seeking to emphasize then, in 1956, was that an age was passing, an age in Malaya and Singapore in which the English and the English-educated ruled the roost. Soon, he predicted, Malay would be accepted as the national language.

Lee was in opposition when he made the speech; he was a nationalist leader. The Bandung Conference had recently been held; Asian nationalism was on the march. He was partly right, in that the English soon did not rule the roost—they had no wish anyhow to continue —but it would have been difficult for Lee Kuan Yew then to have imagined that within ten years the vast majority of the people in Singapore would be sending their children to English schools in preference to Chinese or Malay schools. Malay is the national language of Malaysia and of the Republic of Singapore. In Malaysia it is the sole official language; in Singapore it is one of four official languages, but English is the language of government, the courts, commerce and the University. Lee's PAP Government put an emphasis upon the English language because it is the language of commerce and industry.

This reason for using English was just as valid in 1956 as it is in 1970, but Singapore in 1956 was struggling to become independent of the British through merger with Malaya, and appropriate gestures, such as qualified condemnation of the colonialist's language and an acceptance of Malay in those circumstances, were understandable. But Lee Kuan Yew never expected the Malaysian Government to try to make Malay the sole official language by 1967. He thought that Malayan self-interest would ensure a slow tolerant process spread over many years, because to do otherwise would threaten to disrupt the economy, in addition to causing social stresses among the different races. It is a difficult and, indeed, a profitless exercise to try to imagine what might have happened if the Malaysian Government had tried in 1967 to force the adoption of the Malay language in Singapore, had Singapore remained a part of Malaysia.

In 1956, Lee Kuan Yew held the view that "Nothing that anybody can do in or out of Malaya will alter the fact that there will be two dominant languages and cultures in Malaya. These are the facts in our population figures. The Malay language and the Malay culture will irresistibly become the predominant language and the predominant culture. The Chinese language and the Chinese culture, particularly in view of the tremendous renaissance that it has undergone in China, will occupy a very important place in Malaya... but Chinese culture as it will be in Malaya 200 years from now is not likely to be what Chinese culture will be 200 years from now in China. This is inevitable."

In 1970 it could be argued that Singapore survived as a democracy because the English-educated, led by Lee Kuan Yew, defeated the more Left-wing Chinese-educated to produce an energetic, progressive government which was ready to work, as the government of an independent sovereign state, with Western technology, and with European nations, as well as with non-communist Asia, while maintaining a neutralist attitude towards states of all ideologies. In Malaya, on the other hand, the conservative English-educated Malay leadership, the dominant force in government, more eagerly seeks confirmation of its power from its own people; and the emphasis on the Malay language, Malay rights, and the building of mosques in village and towns is a manifestation of this deliberate policy.

CHAPTER NINE

Leadership and Religion

I

AFTER eight years in office, though still a young man, Lee Kuan Yew in 1967 began to think a great deal about a continuing leadership in Singapore. Undoubtedly he was perturbed by the struggle for power in China and the military coups in Africa. He knew many of the African leaders personally. Unexpectedly, he accepted an invitation in April, 1967, to speak at a meeting on youth leadership training sponsored by the East Asia Christian Conference.

"I have been asked," Lee Kuan Yew said, "to talk about the problems of leadership, particularly of youth leadership, in the context of the unfinished revolutions of South and Southeast Asia. First, there is no such thing as a finished revolution. Nobody really knows when a revolutionary era began, when it ended, when a non-revolutionary era then commenced. But it will make my task simpler if we define this problem in rather prosaic terms.

"So far as modern jargon is concerned, 'revolution' in South and Southeast Asia means the expulsion of foreign dominators, primarily European dominators. That is the beginning of revolution. Does the end of revolution come with the expulsion of these foreign dominators and the assumption of power by local digits? If so, then the revolutions are over, for there is no part of South and Southeast Asia in which non-indigenous or non-Asian powers are in authority.

"But I do know one thing: that whilst in colonial-ruled Asia there was no problem of leadership, whether of a political or a purely social nature, in the Asia that we see today there is a genuine problem of leadership and succession to leadership.

"In the old days, one governor came, served his term, impressed his superiors—in London in the case of the British territories, in Amsterdam in the case of the Dutch-controlled territories, in Paris for the French Indo-China territories, or in Washington in the case of the Philippines. So a constant stream of authority and leadership was provided.

"Now these societies have assumed the right to govern themselves. And, in many of these countries, people, because their glands worked more vigorously than others, or for a diversity of reasons, were dissatisfied with the existing situation, and they upset the system. Now they are saddled with the responsibility—having upset the old order— of establishing a new one that will provide a meaningful life to their own people.

"In South and Southeast Asia, there are societies· which are confronted with the awesome problem—often, the very daunting task—of catching up with 200 to 300 years of somebody else's progress. You have tilled the earth the way your ancestors have always done and eked out a living of some sort. The sun, the rain provided you with some kind of livelihood; some form of irrigation; some primitive instruments with which to get some kind of succour from the earth. And the world has, meanwhile, passed you by. Then, all of a sudden, you decide that you must also join this race to the moon—you believe it to be desirable. These are societies in a stage of transition.

"The first generation, the post-war generation of people who led these countries to independence, are passing away. In some places, they already have. In India, Pakistan and in other parts of South and Southeast Asia, the people who grew up, their whole being just wanting to displace an existing injustice, have exhausted their task. A new generation has grown up, for whom the British Raj, colonialism, and all the rest of it, are but a vague memory: stories from their fathers and grandfathers. Poverty, ignorance, ineptitude, corruption, ineffective administration are what they know. This is the problem of the second generation leadership.

"I came this evening, although I am not a Christian, because I believe that young people—whether they are Christians or otherwise— are always fired with that inexhaustible reserve called idealism, and they have it in greater store than most people. And it is a very necessary ingredient for any sustained human effort. You must believe that certain things are worth the effort. In large parts of the newly-independent countries the easy, soft way comes naturally. You have done your stint, fighting for independence. You are now in authority, and there is nothing to prevent you from putting yourself in a position where, for the rest of your life (at least theoretically), you can fulfil your heart's desires. Acquisition of wealth and the pandering to one's appetite for the good things of life become simple.

"So we are confronted, now, with this problem of succession. The first generation, whatever the reasons which motivated them, have got rid of the past and the people who ruled and ordered that society. But have they got it in them now to create a situation, a system, in which succeeding generations can build upon what they have? This is the problem. Any society needs leadership. The established ones have their system. I am most familiar with the British system because that is where I had most contacts. It had a ruling elite, with public schools, universities, designed to bring forth qualities of leadership. How do you create it, in this area, without tradition, without a past to fall back on? Can it be created? Can you talent-scout? Can you, in fact, prejudge twenty or thirty years before a man matures that he is likely to make a more-than-above-average contribution? My presence here this evening is, in part, a participation in that exercise.

"Somewhere in the church hierarchy or in the Young Men's Christian Association some people are demonstrating more-than-above-average activity, intelligence, verve, drive, ambition, civic consciousness. The wastage rate is very high. No Rhodes Scholar—and they assess these people extremely carefully—has ever become a national leader of any distinction. These scholars are chosen at university level, very carefully. What are the qualities of leadership? Integrity, drive, verve, intelligence, physical and mental discipline. And yet, no Rhodes Scholar has ever become a prime minister or president of any of the English-speaking countries of the world. But a good number of them have become very good second-rank leaders—permanent secretaries, under-secretaries and so on.

"No president of the Oxford Union or Cambridge Union Debating Societies has in the past twenty years become the Prime Minister of Great Britain. Theirs were not the qualities that were required: wit and witticism have their uses, but not in looking after the destiny of a people. What is it then? This is the problem with Asia.

"At least these established societies, whatever their shortcomings, did contrive some system which, in a broad stream of talent, provided every now and again the more-than-average performer to give leadership. Being confronted with this problem myself, I have often asked, 'How do we ensure succession?'—not on the basis of 'I like A, therefore I groom A for leadership.'

"Unless you want long periods of anarchy and chaos, you have to create a self-continuing—not a self-perpetuating but a self-continuing—power structure. Human beings should be equal. But

59

they never are. Some can do more; some can give more of themselves than others. How do we anticipate that? Why is it that often we can't? The Chairman of the Chinese Communist Party is undergoing tribulation at the moment. Who is to succeed him? Hitler tried to designate his successor. It would have been interesting to have known whether his choice was the right one—if, in fact, a successor had become necessary. Churchill lingered on for years as Prime Minister. And it is said by many a diarist that he wasn't quite sure of the qualities of his successor.

"The problem is that the human being is unable yet to assess this thing called 'character'. You can assess a man's intelligence: set him tests, then rate his I Q; and you can say, 'Well, you are 141 as against 100.' Of course, if you have a leader with a good I Q, that helps—because you don't have to go through the memorandum or the minutes with him three times over and explain what it means. You just have to go through three-quarters of the way and he has seen the last one-quarter that you want to lead him to.

"It is amazing the number of highly intelligent persons in the world who make no contribution at all to the well-being of their fellowmen. And it is this as yet unascertainable or rather as yet unmeasurable quality called 'character' which, plus your mental capacity or knowledge or discipline, makes for leadership. . .

"Obviously people like Nehru and Gandhi must have believed passionately in what they wanted to do, to have gone through what they did and survived it and succeeded. How do they ensure that an unending stream of such people are brought forth?

"Hence, you go back all the time to youth. Because that is the age of idealism. You are then fired by what you think to be right and just. But many will fall by the wayside because of personal ambition, personal weaknesses, desire to compromise and to temporize. The problem of all countries in Asia is how to establish some system which will bring forth an unending stream of people with character.

"True, Khrushchev never went to a university; neither did Stalin. Mao, it seems, spent some time in the libraries of Peking University. But if you leave these things to chance, then you are taking chances with your own people's lives and destinies. So it is that in the established societies—in Britain, the United States, large parts of Western Europe, even in Australia—all their leadership comes from a broad stratum of people who have gone to universities. It is so much better if, as well as being an *enfant terrible* like Khrushchev, a person also goes through a systematic course of discipline, learns all the basic norms, what history has to offer and human experience has to offer, and then takes over that leadership. But there are large parts of Asia where this is not the case. The idealism that fired a leader in his early stages,

60

instead of staying with him to the end and making him want to pass the torch on to a younger generation, is corrupted and debased in the process, and leaders lose interest in the future beyond their lifetimes. And so, automatically, you go on to military leadership. When you pass from a leadership, endowed at least with some political motivations, to one which is there as of might, then the future becomes extremely problematical, unless there are other leavening influences which can counteract the corrupting tendencies of power.

"I would like to ask you to ponder on some of these problems. It is not that I have the answers to them. . . These are problems which will beset us for a long time to come. Without values, convictions. . . this was a point which a French Catholic who was kept in Buchenwald Camp made: the people who most contained themselves and survived the experiences of Buchenwald were either those with deep religious beliefs like himself, or those with deep political convictions and dogma, like the communist. . . If they were not communists or deeply religious, they were people with deep and abiding beliefs in certain tenets as to what the human being should and must be. For, in adversity, you fall back on your faith and what you think the human being should be and should do. If you haven't that faith, then you succumb.

"This is the problem with many of the political leaderships in this area. You start off with idealism, you should end up in maturity with a great deal of sophistication giving a gloss to that idealism. But what usually happens is a great deal of erosion by the soft and baneful influence of power, leaving almost nothing of the idealism behind and only the professionalism of political leadership without its leavening values.

"For the Christians who are confronted with this milieu in South and Southeast Asia it is an extremely difficult task. First, they are a minority in a largely non-Christian region. Second, because Christianity is closely identified with the West and Europe, they are therefore —except for very special situations in certain parts of Southeast Asia —suspect. . .

"You may, therefore, ask me the final question: why is it I waste my time with my own Christians if, in fact, they are suspect? If, in fact, they can pose no challenge to the non-Christian leadership? My answer is: because I really do not know what is the ultimate answer. Man gropes forward towards progress. One thing I do know: that it is universal states and universal religions—as Toynbee has analyzed—that really bring the whole of mankind forward. It is only when you offer a man—without distinctions based on ethnic, cultural, linguistic and other differences—a chance of belonging to this great human community, that you offer him a peaceful way forward to progress and to a higher level of human life.

"And I think the Christians, if they understand the milieu in which they are working in South and Southeast Asia, can make their contribution, a ferment, without which it is very difficult, as Toynbee has said, to climb the sharp face of the cliff towards a higher ledge in human civilization. In your own way, you have brought together diverse peoples, diverse cultural, ethnic, linguistic and social backgrounds..."

II

Lee is not a religious man in a formal sense. Speaking at the opening ceremony of the Congregation of Buddhists-from Asia early in 1967, at the Pho Kark See Temple, in Singapore, the Prime Minister said that in many respects "we in Singapore present a unique example of the new society which will manifest itself more and more as human transportation becomes easier and easier and communities of different races, creeds and languages begin to intermix.

"Throughout the history of human civilizations, there has always been a coincidence of the power of the church and the power of the state—from very ancient times, from very tribal conditions to the more sophisticated civilizations of the universal state and the universal church.

"There have always been parallel sets of authorities for the material and the spiritual needs of a society. And sometimes the church has wielded final authority and, sometimes, as in recent times, the state.

"In Southeast Asia, as power is transferred from alien European minorities back to the indigenous population, a problem of transition occurs in which temporal power has been handed to a group of elected representatives who depend upon the support of the majority opinion of the population, who, in turn, are open to influences of prevailing religions which had existed before the Europeans came. And so there is a dichotomy between the state and the church. And where this dichotomy becomes acute, then trials and tribulations are the lot of that society—whether it is prime ministers who get assassinated, or riots which take place in the precincts of the holy walls of a temple.

"In Singapore, we are trying to prevent any recrudescence of the assertion of the right of a majority religious group to dominate or coerce others into similar beliefs. It is true that our constitution means that temporal power is vested in those who are elected and who are, therefore, able to command the support of the majority of the population. It is true that there are one or two religions which would probably be able to command the allegiance of a majority of the population. But it is not true that if we were to allow this to happen the sum total of human happiness would be increased.

"We have seen what happens in other parts of the world where a majority seeks to coerce a minority—whether it is religious, racial, linguistic—into conforming, and seeks to use its influence over the majority of the population to invoke the administrative capacity of the modern state to bring about conformity. The end result then must be a retrogressive one, for I do not believe that we can increase the sum total of human happiness by pushing back the clock. The open society—open to all the influences of a world grown smaller through man's means of rapid communication—must face up to these problems of multi-cultures, multi-religions and multi-languages.

"And, alone in Southeast Asia, we are a state without an established church. There are others, who officially proclaim this policy of the secular state being conducive to the happiness of their community, but who are now facing tremendous pressures from the majority sect to use the powers of the state to bring about conformity and compliance by minorities. Whether their secular societies will continue to progress and prosper and ensure the continuance of tolerance, goodwill and forbearance amongst different groups with different social and religious practices depends upon the capacity of the temporal power to resist these encroachments. But alas, there are other states that actively create and strengthen their religious support.

"We are unique in that all religions are free to flourish. And as with this temple, so it is with all the other churches and places of worship in Singapore. Obviously, to be able to flourish without the revenues of the state backing it, it must tend to the spiritual needs of some sections of the community—and to the good. But where the state exercises its supreme powers of extraction of revenue to solidly back one particular institution, it must mean, in the end, the gradual erosion of the freedoms of the other communities and the adherents of other religions to seek their own solace and their own spiritual salvation.

"It is not for us to prophesy what is to happen in the countries around us. But it is within our capacity to determine that in our society this shall not happen. And whether it is ten thousand Sikhs in Singapore following the practices of a Guru which established them into a separate religious group a few hundred years ago, or whether it is the persuasive, absorbing beliefs of the Buddhist, the Government holds the scales fairly and justly between all. Not because there is any virtue in this, or that there will be salvation from all sects for members of the government in after-life in all the various places for the repose of the soul, but because we are convinced that in this way we ensure the greatest happiness of the greatest number whilst we are here on earth. . ."

III

In a speech at the third centenary birthday celebrations of Sri Guru Govind Singh (14 January, 1967) Lee Kuan Yew again revealed something of his practical approach to religion.

"I am an empiricist," he said. "I start off with what I find I have got. And I know that I have ten thousand people of Sikh descent or Sikh immigrants in Singapore; and I would like all of Singapore to know that they are a valuable contribution to the life, the vitality, the success and the prosperity of our society...

"Like you, I am a migrant. I have left my past behind me. But, like you, I understand that man needs more than bread alone to live. And whilst we are trying to seek the largest number of common denominators amongst ourselves, we should not lightly throw out of the window the virtues, the doctrines which have held whole groups of people together in a righteous and goodly life.

"There are great advantages in rapid assimilation or integration. And all migrant communities must seek this eventual homogeneity— some common milieu which makes you and I—whether you are Sikh and I am Chinese or he is Tamil, or Malay, or Ceylonese—part of a separate society. The Americans did it. It took them some four hundred years." He said that it was his abiding belief that "perhaps in matters of culture, values and moral standards it is best to make haste slowly".

Lee added: "My friends may celebrate the birthday of Confucius. You may celebrate the 330th birthday of Guru Govind Singh... And eventually, that common milieu in which you and I live should give us a sufficiency of being and feeling together to want to continue to live and to be one people. Because, in the end, that is our only way out. I do not believe that these things can be legislated for. Finally, you must feel that this is worth building, this is worth belonging to. If you don't, then it will be very sad because you must look for something else. But, if you do, then, like me, all the time you will be thinking how we can make our future more secure; how we can ensure that what we have built will not go to waste..."

CHAPTER TEN

Can Democracy Survive?

I

THERE has always been, and there still is, a fair amount of scepticism about the survival of the parliamentary system of democracy in Malaysia and Singapore. True, the Earl of Canning in his Minute of 1859 believed that, "democratic in spite of the outward form of their own government, enterprising and persevering", the Chinese in Singapore were "imbued with a strong tendency to self-government", but the Earl must have been thinking more of their talent for looking after their own affairs than of their interest in self-government in the national, as distinct from the clan and community, sense. Indeed, their complete lack of interest in self-government at state level is borne out by the fact that up until the end of the Second World War, the Chinese in Singapore were most reluctant even to lend a hand in governing the Colony. Early efforts to introduce a form of self-government, through participation in municipal work, were actually resisted. In 1910 the Municipalities Ordinance of 1896 was still in force, at least in theory: the town was split into five wards to be represented by Commissioners elected by qualified voters, and by Commissioners appointed by the Government, the advantage being with the elected members in the event of there being an odd number of Commissioners. The intention was that the ratepayers should to a large extent administer municipal affairs. But after fourteen years it was generally agreed that the experiment had failed. There were few men of leisure in the Colony who were also competent to perform the necessary work. People came to Singapore to work hard, to speculate, to make money and go away again. They were not interested in self-government, nationalism, or, in fact, in anything other than conditions which would provide them with reasonable opportunities for the acquisition of wealth.

This early move towards democracy was therefore withdrawn as being unworkable, and the Governor appointed a Board, consisting of representatives of the prominent communities, to keep an eye on municipal affairs. This Board was given limited power, the measure of which can be gauged from the fact that it could not adopt or reject the Budget. It was not until 1949 that Singapore again held elections for the municipality. A short while earlier, Singapore had elected six Assemblymen to the newly-formed Legislative Council. Democracy in all its forms, especially trade unionism, surged forward—an aftermath of the war. A Labour Party came into being in 1948, too late to take part in the Legislative Council elections, but it managed to win a seat in the first municipal election held in April, 1949. The Progressive Party, formed in 1947, won thirteen seats. The Progressive Party won three of the six elected seats in the newly-formed Legislative Council

When Singapore went to the polls in 1955 to elect members to a partly elected, partly nominated legislature, seven political parties sought the voters' favour, including the newly-formed People's Action Party which put up a token number of candidates headed by Lee Kuan Yew. Three were elected. Five years later, in 1959, there were fourteen political parties. Most of them disappeared soon after the elections were held. When the Barisan Sosialis in 1966 decided to abandon the parliamentary struggle, the People's Action Party found itself without an opposition in Parliament. (Barisan Sosialis is Malay for Socialist Front. It is, in fact, a communist-front organization.) By 1967 the PAP, through winning by-elections caused by the Barisan Sosialis vacancies, occupied 49 of the 51 seats. The other two had been held since 1963 by Barisan Members of Parliament gone underground to avoid arrest for subversion. The Speaker revealed that he had received a letter from the two Barisan Sosialis Members of Parliament asking for "leave of absence until such time as the Government can guarantee us security and freedom from arbitrary detention". Both M.P.s disappeared on 8 October, 1963, when the Malaysian Government arrested subversive and anti-Malaysian elements during a strike called by the communists' open-front trade union movement.

In the best parliamentary tradition, the Speaker replied: "In view of your dilemma, I hereby grant you leave to be absent from all future sittings of the Assembly until such time as you are able to be present."

In the 1968 general elections 51 PAP candidates were returned unopposed. Five Independents and two members of the Workers' Party challenged the other seven PAP candidates. All seven PAP candidates, including the Prime Minister, were elected. Once again the Singapore Parliament was a single-party affair, in accordance with the wishes of the electorate.

This state of affairs has caused people to wonder whether parliamentary democracy can survive in Singapore. Lee Kuan Yew's own attitude is that the basic essential of democracy, the right to vote out an oppressive or inefficient or corrupt government, still obtains. By-elections and general elections guarantee the people's inherent right to elect their own representatives to govern them: if they want to elect fifty-one members of the People's Action Party would it be democratic to deny them that privilege? In any case, adds Lee Kuan Yew, the real opposition to the PAP and democracy is the oldest political party in Singapore, and that is the underground Malayan Communist Party.

Both Sir Richard Winstedt and Lennox A. Mills, two knowledgeable scholars, among others, have questioned whether democracy is suitable for the Malays, or liked by the Chinese. Mills, in his book *Malaya: A Political and Economic Appraisal*, came to the conclusion that the mass of the Chinese population (in Malaya and Singapore) are not interested in democracy. They still believe that "governments exist to be placated, to be evaded or to be bought when they are oppressive: to be patiently obeyed at other times". In Mills' view "they do not share the ideas which lie at the root of Western democracy. Whether they will be willing to acquire them and cease to think as Chinese is a question of the future. It is not likely that they will show any sudden enthusiasm for Western democracy." Mills wrote that in 1957. Much has changed in Singapore (and Malaya) in ten years.

Mills had similar views about the Malays. UMNO leaders, he pointed out, were drawn largely from the Malay aristocracy. They were followed by a minority of politically conscious Malays. Mills said the leaders used the language of democracy, but it was doubtful, in his view, whether in doing this they voiced the aspirations of the peasant majority. The peasants had a tradition of leadership by the aristocracy, and they continued to follow their leaders as they had done in the past. They looked to them to defend their Malay way of life. In economics the Malay leaders were conservative: they were opposed to the nationalization of foreign industry, and they hoped to attract more outside capital.

In Singapore, the 1963 elections proved that not all of Mills' conclusions were correct, at least not so far as urban Malays were concerned, for every single UMNO candidate was defeated, in spite of a call from Tunku Abdul Rahman, by an anti-UMNO multiracialist opponent.

Winstedt, in his book *The Malays* (1961 edition), questioned whether democracy, although successful in Europe, suited the needs of Asia. He believed that the only way to see beyond one's nose for the promotion of racial welfare was to "review the effect of past practice and endeavour, and to study the social, political, economic and spiritual history of the race that is to be the subject of experiment". He offered no solution, except to remind his readers that the best government is the best administration.

B. W. Hodder *(Man in Malaya,* 1959) warned that democracy in Malaya could involve the speedy economic and political suppression of the Malays by Chinese and Indians. "Should popular elections on Western lines be fully adopted, Chinese could be in effective control of this key to the Pacific—a fact in which Australia and New Zealand, as well as America and Great Britain, must be interested." The Alliance Government may have had this in mind when in 1960 it amended the Constitution to ensure that Malaya was not divided into one hundred federal constituencies on the basis of the near-equality of registered voters rather than population, which is what the Constitution called for. The Constitution would have given the non-Malay communities a greater measure of political power. The Alliance amended to one hundred and four constituencies which are so drawn as to favour the Malay vote. This perhaps is what Hodder had in mind when he spoke of the possibility of Malay suppression if elections were held on Western lines. The Alliance Government also decided against holding popular elections for town councils in 1965, fearing, with some justification, that they could all be won by the Chinese urban vote for the People's Action Party. The official explanation was that "the country is at war against the Indonesians, the communist terrorists and their sympathizers and agents". No town council elections have been held since Indonesia's confrontation ended.

Derek Cooper, in a BBC broadcast, once asked Lee Kuan Yew what he meant by the word "democratic". Lee said he used the word in the sense normally understood: "that there is some measure of popular will, of popular support; that, from time to time, as accurately as is possible with trying to find out what human beings in a large group want or feel or think, one tries to act in accordance with the wishes of the majority."

Lee's basic belief in democracy is founded on the one-man-one-vote principle for the election of people's representatives. He is also on record as saying that Western-type parliamentary democracy may have to be adjusted to fit the needs and requirements of Asian peoples.

II

Lee Kuan Yew thought out loud about the future of the one-man-one-vote system of government in Southeast Asia at Chatham House in May, 1962. He was not optimistic. He did not think it would come about in Southeast Asia for various reasons. But the present generation of leaders in this particular phase in Singapore and Malaysia envisaged a continuance of the system, and they saw in this a workable solution to prevent communist manipulation of Chinese sentiment on behalf of the communists.

Lee Kuan Yew said that in Malaysia the China-born Chinese were not communists, and that that was important. "They are for themselves, with all their prejudices and pride in their ancient culture and civilization." Ninety-nine per cent of the Malayan Communist Party were Chinese. They had fought for seventeen years, from 1945, to establish a Soviet Republic based on the efforts and sacrifices of the Chinese. They could not conceive of a situation in which communism could come to Malaya without their efforts. And they used the obvious and simple method of winning more people over to communism by pointing to the illustrious example of China. "The result is that they win more recruits from the Chinese into the Malayan Communist Party and present communism to the non-Chinese in Malaya as Chinese imperialism, and so get themselves more and more isolated in this Chinese world. The Malays watching this have a tremendous fear that their position will be jeopardized, and they therefore play around their traditional leaders."

Lee said that Tunku Abdul Rahman, a traditional leader of the Malays, had proved over seven years of his leadership that he was unlikely to be disputed as the Malay leader for a long time, "and certainly for as long as the Malayan Communist Party pursues this stupid policy of augmenting their strength on the basis of the prestige and reputation of China, making an appeal only to the Chinese".

Lee said there were vagaries about the system of one-man-one-vote "which I think makes it an extremely hazardous system to run anywhere in the under-developed and the under-educated world. . . We are not exceptional: we are neither more intelligent nor better educated than many of our neighbours. We have been more fortunately endowed and enjoy a better standard of living, but I do not think the basic factors are materially different. Where the majority of your population is semi-literate, it responds more to the carrot than to the stick, and politicians at election time cannot use the stick, so this leads to a situation where he who bids the highest wins. At a time when you want harder work with less return and more capital investment, one-man-one-vote produces just the opposite. The offer of more return with less work ends up in bankruptcy. I do not think it is a coincidence that it has flopped in Pakistan, did not succeed in Burma, nearly came to grief in Ceylon... It has been abandoned, decried and condemned in Indonesia, and it is not held in esteem anywhere in Asia. It is not a tradition with the Malays nor with the Chinese to count heads: their custom has always been to listen to the dictum of the elder... I think it will endure in Malaya for some time, but for how long, I do not know. I should imagine that with every passing year there will be mutations made on the system in order to make it still work. We all know that barely five months ago the Tunku brought in several basic amendments to the Constitution, a constitution drafted by five eminent jurists from five Commonwealth countries. They settled in Rome and drafted what was jurisprudentially a sensible and an elegant constitution—but it was not going to work. Very wisely, the Tunku decided that he would change bits and pieces. It was my unfortunate burden to attend a Law Society dinner shortly after that in the University, where a somewhat idealistic president of that society decried the fact that the Tunku had already moved 137 amendments, 'more amendments than there are articles in his Constitution'. Gratuitously I defended the need for making something work even if it meant departing from my norms; and I should be surprised if in the course of the next five years there are not as many amendments as there were in the past five years..."

Asked if it were not true that if democratic one-man-one-vote rule is abandoned military dictatorship follows, Lee Kuan Yew said he did not think the proposition was valid. "What I think is valid as a general proposition is that the system of cutting up the country in accordance with the number of adult citizens of given proportions, to elect representatives who then elect amongst like-minded people a cabinet, which then elects a *primus inter pares* amongst the cabinet, is one which presupposes so many basic conditions, which are often non-existent, that I do not think it will ever work. They have all been superseded by systems which give power effectively to one man or a group of men for an indefinite period. Government to be effective must at least give the impression of enduring, and a government which is open to the vagaries of the ballot box when the people who put their crosses in the ballot boxes are not illiterate but semi-literate, which is worse, is a government which is already weakened before it starts to govern." Lee remarked that he said this with no desire to explain away his own problem, but he added: "If I were in authority in Singapore indefinitely, without having to ask those who are governed whether they like what is being done, then I have not the slightest doubt that I could govern much more effectively in their own interests. That is a fact which the educated understand, but we are all caught

70

in this system which the British export all over the place hoping that somewhere it will take root. . . "

The Prime Minister spoke of the difficulties of a one-man-one-vote government in a developing country trying to achieve economic growth through the application of harsh measures. He doubted whether there would ever have been an Industrial Revolution in Britain if there had been a one-man-one-vote system of government. "Mao Tse-tung," he ventured, "would lose his deposit if he had to stand for election today."

CHAPTER ELEVEN

The Malays and the Chinese

I

SINGAPORE and Malaysian politics will be incomprehensible and an appreciation of Lee Kuan Yew as a politician and a leader will be difficult, without at least a rudimentary knowledge of the Malay people and their Press, and something, too, about the Chinese and, to a much lesser extent, the Indians.

The Chinese in Singapore lived for many years in a closely-knit exclusive society, in the sense that Chinese of many different tribes did not mingle with non-Chinese, and there was a great deal of clanishness among the Chinese themselves. In 1857, for example, there were 70,000 Chinese in Singapore, and not a single European resident understood their language. In the beginning, the British colonialists were mainly interested in them as traders, artisans, and colonizers: they were not concerned with their social behaviour, so long as the Chinese did not interfere with their authority and behaved themselves. The Chinese, like other communities, were only too pleased to accept this arrangement, since it guaranteed them the maximum freedom to lead their own peculiarly Chinese lives under the protection of the British.

Serious riots among quarrelling and criminal elements of the Chinese community, however, eventually forced the British to intervene and to provide sound administration for the people of Singapore as a whole. In 1889 the secret societies were suppressed, but it was not until 1920 that the colonial government began to supervise, and give grants-in-aid to Chinese schools.

For many reasons, mainly because of the Muslim religion, few Chinese married outside their own community, even though, for many years, the sex ratio among the Chinese was ten females to every thousand males, a state of affairs due partly to China's unwillingness to let women go abroad, and partly to the fact that a new arrival in Singapore could not afford to keep a wife.

"Why did we come here? To find a livelihood and to get rich. My great-grandfather came here from China to seek a living, just like the others," declared Lee Kuan Yew (in a speech in 1967). But, as Dr Maurice Freedman said (May, 1959), the general economic success of the Chinese abroad could not have been due to any special business training in China because the commercial class played too small a role in the emigration. Most of them were peasants and artisans. The first Chinese bank in Singapore, for example, was established by an emigrant who came to Singapore as a carpenter at the age of sixteen. He was Wong Ah Fook. He became a contractor, then a planter. Soon he was employing a large labour force and he paid them with his own notes. These circulated within the bounds of his extensive estates. Starting a public bank seemed just another natural step forward. Wong was then thirty-six years old: he was already a very rich man.

That is an example of the point stressed by Dr Freedman: that the peasant Chinese was and is above all a hard worker, and that the prosperity of a great many of the first generation of Southeast Asian Chinese generally rested on their industriousness. But, argued Freedman, the ability of Chinese to work hard could not of itself have been a sufficient reason for their progress in the amassing of riches. "They accumulated wealth because, in comparison with the people among whom they came to live, they were highly sophisticated in the handling of money. At the outset, they knew not only how to work themselves, but also how to make their money work." Dr Freedman went on to say: "Shrewdness in handling money was an important part of the equipment which ordinary Chinese took with them when they went overseas in search of a livelihood. Their financial skill rested above all on three characteristics of the society in which they were raised: the respectability of the pursuit of riches, relative immunity of surplus wealth from confiscation by political superiors, and the legitimacy of careful and interested financial dealings between neighbours and even kinsmen." The Chinese were economically successful in Southeast Asia (and nowhere so successful as in Singapore). The Singapore Chinese used their wealth to develop Johore and other parts of Malaya as well as Singapore, "not simply because they were energetic immigrants, but more fundamentally because in their quest for riches they knew how to handle money and organize men in relation to money".

A Malay, according to the Constitution of Malaya (31 August, 1957), "means a person who professes the Muslim religion, habitually speaks the Malay language, conforms to Malay customs..." In Singapore in 1966, a Malay community leader, Inche Ahmad Haji Taff, told a Constitutional Commission that a Malay could be of another race provided he met these three conditions: it did not matter where he was born—Indonesia, England, India, anywhere.

An unexpected witness at this Commission was the Reverend Adam Ibrahim, an Anglican padre, and a Malay. He said that there were not more than ten Malays in Singapore who had become Christians. To his personal knowledge there were four or five. There are some 300,000 Malays in Singapore. The Reverend Ibrahim objected to a Malay being described as a person who must necessarily profess the Islamic faith, because this meant that a Malay would not have the right to embrace any religion of his choice. Besides, it was unfair that privileges normally given to Malays should be denied to those not professing Islam, although they were born Malays, as he was.

In Singapore, he said, "the law may control or restrict the propagation of any religious doctrine or belief among persons professing the Muslim religion". There is, in fact, no law which specifically forbids Christians to propagate their faith among Muslims, but there is a tacit understanding that it is not done. The Reverend Adam Ibrahim insisted that everyone, including Malays, should have the right to profess any religion of his choice. The parson is a most unusual Malay. Most Malays in Singapore would consider that he is not a "real Malay". How could he be if he rejected Islam? Race and religion are closely interwoven, even among progressive Singapore Malays.

Dr Judith Djamour, in her study, *Malay Kinship and Marriage in Singapore* (1950), noted that the Singapore Chinese on the whole considered the acquisition of wealth to be one of the most important aims in life, and also an end in itself. They were indefatigable workers and keen businessmen. Singapore Malays, on the other hand, attached great importance to easy and graceful living. Their attitude, Dr Djamour said, was: what was the use of earning a large salary if one could not rest and have some leisure? Dr Djamour said that the Malays were acutely aware that they were an economically depressed group. They frequently contrasted their status with that of the Chinese. They willingly admitted there were many very poor Chinese, but then they added: "But look at the big houses and the large cars in Singapore. Whom do they belong to? To the Chinese."

On the other hand, most Malays readily stated that their community was not a rich one partly because Malays are not good businessmen and are not sufficiently industrious in accumulating capital and investing it profitably. "They do not like to work hard in order

74

to acquire greater wealth, but prefer to spend what they earn, as they earn it."

Instead of striking at the root causes of this attitude through education, racially inclined Malay leaders advocate, and apparently believe possible, an adjustment, "as in a game of golf", as Tun Razak, then Malaysia's Deputy Prime Minister, put it in a speech in 1965, between ruthless Chinese businessmen and ambitious untrained Malay aspirants. Tun Razak argued that the Malays were economically backward and needed to be helped, "so that they could have the same advantages as the others. In golf, if a player was new, he was given a handicap so that he could enjoy the game." In the interests of "all-round welfare, peace and security," he stated, "we have to make the Malays feel happy". If, Tun Razak added, they did not have special rights they would feel unsafe, and remain backward.

Lee Kuan Yew and the People's Action Party agreed to special rights for Malays when Singapore was part of Malaysia (though they thought they would be of little value to the mass of the poor Malay peasants) and in Singapore they are in a special position (subsidized housing, free education, even at the University). But Lee has always insisted that the Malays must be given a chance to develop through education, and through contact with other races, rather than be encouraged to rely forever on special rights.

In her book, Dr Djamour stressed the importance which Singapore Malays attach to personal happiness. She thought it would be difficult to over-emphasize this attitude: it permeated all fields of human behaviour. Thus, the Malay's primary consideration is not the material advantages to be gained by a change but the serenity of mind which it would be likely to yield. This did not mean that earthly pleasures and worldly goods were despised. On the contrary, the Malay envied the Chinese his large house, car and luxury. Nor did the Malay believe that there is inherent good in renunciation: Dr Djamour said she could find no evidence whatever that asceticism, even in a mild form, was valued for its own sake, or as a means of spiritual joy. On the contrary, she found that the stress was always on gathering rosebuds while one may, and on leading as leisurely a life as possible. Every individual had a right to attain personal happiness by all legal means, and no Malay was expected to treat this right lightly.

These were the factors which produced the constant contradiction which challenged solution: an insistence upon a comparatively unproductive old social order, based upon a philosophy which called for happiness and leisure, conflicting with a human yearning for modern consumer goods and pleasures available only to those prepared to pay for them with long hours of hard work. Fortunately, in Singapore, with education, and the strong leadership of dynamic, progressive Malay leaders like Inche Othman Wok, Minister for Social Affairs, and Inche

Rahim Ishak, Minister of State for Foreign Affairs, the outlook and attitude of Malays in Singapore is gradually changing.

II

Winstedt, no imperialist, examined the effect of what he called "British protection" on the Malay economy. Down to 1941, the British gave the agriculturist and fisherman peace for their labours. British science introduced new forms of cultivation, especially rubber, which requires no large capital expenditure. Roads and railways were built. The exactions of chiefs were replaced by a uniform system of taxation. The British encouraged the emancipation of Malay women and provided Malay children with free and compulsory primary education. All this was to the credit of British influence on Malay material civilization.

On the debit side is the fact that Indian and Chinese immigrants, attracted by British rule in Malaya and Singapore, today outnumber the total Malay population. Britain also introduced to Malaya an industrial and capitalist system alien to Malay experience.

Winstedt contends that the real reason the Malays lag behind the Indian and Chinese is not laziness, but a failure to specialize and a failure to acquire and realize the importance of wealth. The Malay attitude, he says, is that work cannot be counted as a virtue even though it is necessary. "What the European moralist regards as lost time, the Malay regards as time gained." According to Winstedt, the Malay failure to specialize was due first to his isolation in village communities encircled by forests and too small to maintain the specialist, and secondly to a bountiful nature which made living comparatively easy.

For the Malay's failure to save his own capital Winstedt advanced three historical reasons. First, an accumulation of capital was impossible under the tribal system. To demand much more than cost for food was to invite bad harvest. Second, accumulation of possessions was to invite the attention of greedy chiefs. Third, the Muslim law against taking interest also mitigated against a modern use of capital. This attitude, Winstedt thought, was yielding to modernism.

Mills believed the Malays resented the success of the Chinese, an attitude not confined to Malaya: "The same hostility to the Chinese is found in every country of Southeast Asia. . ." Mills said that the final cause of hostility was political. "The Malays fear that under a democratic government they will be controlled by the Chinese. This seems very probable, since most of the Malays are rather naive and unsophisticated. This element of fear must not be underestimated: it is a major driving force in human affairs. Where fear is absent there can be friendship or at worst indifference, but when one individual or race is afraid of another it breeds hostility and, if it is strong enough, hatred."

Inche Rahim Ishak, Minister of State for Foreign Affairs and a member of the Central Committee of the PAP, in a speech which was given wide publicity in June, 1965, dealt with the "inherent fears of the Malays". It was, he said, important that this "emotional factor", this "natural fear and anxiety", should not be dismissed as something trivial. In Malaysia, the Malays naturally harboured certain fears concerning the non-Malays who outnumbered them. Inche Rahim Ishak accused UMNO leaders, particularly the extremists, of playing up this insecurity for the purpose of extracting party political gain. "The truth is that UMNO leaders, in playing on the communal feelings of the Malays, are trying to ensure the perpetuation of their political position of power at the expense of progress and development of the Malays in the rural areas all over Malaysia."

He argued that in the past the British colonialists deliberately "protected" the Malays from the influences of the more aggressive capitalist economy the British introduced. Now, under the pretext of "saving" the Malays, UMNO and Alliance leaders, he said, were perpetuating and extending the semi-feudal and colonial character of the country's economy. "Tunku Abdul Rahman has often said that the Chinese are good businessmen. They should be allowed to carry on as in the past. Indians are good rubber tappers. They should be left alone in this 'blissful state' in the rubber estates to continue to tap rubber. The Malays are a happy people and they should also be left in their present position."

Inche Rahim Ishak considered this "dangerous, if not stupid thinking. This is a deliberate attempt to maintain the status quo and at the same time to ensure the perpetuation of the semi-feudal structure of the economy of the Malays for purely selfish reasons."

III

If references to the very valuable part the Indians have played in the economic development of Singapore and Malaya appear to be limited in these pages this is for no other reason than that this is a book about Lee Kuan Yew, and Lee is of Chinese descent. Modern Indian immigration to Malaya began in 1833 (India had contact with Malaya seven centuries before Christ) when pepper and coffee estates were being developed in Penang and Province Wellesley, and thousands more came later to tap rubber, build roads and railways. In spite of this, the Indian community never made much political impact on the country. In a physical sense they helped to build Singapore, as they helped to develop Malaya: nobody will ever know how many Indians died clearing the jungles in Malaya. In 1888, a thousand Indian labourers working on the railway in Sungei Ujong (now part of Negri Sembilan) were dying at the rate of twenty-three a month. They were paid three times as much in Malaya as they could get in India, but many of them had to pay off a heavy debt for the cost of passage from India. In 1968, thirty per cent of the Indian population in Singapore and Malaya are of the non-labouring class: they are general merchants, money-changers, small shopkeepers, clerks, doctors, lawyers, hawkers, bankers, government servants. Occasionally an Indian political leader has emerged (Singapore's Foreign Minister, Mr S. Rajaratnam, is of Ceylonese descent) and, in recent years, effective trade unionists; but the political influence of the Indians has never matched their considerable practical influence on economic development. Modern Singaporeans and Malaysians are indebted to the Indians for physically constructing what today, in modern jargon, is called the infrastructure—the roads, the bridges, the railways, the clearings in the jungle, the wharfs, the houses, the factories—and there were no bulldozers in those days, and no mepacrin.

IV

In an *Asia Magazine* interview (5 February, 1967), Tunku Abdul Rahman was asked whether in his judgment there was any justification for the "fairly common libel" that Malays are a lazy, indolent people. The Tunku replied that he personally felt that all the nicest people are regarded as the lazy people. "We are extremely kind, warm and friendly. But others have taken undue advantage of our kindness, hospitality and our good, easy-going nature. But to my mind, this so-called laziness, which is in fact kindness, is the thing which makes people happy, which perhaps conditions them to sit back and let others do the work, enjoy the benefits of their labour. But in the final analysis, when it comes to the time when our people must push themselves forward, they are capable of extreme sacrifice, extreme hard work."

In an article in a Tamil newspaper *(Tamil Malar)* in July, 1965, Rahim Ishak wrote that only democratic socialism could correct the economic imbalance between the two major communities and this would ultimately bring about national solidarity and peace. He thought inter-racial harmony in Malaysia, particularly harmony between the Malays and Chinese, "is not attainable within the present scope of a profit-motivated society and system, where the Chinese and foreign capitalists, by and large, reap the profits". Rahim's argument was that, in a non-communal democratic socialist Malaysia, the one community to which would accrue the maximum gain was the Malay community, because "they have nothing to lose, since today they are the dispossessed". He warned that the Malays would need time to adjust, to understand the new concepts and new approaches to their problems. Races and communities lived interspersed with each other: there were no separate cantonments where races and communities lived exclusively, although there were places where one race or community were in the preponderance. "In this respect we are unlike Switzerland: we live together. We work together. We play together. We suffer together. Therefore, the time has come for Malaysians of various races and communities to affiliate themselves to non-communal ideologies or organizations in political parties." To work on the basis of race, as a political party, meant stagnation. This arrangement resulted in a tendency among racial leaders to appeal to communal chauvinism to hold their followers. Communal fears and prejudices were exploited. Strengthening of the communal parties meant their becoming entrenched in communal politics. That could only weaken the prospects for a Malaysian community, not encourage it.

That was the sum of Rahim's argument: neither he nor Lee Kuan Yew wanted to abolish communal organizations at once, or indeed ever: they could always serve some useful purpose as social or cultural bodies. But what was vital if progress was to be made towards multi-racialism was that the races should be encouraged to intermingle politically, that gradually the political-communal pressure upon them should be slackened, eventually dropped altogether. Instead, UMNO told every Malay he must join no other political organization except UMNO. Albar, Senu, Razak and others have made it abundantly clear that any Malay joining another political organization is a traitor to his race and religion. Tunku Abdul Rahman's UMNO crushed Dato Onn's multiracial Independence of Malaya Party ten years earlier by forbidding any UMNO member to join it. In ten years, UMNO's resolve to resist any encroachment on its communalism had intensified. With political power came the firm decision that there was to be no effective intermingling of the Malays with others: their leaders would speak for all Malays.

In July, 1964, UMNO notified the PAP officially of this decision. In Singapore, they organized a Malay convention, attended by some 150 Malay organizations, and there twenty-three Malays were chosen to speak for the entire Malay community in the State, in all future dealings with the Singapore Government. Syed Jaafar Albar, speaking as national Secretary-General of UMNO, appealed to the Malays to unite. "Malays in Singapore have long been oppressed," he declared. "First there were the British to whom the Malays gave their trust. But the British betrayed this trust. Then there were the Japanese with cruel oppression. Singapore is now independent with her entry into Malaysia, but the plight of the Malays remains. Malays must unite to defend their own interest."

More than a thousand Malay leaders, from 114 cultural, social and welfare organizations, met Lee at another mass meeting the following Sunday. No political organizations were asked to attend. As Prime Minister of a State dedicated to multiracialism and a multi-party system, Lee could not accept Albar's demand that his twenty-three-member Action Committee represented the Malay community. He reminded them that the popularly elected Singapore Government (elected in a general election in which the Malays freely rejected all UMNO candidates) had a right, indeed a duty, to solve the problems of all communities, including those of the Malay community. "We would like, before we make any decisions, to consult a wide range of representation in the Malay community. For any group to say that they exclusively represent all persons of a particular community is a claim as extravagant as it is unfounded." He said that for any group to demand the right to represent all the members of a community and so demand the exclusive right to advise what the Government should do "is a challenge to the constitutional rights and obligations of the Singapore Government. We do not intend to abdicate from our right to govern."

Lee promised at that meeting to do what was right and fair. The Government would not be intimidated: they would look after the interests of all the people of Singapore, including the Malays. "They must be trained in the building trade, they must be trained to be skilled technicians. There are just not enough jobs for primary school-leavers as messengers, peons, and other unskilled jobs. But there are openings as fitters, carpenters, masons and semi-skilled labourers in factories and industries... if they are prepared to undergo training." Lee said the position could be improved if Malays could be persuaded to take advantage of training facilities which were available. He was anxious to adjust and remove the imbalance in development between the races. It would harm the unity and integrity of the nation if one section of the community lagged behind the other. Malay problems fell under three headings: education, employment and housing. Education was the most important. If this was solved all other Malay problems would be solved. "Once the Malays are as well educated and qualified as the others, then their capacity to hold better jobs and have a better standard of living will automatically follow." At present very few Malay students went to secondary school, and very, very few went on to universities. The great majority finished their education at primary level. "Somehow we must provide them with a training that will qualify them for industrial jobs."

V

Some historians say that the founding of *Utusan Melayu* in its present form, in 1939, was the first sign of a real nationalist movement in Malaya. Others say that the short-lived monthly, *Al-Iman*, which was more a religious magazine dedicated to Islamic reform, did in fact make the first nationalistic impact, the argument being that "one of the fundamental facts about Islam is that it is not simply a system of religious beliefs, but a political and social blue-print for a good society". The Islamic reformers in *Al-Iman*, therefore, devoted a great deal of their attention to social, political and economic matters, as well as to religious affairs. An article written in 1907, by Syed Sheikh Al-Hadi, caused a stir because of its criticism of Malay leaders.

"Look what has happened to us here in the East," wrote Syed Sheikh Al-Hadi. "The Europeans, better equipped with weapons for the battle of life, have taken over. We, on our part, have remained silent and submissive, like watchdogs or saddle-horses. We are satisfied with the scraps from their tables, and the grass that grows in their compounds. And when other Eastern people, like the Japanese, demonstrate to us the wealth of their knowledge and national glory, what do we do? Do we blame ourselves for our shortcomings? No, we hang down our heads and say it is the will of God." But this attitude, the writer held, was "false and blasphemous. It is we who are to blame for our condition for not following the commandments of God as expressed in the Holy Koran, to strive for ourselves, to assist others, and to pursue knowledge. And the chief of those at fault are our own leaders... Contrast this state of affairs with that of the Chinese who come to this country. They arrive with a mat, a pair of shorts and a singlet. In no time at all, through their own efforts they have become towkays and millionaires. And it doesn't stop at that. The leaders among the Chinese, unlike our own leaders, band together to establish welfare organizations and build schools for their community. If we are blind to the commands of our religion, surely we cannot be such fools as to fail to follow the example set by the industrious Chinese?"

Fifty years later, Malay political leaders blamed the British for the economic backwardness of the Malays. *Al-Iman* concentrated their criticism upon the Malay people themselves, more especially on their

81

leaders. *Al-Iman's* main concern was not to bring about political change, but to improve the conditions of the Malays by recalling them to the true ways of Islam. They criticized Islam as it was practised in Malaya, and while this did not lead directly to nationalist movements, it could not be denied that the reformists of the early twentieth century did much to foster and encourage discussion of the kind of changes which ultimately led to political nationalism.

In the 1960s powerful supporters of UMNO bought control of *Utusan Melayu*. Lee Kuan Yew was legal adviser to *Utusan Melayu* from 1950 until he became Prime Minister in 1959.

CHAPTER TWELVE

Was Multiracial Malaysia Ever Possible?

I

WAS a multiracial Malaysia ever really possible? "The Malays have a deep-rooted feeling that they alone are the *bumiputras*, the sons of the soil," wrote Dr R. K. Vasil, former lecturer at the University of Malaya, in *Quest*, 1966, "and as such have certain special rights over the land." Tunku Abdul Rahman, later to become Prime Minister of Malaysia and President of the inter-communal ruling Alliance, on 30 June, 1952 (a few months after the United Malays National Organization and the Malayan Chinese Association successfully contested the municipal elections in Kuala Lumpur, which laid the foundation of the present Alliance), declared: "Malaya is for the Malays and it should not be governed by a mixture of races." The Malays must safeguard their rights over this land, "which is ours, for the benefit of our future generation".

Dr Vasil went on to quote from an interview the Tunku gave to *The Asia Magazine* in August, 1964 (after the formation of Malaysia), in which the Tunku observed: "It is understood by all that this country by its very name, its traditions and character, is Malay. The indigenous people are Malays and, while they on the whole have been left behind in the economic and professional fields, others have been helped along by the understanding and tolerance of the Malays to be successes in whatever fields they are in. In any other country where aliens try to dominate economic and other fields, eventually there is bitter opposition from the indigenous people. But not with the

Malays. Therefore, in return, they must appreciate the position of the Malays, who have been given land in Malay reservations and jobs in the government... if Malays are driven out of everything, however tolerant they may be, there is a limit. Resentment would build up and there would be trouble, and those who had found prosperity would also suffer."

And yet, according to the PAP and four other Malaysian opposition parties from Singapore, Malaya and Sarawak, after meeting to set up the Malaysian Solidarity National Convention: "Malaysia was conceived as belonging to Malaysians as a whole and not to any particular community or race."

In a statement put out after the meeting (on 9 May, 1965) the representatives of five parties explained that by stressing a Malaysian Malaysia they underlined the fact that the nation and the state could not be identified with the supremacy, well-being and the interests of any one particular community or race. "A Malaysian Malaysia is the antithesis of a Malay Malaysia, a Chinese Malaysia, a Dyak Malaysia, an Indian Malaysia, or Kadazan Malaysia, and so on." It was because the concept of a democratic Malaysian Malaysia had been challenged by "certain leaders" that doubts and fears arose about the future of Malaysia. "Certain political leaders have allowed their resentment of criticism and opposition to some of their policies to degenerate into threats that if such criticisms are persisted in then parliamentary democracy might be brought to an end. Others have gone so far as to enunciate the doctrine that the existence of democracy and Malaysia is conditional only on their unchallenged right to be the rulers of Malaysia, and that, therefore, other groups should desist from trying to win following and support by constitutional and legitimate means. If they do not, then dire consequences are predicted. These vary from the ending of democracy to warnings about communal disturbances."

The Malaysian Solidarity Convention deplored the "growing tendency among some leaders to make open appeals to communalist chauvinism to win and hold their following". Such appeals were a repudiation of the concept of a Malaysian Malaysia. The Convention did not deny the fact that communal fears and prejudices still influenced popular political thinking, and that the emergence of a Malaysian outlook might take time to develop. "We are realistic enough to recognize that until such time as a Malaysian outlook takes strong root, substantial sections of our population will be inclined to express themselves through communally organized political parties." But what dismayed them was the "viciousness" with which attacks were launched against those who, of whatever race, abandoned communal forms of politics for non-communal politics. "One would have thought that the more the people affiliated themselves to non-communal ideologies and organizations the nearer we are moving to our goal of a Malaysian Malaysia. If people are discouraged and denounced for abandoning communal loyalties because they have found common ground for political action with Malaysians of other races then the professed concern for a Malaysian Malaysia is open to serious doubts." The Convention warned: "Assertion by one group of chauvinists must lead to counter-assertion by other chauvinistic groups and in no time a multiracial Malaysia must be rent asunder by communal conflicts."

II

By the end of 1966, Tunku Abdul Rahman was quoting as an historic fact his belief that Lee Kuan Yew was entirely responsible for the separation of Singapore from Malaysia. In an interview published in *The Asia Magazine* on 5 February, 1967, the Tunku said the reason for the breakaway of Singapore was "because the Prime Minister of Singapore wanted to be a Prime Minister. There can never be two Prime Ministers in one nation. Therefore the break had to come about sooner or later. The reason for the split, the separation of Singapore from Malaysia, was because of the danger of communal differences which was being encouraged by the Prime Minister of Singapore. It was being worked up to the extent that I feared that unless Singapore separated from Malaysia, there might in fact be real racial trouble between the Chinese and the Malays."

Pressed to recall the background, the events, which eventually led to the separation of Singapore from Malaysia, the Tunku said: "Well, at that time, Singapore was talking about the various differences among the races: the advantages the one enjoyed over the other. Things were really getting bad. I was in England at the time in hospital. I had a lot of time to think. My mind was clear. I gave all my thoughts to the problems facing this country. After long consideration I felt there was really no alternative. Singapore could not be in Malaysia. I wrote to Tun Razak. I told him the only alternative was to break with Singapore. When I came back from London I called a meeting of the Cabinet. I gave them the reasons behind my thinking, the need to break away. They agreed with me. I informed Mr Lee Kuan Yew, Prime Minister of Singapore. I don't think it came as a surprise to him. He knew almost a year before that. When he made many requests and demands I told him things could not go on like this. I pointed out to him that the only way out was for Singapore to be independent. In fact I did mention earlier to Mr Goh Keng Swee, who was acting as Mr Lee's agent, that separation was the only alternative. We had all these discussions either on the golf course or here in my drawing-room. So in the end, the final decision did not come as a surprise to the Prime Minister of Singapore. He was ready and willing to accept separation."

III

What happens to Malaysia is of vital concern to the Republic of Singapore (and, of course, what happens to Singapore must have a considerable impact upon Malaysia), and in 1967 not only Lee Kuan Yew, but others further away, were anxiously assessing Malaysia's future.

Malaysia's great neighbours, China, India and Indonesia, ancestral homes of most Malaysians, were themselves in the midst of social revolution, and no one could judge what influences these changes, some of them sudden and far-reaching, might have upon the destiny of Malaysia. Of more immediate concern was the rationalization of Malaysia's own internal contradictions: if they remained unsolved, they could wreck the whole concept of multiracialism, the rock upon which the entire experiment was based. These contradictions stem from the disparity of the two communities, the leisure-loving Malays, followers of Mohammed, and the industrious, materialistic Chinese.

Inter-marriage among them is rare: Muslims are forbidden by Islam to wed an infidel. Islam does not attract the Chinese, most of them being Buddhists, and the Malays show no signs of abandoning their religion. On the contrary, never have more mosques been built, mostly from public funds. Malaysia boasts the most modern, probably the largest, certainly the costliest, mosque in the world. The possibility in the foreseeable future of Malaysia producing an assimilated breed of Malaysian nationalists, must therefore be considered remote. Religion, if nothing else, will ensure the continuance of separate communities.

This means that to survive as a coherent nation, Malaysia's unlike citizens, dissimilar in character, speech, education, diet, religion, and political and social philisophy, must study and practise the art of living together in harmony. Upon their ability to do this will depend the existence of the state as conceived, and, in the final analysis, their own lives.

Perhaps fortunately, no single community numerically dominates the others. In a population of nine million (Singapore, which became part of Malaysia when the state was formed on 16 September, 1963, was detached on 9 August, 1965) the Malays are the largest group: they are outnumbered by the Chinese, Indians, Dyaks, Ibans and others together. Political control is largely in the hands of the Malays, and

86

At the Five-Power Defence Conference in Canberra, 1969. Dennis Healey, then British Defence Secretary, Tun Abdul Razak, then Director of Operations, Malaysia, Lee Kuan Yew, and Gordon Freeth, then Australian Minister for Defence

A Canadian Broadcasting Corporation television interview in London. Pierre Trudeau, Prime Minister of Canada, Lee Kuan Yew and President Kaunda of Zambia

Socialist Conference in Geneva 1968

Before the television cameras in Cairo

they oppose any innovation which they feel might change this ("The position of the Malays in politics is unassailable," said Tunku Abdul Rahman, Prime Minister of Malaysia, in 1964); whereas the Chinese, the Indians and the overseas British companies own the greater part of the available wealth, a state of affairs which the Malays would wish to amend in their own favour. This must be done, they believe, if Malaysia is to survive—where else in the world is the economic power of a state not in the hands of those who exercise political control? Lee Kuan Yew believes that socialism is the only solution to that problem, not the artificial, forced creation of Malay capitalists, which is the positive policy of the Alliance. "You must help the Malays to share in your trade and industry," Tunku Abdul Rahman told Chinese merchants and industrialists in Parliament in 1965.

Experience in Indonesia, where, soon after independence, President Sukarno gave away millions of state money in a disastrous and hurried attempt to create Indonesian capitalists, proved that more than capital is required to set up a flourishing industry or business. Probably bearing this in mind, the Alliance Government decided to provide, as well as substantial loans, expert advice, and short technical training courses. What no organization or government has yet been able to produce, however, is an aptitude for trade; an aptitude which combines forcefulness with accurate judgment, an ability which forms the very basis of a capitalist's character. In the same way that an artist must possess a feeling for form and colour, an embryo capitalist must possess qualities which will fit him for participation in what is undoubtedly a skilled, aggressive and highly competitive manner of earning a living.

Inche Rahim Ishak, when Singapore's Minister of State for Education, argued that the "British policy of divide and rule" created a situation where the Malays remained in the rural areas, "kept down as padi farmers and fishermen" (*Petir*, June, 1956). Rahim Ishak said that the Malays were pushed further and further into the undeveloped hinterland "with the expansion of capitalism and the taking over of vast tracts of land for mining and rubber planting". The British allowed and encouraged capitalism "to penetrate the rural areas" thus "helping to destroy the old structure of Malay feudal economy". Ishak reasoned that as a result of this "deliberate policy" the Malays, by and large, were not drawn into the more aggressive capitalist economy. They have now emerged after independence, out of the "shattered" fabric of semi-feudal economics only to discover that there are "less and less economic opportunities for them in commerce and industry".

The logic of this argument is not easy to follow. Dato Abu Bakar bin Baginda, Menteri Besar of Selangor, may have been nearer the mark when, in a speech to Malay retailers in 1963, trying to find an explanation why Malays "lag behind in the race for economic progress and advance", he suggested that the reasons "may be historical or inherently psychological and sociological". Whatever the correct explanation of the Malays' backwardness in business, Dato Abu Bakar, and many other Malays, consider that the Government is responsible for putting the matter right.

Now in a position of political dominance, Malay leaders believe it to be their duty to establish a Malay capitalist class as quickly as possible. They see nothing odd that they should be trying to do this at a time when the tendency throughout the world is for newly developing countries to turn towards some form of socialism.

Most nations emerging from colonial control equate capitalism with colonialism, and this has been sufficient for some countries—Burma for instance—to abandon the remnants of capitalism left behind by the colonialists, and to endeavour to substitute foreign capitalism with socialism adapted to meet local conditions and requirements. In Burma, all forms of capitalism, native and foreign, have been crushed. Burmese socialism controls every aspect of the nation's entire economy.

In Malaysia, not only has capitalism not been rejected. In spite of their lack of experience, the Malays, as the nation's political masters, though fully aware that economic power (which developed Malaya in a hundred years far beyond their own expectations) remains in the hands of European, Chinese and Indian capitalists, conscious of their own past disinterest and inaptitude for capitalism, nevertheless embraced free enterprise as an economic national policy as soon as they assumed office after independence. Having done that, they forthwith set out to design a form of protection and safeguards which would safely allow Malays to join in the capitalist game, and, like the successful Europeans, Chinese and Indians, achieve wealth and happiness and, accordingly, somehow (though this was not defined) contribute towards the general uplifting of the standard of living of all Malaysians, especially the Malays.

Many reasons have been advanced why the Malays have never been capitalists. Wallace in 1869 wrote that the Malay does not quarrel easily about money matters, dislikes asking too frequently even for payment of his just debts, and will often give them up altogether rather than quarrel with his debtor.

In a hundred years, the Malay, like most people, has developed through modernism; and some of his attractive qualities, which ill equipped him as a capitalist, may have become more attuned to present-day hard realities, yet Hodder in 1959 continued to describe the Malays as a "charming, pleasure-loving and easily contented people", their "so-called indolence and improvidence" being but an expression of their social and economic philosophy. In fact, every modern reference to the Malays agrees that they are, as a race, polite, unaggressive, kind and gentle, more interested in leisure than the accumulation of money, generous, not greedy, lacking, in brief, the very acquisitive urge, and other characteristics, not all of them pleasant, without which capital cannot be saved and capitalism practised. On the contrary, the most strongly developed trait of the Malays is their belief in, and their constant practice of, co-operativeness. They call this *gotong-royong*. Modernists call it socialism. Call it what you like, this system of mutual help will have to be stamped out if the Malays are to become capitalists. The basic character of the Malays will have to be changed.

IV

Malaysia made a slow start, and conditions worsened. At the end of the first two years there was probably as much disunity within the Malay community because of quarrels over Malaysia, as there was between the Malay and the Chinese communities. There are three groups of political thought among the Malays, ranging from the extreme Right, which believes that Malaya belongs to the Malays and no one else, to the sophisticated urban Malay on the Left. In the middle is the mass of moderates now led by Tun Abdul Razak. The Malay Right, or ultras, argue that, since the Malays originally surrendered authority to the British, the Malays must inherit the power relinquished by the British. They say non-Malays should be grateful for being allowed to live in Malaya, to make themselves rich. Non-Malays are not persecuted: they should not talk of rights: they should consider themselves fortunate to be allowed to live peaceably, as well-behaved guests—distant relatives perhaps—in somebody else's home.

Most Chinese accept the Malaysian concept of Malaysia at face value: they want to share, and there is a willingness to accept the principle that the Malays need help for the time being. Within the Tun's mass of moderates, inside UMNO itself, is a strong element of extremists. Tunku Abdul Rahman, sixty at the birth of Malaysia, was Prime Minister of Malaysia and also leader of the Malays, and this dual status, in a plural society embarked upon the establishment of a multiracial democratic nation, added to the Prime Minister's difficulties. As a Malaysian, the Tunku had to reject the "Malaya belongs to the Malays" demand and speak of tolerance and progress, of a Malaysian citizenship which embraced those qualified by birth or residence to call themselves Malaysians. Here was equality and justice for all, certain privileges being extended to the Malays to help them economically and educationally. Speaking at a meeting of UMNO in 1964, the Tunku insisted there was no hatred between Malays and Chinese. Trouble between them broke out only when "our enemy and their agents and saboteurs" stirred it up (the Tunku was speaking shortly after race riots in Singapore, started, it was believed, by President Sukarno's Indonesians). The Tunku argued that, while there was "healthy rivalry in many spheres of activity in the life of this country, the Malays and the Chinese, on the whole, were content with their respective positions". He said that "people take for granted what each as a race are capable of, and able to do better than the other. In politics, administration and perhaps service in the armed forces, the Malays are unrivalled, because their needs and ambitions are clear-cut. They know what it is they can do well and what it is they cannot do quite so well, but, given time and wise planning, I have no doubt that they can do many things. In a country of free enterprise, opportunities must be open to all, and at the same time there must be a feeling of give and take. A serious effort must also be made to improve the lot of the Malays, or have-nots, in the fields of commerce and industry. On the other hand, the Chinese and others do not aspire to giddy heights in politics, administration and the armed forces because in these fields the opportunity to make money is limited: they therefore go in for business, big or small, and work laboriously without regard to all the risks involved." The Tunku warned that "any attempt to try and force one side to give up their place in favour of the other is bound to meet with trouble".

In this frank statement of Malay intentions and aspirations as he saw them, the Tunku held that the Malays must retain their political and administrative advantages, their control of the armed forces and the police, and use this power in a reasonable manner to improve the lot of their community, while allowing the Chinese a free hand to "work laboriously" and to enrich themselves, but not to try to force a change in basic Chinese-Malay relationships. This prescription for a continuance of the Tunku's "happy Malaya" is accepted by most Malays, and also meets with the approval of the rich Chinese merchants. They are content with economic power. Malay rule is not oppressive, and they have no political ambitions: they prefer to be left alone to increase their wealth.

This argument and outlook was not acceptable to Lee Kuan Yew when Singapore was part of Malaysia, nor to the mass of the non-Malay Singaporeans (the organized workers and the peasants). So long, therefore, as these basic economic and political contradictions obtain—the Malays having the political power and intending to retain it, and the non-Malays possessing the nation's wealth and facing pressure from the Malays to share it with them—stability within Malaysia must be threatened and the very survival of Malaysia in its present form a matter for grave concern to the Republic of Singapore, indeed to the whole of Southeast Asia. There are additional problems of state nationalism in East Malaysia.

Part Two

CHAPTER THIRTEEN

The Year of Power 1959

IN 1959, Singapore became an internally self-governing state with a fully responsible parliamentary government based on a mass electorate. Britain was still responsible for foreign affairs and defence. Lee Kuan Yew's People's Action Party won forty-three of the fifty-one seats. They secured 53.4 per cent of the total votes cast. The former Chief Minister, Mr Lim Yew Hock, was one of two former Ministers re-elected to the Assembly. He became leader of the Opposition.

On 4 June, Lee Kuan Yew formed his Cabinet, and nine days later flew to Kuala Lumpur with four of his colleagues to meet the Prime Minister of Malaya and his colleagues. The official communique gave special emphasis to the need for communal harmony.

Preparations for the Development Plan were immediately set in motion and a bill enabling the Government to raise a $100,000,000 Development Loan was passed. Steps were taken to form an Economic Development Board to carry out the planning and construction of industrial sites. Talks began with the Malayan Government regarding the creation of a mutually advantageous Common Commodity Market.

The TUC was reorganized under a new constitution to provide cohesive policy and steady leadership. The Government launched an anti-yellow culture campaign, and many juke-box and pin-table parlours were closed down. A strip-tease show was banned as the first move in a policy of "eliminating sex-obsessed culture and all activities which are detrimental to the growth of a new and healthy society and culture". Hundreds of secret society gangsters were arrested. The birth-rate showed a natural increase of 39.8 per thousand, one of the highest in the world. During 1959, the cost of education rose to $63,000,000, almost twenty-four per cent of the budget. Towards the end of the year the National Theatre Fund was launched. Yusof bin Ishak became Singapore's first Malayan-born Head of State. Zubir Said wrote the new national anthem, and the new state flag of red and white, incorporating a crescent moon and five stars (the red representing universal brotherhood and equality, and the white purity and virtue, and the five stars democracy, peace, progress, justice and equality), proudly flew over public buildings. The year of revolutionary transition from colony to state ended peacefully, and hopefully.

94

I

LEE Kuan Yew became Prime Minister of self-governing Singapore on 5 June, 1959. The election campaign, which lasted several weeks, had been strenuous but orderly. One hundred and ninety-four candidates, including fifty-one from the PAP, were nominated by ten political parties. There were up to 200 meetings a night throughout the island and when Lee spoke ten thousand people turned up to hear him.

The PAP won forty-three seats and collected 53·4 per cent of the votes cast. During the campaign the PAP declared they would not take office until eight of their former leaders, including Lim Chin Siong, detained under the Preservation of the Public Security Ordinance, were released. On 1 June, Lim Yew Hock resigned as Chief Minister. The Governor, Sir William Goode, invited Lee Kuan Yew to form a government. Lee promptly made his formal request for the release of the detainees. On 2 June, the Governor announced that "in the changed political situation", and "in order to achieve a swift and smooth introduction of the new Constitution", they would be released on 4 June. Lee then agreed to form a government and on 3 June the new Constitution came into force.

That night, Lee Kuan Yew spoke at a mass rally on the Padang. "Once in a long while in the story of a people," he said, "there comes a moment of great change. Tonight is such a moment in our lives. Last Saturday saw the end of an era. This morning the new Constitution was promulgated. We begin a new chapter in the history of Singapore. The powers of the people through their elected government is limited to our internal affairs. It is not what we really want. It is but a step forward towards merger and *Merdeka* ... This rally tonight is symbolic of the nature of your Government, a people's government ... We have no personal future apart from your future. Your joys and your sorrows are ours. We share the same future, be it good, indifferent, or bad ... "

On the afternoon of 5 June, Sir William Goode, as Yang di-Pertuan Negara of the new state, drove down from his palace on the hill to the City Hall, a symbolic gesture, there to witness Lee Kuan Yew and his eight Ministers take the oath of office.

Sir William read a cable from the British Prime Minister, Mr Harold MacMillan, offering "any help that lies in our power". Lee Kuan Yew read his reply: "My Government will require all the goodwill and help from all those who wish our people well." Shortly afterwards, Lee Kuan Yew went to the radio station to give his first message to the people as Prime Minister. He said:

"We have taken office because we believe that the PAP is the

95

party most capable of discharging the duties and responsibilities of the government. We are the best organized and the most coherent political leadership in Singapore. Every one of my Ministers has gone through years of political struggle before we reached this position. If we were weak or insincere we would not have survived the stresses and strains of the political struggle that we underwent. The business of a government is to govern and to make firm decisions, so that there shall be certainty and stability in the affairs of our people. We shall do our best to give you not only firm and stable government, but one which will carry with it the support and co-operation of the majority of the people.

"During the elections our opponents tried to frighten you against a PAP government. They spread vicious rumours that polling day would be accompanied by unrest and civil commotions; that there would be a curfew; that buses would stop running. None of these things has happened. The events of the past six days have proved the falseness of these lies. The people of Singapore went to the polls in a peaceful and orderly manner and voted in the government they wanted, a PAP government. They celebrated their victory in the constituencies and on the Padang in a joyous, sometimes boisterous, but always orderly and peaceful manner.

"In the same way their other predictions about the terrible consequences of a PAP victory will be proved equally false. In the next five years there may come times when we shall face difficulties and tribulations. The tasks ahead of us are not easy to accomplish. We have never pretended they would be easy. But we shall not deviate from our declared objective of bringing about a social revolution by peaceful means. . ."

Lee Kuan Yew had hardly been in office a week when he went to Kuala Lumpur, with a small delegation of Ministers, to pay his respects to the Prime Minister of Malaya, then, for a brief period, Dato (later Tun) Abdul Razak. (Tunku Abdul Rahman had vacated office for a few months to give all his attention to the reorganization of his party, the United Malays National Organization.) An official communique gave special emphasis to the need for communal harmony. "Both Prime Ministers and all Ministers present were firmly agreed that under no circumstances would they countenance any attempts to arouse racial or communal friction."

Later in the year, Dr Subandrio, the Indonesian Foreign Minister, visited Singapore to express his determination to "restore good relations between Indonesia and Singapore". Relations had become somewhat strained as a result of Indonesia's accusations that Singapore had harboured instigators of the revolt in Sumatra. When Lee came into office a certain number of Indonesians were told to leave.

96

In July, Lee Kuan Yew spoke at a dinner given by the University of Malaya Society. It was to honour graduates from the University in Singapore who had been elected Assemblymen. This celebration in effect underlined the achievement of the English-educated leadership in wresting political power from the Chinese-educated leadership through the votes of the non-English-speaking people. Lee Kuan Yew said the PAP had never been more confident than it was when winning the elections.

He said: "Let us never forget, that we, the English-educated elite, merit our place in society so long as we are able to do a service to that society... We exist because of special conditions in the past which threw out our forebears... all those who belong to our generation are here because of an accident of history. The British Raj transferred power... the British Raj nurtured the English-educated class... My colleagues were specially educated on this theme. They went to Oxford and London at the expense of the British Raj... Despite the fact that it was in their power to slide into the system and make the world for themselves, they had not only the courage and strength of their convictions, but a social conscience that made them discard the privileges that were theirs for the asking, and ask for those privileges to be shared amongst the bulk of the population. They were ready to discard all positive personal advantage for a cause."

Lee spoke to the workers on 28 June. He told them that his mandate was clear: to bring about by peaceful and constitutional means an independent, democratic, non-communist, socialist Malaya. He said many people in Malaya had not yet grasped the significance of the stand taken on 4 June when Lim Chin Siong, Devan Nair and others were released from Changi Gaol, and issued their political manifesto which they called *The Ends and Means of Malayan Socialism*. Lee told the trade unionists that "some political experts in their hard-boiled cynicism" dismissed the manifesto as a temporary tactical change of life (which so far as Lim Chin Siong was concerned was the truth). Lee said he knew it as a completely sincere document (as it was to Devan Nair) which a group of courageous men had drawn up while in prison for the explicit purpose of making a clear-cut stand on the PAP ideology when the time came for their release and re-entry into active politics. "The thinking that went into the document was spread over a period of one year. And these words were very carefully weighed before they were pronounced on 4 June. The words were—and here I quote: 'It is necessary to state categorically that we are democratic socialists, and that we subscribe without reservations to the theory and practice of democratic socialism on which the PAP is based.' "

Lee declared to an enthusiastic, cheering gathering: "There is no going back to the past. Such mistakes as have been committed are over and done with. We move forward into the future confident that we shall advance the cause we all stand for, a more just and equal society in an independent, democratic, non-communist, socialist Malaya.

"It is imperative that the trade union movement, which will grow and expand under the PAP Government, should be imbued with the same democratic, non-communist, socialist ideals. Otherwise there are bound to be frictions and collisions between the labour movement and the political movement."

This is precisely what did happen. Lee had been deceived. In the end, only Devan Nair kept faith with democratic, non-communist socialism. It is unlikely that the others ever abandoned communism. They revealed their hand in 1961 when, after failing to capture control of the PAP from within, they broke away and formed the Barisan Socialis, later exposed as a communist-front organization.

Though a socialist, Lee Kuan Yew knew that those engaged in trade needed to be reassured that no revolutionary measures were intended which might be inimical to their livelihood. His revolution was against colonialism, and for a better standard of living. He spoke (on 8 August) to the Chinese Chamber of Commerce, and thanked them for "the tribute they had paid to the first elected government of Singapore".

He said: "Although we are a socialist party, we fully recognize that socialism cannot be implemented in Singapore before merger with the Federation of Malaya. We are an island of 220 square miles. We have been living for the past 100 years by the hard work of our people and the skill of our traders. There is no doubt that with better relations with our neighbours like Indonesia our trade may still increase. But we would be blind if we did not recognize the tremendous change in the pattern of trade and commerce in Southeast Asia. Both our two closest neighbours—the Federation of Malaya and Indonesia—have, not unnaturally, since they attained their independence, set themselves out to build up their own industries. They want to establish their own trade lines with foreign countries without having to go through the merchants and brokers in Singapore. We must adjust our position before they begin to succeed in doing this. It is unlikely that we shall be able to support our ever-increasing population just by trade alone."

Lee assured the Chamber that his Government did not seek to destroy Singapore's trade: industrialization would go on at the same time. He said that co-operation and not competition was what was needed between Singapore and the Federation in the fields of commerce, industry and finance.

A careful study of events in Southeast Asia confirmed Lee Kuan Yew's belief that a sympathetic and efficient civil service, one that was politically aware, was vital if the PAP's ambitious plans for development and progress were to be carried out properly. It was one thing for politicians to prepare a broad outline, to plan, to exhort the masses and to win elections. Making policies work, translating election speeches into material progress, into housing estates and new schools, demanded an efficient and incorruptible administration.

At the opening of the Civil Service Political Study Centre on 15 August, Lee Kuan Yew admitted that for several years he and his colleagues had discussed the problems which a democratic socialist party, committed to a dynamic social programme, would have to face if it assumed power in Singapore. "And one of these problems is the civil service through which we have to translate our policies. . .

"This Civil Service Study Centre is in part an attempt to telescope into a study course the main elements of the political and social forces which caused the postwar revolutions in Asia. If nothing else you will at least understand what was the genesis of the forces that have shaken the British Raj under which nearly all of you were recruited, and under which you were guaranteed a lifetime of service with a pension at the end.

"Some of you may be bewildered and perplexed by what you may consider the impatience with which we are asking for things to be done. If so, then I hope that at the end of your course in this Study Centre, if you do not share our impatience, you will at least understand it. You will at least appreciate why we consider it so vital, if the democratic state is to survive, for the machinery to be in tune with the temper of the people and tempo of political change in the rest of Asia.

"Whether an administration functions efficiently and smoothly in the interests of the people as a whole or in the interests of a small section of the people, depends upon the policies of the Ministers. But it is your responsibility to make sure that there is an efficient civil service.

"If you look around you in South and Southeast Asia you may be disturbed by the phenomena of newly independent countries passing from the first phase of democratic constitutions into military or semi-military dictatorships. Pakistan, Indonesia and Burma are grim reminders to us that the democratic state is not something which will look after itself just by the setting up of a democratic constitution. There are many reasons why in South and Southeast Asian countries like Pakistan, Indonesia and Burma the democratic system has broken down, and why in India and Ceylon it has, relatively speaking, succeeded. One of the reasons is that both in India and in Ceylon they had the administrators to run the machine of the democratic system. India had more civil servants than Pakistan. In Ceylon they had a long time to build up their civil service. And so, despite all the stresses and strains of racial, religious and linguistic clashes between Tamils and Sinhalese, Buddhists and Hindus, the administration did not collapse. . ."

III

The Prime Minister dealt more fully with the role of the English-educated in the social revolution of Singapore and Malaya when he spoke to the Singapore Union of Journalists (on 16 August). He said that no single factor had so great an influence on the minds of the English-educated as the Press. Those who worked on newspapers, therefore, had a heavy responsibility not to allow those who owned newspapers to distort problems confronting Singapore and Malaya.

Lee Kuan Yew defined the phrase "English-educated" in the Malayan context. "By English-educated I do not mean just somebody who can speak, read and write the English language. I refer to that group of people who have gone through the Government or Mission English schools in Malaya. They are not merely English-speaking. They have also acquired certain definite characteristics as a result of going through the English schools. There are others in Malaya who are English-speaking, like Englishmen, Australians, Americans—even Frenchmen. And there are Chinese who have learned English in China or Hong Kong or elsewhere. But they are not the Malayan 'English-educated'. They are different. Not only do they speak with a different accent and have different slang and idioms but they have also different standards of behaviour, different scales of values, different characteristics from the Malayan 'English-educated'.

"We may not be conscious of the Malayan English-educated group as a homogeneous one. Let me give you an illustration. When I was a student in England we used to go—my friends and I from Malaya—to a club called the China Institute where Chinese people from all over the world forgathered. There we met Chinese from China, from the West Indies, Mauritius, Malaya and other places too. All spoke English. All had learnt it in China or the West Indies or Mauritius or Malaya. But the Malayan student could unerringly pick out another Malayan by the way he dressed and talked, and by his mannerisms. The Malayan English-educated was a definite type. And another strange thing was that the English-educated Chinese from Malaya found that he had more in common with the English-educated non-Chinese from Malaya, than with the English-educated Chinese from Mauritius, the West Indies or China. Having thus defined our term 'the English-educated', let me list their characteristics. Their good points are, first, they are homogeneous. Next, they have ceased to think of themselves primarily as Chinese, Malays or Indians. They are loyal to the community, honest and well-behaved, if somewhat too obedient to colonial authority. Their weak points are, in the case of the Chinese and Indians, that they are devitalized, almost emasculated, as a result of deculturalization. The syllabus in the English schools in pre-war Malaya had pumped in a completely English set of values

100

and ideals. They have not taken to those, but they have lost their own sets of values and the ideals of their own cultures. And because they have not quite worked out, as the Chinese, Indians and Negroes in the West Indies have, new patterns of their own cultures, there is a certain loss of confidence in themselves. When you see the Chinese-educated products from the Chinese schools, particularly when they speak on public platforms, you will understand what I mean. The English-educated is somewhat uncertain and hesitant, speaking and thinking in a language he has learnt all his life but which is not part of his own being. The other is supremely confident, speaking and thinking in a language which is part of his being and his cultural world.

"Next, and this is a serious disadvantage in a democratic system, the English-educated have lost touch with the mass of their own people who speak the vernacular languages. The only exception are the Malay English-educated. They first go to a Malay school before they go over to English. Hence the difference between the English-educated Malay leaders, who have not lost touch with their ground, and the English-educated Chinese and Indians who have, broadly speaking as a class, lost touch with the mass of the people from whence they came. I have not yet come across a Malay who is unable to speak or read and write in Malay. But I have come across many Chinese and Indians who are educated in English but are unable to read and write or even speak Chinese or Tamil or Malayalam or whatever their native tongues may be. Of course there are exceptions. Many, for instance, of the Chinese who are educated in the English schools are also educated at home in Chinese or have been to Chinese schools. But they are the exceptions.

"What is the future of this class? In the past they have been those most favourably placed and treated in colonial Malaya. The British, not unnaturally, preferred to deal with people who could speak their language and who understood their manners and mannerisms. Therefore the English-educated had risen to the highest positions, both in government service and in the professions, as doctors, lawyers, teachers, engineers, and in trade and commerce. They were the elite—the elite of a colonial society. They got the best jobs in the commercial firms. They were paid more in the English commercial firms than their counterparts were paid in the Chinese or Indian firms. In government service only the best of the English-educated were admitted. The local university, which then consisted of two colleges—Medical College and Raffles College—only admitted the English-educated. There were no English-educated trisha riders or ricksha pullers, labourers or coolies, as they used to be called, because whoever became English-educated need not become a coolie or a trisha rider. Other more profitable avenues of employment were open to them.

"How closely the social and economic position of the English-educated was related to the political power in the country was shown when the Japanese took over in 1942. Then, all of a sudden, the English-educated lost their special position. The people who rose to high places and who could do business and make profits with the Japanese merchants and the Japanese Government were those who could speak and write the Japanese language, or, at second best, the Chinese *Kanji* characters.

"And so the Chinese-educated did better than the English-educated in Japanese-occupied Malaya. Suddenly the English-educated discovered that they had lost their foster-parents. And they had to compete in the hard, cruel world on equal terms with everybody else. But we should all be cheered to remember that, although they did not do as well as when the British were there, in open competition with the other language groups they did not go under. Then in 1945 the British returned and the English-educated once again assumed their pre-eminence. Well, so much for the past.

"Now, for the present. Those who want to defend and extol the qualities of the English-educated can easily point out that the leadership of both the Federation and Singapore are in English-educated hands. Most of the members of the Government of the Federation of Malaya are English-educated—the Tunku went to Kuala Kangsar and Cambridge, Dato Razak went to Kuala Kangsar and London, and so on. Similarly, in Singapore. But I would like to suggest to you that this is not proof of the superlative qualities of the English-educated. It is proof that in a given historical situation the English-educated nationalist has a useful role to play. In colonial revolutions in all the territories of the British Empire, when independence was won from the British Raj, power was handed over to the English-educated local nationalists. So it was in India, Pakistan, Burma, Ceylon, Ghana and Malaya. But, having won power, the role that they have to fulfil depends upon the circumstances and conditions of their people and their country.

"I suggest that the role of the English-educated leadership in Singapore and in Malaya is the role it is playing in India. It is for them to carry the social revolution one step further by extending the rights and privileges that they have wrested from the British to the mass of their own people, the majority of whom are not English-educated. . .

"Nobody disputes the usefulness of the English language. India, after twelve years of independence, is doubting whether she should discard it as the official language. The whole world of the sciences and technology is opened up through this medium. The trends are that in ten years' time there will be a higher percentage of our population proficient in English, for they will have learnt it not only in the English-language schools but also in the Chinese, Tamil and Malay schools.

"But I suggest to you that the English-speaking student who will emerge in ten or twenty years' time from today from the English, Chinese, Malay or Tamil schools will be a completely different person from the English-educated person of the past. He will not be deculturized or devitalized. He will have vitality and confidence and a sense of dedication to our own country and our own people. So, in a way, the present English-educated type will disappear and a new English-speaking group with different characteristics will emerge.

"This is the historical process of Asians who first became Western-educated and ceased to be Asians giving way to Asians who have learned Western languages, techniques and sciences but remain Asians and are proud to be Asians. What the English-educated of today must do is to help create a people who are Malayan-educated but are also proficient, amongst other things, in the English language. That is the way to the future."

Two weeks later, Lee Kuan Yew addressed the Chinese Union of Journalists (on 1 September). He urged all journalists in the state to form one single union, not to continue with unions which separately catered for racial groups. In Singapore there were English language newspapers, Chinese language newspapers, Malay 'language newspapers and Tamil language newspapers. Although they used different languages to express their thoughts, the duties and responsibilities of the journalists were the same. Whether he was a reporter from the Chinese Press, the English Press, or the Malay Press, his duties were the same: to report facts, to arouse and enlighten the mass of the people and to educate them. Since they had the same responsibilities, there was no reason why they should not form a united and strong journalists' union.

Lee said that the term "Singapore Chinese" contained an element of chauvinism. In Singapore there were still many organizations, guilds and schools using the terms "Singapore Chinese" or "overseas Chinese". The organizations registered under such names implied that they would protect the interests of the Chinese, and that other races were barred from joining them. Such terms were detrimental to racial unity. Lee said: "If every race adopts this closed-door policy and forms small cliques or associations to protect its own racial interests, then it is difficult to talk of establishing a Malayan nation. For, although by what name one calls oneself is a small matter, it nevertheless reflects the shape of one's thinking. We must realize that the position of the local Chinese here today is completely different from, say, that of ten years ago. Previously, the majority of the Chinese did not regard this country as their permanent home. They regarded this country as a place to earn a living, make money to send back to China to buy land, farms, build houses, schools, and so on. This situation has changed since the war, particularly since the establishment of the Communist Republic of China. Travel restrictions between Malaya and China

103

were imposed. This forced the Chinese to decide which of the two places they regarded as their permanent home and the object of their loyalty. The Chinese here have chosen Malaya as their permanent home and object of their loyalty. Therefore, we must approach all problems from the point of view of Malayans. That, for many, means actively to cultivate a Malayan consciousness."

The Prime Minister conceded that Malayan consciousness for many Chinese was a new thing. He said: "Many still do not understand it and some find it difficult to accept. They may even feel that Malayan consciousness is being used as a pretext to eliminate Chinese culture. Thus, as journalists, it is your responsibility to educate the Chinese so that they will understand our Malayan nation and the meaning of Malayan consciousness. What we need is not a paper to convey the Chinese point of view, but a paper using the Chinese language as an instrument to convey the Malayan point of view. We have only to look at countries in Southeast Asia to realize that the Chinese and the Chinese newspapers are being suppressed and victimized. Only in Singapore has such a situation been avoided, because the Chinese here have, through their predominance in population, gained a limited political security. But the lesson of Southeast Asia is that if the Chinese Press wish to continue to survive, they should identify themselves as part and parcel of the national culture. . . "

IV

In merger with Malaya, Lee Kuan Yew saw Singapore's only hope of complete freedom from colonial ties. He explained why in a speech to the Foreign Correspondents' Association on 16 September, when he also expanded on his theory that the Malay peasantry, not the Chinese urban-educated, must decide the pace of Malaya's development. Lee also warned of the dangers of communalism.

"In the fourteen years since the end of World War II in 1945, the political face of Asia has undergone more change than during any other equivalent period in Asian history. Events have taken place which are likely in the next few decades to shift the centre of world gravity from Europe and the West to Asia and the East. The massive potential greatness of India and China dominates the Asian scene. Events in Malaya must be looked at against this background if we are to see them in proper perspective. What happens to the rest of Asia is bound to affect Malaya. With one exception, the problems that we face are the problems common to the whole region—the problems of under-developed territories seeking ways of rapid industrialization and progress. The one exceptional problem is that caused by the plural society of Malaya. It was because the Malayan Communist Party misjudged the situation caused by this plural society that their revolt failed. And other political movements, besides the Malayan Communist Party, ignore this factor at their own peril.

"Put briefly it means this—that the pace of the social revolution in Malaya is as fast or as slow as the Malays in the kampongs want it, not as the Chinese in towns desire it. The towns can act as a catalyst on the kampongs, but it is the kampongs that decide the pace... In Malaya, if we include Singapore in the name. the Malays and the Chinese are about equal in numbers. Broadly speaking, the majority of the Chinese live in the big towns and the majority of the Malays in the kampongs in the countryside. Even more broadly speaking, the Chinese constitute the urban proletariat, and the Malays the peasantry. If there were a free-for-all in Malaya it might be possible that a movement of the Chinese urban proletariat could assume power and dictate the course of the revolution. But this is impossible. For the British and the Americans will never allow a free-for-all in Malaya. Now if the Chinese People's Republic and the Russians were prepared to intervene, as in Indo-China, and throw their weight on to the communist side, then the position would be different and a small militant party might succeed in capturing power. But they are not, and will never be, so stupid as to intervene. They want to win over eighty million Indonesians, and many more millions of the uncommitted people in Southeast Asia. And nothing is more likely to make the Southeast Asian countries more anti-communist than the spectacle of China's might coming to the aid of Chinese minorities in Southeast Asia. The fact that the Chinese are numerically not a minority in Malaya does not alter the position. Constitutionally the Chinese are in the minority, for not all have citizenship. And so it is that it is the Malay peasants in the kampongs who decide and set the pace.

"For this reason I believe that the immediate danger to Malaya is not communism but communalism. There can be no communist Malaya until there is a Malay-led Malayan Communist Party. That follows from the hypothesis that it is the Malay peasantry and not the Chinese urban proletariat who can and will decide the pace. There can be no Malay-led Malayan Communist Party until there is a disgruntled Malay educated elite to lead a discontented Malay peasantry. But there is no likelihood of any significant Malay educated elite becoming disgruntled anywhere in the foreseeable future. For many, many years there will be more important and valuable jobs than there are Malay candidates for them. And there need never be a discontented Malay peasantry so long as the Federation Government keeps up social advance and progress in the kampongs.

"But in the meantime the communal tensions can easily increase.

105

The Chinese urban population may chafe at what they consider the slow pace determined by a Malay-weighted government. And there are bound to be groups who are prepared to exploit the dissatisfaction of the urban Chinese by making communal appeals.

"On the other hand, the Malay sector is equally open to exploitation by communal and—this is more serious—by religious appeals. Groups are bound to emerge which will exploit the natural desire of the Malay to be dominant in his own country, not only in the political but also in the economic and social fields. A Malay-weighted government which openly declares its desire to foster inter-racial co-operation and makes concessions to the Chinese on economic, cultural or educational issues can be accused by communal-minded groups of selling out Malay rights.

"And so the country can easily drift into communal conflicts. Unlike communism whose dialectics have to be taught and learned before loyalties to it can develop, communalism makes a direct primitive appeal to emotional loyalties whose response can be immediate and spontaneous. Anyone who lived through the Maria Hertog riots of 1950 and the Hock Lee riots of 1955 can remember the difference in intensity of the emotional hysteria generated in the first as against the second.

"What is to happen? Does the existence of a Left-wing Government elected by a largely urban Chinese population in Singapore aggravate or alleviate the situation? I suggest the answer depends upon how the Government in Singapore conducts its affairs. If it panders to Chinese chauvinism and uses its position to give encouragement and expression to Chinese greatness then it is bound to aggravate the situation. For every major event in Singapore is carried by the Press and the radio to every Malay kampong in the Federation. And this will still be the case, whether or not the Press produces different editions in the two territories, or the radio news is separately and differently presented by Singapore and Kuala Lumpur. For there is no possible way of ensuring that the Singapore situation can be isolated from the Federation. For this reason if the Singapore Government so conducts its affairs as to convince the Malays in the Federation kampongs that the Chinese in a big city like Singapore are prepared to be assimilated as one Malayan people, and to convince the Federation Chinese in the towns that there can be a happy medium between the tempo of the Malay kampong revolution and the Chinese urban revolution, it cannot but have a healthy effect on the whole Malayan situation.

"1959 marks a new phase in the history of the Malaysian Archipelago... Broadly speaking, the old anti-colonial phase is over. Now all the differences in our peoples, differences which were muted in the common desire to unite for freedom, have come back into their own.

106

But in a way it is a healthier situation now. For all the main issues have been brought out into the open. Issues not clearly defined before, are now presented to the people in clear terms—the problems of nation-building and industrial progress in a multiracial, multilingual and multicultural society. Now for the first time the questions of national language, Malayan culture, Malayan-centred loyalties have been posed to the people not as theoretically desirable ideas in the distant future, but as immediate issues which can become literally a matter of life and death.

"On all sides other than in the opportunist camps, there is sober rethinking and reappraisal. Our social revolution is complicated by the lack of national solidarity. If the period ahead is not made into one of national consolidation, then we are in for a troublesome future.

"I wish to end on a note of optimism. Whatever the differences of political philosophy or ideology between the Federation Government and the Singapore Government both are acutely conscious of this problem. Both desire a national, not a communal, solution to it. For that reason we can look confidently to the problem being tackled in a firm and courageous manner on both sides of the Causeway. If we succeed then there will be no headlines for the foreign Press. But these are the headlines we can well afford to miss."

V

On the Prophet Mohamed's birthday on 17 September, Lee Kuan Yew spoke to representatives of the Muslim community. He reminded them that Singapore was a multiracial and multireligious society which could not survive without religious tolerance. All the major religions of the world were represented in Singapore. Lee said that one of the most arresting and hopeful features was this spirit of religious tolerance. Hindus, Muslims, Buddhists and Christians worshipped side by side without rivalry or jealousy. "We are," he said, "fortunate in that we have escaped the religious tensions and conflicts that have convulsed less fortunate countries in Europe and Asia. There is no reason why this spirit of tolerance should not continue. We can maintain this spirit of tolerance provided religious and secular leaders do not commit the tragic error of dragging religion into the political arena or using it as a cloak for political ambitions. For once a religious creed is identified with a particular political movement, then every normal and legitimate political conflict is immediately transformed into a religious conflict as well. We should guard against this danger because there are politicans who see in the exploitation of religious sentiments a short cut to political popularity.

"The true men of religion will, on the other hand, stress the essential principle underlying all religions—that mankind is one and that, whatever the doctrinal differences, all religions teach that all men are brothers and should live peacefully together. All religions strive to bring out all that is best in man—love, decency, charity and understanding. These are qualities necessary not only for the spiritual advancement of the individual but also for the well-being of society."

VI

When nationalists in newly independent countries assume responsibility for government they are at once confronted with an urgent security decision: should they retain on the statute book laws which they strongly condemned as inhuman, unjust and oppressive when fighting colonialism? India was faced with this problem, as other countries have been. Not only did India retain all the British-made emergency regulations: more were added.

Lee Kuan Yew was probably unusual, if not unique, in that he was a nationalist leader of what he knew was a communist-backed, anti-colonial, nationalist front, who announced before the elections, on the eve of self-government, that if his party won control they would retain the hated Emergency Regulations. In other places leaders have not been so frank. Perhaps the circumstances were different.

Lee first explained his party's stand in the Assembly on 8 October, 1958. He said then that after the general elections the Federation of Malaya would be represented on Singapore's Internal Security Council under the new Constitution. It would have the decisive vote. What happened to the Emergency laws was a matter of some considerable importance to them, because there were two political situations; one in the Federation and one in Singapore, both distinct and separate and self-contained, with a cordon sanitaire in the Straits of Johore.

Lee said: "As a party of the Left, we may not always agree or see eye to eye with a party of the Right, as the Tunku has once called the United Malays Nationalist Organization. But we can assure them that their views and susceptibilities will be given the most careful consideration by us. We state our stand now on the question of the Emergency laws, and it is this: that as long as they are necessary for the maintenance of the security of the Federation, so long will they be necessary for Singapore. We state this now in the full knowledge and anticipation that there will be political bankrupts and charlatans . . . who will make promises to abolish them in the next elections. We have met these types before, and we expect to meet them in the next elections. When that time comes, we shall justify our view and our stand, that there will be no abolition of the Emergency laws in Singapore until they have been abolished in the Federation. Those who want the Emergency laws abolished in Singapore should try to help to establish conditions of peace and security in the Federation so that they may no longer be required there.

"But we also wish to say that the use of these Emergency powers depends upon the stand of the persons who are equipped with them, and we stand for an independent, democratic, non-communist Malaya. Within this democratic system everyone has the right to compete, to preach his political views, but the competition must be for the purpose of working the system, not destroying it. These powers will not be allowed to be used against political opponents within the system who compete for the right to work the system. That is fundamental and basic, or the powers will have destroyed the purpose for which they were forged. If in using these powers you, in fact, negate the purpose for which you made them, then you will end up with a situation where force, and more force, will become increasingly necessary.

"In our definition, 'subversion' is any political activity designed to further the aims and interests not of our own people but of foreign powers: and by foreign powers we mean not just Russia and China, but also America and Formosa, and the Western bloc... We in the People's Action Party would prefer to lose an election rather than win it on false premises and promises."

When the Assembly met on 14 October, 1959, Lee Kuan Yew claimed that the people had given him a mandate to continue the regulations. "But," he said, "let me be the first to remind this House that the ultimate answer to the communist challenge is not provided by this type of legislation giving the executive emergency or extraordinary powers. Ultimately it is the economic, social and political conditions and the battles on these planes that will decide whether Singapore, and indeed Malaya, will grow from strength to strength as a democratic state in which the more tolerant features of human civilization are preserved whilst the economic needs and necessities of the people are rapidly met, or whether a more totalitarian system will succeed the democratic system to cater for these economic needs. These powers can only provide a temporary damper against those who set out to wreck the democratic state..."

VII

"A man is as good as he is, and the degrees and titles he has after his name do not make him a better or a lesser man. In the last analysis, it is what a man is worth—his innate ability, his intellectual discipline

109

and his drive—which determines his effectiveness and usefulness in society. But because it is not practical to measure the ability of human beings individually when you have to deal with them in large numbers, they have to be classified into broad categories. One of the ways of classification is to denote a man's educational standing—he has passed primary school, secondary school, or university."

This was how Lee Kuan Yew began his speech at the Nanyang University on 28 October. Nanyang University (sometimes called Nantah) was founded in 1955 mainly through the efforts of a rich rubber merchant, Tan Lark Sye, who became chairman of the University. The main medium of instruction is Chinese. In July, 1964, the Singapore Government deprived Tan Lark Sye of his citizenship on the grounds that "out of extreme racialist sentiments he knowingly allowed himself to be used by his associates to advocate the communist cause in Malaya".

In his speech, Lee warned teachers and students of the dangers of making the University a symbol of Chinese excellence and of the supremacy of Chinese and not Malayan scholarship. This, he said, could aggravate the position of the overseas Chinese in all the other places in Southeast Asia. Lee Kuan Yew told them:

"Over a long period of time the academic standing of a school or a university acquires a reputation which is either good or bad. It is a reputation based on the sum total of opinion as a result of the performance of the graduates of either the school or the university, an indication of the degree of intellectual discipline and the breadth of knowledge which that educational institution has infused into its pupils. And so it is that the old universities in the world, like Oxford or Cambridge in England, or Harvard and Massachusetts Institute of Technology in America, or Leningrad University in Russia, or Peking Union Medical College in China, do not bother to ask other countries or other governments to recognize their degrees.

"People know the value of these degrees and it is universally accepted that their standard of training is high, and that a graduate who holds a degree from one of these old universities is a person who has attained a reasonably high degree of intellectual discipline and professional skill. Hence it is that these old universities did not have to ask their governments to pass laws to acknowledge and recognize their degrees. Their degrees won recognition through the process of time, for the acid test of the value of their degrees was what those graduates who held degrees made of themselves after graduation, either as captains in trade or industry, or by becoming leaders of men in other fields of human endeavour. The other major yardstick of the worth of a university is the contribution to human knowledge that research workers in the university have made in their pursuit of knowledge and truth. The bigger the contribution, the higher the reputation of the university.

110

"In the long run it is not whether the Singapore Government or the Federation Government recognizes your degrees that decides the opinion of people on the value of the Nanyang University degrees. In the end it is what the graduates of this University do in the outside world and by way of research in this University which will determine its status in the eyes of all people.

"Ultimately, it is what Nanyang graduates are really worth, and not what the Government says they are worth, which counts. However, in the meantime you have to face the problem of earning a living with the degree that you have got from this new University, and so to that extent official recognition of your degree can be of some assistance in helping Nantah graduates find their feet...

"You must appreciate that Nanyang University can best succeed and flourish if it is accepted as a Malayan university and not just as a Singapore university. In other words, by your efforts and performance you must slowly convince the people of the Federation that you deserve approval and recognition from the Federation Government...

"All around us in Southeast Asia are examples of countries where the local peoples, having wrested power from their colonial rulers and obtained the right to govern themselves, have decided to root out or suppress the Chinese distinctiveness in language and culture of the Chinese immigrants who have come to reside in these countries. Throughout the whole of Southeast Asia, where about fifteen million Chinese are scattered, they are being discriminated against because they are considered as having remained distinct and separate from the local communities, both in the use of their language and in the observance of their customs, habits and culture.

"At this moment in Indonesia a full-scale campaign has been launched to assimilate or else eradicate the Chinese people living there. Let us never forget that Singapore is part of Southeast Asia; that we are in the centre of a Malaysian people; that despite the fact that eighty per cent of our population are Chinese we cannot escape from our environment. The isolation from Indonesia and now from the Federation, which the British colonial system has imposed on Singapore, is a man-made one and can easily be unmade by man. Our geographical and ethnological positions are realities which we must face... A resurgent China is already the object, not just of admiration, but also of apprehension amongst the peoples of Southeast Asia. And if Nanyang were to become symbolized as an outpost in Southeast Asia of Chinese dominance, then we will only have ourselves to blame if we find the position deepened and embittered.

"But if you, by what you say and do, are able to demonstrate to the peoples of Southeast Asia that Nanyang is a beacon for the peoples of Southeast Asia for the pursuit of truth and knowledge, which has been founded by persons of Chinese descent, then

111

you will have made a signal contribution to the cause of inter-racial harmony and peace in this region.

"If you, by your deeds, after you have graduated, prove that this is not just a tactical move, but a demonstration of deep and sincere convictions that Nanyang is part of Southeast Asia, and is dedicated to the furtherance of progress and prosperity for the peoples of Southeast Asia, then, in the years to come, those who follow in your footsteps as graduates of Nantah, will be respected and honoured as products of an institution for higher learning which has made a contribution to the pursuit of knowledge and human happiness in Southeast Asia. Your immediate worries are elementary ones, like finding a job and making a living. But your long-term problems are the ones that really decide what happens to you and to the peoples of Southeast Asia, of whom three and a half million of Chinese descent are living in Malaya and Singapore. We are living in a Southeast Asia which is rapidly changing, and it would be folly to shout slogans coined in old battles. Our problem is the future. The past are lessons from which we learn to avoid the pitfalls in the future."

VIII

3 December was a historic occasion and Lee Kuan Yew with his pronounced sense of history made the most of it. Singapore's first Malayan-born Head of State, Inche Yusof bin Ishak, a former journalist and founder of the modern Malay newspaper *Utusan Melayu* (now owned by leaders of UMNO in Malaysia), was installed in office. This was not then an elective post. Singapore's first President was appointed by the Cabinet. He was a constitutional President and must accept the advice of the Prime Minister.

Lee Kuan Yew spoke after the installation ceremony from the steps of the City Hall to a large crowd massed on the Padang, the grassy battlefield of many football, rugby and cricket encounters since Raffles' days.

"Exactly six months ago," he said, "on 3 June, with the promulgation of the new Constitution of the State of Singapore, the office of British Governor and Commander-in-Chief of the Colony of Singapore was abolished. Gone was the cocked hat with the white plumes, the symbol for over 100 years of our British overlord. On that memorable evening six months ago we, the people of Singapore, gathered here to rejoice in the step we were taking, away from the colonial past, towards an independent future and our tryst with destiny. But the man who used to wear the cocked hat with plumes on top did not disappear. Quietly and unobtrusively he put away the symbols

112

of his once great office. As laid down by the Constitution, he became the constitutional Head of State, to help transfer smoothly the reins of power to a government elected by the people. Yesterday he departed, and with his departure goes the last of the powerful British Governors who once held sway over our lives.

"This morning, a few minutes ago, our own Yang di-Pertuan Negara was sworn and installed in office. It is a milestone in our brief history. He is not a powerful man with power of life and death over us. His role is that of constitutional Head of the State of Singapore. He is the personification of the state of which you and I are members. Abstract concepts like 'the state' do not easily arouse mass enthusiasm and loyalties. From tribal chiefs to kings and emperors, through the ages down to present-day dictators and presidents, it was the individual leader who personified the state.

"But our Yang di-Pertuan Negara is no such potentate. As human civilization advances, forms of government also change. No individual is perfect. So the search for more perfect forms of government has moved from the rule of the autocrat to that of the collective leadership. But again collective leadership is an abstract concept, and cannot easily invoke mass enthusiasm and loyalties. So over and above this collective leadership of the elected Government, is the titular Head of State. He symbolizes all of us. To him devotion and loyalty are due.

"It is my privilege to introduce to you our Yang di-Pertuan Negara, Inche Yusof bin Ishak. It is not his high birth which has commended him for this high office, for he is a commoner. It is only that he is one amongst us whose deep understanding of the hopes and fears of our people, and whose natural dignity, ensure that the duties of his high office will be discharged honourably and well.

"With his installation as our first Malayan Yang di-Pertuan Negara, we have also adopted new symbols. The flag, the coat of arms and the anthem, they serve a powerful emotive function. Men have died for the honour and glory of their flag. Men have rallied and united in instinctive response to their anthems. Small country though we may be, it is nevertheless necessary that we develop these instinctive emotive responses so vital to the survival of a people. Singapore is unique in many ways. An island city state of one and a half million people with a constitution of semi-independence, we must be unique in this world in having as our adult citizens less people who were born and bred here, than those born and bred elsewhere. Of our nine Ministers, only two were born and bred in Singapore. And so it is with the bulk of our adult citizens. In the last elections, of about 600,000 voters, only about 270,000—less than half—were people born and bred in Singapore.

"I have mentioned these facts to emphasize the urgent need for inculcating common values, common loyalties, common responses amongst our people. The sense of belonging together, belonging to one entity, one unity, is a must in our task of nation-building. An old nation with an ancient past has long historic experiences to bind its people together. Indeed, it is their long history that permitted the evolution of a common language and a common cultural heritage. We may not be able to afford such a long time to evolve a common heritage for our people. There are forces let loose in Asia, and in the whole world, which make it dangerous and foolish for us to count on several decades in which to accomplish our task of building one nation and one people. We must go about our task with urgency. The racial and cultural conflicts engendered by the differing economic status of the indigenous peoples and the Chinese settlers in neighbouring countries are grim reminders to us to accomplish our task of integrating our peoples now and quickly. We cannot afford the tragedies that have taken place amongst some of our neighbours. . . .

"In a world where all the city states have disappeared, in a century where only the big and the powerful nations count, there may be a touch of pathos in our attempts to inculate local loyalties in 1·5 million people. It is always useful to keep our sense of proportion. Whilst we are searching for that vital sense of oneness in a common destiny, let us not forget that what we have always inculcated is a sense of belonging to Singapore as part of a larger Malayan whole.

"Today, here on this Padang, and also in the thousands of homes listening with us here, let us renew our faith in ourselves and our future; let us resolve to be loyal to the interests of our people; let us pledge ourselves afresh to make this island a happy and peaceful place of plenty for all those who have sworn to be one with us. May our new symbols endure and evoke in our hearts those sublime feelings of dedication and sacrifice to a cause bigger than our individual selves. Finally, let us give to our Yang di-Pertuan Negara the loyalty and affection due to him as the symbol of the unity of the people who constitute the State of Singapore."

That night Lee Kuan Yew went to Radio Singapore to broadcast on the implications of Loyalty Week. Loyalty to the State, he said, was imperative if the people of Singapore were to forge ahead as a united, coherent, purposeful people. "Without this quality, we shall never build the foundations of a stable society.

"Few people in the world have ever been asked to undertake a more difficult task. In the centre of a Malaysian archipelago inhabited by about ninety million Indonesians and Malays living mostly in a peasant economy, Singapore is a city of one and a half million Chinese, Malays, Indians, Ceylonese, Eurasians and others: a city of traders and merchants and workers living a sophisticated city life. Only less than half our adult population was born and

114

bred in Singapore. The others have come from the Federation, from China, India, Ceylon and Indonesia as immigrants. And immigrants they would have remained all their lives but for the tremendous upheavals throughout Asia in the past ten years. The immigrants have decided to stay and make this their home. They have taken Singapore citizenship, acquired the rights and privileges of being citizens, and promised to share the responsibilities of the state. Diversity of race, language and culture is part of the richness of Singapore. But in one thing we cannot afford diversity—diversity of loyalty. If our new citizens are loyal not to Singapore but to the countries of their origin, then the state will run into difficulties. To emphasize this paramount need for singleness of loyalty, we have called our week of rejoicing Loyalty Week. Since the PAP Government took office exactly six months ago the emphasis has been on hard work, for without sustained effort there can be no progress. But all work and no play makes for a dull life. We must never overdo things. Whilst we live and work and sacrifice for the next generation, let us not banish all pleasure and happiness from our own. So let us make this a week of rejoicing and relaxation."

CHAPTER FOURTEEN

The Year of Power 1960

"WE become a nation," the Head of State declared in his 1960 New Year message *"without the prerequisites of a nation—a common language, common loyalties, and a common psychological make-up—to bring about that unity which we all desire."* 1960 for the new state was a year of reorganization, consolidation and preparation for the tasks ahead.

The Prime Minister visited Indonesia, and this was followed by an Indonesian cultural mission to Singapore, and visits from General Nasution and Dr Subandrio, Indonesia's Foreign Minister. Relations with the Federation of Malaya were good, and every initiative was taken by Singapore to promote co-operation in all matters of joint interest to the two territories. Singapore citizenship was clearly defined by new legislation. Henceforth a Singapore citizen's allegiance was to Singapore and no other state. The Industrial Arbitration Court was established. A new Factories Ordinance was introduced. Four new schools were completed. Work on thirteen others was started. Education was still the largest single item in the budget. Free education was provided for Malays *at all levels up to and including university. On 2 April Nanyang University held its first graduation ceremony. The People's Association was set up to organize leisure and promote youth activities. The new National Library was opened in October.*

In the Cabinet there was a clash between Ong Eng Guan, the Minister for National Development, and his colleagues. Later, Mr Ong was expelled from the PAP. In the Assembly, he continued to attack PAP leaders, and specifically charged the Prime Minister and Minister of Labour and Law with nepotism. A few minutes before he was due to be called before the Assembly to justify his allegations, he resigned.

Singapore's population (nearly half of the people under the age of fifteen) continued to grow, and statistics showed that Singapore's earning power depended on thirty-two per cent of its population gainfully employed, one of the lowest proportions in any community in the world. Economically, 1960 was a good year of expanding trade and industry, and a record year for the seaport and airport. The Post Office handled a record of 123 million letters and parcels.

I

A CONFIDENT Prime Minister went to the microphone at Radio Singapore on 1 January, to "wish and will ourselves a happy and prosperous New Year". The first half of 1959, he said, had been months of excitement and uncertainty. Everyone knew that change was in the air. Everybody marked time while they waited to see what was to happen. The second half was the aftermath, as fears proved largely unfounded and hopes were not completely realized. But by the end of the old year the heat and dust had settled. The shape of things to come had become clearer. "Not all are strange shapes. A good number of the good things in the past still find their places in the future. If 1959 was a year of decisive change, let 1960 be a year of consolidation." After seven months of the PAP, since June, 1959, everyone had had the measure of the Government, and the Government the measure of its problems. "Let us look forward to progress in the year ahead. Through hard work, faith and a little good fortune, may 1960 bring more happiness to more of us. Let us all make this our resolution for the New Year: to stop fretting and grumbling and doubting—to get on with the job in hand—do it well and the future will look after itself. . . "

Nobody then, not even the communists, could have imagined that, before the year was out, the extreme Left in the People's Action Party would try to capture the party. They were repulsed, and expelled. Later they formed the Barisan Sosialis. The break between the communists within the PAP (formed as a nationalists' front), and the non-communists led by Lee Kuan Yew had to come sooner or later. What was surprising was the communists' mistiming and their mistaken belief that the English-educated leadership would accept their direction rather than lose office, or that the Lee Kuan Yew group would not be prepared to fight to the finish.

It started with a clash between Ong Eng Guan, the Minister for National Development, and the rest of the PAP leadership. At the PAP Conference in June, Ong proposed sixteen resolutions in fundamental criticism of the Government of which he was a member, and its policy. After discussion the Conference recommended that the Central Executive of the party should consider his expulsion "after hearing evidence of his attempts to disrupt party unity and destroy collective party leadership". At the end of the month Ong was expelled and he then took his attacks on PAP leaders to the Assembly. There he accused the Prime Minister and the Minister for Labour and Law of nepotism. Ong resigned from the Assembly a few minutes before the Assembly was to meet in Committee to hear him justify his allegations. A Commission of Inquiry, headed by a judge, found there was no truth in his allegations.

Press conference

ı London. Facing the Press

ı Warsaw. Inspecting the guard of honour with the Prime Minister of Poland, Mr Cyrankiewicz

At the 1966 Commonwealth Prime Ministers Conference, listening to the Tunku

In January, Lee Kuan Yew made his first official visit abroad as Prime Minister. He went to Indonesia. At Jakarta airport he said that, but for the accidental divisions of the European colonial empires, the history of Malaya, Singapore and Indonesia might well have been more closely knit. The Portuguese, the Dutch, the British and the French came to Southeast Asia and divided it up amongst themselves, much in the fashion of modern gangsters who demarcate their respective territorial jurisdictions over a city. Geography they condemned. And the course of history they distorted. During that colonial era, the links between Jakarta and Amsterdam, between Singapore and London, were closer than the links between Jakarta and Singapore. Such were the absurdities of European colonial domination.

"That era," said Lee, "the dark ages of Asia, is slowly disappearing into the limbo of the past. But it may take some time before we can completely rectify or eradicate the evils of the past. Your great country nurtured a high level of civilization in the past. Borobudur and the relics of the Hayam Wuruk and Gajah Mada governments are traces of a golden age. Your struggle against the Dutch to establish your independence was a source of inspiration for the nationalists in Singapore. And we watch with even greater interest your efforts to make up for past decades of stagnation under Dutch colonial exploitation.

"You are our great neighbour. You have asserted your right to independence fourteen years ago. We are a small country and we have yet to rid ourselves of the last vestiges of colonial domination. But as we emerge from the stupor of the colonial era we must renew our links and our friendship with our neighbours. I bring you the goodwill and fraternal greetings of the people of Singapore."

At the state banquet, the Prime Minister submitted that "our friendship and desire for co-operation spring from the hearts of the people of Singapore. There is nothing that the people of Singapore would like more than to have more friendly and closer relations in cultural and trade matters with our second closest neighbour—the Republic of Indonesia...

"I feel that our relationship has undergone a fundamental change for the better. Our relationship will not be of the nature it was when a colonial power dealt unsympathetically and in purely commercial terms with the Indonesian nation. Co-operation between us will be to our mutual benefit. It is our intention in our trade with Indonesia, not just to make a profit out of her, but to serve her needs for as long as we can perform a useful function as a collecting point for disposal of Indonesian products, and for purchases of finished goods. As your economy develops and our own industries are established, it is inevitable that the pattern of trade between us will change in its complexion. But I am confident that we will always be able to benefit from trade with each other."

Lee Kuan Yew concluded his speech with the assurance that Singapore would not allow anything detrimental to the security of Indonesia to be committed in any territory over which it had control. "This is the basic friendship which we have towards our neighbours, the people of Indonesia. May that friendship strengthen and grow in mutual respect and mutual prosperity."

III

To the surprise of its members, the Prime Minister accepted an invitation from the Rotary Club to dine with them on 24 February. He had refused invitations while in opposition. He explained why, and he told them of the considerations which prompted him on this occasion to accept. The speech made a considerable impression on the trading community, who looked upon it as a major policy declaration.

Lee said that the political beliefs of the PAP would not normally commend themselves to a group of people who were successful in a given order of society. "By the very nature of your constitution, your members are those who have succeeded in life... It was not unnatural to infer that your membership consists of people who, having done well under an existing social order, are satisfied with that social order and therefore extremely anxious that nobody should alter things in case they may not do so well under a new order. Not wanting to arouse more animosity from those who are not likely to be politically sympathetic to the PAP, I did not take advantage of the opportunity you offered me in the past to inflict my political views on your members. However, now that the PAP is the governing party, although you probably still do not agree with its political objectives, you may be interested to know what these objectives are."

Lee said that a whole set of political principles and socialist beliefs had often been summed up in the PAP phrase "a more just and equal society". By this the PAP did not mean that all men were equal and would be rewarded equally. "Men are not born equal in either physical or mental capacity. But a socialist believes that society as a whole will benefit, and there will be more happiness for more people, if all are given equal opportunities for education and advancement regardless of class or property. It therefore follows that, even under the new social order, there will be some men who are more successful than others, but with this fundamental distinction: that they have become more successful after free and equal competition and effort."

It was by now generally accepted, Lee said, that a revolution had taken and was still taking place throughout Asia, and that Malaya and Singapore were a part of this revolution. The revolution began before the PAP was ever thought of, but the PAP hoped to endure to see it through to its fulfilment. "Last year, before we assumed power, we expounded the theme of the social revolution. . . "

Lee said that the PAP was basically a revolutionary, and not a reformist, movement and that the social and economic forces which brought the PAP into power had not altered. Although it was not practical or possible to have a profound change of social organization through a major shift in the relations between social classes because of the entrepot economy of Singapore, it was nevertheless important to remember that the have-nots—who formed the mass of the workers —the under-privileged, the under-employed and the unemployed, were seeking a change in their position in society. A government of Singapore which represented these urges could not modify its social programme or political principles without forfeiting the trust and confidence that had been placed in it by the under-privileged. "Such a government can trim its economic programme to fit into the limitations of an entrepot island economy only if a strenuous effort is made to redress the economic balance by a redistribution of social and economic benefits. . . "

For some time before a revolution, said Lee, the ruling class finds itself in a position of a minority, isolated from the rest of society. If the British colonial government had persisted in maintaining its domination, then the machinery of the state would have given way and there might well have been a complete breakdown by a concerted attack of revolutionary forces from the ground. "We have been saved this inconvenience by Britain's policy of withdrawal from positions of open colonial rule in Asia."

After the recent elections, the Prime Minister explained, the political system changed, and power passed from the last legitimate colonial government to the first representative government of the people, thus for the time being bridging the gulf between the rulers and ruled. It was important that, if the gulf was not to re-appear, the Government's social and political policies should reflect the sentiments and attitudes of the revolutionary mass from whence it drew its strength. But, on the other hand, he warned, a revolutionary government which attempted to upset the structure of Singapore's island entrepot economy would only bring deprivations upon the people and disaster upon itself. "So the art of government in

Singapore, through this phase of its history, can be summed up in two guiding principles: first, to work to the best advantage the present entrepot economy whilst slowly encouraging industrial expansion, partly through government capital but largely through private investment; and second, to satisfy the revolutionary urge of the mass of the people for a fundamental change in the relationship between social classes, and this in spite of the fact that there can be no fundamental change in the immediate future in the economic base of society. An orthodox Marxist will say that is an impossible task. The business of the PAP, as a democratic socialist party, is to show that, difficult and delicate a task though it may be, it can be done. In the long run, it is inevitable that the economic base itself will be transformed."

The Prime Minister said that those who feared disastrous changes in the economic system with the advent of a PAP Government, but who were now agreeably surprised that the world had not collapsed, should remember that the PAP's political opponents were frequently not truthful. "Never at any time did we consider, or pretend, that drastic changes in economic relationships were possible in our given set of political circumstances. It is not for lack of revolutionary purpose that we have not made more drastic change in the relationships of the social classes. It is more the appreciation of the limitation of the Singapore situation which has predetermined our line of policy and action. Basically we are not reformists. We do not believe that changes in the social order can be accomplished through the alteration of some particular institution, activity or condition. But, revolution aside, the first business of a government is to govern firmly and wisely in the interests of the whole community. And the interests of the whole community in our entrepot situation require the active participation and co-operation of the managerial and professional elite. We understand how you came to be leaders of trade and commerce, or captains of industry, or distinguished yourselves in the professions. We also understand that the incentives were material ones. And since it is our desire to see that the system continues to operate effectively and efficiently, it must necessarily follow that we are prepared to allow the old incentives to continue."

The problem of the Government, he said, was how best to utilize the existing social order to produce the maximum results. This being so, Government's only intervention in the economy envisaged in the next four years was a redistribution of the results of the fruits of the economy. "At the end of our tenure of office, it is our intention that there should be more equality of opportunity for education and advancement. To fulfil this intention will require a tremendous expenditure of the national revenue on education, expenditure which cannot be made unless there is an expansion of the whole economy. And if there is one overriding problem which we must resolve, it is that of creating sufficient expansion in the economy (1) to provide the jobs for a growing population, and (2) to provide the revenue to educate the younger half of that growing population."

The curious position now was that a socialist government was entrusted with the responsibility for industrial expansion in what was still essentially a free enterprise, and capitalistic, system. "To the extent that you help the expansion of that system, you will have the support of the Government. And the message that I would like to leave with you this evening is this: regardless of our differing political beliefs, we have enough common ground, albeit for different reasons, in desiring a rapid economic and industrial development in the immediate future. For this phase of our social revolution, the better business you do, the more things you buy and sell to and from Singapore, the more shops and factories that you open, the happier we are. Where we might not be in agreement is the way in which we hope to spread the benefits of prosperity. But so long as your activity assures not only your own prosperity but the prosperity of the whole community, you will find the apparatus of the Government willing and ready to assist you in your enterprise."

IV

Multilingualism may well be a symbol of racial tolerance in a multiracial state, but it has its own peculiar problems, and the impact of several tongues upon a debate in the Assembly was remarked upon by the Prime Minister at the election of the Speaker on 1 June. Lee said that the task the Speaker had been invited to discharge was not the simple one of following traditions and precedents. He was faced with some of the complications which a chairman of an international conference must face. "Can we maintain decorum and an air of intimacy in debate in spite of the fact that the Chairman and many Members of the House will not know what is being said until it is irretrievably recorded on the official tapes? Can such a chairman develop the powers of intuition to sense and fathom the evil intentions of wicked tongues before the words have been uttered? Can there be a sense of humour and an atmosphere of conviviality as one is being harangued in a language not understood, even through an interpreter not always clearly understandable? The past year has given us some experience of the problems which we have to resolve if we are to maintain this House as a debating and thinking Chamber, and not just a forum for declamations and denunciations."

123

Lee Kuan Yew realized that multilingualism had its limitations, but he strongly resisted any move to abolish it. Whenever occasion demanded he continued to speak, in the House and outside, in Chinese, Malay and English. He encouraged everyone to learn at least two languages in addition to their mother tongue.

V

From March onward, Lim Chin Siong and other pro-communists began to build up their strength in the unions and set out secretly to undermine the prestige and influence of the Government. To embarrass PAP leaders, Ong Eng Guan, expelled from the party for unprincipled activities, also voiced ultra-Left slogans. Lee Kuan Yew faced up to all this in a speech in the Assembly on 3 August, when he spoke of "new factors which have entered the political arena". Against the PAP and what it stood for—an independent, democratic, non-communist, socialist Malaya, of which Singapore would be part—there was only one organization, the Communist Party, which could challenge the Government in a bid for ultimate power. The Right-wing forces were "inert and ineffective", but communist sympathizers and activists, who had scattered and gone underground before the election, had begun the work of regrouping and reorganization.

Lee dealt with the contradictions between the PAP and the pro-CP forces. "I would like to restate in simple language for the benefit of the Opposition, both in the House and outside the House, that the policies of the PAP were evolved out of its own experience of struggle under local conditions, not out of doctrinaire principles. And it has been successful up to date and will continue to be successful so long as it adheres not to doctrinaire principles, in complete disregard of local facts and conditions, but to the principles evolved in the context of the Malayan revolutionary situation. We believe in an independent, democratic, non-communist, socialist Malaya. What is the alternative for all Left-wing forces in Malaya? To this affirmation of faith, does anybody seriously stand up to say that they believe in the establishment of an independent communist Soviet Republic of Malaya? In the context of the present situation, do they hope to carry with them the mass of the Muslim Malays, the English-educated, the Indian-educated? Surely all have conceded that there can be no communist Singapore until there is a communist Malaya, and that there can be no communist Malaya unless the Malays are sufficiently softened from neighbouring territories."

Lee chided the English language Press, which he said confused and deluded the public. "The irony of it is that, basically, anti-communist local journalists, through European, imperialist, colonialist newspapers, have helped to build up confusion in the minds of the people. All this talk of democratic rights, *laissez-faire* liberalism, freedom, and human rights, in the face of the stark realities of an underground struggle for power, can only confuse the English-educated world."

The problem that confronted them was not, he suggested, a simple one of allowing absolute liberalism and democratic rights to prevail, but of exerting that right amount of restriction on absolute rights so that a tolerant democratic society could endure and not turn into a totalitarian state. "In other words, the Government can, and where necessary must restrict the rights of individuals, but if it does so to a point where it becomes in fact a totalitarian society, then the purpose of the restriction has been negated. These restrictions are bearable only because without them a more intolerant system would triumph."

Winding up the debate a week later, the Prime Minister returned to what he called "the ideological battle and political realism". He said that a big mistake which the Left-wing adventurers were making in Singapore was that they thought they could use Singapore as a base, a Yenan, from which to liberate the rest of Malaya. "As the top leaders of the MCP know, independence for Singapore can only come with merger... the task is not to build up tension and strife, but to lay the foundations for merger. For independence is no longer the simple business of fighting the British. All these attempts to try and swing the political line back to the fluid, confused, uncertain position of the 1955 elections can never succeed, for these Left-wing adventurers cannot find the arguments to counter the logic and the realism upon which our analysis is founded."

To summarize the PAP's ideological stand, Lee Kuan Yew read out what five persons closely connected with the Party leadership, S. Woodhull, Fong Swee Suan, Lim Chin Siong, C. V. Devan Nair and Chan Chiaw Thor, all of whom were in prison for two and a half years, from 1956 to 1959, had had to say immediately after they were released on 4 June, 1959: " 'In most other countries, socialist programmes rest on an already given historical foundation of an unitary national consciousness and solidarity. We have to struggle not only for socialism, but for the nationalist basis of socialism. The real struggle for socialism in Malaya can only begin when our people, Malays, Chinese and Indians, are able to transcend the communal, cultural and linguistic barriers and loyalties which at present divide them, and embrace a common Malayan loyalty and cultivate a common national consciousness.

" 'Once the problem of linguistic and cultural unity is on the way to being resolved, fears and suspicions will fade away. We must face the facts. So long as the fight was against British colonialism the differences between the peoples of Malaya were muted and dulled in the desire to achieve the common goal of freedom by common effort. Now that this freedom has been won in the Federation all the differences come back into their own. They can and must be resolved. And we in Singapore can set the way to the solution of these important differences in language and culture. That is what we can and must do in this next phase of our struggle for freedom, the struggle for merger.

" 'It was not the might of British arms which defeated the armed revolt led by the MCP, but the failure of the MCP to establish itself as a nationally-based movement. And thereby hangs a lesson which Malayan socialists will ignore at their own peril. But genuine socialists will oppose, positively and on the basis of principle, all those who attempt to negate and destroy either the ends or the means of democratic socialism in Malaya.

" 'With the achievement of political independence by the Federation of Malaya, a new phase has begun. And the most important task of socialists in this new phase is to achieve complete identification with the ideal of a United Malayan nation, and to struggle by peaceful, democratic and constitutional means for the enduring objective of an united, independent, democratic, non-communist and socialist Malaya.' "

Lee said this had been a declaration of political faith and principles which was in complete accord with the policies and programmes of the PAP. On the strength of this political stand four of the five authors were appointed Political Secretaries. Lee assured the House that, if any deviation was made from this stand, then the working basis was gone. "We are not going to harbour those who are not sincerely with us.

"One thing," added Lee, "we have achieved in greater measure than any other political party since 1948: we have won over the masses of people who might otherwise be sympathizers or supporters of the communist cause by our positive approach—the non-communist, democratic, socialist approach. As long as we keep on doing so and succeed in doing it, we shall remain a virile and vigorous force, and a movement to be reckoned with in the Malayan political situation..."

VI

What suddenly became known beyond the frontiers of Singapore as the Professor Enright Case, brought to the fore once again the question of academic freedom. At the end of November, Professor Enright,

Johore Professor of English at the University of Malaya in Singapore (now the University of Singapore), publicly presented his inaugural lecture. After reading a *Straits Times* report of this, the Minister for Culture came to the conclusion that Enright had interfered in state political affairs and angrily and publicly rebuked him.

Speaking to the Students' Union on 25 November, the Prime Minister said it was unfortunate that the Professor had become the unwitting trigger of the larger question of academic freedom. "Several of my contemporaries who are now teaching at the University tell me that he is one of the best type of teachers that the University should be recruiting, and a distinguished scholar and poet." Had the Professor explained that the report in *The Straits Times* was "tendentious", and that no sneer had been intended against "sarong culture", then no letter would have been necessary. There was no issue of academic freedom as such at stake in this case. "And whilst I sincerely congratulate you on your high resolve to defend the principle, I think you have rallied in defence of a principle that was never challenged. The simple point the Minister of Culture made is that no alien has a right to intervene by comment or action in the political issues of this country. Academic freedom does not confer this right on a visiting professor. And this right the Professor never intended to exercise."

Lee argued that academic freedom was founded upon three principles. First, that the teacher was a technical expert in his field. Second, that his search for truth and knowledge was disinterested. Third, that teachers in a university did not just transmit knowledge to successive generations: they were expected to advance the frontiers of human knowledge and widen the dominion of man's mind. His freedom of inquiry, research and exposition on the subject of which he was a competent and disinterested explorer and mentor should not be challenged by either governmental or even university authority. Within his province, his freedom was supreme. But his special status did not extend to fields where he was not the competent disinterested explorer. And one of those fields was the heat and dust of the political arena. Of course there was nothing to prevent him from going into this arena if he was a citizen and so entitled. But he entered this field not as a university teacher but as a citizen, and must therefore be ready for the hurly-burly in which other citizens entering this arena indulged.

Lee said: "Indeed, if they are citizens, it is their duty as respected and educated members of our society to express and canvass their views on what should or should not be done in the government of their country. They are citizens who, at very high cost to the state, have had their minds trained and sharpened in their various disciplines. They should and ought to undertake the responsibility of leading and formulating opinion on the political issues of the country. As I said to some friends teaching in the University, whether you are a trained physicist, or scholar of English literature, if you are a citizen it is your duty to contribute your share in the running of the democratic system. In England, before the days when egalitarian principles were carried to their logical conclusions, the English Universities of Cambridge and Oxford had special representation in the House of Commons, in recognition of the special contribution which trained scholars were expected to make to the deliberations of the country. But only those who were British subjects, citizens of Britain, could be elected to represent the Universities in Parliament.

"What then are the limitations on the university teacher who is not a citizen? None whatsoever as a teacher, but a definite prohibition against participation in the political issues of the country. How are we to know where the bounds of academic freedom end and the boundaries of political issues begin? I say common sense and academic judgment can be left to mark out these bounds. In the large majority of cases the question of whether it is wise for an alien teacher to canvass his views publicly on a political issue of the country in which he is a guest is quite simple. If you are an authority on Greek literature but a non-citizen, then you would be wise to leave the question of whether or not Malay should be the only official language to those who are citizens. The best thing is to stick to your subject. Now if you are an authority on economics and your research shows that a certain type of industry cannot be successfully established in Singapore, then by all means propound the results of your research and your conclusions thereon, even if it should conflict with a pet scheme of the Minister in charge of industrial development. And if you are an economist of repute the Minister would do well to read your exposition of the subject...

"Good sense should not be lacking where there are good brains. We need and will continue to need these good brains from abroad. In the past my colleagues and I have had occasion to state in no uncertain terms what we would have to do to expatriates who meddle in local politics, to colonial-owned newspapers and the expatriate newspapermen employed on the local paper. They took heed of our views. But they seem to have found a new way of meddling with local politics by publishing tendentious and sometimes completely distorted reports of speeches, making mischief all round. We trust these misreportings so far were not deliberate. If they persist we shall have to revise our views. On the whole, however, good sense has made any unpleasantness unnecessary so far. So I am sure good sense will prevail in other fields. For no one can be upset by the language of a scholar erudite in his branch of human learning, however polemical the views propounded. It is the language of the partisan that offends, and no great scholarly effort is required to avoid this."

128

CHAPTER FIFTEEN

The Year of Power 1961

IN 1961, the Government suffered defeat in two by-elections. The first created political uncertainty and provided opportunities for exploitation by pro-communists and communalists. Concerned with this, the Prime Minister of Malaya, in a speech in Singapore on 27 May, suggested the creation of a new State of Malaysia with the merger of Malaya, North Borneo (Sabah), Sarawak, Brunei and Singapore. This proposal became a critical issue in the second by-election. It was during this contest that a group of trade union officials led by Lim Chin Siong (secretly a member of the Malayan Communist Party) set out to prevent Singapore from merging into Malaysia. He was supported by Dr Lee Siew Choh, Parliamentary Secretary to the Ministry of Home Affairs. The PAP was defeated, the TUC was split, and the Prime Minister offered his resignation as Prime Minister to the Chairman of the PAP. This was refused, and the PAP confirmed its faith in Lee Kuan Yew's leadership.

Lee demanded a show-down in the Assembly. The

issue was nationalism as against communist united-front tactics. The Government held its position by twenty-seven to eight with thirteen PAP Members (including five parliamentary secretaries) abstaining. Having failed to capture the Government, the extreme Left of the PAP, led by Lim Chin Siong, Fong Swee Suan, S. Woodhull and Dr Lee Siew Choh, broke away from the PAP to form the Barisan Sosialis. On 24 August, Lee Kuan Yew met Tunku Abdul Rahman for the first formal discussion of the details of merger. The TUC was dissolved, and two new trade union organizations emerged, one of them grouped around Lim Chin Siong. Two major strikes marred the labour scene, a disturbing effect of the political conflict between the two groups. Pro-communist elements organized student demonstrations. The year ended with the issue of merger and Malaysia still undecided and Lee Kuan Yew, with a majority of one in a House of fifty-one, determined that the two territories must be reunified.

I

IN Asia, as in most other parts of the world, emotions were aroused by the murder of Patrice Lumumba in the Congo. In the Singapore Assembly, on 22 February, the Prime Minister moved a resolution expressing abhorrence at the "cold-blooded murder", called upon the United Nations to bring the murderers to justice, condemned the presence of Belgian troops and agents in the Congo, and supported the proposal to expel from the Congo all foreign troops not under United Nations command. At the same time, Lee Kuan Yew warned the people of Singapore to "restrain their righteous desire to show the Belgians what they think of them". Lee said that when the news broke upon the world that Mr Lumumba was said to have escaped, and ten nations immediately signed a declaration that they believed that he had been murdered, millions of angry, indignant words were uttered and millions more went out over the air carrying the righteous indignation and anger of people with any sense of decency throughout the world. But it illustrated, he said, that we live in one world, that there was only one peace and that it was indivisible, and that what happened in the Congo affected everyone sooner or later. Lee continued:

"In a world shrunken in size as a result of man's scientific and technical advance, new problems emerge, and, just as in the case of the Algerian conflict, since total war means total annihilation, new forms of combat for partial or complete victory in limited fields have to be evolved.

"It is the intention of the Government in bringing this matter for debate to put on behalf, I hope unanimously, of the people of Singapore a little more weight in the balance in favour of what is right and just, and also to set the tone of the talking that has been going on and will be going on in Singapore and around us and, what is more important, to set the pace of the thinking...

"There are really very few new things that can be said on the subject of the death of Mr Lumumba. Everything that need be said has been said so well and eloquently by so many other eminent people with more powerful pens and eloquent voices than our own. All I wish to do is to draw attention from our point of view to a few salient facts.

"There are really two issues—Lumumba the man when he was alive and Lumumba the myth that has been created by his murder. As for Lumumba the man, we never said anything. We stood for the freedom and independence of the Congo. If the Congolese people chose Mr Lumumba as their Prime Minister, then it was their right to do so, and he should have been given the opportunity to carry out his duties as Prime Minister. Whatever he was, the stupidest thing that could have been done was to have killed him and created a myth. The myth is becoming stronger day by day. It is the biggest united front issue on a world basis created since the Spanish civil war. Whether you are Right-wing, liberal, Fabian, social democrat or democratic socialist, or whether you are a communist, willy-nilly if you believe in decent behaviour, certain standards of honesty, certain standards of what people should do or should not do, then you must be against what has happened...

"We add our voice to the rising chorus of indignation... In Singapore, I hope we can give the lead to the thinking that should be done by people in a position to influence public opinion. One can get hysterical over this. One can get very angry. But what I am asking this House to do is soberly, albeit we are angry, to say what this means to us, what it is doing to our people, and how we, as elected representatives of the people, should lead them in the expression of their views of what is right and wrong in matters which concern us, although these matters take place some thousands of miles away in some country unknown to us, but so vitally important for the survival of all of us."

II

In 1960, the Minister for National Development, Mr Ong Eng Guan, was expelled from the People's Action Party. He resigned from the Assembly, contested a by-election, won, and became a member of the Opposition. He at once began to attack the PAP, and PAP personalities, especially the Prime Minister.

On 29 December, 1960, seventeen minutes before he was expected to appear before the Assembly, meeting in Committee, to substantiate serious allegations he had made of corruption and nepotism against the Prime Minister and another Minister, Ong Eng Guan resigned. The Assembly thereupon voted to set up a Commission of Inquiry, headed by a judge. This Commission met, and the Prime Minister gave evidence and took part in the proceedings. On 2 March, 1961, the Assembly "took note" of the report which said that Ong Eng Guan was a person "not to be believed". The report stated that all the allegations against the Prime Minister and the Minister for Labour and Law were "untrue, groundless and reckless". The Opposition decided not to vote on the Government's motion to condemn Ong for his "dishonourable conduct" in using his Assembly privilege "as a cloak for spreading malicious falsehoods". Lee was contemptuous of the Opposition's behaviour and in a scathing attack said that on several occasions in the past "we have had to underline the fact that Western-type parliamentary democracy has to be adapted and adjusted to suit the practical realities of our position. The system of one man one vote, which ensures that the interest of the majority prevails without having to crush and destroy all opposition, can only work if adjustments are made to preserve not the forms, but the essence of a tolerant political system which ensures change in the social and economic order without violence.

"One curious fact which emerges from the experiments in parliamentary democracy in Asia is that it works only when the governing party has a clear majority and is strong and decisive. Where a government is weak and has not got a clear majority or is composed of coalition factions, then the system breaks down. This happened in Indonesia; in Burma, where the governing party AFPFL split and the Army took over; in Ceylon in the last Government of the late Mr Bandaranaike, when he led a coalition because he did not have a clear majority; and lest we forget, in Singapore from 1955 to 1959, with the David Marshall Government and later the Government headed by the present Member for Cairnhill," (Mr Lim Yew Hock) "neither of whom had a clear majority and both of whom depended on unstable alliances all of an opportunistic nature. Only in India, where the ruling Congress Party has a decisive majority, and in the Federation of Malaya where UMNO has a clear majority, are there governments successfully working under the democratic parliamentary system... And the conclusion one is forced to draw from these facts is that one of the problems that bedevil Western-type parliamentary democracy in its workings in Asia is that the Opposition is unwilling or unable to play its role within the constitutional framework. And when the Opposition is strong it can and often does foul up the work of the government. A proper Opposition opposes the policy of the government by offering to the people its own alternative remedies for economic and social problems, whilst at the same time upholding the institutions upon which parliamentary democracy is founded. One of these institutions, of course, is the elected legislature itself. Unfortunately, most, though not all, Oppositions in Asia are negative in that they have no alternative policy to offer to the electorate, and oppose for the sake of opposing not only the party in power but, as in the case of Singapore, also the institutions of the state.

"Our Opposition is feeble not just in numbers. We have tried and will continue to try to make it possible for our Opposition to play its proper constitutional role, albeit limited, to criticize Government policies and to offer their own alternative policies to solve our economic and social problems in order that the people can decide between them and us when the time comes for general elections again. But one

133

thing the Ong Eng Guan issue proved is that this opportunity we have offered the Opposition to play up to its proper constitutional role is wasted. It is wasted because it is an Opposition with no principles or fixed beliefs. It opposes on the basis of opportunistic opposing. It has no firm policies, let alone principles, to offer to the people as an alternative to the PAP...

"Mr Speaker, a grave charge was made against the Government which, if true, must mean the resignation of the Government and fresh general elections. And it is the duty not only of the Government but also of the Opposition to see that the truth is uncovered and placed before the people..."

"This motion formally condemns a proven liar, but more important, it condemns all those in the Opposition who tried to cover up Mr Ong Eng Guan's lying tactics by confusing the issues."

III

May Day for the People's Action Party has always been an important occasion. It is a national holiday. Traditionally, the Prime Minister addresses a mass rally. In 1961, the Lim Chin Siong group was moving secretly among the workers' organizations, scheming to capture the PAP from within. Two days earlier, the PAP had suffered defeat at the Hong Lim by-election. There was now a grave danger that "irresponsible people" could create a state of political chaos. Lee was anxious to prevent that. He believed people would listen to reason if they knew the facts. He said: "Every one of you must know that never in the history of Singapore has there been a Government more sympathetic, more actively sincere in trying to better the working class. However, over the last twenty-two months, not unnaturally, many people have tried to get the best of both worlds. On the one hand, they are quietly pleased, if not grateful, that there is a Government which is prepared to hold the fort against those who would like to see the old order continue. They are pleased that there is a Government working definitely on fixed principles in the interests of the working class, a Government which keeps the predatory instincts of the employer, be he a local or a foreign one, keeps his avarice and his greed in check, a Government which ensures within the limits of its power the maximum amount of political freedom amongst the working class, the maximum amount of political · exercise of mass cohesion of workers in the interests of the working class.

"But, on the other hand, there has been constant and carping back-biting and criticism. Whilst acknowledging to themselves that the Government was generally trying to better the interests of the working class, they publicly tell the rank and file half-truths designed to maintain an atmosphere of discontent, an atmosphere that all could be better if only things were different, if only fiercer men were in the saddle, if only the British colonialists were wiped out, if only independence were obtained, if only the Government did a 1,001 dreamy, starry-eyed impracticable things. . ."

Lee blamed all this on the wild talk during the Hong Lim by-election. He admitted that the position had undergone a definite change. Now was a moment of decision not only for the workers but for all the people of Singapore to decide "whether they stand for or against the PAP. Nobody can have it both ways. . . We of the PAP are of use to you, the working class of Singapore, in so far as we can establish conditions of certainty, to ensure not only the maintenance of living standards, but the sufficiency of industrial expansion which will ensure your jobs, better working conditions, more work for more people with more pay and better terms of service. Uncertainty, a state of stagnation in which there is no expansion of industry, no more employment opportunities are being created, and there is a gradual worsening of the present position for the workers—all these must come back to roost, whoever is in government. Therefore, everybody in Singapore, including us, must, I think, make a careful reappraisal of where we stand and where we are going. It's no use just saying 'support the anti-colonial movement'. Those are obvious things. Tun Lim Yew Hock says he represents the anti-colonial movement, David Marshall says he represents an anti-colonial movement, Ong Eng Guan says he represents an anti-colonial movement. The PAP also represents the anti-colonial movement. Positions must be taken in which those who believe they can lead the people better than the PAP must come forward and lead.

"It is not possible to tell the PAP 'do this, do that, do the other,' knowing full well that the objective and realistic conditions have to be faced by any Government in power with the interests of the people at heart. Therefore to those who say 'seek concord amidst or whilst maintaining differences' I say to them and to their supporters: the PAP has clearly stated where it stands. Seek concord if you will with the PAP on the PAP stand. Maintain your differences and seek no concord if you find that the PAP stand is against your stand. But I say this: that it is our duty to convince the people that the PAP stand is in their interests; that in the long-term future the PAP road is the best road that they can travel to a peaceful and prosperous, a happy and a united society."

Everyone knew what Lee Kuan Yew meant when he said "We had believed that perhaps decisions of principle, of grave political policy, could be left open till 1963 when the constitutional position has to be reviewed." He was referring to the decision which he always said would have to be taken when Singapore was free of colonialism: communism or non-communism? Right from the beginning, it must be remembered, the PAP was a nationalist front more than a socialist party. "But, " he said, "developments that have taken place make it necessary that decisions have to be taken earlier and not later, for the interests of everybody. Those who say they stand for outright independence, let them seek concord whilst maintaining differences with Tun Lim Yew Hock, David Marshall, Ong Eng Guan and all the others who say 'Independent Singapore'. Those who genuinely believe that that is the road to perdition and who know that our political future lies in merger into a larger entity, into a Malayan whole, then it is their business, as it is the business of the PAP, to convince the people, whatever the temporary setbacks, whatever the temporary misunderstandings, that this is the road ahead. Anti-colonialism as a slogan is a necessary slogan. But the direction of that anti-colonialism, the road that we are to travel to independence, are objectives which must be clarified in no uncertain terms.

"In the coming weeks, it is not unlikely that events will unravel themselves with greater lucidity in order that everybody should know where everybody stands. We should be honest to ourselves and to our people. It is my hope that when that moment of decision comes, when the lines which are at present being blurred have to be drawn, we shall be able to convince the majority of the people to stand on that side of the line which stands for sanity, for national unity, for independence through merger in a larger political whole. On the other side of the line is the easy way out—the easy appeal to impatience and frustrations, the slogans that for years have always aroused an atmosphere of excitement and, in some quarters, of hysteria; slogans which appeal to the different communities, different slogans on different wavelengths, bring about different results, the results of all of which must mean national disunity, unhappiness and chaos. It is therefore, your duty as members of the working class to take up your stand. For us, as those who are supposed to guide your destinies in the Government, it is our business to see that you are brought along a road which leads to national happiness, national unity and national independence.

"The history of a people is not decided in one or two election defeats or victories. It is a long and relentless process not dependent on persons and personalities but on the political and social and national forces at work within a given milieu. And it is only a question of whether one can analyse and decipher and discern the forces in play and calculate the resultant direction of all these forces. They are factors more enduring, more decisive than all the slogans that men or politicians or trade unionists can coin. So let us therefore, if we are to survive the test of history, regardless of temporary setbacks, coin slogans which will stand the test of time. That is our business and we hope that is also your business."

136

The PAP's defeat in the Hong Lim by-election created a political shock, and Lim Chin Siong and his group, though still members of the PAP, exploited the situation subtly to put across communist propaganda. Lee Kuan Yew thought of resigning, of going back to the people for a fresh mandate. *The Straits Times* came out with an editorial saying that it was the scale of Ong Eng Guan's victory that shocked and dismayed. Ong polled more than two and a half times the votes cast for his opponent from the PAP. *The Straits Times* attributed the PAP defeat to Ong's personal popularity. "They have chosen to overlook the failings of Mr Ong, the Minister for National Development, the man who all but wrecked the municipality, who did not get a house built in twelve months, who planned nothing, built nothing, developed nothing." *The Straits Times* referred to the PAP's record of solid achievement and urged the PAP to remain in office. "The Government must stay on the job and get on with it."

Lee Kuan Yew later went to Hong Lim to explain why he thought the PAP had been defeated. It was, he said, because the Government had not sufficiently explained its plans to help them. The Government had failed to explain why certain things had to be done, why other things could not be carried out. Lee realized that Ong Eng Guan spoke Hokkien to the Hong Lim voters, and could thus get his message across to them direct. Lee at once set about learning Hokkien.

Unexpectedly, there was another by-election caused by the sudden death of the PAP Assemblyman for the Anson constituency. Nobody realized it then, but this was to be the instrument which the communists were to seize, and to try to use, in an effort to capture the party. They nearly succeeded.

Singapore's political uncertainty, and the opportunity it appeared to provide for pro-communist and Chinese communal policies, caused Tunku Abdul Rahman, Malaya's Prime Minister, to make his historic proposal on 27 May for the building of a new State of Malaysia out of Malaya, Singapore, Sarawak, Sabah and Brunei. Lee Kuan Yew welcomed and supported the Tunku's plan. Lim Chin Siong and the pro-communist group opposed Malaysia: the showdown between the communists and the nationalists was fast approaching a climax.

Lee made two speeches to celebrate National Day, on 3 June. Over the radio he suggested that the salient feature of the past two years of PAP Government had been an absence of hysteria and general unrest (which had been a feature of previous governments) and the presence of an effective government prepared to enforce whatever measures were necessary in the general welfare. "Never," he declared, "had there been more freedom in the exercise of democratic rights of association for trade unions, cultural and civic associations. Rather than repression, persuasion has been the guiding principle. But we have had to suppress secret society gangsters. We had also to suppress known destructive and communal elements... But on the whole, oppression as a method of government is disavowed and the general atmosphere is much healthier."

Lee dealt with progress in housing and the building of schools. He said there had been a change for the better. "But let us not deceive ourselves. The change has not been large enough or fast enough. The recent by-election which the PAP lost has been useful, for it revealed the sectors where there is dissatisfaction..."

Some of these problems, Lee said, could and would be solved. Some problems would take longer to solve. Problems there would always be. "And we will continue to solve them; though it is not possible to please everyone. But let us take heart from our fortunate position of having one of the best-fed and best-clothed cities of the whole of Asia..."

The next day, at the National Day mass rally, the Prime Minister spoke from the City Hall steps to thousands of supporters. He said that the years which had gone by defined in sharper outlines the problems they had to face. "They have also defined more clearly the great future that awaits us when we overcome our present problems...

"We share a common destiny with our people in the Federation. No one doubts this any longer... This coming together must ultimately be decided by the collective will of the people... We welcome and support the declaration of the Prime Minister of the Federation of Malaya that it is inevitable that we should look ahead to this objective of closer political and economic association between the Federation, Singapore, Brunei, Sarawak and North Borneo. This declaration should accelerate the speed of political progress towards complete independence for us... We have shared a common colonial past. We were part of the same British Empire in Southeast Asia. If we can keep together in close political and economic association as we find our place in the comity of independent nations, it will be to the advantage of all of us, and to the advantage of peace and stability in this region."

Lee found time during the National Day celebrations to remind school children that the size of a country was not all that important. "If," he told them in a special National Day message, "size is what determines the importance of a country and its people, then Singapore would be of little importance to anyone other than to ourselves. Fortunately it is not size but quality which counts. Ancient Athens was a small state, but its vigorous and alert people gave birth to ideas and philosophies which are as alive today as they were 2,000 years ago..."

July was a month of crisis for the People's Action Party. David Marshall, the former Chief Minister (making a return to politics after "leaving politics for ever", and forming the Workers Party, which soon became heavily infiltrated by communists) snatched victory in Anson (on 15 July) with a majority of 546 seats over the PAP candidate, Inche Mahmud bin Awang, a bus conductor and President of the TUC. In his brief and unexpected hour of glory, Mr Marshall called upon the Prime Minister to resign. This was the second defeat of the PAP in two by-elections in three months. Lee Kuan Yew did in fact offer his resignation to the Chairman of the PAP, Dr Toh Chin Chye. Dr Toh in his reply expressed the confidence of the party in Lee.

"We lost Anson by the treachery of three political secretaries and eight Assemblymen who worked in concert with the trade union leaders against the PAP candidate," said the PAP in a statement analysing its defeat. "At a critical time they deliberately set out to divide the party and confuse the voters... All those loyal to the genuine aims of the party (the creation of a democratic, socialist, independent, non-communist Malaya including Singapore) must rally round the party and Government, and close our ranks."

More than 1,500 people abstained from voting in the Anson by-election. Lee said they had been disillusioned by party dissension. Lee called for a special meeting of the Assembly to clarify the whole issue by a vote of confidence: the time had come for the nationalists and communists, now moving towards different objectives, to stand up and be counted. Control of the PAP was now at stake. Meanwhile, a delegation from Lim Chin Siong's group dropped in on the United Kingdom High Commissioner, Lord Selkirk, for a cup of tea, and assurances that the Constitution would not be suspended "to prevent them garnering the fruits of the defeat they expected to inflict upon Lee Kuan Yew's government".

The Assembly met in the afternoon of 20 July, and the dramatic and crucial debate went on until four the next morning. Lee posed the issue in terms of nationalism as against the communist united front tactic with the "connivance of the Colonial Power". In a House of fifty-one, the PAP held their position by twenty-seven votes to eight with thirteen PAP members abstaining while still sitting on the Government benches.

Lee said: "After Hong Lim, when we were defeated badly, I felt that if the people desired it, there should be a reference back to the people. However, it was decided by a majority opinion of the party that we should first fight Anson and then reconsider the position. At that time Mr Lim Chin Siong and all his trade union friends strenuously opposed any talk of our resignation. After losing Anson by a narrow majority and because of this attempt by the six trade unionists and eight Assemblymen to capture the Government and the party, we are resolved not to abdicate our position in order that the party and the Government does not pass into the hands of people who intend to use it for purposes for which the people did not vote the PAP in. The present leadership of the party was responsible for winning the mandate of the people in the last elections, and it is our duty not to give Mr Lim Chin Siong any opportunity to take over this Government in order to run it as a communist front government.

"Their first plan now, since they are unable to capture the Government, is to get me to resign in order that someone whom they believe they can manipulate could be elected Prime Minister. They hope in this way to force a compromise in the policy of the Government so that they can extend communist influence in Singapore and prevent us from fulfilling our declared objective of independence through merger with the Federation, with or without the Borneo territories, in 1963. This move has now been frustrated by the unanimous decision of the party's Central Executive Committee to stand collectively together against any change. This stand has been endorsed by a majority of PAP Assemblymen.

"This motion is one of confidence and the motion will have to be carried as it stands without amendment or the Government must resign and general elections follow. On a motion of confidence, any amendment is tantamount to a vote of no confidence. As for the Honourable Members on the other side of the House may I say on behalf of my colleagues and I, that if they want general elections they can vote against the Government.

"This extraordinary session has become necessary because of the sudden turn of events over the past few weeks. Eight Assemblymen on the PAP side have openly defied the party leadership. Demands for my resignation as Prime Minister have been made and it has become necessary that the House should clearly give us a mandate to carry on. . .

"The time has come for the unvarnished truth to be told. For two years the British Government has tried to manipulate the PAP into a position where we will become the successor to Lim Yew Hock's policy, where the communist party will be attacked not by British imperialism, which is the supreme power in Singapore, but by us, the locally elected Government with limited powers. To achieve this end every blandishment and argument has been put forward, and every device and seductive manoeuvre practised. After two years the British have decided that the PAP is impervious to such blandishment. Perhaps they have decided that we are men who are not influenced by personal considerations of wishing to stay in power. We are

140

prepared to lay down office at any time at the behest of the people and we are not going to be manipulated by any power.

"The big scheme we have only been able to piece completely together after the Anson by-election. The plot, counter-plot and sub-plots that have been going on would make an Oppenheimer thriller read like a simple comic strip cartoon. The diplomacy, skill and cunning derived from some 300 years of building and running the British Empire, and from the manipulation of men and their motivations, have in great part led to this curious position, daily growing curiouser and curiouser. The British, as I see it, had two objectives. The first was to engineer a collision between the non-communist Left in the PAP and the communist Left. Their second objective was to ensure that the Borneo territories are put into a position where they will come together immediately in a federation under British tutelage, but in a state of readiness, if the international situation turns delicate, to be transferred to a nationalist government of 'Greater Malaysia'.

"I congratulate the planners of this scheme for having succeeded this far. Day by day, on the basis of British blandishments and manoeuvre, all parties—the communists, the PAP, the Federation and the leaders of the Borneo territories—have been mounting the stakes at the poker table. To the pro-communists in Singapore the British say that the British are liberal and democratic, that if they have released men from prisons to be Prime Ministers, and only recently they have done so again in Nyasaland, why should they want to keep detainees in gaol? It is darkly hinted that it is the wicked Singapore Government that wanted to keep them in gaol.

"These insinuations started slowly. After the Hong Lim by-election they were intensified. The British were unhappy that in Hong Lim the communist Left rallied to the PAP united front. So some plan had to be found to ensure that the PAP would come into collision with the CP Left. Dinner parties, cocktails, luncheons led to friendly fraternization between the British lion and Messrs Lim Chin Siong, Woodhull and Co. The pro-communists were led to believe that the PAP were the wicked obstructionists, and the British, wise and statesmanlike people, were prepared even to envisage a new 'Left' government emerging in Singapore, even more Left than the PAP, provided their military bases were not touched.

"The British have become their own *agents-provocateur*. How well they have succeeded! Quietly and insidiously they instigated the pro-communists to attempt the capture of both the PAP Government and the party. Young, inexperienced revolutionaries were so taken in that in a crisis Lim Chin Siong, Woodhull and Fong Swee Suan looked up the UK Commissioner for consultations on Tuesday 18 July at the Eden Hall home of the UK Commissioner. We felt that

141

something curious was going on and we therefore kept observation of the residence of the UK Commissioner. Lo and behold, the great anti-colonialists and revolutionaries turned up for secret consultations with the British lion! I am now convinced that some funny things are happening when in a serious crisis this revolutionary trio get into consultation at Eden Hall with the UK Commissioner, instead of with the PAP.

"Having led the pro-communists into believing that a non-communist government was no longer necessary and that a pro-communist government was possible, obviously these men were going to try and capture the PAP party and Government. And the British may also have hoped that under attack and threat of capture the PAP would fight back and finally suppress the communists, something they so far failed in persuading the PAP to do. Meanwhile to the PAP the British has suggested that we should take firm action against the mounting subversion. In fact, a plan was to have been drawn up which would have culminated in an act leading to open collision with the communists in which the PAP either remained in office and so became committed for ever to defend British colonialism, or resigned, in which case a non-communist government not amenable to British pressure would have been got rid of.

"Meanwhile, the Federation began to believe that they could get the Borneo territories, together with Singapore, merged in a larger federation. The Tunku came down on 27 May, a week before National Day, and announced to a group of foreign correspondents that he recognized that there must be closer political and economic ties between the Federation of Malaya, Singapore and the three Borneo territories. I answered on 3 June, National Day, that in principle we welcomed the Tunku's plan for a larger federation, if thereby, merger between Singapore and the Federation was made easier.

"The communists, on the other hand, propounded that there was no need for independence through merger and that the next step should be to abolish the Internal Security Council in order that there would be expansion at all levels of human activity on behalf of the communist cause. Six trade unionists came out with statements openly supporting the communist line on 2 June. Forty-two trade unions also supported this CP line and literally put their rubber stamps on the statement without convening any meetings or consulting the rank and file. On 9 June, the PAP Chairman, Dr Toh Chin Chye, announced that the Government would demand complete independence through merger with the Federation, or merger with a larger federation, when constitutional talks reopen in 1963. The PAP, which was not amenable to manipulation by the British, is not going to be manipulated by the communists.

142

"We took our stand and the battle then began. Three days later, six trade unionists demanded immediate release of the detainees, implementation of the reunification of trade unions, granting of citizenship rights to all those loyal to the anti-colonial struggle, communist or non-communist, and more freedom of speech, Press, assembly and organization for the advancement of the anti-colonial struggle.

"Meanwhile two Governors and one High Commissioner flew in from the Borneo territories to add impetus and mystery to the vast developing plot. All these events incidentally lent credence to the false rumours that the PAP had sold out Singapore to an imperialist plot. The UK Commissioner for Singapore left for London, the Tunku and the Yang di-Pertuan Agong went to Brunei. Everyone started his own analysis and adopted his own counter-measures. Mr Marshall said all this was for the purpose of the Anson by-election. But the communist Left believed differently and decided that this was an evil conspiracy to which the PAP was a party. They mounted the offensive and intensified their campaign. The TUC six openly attacked the PAP; three political secretaries in receipt of Government remuneration flagrantly flouted all rules of decency and attacked the Government they had promised to serve. Forty-three unions came out against merger, supporting the TUC six, to make the PAP lose in Anson. Finally, when, in spite of everything, the PAP looked like winning, they engineered the betrayal of the party by eight Assembly-men issuing a statement of discord on the eve of poll. These pro-communists had been duped into believing that the PAP had sold out the rights of the people of Singapore.

"It will take some time for me to tell you the story right from the beginning. But I feel the people must know the truth in order that when the mandate is returned to the people they will make their choice in full knowledge of the facts. And the choice will be—do you want your future to be a Singapore merged with the Federation of Malaya, or do you want to follow people who ask for the abolition of the Internal Security Council and full self-government, as a first step to an independent communist Singapore? We saw these problems looming over the horizon, even whilst the Hong Lim by-election was on, and I stressed over and over again why the PAP does not stand for an independent Singapore and why our future must lie in a merger with the Federation.

"Mr Lim Chin Siong and his friends took fright and alarm when rapid development began regarding merger. They were alarmed because merger is no longer a mirage over the horizon but a reality which will take place in 1963. . . Why do they oppose this? Why do they want to capture the Government and the party to prevent this, when for years they have always endorsed and supported the PAP

143

plan of independence through merger? Mr Lim Chin Siong, Mr Woodhull, Mr Fong Swee Suan came out of prison because we won the elections and demanded their release as a condition before we assumed office. Although we knew that politically our opinions differed on important points from some of theirs, we were openly comrades in a united front and we did not betray them. Yet in the middle of a by-election, which was crucial to the Government, for their own reasons and for the purpose of preventing merger, they betrayed us openly at Anson, causing dissension in the party ranks and confusion in the minds of the people.

"Day by day the chips on the poker table are mounting. The game as played has gone so far now that no side can afford to back out; some time in the near future all cards will be called and seen. Whoever is bluffing will lose bitterly. I say now on behalf of my colleagues and my party, that we are not going to fit in with the scheme to beat up the CP for the benefit of British colonialism. If we get no independence through merger we will leave the British with the predicament of having to deal with the communists them-selves, even in an elected government. The communists, on the other hand, have mounted their offensive in order to capture the PAP party and the PAP Government. We shall resist them. We advise them not to try it and not to provoke us into unnecessary collision. If they want to win and take over power in Singapore they may try to do so in the next general elections. We on the other hand must let the people know the truth—plain, simple and unvarnished—so that all will realize the hazardous course they will travel with these men.

"Our battle with the communists must be won by argument. We will prove that the democratic socialist forces in Singapore are honest and sincere to the people and have not and will not sell out their rights to anybody. It will also be shown that the communists have not only been duped by the British but duped to the extent that they betrayed their PAP comrades in the nationalist Left united front. The battle for men's minds cannot be won by simple smearing of a man as either anti-communist and reactionary, or a wavering bourgeois, social democrat or communist. Not all those who oppose the British are nationalists. Some anti-colonialists are nationalists and some are communists. We must also see this distinction: that not all who oppose the PAP are communists; some are communists, some reactionaries, some opportunists and some merely confused.

"Therefore, in this battle of ideas it is necessary that we should call a spade a spade and put across truthfully and honestly the respective position of everyone. Our purpose is to build a movement for a united, independent, democratic, non-communist Malaya. Our business is to strengthen the forces that help to create this united Malaya. In the past the communists may have for their own reasons assisted us in this task. If so, they did so in the full knowledge that we are non-communist, not communist. We are firmly convinced that the survival of the PAP depends on a strong adherence to this line of non-communism to prevent perversion of our party, either by the British getting the PAP to openly repress the communists or by the communists making the PAP the vehicle of their communist line.

"As the game has been played so far, beyond any doubt the really able and skilful player has been the British. Even we were at first puzzled by this development of events. On the one hand we were asked to be tough and to take firm action. On the other hand the British lion was asking the revolutionary Messrs Lim and Woodhull and Co to dinner and telling them that all the detainees can be let out. And then their fellow-travelling friends come and tell us that they have a first class pipe-line with the UK Commission and are convinced that all that the British wanted in Singapore were their bases and quiet, peace and stability, and even if a communist government can be popularly elected, all is well.

"For all sides the events of the past two months have been irrevocable ones. Such conflicts as have appeared between the pro-CP elements and us cannot just be laughed off and forgotten. The British are still hoping that we will come to open collision and we will use draconian methods of suppression to establish our position as a government. As I have explained, we are completely unmoved by considerations of staying in office, pomp and power, for these were not the considerations that made us seek office in 1959. We can therefore afford to ignore these blandishments and present to the British the dragon's teeth they have been sowing. But we shall fight to save the Government and the party from capture. In many ways the events of these last two months bear resemblance to the crisis in the PAP in 1957. There again the pro-CP Left, whom we had called Left-wing adventurers, miscalculated their position and tried to capture the PAP and force us to follow their line. Very prudently we calculated differently and abstained from office, thereby saving the PAP and ourselves a great deal of unnecessary trouble. As a result we were able to survive, grow to greater strength and after succeeding in the last General Elections we were able to rescue Mr Lim Chin Siong and seven others from prison, before we assumed power.

"Now again, in 1961 as in 1957, it is believed that the PAP can be captured by communists and used for communist policies with impunity. Some of the lesser souls in our party have decided to take the easy way out—this short cut to peace in our time and popularity in our time. Little do they realize that this short cut can lead to peace only for a time and popularity only for a time. We have decided to stay in office to prevent this criminal folly from being perpetrated on the PAP for the second time. I only hope these gamblers will not have to pay too bitter and high a price when the cards are down. . ."

Lee's motion of confidence was put to the House at ten minutes to four in the morning after a late night sitting. Twenty-seven members of the PAP supported the Government. Eight Opposition voted against. The thirteen PAP rebels abstained. Later they formed the Barisan Sosialis.

VI

After the Anson by-election dust had settled, Lee Kuan Yew went to the radio station (on 26 July) to tell the people "what the principal forces engaged in battle" were trying to do, and with what success. He said that the thirteen PAP Assemblymen who had failed to support the Government fell into two groups—eight who were ostensibly led by Dr Lee Siew Choh, and five who recognized Dr Sheng Nam Chin as their spokesman. "Neither Dr Lee nor Dr Sheng is a communist. They both joined the party in 1959 when the PAP was in the ascendant. They were both upset by the PAP defeat in Hong Lim. Dr Lee was persuaded that the way to popularity and success was openly to seek communist support from their cadres in the unions and the mass organizations. He had several discussions with me and with Dr Goh. The gist of his argument was that since the communists cannot directly take power in Singapore so long as they have no communist government in the Federation, there will be no harm at all in espousing their cause, co-operating with them, and depending on their support. "What's the harm?" he asked me. I explained that this would leave him a prisoner of the communists. But all this was of no avail and he set out on this perilous course. Dr Sheng, on the other hand, felt that the communists would win in the long run because of the international situation and he was not prepared to resist them. . . He was offered the Deputy Prime Ministership by the group that wanted to take over power and stay on."

Lim Chin Siong and his group were expelled from the PAP and fourteen branch secretaries were suspended. Shortly afterwards, Tunku Abdul Rahman invited Lee Kuan Yew to begin discussion on merger and Malaysia.

Finding they could not win over twenty-seven PAP Assemblymen to their side, the communists tried to bring the Government down, if not by constitutional means, then by fomenting industrial strife and mass agitation.

Lee Kuan Yew meanwhile continued to govern. A young

developing nation, he told the teachers on Teachers' Day (5 August), needed guidance and this must be firm. But, at the same time, an independent multiracial society could only come about through tolerance and democracy. Lee said it was most important that the problems of language and education be resolved by the free will of the parents, not by the orders of a government. "It is our duty to point out the road to national unity by offering equal opportunities of learning all mother tongues while encouraging the learning and use of the national language. Then it is up to the fathers and mothers of our community to decide how their children should be taught and trained."

VII

Having failed either to capture or destroy the PAP Government, the communists, with the thirteen defectors from the PAP, on 26 July formed the Barisan Sosialis. Dr Lee Siew Choh was Chairman and Lim Chin Siong, the Secretary-General. It obtained registration as a party on 13 August, and that evening held a rally. Eleven days later Lee Kuan Yew went to Kuala Lumpur for formal talks with the Tunku about merger and Malaysia.

The open fight between communists and nationalists was now on. Trade unionists grouped around Lim Chin Siong formed the Association of Trade Unions. The TUC was dissolved. PAP trade unionists formed the National Trade Union Congress.

The Barisan were a definite political threat to the PAP: from the beginning the new party employed those very techniques which had brought the PAP to power in 1959—appeals to anti-colonial feeling, criticism of Britain, and a determination to dominate the trade union movement.

In September Lee took the offensive: opposition to the PAP's plans for independence and merger leading to the creation of Malaysia had to be met head-on. In a series of radio talks he set out to show that the Barisan Sosialis rejected merger because it was a communist movement bent upon establishing a communist republic of Malaya including Singapore. The original plan of the communists was to capture power in the Assembly by co-opting twenty-six Assemblymen and forming the Government. This plan failed. Their second plan was to persuade twenty-six Opposition Assemblymen to vote the Government out. This also failed. In another radio talk on 6 October, Lee said that their third plan was to "make it so hot and uncomfortable for the Government all round that they would quit before merger was accomplished. We shall be patient and forbearing, and we shall see merger through." "The communists are on the surface playing the

147

game constitutionally and softly for the time being... At the moment the communists are putting on relatively mild pressure through persons and organizations which they hope cannot be attributed directly to them... The communists always do this. Exploit a real or imaginary grievance through cadres and sympathizers not generally known to be connected with them... One difficulty the communists are facing at the moment is the complete absence of tension or uncertainty or anti-Government feeling. For them to succeed, a state of uncertainty and unrest, and a belief that revolution is just around the corner, is most necessary..."

VIII

When the Malaysia Solidarity Consultative Committee met, on 18 December, in Sarawak, Lee Kuan Yew reported progress. He said: "Each of us has his own ideas of the form and the content Malaysia should take... but all of us acknowledge that the only logical course is to come together for our stability and survival in the midst of the shifting balance of forces in Southeast Asia. So long as we accept the necessity and inevitability of Malaysia, the differences of view we may have as to the form and content of Malaysia can be resolved. We all recognize that, before a period of rapid and far-reaching changes, there must be some hesitations, doubts, and anxieties. These are the natural reactions to swift changes. It is right, and all to the good, that all of us should speak our minds freely and frankly, for only by understanding each other can we help to resolve our mutual problems. What is wrong is to allow anxieties for local interests and ambitions to become excuses for resisting changes which are inevitable, or to stall solutions which in the long run are to the benefit of all of us...

"Having enunciated the principle of Malaysia we should now find ways and means of expediting the realization of Malaysia. The pattern of Malaysia cannot be dictated by any one of the five partners to the exclusion of the others. It cannot be fashioned to fit the exclusive interests of any one partner. We must all uphold the essential interests of Malaysia, the basic and fundamental interests of all of us collectively, whilst at the same time we must take into account the special local interests and conditions of our respective territories. Malaysia is our creation. It is our own nationalist answer to our problems of viability and survival in one of the most contested regions of the world..."

Over Radio Sarawak the next day Lee Kuan Yew said that the speed of political development during the past few months was a reflection of the speed with which ideas travel in a world of jets, rockets and sputniks. The three territories of Sarawak, Brunei and North Borneo were the last of the colonial possessions in Southeast Asia...

"Colonialism is on its way out and the sooner it is out the sooner we begin to grapple with our real problems of social change, of building a more just and equal society. The longer colonialism goes on, the more will we accumulate these problems and the more intractable they will be, because in the process of the anti-colonial struggle, in the name of freedom, the communists in Singapore and in Sarawak, and later, no doubt, in North Borneo, will expand and increase their strength. People everywhere in all colonial territories want freedom. It is easier for the communists to get the people to fight with them for freedom than to fight with them for communism. The communists are the only people who profit by having colonial territories malingering in a stage of semi-independence... "

"Malaysia is simply the nationalist answer of cutting short the period of gestation from colonialism to independence in order to deny the communists the use of the time spent in a protracted struggle to build up, not our forces of democracy, but their forces of communism. The communists have seen what happened in the Federation of Malaya. Once independence was achieved in August, 1957, the communists had to face a local, nationalist, elected government, and not a colonial government. Then their armed revolt collapsed and their organization was broken up. From time to time, as they expanded their front organizations and created discontent, a nationalist Federation Government punctured it. So the relentless process of struggle goes on; but now not for freedom, for independence has already been won, but for what we should do with the freedom that we have won for ourselves... "

"Constitution-making is the art of making forms of government practicable by taking into consideration the practical realities of a given situation. Those of you who have read our agreement between Singapore and the Federation can see how we have been able to resolve our problems to our mutual satisfaction, fairly and reasonably. But at the end of it all, we have one mutual interest which overrides everything else, namely, the need to survive together in a troubled and changing world, and to create prosperity and stability despite the rapid changes of our social order.

"As one who is a descendant of a Chinese immigrant and who firmly believes that the future of all our peoples in Malaysia depends upon our being united in one nation, I would like to see a fair balance of interests maintained between the indigenous people, the Dayaks, Dusuns, Muruts, the Malays, and the immigrant Chinese and Indians. Naturally I would be most unhappy to see any of the discrimination which is practised against the Chinese in almost every country in

Southeast Asia except our five territories of Malaysia. And Malaysia offers us this hope of finding a just balance of interest between the descendants of the immigrant people and the indigenous people.

"If we remain fragmented and in isolation then surely survival will be a dangerous business. But if we come together to form a strong Federation of Malaysia, with our record of reasonableness and tolerance between Dayaks, Dusuns, Muruts, Malays, Chinese, Indians and others, there is every reason for our multiracial society, with stable and happy relationships between its many races, to survive and continue to prosper. If we had the time, perhaps Malaysia could take five or six years for formulation, re-formulation and final creation. But the second half of the twentieth century is the age of rapid change and advance. Ideas and ideologies move with fantastic rapidity. We have to move as fast as events around us are moving. We have to ensure that we are not overtaken by events, and that our future is what we wish it to be. The days of the protecting British Raj are over. We, the peoples of Malaysia, must provide the leadership to solve our own problems before they become intractable..."

CHAPTER SIXTEEN

The Year of Power 1962

DECISION was the keynote of 1962, a year in which issues were clarified and put to the test of public opinion. Seventy-one per cent of the people in a national referendum voted for Malaysia. Early in the year, on his way to London for discussions, Lee Kuan Yew went to Burma, India, the United Arab Republic and Yugoslavia, personally to explain the significance of Singapore's plan to merge with Malaysia. In July, a PAP Assemblywoman announced her resignation from the party and crossed the floor of the House, where she sat as an independent. Her resignation deprived the Government of its majority, reducing its strength to twenty-five in a House of fifty-one. Lee declared the Government's intention "to govern and to see Singapore's destiny in Malaysia secured". He added: "Until the Opposition outvotes us we are constitutionally the Government. We shall see the referendum and merger through." Fortunately for Lee Kuan Yew, the Opposition was divided, consisting of the Right and the pro-communists.

In July, the debate on Malaysia was transferred to the United Nations Committee on Colonialism. David Marshall, Singapore's first Chief Minister, argued for the Barisan Sosialis. Lee Kuan Yew and Goh Keng Swee presented the Government's point of view. Mr Marshall won Russian and Polish endorsement of his view that the referendum was a "gross deceit", but the Committee declined to reverse its decision not to send an observer to Singapore.

In August, the Government again had twenty-six votes when a former PAP Assemblyman retraced his steps across the floor, and rejoined the party. But before the end of the month the Minister for Labour died, thus reducing the House to fifty, and leaving Government and Opposition with equal votes. This did not affect the coming of Malaysia, however, for the seven Alliance Assemblymen used their votes to sustain the Government at least until its realization.

Meanwhile, on the economic front, considerable progress was made on the Jurong industrial project. Factories began to go up. Elsewhere, huge blocks of flats began to change the Singapore skyline. Singapore's trade continued to increase. Fifteen new schools were built. Attendance in Malay secondary schools increased seventy-five per cent.

I

LEE Kuan Yew greeted 1962 with an appeal to the Right nationalists to rally with the Left nationalists to fight the Malayan communists. In his 1962 New Year message, he said that 1961 had not been so bad a year after all: it had been memorable for the "drawing of the line between the communists and the nationalists.

"We, the under-developed countries, must continue to seek our own salvation. We do not want the communist system to spread and envelop us. Nor do we want to be pawns of the Western powers for the defence of their own interest. We have to fight and win our own place under the sun. And it is our duty to fill the power vacuum which the withdrawal of colonial rule will leave in this part of the world. . .

"1962 will see events begin to unfold to their logical conclusion. In this round of the struggle between the communists versus the nationalists, victory is assured to us, the nationalists. Malaysia will triumph, whatever the communists may try to do. But we must be prepared to see them come back for another round. We, the nationalists, whether of the Left or of the Right, must study the twists and turns of communist tactics—for example, how they support Malaysian solidarity in principle, while working against it in practice. For it is in the practice that they hope to break up the nationalists and devour us in small morsels.

"So let us rally together for our own survival, not just this once, but for all time, for the struggle by the communists for a communist Malaysia will go on. May 1962 bring us more unity in Malaysia, for unity brings more strength and security to ensure our survival and prosperity in a troubled world."

In April, Lee Kuan Yew undertook a tour of Afro-Asian nations to meet uncommitted leaders and to explain to them the meaning of Malaysia. This was to counter communist propaganda abroad, mainly through the Peking-oriented Indonesian Communist Party, and the communist-dominated Secretariat of the Afro-Asia Solidarity Organization in Cairo. Lee's tour was highly successful: the myth that Malaysia was a neo-colonialist plot was destroyed.

Upon his return, Lee Kuan Yew relentlessly pursued a policy of open confrontation with the Barisan Sosialis through radio forums and public debates. Soon the communists were avoiding debate. Refusing to resign, the PAP declared it was prepared to submit the issue of merger to referendum, and this was the question which dominated the political life of the state for the first eight months of 1962, until the referendum decided the issue on 1 September, when, by a seventy-one per cent majority, the people of Singapore decided to become part of Malaysia.

Up until the end of 1961, the Barisan line had been to support Malaysia in principle provided internal security was left outside the hands of the Central Government. On 30 December, 1961, the Partai Kommunist Indonesia held its conference and denounced Malaysia as anti-Indonesian. This was now the line followed by the Barisan Sosialis.

In the Assembly on 29 January, the Prime Minister asked: "What are the long term aims of the communists? Surely it cannot be to create an independent communist state of Singapore for that would be impossible both militarily and economically. The declared aim of the Malayan Communist Party is to set up a communist Soviet Republic of Malaya and Singapore. And yet they do not want merger, although for all these years since 1945 they have condemned the separation of these two territories as being the responsibility of the British colonialists and later of the Federation reactionary feudalists...

"The tragedy of the MCP is that, contrary to Marxist–Leninist doctrine, it is trying to bring about a communist revolution working not through the indigenous races, the Malays, the Dayaks, the Dusuns and the Muruts, but through the active immigrant section, the Chinese... the inspiration, the impetus and the organizational techniques are those of the Chinese communist revolution. The communist revolution in China is one of the greatest that has ever taken place in the history of China, and has given coherence, discipline and a sense of purpose to replace the warlordship and corruption which had reduced China to anarchy for so long. But even according to Marxist-Leninist doctrine, for a revolution to succeed it must be locally based, and the MCP will not be locally based for as long as its inspiration cannot pull at the heart strings of the indigenous people of Malaya and Malaysia. If ever one day communism were to hope to make a really massive appeal, it must be home-based and it must be able to draw the Malays, the Davaks, the Dusuns and the Muruts, together with the Chinese and the Indians, into its whirlpool. And that day can only come if the leadership of the Communist Party passes into the hands of local Malays, Dayaks, Dusuns and Muruts, and the inspiration of revolution comes from a close neighbour like Indonesia with a people and a country more like Malaysia.

"Hence the significance of the PKI's statement about Malaysia being anti-Indonesia. It is easier to make Malaysia accept communism from Indonesia through the Dayaks, the Dusuns and the Muruts on the Indonesian side of Borneo appealing to their kinsfolk on the Malaysian side, and through the Malays from Minangkabau and Sumatra appealing to their kinsmen in Malaysia, than to get Malaysia to go communist from an appeal thousands of miles away, from China..."

II

Although the PAP Government in June 1959 received a mandate in the Assembly to proceed with merger and Malaysia, Lee Kuan Yew insisted upon holding a referendum to ascertain "the mode and manner of the inevitable reunification of Singapore and Malaya".

Lee's majority in the Assembly when merger and Malaysia was again discussed in 1961 was thirty-three, but he believed he had to hold the referendum to take away from the communists any hope that, after Malaysia, they could exploit the fact that eighteen Assemblymen abstained from voting. Lee wanted Malaysia to get off to a good start. He wanted to be able to say with unchallenged confidence that Malaysia was strongly supported by the majority of the people of Singapore, and he wanted figures to prove his contention. In the Assembly on 16 March, he was caustic as usual with Assemblymen on the opposite side of the House. "In the past two days in this Assembly there has been a great deal of hypocritical exhortation about democracy and the democratic process made by the Barisan Sosialis who are the least qualified to talk about democracy. They have invoked democracy to establish the right of communists to cause confusion, spread falsehood and try to prevent merger, they the people who are furthest removed from the ideals of government by the free will of the people. Perhaps the Member for Thomson has forgotten that, during the PAP Conference in May last year, after the Hong Lim by-election, he was the strongest advocate for taking the Cuban line, and, like Fidel Castro, he strongly advocated the abolition of all future elections as being unnecessary and stupid. The Member for Upper Serangoon was then trying to dissuade my colleagues and I from ever contemplating resignation and returning the mandate to the people... He went so far as to say that what was important was not whether the people knew that what we were doing was good for them, but whether in fact we were doing good for them, and he capped this argument by saying that had Mao Tsetung stood for elections after the hardships of the Chinese communes in the past few years he would probably have lost his deposit..."

All the thirteen Barisan Sosialis Assemblymen, Lee reminded them, were elected on the PAP platform, the main plank of which was merger, and had signed solemn pledges that they would resign if they were expelled from the party...

Lee went on to say: "We have a mandate from this Assembly of thirty-three unanimous votes, with no Assemblymen being bold enough to be present to vote against the proposals for merger... Lim Chin Siong, the communist front leader, who is manipulating and

155

co-ordinating communist policies in Barisan Sosialis and the communist front unions, has openly told a meeting of committee members of several union officials who taxed him on this point that the Government has full legal and constitutional rights, once the proposals have been passed in the Assembly, to carry out the merger. Therefore, let us be clear in our minds that the Government is under no compulsion to have this referendum and there is no necessity to resort to trickery, as the Member for Queenstown has suggested... The final position which we want to achieve is not just merger, but a merger under which the various races in Malaya will live in peace and harmony... It is the duty of the Government to try and bring merger and Malaysia about peacefully by consent with the maximum of goodwill and of give and take... "

The Bill authorizing the referendum was approved on 6 July after a debate which lasted for eight days of midnight sessions.

III

On the eve of his departure for the Afro-Asian countries, on 19 April, Lee Kuan Yew spoke to the Foreign Correspondents' Association. He recalled the three points he had made in 1959. One, that if there was a free-for-all in Malaya then the course of political and social revolution in Malaya might be dictated by the Chinese in the towns. But there could never be a free-for-all, and that being the case, the course and the pace of the revolution must be as fast or as slow as the majority of the Malay peasants desired. Two, there could be no communist Singapore so long as there was no communist Malaya. The third was that, for the time being, the threat to peace, stability and prosperity in Malaya was greater from communalism than from communism. Lee said these three points were as valid in 1962 as they had been in 1959.

IV

Lee Kuan Yew landed at Belgrade's international airport on May Day. Normally, President Tito left for the country after taking the salute at the Labour Day march past, but he agreed to give Lee half an hour of his time and catch a later train. President Tito received the Prime Minister at his official residence on 2 May. The scheduled half hour expanded into an hour. Lee left the President believing that Tito understood (as did other Afro-Asian leaders including Ne Win, Nehru, and Nasser) that Malaysia was a development of Asian nationalism and not neo-colonialism.

At the airport just before he left, on 4 May, Lee Kuan Yew was asked by the Press about his talk with President Tito. Lee said he had formed the impression that President Tito fully supported Malaysia. "Is that not so?" Lee asked Yugoslavia's Secretary for Agriculture, Dr Slavko Komar. The Minister nodded his agreement.

Before Lee met President Tito, Yugoslavia had been highly critical of Malaysia.

V

On 20 May, from the BBC in London, the Prime Minister broadcast to Singapore an account of his visit to some of the Afro-Asian non-aligned nations. Lee said his purpose in visiting these countries was to tell them of the facts of Malaysia and the problems in and around Malaysia. . . Since November last year, he said, there had been a consistent campaign to damn Malaysia even before it was created. The communists in Malaysia and the Communist Party of Indonesia had been selling the line that Malaysia was neo-colonialism; in other words, that Malaysia, when created, although nominally independent, would in fact be a stooge regime of the British. This line was echoed by communist radio stations throughout the world. They were able, through their communist representatives on the Afro-Asian Secretariat in Cairo, to move a resolution condemning Malaysia as neo-colonialist. Lee said this was bad for Malaysia. "It meant that even before we were born we would be regarded as an illegitimate offspring of British colonialism and not as nationalists, rightful heirs and successors to the British colonial empire in Southeast Asia. The communists had two motives for taking this line. First, by throwing cold water over the plan, they hoped to prevent or impede its fulfilment. Second, if Malaysia were to come into being, in spite of their opposition, then they hoped to isolate Malaysia from the Afro-Asian nations, and make it appear to the world as a stooge regime of Britain. And then, from time to time, when the independent Government of Malaysia takes action against communists in Malaysia, they hoped, through the Afro-Asian nations, at meetings in Cairo, Belgrade or Casablanca, to mobilize world opinion for the communists and against the Malaysian Government. They would represent actions against communists as being in the interests of the British imperialists, and in suppression of the freedom movements of the peace-loving peoples which the Communist Party of Malaya claim for themselves. And so I spent a few days in each place to talk things over with the men whose names are household words not only to us in Malaya, but also to the peoples of the non-aligned bloc, and of the communist and anti-communist bloc as well. . .

"Has my meeting the leaders of these countries made any difference to us in Malaya? Politically, yes. Economically, not immediately. Our trade and economic links are still largely with the West. We are dependent on the West for our economic development. But more and more in the future, the Afro-Asian bloc of non-aligned countries will make a great difference to us in our march towards our own machine age. To begin with, all this talk of Malaysia being a neo-colonialist plot has been debunked. And if the communists in Malaya and Indonesia continue to decry Malaysia as neo-colonialism, they will find theirs a lonely cry. The Afro-Asian world of newly independent nations will welcome Malaysia into its ranks as an honourable member. We will not be isolated. Nor can the communists use the prestige of the Afro-Asian nations to attack Malaysia for their communist ends. All of us have just emerged from a colonial society largely agricultural, producing the raw materials to build up the wealth and strength of the industrial societies of Europe. We are all tired of being backward, under-developed peoples. All of us want to make our own manufactured goods, acquire machines and build more machines so that our workers can raise the material and cultural standards of our people. The acquisition of political independence is only a first step towards our goal of a better society. . ."

VI

Back again in Singapore, Lee Kuan Yew on National Day (3 June) restated to thousands assembled on the Padang, the basic attitude of the immigrant communities, especially the Chinese, towards the concept of Malaysia. He stressed the contributions the Chinese had made to Singapore and Malaya, and could make to Malaysia. Neither did he forget the Indians. And he reminded the Malays that they must weld into the new society as Malaysians and stop thinking of themselves as a separate and distinct group.

On 3 July, another PAP member, a woman member of the Assembly, crossed the floor and joined the Opposition. The PAP Government then became a minority government with twenty-five seats to the Opposition's twenty-six. But the Opposition consisted of the Barisan Sosialis and the Singapore Alliance, and the anti-communist Alliance would do nothing at this stage to bring down the Government. Lee Kuan Yew put out a statement clarifying his Government's position. "It is the business of the Government to govern and to see the country's destiny in a Federation of Malaysia secured. That is the primary duty of the Government and indeed the duty of all citizens who want to see racial peace and harmony prevail. We are on the final phase towards our goal. There is no question of our quitting and leaving the job unfinished. Until the Opposition outvotes us, we are constitutionally the Government. It is a pity Madam Ho Puay Choo, under pressure, lost her nerve at this late stage. We went through the worst in July last year and there are no troubles that can confront us now which can be worse than what has happened. We shall see the referendum and merger through. There will be merger, there will be Malaysia, in or before June, 1963."

Lee Kuan Yew's confidence did not intimidate the Barisan Sosialis. In a bold and desperate move they decided to take the issue into the international arena. They persuaded seventeen Assemblymen (fourteen of them Barisan Sosialis) to petition the United Nations Special Committee on Colonialism. In New York on 26 July, Dr Lee Siew Choh laid their complaint before the Committee. Lee Kuan Yew appeared in person to argue for the Singapore Government. He answered Dr Lee's charges in detail. He traced the political history of Singaporē and Malaya, pointed out that Malaysia would mean that four former territories of the United Kingdom, all of them colonies, would achieve independence and nationhood through merger. The new nation would cover an area of 130,000 square miles and have a population of ten million. Malaysia would become a viable economic and political unit. Instead of being warmly acclaimed by all patriots and nationalists anxious to see an end to colonial rule in that part of the world, the ultra-Leftist Barisan Sosialis resisted Malaysia and demanded that the Singapore Government negotiate with the British Colonial Office terms whereby Singapore would still remain a semi-colony. Lee said that only David Marshall had ever suggested that Singapore should be independent by itself. "It is a political, economic and geographical absurdity," he added, believing that at the time. He was forced to change his mind later.

Mr Marshall had once suggested that Singapore should be independent and guaranteed by the United Nations, such guarantee being underwritten by the United Nations moving its headquarters to Singapore.

"It was," Lee Kuan Yew told the United Nations Special Committee on Colonialism, "the perfidy of the British, in their desire to hold on to a military base at the tip of the Malayan Peninsula which would give them a command of the whole area, that decided them on this cruel political amputation (of Singapore Island from Malaya), one from which the logic of geography, economics and military necessity compels them now to withdraw. Unlike the Portuguese, the French and the Dutch, the British are the people who most gracefully withdraw from an already untenable position. For that reason I have not had difficulty in the midst of my negotiations with the Federation Prime Minister in getting the British to agree that, on our agreement with the Federation of Malaya Government, sovereignty over these bases and over the whole island will pass into the hands of Malaya."

Lee questioned the inner purpose of the Barisan's appeal to the United Nations. What was it they wanted? Lee said all they sought from the Committee was an observer "who may deter major active perfidy being perpetuated against our people". Lee then set out the PAP Government's case, and point by point demolished the Barisan's arguments. It was a skilful performance. The Government was properly elected, had received a mandate for merger, but even so was planning to hold a referendum. "The anti-national Left, having failed in attempts to oppose merger and subvert the national referendum, have now submitted a petition to the United Nations Committee over an internal issue in the hope that somehow, first, they can boost the morale of their followers after their internal defeat in Singapore through intervention of some sort, and secondly, to prolong and delay the inevitable reunification...

"The supreme humiliation of the petitioners came last week when they went cap in hand to the office of the British High Commissioner in Singapore to petition the United Kingdom Government not to transfer sovereignty over Singapore to the Government of an independent Federation of Malaysia. They do not allege that the coming referendum will be carried out other than in accordance with the provisions of the Ordinance. They do not, for instance, express any fear that the Government will resort to illegal and unfair manipulations. Our general elections and by-elections have been conducted in a peaceful and orderly manner, and there have never been any instances of kidnapping, murder, violence or any of the other forms of irregular conduct which are not altogether unknown in some parts of the world. The coming referendum will be conducted scrupulously and in accordance with the law; and the petitioning Opposition has never questioned this. What then can an observer from the United Nations Committee of Seventeen do? I suggest that by this move they have demonstrated that their case is weak, hollow and empty. If they request an observer and if an observer were granted, he could do no more than observe and eventually he must report that the referendum was carried out strictly in accordance with the laws. What is the purpose of this request? I repeat: it is that they are now so thoroughly demoralized at their defeats in Singapore, and at their repeated failures in their attempts to unseat the Government through various anti-democratic campaigns that they have waged in the past twelve months. If the United Nations were to take notice of this petition, that would of course boost their sagging morale, for this means that an international organization would have been dragged in on their side in an internal, inter-party quarrel waged between the governing party of Singapore and the anti-national Left, the elements which deserted the governing party because they feared independence for Singapore through a merger in the Federation of Malaysia."

Lee Kuan Yew concluded his speech with these remarks: "It is my understanding that appeals are made to this United Nations Committee by colonial subjects who desire freedom and who fight for freedom but who are denied that freedom by a colonial power. If my understanding is correct, then this petition before the Committee must stand unique in the annals of this Committee, as it comes from a group of politicians in Singapore who do not want to see the country free and independent. Their sole purpose in fighting merger in Malaysia is to retain Singapore's semi-colonial status for political reasons of their own. This is the paradox on which these persons have claimed the assistance of the United Nations Committee of Seventeen and this is the position in which they find themselves today through their own follies."

The United Nations Special Committee on Colonialism did not send an observer to Singapore. Lee Kuan Yew's arguments prevailed.

VII

Lee Kuan Yew wept when the result of the referendum was announced late on 1 September. He had been working at high pressure for weeks. Malaysia was his political ambition. He admitted that in a sense the referendum had been a calculated risk. The communists had put up a fierce fight, but they had in the end been rejected by the people and Lee's tears were of relief and joy.

Three days later, over Radio Singapore, Lee claimed that the battle for merger, for all practical purposes, was over. All that remained to be done was to finalize the Constitution of Malaysia and sign a formal treaty. Over seventy-one per cent of the poll wanted merger on the lines of the PAP proposals: twenty-five per cent cast blank votes. Lee reminded his listeners that in 1959 in the general elections the PAP secured only fifty-three per cent of the votes. But on this national, not party, issue, seventy-one per cent of the people rallied round "to defend our future for ourselves and our children. And," he added, "the communist-manipulated, united-front organizations, aided and abetted by cranks and opportunists, can only temporarily deceive a quarter of the electorate. I must emphasize that the majority of this twenty-five per cent did not vote for communism.

"The calculated risk is now over. The people have declared their will. The front men of the Malayan communist united front are now threatening a continuation of their struggle. After your verdict, it is our duty to tell them that, if they continue their anti-national struggle against merger and Malaysia, they will have to face the consequences, backed by the clear endorsement of the overwhelming majority of the people. And if the tough men in their midst take to direct action, they face direct consequences. Before 1 September our firmness could have been misrepresented as Fascist repression of a so-called colonial liberation movement. After 1 September I am sure you will want my colleagues and me to do what is right for the security and well-being of all in Singapore and Malaysia. . . ."

VIII

In September 1962, on his way back to Singapore from London, where he had attended the Commonwealth Prime Ministers' Conference as "an adviser", Lee Kuan Yew visited Moscow. Malaysia's Prime Minister said that the trip nullified all that Mr Lee had said about communism. At the Singapore Airport upon his return Lee Kuan Yew told a large crowd of party supporters that he had not been contaminated by communism, a suggestion made in "certain quarters", *The Straits Times* reported, in Kuala Lumpur. "I am what I am and the Russians know it. They know the PAP, they know the Singapore Government, and they are prepared to deal with us as such. They are prepared to trade with us." Lee said it was an advantage to get to Russia, to know the Russians and "tell them where they get off here". The Prime Minister said he had also gone to Moscow to learn. Stressing that he had not been contaminated, the Premier said that his stand was like those of Prince Norodom Sihanouk of Cambodia, whom he had just visited, and Abdul Gamal Nasser of Egypt. "We will defend our territorial integrity, our ideas and our way of life to the last drop and I don't think anybody can doubt it."

Lee also spoke of his three-day official visit to Cambodia, whose leader, Prince Sihanouk, he said, shared the same views. "We are neutral where it is a collision of the big power blocs because we are not sure who is on our side, but we are not neutral where our interests are concerned. And if we are threatened, we shall defend our interests."

When Singapore became an independent republic, the Russians were invited by Lee Kuan Yew to set up a trade commission in Singapore. In 1967, Tunku Abdul Rahman announced that Malaysia and the Soviet Union would exchange Ambassadors, and the Moscow magazine *New Times*, commenting upon this rapid development, remarked that this would mean that Malaysia and the Soviet Union, in trading, would be able to cut out the middlemen, presumably referring to London and Singapore. The wheel seemed to have gone the full circle.

IX

For a while, the Barisan Sosialis lay low after their referendum defeat. They turned more and more to clandestine activity, and became involved with Sheik Azahari, leader of the Party Raayat in Brunei. He was preparing an armed revolt in Brunei, and this was to be backed by communist demonstrations and other forms of direct action in Malaysia. The hope was that the Malaysian plan would collapse amid armed action and civil disorder.

The revolt broke out on 8 December, but was contained within a few days. Even before it started, Azahari fled to Manila. Before the Brunei uprising began, Azahari had been in touch with Barisan Sosialis leaders, including Lim Chin Siong and Syed Zahari, and prominent Indonesian politicians. The failure of the Brunei revolt was the signal for an open campaign against Malaysia by Indonesia. On 14 December, the Indonesian Government issued a statement denying implication in the revolt, accusing Tunku Abdul Rahman of an unfriendly attitude towards Indonesia, and supporting Azahari's revolt as a movement for independence against imperialism and neo-colonialism. Four days later the revolt was over.

Lee Kuan Yew took all this in his stride. He went about his business as usual, confident that Malaysia would be created and would survive. On 10 December, he opened an Asian Seminar on Urban Community Development. He pointed out that more than eighty per cent of the population of Asia lived in villages in the country where the forms and patterns of a traditional peasant society had persisted for centuries, oblivious to the great changes to the city civilization of the modern world.

"However, two factors—the industrialization programmes of the new governments in Asia, and the landlessness of the younger sons—are bringing about the inevitable drift from the country to the towns. As they leave the country behind, so they leave behind the traditional village and family ties, ties of mutual insurance that go with a tightly-knit peasant community, the oldest form of social insurance against hunger and poverty. In the higgledy-piggledy tenements of the city new problems arise, not only of re-housing them but of re-forming them in new group patterns to create a community which ensures a satisfying social life and effective forms of social organization to help co-ordinate with, and supplement, welfare programmes of government departments.

"In Malaya, because of the highly developed plantation and mining economy of the past fifty years, with its extensive road and rail transport, about half the population lives in towns. Broadly speaking, the Chinese and Indian communities, either first generation immigrants or the descendants of immigrants, live in the towns and cities, and the Malays, who are the peasants, live in villages or kampongs in the countryside. Singapore is the first large town to develop in Malaya and fairly presents the problems of urbanization throughout Malaya, albeit in an advanced stage.

"Over eighty per cent of the population of Singapore are Chinese and Indians, immigrants or descendants of immigrants. About twelve per cent are Malays. Only recently, with widespread primary Malay education in the countryside, is there a drift of the Malays from the country to the towns of the Federation of Malaya. From the towns of Malaya there is a drift to Singapore, the largest town of all.

"The Chinese and Indians are those who were adventurous and adaptable enough to leave their homelands to seek a better life in Malaya. From the villages of Southern China and Southern India they have grown new roots here. They carried over from China into Malaya their clan and village associations. These were their closest knit non-governmental organizations. Through the clan associations, and the Chambers of Commerce formed of trade guilds and clan associations, they maintained a substitute pattern for the old social ties of the villages of their homeland. Their *tontines* and mutual aid and insurance relationships of the early clan associations took the place of the traditional village social patterns.

"After a hundred years the pattern gradually changed. As the immigrants and descendants of immigrants became the settled community, new forms of social association developed. Gradually, sporting clubs and benevolent societies began to mean more to the active social life of the descendants of the immigrants than the old clan associations which helped their fathers to settle here.

"Now, in a new phase, with self-government and independence,

164

the clan associations, guilds and Chambers of Commerce have changed their roles and are gradually ceasing to be the only points of contact between the immigrant communities and the Government. With direct representation in the legislative chamber the people have learned quickly to adjust themselves to a new situation. The old forms of contact and co-operation between the immigrant population and the colonial power have given way to new forms between a settled community and its elected leaders. Political parties, community clubs and recreational groups, welfare bodies, are all in the process of becoming the new medium of co-ordination and co-operation between government activity and the people. What is interesting to note in the urban community in Singapore is the difference between the high mobility and adaptability of the Chinese and Indian immigrants as against the indigenous Malays. The Chinese and Indians, being immigrants, were people who had psychologically prepared themselves for change, and they took to the urban life in Singapore easily and without tears.

"The Malays, on the other hand, being a settled rural community in Singapore, are reluctant and resistant to sudden change in their living habits. They still prefer to live in kampongs or villages in the country. They prefer wooden houses on stilts with land around them for poultry, fruit and vegetables, to concrete flats in the city. As the city expanded, rather than be absorbed into it, they have gone or been pushed to the outer rural areas. They have preferred this, although it has meant fewer amenities. An example can be seen in the Southern Islands where about 4,000 to 5,000 Malays eke out a precarious existence on what must have been the traditional fishing village economy over 100 years ago when Raffles landed here. Living in houses built on stilts over the sea, with the tides acting as a natural sewerage, they have preferred it and have adjured the amenities of pipe-water, electricity, schools, medical services available in Singapore City itself. For, with the Malays, it is not just an economic adjustment between a cheap attap hut and a dearer city flat. The greater problem is the psychological one of making them willing and happy to give up their traditional forms of kampong society, for the impersonal life of the city...

"Fortunately, here and there in the city proper there are pockets of Malays who, because of their employment either in the police, army or government departments, are in institutional quarters, most of which are modern flats. They are examples of Malay adjustability to urban life once the psychological resistance to change has been overcome. Their resistance to change is not just because they are changing from wooden houses on stilts with attap roofs to a cell in a concrete beehive, but, more important, because it has meant the breaking of old social ties in community patterns which provided a satisfying life in a complete society as they understood it..."

165

CHAPTER SEVENTEEN

The Year of Power 1963

ON 16 September, 1963, Malaysia was established: five days later the anti-Malaysia, anti-national and pro-communist elements were soundly beaten by the People's Action Party in a snap general election.

The year started badly. On 20 January the Indonesian Foreign Minister publicly proclaimed Indonesia's policy of confrontation against Malaysia. The Indonesians explained that this amounted to "direct offensive" in the economic and social fields, not the military sphere. Within three months, however, Indonesian troops had penetrated Sabah and Sarawak, and Indonesian saboteurs and guerillas were sent to Singapore and Malaya. In February, more than a hundred pro-communist and anti-Malaysia leaders in Singapore, including Lim Chin Siong, were arrested.

In the same month the Government introduced the world's most remarkable television service, with programmes in all four official languages (Malay, Chinese, Tamil and English) as well as in Cantonese, Hokkien and Hindustani. In July, Lee Kuan Yew went to London where the leaders of all the proposed states in Malaysia, excepting Brunei, signed the

Malaysia Agreement. In a television report on his return to Singapore, Lee spoke of sharp exchanges between Singapore and Malaya "which had demonstrated the differences between the two states in the economic situation and the political approach. These differences cannot be wiped out overnight on 31 August just by the promulgation of independence." President Sukarno and the Barisan Sosialis condemned the Agreement.

As predicted by the PAP, the electoral fight was between the PAP and the communist-front organization, the Barisan. All other political parties failed to return even a single candidate to the Assembly. The pro-communists polled 32·1 per cent of the vote and won thirteen seats. The People's Action Party polled 47·4 per cent and won thirty-seven seats. Ninety-three per cent of the electorate voted.

During the year another twenty-one schools, including technical schools, were completed, seven more were under construction and a further twenty-four planned. By the end of the year 45,000 citizens were living in Government-built flats. Despite Indonesia's confrontation trade continued to increase.

167

IN his 1963 New Year Message, Lee Kuan Yew said that 1962 would always be a memorable year in the history of Malaysia. "A year ago it was popularly believed that Singapore was a troublesome place and Brunei a peaceful and prosperous oil kingdom. It was said that Singapore, mainly Chinese, would oppose Malaysia, and Brunei, mainly Malay and ruled by a Sultan, would fit neatly into the Federation. But the prophets were proved wrong. In 1962 it was all peace and tranquillity in Singapore and people got down to working and planning for more prosperity in Malaysia. But in Brunei, some 2,000 of the 45,000 Malays—less than half the number we have in Geylang Serai and Kampong Melayu—attempted to set up the United States of Kalimantan Utara (in North Borneo). These rebels, armed with shotguns and *parangs*, in green uniforms with buffalo-head shoulder flashes, probably believed they were out to shake the world. But it needs more than the Ruritanian flamboyance of their leader, Sheik Azahari, to make a revolution. It needs more than cash to buy arms and weapon-training to stop the course of history in Malaysia. Indeed now it will take more than volunteers from Kalimantan Utara to stop it.

"The year 1962 saw two agreements, the first that West Irian would be liberated by May 1963, and the second that Malaysia would be established by August 1963. A bare three months will separate these two events which is perhaps just as well. For even before West Irian is liberated and Malaysia established, events have moved to show that nations in Asia are just like nations in Europe—they all like to grow bigger and more important and more prosperous. The solidarity of Asia was and is a solidarity against European colonialism. Once this common enemy is pushed out of the ring, the struggle for supremacy between themselves resumes. And now, even before British colonialism is pushed out of North Borneo and Sarawak, we find some groups in foreign countries pledging support to help Azahari and some 45,000 Brunei Malays he claims to lead to 'liberate' North Borneo and Sarawak."

On 2 February, Lim Chin Siong and his intimate group of communist-front men were arrested. A week later, in the Assembly, Lee Kuan Yew explained why. He said that the Internal Security Council (consisting of representatives of Singapore, Malaya and Britain), which Lim had so long insisted must be abolished, met in Kuala Lumpur. It decided that action should be taken immediately to safeguard national defence and the security of Singapore and the other territories of Malaysia. It decided that certain of those known to the three security authorities to be deeply implicated in the united front working for communist and foreign interests must be arrested. In the early hours of Saturday morning, 2 February, operations were launched from Johore by Singapore and Federation Special Branch officers. A number of persons were detained. "I don't think the public were surprised that action had been taken against these communists and their united front cadres. For that matter the communists were not surprised either."

Lee explained the background to the arrests. "The communists preferred Singapore not to merge with the Federation. They wanted to make it into a Cuba, from which they hoped to mount an offensive against the Federation of Malaya. When they lost the referendum, and the overwhelming majority voted decisively for merger, for a peaceful and stable future in Malaysia, they knew that after 31 August they would face security action. Their first team—the open leaders—were so well known they could not easily withdraw and go into hiding. Also, if they had done so, their rank and file would have lost heart and melted away. So their first team of open united-front cadres in the political parties and in the unions and in the rural associations and cultural associations had to be sacrificed. The communists treated them as 'expendables' to be sacrificed. However, there were other less well-known expendables, cadres whose names and faces were less well known to the public..."

There were urgent reasons why security action was taken on the morning of 2 February. On a previous occasion, when intelligence reports came to the notice of the Federation Government of an impending revolt in Brunei by persons trained in Indonesian Borneo, no action had been taken. The Tunku has said that, although he informed the British, they took no preventive steps. British Intelligence did not altogether accept the imminence of the danger. Had the report been acted on, perhaps the Brunei revolt, which cost money, involved the movement of troops and arms, caused deaths and built up an atmosphere of crisis with some of Malaysia's neighbours—all this might not have happened. This time, however, none of the three governments represented on the Internal Security Council was willing to be caught napping a second time. Captured rebel leaders in Brunei revealed that Azahari had told them that he had arranged for a simultaneous uprising in Singapore at the same time as they attacked in Brunei, Sarawak and Sabah. These men knew that they had lost the battle in Singapore against Malaysia. So they resorted to every available device, and exploited every opportunity to create trouble in the other territories, particularly in Sarawak and Brunei, in order to stop Malaysia. Lee warned that after the experience of the Brunei revolt, it would be a mistake to underestimate communist intention or capacity for harm. They said in the past that there would be bloodshed and violence if Malaysia were pushed through. "This was said by some of their leaders now in detention, Lim Chin Siong, Fong Swee Suan and Sandra Woodhull. Subsequent events have shown that they were prepared to

169

use the Brunei Malays and involve themselves in conspiracy with foreign groups to precipitate armed revolt in the Borneo territories to stop Malaysia. Action could not be delayed any longer. Already, relations between the Federation and neigbouring countries are gravely strained. We can only hope that goodwill from all sides, with the help of conciliation and mediation by disinterested officials of international organizations, will ease the situation . . .

"But the most dangerous aspect of this purge of communist-front organizers is that the country may be lulled into a sense of false security. Without the leading communist-front figures in the open, with their wild postures, their fierce statements, their strikes and inflammatory speeches, people may believe that the communist threat is gone. Let us never deçeive ourselves that this action has removed the communist threat. Even if the Internal Security Council were to arrest all the other united-front cadres and ban their organization, the problem would be only slightly further diminished. The basic threat remains.

"There are two reasons. First, the underground party is still there. . . Second, the united-front framework is still there. . . All those detained should remember that it is up to them to decide if they want a decent place in our society. If they give up this dangerous nonsense of revolution for a communist Malaya, and stop taking their directives from foreign groups, they can be released immediately. We have no desire to keep anybody out of a fair share of the fruits of our society, whether Chinese-educated, Malay-educated, Tamil-educated, or English-educated. Everybody can share in the fruits of freedom and join in building the nation. But let me remind those who are still determined on violent revolution and the setting up of a communist society, that this time they face nationalism, a much more formidable opponent than colonialism. Colonialism is on the way out. Nationalism will stay and triumph."

II

On Tunku Abdul Rahman's sixtieth birthday, Lee Kuan Yew issued a message: "After eight years as Malaya's leader, the Tunku has become the symbol of a tolerant, happy and prosperous country. Of the leaders that have emerged in Afro-Asia since the end of World War Two, some would wish to leave their mark behind as great revolutionaries, some as great orators, and some as great nation-builders. Unfortunately the pretensions to greatness of a few of these leaders have led them into curious ways. But the Tunku has not proclaimed himself after the style of the ancient emperors 'great saviour of the nation', 'divine genius', or 'infallible leader'. There are no busts or statues in every park and square. No face stares up from every coin and stamp. Instead, every time the Tunku appears, it is always the tolerant, cheerful personality—moving easily amongst all races and classes—a man completely at ease, relaxed, at peace with himself and with the world, practical, and, most important of all, successful. For that is what Malaysia will be—a country with a practical and realistic approach to life, and, most important, successful.

"On his sixtieth birthday, may we wish him many happy returns, for the more happy returns he has the more years there will be in which we can find more permanent solutions to the problems of our multiracial and multicultural society, where intolerance and bigotry could so easily take over and wreck everything. We know if he is in charge he will never let this happen."

III

The rate of growth of Singapore's population when the PAP Government came into power in 1959 was a world record of nearly four per cent per annum. "Here, in a relatively modern city, in an Asian context," Lee Kuan Yew told the Seventh International Conference on Planned Parenthood, held in Singapore on 13 February, "you will find a microcosm of the problems of population control. Modern science has checked the ravages of disease and pestilence. Floods, drought and famine no longer occur. But old habits and ancient traditions built out of centuries of experience of natural disasters and uncontrollable plagues, still prevail. Old cultural patterns and family values, designed to meet conditions which prevailed hundreds and thousands of years ago, still persist, with grave consequence to the problems of economic and industrial growth.

"Quite apart from religious principles, by and large, Chinese and Indian families believe that the more children a man has the greater is his good fortune. In the old days the more wives a man had, the higher his status. Just like motor-cars, wives and children were a status symbol. All this proliferating made sense in an age when periodic plagues, drought, floods and famine regularly decimated the population. But the same habits in a relatively affluent society, whose public health standards are high, lead to a phenomenal increase in population growth that cannot but dampen the spirits of those who are entrusted with our problems of economic growth, industrial expansion and the maintenance of standards of living. . .

"I have assumed that Asian governments want to increase industrial growth by population control. But perhaps this is an assumption which is dangerous to make. For us, a small people, the decision is obvious. There is no hope of fulfilling any expansionist ambitions. It is disturbing, however, to think that there are some bigger nations in Asia whose population expansion can become phenomenal if health, nutritional and social conditions, which modern science has brought to Singapore, were also to prevail. What happens if one nation controls its population growth and others do not? What happens in the long run if one country becomes overwhelmingly more numerous and more powerful than the other? The problem of the balance between nations is a delicate and sensitive issue. Sometimes even the balance of population within a nation can also become a sensitive issue. I have read that in a particularly advanced country one religious group which does not permit birth control has expressed its confidence of gaining political dominance because numerically it is growing in proportion to the rest of the population. Is the world, then, to be finally inherited by those nations whose religions do not permit the practise of birth control?

"These are the wider imponderables with which, fortunately, we in Singapore need not concern ourselves. We have decided that it is in our interest to check our population growth. Our only problem is how to disseminate knowledge of simple birth control methods as quickly as possible, and how to educate our people to new social values to meet our social and economic conditions. If we do not, then we shall face grave problems affecting our living standards. . . When you see so many little children and young people during your stay in Singapore, you can recall that sixty per cent of our population are below eighten and are being fed and housed and schooled by the efforts of some twenty-five per cent of the total population."

IV

Discovery (during house-building excavations) of another cache of human bones, evidence of yet another unrecorded massacre of Singapore Chinese by Japanese soldiers during the war, again reminded Singaporeans of their sufferings during the period of occupation, and reawakened their determination that Japan should atone for the crimes of her soldiers. At a meeting (on 21 April) called to make arrangements to build a memorial "to an unhappy incident in which many tens of thousands of all races died at the hands of a brutal invading army", Lee Kuan Yew said the incident left a scar which after more than two decades was still sensitive.

"Many of us here today have friends or relatives who simply disappeared soon after the fall of Singapore in 1942, and have never been heard of since. Today we stand in silence to pay respect to those who died for no crime whatsoever except the misfortune of being in Singapore at that time. There is one reason why, although twenty years have passed, this matter has never been resolved in our hearts, whatever the legal situation may be. Legally, it may be argued that the Treaty of San Franciso has settled everything, and that all things should be past and forgotten. But this was settled by a colonial government that did not represent us, and never understood the depth of our feeling at the atrocities and humiliation an occupying invader inflicted on us, then a subject people—the tributes in cash and kind exacted, the senseless brutality and the futile humiliation. It is this feeling that we, as a government representative of the people, now seek to resolve peacefully and quietly.

"It was my duty to make known the depth of the feelings of the people to the Japanese Government. This I have done. They have assured me that they are genuinely sorry for what happened and that they are prepared to make a gesture of atonement. They have made a certain proposal. The Singapore Government in turn has put forward another proposal. . .

"Meanwhile, we must be patient, and, above all, we must be realistic. You know that in our industrialization programme the participation of Japanese industries in the development of our Jurong industrial complex would help. They have sent several missions to Singapore to survey the prospects. Already several enterprises, including an oil refinery, have been set up. The amount of trade, technical co-operation and industrial development that they could take part in in Singapore and the rest of Malaysia would be out of all proportion to any gesture of atonement they can make. For that reason I understand the views of the representatives who have organized this meeting that a parsimonious gesture would be worse than nothing. The Japanese are hard-headed businessmen. And because they are hard-headed businessmen, I think they understand that in the long run it is worth their while to make a magnanimous gesture of contrition."

In 1966, the Japanese offer of a grant of $25 million and the loan of another $25 million on very liberal terms was accepted by the Singapore Government.

The memorial, a concrete pillar, at the base of which were buried the bones of thousands of victims, was completed in early 1967.

V

Would Malaysia succeed? Lee Kuan Yew told the Singapore National Union of Journalists, on 24 May, that Malaysia was inevitable. But no one could say that the success of Malaysia as an economic and a political unit was inevitable. "It is dependent upon what we, the people and the leaders in Malaysia, do in fulfilling the basic pre-conditions for success. I would list some of these pre-conditions:

(1) National unity of all the races comprising Malaysia with undivided loyalty to the elected Central Government of Malaysia;
(2) An effective, honest administration which can extend its writs throughout the length and breadth of Malaysia;
(3) Stable political leadership that will infuse confidence, bring about capital accumulation investment in the country, and attract foreign loans and investment capital without political strings from abroad for the development of industries;
(4) The maintenance of a representative system of democratic government in which the interests of all racial and economic groups are fairly balanced by this leadership.

"One factor is fundamental to make Malaysia successful economically and politically, and that is a spirit of tolerance between all the races in Malaysia with all their interests reasonably balanced. Malaysia will begin with political and administrative power in the hands largely of the Malays and economic power in the hands of Chinese and Indians. But it speaks volumes for the wisdom of the Tunku and his colleagues, like Tun Razak, his deputy, that the power which the Malays have in the Federation is not misused. More and more non-Malays are being introduced into the higher echelons of the army, navy, air force, police and administration. Non-Malays may sometimes feel that the progress is too slow, but we must always remember the problem of the Malay leaders in not going faster than their own Malay opinion will allow them. . .

"The art of successful government in the Federation and in Singapore is in part the art of balancing competing interests and not allowing the racial preponderance of any group to conscribe the economic opportunities of the others. The Federation, with a Malay-based political majority, has allowed free Chinese and Indian enterprise, and has employed Eurasians and Ceylonese in public office. In the same spirit Singapore, with a Chinese-based political majority, accepts Malay as the national language and ensures that the Indians, Ceylonese, Eurasians and others, though they may not have the special privileges of the Malays in education, are in no way handicapped when competing for jobs and businesses by the fact that they are racial minorities. This balance of competing interests is an essential precondition for an economically and politically successful Malaysia. . .

"I would like to analyse the problems of Malaysia into two phases —short term and the long term. In the short term, it is impossible for any political party in the Federation to govern without carrying the Malay mass base with them. The Malay mass base, being apprehensive of the commercially and socially more advanced Chinese and Indians, have rallied together around their traditional leaders—

174

their Sultans, their Tunku, and Dato Razak, respected as one of the traditional ruling chiefs of Pahang even before he became a Tun. It is fortunate for Malaya that the Malays should have thrown up traditional leaders to lead them who are also men of good judgment and ability. They see in their solidarity their only protection against being overwhelmed by the more economically and socially advanced immigrants, who are mainly Chinese and Indians. Nothing will change this in the immediate future, and they demand that their leaders should protect their interests under the Constitution, particularly their rights to land and executive positions in government service, so as to ensure that they have the State apparatus in their hands and can thus prevent themselves from being overwhelmed . . .

"In the short term there is no escape from this. There is no person who has yet emerged in Malaya as a complete Malayan national leader, in the sense that he enjoys support equally strong from all the communities. For how can there be one when there is not yet a completely Malayan national opinion, from which such a leader can draw his strength? The Tunku is the leader of the Malays. The Chinese in the Federation, realizing that the Malays are in the majority, are relieved that they should have a fair and non-communal-minded leader. Of all the Malay leaders there is no doubt that the Chinese and Indians, Ceylonese and Eurasians support the Tunku first. Of course, if the Chinese were in the majority in Malaya, then we must be honest and say that, as they are at present, before a new generation has grown up, born and educated in the Malayan national spirit, they would probably choose a Chinese leader. They have done this in Singapore where the Chinese are in the majority. Only the English-educated are completely Malayanized in their political outlook, but they are not in the majority. . .

"Any analysis of the short-term phase must take into account these communal factors. But, in the long run, the only way to a peaceful, democratic and successful Malaysia is to have political loyalties rallying around competing economic policies and competing political ideologies, rather than to strike a balance of communal forces. After Malaysia, as the years go on, more and more of those born in Malaysia will come of age and acquire the right to vote. Then no purely pro-Malay or pro-Chinese party can ever win power. In the Federation today, it is theoretically possible to appeal only to Malay votes and win the right to govern. Similarly, in Singapore, theoretically one could appeal purely to Chinese votes and form a government. But in Malaysia, with forty-four per cent Malays and indigenous people, about forty per cent Chinese, about ten per cent Indians, and the rest Pakistanis, Ceylonese and Eurasians, to secure the right to govern the appeal to the electorate must cut across communal barriers.

"As a democratic, socialist, non-communal party, I consider the role of the PAP to be in a small way a forerunner of this new order of things. We can set the pace for change and progress gradually through persuasion and example, provided in the next ten years of flux and change there is a strong Central Government with a leader like the Tunku or Tun Razak, whose national image can weld the people together. In any case, the events of the past fifteen years in Singapore since elections were first introduced show clearly that only a party with a radical and non-communal programme can hold the loyalty of the people. Any attempt to introduce communal politics would be a retrograde step unlikely to succeed. All it may succeed in doing is to arouse communal friction to the detriment of Singapore and of Malaysia. For without a healthy, stable and prosperous Singapore, the centre of gravity of Malaysia would be severely rocked. The fight in Singapore for the hearts and minds of men is between the communists on the one hand and the democratic socialists on the other. There is no third alternative. . .

"What are the chances of success for Malaysia? I rate them reasonably good, provided racial extremism in any of the major races is kept down, and tolerance and amity preserved. There is a sound administration throughout all these five territories and a sound economy, with confidence established among both home and foreign investors, and international credit high. . . But if racists and communalists take over, then we must be prepared for a sudden and dramatic change, for then I have no doubt that whoever succeeds the Tunku as leader of the Malays must, in order to retain supremacy, exercise his authority to govern through the strength of the army, police and the symbol of the monarch. This would mean there would be a less balanced representation of competing economic and political interests. This in turn would lead to growing resentment among the Chinese, Indians, Ceylonese, Eurasians and others, with all its incalculable effects on the politics, economy and prosperity of Malaysia. The chain of consequences that such a course of events would set in motion is so gruesome as to make one flinch even to contemplate it. It is one thing to mount an anti-Chinese campaign where the Chinese are a minority of three to four per cent of the population: it is another thing to mount an anti-Chinese campaign where they constitute nearly forty per cent of the population, as they will in Malaysia.

"The alternative to success, which is dependent primarily on communal harmony and firm but wise leadership on non-communal policies, is so terrifying that no government can afford to allow any communalist to get out of hand and trigger into motion communal passions, the end result of which nobody can control. But, on the whole, I am hopeful for the future of Malaysia as a developing nation, prosperous and stable, with more and more equal opportunities for its people, regardless of race, language and religion. Malaysia will succeed if we all know what are the dangerous issues and where the danger points. . . "

VI

Malaysia had been agreed upon in principle and most of the details had been settled, but sharp bargaining over finance, in which Tan Siew Sin, Malaya's Finance Minister, was personally involved, led to recriminations. In the end common sense and realism prevailed. Lee Kuan Yew persuaded the Tunku to discuss the matter in London, where they were due to meet the British Government to finalize Malaysia. At the eleventh hour agreement was finally reached, and the Malaysia Agreement was signed by Malaysia's Prime Minister, Lee Kuan Yew, and representatives of Sabah and Sarawak at 11.30 p.m. on 8 July.

At the signing ceremony at Marlborough House, Lee Kuan Yew briefly made the point that "nations do not depend on legal documents, but on the hearts and wills of the people, and the quality of the leadership". It was, he said, his trust and his confidence in the quality of the Prime Minister of Malaysia that had made a very difficult decision possible. "We append our faith and confidence in this document which we shall be initialling to put our lives together for better or for worse."

In the Assembly on 30 July, Lee Kuan Yew formally moved the motion to bring about merger and Malaysia. He said that the debate would end an era which began in 1945 when "British troops returned to Malaya and, by a unilateral act of the British Government, Singapore was severed from the mainland". In 1948 the Malayan Communist Party launched its armed revolt. The struggle reached a turning point in 1957 when the British granted Malaya independence, but not Singapore. "Singapore, it seems, was ordained to remain forever in semi-tutelage with internal self-government but with supreme authority in matters of defence, foreign affairs and, for that matter, internal security, in the hands of the British raj.

"I do not wish to detail an account of the years 1945 to 1948 or, even more unpleasant, the years 1948 to 1957. Suffice it to say that this unilateral division of the country was never accepted by the peoples of either the Federation of Malaya or of Singapore. In Singapore. . . for us, the last chapter to merger really began with 1959. Then for the first time power, other than responsibility for defence, foreign affairs, and internal security, which was shared with Malaya and the British, was bestowed on a wholly elected government. The history of Singapore, and indeed the history of Southeast Asia might well have been different had we decided any other way . . . In 1959 we were quite convinced, even before we assumed office, that there was no other way . . . In 1956 . . . I urged the then Secretary of State for the Colonies, a very able and forceful character, who decided to give independence to Malaya, that he should, despite the advice of his officials, tie up Singapore with the Federation, for there was too much at stake . . .

But it took another two years—from 1959 to 1961—before the British were convinced of the next step in the argument: that if Singapore was not in Malaya, then Singapore and Malaya would ultimately be lost to the communists ... Slowly the unpleasant and brutal facts were placed before the Federation Government. What had been publicly known was that Malaya was vital to Singapore, but what we did not emphasize, lest we offend our friends across the Causeway, was that Singapore was vital to their survival.

"Quietly over the golf course, sometimes even across the poker table, and sometimes over a meal, friendly discussion always came. It had one theme song: merger is inevitable, either by consent or by force of one territory over the other. Let me say, Mr Speaker, that the possibility of Singapore overwhelming the Federation is not a possibility to be altogether dismissed. Being what we were, having regard to the susceptibilities of our friends in the Federation, the line was put over softly, gently, and politely. Finally a note was struck in the hearts of the Federation Ministers. On 17 May, the Tunku came down to announce that he had decided that there should be a closer political and economic association of the Federation of Malaya, Singapore, and the three Borneo territories."

For another hour the Prime Minister went into details about the arrangements for merger and Malaysia. He ended his long speech by insisting that two things were required of anyone who wanted to inherit the 400 million dollars stacked away for the country to carry out the building plans, the industrial projects in Jurong nearly completed, harbour, railroads, water, power — integrity and determination. "Absolute and utter integrity that can stand the closest scrutiny at any time. And determination to see that right is done. I do not know whether the same Assembly will meet again, Mr Speaker. I am not in a position to tell my opponents these things, but I hope in the next Assembly you will find a government worthy of an industrious and able people."

Winding up the debate, on 1 August, a disappointed Prime Minister said he had hoped, somewhat forlornly, that before the end of the Assembly the House would rise to the occasion. "We are," he said, "deliberating not the future of the PAP, or the future of the Barisan Sosialis, or the Singapore Grand Alliance. We are taking a decision of momentous proportion." He expected the communists to take the same consistent anti-national, anti-Malaysia line, but he had expected more from the rest of the Opposition, whom he accused of playing party politics. He appealed to David Marshall and the others to stop this. "Why not rise above this pettiness? This is something bigger than ourselves. This is going to ensure our survival."

At the same time, Lee Kuan Yew urged everyone not to misjudge the situation. Two thousand communists were under training in Sarawak, along the border. They were being supplied with arms. "I for one," declared Lee Kuan Yew, "and I am sure my colleagues with me here, will stand up and fight for Malaysia."

VII

Determined if they could, to frustrate Malaysia even at this late stage, the Malayan Communist Party, through the Barisan Sosialis and the extreme Left trade unions, decided to exploit the Japanese blood debt issue to turn the people against Lee Kuan Yew. Lee understood the people's anger and bitterness, but he was more interested and concerned with the future than with the past, more worried about new factories than old bones. He knew the Japanese must make a suitable gesture of atonement, and he expected they would, but he did not want to damage Singapore's plans to industrialize, for these included high hopes of Japanese participation.

But the blood debt was a popular issue: it was sponsored by well-meaning Chinese connected with the Chinese Chamber of Commerce. Tension mounted. People became more interested in the Japanese blood debt than in Malaysia. This was a situation which the pro-communist anti-Malaysia elements could exploit: here were capitalists and communists in harmony against the popularly elected Government which did not, on this issue, apparently, reflect the true feelings of the masses. Lee's dilemma was that if he stood aside the anti-Malaysians would magnify the issue out of all proportion: if he took part in the growing anti-Japanese agitation he might ruin the prospects of Japan helping Singapore to industrialize, and in the process might find himself a captive of the joint communist-capitalist leadership.

Lee recognized that there was only one move he could prudently make. He must take over the direction of the blood-debt issue himself. He knew that both the capitalists and the communists, for their own separate reasons, would resist. He knew that what the communists wanted to do was to create chaos and confusion. By taking this step Lee realized he might force their hand in what was a highly charged atmosphere of emotion and tension. This was danger he felt he could not avoid. He could no longer stand aside. Accordingly, he notified the blood-debt committee that the Government had decided to throw its weight behind the campaign and to take certain anti-Japan decisions in an effort to convince the Japanese that some gesture of atonement was necessary. He told them he would address the rally.

On Sunday night, 25 August there gathered on the historic Padang the largest crowd ever assembled in Singapore. Lee expected trouble. He knew the temper and desperation of the pro-communist, anti-Malaysia elements. Elaborate security precautions were taken: Lee himself had a revolver in his pocket when he addressed the silent crowd. "You all know," he said, "that my colleagues and I have placed great emphasis on the rapid industrialization of Singapore. It is our policy to invite technical and industrial skills from the rest of the world to come to Singapore to heighten the tempo of industrialization. The cheapest technical and managerial skills that can come to Southeast Asia are from Japan. But after tonight's meeting, and the adoption of the resolutions of non-co-operation until a fair and just solution has been found, no more visas will be issued for more Japanese on new industrial or commercial projects in Singapore. And, indeed, with the solidarity now shown by the Chamber of Commerce in Kuala Lumpur and the response from the people in North Borneo and Sarawak, it means that non-co-operation with Japan will be extended throughout Malaysia. . . I am not unhopeful that, being a practical people, the Japanese will come to realize the wisdom of coming to terms with the national representatives of the people of Singapore, Malaya, North Borneo and Sarawak, and even Hongkong. It is now up to them whether they wish to participate in the lucrative commerce and industry of Malaysia. I say Malaysia because, as you can see from the development of events over the past few weeks, even though the Central Government will be in charge of foreign affairs and immigration, it will make no difference at all. For on this issue there is Pan-Malaysian solidarity. . . In other words, Japan must come to terms with us in Malaysia, or else lose the Malaysian market—at present and in the future potentially one of the wealthiest markets in this part of the world.

"Let me add that calm deliberation and cold calculation do not mean that my colleagues and I have no feelings on this issue. Indeed, it is a highly charged issue for many of us. My colleague, Dr Goh Keng Swee, was a member of the Singapore Volunteer Corps, together with my wife's brother. My brother-in-law was shot and killed, but, by an inexplicable chance of fate, Dr Goh escaped this unhappy end to play his part in the history of Malaysia. The Japanese Consul-General and his predecessor, who discussed these matters with me, or indeed the Japanese Prime Minister and his Foreign Minister, with whom I had brief discussions in Tokyo, did not know how I, but for a chance of fate, would have been one among those massacred in February 1942."

Lee told how he escaped from a lorry taking young men to be executed. He hid. "Those who were put on the lorry never came back. Such was the blindness of their brutality. They would never know what they did to a whole generation like me. . . Now, in a matter of days, we shall be a free people. We are not going to change masters from time to time. We have had enough of all that. We shall be our own masters in our own country. Rather than have a new master, death would be preferable. But I believe that the solidarity of the people of Malaysia, the desire to unite and live in peace and tolerance with each other, the desire to prosper in freedom, to be friends with our neighbours,

180

friendly, fair and firm, will ensure our survival and prevent the repetition of the horrors of enemy occupation and re-occupation. Humiliation and degradation by foreign European powers is bad enough. It was worse at the hands of a conquering Asian nation like Japan—and it will be even worse if it should be by a neighbouring power in Southeast Asia.

"I speak for one and all of you when I say that we have had enough of being the pawns and playthings of foreign powers. We have a will of our own, and a right to live in peace on our own. So let us unite in Malaysia and prevent it ever happening again. And let us settle these legacies of World War II peacefully if we may, but otherwise if we must."

Pro-communists in the crowd tried to agitate, to start a riot, but Lee's words fell on receptive ears, and there were no more than a few scuffles with the police. The people went away prepared to have confidence in his handling of Japan.

VIII

On 4 September, Lee Kuan Yew announced his decision to hold general elections. Nominations closed on 12 September. The legal minimum notice was given, but the PAP had indicated on 25 July that elections would be held after Malaysia. Polling day was fixed for 21 September. Nine days' campaigning was sufficient, it was thought; people were getting tired of politics and the climate of tension. For the communist-dominated Barisan Sosialis these general elections were a matter of life and death: here was an opportunity for them to prove to the world that the people of Singapore did not, after all, want Malaysia. They marshalled all available forces to smash the PAP and to win the elections. If they did that they could stop merger and wreck Malaysia, all in a constitutional manner.

Early in the morning of 22 September, Lee Kuan Yew knew that the People's Action Party had been returned to office with a substantial majority. Over the radio a physically almost exhausted Lee described the result "a vote of confidence which will resound throughout Malaysia. It was more than just an act of faith that made us hold these general elections at this moment with the communists out in the open. We knew that they were the real enemy. Our problem was to convince you that they were really the enemy, and that the others were clowns and were just confusing the issues, clouding the sharp definition of issues in all the main towns in Malaysia. We have proved in Singapore, long abandoned by many a professional political commentator as a lost city, lost to the communists, that it was not lost, never had been.

What was required was an honest and effective leadership to work the democratic system. And after four and a half years, of which the last two and a half have been for you and for me years of acute conflict and anxiety, we reached this morning what is for the communists their moment of truth. That their masses were mythical, that the invincibility of the communist organization—the claque, the cheer leaders, the slogans, the posters which they stuck up over everyone else's, their attempts to smother everybody else with a sense of inordinate numbers—was false. . . ''

IX

In August, the Prime Minister received the only known official communication from the People's Republic of China. It was a letter addressed to him by the Prime Minister of China, Chou En-lai.

Then, at least, China recognized the existence of independent Singapore. In later years Peking Radio was to quote reports from the Barisan which denied Singapore's separate existence. These reports also denied Malaysia and referred to "Malaya including Singapore".

On 17 December, Peking Radio broadcast the following: "Lee Kuan Yew, Singapore Premier, on 30 November, 1963 wrote a message to Chou En-lai, Premier of the State Council of the People's Republic of China, replying to the Chinese Premier's letter dated 2 August, 1963. Premier Chou En-lai in his letter proposed the complete, thorough, total and resolute prohibition and destruction of nuclear weapons by all countries and a conference of the government heads of all countries of the world to discuss this question.

"Lee Kuan Yew's letter said, 'The letter from your Government dated 2 August, 1963, has been received. Due to various reasons, the reply message was only posted today. The Singapore Government holds that all efforts for the abolition of nuclear war deserve support. Mankind will be overjoyed should all nuclear weapons be eliminated and the danger of nuclear war be thus lessened and removed. Any step towards this lofty ideal will have our positive response.' "

X

When he opened a UNESCO symposium at the University of Singapore (on 8 December), Lee Kuan Yew said he could think of no more fascinating subject for scholarly analysis and discussion than patterns of authority and leadership in traditional and modern societies. Since 1945, over fifty new nations had emerged, and the patterns of authority and leadership that they presented were a rewarding subject of study. Surely some universal truths and principles emerged from a systematic comparison of the forms of authority and leadership and their relative efficacy as intelligent and tolerant forms of government?

"As one who is actively engaged in this quest for benign authority and yet effective leadership, immersed in the day-to-day task of resolving specific problems in the given situation obtaining in Singapore and Malaysia, I have often wondered which of these problems are universal and whether solutions have not been found in other similar situations elsewhere which I could profitably amend for use in Singapore.

"Most of the nations that have emerged since 1945 have never before existed in history with those exact geographic boundaries and demographic content. A few, like India or Burma, re-emerged, but not altogether in the form they were before colonialism engulfed them. Pakistan is new; so is Indonesia; so is Malaysia. Whether these countries will endure as coherent nations, providing the political framework for economic and industrial development to raise standards of life to levels comparable to those prevailing in Europe and America, depends in large measure upon the quality of the leadership.

"Basically, the problems presented to all these new nations are the same. In the period of European colonial rule, there was centralized institutional authority. The Viceroy or the Governor held his power by virtue of external authority, and was, in fact, the agent of external authority. The people he governed consisted not of followers, but of subjects. In this colonial-type society some forms of traditional leadership of maharajas, sultans and chieftains were sustained as useful adjuncts to the authority of the metropolitan power. But leadership which rests upon the capacity to articulate the hopes and fears, the wishes and grievances, of the mass of the people was actively discouraged.

"In the phase just before colonial authority relinquished its power, it was this second kind of leadership which forced itself into the fore and asserted its right to authority. In other words, it had to have the capacity to exercise ascendancy over the people. In some countries, like India, the development of this leadership is a long process stretching over more than seventy years. Where popular leadership took some time to mature before emerging, and the traditional rulers had been associated with the colonial power in trying to stifle its emergence, then they were cast aside by the popular leaders. This was the fate of the Indian maharajas.

"But in most countries the spark of freedom only flared after the end of the Second World War. In many, where the European colonial power in its own enlightened self-interests withdrew more rapidly than the nationalist leadership could oust it, curious combinations of the traditional leadership of sultans and kabakas and other chieftains, found accommodation in the pattern of authority.

"Another common feature of these new nations is that the pattern of authority and government invariably follows that of the metropolitan power. The Philippines copied the American presidential system. The French colonies in Africa have variations of the Fourth and Fifth Republics. The British Commonwealth nations have moulded themselves after the pattern of the Houses of Parliament in Westminster. This inevitably happens when there is legitimacy in colonial revolutions, where the new nationalist government takes over with consent of the metropolitan power. Partly as a condition precedent, and partly because of general acceptance in the colonial territories of the value of the institutions of the metropolitan power, since it was the only pattern of authority that the leaders were familiar with, the pattern was repeated in the new nation.

"But soon afterwards, confronted with the stresses and strains of social and economic problems, in a society where the people have no abiding loyalty to the new institutions of authority that have been adopted, there is a rapid return to the centralization of power in the person of one leader, much after the fashion of the centralized power of the imperial Viceroy or Governor. And so many of the former British colonies in Asia and Africa have abjured the British parliamentary system and have established the centralized power of the presidential system. There must be a common denominator of factors which has brought this pattern about in countries where national, racial and situational peculiarities are as divergent and far apart as Pakistan and Ghana, or Burma and Tanganyika.

"One possible explanation is that often in new nations the loyalty of its people is to individual leaders and not to the institutions of the state. In an established society, the institutions have endured over a period of time and have become the objects of loyalty. The Houses of Parliament and the office of Prime Minister in Britain, together with the symbol of the monarch, provide whoever attains the office of Prime Minister with a ready-made set of loyalty symbols, and changes in the personnel of the leadership do not affect the pattern of authority or the order of society. Whether it is Churchill or Attlee or Eden or Macmillan or Home, the pattern of authority, set and established long before the incumbents of the high office, endures. But the loyalty to Pandit Nehru in the hearts of millions in India is certainly greater than the loyalty Indians feel towards the Indian Parliament, the Lok Sabha, or to Dr Radhakrishnan, constitutional Head of State, who resides in the former Viceroy's palace. In other words, in such a situation, the pattern of authority can so easily be changed, and usually is changed, with changes in the personnel of the leadership.

"No doubt ultimately, if these new nations survive and endure, their societies may become established and their institutions of authority acquire a capacity to attract loyalty greater than that which their occupants now attract ... The loyalty those leaders personally command is much greater than the loyalty that their high offices command. Their successors, however, may not command the same loyalty, affection, reverence and obedience. But eventually, as the pattern of government becomes established, so loyalty accrues more to the office than to the person. . .

"If the leadership of these new nations is successful, then the pattern of authority, through which the leadership governs, becomes established and institutionalized. Continuity is then ensured for some time. If, on the other hand, failure, not success, is the result, then, even during the lifetime and ascendancy of the leader, experiments proceed on new and other patterns of authority. Innovations are made in the constant search for a magic solution that will provide material success. Strangely enough, in most cases, it is not the pattern of authority that guarantees success, but the quality of the leader and the men around him—whether they have the ability, dedication and the executive drive to achieve success for the new nation. . .

"When success comes, as it did to Malaya over the years 1957 to 1963, the pattern of authority is maintained. The constitution drafted for Malaya by five constitutional jurists from five British Commonwealth nations has had a few hundred amendments, mostly of a minor nature, and a few quite fundamental, all in order to make it suit the national, racial and constitutional peculiarities of Malaya, and now of Malaysia. But the broad structure has been retained, for success had come whilst this pattern of authority was in operation. But I feel that research and analysis will probably show that success or failure was quite unconnected with the constitutional pattern of authority, and more closely dependent upon the quality of the leadership—the first leader and the men immediately around him. If, together, they constitute a balanced team, in which ability and intellect are matched with imagination and executive capacity, success is more likely. When success is achieved, reliance on demagogy, and on fear and hate fetishes, diminishes. In its place is the halo of success, the magic touch of the leader ... But when the team in the leadership is unable to produce results, then the leadership is either changed, and with it the pattern of authority, or it sustains itself in power and holds its following by demagogy, and the stimulus of real or imaginary threats to the new nation. The problem of authority and leadership is as old as the history of man. But what is new and fascinating in the eighteen years since the Second World War is the great number of experiments being made in Asia and Africa with patterns of authority copied from a wholly European historical experience.

"All these nations share a first common problem—that of creating unity in a new nation which has come into being for the first time in history. A second common problem is how to raise standards of living quickly enough to meet the expectations which political freedom has stimulated in the people, who vaguely believe that freedom should entitle them to the standards of living of their former European rulers.

"This must be achieved in spite of the backwardness of the colonial economies, geared by and large to be feeders of raw material for the industries of the metropolitan power. Further, the new nations lack trained administrators, technicians and professional men. They need to re-establish the obedience and respect for authority and discipline which the very same leaders, in their struggle for independence, had to destroy only a few years before. There must be some universal truths which could be of immense value in helping the leadership of these new nations to avoid the mistakes committed by others, and which could provide answers already proven in similar situations elsewhere... All these new nations are in a state of flux, patterns of authority and leadership are fluid, changeable and changing. It would be a valuable contribution to the problems of authority and leadership if systematic research could provide an insight into the mechanics of power which can make or break the most idealistic and well-intentioned leadership in the new nations of Asia and Africa."

XI

Singapore's new Assembly met as a State body within Malaysia for the first time on 9 December, 1963. "It is," recalled the Prime Minister, "nearly two and a half years since the communists broke away from the united front with the nationalist Left in the People's Action Party to form their own front organization, the Barisan Sosialis, to prevent Malaysia." Ultimate power, he reminded Members, was now vested in the Parliament of Malaysia, and it was still true that Singapore could not become communist until the communists first captured power in Malaya. Lee said: "The division between this side of the House and the Opposition is deep and abiding. They represent the minority, but a militant and tightly knit minority, determined to bring the democratic state down and establish a communist regime. We, on this side of the House, are privileged to have been chosen to represent the majority, the rest of the people who want Malaysia to live in peace and to progress unmolested. We are a party dedicated to democratic socialism. But it is our duty to recognize that the only long-term basis on which national unity can be forged and stability ensured is for us to bind all those sectors of society who reject the soulless creed which offers communist dictatorship as the only answer to our undoubtedly many social evils. We are proud that, in the process, we have been able to convince large sectors of the community, from working-class labourers to wealthy merchants and the professional and middle classes, that the long-term answer to the communist challenge lies in an honest and effective government whose social and economic policies can bring about appreciable and visible equalization of opportunity.

"We would be breaking faith with the mass of the people who voted for us this time if we did not recognize that we represent, as the governing party, a broad cross-section of the community. We must recognize further that their aspiration is to create a more equal society by the more difficult process of levelling up rather than levelling down. In this city of pushful people, energetic and hard-working, largely of immigrant stock, the desire that there should be more opportunities for everyone to work harder and do better and increase the size of the national cake is as great, if not greater, than the desire to share the cake more equally.

"We would be doing a disservice to the country if we misled people into believing that just because this last time the communists were defeated they will thereby remain an impotent force. There are already signs of their picking up the bits and pieces left of their organization, wrecked by the disastrous policies they pursued. We cannot expect them always to be so accommodating in the next round, to continue to make false and erroneous assumptions. . .

"We are," claimed Lee Kuan Yew, "realistic enough to anticipate that the Barisan Sosialis and their communist-front organizations will become more skilful in their tactics to obstruct and prevent Singapore's success. In thwarting industrialization they can create unrest in labour unions and a sense of insecurity to prospective investors. . . The stage has been set for the next five years. We can and will succeed. The constitution and responsibilities of this Assembly have been changed—if anything, for the better. Whilst the State Assembly may not have so many matters to look after, we have enough of the constructive side left to make our meetings useful occasions, when progress can be reviewed and faults remedied. It would be useful if at these meetings criticism of shortcomings, either in policy or implementation, were aired not only by the Opposition but also by our own back-benchers. It can serve a useful purpose in focusing public attention on the way in which things are done, on how they can be done better, or on why an apparent ineptitude has in fact a rational and valid explanation. . . We must never be afraid of departing from accepted and habitual practice, either in this Chamber or without. And it is for this reason that I invite our own back-benchers to criticize the Government in this Chamber for what they consider to be its shortcomings, even though this may not be the practice elsewhere. For all of us inside this Chamber must realize that the mental attitudes and responses of the mass of the people outside are very different from those of the people who elect representatives to the House of Commons in Britain.

187

"We have gathered valuable experience from our difficulties over the past ten years. To ensure that the democratic system prevails we must not only ensure that there is an honest and effective government that produces results. What is more important is that we must also ensure that it is able to keep in touch with the mass of the people, to produce those results in the form and manner the people consider desirable, and to prevent the communists from distorting the success of the Government or subverting public loyalties by pressure and manipulation.

"In the next five years we will see the growth in my office of a special department which will help to create and build up a whole series of grass-root organizations in every village, in every street, and in every community. All those active in the interests of their fellow-citizens can find rewarding work and recognition in Citizens' Consultative Committees. For in the end not only must we succeed in making Singapore a better place, but we must also succeed in building up an organizational structure within the country that can help strengthen the links between the people and their government, so that the best that can be done will be done in their interests. Only in this way can we ensure stability and progress towards a more enlightened and healthy society."

In spite of his analysis of Barisan Sosialis intentions, Lee Kuan Yew still hoped that the Opposition would contribute something to the Assembly's proceedings. He was disappointed: his analysis had been accurate. The Barisan continued to be destructive. "The tone and tenor of debate set in the past week," he said on 18 December, winding up the discussion, "is a depressing reminder of the futility of these meetings, when the purpose of the Opposition is not to debate, to criticize and to improve. Their purpose is to read out, under cover of privilege in this Chamber, long and dreary extracts repeating the communist united-front line, anti-Malaysia, and anti-any plan or policy or action that in any way makes things difficult for the communists to strengthen their ground... They talk of the death of freedom and democratic rights, of merger and Malaysia being a sell-out, all as if the referendum never took place in September last year, and the general elections had been a triumph for Barisan Sosialis. For it appears that, every evidence to the contrary notwithstanding, only they can speak for the masses... We would do well to always remember that if they, the Barisan Sosialis, were in charge of the country it is very unlikely that we the Opposition would be allowed to say the things of them that we have allowed them to say of us. It is also unlikely that, either in the unions or in the civic organizations we would be allowed even one hundredth part of the opportunity that we are now giving them to organize and preach their gospel against the nation. Our failing is not that we have stifled democratic rights and liberties, but that we have been too tolerant with a group of men who interpret our tolerance as a weakness to be exploited and abused.

"We can all remember what happened throughout Malaya and Singapore in the few weeks immediately after the defeat of Japan and before the re-occupation by the British Forces. The communists were in charge in some towns and districts. Members on the other side have been talking about the right to free and open trial. The unreasoning, unceasing screech of hatred which they have preached leads us straight back to the summary methods of justice the people's courts then enforced. They had even less regard for the niceties of the rules of evidence and of trial by jury. On this side, we must never forget that, if ever we lose this fight, we shall be stupid indeed if we expect them to concede to us what we have conceded to them, even after their defeat.

"But it is worthwhile pointing out to them that, whilst the democratic system concedes the right of opposition to the new nation before it is formed, once it has been formed, to preach disloyalty and incite disaffection against Malaysia is treason, and punishable as such... To talk of Malaysia being imposed upon the people after the people have endorsed it, both at the referendum and, again, in the general elections, is not just to perpetrate a lie, but to actively help hostile forces around us to intervene against Malaysia...

"The question we have asked the Opposition is: whose side are they on? They have not answered. They have remained silent. They have never admitted the existence of Malaysia. So how can they admit they are Malaysians? And how can they defend Malaysia if they are not Malaysians? But let me give them this piece of advice: whatever their intentions, if by any overt act they help the enemy against Malaysia, then they must bear the full consequences of being treated as traitors to the nation.

"The fact that Indonesia is now prepared to use agents and fifth columnists to disrupt our economy puts a sombre hue on our responsibilities. We are now in the midst, literally, of a battle of life and death, a battle for survival, our survival as a separate entity to live our own lives in our own way in Southeast Asia, unmolested by bigger and more powerful neighbours. We have always feared that the temptation of the big to be bigger and to absorb the smaller would be too great to resist. But now we know this for a fact, in that confrontation includes fifth columnists and trained saboteurs, trained to wreck the economy of Singapore and, even more important, to weaken the will of the people of Singapore and of other parts of Malaysia to resist absorption.

"Our chances of survival are ten times better in Malaysia than if we were by ourselves. Malaysia has been followed by a trade boycott and a loss of 8·7 per cent of our national income. But this was not the logical consequence of Malaysia. It was the consequence of a conscious act of the Government of the Republic of Indonesia to inflict damage on all the parties in Malaysia, either by economic sanctions, even if it cost Indonesia four times our losses, or by military pressure along our borders and sabotage from within. If ever it appears to have a chance of success, then direct military action cannot be altogether ruled out. We must resolve to defend ourselves to the last man; death is preferable to conquest and absorption. When our neighbours, both friendly and unfriendly, understand this, then peace in Southeast Asia is more likely to be preserved. Whatever the economic pressures, whatever the harassment by sabotage, whatever the psychological tensions, let no one mistake our right to be masters in our own house. We cannot afford to be befuddled or bemused into weakening in our resolve for Malaysia. What is at stake is not just 8·7 per cent of our national income, but literally our survival as a separate people in this part of the world. When our survival is at stake, those who help the enemy to weaken the nation will find to their cost that the nation is prepared to defend itself against the enemy without, and also against the enemy within. If ever the communists succeed in weakening our resolve for Malaysia, then verily first Sarawak, then Sabah, then Singapore, and finally Malaya itself will be slowly absorbed into the Indonesian orbit. If this happens, perhaps then even the Barisan may look back to this era as a golden age compared to what is in store for all of us in that situation."

Activities of Indonesian saboteurs and local fifth columnists in Singapore, with plans to disrupt the economic life of the State and generally to cause alarm and despondency through terrorism, were reported by the Prime Minister to the Assembly on 18 December. He also revealed that, in their operations in Singapore, the local representatives of an Indonesian intelligence organization at Tanjong Sekupang (an island in the Rhio Archipelago, a few miles south of Singapore) used three dummy commercial organizations as cover for their intelligence operations and for the finances required. They were:
(1) Gerakan Ekonomy Melayu Indonesia (GEMI)
(2) Duma Corporation, in Bussorah Street, and
(3) Malaysia Indonesia Corporation (MIC), in Beach Road.

"The training of these fifth columnists at Tanjong Sekupang consisted of military close combat, sabotage, and political propaganda against Malaysia. Their instructions on return to Singapore were to sabotage petrol dumps, railway lines and, in particular, the Tebrau waterworks and the water pipeline to Singapore, and the Pasir Panjang Power Station. In the event of their being unable to reach these targets, they were instructed to explode their charges anywhere in Singapore, with the object of causing damage and public alarm." The Prime Minister called upon the public to report to the police any suspicious movement of persons or vehicles.

XII

Lee Kuan Yew's first speech in the Malaysian Parliament, as one of the fifteen Singaporean MPs, was on 21 December. He said he spoke not as a Singaporean, but as a Malaysian, in the Budget debate. He would have preferred, he said, to have talked about a more neutral issue "on which pleasantries would have been more appropriate". He congratulated the Finance Minister on a business-like Budget, even though he had to criticize certain tax proposals. He also congratulated the Minister "on having considerably scaled down what his military advisers wanted him to do, and what we in Singapore were originally expected to pay for... Far from joining the cry of the Opposition on wasteful defence expenditure, I congratulate him for having kept the ambitions of the armed forces within very realistic limits. I say that it is not altogether without a certain degree of self-preservation on the part of those who determine these things, because I remember once recounting to one of his ministerial colleagues that there is no army or air force or navy in Asia that has been expanded and subsequently demobilized. Armies have been expanded in Europe, wars have been fought, armies have been brought back to size. But in Asia, particularly in Southeast Asia, armies when expanded have a tendency ultimately to take over, whether it is in Burma, Pakistan, or in some other of our neighbouring States, and we should be extremely chary about an unnecessary expansion of the army. We can count ourselves lucky that the Finance Minister, whatever his other idiosyncrasies, is not a man with great military ambitions for Malaysia."

Lee predicted that "the next few years will test the capacity for survival of Malaysia—whether we have enough national and social cohesiveness to be a nation. If we haven't, then, as I said before on some other occasion, history will write us off in one paragraph as a polyglot community, which, by an accident of British imperialism, came together with Malaya and Sarawak and North Borneo, and looked for a momentary fraction of history like succeeding... I say to Members opposite, our problem now is not that the British will dominate us, but whether they have the will and the capacity over the next decade to manifest the same determination to see that Malaysia, which they have helped to bring into being, survives. Is there all that amount of vested interest—in tin and rubber, and in other commodities in Borneo—for the British Government to find it worth its while to face a recurrent annual drain on its budget? If not, where is the cancelling force which we ourselves are unable to produce? If ever it happens in the immediate future, that these 'neo-colonialist, imperialist forces' suddenly withdraw from this region, I suggest that the only people in this Chamber who will take any joy from that are those who, from the very outset, have contemplated the possibility of power based on the armed strength of the friendly communist parties in this region—nobody else..."

Lee Kuan Yew went on to say unreservedly that, "having played our part in bringing Malaysia about, we have every intention of playing our part in making Malaysia succeed—and I would like to define success in this context, not as a struggle for power between political parties, but as the social and economic objectives which our nation must pursue if we are to be successful in the modern sense of that word—an emerged, developed nation... Now, Sir, what I do propound is this: that whether or not our tolerant society—multiracial, multilingual, multicultural, multireligious — survives depends so terribly upon a tolerant and reasonable leadership of the Malay rural population. Whether it be the present Prime Minister, or whoever succeeds him, I say without reservation that we would be fools, in our own self-interest, not to sustain in leadership a group of men basically tolerant in racial, religious, linguistic and cultural matters. The problem, as I see it, is how do we ensure that the leadership that emerges from this Malay rural base is always reasonable and tolerant? If they do not produce results for the mass base that has thrown them up, then I say verily that mass base will be tempted to throw up new leaders, not necessarily so reasonable or so tolerant, and my fear is that the fiscal policy of the Finance Minister is inadequate to produce rapidly enough a visible and appreciable change in the conditions of the have-nots in both the rural and urban areas. That is the core of the matter. If this leadership were replaced, then I say it can only be replaced for the worse. We have seen glimpses of what it could be: people, who, in the name of God and the scriptures, literally lose perspective and sanity...

"The totality of my argument really amounts to this, Mr Speaker: assuming that we survive this first impact of confrontation—and I think there is a fair chance that we will do that—are we able in five, at the outside in ten, years to reshape the structure of our society to equalize opportunities within the country? Does one really solve rural poverty and distress by the creation of a counter group of 'haves' in the Malay world? You have got it in the Chinese world—a group of 'haves'; you have not got it in the Malay world. Is the problem resolved by creating—assuming that it can be created—an energetic and pushful group of entrepreneurs who move from the acquisition of bus licences to the running of aeroplane companies, and so on? Is that the solution? My humble submission is that it is not—and never will be—and the dilemma with which we are all confronted is that for various reasons an education policy has already been implemented in the Federation, in Singapore, and is soon to be implemented in Sarawak and Sabah, by which literacy becomes universal. In other words, the revolution of rising expectations has already been set in motion, and it will no longer be possible, when this generation grows up, to prevent

192

a social revolution—a remodelling of opportunities and the structure of power in our society. And my indictment of this Budget, as of all the other budgets, is that it has not set into train what one would call, euphemistically, social change for the better, social change to create a more equitable society, where rewards are based on performance and efforts, and not on property and rent . . ."

CHAPTER EIGHTEEN

The Year of Power 1964

1964 was Singapore's first full year of life in Malaysia. On behalf of the Malaysian Government, Lee Kuan Yew led a delegation from Singapore, Sabah and Sarawak, the three former colonial territories which had won their freedom with Malaysia, to seventeen African states. He convinced them that Malaysia was not a neo-colonialist plot.

But dark clouds began to appear on the horizon. During March, the PAP as a non-communal Malaysian party took a token part in the election for the Malaysian Parliament. The PAP intended to co-operate with the United Malays National Organization in fighting the anti-Malaysia parties. The PAP put up eleven candidates and all except one were defeated. PAP's motives for participation in the elections were misunderstood and a great deal of communal tension in consequence was generated by Malay extremists. In Singapore, UMNO spokesmen, seeking to regain Malay support—lost to the PAP in the 1963 general election—accused the PAP Government of deliberately plotting against the Malays. Syed Jaafar Albar, Secretary-General of UMNO, declared in Singapore that there was enough evidence to send Lee Kuan Yew to prison for oppressing and suppressing the Malays. Racial rioting broke out in Singapore, on 21 July, and went on for the rest of the month. In all, twenty-two persons were killed and 461 injured.

Indonesia's confrontation continued to pose an economic threat, but the Jurong Industrial Project made major advances. A further twenty-six factories were under construction. The Housing and Development Board was now building low-cost flats at the rate of one flat every forty-five minutes. More people now earned as much as 150 dollars a week.

The unity of the non-communist democratic socialist trade unions was consolidated and strengthened by the setting up of the National Trade Unions Congress.

I

LEE Kuan Yew, in his 1964 New Year Message, thought that 1963 would probably "go down in history as the most eventful year of our lives". Had Malaysia been formed in 1957 and not 1963, at the time when Malaya was proclaimed independent, Malaysia's emergence as a nation would have been welcomed by the whole world "including our immediate neighbours". But seven years later, the mood had changed, and Malaysia's neighbours grudged her the territorial integration and economic success they desired for themselves.

"So from a 'confrontation' of propaganda and villification commenced at the beginning of the old year, they ended up with an economic boycott and military pressure by the beginning of the new year.

"1963 saw the two world powers reconciled to living with each other's strength, witnessing the first real thaw of the cold war with the test ban treaty... But, paradoxically, 1963 saw us in Malaysia having our first experience of prolonged tension and conflict with our neighbours. It is difficult to believe that only three years ago all appeared to be well with Malaya and the other territories now in Malaysia... But, however tantalizing the prospect of moving the hands of the clock back, it can never be the same again. Whatever the immediate causes of conflict, and however the blame is to be apportioned as to who precipitated it so quickly and acutely, the fact remains that we have now got to get used to living with a big and difficult neighbour...

"Life for all of us would have been so much more pleasant if we could have Malaysia, and also Indonesia's trade, with generally amicable relations. But this was not on the cards. Perhaps we can take philosophic comfort at having avoided an even more unpleasant alternative to 'confrontation'. For the alternative was never the *status quo*, the old easy relationship of trade and cultural exchanges. Had the Indonesians not persisted in 'confrontation', we would be now engaged in the more trying process of erosion and absorption through Maphilindo. For Maphilindo cleverly developed and skilfully operated would have gradually dissolved our distinctive identity in Malaysia. It would have been so much more difficult to counter—no visible enemy, no hostility, all cultural exchanges and co-operation, in which eventually the smaller nation would have been absorbed. Imagine the proportions these embryonic organizations for cultural and ideological penetration would have grown into in five years' time with the stimulus of Maphilindo...

"Historians will wonder why, after the Manila accord, Indonesia swung back from Maphilindo 'confrontation', from the line of penetration and absorption to open hostility and conflict. Having settled for Maphilindo at Manila in July, it appeared inexplicable that they should go back on it, reject the United Nations Secretary-General's assessment, and pursue a hard line which was not likely to produce comparable dividends.

"But that assumes that there were no internal conflicts within Indonesia. Dr Subandrio was Maphilindo's foremost protagonist. The PKI (Partai Kommunist Indonesia) was its fiercest enemy. Maphilindo meant, among other things, a preoccupation with Indonesia's internal economic and political problems. This, together with the Indonesian Army's civic action programme, may well have led to a major setback for the PKI...

"What of 1964 and the future? First, we must stand up to the sharp and acute test to national unity and security. If we do not, if we allow wishful thinking to undermine our resolve and unprincipled opposition to divide the nation, then that is the beginning of the end. On the other hand, if we assert our will to be a nation and establish our capacity to progress and prosper in spite of everything, then our relationship with our neighbours will settle down at a new equilibrium.

"We are not the only nation in Asia with strong and ambitious neighbours: India and Pakistan dispute over Kashmir, India and China over the barren Himalayas, Cambodia and Thailand over the ruins of a temple, Cambodia and South Vietnam over a. few islands—yet they are all learning to live with each other...

"Perhaps it is not too late for us to learn the devious ways of men and nations. But first we must ensure our right to live in peace in Southeast Asia. We must be firm on this. But at the same time we can afford to be friendly and fair. We must never by word or deed allow ourselves to be presented by the propaganda of our neighbours as an obstinate and obdurate people...

"Finally, let us resolve to make 1964 a year of consolidation. If we are realistic and practical, we can hold our ground internationally, and thoroughly expose the hollowness of the neo-colonialist line. If we, the states within Malaysia, are united and prepared to help each other, we adjust our economy and make good any losses. If at the end of 1964 we are stronger internationally and internally than at the beginning, the prospects for a permanent settlement will be bright. But in any event no one can prevent us from making good on our own. We have the capacity and the wherewithal to succeed. Given the effort we will."

II

Lee Kuan Yew left for Africa on 20 January. He was to be away five weeks, visiting a dozen countries in North, West and East Africa.

Over the radio and television the night before he left Lee spoke of the importance of international understanding and sympathy. "The impression other nations have of Malaysia depends on her policy, her stand on so many issues in the world—the freedom movements of Asia and Africa, apartheid, military treaties, and power blocs and so on. We have got to be constantly aware of the danger of isolation. For, if our only friends in Afro-Asia are South Korea and South Vietnam, then even Australia and New Zealand may find it difficult to be actively committed to our side, and this in spite of the fact that they know their future is intimately connected with preventing any further erosion of national boundaries in Southeast Asia.

"Half the problem of international survival is to win friends who understand and sympathize with us. There are many new nations in Africa who, like us, have just become independent, emerging from colonial rule. Like us, they are against the perpetuation of colonial domination in any disguised form. Like us, they believe that a nation, big or small, should be allowed to develop, to raise its standards of living, to live in peace and harmony with its neighbours.

"Many of the countries in Africa have no intimate knowledge of Southeast Asia. Like us, they cannot afford to keep embassies all over the world. But somehow we must get them to know us, to understand us, to see us for what we are. Then we can debunk all this talk that we are a neo-colonialist plot, designed to encircle Indonesia, a nation ten times our size. And then there will be less sympathy for this slogan of anti-neo-colonialism behind which foreign intervention becomes more and more blatant. This is a continuous and a continuing task. The effort must be made all the time. National independence, which has come to so many of the countries of Asia and Africa, is not the end of our problems. It is the beginning of new ones... History marches on. We have got to make sure that we are marching abreast of history."

Lee Kuan Yew returned from his highly successful African tour on 26 February. While he was away, the PAP Central Executive decided "as a non-communal Malaysian party" to play a "token" part in the elections for the Malaysian Parliament in order to "co-operate with UMNO in fighting anti-Malaysia parties". Dr Toh Chin Chye, the party chairman, announced this on 1 March. He said it had been decided that the party which had played an important role in the establishment of Malaysia should now show itself to be a national party.

On 20 March, the PAP, in its election manifesto, declared that it aims were to assist in the "building of a united democratic and socialist Malaysia... and to ensure that the Socialist Front does not benefit from substantial protest votes against the MCA".

It is a fact that on 19 November, 1963, Lee Kuan Yew told a PAP gathering that the PAP would not take part in the Federal general elections. He then visualized the role of the PAP in the Malaysian

Parliament to be that of "a friend, loyal opposition and critic". He added: "We are a loyal opposition whose aim is to improve the working of the democratic system." Within four months, the PAP had decided to test their strength as a national party in Malaysia for a variety of reasons which Lee Kuan Yew advanced in his election speeches.

Lee Kuan Yew analysed the forces involved in the Malaysian general election in a speech on 15 March. He was critical of "the touch of emotionalism" generated by the Government party leaders, "made worse by pro-communist opposition leaders", which, he argued, prevented the people from realizing what the threat from Indonesia really meant. "What is at stake is literally the survival of Malaysia as a separate entity with a high level of prosperity in a fairly liberal and tolerant society." The alternative was the liquidation of Malaysia and its absorption in a not-so-prosperous and not-so-tolerant Indonesia. When the elections were over and people realized the nature of the threat, said Lee, "then our chances of meeting this threat successfully will be much better. There is no quick solution to this threat, like a full-scale war in which the outcome can be swift and decisive. If we had no mutual defence pact with a power that could more than match Indonesia's military might then war would have already taken place. But, because the Indonesians realize their inability to wage such a war successfully, we must expect this relentless process of attrition, of guerilla penetration, of hitting and running, and sabotaging.

"But the situation could easily become serious if, because we are bogged down in heavy military expenditure, rural developments do not keep pace with urban developments. Then the challenge to the present Malay leadership of the Tunku and Tun Razak in UMNO could become intense... If nothing else, our enlightened self-interest demands that we should do nothing to hinder or embarrass the present Malay leadership of the Tunku and Tun Razak. Indeed, if we are wise we should help them demonstrate to the Malay masses that Malays are infinitely better off in Malaysia, where progress and prosperity is high because of the co-operation of all the races in the economic and social life of the country.

"But, whilst the present Malay leadership of the Tunku and Tun Razak in UMNO is vital to the survival and success of Malaysia, the Chinese leadership in the Alliance as represented by the MCA is replaceable. Over the past ten years the image the MCA has created has been such that even on the eve of general elections their president was talking of the need to build a new image and to scrap the old. In the urban areas in Malaya the antipathy that has grown towards the greed and ineptitude of these men has reached such proportions that, despite the obvious communist links of the Socialist Front, the Socialist Front may still make election gains, if for no other reason than that there would be no other way to register a protest vote...

"To sum up, for Malaysia to survive and endure, there must be

199

cohesion and unity of purpose amongst its various communities. The most important community that decides whether Malaysia survives as a separate entity or is absorbed into Indonesia is the Malay community. The only coherent and effective leadership that can build Malaysia into an enduring unit in a liberal and tolerant society with our various communities participating in full in the political, economic and social life of the country is that in UMNO led by the Tunku and Tun Razak. If their policy of a separate Malaysia appears, or is made to appear, to lead to the Malays' losing their dominant political position, then the way is open for a pro-Indonesian leadership, either inside or outside UMNO, to challenge and replace them. Further, this new leadership could point out that to dilute the four million Chinese among 100 million Indonesians would provide for permanent Malay dominance, even if everyone became poorer and worse off in the process.

"Hence, it is important that the urban population realizes the problems and the possible challenges that face the Malay leadership in Malaya. For Malaysia to succeed, we must help the Tunku's leadership to succeed. It can only succeed if it can be constantly demonstrated to the people that this policy of multiracial co-operation not only ensures a better life for all, including the Malays, in Malaysia, but in no way affects the rightful place of the Malays and the indigenous people, with all their constitutional safeguards to see that they are not displaced from their honourable position in Malaysian society.

"In other words, the urban population must understand that what is at stake is, first, Malaysia's survival as a separate entity. To ensure this the over-riding interest of Malaysia demands that the Tunku and Tun Razak be supported, and that, however strong their disaffection to the present MCA leadership, they should not cast their votes for the Socialist Front, even in protest. If the Socialist Front were to win more seats it would encourage that school of thinking in America which wants to save Indonesia from communism even if it means sacrificing Malaysia. Their argument will be that in any case such a sacrifice cannot be considered too high a price since Malaysia has basically been shown to be weak... In short, it is in Malaysia's national interest to see that every UMNO candidate is supported in all the rural areas of Malaysia, and in all the urban areas the non-communist, pro-Malaysia opposition parties should be supported, so that the protest vote against the present MCA leadership does not go to the pro-communist Socialist Front."

Two days later, Lee Kuan Yew said: "We must help Kuala Lumpur to succeed, in order that we may succeed even more." He added: "It is this knowledge that we are closely linked to the political and economic health of Malaya that decided us to field a token number of candidates in the present elections. If it can be shown that the people in the bigger towns in Malaya support Malaysia by supporting pro-Malaysia parties—better still, if it can be shown that they support an economic and social policy similar to that of Singapore—it will give us added strength in convincing the UMNO leadership that this policy should be adopted for Malaya, particularly when these policies will benefit the rural Malays even more. For the present taxation policy does not set out to close the gap by taxing the rich more than the poor to pay for education, health and social services provided for all.

"It is not the desire to shirk the responsibilities of office in the Central Government which has made the PAP field only a token number of candidates. It is true if we wish to demonstrate the desire of the urban population of Malaysia to support the economic and social policies designed to provide more equal opportunities, we should field as many candidates as there are seats in the urban areas. We will not do this for very compelling reasons. We believe that any massive intervention in the elections can easily be misinterpreted and will be presented to the rural Malays as an attempt to challenge UMNO. This will be bad for Malaysia, for it will encourage extremist Malay elements to work up feeling that, with merger and Malaysia, the position of the Malays has been endangered and the Chinese in the towns are making a bid for power..."

Lee Kuan Yew's hope that responsible Malay leadership would welcome (or at least not violently attack) the PAP's token intervention was not sustained. Extremist Malay elements wildly accused the PAP of starting a campaign of infiltration into Malaya, and, for most voters, the subtlety of the PAP's arguments failed to register. They could not understand how, in one breath, Lee Kuan Yew could urge them to support the Tunku's leadership, while also asking them to vote for the PAP against the Tunku's own Alliance Party candidates.

"Stop antagonizing the Malays, and stop provoking them," demanded the Secretary-General of UMNO, Jaafar Albar (4 April), "otherwise the Malays will throw democracy overboard and start using fists to teach the PAP democracy." Albar said all the PAP Ministers were corrupt. This charge was made in reply to a PAP challenge. The PAP Ministers were willing to have their bank accounts examined if Jaafar Albar and other Ministers agreed to the same scrutiny. Jaafar Albar ignored the challenge. He accused Lee Kuan Yew of Chinese chauvinism.

At a mass rally in Kuala Lumpur (on 22 March), the Prime Minister predicted that a victory for the nine PAP Parliamentary candidates (five in Kuala Lumpur and one each in Penang, Seremban, Malacca and Johore) would "trigger off the social revolution in Malaya". Had the PAP captured the capital of Malaysia, by winning all five Kuala Lumpur seats, the Alliance Government might have been considerably embarrassed. In the event, the PAP won only one seat in Kuala Lumpur and none anywhere else. In the other eight

201

constituencies the PAP candidates were all soundly beaten.

Lee explained at this rally, which attracted probably the largest crowd ever to attend a Malaysian political meeting (for the first time a Kuala Lumpur rally was addressed by a speaker in two Chinese dialects, in Malay and also in English), that to have fielded PAP candidates in all the urban constituencies would have upset the Malay leadership and risked misunderstanding with the rural Malay mass base.

"For our purpose, to prove that the urban population in Malaya wants social change, wants a more just and equal society, the nine candidates are good enough. If Kuala Lumpur supports the policy of the PAP and so does Penang, Seremban, Malacca and Johore, UMNO leaders must adjust their social and economic policy to take into account the wishes of the people in the towns. . . "

Lee Kuan Yew, speaking to the Chambers of Trade in Singapore (on 17 April), said "It is not unlikely that after these elections people will see that the choice for the towns in Malaya is between an anti-Malaysia, pro-communist party like the Socialist Front, or a pro-Malaysia, non-communist party like the PAP."

Lee miscalculated. The Chinese in the towns in Malaya had never thought much of the Malayan Chinese Association, but almost to a man they looked upon the Tunku as a man they could trust. He did not oppress the Chinese and he contained the Malay religious fanatics in the Pan-Malayan Islamic Party. They voted for the Tunku, not the MCA.

In his eve of poll message (on 24 April), Lee said: "Parliamentary democracy of the one-man-one-vote will work only if people choose rationally between the alternatives they are offered in an election. The democratic system breaks down if people make a choice which is irrational. . . The rational choice for Malaya at present is a party which can hold the rural Malay mass to build a Malaysia distinct and separate from Indonesia, and at the same time can work with a non-communal party representing the urban areas. Together they can implement economic and social policies which will make opportunities more equal and give fair shares to all according to their contributions to society. . . The Tunku knows that good leadership is the reconciling of ideal solutions with the realities of life. If the urban areas constituting more than half the people of Malaya give their verdict for the winds of change, no leader can afford to ignore it. . . The rational choice in these elections is to vote for UMNO in the rural areas, and to vote for the PAP in the urban areas. Where there is no PAP, vote for other pro-Malaysia opposition parties. Where the choice is between only the MCA and the Socialist Front, then out with the Socialist Front. For, whilst the MCA has been a bane on our society, the Socialist Front will be a blight on Malaysia. With your votes counted on Saturday night, a new chapter opens in the history of our nation. If your choice is practical and realistic, we can make this new chapter one of achievement and progress."

To Lee Kuan Yew's amazement all but one of the PAP's nine candidates were heavily defeated. He issued a statement in which he said with frankness that he was disappointed that the nine PAP candidates did not fare better. "But I take great satisfaction in the fact that, far from being a disruptive force, we have helped to bring home the dangers of Indonesian confrontation and subversion and have contributed to the rout of the Socialist Front. The results could not have been better for international effect. No government in the world can now doubt that Malaysia exists by the free will of its people— Sabah, Sarawak, Singapore and Malaya. All the strident voices raised against it over the past few years were those of reckless adventurers and traitors.

"My one concern at the election results is that it means the old order will carry on—the same old economic and social policies in the same old way ... We had hoped that our token participation would have given the people of the bigger towns an opportunity to endorse our economic and social policies towards a more egalitarian society. But I am afraid the token participation was too subtle a method of doing it. Since we said 'back the Tunku' and since the Tunku said 'back all my colleagues in the MCA and MIC', we had to accept the fact that this situation might arise.

"Every analysis I have made of the basic political situation in Malaysia remains undemolished. The people have decided to back the Tunku in the fight for Malaysia's survival. All the other problems of economic and social change will come back to the fore later when Indonesian confrontation has been resolved or contained. Between now and then we shall build up our organization and recruit able and honest men in Malaya to help carry on the battle for a more equal and more just society."

Lee also despatched a telegram to Tunku Abdul Rahman, in which he offered his "warmest congratulations on your stupendous victory. No one in the world can now doubt that you lead the people of Malaysia in their desire to build an independent and democratic nation separate and distinct from Indonesia. The severe reverses of the Socialist Front, PMIP, and other anti-Malaysian elements have strengthened Malaysia's position *vis-a-vis* Indonesia. Whatever our party differences, you can count upon us to support you on all national issues. Malaysia will triumph over confrontation under your leadership."

III

When the new Malaysian Parliament met for the first time on 21

May, Lee Kuan Yew contributed what many thought was a statesmanlike speech. Lee said that whatever else the votes on the morning of 26 April did or did not prove, they nailed forever the lie that Malaysia did not enjoy the support of the people. One by one, Sabah, then Sarawak, then Singapore, and now the eleven states of Malaya had endorsed the new nation... "I hope I will be forgiven if I sound a note of caution in the midst of the renewed self-confidence and euphoria on the Government side. The new lease of life they have been given for another five years could well be frittered and squandered away if they interpret the result as a blanket approval for carrying on in the same old way. Malpractices, inefficiency and ineptitude, unless eradicated, will lead to a very different situation in the next five years... We share these Opposition benches with some parties whose differences from ourselves are more abiding than the differences between us and the Government... We are a loyal Opposition, loyal to Malaysia and the democratic system of government that obtains in Malaysia. Our criticism will therefore be directed to pointing out the dangers of policies which could lead to failure, and to checking the lapses of political leaders and administrators which could lead to a breakdown of the whole system. But a loyal Opposition does not mean a subservient Opposition. Criticisms, however unwelcome, will have to be made, seriously and in good faith. We hope they will be taken equally seriously and in good faith.

"On all external matters, on foreign policy, on confrontation, on questions of national integrity and survival, there are no differences in either objectives or attitudes between us and the Government. We may differ on what is the most effective way of securing our integrity and survival, but we are at one in achieving the same goal. Even on domestic issues there is a large measure of common agreement on the tolerant approach to cultural, racial and linguistic problems. Our differences will arise over questions of economic and social policies, over issues of taxation to provide the amenities of a modern civilized community—education, health, housing, welfare benefits, and so on, and how they are to be paid for. How acute this conflict will be depends on how far the Finance Minister and his colleagues are able to bring themselves to view the world, not from the point of view of a rubber estate owner or a holder of stocks and shares, but also from that of the rubber tapper and the workers in companies who provide profits for the stockholders and shareholders. We consider it our duty to help to open windows for the winds of change to blow through. We are not pessimistic. We believe that criticism and example can set off a change... It is inevitable that the newly independent nations of Asia and Africa should move towards a more egalitarian society. For, having stimulated men's minds for more equal opportunities, and mobilized men's energies and loyalties to be rid of the inequities of the colonial system, there is no stopping the process after independence. This is the tide of history. It would be foolish to stop it. We deem it our duty to ease the way forward towards a more just and equal society."

Lee Kuan Yew went on to say: "One of the reasons why Western-style parliamentary democracy has failed to take root in the newly independent countries of Asia and Africa is that the Government in power does not contemplate with equanimity the passing of power to the Oppositions and also because the Opposition opposes merely to bring the Government down, regardless of the harm inflicted upon the country. We in the PAP have played the role of Opposition as well as of the governing party in Singapore. We bring to our duties as the Opposition in Parliament an understanding of the difficult and delicate problems which the Government party faces."

IV

Nehru died on 27 May. Lee Kuan Yew knew the Indian leader, and liked and respected him. "Nehru," said Lee in a tribute, "was one of the great men Asia has produced. For more than three decades he has been a legendary figure to the people in the colonial empires of Europe. For the past seventeen years, since India's independence, he has set the pace of international policies and relations for the rapidly growing band of newly independent countries of Afro-Asia. Perhaps the most grievous blow that ever struck him was when his foreign policy, based on positive neutrality and non-alignment, reeled under the pressures of conflict over the Himalayas. That conflict over the borders of India marked the end of an era. But he lived on for a further two years. That he was able at his age to take this blow with considerable restraint and dignity and to adjust his policies without renouncing his basic tenets of non-alignment was a tribute to the greatness of the man.

"It was sad to watch his gradual decline over the last few months. It was not fair to him, to India, or the world. But it gave time for the various contending forces in India to prepare themselves for the tremendous change that must come with the end of the era in which the image of one man held a vast nation in unity for so long. The weeks ahead will show what kind of new leadership the second biggest nation in the world will have, and where its leaders intend to take it. Its consequences to us in Southeast Asia will be momentous."

Lee had met Mr Nehru in Delhi, in London and elsewhere, on several occasions. They became friends. At a mass meeting in Singapore, on 30 May, Lee Kuan Yew said they had gathered to pay

205

homage to a great man whose life and work has helped to change the course of history, not only in India, but throughout the world.

"Nehru was the first of the Afro-Asians. He started on the anti-colonial struggle fifty years ago when joining an anti-colonial movement meant not the glory of quick independence and high office, but a grim prospect of interminable hardship and repression with no prospect of easy victory. It was different for those who joined anti-colonial movements after the Second World War. By then India had become free, to the achievement of which he contributed in no small measure. And he gave his unceasing support to all the anti-colonial revolutions elsewhere in Asia and Africa, against the British, Dutch and French. We in Malaysia also received his support and were inspired by India's own successful struggle for freedom.

"It was his vision of a better world that led Nehru to untiring support of other people's freedom. Small wonder that he won so much admiration and respect from so many of the nationalist leaders of Africa and Asia whose countries became independent after India. He pressed for Indonesia's independence. At Bandung in 1955 he introduced Mr Chou En-lai to the non-communist world and sponsored China's re-entry into the comity of Asian nations. He threw the weight of India on the side of Egypt when Britain and France resorted to force to undo the nationalization of the Suez Canal.

"At home in India he governed the second biggest nation in the world through democratic institutions. How easy it would have been for him, with the adulation Indians had for him, to have resorted to autocratic rule. But he was determined to establish the foundations of democratic government for India. A Brahmin from an elite family, he set out to build a modern India, secular in its approach, socialist in its structure. It was a task not to be finished in his lifetime. But when, in the years ahead, India emerges as a modern industrial nation free from the bonds of caste and privilege, it will all have been because he laid the foundations of modern India in the last seventeen years of his life, which were the first seventeen years of the life of new India. India has lost her most illustrious son, Malaysia has lost a staunch friend . . . "

V

In a speech in the Malaysian Parliament on 13 July, the Prime Minister supported the Internal Security (Amendment) Bill which sought to give the Government power to insist upon security clearance before students could join the university. Lee said there were in the House "those

206

who represent abiding communist interests", who, however genuinely, however sincerely, however much in good faith this Bill may have been introduced, and however scrupulously honestly it may be implemented, must be opposed to the principle that communists should be excluded from higher institutions of learning, centres for talent-scouting and recruitment.

Lee said he was concerned that honest men—and there are large numbers of honest men—should be reasonably satisfied in their minds first, that what was to be done was necessary, second, that there was no less obnoxious way of doing it, and, third, that all proper precautions against abuse had been taken.

The problem arose because no government was perfect, no minister was infallible, no Special Branch or intelligence organization was beyond reproach, and, therefore, the dangers of abuse or misuse loomed very large in the public mind.

As with the Internal Security Act itself, whether this Bill would succeed in its objective of minimizing the communist use of universities as centres for breeding and spawning and recruitment, or whether it succeeded in augmenting the already frustrated, both in numbers and in intensity of frustration, depended upon its implementation.

"First we must ask ourselves: is there no other way? If I believed that there was some other way, then I would have been reluctant to support what is undoubtedly an encroachment on established practice. Unfortunately my view is, knowing the complexities of this problem, that as of this given moment, there is no other way... Over the past forty years, the Malayan Communist Party has successfully established a caucus in the Chinese Middle Schools of this country, using first the teachers, who were originally recruited from China, and next the converts that they make in the schools. Finally, they have established a self-perpetuating core of trained communists in the schools. It is one of the hard facts of life...

"The ultimate answer to the communist challenge is to provide a better life without the communist method. Whether finally we achieve that answer depends on so many imponderables, one of them being how we survive confrontation, and the other being whether we have the will and capacity to integrate our peoples into one Malaysian nation. But for the time being, this is a sector of communist recruitment that must be contained.

"It may sound something quite outside this world, Mr Speaker, to those of us who have had experience, as some of our friends in the Barisan Sosialis in Singapore undoubtedly have, of the intensity with which revolution is being pursued by young men. I cannot but concede their dedication. I am convinced that they must be met with equal resolve, and I am convinced that they should not be let loose amongst the innocent..."

VI

Lee Kuan Yew took the opportunity, at the opening of a secondary technical integrated school, on 18 July, to warn of the growing dangers of Malay chauvinism. He said: "New problems have arisen. That is in the nature of life. Three years ago, you would not have imagined that Nanyang University could have been reorganized with so much peace and tranquillity and public understanding. There could have been real riots, real trouble; and it is not the force of authority that prevented a riot. It was the absence of anger, an abiding understanding that this was inimical to society, and must be put right. Chinese education and culture cannot be exploited for communist ends. Hence, the tranquillity with which the reorganization has gone through. We put down Chinese chauvinists using Chinese sentiments for communist ends; now we have rearing on the other side, Malay chauvinists playing on Malay sentiments for equally dangerous ends. I say we must be prepared to fight both extremes, or Malaysia will perish. The concept of Malaysia was conceived as a Malaysian nation not as a Malay nation . . ."

The following morning, in the Victoria Theatre, Lee Kuan Yew addressed a thousand Singapore Malays. They represented Malay non-political organizations. "First I would like to explain what made the Government arrange for today's meeting of 103 Malay cultural, sports, social and other non-political associations, together with about 300 *ketuas* and *penghulus* from the various kampongs throughout Singapore, and Malay members of all consultative committees. In the past nine months since Malaysia, there has been intensive propaganda by Indonesia directed at Malaysia, intended to cause friction and conflict between the Malays and the Chinese, and Singapore, as the largest city with the largest number of Chinese in Southeast Asia, has formed the target of Indonesian fire in their anti-Chinese propaganda. They have tried to present their 'confrontation', which is an aggression by Indonesia against Malaysia, as a policy by which they are trying to help the Malays take over the wealth and position of the Chinese, as represented in Singapore. On 5 June, Radio Indonesia, in a broadcast directed to Malaysia, said the Chinese Government of Lee Kuan Yew is deliberately forcing the Malays out of the city so that the Chinese can be in control.

"Then, in the past few weeks, for diverse reasons, UMNO has joined in this propaganda campaign. UMNO charged that the Government was deliberately expelling Malays from the city—for example, the Malays in Crawford—but not the Chinese in Chinatown. The Malays in Crawford have had to move out because of the urban redevelopment programme. The 200 Malay families there represent about ten per cent of the people who have to move.

"I thought that it was in the best interest of the country if we could divorce the genuine problems of education, social and economic development from complication by political rivalry. Hence I have left out all political parties in this gathering, so that nobody can take political advantage of any policy which will result from these discussions. I wish to make it clear that the policy will be that of the Singapore Government alone: the Singapore Government accepts full and sole responsibility for all policies it implements.

"There are two aspects to the Malay problem now. First, the propaganda aspect, which the Government is confident it can wage successfully not only against other political parties but also against Indonesia. We have done nothing which is dishonourable or wrong to the Malays, and we are prepared to have our record put to the closest scrutiny. That is a battle which is best left to the political parties to slug out.

"But the other and more important aspect is the genuine difficulties caused in our society by unequal development between the Malays and the other non-Malay communities in Singapore. The Government has a responsibility not only because of the special position of the Malays, recognized in the Singapore Constitution, but also because harm will be done to the unity and integrity of the nation if one section of the community is lagging behind. It is in the sincere effort to adjust and remove the imbalance in development that I have invited you all to give me your views.

"You need not worry about its being said that you have compromised Malay rights in any way by making your views known. The Government's decisions will have to be based on a balance of all interests, that of the special position of the Malays and also of the legitimate interests of the ninety per cent non-Malays in Singapore, which it is also the duty of the Government to advance."

Lee said there were three problems: education, employment and housing. In the opinion of the Government, education was the primary problem, because if this was solved then all the other Malay problems would be solved. "Once the Malays are as well educated and qualified as the others, then their capacity to hold better jobs and enjoy a better standard of living will automatically follow. Unfortunately, as a result of a different cultural development, and many years of British colonial education policy, the Malays have not as yet achieved the same level as the other communities. The Government is prepared to consider all practical suggestions as to how the level of education of Malay youth can be raised in order that they can come out into the world as well equipped and trained as those from other communities.

"The second problem, employment, is the direct result of the education policy in the past... Malays have difficulty in finding openings in fields for which skills and training are required. Somehow we must provide them with training which will qualify them for jobs which are being created as a result of our industrial development.

"The third problem is housing. I understand that Malay desire to continue their old traditions and live in a traditional Malay *rumah kampong*.. But the problem arises because there is an acute shortage of land in Singapore ... The Government would be prepared to build flats and offer them at special subsidized rentals to the lower income groups if it were sure that the Malay community would adjust itself to accept these flats as a mode of life in a modern city.

"These are the three main problems. There are probably many more which I would like you to tell me about. I would like you to suggest to me what can be done, so that we can consider how best to tackle these problems. This is not a job which can be resolved in one, two or even a hundred meetings. It is a long and continuous process which will go on for years, for the imbalance in the speed of development in the different communities will take a whole generation to redress. But if we are always striving to provide solutions people will know that things are getting better and will get even better. Then peace and stability in Malaysia will be assured. We must be prepared to go oh doing everything reasonable and practicable to solve these problems. But we must never forget that, whatever we do, the Indonesians will never cease in their propaganda war against us, to break up Malaysia by making the Malays and Chinese split apart, grow jealous, and suspicious, and finally hostile to each other ... "

VII

Lee Kuan Yew's warning to the Malay extremists went unheeded. An atmosphere charged with tension was being created by racial exhortations uttered by politicians and given prominence in *Utusan Melayu*. On 21 July, the Prophet Mohammed's birthday, there was a serious communal clash. Over radio and television later that day, the Prime Minister pleaded for an end to "this stupidity". He said: "What or who started this situation is irrelevant at this moment. All the indications show that there has been organization and planning behind this outbreak to turn it into an ugly communal clash. All that was needed was someone to trigger it off. Then the news spread like wildfire, with each attack followed by a counter-attack. We can and we will sort these things out later on ... "

Lee spoke again over the radio and. television on 26 July, five days after the riots started. He said that order had been restored, and sanity was returning. Now came the long and delicate process of getting people to resume the even tenor of their lives. Goodwill committees, he said, were being set up, but he issued a word of warning. "We must not assume that those who were out to create mischief only a few days ago have suddenly been overcome by remorse and are now filled with the milk of human kindness. Care and caution must be exercised in deciding who can be relied upon to help spread confidence, goodwill and amity. If we keep up the progress we have made in the last two days, conditions should return to normal before the end of the week. We should not have made this progress if there had not been a real desire among our various communities to live together in peace and harmony. We must never let last week's events recur. Squash all talk of communal hatred or revenge. Let us instead get on with our work in peace and amity."

In all, twenty-two people were killed and 461 injured.

Tunku Abdul Rahman, on his return to Kuala Lumpur from the United States on 12 August, said: "I have always asked that leaders be careful in what they say to avoid any quarrel among themselves. But some of them have been careless in the speeches leading to the incidents."

VIII

Partial curfew was still on when the Prime Minister kept a month-old promise to talk to the Consular Corps. He said on 30 July that he had decided to speak to them honestly about the prevailing situation, but without exacerbating the situation. "Over a year ago, before Malaysia was formed, I said: 'Malaysia is inevitable. But no one can say that the success of Malaysia as an economic and a political unit is inevitable.'

"I did not realize then how quickly after its formation Malaysia would be put to the test. Will Malaysia, after the events of the past few weeks leading to the riots, show that spirit of tolerance between all races with all their interests reasonably balanced? The answer to this depends on whether extremists can be kept out of the leadership of both the Chinese and Malay communities. If the extremist elements gain dominance on one side, it must lead to the emergence of extremist leadership on the other... To succeed, therefore, rational and moderate leadership must smack down extremist elements on its side and co-operate with rational and moderate leadership on the other side..."

At a goodwill gathering, on 15 August, held at a large government-built housing estate, where nearly 10,000 of the 50,000 flat-dwellers were Malays, Lee remarked that there had been no disturbances there. He said the reason was their outlook on life. The people had hope for the future, they had a new outlook, a new breadth of vision. If this was spread to other areas in the island "a lot of all this communal mumbo-jumbo can be dispelled. We must," said Lee, "make up our minds whether we want to make Malaysia succeed, or let it drift and collapse."

Lee confidently expected "that in the weeks to come you will see all extremists, all people who preach hatred, ill-will, who say things which will work up the feelings of one race against another, dealt with. If we don't do that, then this country will go down the drain..."

IX

Shortly after the Tunku's return to Malaysia he paid a two-day visit to Singapore "to see how best confidence could be re-established among the people". On 19 August, Lee Kuan Yew accompanied him on a tour of the areas where the disturbances had taken place. In a brief speech, Lee, in the presence of Tunku Abdul Rahman, said: "We stand at the crossroads of Malaysia." Lee told the crowd that, a year before, in London, at the time of the signing of the Malaysia Agreement, Singapore had confidence in the Tunku's leadership. "We have faith and trust in his ability to see that justice is done to all. Whatever guarantees we have in the Constitution, in legal documents, finally it is faith in the persons who have to translate and implement these documents which is more important than the written word."

Demonstrating their respect and affection for the Tunku personally, the people of Singapore gave him a tremendous, and an affectionate, welcome. All fifty-one parliamentary constituencies collaborated in giving him a big public dinner—hundreds were present—in the grounds of a school on the East Coast Road. He spoke without notes. He believed the trouble on the Prophet's Birthday had been instigated. It must never happen again. "Let each one of us enjoy life according to his own custom and religion, because this country has guaranteed that every race can follow its own customs and religion. We have our mosque, the biggest in Southeast Asia... and eighty per cent of the money for its construction came from the Chinese, and the other twenty per cent from other races, including the Malays. Now this shows religious tolerance."

Speaking specifically of "our beloved Singapore" the Tunku ended his speech, cheered wildly, with these words: "Malaysia is with the wishes of you all. In the referendum all of you accepted Malaysia. After the establishment of Malaysia you had the general elections, and all of you voted the PAP to govern this State of Singapore because it wanted Malaysia, and not one of my UMNO candidates was voted in. I say never mind, so long as there is Malaysia. Therefore, strengthen Malaysia, bring peace to Malaysia, make Malaysia independent forever."

The Straits Times, on 21 August, commented that the Tunku's visit had done much good. There should be "positive steps" to blunt the force of communal agitation. And only the Tunku possessed "the strength and authority" to effectively deter and silence the voices of communal dissension.

If, as Lee Kuan Yew was to say sorrowfully a year later, the Tunku had then "smacked down the six mad Mullahs", had stopped the fanatical cry 'Malays unite' and had encouraged progressive Malays to mingle with others, politically as well as socially, Malaysia would have progressed. History may well judge that this was the Tunku's hour of decision, wherein he faltered. Having escaped condemnation or punishment, the extremists maintained their campaign, increased it with vigour for another year, until the Tunku was forced to shatter his dream and drive Singapore out of Malaysia.

Lee Kuan Yew understood the Tunku's difficulties. "He has assured all the races in Malaysia, the Chinese, the Indians and the others," he declared in a speech on 23 August, "that they have, together with the Malays, a permanent place in the country. So the Malay extremists and racists were not pleased. Instead of taking sides and joining the racists, the Tunku calls for goodwill, patience, and tolerance, seeking ways to put things right..."

Not until 2 September (the day riots broke out again in Singapore) did the Malaysian Government announce its intention to set up a Commission of Inquiry into the July riots. And not until 9 October did the Government announce the composition of the Commission. It consisted of two Malays and two Chinese and one Indian. The Commission never published its findings, and, upon Singapore's separation from Malaysia in 1965, the Commission ceased to exist.

X

Lee Kuan Yew was in Europe when the second riots broke out. As Secretary-General of the People's Action Party, he was making his first venture into international socialism. He took part in the debate, on 3 September on East-West relations, at the Socialist International conference in Brussels. It was the centennial conference. Lee described himself as a democratic socialist of a rising generation of the newly emergent nations. "What we will emerge to, what we will inherit, depends upon how quickly we can learn from the experiences of those who have travelled similar roads before us, and have found themselves confronted with similar situations in Europe and elsewhere.

"For many years, socialists who are not communists in the colonial empires of Europe have looked upon the Socialist International with cynicism and disdain. Partly because we did not believe that there was something innately decent in human beings to rise above his own national interests; partly because the prospect of a socialist in an anti-colonial movement being associated with French or British socialists, who were oppressing Algerian and other freedom-fighters in other parts of the world, was so abhorrent that we stood by on the sidelines.

"Hence the emergence of what has been loosely called the non-aligned or the neutral group of nations. We are non-aligned if we are asked to choose between competing power blocs. We are non-aligned if we are asked to choose between the interests of the competing ideologies of communism or capitalism. But we are not non-aligned, nor can we afford to be neutral, when our own existence, our happiness, and our future are at stake.

"We are moving away from the first flush of the freedom movement. We are facing problems which are fairly well known to all of you. Having acquired freedom, partly as a result of holding out prospects of a socialist paradise almost immediately after freedom, we have to resolve the problem of meeting rising expectations of better living when the only answer is the more equal distribution of poverty and more hard work to produce some of the things worth distributing.

"Fortuitously, the discussion today was opened by a German democratic socialist, two Japanese and a Britisher. I am here today because of what the predecessors of these three parties did, or did not do, some twenty-five years ago. Had there been men like Comrade Willy Brandt in charge of the German nation, then perhaps there might not have been a Second World War in Europe. In which case, it is conceivable that, if there had been social democrats responsible for the destiny of the German people, perhaps Japanese militarists would not have been in power in Japan, and Japan would not have unscrambled the empires of the British, Dutch and French in the Far East. But that was not to be. Social democratic forces in Germany were stifled, and in Japan were unheard of, and in Britain they were in alliance with reactionary forces fighting a patriotic war. Now this is all over.

"In Asia and Africa today, there are over sixty new nations which have emerged and obtained independent membership of the United Nations. In the majority of cases, the metropolitan power had a limited choice in selecting who was immediately to inherit the apparatus of the state, or at least in deciding who should not inherit it. Whether the successor government in the newly independent country can live up to the original hopes which the metropolitan power had when power was handed over can only be determined by the degree of assistance in wisdom and expertise, which distinguished social democrats or

214

democratic socialists, such as you, can decide.

"Let me explain. Throughout Africa and Asia, the European empires were determined that the communists—local communist parties —should not take over from them. There is only one instance where this happened. That was in North Vietnam, on the battlefield of Dien Bien Phu, where power was wrested from the colonial power by force. The lesson was learnt by all the other colonial powers, and power was handed over by consent before colonial freedom movements wrested it by force. So that left a limited freedom of choice as to who should succeed, and, in the majority of these countries, there were parties of the Left embracing socialism in varying degrees of crispness or vagueness in their socialism—but, nevertheless, Left-wing parties, non-communist in their affiliations and in their ideological beliefs.

"Now they are faced with the business of making their anti-colonial revolutions succeed. They are faced with the problem of preventing the revolution from going one step further, until what remained of the colonial state would be dismantled and a communist republic installed in its place. How is that to be prevented? By ideological contest, by talk of human values and humanism to a hungry and sometimes angry people, or by giving them all the things that they could hope for under even the most benevolent of communist regimes and, at the same time, having a system of government where human values are not trampled upon by an intolerant regime?

"I was impressed by the vehemence with which our first speaker, the famous Mayor of Berlin, stressed the importance of Berlin, of German reunification, of attitudes of firmness and flexibility in dealing with the East, by which he meant Russia. I would like to take a little bit of your time this morning to ask you to cast your eyes to a similar situation in some different dimensions in Southeast Asia.

"In Berlin you had, on the Western side, complete cohesion, understanding of the problem, and definition of the objectives of the Western alliance, and unity in its policies. Sixteen or seventeen years ago, when the first fight over Berlin broke out, I did not understand how that conflict had anything to do with me. I was not aligned. Today, I understand that had that fight been lost, I would not perhaps have emerged in Southeast Asia.

"The problem that worries me is that I think the West is not sufficiently aware of the acuteness of the conflicts which have now shifted to Southeast Asia. There you find the West in disarray. The Americans are committeed to contain. There are military bases in Formosa, South Korea, Vietnam, the Philippines—to contain what we sometimes fear is the uncontainable. The British play a secondary role, partly committed to contain, partly hoping to strike out in some new more positive direction. They tentatively made what was an intelligent move when they exchanged diplomatic representation with China,

215

recognizing China, hoping to open up windows in the Chinese mind to other ideas and other perspectives in the world. Perhaps, had the Americans embarked on that policy, there might be very little to choose today between President Ho Chi Minh and President Tito of Yugoslavia.

"Conflicts have arisen and our situation is bedevilled by a rift even in the Eastern camp. The Dutch, the Germans, the French have different and divergent assessments of the situation and of what is to be done. The French President, in his wisdom, has proclaimed neutralism as the panacea for all the ills of Southeast Asia. Whether this simple pill will work in such an advanced state of cancer in Southeast Asia is dubious. Nevertheless, it illustrates differing assessments of what is wrong with the patient, and whether he needs medical or surgical treatment . . .

"I listened to the first four speakers with great attention on the urgent need for disarmament, for containment of armaments, for the abandonment of force as the decisive factor in determining international problems. Perhaps in the developed countries of the West, governments are abashed to embark on a gun-running policy to pursue their own nationalist ambitions. But in Southeast Asia, whilst Mr Khrushchev preaches disarmament and the banning of nuclear weapons, he sends to Indonesia out-dated cruisers such as the one that took him to Britain one decade ago—and out-dated guns, but guns good enough to kill socialists, or others, effectively and without discrimination. He has now helped to build up a force in Indonesia that may make for instability and unhappiness, leading ultimately to localized wars, which must in turn lead to wider conflicts.

"I have no solutions to these problems. All I wish to say is that they are not new. They are variations, different permutations and combinations of the age-long problems which you have already faced in Europe. Perhaps if democratic socialists who have had more experience in these matters were to allow us to compare notes with them in a more systematic and effective manner, we might avoid some of the pitfalls which otherwise are waiting to ensnare so many of the over sixty new nations.

"They can be won over to your side, and to my side. They are like-minded men and women who seek salvation for their own people, who are increasingly conscious of the fact that they live in a very small world, growing ever smaller, and that the problems of the East and West, the problems of nuclear war, of disarmament, are so closely tied up with their problems. They seek development, technical skills and industrial capital to create more of the material things of life, which can make their people travel the democratic and socialist path to prosperity and happiness.

"If democratic socialists, or social democrats, as we used to call them, are only pre-occupied with their own little problems, are only concerned with their own immediate neighbours, then the over sixty new nations, non-aligned, neutral though they may be, must eventually drift to the other side. Polarization is almost inevitable. What is not inevitable is that they should drift that way. If you give them sustenance, succour not only in ideas—although they are important—but, even more important, in intelligent policies by which the have-nations help the have-nots to reach a fair level of economic development without undergoing the tribulations of violent communist revolution, they will be tempted to go along with you."

Two days later, Lee Kuan Yew was invited to speak for Asia at the centenary celebrations of the Socialist International. Clement Attlee spoke for Britain.

Lee said that since 1945 more than fifty independent nations had emerged in Asia and Africa, and in nearly all of them the political leadership professed socialism of varying shades. The appeal of an equal society to the dispossessed millions in Asia and Africa was so powerful that no regime emerging from colonial rule dared call itself a party of the Right.

"In the first flush of the transfer of power to local nationalist leaders, a number of democratic socialists assumed authority over the apparatus of the state and the fortunes of their people. The history of the past two decades, however, was a sad commentary on their lack of understanding of the mechanics of power, and worse, their lack of expertise in the exercise of power...

"In sharp contrast is the subsequent emergence of communist leaders in Asia. When they come to power, they stay in So it is with the Chinese People's Republic under Chairman Mao Tse-tung, North Korea under Kim Il-Sung and North Vietnam under Ho Chi Minh. There is a marked distinction in attitudes to the exercise and mechanics of power between the communist and the democratic socialist. The communist, with his dialectical catechism and his instruction manual on how to organize and seize power, poses the sharpest challenge to socialism and democracy in Asia.

"Whilst the democratic socialist weaves neat and attractive patterns for an egalitarian society, often he does not give as much time and effort to building up the organizational instruments which alone can give flesh and blood to egalitarian ideals. The contest for power, the right to shape the destiny of nearly 1,000 million people in Asia, as yet uncommitted, depends upon whether the democratic socialist can meet the challenge that communist organizational and propaganda techniques pose in appealing to the dispossessed millions in Asia...

"Democratic socialism has survived in Asia only where living standards are above the rice line and where the administrative organs of the state are effective. In Ceylon, in spite of setbacks, democratic socialism still persists in trying to find a new formula to solve old

217

social and economic problems. And India, after seventeen years of Nehru's interpretation of socialism for the Indian Congress movement, will not succumb to communism even though there are temporary difficulties over grain distribution. In Singapore it was affluence, relative in Asian terms, spread out more widely by social and economic policies, that checked a hot-house revolution carried on the backs of teenagers, who in other communities take to more flamboyant and less dialectical pursuits. Where these two conditions, reasonable living standards and an effective administration, do not exist, democratic socialism cannot provide an answer. The conflict then invariably becomes one between a reactionary regime backed by military force and a totalitarian communist movement backed by terror. It is doubtful whether such a regime can become less reactionary and so make possible a political solution other than communist dictatorship. This is an exercise in human ingenuity which so far has outwitted all local talent in South Vietnam, even when backed by massive American aid.

"All these newly independent countries are not economically developed. With independence comes no immediate socialist paradise to satisfy the rising expectations of their people. Instead, if things are to get better there must be increased effort to increase productivity. Otherwise, poverty is all there is to share out equally. The acid test is in performance, not promises. The millions of dispossessed in Asia care not and know not of theory. They want a better life. They want a more equal, a more just society. He who gives them this is their saviour...

"The democratic socialist can provide these answers quickly enough only if he can draw on the technical and industrial skills of the developed industrial nations. The communists also do this. And people in Asia are only too acutely aware of the adverse effects on the industrialization programmes of certain Asian countries when the Russians withdraw their experts and machines.

"There is a growing cynicism amongst the have-not nations of the world that the haves, whether capitalists or communists, are not prepared to help them become have nations. Not only are industrial skill and capital not forthcoming in a manner to make any appreciable difference but worse, trade barriers are put up against the simple manufactures that the have-not nations manage to produce. This cynicism can and should be banished. The democratic socialist parties of the advanced countries can help a new atmosphere of hope and co-operation in this endeavour to lift the lives of the millions in Asia and Africa into something more akin to what the have-nots in the have nations of Europe and America enjoy.

"The events of the past two decades have in many ways mocked the communist claim that communism is inevitable. If democratic socialists help each other, they can write some illustrious chapters of history about the newly independent countries of Asia and Africa."

XI

Early in November the Quakers held a conference of Young Asian Leaders in Singapore. Lee Kuan Yew was among the speakers. He said: "I am asked to say a few wise things about 'Unity and Diversity, and Sources of Tensions in New Nations'. Well, unity is what we are striving for, though God knows what a dull world it would be if we were all uniform. Diversity, and too much of it, is what we are suffering from in Malaysia, and in this region. And I am not quite sure whether it is our affinity to our neighbours, or our diversity from them, that has attracted this tremendous attention from them to our fortunes, and has created tension in this part of the world. Suffice it for me to say that a process of unity and diversity in the history of tribes and nations is an unending one.

"But we have always to remember this when we talk about Asia: the erosion of communications; the lack of contact; the isolation of the intellectual elites in the various new nations emerging in South or Southern Asia. When we talk about Southern Asia, we must remember that we are not talking in European dimensions. Europe, with its easy communications, is about the size of India and Pakistan put together. When we talk of South Asia perhaps we also include South China.

"I see some delegates have come from as far afield as Manila and Tokyo. This is a vast area with a population twenty times that of Europe; people with more divergent cultures and civilizations than the Europeans and people, for the first time, now finding their own avenues of assertion and expression in a vastly awakened world. Hence, tension is only to be expected after all these centuries of closed communications. In spite of belonging to fairly similar racial groups, all Caucasians, whether they are Anglo-Saxons, or Latin types, or Nordic types, have not united politically. Is it any wonder then that we in Asia should be so different from one another? Is it any wonder that, for the time being, we, who are supposed to represent the educated intellectual elite of the various new nations in Southern Asia are present here today as a result of the initiative of an American Quaker organization? . . .

"I do not wish to exaggerate the importance of the intellectual impetus which will determine the intellectual content of the various ideological drives behind the different governments in Asia, but one of the besetting ills of Southern Asia has been a lack of comparative analysis.

"So many of the problems we face here in Singapore, in Malaysia, are problems which have been encountered in India, in Pakistan: different peoples, different cultures, speaking languages completely diverse from one another, having to live in ever-growing proximity as a result of modern means of communication. What is the end result of this? Does Asia go through this painful process of deciding which is the bigger hen to peck the smaller hen before the hen-pecking order is accepted? How much is it to be bedevilled by East-West ideological conflicts? What is the end result? Definitely not the United States of Asia. What then? I would say a period of great trial and tribulation. But there is a fair chance that at the end of it all, if the present Western-type leadership survives, after the first impact of pressures and conflicts for hegemony in this region, a new equilibrium will be found in which each country understands the respective power strength of the other. Nations are that way. Tribes were that way. Modern Europe was created out of the conflicts of national ambitions, and Asia is undergoing such a conflict of gigantic proportions...

"There is one advantage which Asia has enjoyed in the past decade: that its first-generation leaders share certain common Western or European values, because most of them, for diverse reasons, had their training in Western traditions. Even if they do not accept them, they are used to them... As countries emerge, their leadership reflects more and more the real ground position. The Western veneer of the first-generation leaders may disappear. It is not unlikely that in the next decade, in the seventies or the eighties, Asia will be led by men who not only do not speak each other's language, but who probably will not understand a common language. That is the depths and the dimensions of this problem. To travel from here to Rangoon is not the same thing as to go from Dover to Calais. There are different dimensions in space and time, in cultures, and peoples, and languages. French and Latin and English have something in common. But the Burmese script has nothing in common with Chinese characters, let alone with Malay written in the Arabic script. And yet we talk of Asia as one entity. In fact, it never has been. It was only one in so far as the West came here and carved it up. One of the things that struck me about Africa was that, in fact, the peoples there are more akin to one another. It is one continent, nearer one people racially than the Asians are. And because very few of their languages had been scripted, today there is, in fact, a second generation of leaders being brought up with a common, either English or French, language.

"So there is an organization for African unity. So the Africans meet if for no other reason to agree not to disagree. But in Asia they do not meet all together, but they have bilateral talks, in order to keep up formalities, knowing full well that the problems are insoluble and that neither side can afford to concede...

"But everybody is beginning to understand that behind all this show of great Asian oneness and solidarity is the crude, brutal conflict of force: the assertion of dominance, of hegemony. And one of the comments in the recent turn of events was from the Tunku. He said, 'Asia was proud that China exploded a bomb.' Perhaps he was right, but in that explosion you have the stage set for the final phase of modern Asia: the power situation. Who is who in Asia? Who becomes what by leave of whose assistance?

"If such a gathering as this were to meet again in twenty years, first I hope that it would take place on Asian initiative. The Americans and the British, however well-intentioned, are not Asians. And second, when we come together, I hope it will still be possible to meet and talk in some common language, be it Asian, be it African, be it Western. But the ever-growing feeling which one gets of the drift of events is that twenty years from now, if such a gathering were to take place, very different types of people would come together under very different circumstances. How very different they would be is to a large extent beyond our control. The pace is being set, for better or for worse, by those who have determined that they will play the European game of power politics efficiently, scientifically, with all the panoply of modern diplomacy—its propaganda sinews of radio and television, the world Press. So, behind all the sweet talk, we should never forget that this is what we are in for: the reality of power positions."

XII

On 21 November, the People's Action Party celebrated its tenth anniversary. In a party souvenir booklet, Lee Kuan Yew, as Secretary-General of the party, looked to the future. The old battle cries, he said, were no longer valid. British colonialism was no longer the main enemy, as it was when the party issued its manifesto in 1954. "Then the people, whatever their shades of political beliefs, from extreme Right to extreme Left, were on the same side fighting the colonial regime. Today it is our only recently independent and expansionist neighbour who presents the biggest threat to our existence. Against this threat we would probably be defenceless without the military help of the former colonial power.

"Ten years ago a handful of stooges stood up against the united strength of the people demanding freedom. Today, there is a small but well organized segment of the population standing out against the popularly elected Governments both in Singapore and in Malaysia. They are the militant communists who follow the international communist line, and work hand in glove with the pro-Indonesian irredentist groups that see their only chance of getting power through collaboration with Indonesians.

"For, as long as Indonesian confrontation remains acute, the urge for social revolution, for a better life in a more equal society, will be relatively muted, as Malaysians rally to defend the country from

221

destruction through external aggression and internal subversion. Confrontation will go on for some time, because it has become part of the balancing of political forces in Indonesia. But, sooner or later, as they learn that Malaysia cannot be destroyed and absorbed, and as the present equilibrium of political forces gets disturbed, either through the ascendancy of the communists or through the decline of any one of the forces that President Sukarno now holds as a counterbalance to communist strength and pressure upon him, so their attacks will become more formal and less acute. When that moment comes, the desires of the people for social change will once again come to the forefront. It is difficult to predict when this moment will come. But it is reasonably safe to affirm that when it comes the changes that it will set in motion will be all the greater, to make up for the years lost through preoccupation with Indonesian aggression. . .

"For the moment we anxiously watch and analyse the attempts by the main parties in Malaya towards a vertical division of loyalties on communal lines. They are trying to reverse the healthy horizontal division of loyalities in Singapore along the lines of economic and class interest. Not unnaturally in Malaya, where the Government party runs its politics throughout the country along communal lines, there is some apprehension and uneasiness when they are confronted with Singapore's urban politics along horizontal class lines. There have been attempts to reverse this pattern in Singapore so that it conforms to the one with which they are more familiar in Malaya, where even the common interests of the workers, whether in kampongs or towns, have been overwhelmed by the pulls of loyalty to their community. But in the end, if Malaysia is to progress and inequalities of wealth and opportunity are to be narrowed, then class interests and economic groupings, not racial groups, must prevail . . . "

On Sunday, 22 November, the National Theatre was filled to capacity when Lee Kuan Yew, at the party's Tenth Annual Congress, set out the tasks for democratic socialists in the next ten years in Malaysia. Lee spoke as Secretary-General of the PAP. He said they had to bring the country together, isolate the enemy (the Indonesians and those who helped Indonesia divide Malaysia), and build that climate of opinion on which they could mount a movement comprised of all the have-nots in Malaysia, regardless of race, religion and language, to bring about a more equal and just society. Lee Kuan Yew stressed that once this message got through to the have-nots, who shared a common destiny, then the democratic socialists must triumph. He said those who were against a socialist society knew that this message could beat them once it was understood. This was why a great deal of effort and time was spent to prevent the message from getting through, "and a shindy of so many extraneous issues raised so that this one vital, unifying message would be dissipated and prevented from galvanizing the people".

222

Lee Kuan Yew said that one of the most important tasks of a democratic socialist party was to maintain basic faith and conviction in its ideals. It had to struggle to establish socialist values in a very capitalist system. For nearly six years, as the Government of Singapore, the party had been confronted with a completely capitalist economy, which it could not convert into a socialist economy without disastrous consequences to everyone. It was not possible to do this with Singapore's entrepot economy. That was the reason for the fight for reunification, for the broader and viable base .of Malaysia.

Lee said that a party running the mechanics of the state in a capitalist society which gave unjust rewards on the basis of possession of wealth or acquisition of status and rank was one which was easily corrupted. This had happened in many newly independent countries. A government came in with revolutionary fervour, soon to be worn down by the blandishments of an experienced capitalist system. "The capitalist system buys the politicians as individuals and it is easy for those in authority to establish paradise for themselves." Very few governments had been able to resist the temptations inherent in a capitalist system. But, Lee declared, the People's. Action Party had managed to do so. This was because of its ideological conviction that, while working a capitalist system, while forced within limits to redistribute the rewards of labour through social welfare, educational opportunities, housing, and the raising of living standards, rather than by a basic reorientation of the economy, it had retained the purity of its ultimate beliefs, and had resisted the temptations of the moment. There were many more years before the democratic socialist movement gained authority to reorder the shape of things in Malaysia. It was necessary that democratic socialists "inspire and infuse the coming generations to join their ranks with the same dedication and conviction that set them off ten years ago".

If there was one thing which democratic socialists in Singapore could be proud of (apart from having worked the capitalist system in Singapore efficiently), it was that, although ten years had passed, although the youthful zest was now tempered with more mature judgment, the idealistic drive to establish a more equal and just society, "where man does not exploit man, where wealth and rank is not the arbiter of a man's family fortunes and the fate of his children", still burned in them.

XIII

"One of the significant developments of the past decade," said Lee Kuan Yew at a Far East Scout Training Conference, 'on 2 December, "is the emphasis newly independent countries put on youth movements. In these countries where the vast majority of people are not literate, and where many of school-going age are not receiving formal instruction, it is so important that there should be proper active organization and training of those who are in schools.

"There are two broad patterns on which these newly independent countries can mould their own youth movements. First those existing in the Western democracies—boy scouts, boys brigades, cadets, youth clubs. The second is that of the young pioneers and communist youth movements of the Eastern bloc. In the latter, emphasis is not just on vigorous, physical activities, but on the systematic inculcation of communist doctrines and values. This is not to say that the youth organizations of the West, like the boy scouts, do not impart their own values of what an upright and useful citizen should be. In fact they do. They emphasize orthodoxy—upholding the king, the country, and being an honest citizen. These values no doubt help to sustain society. Loyalty and obedience to traditional institutions and democratic leaders, civic consciousness and resourcefulness help to make living in a civilized community congenial to all. But the ideological content is not as systematic and thorough as that of the communist youth movements.

"From my experience, now nearly three decades ago, of the scouting movement in Singapore, I believe it has a useful role to play in helping to organize part of our youth. Most young men or women find glamour in uniforms, organized discipline and opportunities for leadership. But if the scouting movement here will make adjustments to its style of dress and activity, it can make a far wider impact. The former wide-brimmed hat, the scarf, the lanyard and whistle, and a staff, invoking vistas of adventure in some wooded valley in Europe, may stimulate a sense of adventure, but they evoke a completely different response here, where dress and styles and climate are different. And so I am happy to see that innovations and improvements have been made over the years.

"I have found it difficult to understand why certain countries in Southeast Asia regard the scouting movement as subversive and as an imperialist tool. The criticism I would make is just the opposite, that its emphasis is almost wholly on healthy physical activity and creative work with the hands: the ideological content is conformity and orthodoxy. However useful these values are in established societies, they are less than sufficient for an effective youth movement in Malaysia.

"There are two forces in Malaysia, both anti-democratic, that are making a bid for recruits. First, the communists, second, the communal bigots. If either of them gains ascendancy over our youth, then as a nation we will disintegrate. Our chance of survival, of preserving one of the highest forms of civilized life in Southeast Asia, is to have tolerant democratic values triumph, where people accept that the majority will not only prevail, but also respect the need to accommodate a large dissenting minority.

"When young pioneers in communist countries graduate, they are budding young cadres for the communist party. I do not advocate slavish imitation, but if we give to our youth the values of a tolerant democratic society, aware of the great perils the country faces from the challenge of communists and communalists, who preach intolerance and suppression of dissenting views, if you help them to recognize that there are heresies in a democratic state, and that they should be inured against them, then you will have done your duty to your King, your country and your fellow citizens."

XIV

By the end of the year, Lee Kuan Yew was getting seriously concerned about the future of Malaysia. He told the Democratic Socialist Club at the University on 13 December that there was a growing awareness that, if things were not looked after carefully, "if there is not sanity, but more appeal to emotion," then there could easily be a drift to disaster. "We must learn how to live with each other. If you can remove that problem from the political arena then you can begin to face your real, other problems—the economic problems—and they are becoming more and more acute."

Lee said: "Free enterprise in Malaya, and now in Malaysia, has meant rapid urbanization, a gradual drift from the countryside to the town, development in the towns on the basis of free enterprise, new factories, new roads, new housing estates, and so on. Meanwhile, in spite of massive expenditure on rural development, roads, the breaking up of large tracts of jungle into smallholdings of ten acres each, part for rubber, part for mixed crops, cash crops, the real cash earnings of the rural people have not risen as quickly as those of the people in the towns. This is the first major problem; that is a fact. So you get adrift. Now, with good roads in the countryside linking it up with the towns, the young men begin to leave the country and drift into the towns and set up shanty towns around the suburbs of Kuala Lumpur, Ipoh and the other towns. In Singapore there is a constant drift of Chinese, Malays, Indians, from the Federation coming to stay with friends and relatives, looking for jobs.

"How do you resolve this? I believe you can only resolve this on the basis of socialist planning, not on the basis of free enterprise. Free enterprise, however suitable it may be in the early stages of industrialization in your urban areas, when it's a relatively efficient way of acquiring industrial skill and capital, is just not working to alleviate rural poverty. This curious alliance between representatives of rural have-nots working in conjunction with the urban haves has so many contradictions that it is unable to produce the answers for either the rural have-nots or the urban have-nots .

"I am, to a certain extent, inhibited in putting this analysis by the thought that a wrong phrase, or a wrong turn of phrase, might give rise to another round of emotionalism and a great deal of unnecessary agitation. But, looking at it coldly and in talking to a group of university students, I think I am entitled to put the problem in completely cold and dispassionate terms in this way: we have now a completely new situation in Malaysia in which the group loyalties of the various peoples, races, are intermixed with their class and economic loyalties. We are not quite sure now how the pattern will work out in the end...

"We are bedevilled by this racial line between country and town: country and town more or less coincides with the Malays and non-Malays. And the towns are advancing under free enterprise, but the country is not. The answer to the country's problems in my party's analysis is this: systematic and sustained scientific research, and an economic evaluation of the possibilities of profitable economic crops which can be grown by the Malay peasantry; the extension of adequate credits to peasants to introduce these crops; extensive training and education of the peasantry in modern techniques of agriculture and animal husbandry; an effective system of agricultural co-operatives, for the purchase of fertilizers, feeding stuffs, agricultural implements as well as for the marketing of their products. This is the answer for the countryside, which the capitalist system cannot produce. And, if the gap between the country and the town widens over the years, then racial conflicts will become deeper as advance is associated with the urban areas and with the people of immigrant stock—the non-Malays —and stagnation with the countryside, largely with Malays..."

XV

Lee Kuan Yew was deeply disappointed with the first really comprehensive Malaysian budget. The tax proposals heightened Lee Kuan Yew's growing fears that Singapore was not going to get a fair deal in Malaysia. In Parliament, in December, he criticized the Government for allowing only two days to examine a budget and study the implications of the tax charges "upon which the Finance Minister and his Ministry must have spent long months of cogitation and planning. The classification of direct and indirect taxes has been less than frank... He has classified turnover tax, estimated at $45 million, and payroll tax, estimated at $21 million, under direct taxation.

"A careful scrutiny of the incidence of these two taxes has led my colleagues and me to the conclusion that both turnover and payroll taxes in the majority of cases will be passed on to the consumer and their incidence has no relation to the capacity to pay of the person who is being taxed. If we are to help to narrow the gap between the haves and the have-nots, to equalize opportunity, the cost of running the Government, the provision of social, medical and educational services must more and more be paid by the haves, than by the have-nots. The way this is usually achieved is by having taxes based on the capacity to pay, such as direct taxation on income, capital gains and profits, rather than by choosing taxes because of facility of their collection, such as indirect taxes which are spread over the whole community equally, thus making the have-nots pay more in proportion to their incomes . . . "

In Committee of Supply, Lee Kuan Yew, commenting upon the Defence Estimates, warned of the danger of a large standing army, and pleaded for the organization of a territorial army of volunteers (which would, of course, have consisted of Malays, Chinese and Indians: the standing army is largely Malay).

In Singapore, employers and workers alike protested against the proposed taxes. Meetings of protest were held; some were banned by the Kuala Lumpur authorities. Lee Kuan Yew became alarmed at the Malaysian Government's attitude. Was this going to lead ultimately to the collapse of Malaysia? Lee posed this question at a conference held by the National TUC on 14 December. He felt the time had come for some plain talk. "By the time you cannot hold a meeting," he said angrily, "to protest against the budget, to protest against Government revenue proposals which will hurt or injure your interests, then there's something gone wrong with the country.

"This is the problem we have to face. I do not believe that sane, rational leaders want to stifle criticism; but we must prepare for the possibility that not rational and not very sane leaders may ultimately come into power. Then there will be a lot of trouble. Then the situation will get very serious and there will be real disintegration in Malaysia, and all the police and troops cannot keep Malaysia together . . . Our job is patiently and persistently to put across the sane, rational solution for the country, and give encouragement and help to moderate, rational leadership so that they will triumph. . ."

"Let us get down to fundamentals. Is this an open or a closed society?" demanded Lee Kuan Yew in the Malaysian Parliament on 18 December. "Is it a society where men can preach ideas—the novel, unorthodox, heresies, established churches and established governments—where there is a constant contest for men's hearts and minds on the basis of what is right, of what is just, of what is in the national interests? Or is it a closed society where the mass media—the newspapers, the journals, publications, TV, radio—either by sound or by sight, or both sound and sight, feed men's minds with a constant drone of sycophantic support for a particular orthodox political philosophy? That is the first question we ask ourselves.

"And let me preface my remarks with this: that it is not only in communist countries where the mass media is used to produce the closed mind, because the closed society must produce the closed mind. I believe that Malaysia was founded, if you read its Constitution, as an open society, constituting peoples of various communities, of various religions, of various languages, of varying political beliefs, in which the will of the majority will prevail, and in which a large dissenting minority will not be crushed and intimidated and silenced.

"I believe in an open society, and for that reason we are here. Not to be abused, for abuse carries us nowhere; not to be intimidated, for the Members on the other side, like ourselves, are brave and gallant men not to be easily intimidated by words. What are at stake are the lives of eleven million people, and foolish words uttered either in anger or in haste can bring about great trials and tribulations all round . . .

"We have been in this Chamber now for over a year. We were new boys when we came in last September. I think we now know the technique, the form, the style, and we were prepared to adjust. This is a different form in a different forum, in a different context against the broader canvas. We played it on a low key. The piano was muted, Mr Speaker, in order that we shall first get the measure of each other and the measure of our wills, areas of agreement and areas of disagreement. What has happened? There is now a set pattern and a set technique: from the press controlled by them vituperation, vilification is the daily bread to hold the faithful." (Lee was referring to the Malay extremists).

"We read it, we watch it with a lot of patience, otherwise this thing will not hold; vilification, falsification, vituperation is the daily bread they feed a lot of innocent minds on, to sour up a whole nation. We do not make wild allegations. There is a commission of enquiry (into the riots in Singapore) which has been appointed, gazetted in October the day before a motion tabled by my colleagues and myself was to be debated. It has not even sat. The secretary has not been appointed. Perhaps this Chamber may be dissolved before this Commission of Enquiry even begins its work, the open debate, the careful, scrupulous scrutiny of facts as against fiction.

"And in this Chamber the same technique—not the big men, they are gentle figures, but from the small fry, the hatchet men—howls of vituperation and abuse. Is this the open encounter? Is this the democratic system in which ideas compete for ascendancy? Not brawn or the strength of one's pharynx, but ideas—they cross frontiers, they have brought men into space—and if we try to keep our men rooted, glued to the ground, fixed in an orthodox political society which

228

resists change, the world will pass us by. One day it will come down like a house of cards. It has not the resilience, the sturdiness, the stamina to survive.

"Let's be honest amongst ourselves, and in this Chamber many things can be said which Members dare not mention or whisper outside. This is a privileged Chamber. Here let us be honest to ourselves. The issues are a matter of life and death. They have triggered off something basic and fundamental—Malaysia. Who does it belong to? To Malaysians. Who are Malaysians? I hope I am, Mr Speaker. But sometimes, sitting in this Chamber, I doubt whether I am allowed to be a Malaysian. This is the doubt that hangs over many minds. So I beseech Members of this House to pause and think of the immeasurable consequences of their actions. Once emotions are set into motion, men pitted against men, not on the basis of interests and ideas—class warfare, that will not break Malaysia. No danger of that. Not the slightest risk of it. But everybody in this House knows, without it having been uttered, what kind of warfare will split the nation right down from top to bottom and unzip Malaysia. Everybody knows it. I do not have to say it. It is an unspoken word. The Press know it, the public know it. Everyone in the coffee shops speaks of it. But to us in this Chamber it is taboo. Why? Make-believe! But for how long? Even the make-believe is wearing thin. I say let's pause and ask ourselves ... I am talking of the principle of the open society, the open debate, ideas not intimidation, persuasion not coercion."

CHAPTER NINETEEN

The Year of Power 1965

*"UNEXPECTEDLY, without choice, and reluctantly",
Singapore in 1965 was separated from Malaysia, and
became a sovereign independent nation. During this
dramatic and decisive year, Indonesia's confrontation
continued unrelaxed, but without major impact on
Singapore's economy.*

*In his New Year's Message Lee Kuan Yew had
warned that if the follies of 1964 were repeated in
1965, Malaysia might well break "not through external
aggression but through internal disintegration". In all
his speeches he stressed the urgent need for racial
harmony. Lee sought to apply the logic of Malaysia
not only through internal adjustment but also by external support. For four weeks he toured New
Zealand and Australia and repeated his view that
Malaysia would win "provided everybody understands
what the problems are, and is prepared to accommodate each other". Lee's speeches aroused severe criticism in Kuala Lumpur.*

In Singapore, upon his return, Lee Kuan Yew said that no one race was more entitled to be called Malaysian than any other. Malay spokesmen reacted strongly, and Tun Abdul Razak, Malaysia's Deputy Prime Minister, urged the people of Singapore to replace Lee Kuan Yew with "another leader who is sincere". To save Malaysia, the Malaysian Solidarity Convention was established by Opposition political parties in Singapore, Sarawak and Malaya. The substance and significance of Malaysia was debated in the Malaysian Parliament. Moderate speakers accepted the idea of a Malaysian Malaysia, but accused the PAP of seeking non-communalism too quickly while the first task should be to create racial harmony. Other speakers followed the Malay communal line and accused the PAP of being a Chinese communal party. A week later, Malaysia's Prime Minister left for London, for the Commonwealth Prime Ministers' Conference. Illness delayed his return until four days before Singapore, on 8 August, was separated from Malaysia "to prevent bloodshed". The Tunku said that separation had been made on the understanding that "we shall cooperate closely on matters of defence, trade and commerce". On 9 August Lee Kuan Yew proclaimed Singapore "a sovereign democratic and independent nation". Lee said: "We are going to have a multiracial nation in Singapore. This is not a Malay nation, not a Chinese nation, not an Indian nation. . ."

In Kuala Lumpur, the secretary-general of UMNO resigned his post "to save the Tunku from embarrassment". He opposed separation. On 21 September, the Republic of Singapore became a member of the United Nations. The following month Singapore was admitted as the twenty-second member into the Commonwealth.

I

LEE Kuan Yew's 1965 New Year's Message reflected his awareness of a grave situation and of impending storms. "The year 1964," he said, "was a turbulent year for us in Malaysia—race riots in Bukit Mertajam and Singapore, a crisis in Sabah, closure of the barter trade, and the year ended on a wrong note with an unhappy budget. But the country ticks on and people by and large are in good heart.

"It will be foolish, however, not to realize that if in 1965 we set out to repeat all the follies of 1964, then Malaysia may well break, not through external aggression but through internal disintegration. Confrontation, after fifteen months, has succeeded only in so far as it has accentuated divisive tendencies within the nation. Hence, for the coming year, we must resolve to halt this drift to perdition, resolve to dispel this atmosphere of growing intolerance, resolve to expose the communalists and isolate the extremists, resolve to banish fear and hatred from our hearts, and give the people faith in the future and in each other's good intentions. . .

"The experience of the first fifteen months of Malaysia, if nothing else, should teach us that, if the different leaderships in the different territories of Malaysia persist in wanting to get their own way as they were accustomed to in the old Malaya, Singapore, Sabah or Sarawak, then there is a danger of collision, not just of political leaderships, but of their followers in the different communities throughout Malaysia. We can make or mar our future; make it by accommodation and tolerance, or mar it by throwing a tantrum every time we do not get our way. We have to learn that the world does not owe us a living and that tantrums do not pay."

On 24 January, six months after the riots, Lee·Kuan Yew, now seriously perturbed at the worsening conditions, spoke at a mass rally and drew attention to the group represented by the Malay language newspaper *Utusan Melayu*. "This group," he said, "started off by attacking the PAP, then the Singapore Government and then Lee Kuan Yew." Finally there were riots in Singapore. "Now the attack has widened over a broad front. Now they are attacking the MCA." Dr Lim Swee Aun, Minister for Trade and Commerce, had been accused of being un-Malaysian because he had said that Malays must help themselves in business. Then they attacked Wong Pow Nee, Chief Minister of Penang, also of the MCA. "Now," continued Lee "the Muar Branch of the MCA passes a resolution and says *Utusan Melayu* is playing a dangerous, communal line, everyday pumping up people with poison."

Lee warned of the dangers of communal strife. He said there were two possible developments for Malaysia. "One, progress. To progress you must have peace and solidarity in the country. To have

232

peace and solidarity in the country you must act in accordance with what has been agreed in the Constitution. If you want to change any of these things, then you must get the consent of the people.

"The other way is sure disaster, not just for Singapore but for the whole of Malaysia. That is, to do whatever you like: I want to do this, I do it. Have you really got the power to carry the people with you? To act contrary to the wishes of the people, contrary to what has been agreed, will make us like South Vietnam."

In 1965, for the first time in thirty years, the Malays and the Chinese celebrated their New Years at the same time, and in Kuala Lumpur, Tunku Abdul Rahman made use of this opportunity, on 27 January, to strike back at Lee Kuan Yew. There were some politicians, the Tunku said, "whose minds are obviously distorted, polluted. Their thoughts and talk appear to be so. They talk about Malaysia with gloomy forebodings. They talk of strife and strain, of trouble and bloodshed ahead, they talk of war, they talk of calamities. They predict that Malaysia is on the road to ruin and destruction and yet they are the ones who wanted Malaysia. They produce gloom in the minds of the people wherever they go. They strike fear and despondency in the hearts of men who hear them, though with their high office they should be talking of peace and happiness, of goodwill and friendship among the people in Malaysia. In this hour of trial and tribulations, such talk is indeed foolish and harmful and dangerous, and I say shame on them... responsible citizens of this country must not indulge in such talk, and politicians more so cannot afford the luxury of such talk. Our thoughts, our every word, our movements, our talk must be directed and subjected to the needs of our country. Our country's needs at this moment are the loyalty and the dedicated service of her citizens. Therefore, minimize rather than widen the differences between the various people in the country. Loose talk can only cause disunity and misunderstanding. Divided, we shall go under and be swallowed by waves of terror and subjection under such tyrants as Sukarno or terror such as only the communists know how to inflict upon mankind. This is the most appropriate moment to achieve unity: make it our resolution on this day when we are celebrating jointly Hari Raya and Chinese New Year. This is more than coincidence. It is the will of God that it should be so. It is His command that we should celebrate the joy of these festive occasions as one people. In our diverse ways let us work for peace, harmony, and goodwill to all ..."

Lee Kuan Yew's Chinese New Year and Hari Raya Puasa Message reflected more upon material matters. He said: "Amidst all the festivities, the new clothes and the good things to eat, perhaps there is time for reflection on how it is that eleven million Malaysians eat the best and have the most clothes to wear in Asia—not to mention the good roads, public buildings, private housing, telephones, street lights and drinking water.

"We can continue to enjoy all these provided the foundation of this economic well-being is never shaken—harmony between the races, peace and order in the country, constructive endeavour in a tolerant society. Take away tolerance and substitute extremism, in place of peace and confidence put excitement and anxiety, and in no time at all we shall be lucky to be eating as well as the Indonesians, for this country is not as fertile as Indonesia. But it has a well developed plantation, mining and trading economy and the men with the skills to run the system. If all in Malaysia understand and always remember this then there is no reason why we should not always continue to eat and live better than others in Asia."

Some people read into this message a subtle warning to Malay extremists as to what could happen to their standards of living if there was conflict with the Chinese, who mainly controlled Malaysia's economy. Indonesia's economy suffered when Chinese retailers in the rural areas of Indonesia were persecuted.

"Nations, like men," declared Lee Kuan Yew, at a Symposium on Scientific and Technological Research in Malaysia, organized by the University of Singapore, on 10 February, "can be divided broadly into two groups: the elite, consisting of the workers by brain, possessing the scientific and technological skills which give them in return high standards of living; and, second, the hewers of wood and drawers of water, who obtain the satisfaction of an active physical existence without the same high rewards. This division does not coincide necessarily with rich and poor nations or, for that matter, with rich and poor people. Some nations, like the oil kingdoms, are wealthy by any standards, by reason of their possession in abundance of scarce natural resources. But their lack of human resources must always condemn them as a people to the category of hewers of wood. A nation will be perpetually developing if it is unable to produce men who can learn and catch up with the more efficient and effective techniques of getting fuel other than by hewing wood...

"So it is that, to date, very few countries in receipt of aid programmes look like ever emerging into industrial societies as of their own right. For before they can discard the props of foreign aid and rely on their own sinews to give their people the standards of life of a modern industrial society, the first basic requirement is an infrastructure of skilled scientists and technocrats who can not only work the mechanics of a modern scientific and industrial society, but create innovations and ensure self-generating advance in creating more and more of the commodities that make for gracious living with less and less physical effort.

"Newly independent societies have always found it easier to produce politicians and administrators who could pass themselves off as their counterparts in the modern industrial societies. Administrators and, even more so, politicians seem to require no special training or discipline, and the pretence of competence can be kept up without danger of discomforting exposure. One might even pretend to be a doctor without having been properly trained and get away with it for some time. But to pretend to be a structural engineer or an industrial chemist and undertake the building of a suspension bridge or a fertilizer plant is a hazardous operation even for the most debonair of confident men.

"And so, as we go up the scale to the research scientist, it becomes more and more difficult to keep up appearances other than by having many men of quality available for training. And a country that has these trained and disciplined men of quality in abundance cannot be kept down, as Western Germany and Japan have proved in the twenty years since the Second World War. If you have the human resources, the skills, the disciplines and techniques of modern science and technology, you can overcome whatever lack of natural resources your nation suffers from. It is not mere accident that the greatest nations in the world are the Americans and the Russians, who are the only people who are now able to afford to explore the universe.

"The capacity for original research to add to the sum total of new knowledge is the final culmination of a people's triumph and greatness. Between the process of learning for the purpose of straightforward imitation, and the process of competing may lie decades of hard work. The Japanese proved to the world that it could be done, that the trade mark 'Made in Japan', which once connoted cheap, shoddy imitation goods, today invokes a different image of a finished product of quality as good as any other in the world in some particular types of manufacture.

"Malaysia is some way off from the Japanese situation. But that we have the capacity, first, to acquire the knowledge which the industrial nations have, and, next, having assimilated it, to generate new ideas and techniques of our own is, I think, being demonstrated. If anyone donates us a nuclear power station or a submarine, the donor can be assured that in no time we shall be able to run it ourselves."

By 24 February, Lee Kuan Yew was talking about "the turning point in Malaysia". In Kuala Lumpur, he said that the previous three weeks, starting with the Tunku's Chinese New Year Message had marked the beginning of a new phase of Malaysia. It was a turning point, for recent Alliance speeches had given expression to a fundamental decision, which must have been taken by its leaders, to write off any hope of winning over large urban areas like Singapore. By its series of public pronouncements it had disabled itself from competing for mass support in Singapore and other sophisticated urban areas in Malaysia. Its primary interest now was to hold on to its rural base in Malaya. . .

To arouse Malaysians to the growing dangers, Lee Kuan Yew visited several towns in Malaya. He spoke first at Seremban on 2 March. "Would," he asked, "a multiracial Malaysia be achieved more quickly and better through communal bodies meeting at the top, or through inter-racial political organizations meeting at all levels?" This, Lee said, was becoming the issue. Lee Kuan Yew said he believed in multiracialism at all levels. He referred to a Chinese Minister of the Central Government who had gone to Sabah and advised the Chinese (who constituted twenty-three per cent of the population in Sabah) to unite in one communal political party. This Minister advanced the theory that if all the Chinese united along the lines of the Malayan Chinese Association they could assume greater importance and become the balancing factor in Sabah politics. "I cannot think of anything more disastrous for the Chinese in Sabah, or indeed anywhere in the rest of Malaysia, than to get themselves isolated together in a communal party and then negotiate and bargain for advantage from such an isolated position.

"Recently Alliance leaders have tried to explain why their pattern of politics through communally segregated political parties, organized along exclusive racial lines, will make for Malaysian unity. They say that first they have three little unities: 'Malays unite', 'Chinese unite', 'Indians unite', and then the three unities unite into one big unity. They have been doing this in Malaya for the past decade and have successfully maintained the privilege and power position of a few privileged Malay traditionalists sharing the spoils of office with a few wealthy Chinese and a few fortunate Indians who were chosen to represent the Chinese and Indians respectively.

"The first fallacy in this scheme is that it falsely assumes that in fact the Chinese and the Indians are allowed to unite and choose their leaders. On the contrary, if any Chinese or Indian ever attempted to unite all Chinese and Indians he would be branded a dangerous racist. The segregated communal party arrangement in Malaya was a situation where the traditionalist leaders, who had the majority of the Malays, in fact nominated who should represent the Chinese and who should represent the Indians respectively.

"Now they are trying to apply the same technique of the segregated communal party to Singapore, Sabah and Sarawak. They think that it will produce the same results, that the traditionalist leaders, by getting the majority of Malays to support them, can manipulate the others and perpetuate their facade of inter-communal co-operation through segregated political parties.

"The difficulty for the Alliance leadership is that this formula cannot work either in Singapore, Sabah or Sarawak. And in the long run it will not work in Malaysia as a whole. The demographic composition of the three new states is different, and the people have different traditions and group loyalties. The only state where the Chinese, uniting into a communally organized party, can get results is in Singapore, where they constitute seventy-five per cent of the population. And, ironically, it is in Singapore that the Malaysian nationalist has defeated the Chinese chauvinist. . .

"A Chinese communal party, however well organized, must always fail. For out of 104 seats in parliament in Malaya, a Chinese communal party can only win twenty seats. It could probably win fifteen out of fifteen seats in parliament from Singapore. In Sabah, depending upon the way constituencies are drawn for direct elections to parliament, they could win three or four out of the sixteen seats. In Sarawak they might win five or six out of the twenty-four seats. So those who advise the Chinese to assert themselves politically through a Chinese communal party are giving wrong and dangerous advice. . .

"For the Indians it is even worse to be organized along completely communal lines, as has been suggested by the Malayan Indian Congress. In Singapore they will get zero seats out of fifty-one for the state assembly and zero out of fifteen for parliament. Similarly, in Sabah and Sarawak both for state and parliament there are so few Indians that they will get zero seats. And in Malaya, whilst in some of the state assemblies they might get one or two seats where Indian estate labourers are gathered together, for parliament the Indian communally organized party on its own will get zero out of 104 parliamentary seats.

"And Malays also stand to lose in the long run in backing parties on the basis of race and not policies. It is only the traditionalists who will obtain a temporary advantage from communal segregation in the political life of the country. But only for the time being. But it is inevitable that over the next decade, as more and more of the people in the country will have been born and bred here and have citizenship and the right to vote, it will not be worth while playing communal politics, even for the traditionalists.

"If, instead of getting caught in the stupidities and dangers of communal politics, the Chinese, Indians, Pakistanis, Ceylonese, Eurasians, Dayaks, Kayans, Ibans, Kadazans and others, and, most important of all, the Malays, get together on the basis of their collective economic and social interests, then the majority of the people, the majority of Malaysian have-nots, which will include the majority of the Malays, Chinese and Indians and others, will all win. . ."

In Malacca the next day, Lee Kuan Yew summarized the strains and tensions within Malaysia and laid the blame for an unhappy and dangerous internal situation squarely upon "secondary leaders within the United Malays National Organization". Lee said: "We had all

237

expected that after Malaysia there would have to be adjustments of attitudes and policies, not just in the new territories but also in Malaya itself, in order that there could be a harmonious whole. So we all anticipated some teething problems. But what we did not anticipate was the campaign that was mounted, particularly in Singapore and Sabah, by a small but influential group of secondary leaders in the Alliance, to assert their pattern of segregated communal parties throughout the new states, in order to ensure that whoever has the support of the majority of the Malays in Malaya automatically has supremacy, not only in the Central Government of Malaysia, but in all the constituent states, including the three new ones. This campaign has altered and accelerated the re-alignment of political forces within Malaysia. . .

"In Singapore the campaign to get all Malays segregated into one party has had grievous results. The only consolation is that it has not succeeded in breaking multiracial politics and solidarity in one political party, and is unlikely ever to succeed. But the repercussions throughout the other states of Malaysia have been so severe as to cause a fundamental re-thinking of the position of all political parties and groups. All groups have now to make up their minds, now that Malaysia is formed, whether they want a Malaysian nation or a communally segregated nation dominated by one of the constituent parts. . ."

II

In their memorandum dealing with the causes of the 1964 Singapore riots, submitted in March 1965 to the Commission of Inquiry, the Singapore Government explained the background which made it possible "for irresponsible political elements to manipulate the explosive forces of communalism". The Government said that the potential for racial tension and conflict had always been present in a multiracial Singapore, but they had never come to the surface because, neither under British rule nor under the conditions of self-government (which lasted fom May 1959 to September 1963) did the major political parties and their leaders openly and deliberately exploit communal fears and prejudices. "There had been sharp and bitter political rivalries and indusirial conflicts, but these had never provoked racial animosities simply because political parties in Singapore had never made direct and inflammatory appeals to racial emotions."

The trend away from communal parties was amply demonstrated in the general elections of 1963, when none of the communal parties, including UMNO, were returned. The three traditionally Malay constituencies withdrew political support from UMNO in favour of the non-communal PAP. The Singapore Government argued that this was resented by UMNO leaders, and their speeches and statements "contributed in no small measure to the events of July and September". The Government submitted that "unlike in the past, influential political leaders and newspapers were allowed to carry on open and sustained communal and racial propaganda for many months... propagandists of aggressive communalism included people and newspapers closely associated with the Malaysian Government and the ruling party of Malaysia... local communists were using racialism as a cloak to enhance the influence of their party among Malays in Singapore. Statements by UMNO leaders, before, during and after the two riots show clearly that racialism was used as a weapon to beat the Singapore Government into submission.

"It may well be," continued the Singapore Government memorandum, "that in the present stage of our political history communally organized parties are unavoidable, and that political competition between them and non-communal parties are equally unavoidable. But if such competition is not to lead to acute race conflicts, there is a responsibility, particularly on the part of the communally organized parties, to avoid recourse to crude and dangerous types of communal propaganda in order to retain their hold over the racial group over which they claim monopoly. In so far as individuals of any race show enough political sophistication to support non-communal ideologies and movements in preference to communal policies, they are to that extent moving gradually towards a Malaysian outlook and loyalty. Many communal leaders claim that this is also their goal. Their justification for communally organized parties is that the politically unsophisticated are not yet ready to support non-communal parties. To the extent that such masses exist they will no doubt give their support to communally organized parties. But leaders of communally organized parties should show enough tolerance for an understanding of those who drift into non-communal movements, because such a drift strengthens rather than weakens the sense of Malaysian identity. To combat this drift by deliberately inflaming communal animosities is not only to invite race conflicts, but also to throw doubt on the professed claims of communal leaders that their ultimate goal is a Malaysian Malaysia."

The memorandum said that the defeat of UMNO in the Singapore elections came as a shock to UMNO leaders. It was attributed to Malay "traitors". Singapore UMNO held a meeting shortly after the elections and Jaafar Albar made a fiery speech against the Government and Lee Kuan Yew. Other speakers urged the meeting to march on Lee Kuan Yew's house. An effigy of Lee Kuan Yew was burnt... Tunku Abdul Rahman was present and advised the meeting to refrain from any stupid action. Except for occasional rumbles against the PAP there matters were allowed to rest until March 1964, when, for the first time, the PAP were accused of oppressing the Malays. The PAP had been in office for five years. This was the first communal charge made against them, and after three Malay constituencies had returned PAP Assemblymen. This could not have happened if the Malays were oppressed. The Singapore Government submitted that this myth of "oppression of the Malays" was deliberately built up and sustained with increasing ferocity as a political weapon against the PAP Government. "It was a clear warning to the PAP that certain UMNO leaders were quite prepared to counter the PAP'S ideological influence with the dangerous weapon of racialism."

The memorandum quoted extensively from editorials in the *Utusan Melayu* and other Malay papers, and from reports in these papers of inflammatory speeches by Jaafar Albar and other Malay extremists. *Utusan Melayu* in one instance reported an UMNO leader as saying that Lee Kuan Yew wished to damage something the Malays "love and cherish, for instance, their religion and their traditions, or to oppress the Malays as he pleases".

Jaafar Albar came down to Singapore again in July and made another fiery speech, during which he said there were reasons for keeping Lee Kuan Yew in prison. "Whether he will be kept inside or not, only time will tell." The assistant secretary of UMNO in *Utusan Melayu*, "revealed" that the PAP Government was trying to create an Israel state for the purpose of suppressing the Malays.

On 13 July, there were racial clashes in Malaya, in the Bukit Mertajam area. Two persons were killed and thirteen wounded. Prior to this there had been racial clashes in Labuan. The memorandum said: "A sustained campaign of nearly three months, spread all over Malaysia through a pan-Malaysian newspaper, in which Singapore Malays were depicted as being hunted down by a non-Malay, PAP Government in a predominantly Chinese city like Singapore, must have made an impact on the sensibilities of the various races, more so as this campaign was carried out by influential and responsible UMNO leaders and publicized through *Utusan Melayu*. However, the warning light from Bukit Mertajam was unfortunately ignored. On 15 July, *Utusan Melayu* came out with an editorial where mischievous falsehood was compounded with the warning that 'Malays will lose their patience'. The ｜PAP had planned to hold a meeting of Malay cultural and social bodies on 19 July. *Utusan Melayu* warned that if the Singapore Government persisted in 'its efforts to split the Malays and carry out discussions with individual organizations... then neither the Malays or Jaafar Albar should be blamed for the consequences'." In spite of this threat eighty-three Malay organizations attended the meeting. It lasted three hours and was carried out in an atmosphere of calm, free and frank discussion.

On 20 July, the day before the riots broke out, *Utusan Melayu* carried three news items. One reported that the Secretary-General of Singapore UMNO had asked the PAP Government to stop the plan to move the Malays in Singapore if the PAP did not want the Malays to make a "noise". Another item quoted a speech of an UMNO official who reminded members of the anti-Malay campaign being carried out by the PAP. The third item had the following headlines: "Challenge To All Malays—UMNO Youth. Lee Kuan Yew Comdemned. Teacher Forced Student To Smell Pork." The headlines suggested that there was some connection between a teacher forcing a student to smell pork and the condemnation of Lee Kuan Yew. Only those who took the trouble to read the news story in full would have discovered that the third headline referred to a story which had nothing to do with Lee and constituted the last paragraph of the lengthy news item. "This juxtaposition of headlines was mischievous as well as dangerous, in view of the fact that the following day was Prophet Mohammed's Birthday, a day of great religious significance to the Malays". The same news item also quoted an UMNO youth leader as saying "Lee Kuan Yew's moves to cause the races in Malaysia to fight one another... constitute a challenge to the Malays as a whole. It also constitutes a threat."

The Singapore Memorandum pointed out that all these news items came out on the eve of the Prophet Mohammed's birthday when it was known that thousands of Muslims were intending to stage a procession through the streets of Singapore. For three months certain Malay leaders and the *Utusan Melayu* had maintained an unceasing campaign depicting Singapore Malays as victims of a cruel racial persecution by a PAP Government. Nor was there a let-up of agitation at the ceremony at the City Hall from where the procession was to start. Speeches were supposed to have been religious. This was not so in the case of speeches made by some UMNO representatives. Dato Syed Esa Almanoer, secretary-general of Singapore UMNO, spoke about Muslims being friendly with non-Muslims "who are friendly with us... but in everything that we do there must be a limit and if it has come to that limit that such people who are non-Muslims, who have disturbed our religion and who have driven us from our homes then Islam says such people are cruel wrong-doers." After calling for understanding and patience in a multiracial society, the Dato went on: "Be it so, here again, patience and understanding cannot stand the limit when people have come out from within or without to disturb our castle, our place to live, and our religion. When it comes to such a climax it is the duty of all Muslims to sacrifice their lives and properties..." The Memorandum suggested

241

that, coming from a Malay leader, this was more like an invitation to trouble than a religious speech appropriate to the occasion.

Trouble began during the procession, when several Malay youths attacked a Chinese policeman on duty at a corner. The policeman was alleged to have pushed a Malay steward. This was the incident which led to the death of twenty-two people in riots which lasted eleven days.

In their Memorandum, the Singapore Government observed that, though security was not in the hands of the Singapore Government, Lee Kuan Yew had on several occasions asked the police whether, in view of the communal agitation that had been going on for months, anything was likely to happen on Prophet Mohammed's birthday The police said no.

Even while the riots were going on, *Merdeka*, the official organ of UMNO, was calling upon the PAP to change its leadership. This editorial, said the Singapore Government's memorandum, "betrayed itself by revealing what had always been at the back of the minds of those who had been carrying their virulent communal propaganda against the PAP Government". Extracts from the editorial were reproduced in *Utusan Melayu*. "The implications of the editorial are clear. The price of their stopping their campaign based on racialism was the replacement of the duly elected leaders of the PAP Government—and the Malaysian Government should if necessary act firmly in this regard."

Utusan Zaman, on 26 July, found it necessary to fall back on the *Indonesian Herald* for support. It reprinted a story headed "Lee Responsible For Riots". The report said that the riots were anti-Islam. Jaafar Albar in Kuala Lumpur, made a speech during which he said, "There is a devil in Singapore who sets the Malays and the Chinese against each other." Albar said, "Lee Kuan Yew hid himself during the riots in a steel trunk... after peace had been restored he came out, the cowardly leader." This, remarked the Memorandum, "is typical of Albar's reckless disregard for truth and of his habit of inventing any story to work up emotions". He ended his speech by saying: "Personally, I would prefer an Inquiry Commission to be set up" (the Tunku had opposed this) "to find out why the incidents occurred, so that the world may know that Lee Kuan Yew's hands are stained with blood." In their Memorandum, the Singapore Government produced signed affidavits by witnesses present during the procession to show that the disorders were deliberately provoked. The Memorandum summed up: "The riots were willed by irresponsible and reckless propaganda based on falsehoods and distortions of facts. Their purpose was principally to re-establish the political influence of UMNO among the Malays in Singapore. An even more important objective was to use the Malays in Singapore as pawns to consolidate Malay support for UMNO in Malaya. By placing the blame for the riots on the Singapore Government and depicting it as oppressing the Malays of Singapore, Malays outside Singapore could be terrified into rallying around UMNO for protection."

In an attempt to remind the extremists that there were limits even for politicians, Lee decided to sue Albar for libel. Before instructing his lawyers, the Prime Minister informed the Tunku of his intentions. Realizing the implications, the Tunku asked Lee to hold his hand while he approached Albar to seek an apology for Lee and an assurance that attacks upon him would stop. Lee waited for months. Then he saw the Tunku again. More time passed, and Albar's speeches, all fully reported in the Malay Press, became even more inflammatory. At the end of April, 1965, Lee decided to take action. Two writs were filed in the High Court. In the first suit Albar was alleged to have libelled in an open and undated letter to Dennis Bloodworth, Southeast Asia Correspondent of *The Observer*, on or about 7 August, 1964. In the second suit, against Syed Jaafar Albar, the *Utusan Melayu* and Inche Melan bin Abdullah, editor of *Utusan Melayu*, libellous statements were alleged to have been contained in *Utusan Melayu* on 25 March, and 27 March, 1964. According to the writ, the articles were headed: "Lee is Accused of Being an Enemy of Malaysia and an Agent of Indonesia" and "Albar Accuses Lee Kuan Yew of Being an Agent of the Communists". Albar refused to apologize and announced his intention of contesting. *Utusan Melayu* announced that UMNO branches were raising money from members and others for an Albar Defence Fund. Donations from time to time were listed in the Malay Press.

Lee decided to pursue the case after separation, and it was set down for hearing in Singapore in September 1967. Judgments in Singapore are valid in Kuala Lumpur and vice versa.

On 22 September, 1967, in the Singapore High Court, Lee Kuan Yew's Counsel read an agreed statement concerning Jaafar Albar's withdrawal and apology.

Counsel said that the first of the statements complained of was made in the course of a speech delivered by Tan Sri Syed Jaafar Albar at a public meeting in Kuala Lumpur on 23 March, 1964, and was in substance an allegation that Lee Kuan Yew was "an enemy of Malaysia and an Indonesian agent". The speech in which this comment was made was subsequently reported in *Utusan Melayu* on 24 March and 25 March, 1964.

The second of the statements complained of was made in the course of a speech delivered by Tan Sri Syed Jaafar Albar at a public meeting in Besut on 26 March, 1965, and contained an allegation that

243

Lee Kuan Yew was "an agent of the communists and the Jakarta regime who had the evil intention to destroy Malaysia and to pit the Malays and Chinese against each other". This statement was reported in *Utusan Melayu* on 25 March, 1965.

The third and most serious of the statements complained of was contained in the open letter written by Tan Sri Syed Jaafar Albar to Mr Dennis Bloodworth. This letter was written with a view to publication, and contained the following words:

"As you know the Malays are having a rough time in Singapore and are now being oppressed by the PAP. Lee Kuan Yew is continually challenging their national sentiment with provocative statements, yet in spite of all these it is not the Malays who started the riots. The riots were started by *agents provocateurs,* who may even be in the pay of Lee Kuan Yew. Lee's intention is to create disorders in Singapore at a time when the Malays are gathering to celebrate the Birthday of Prophet Mohammed, so as to give the impression to the world outside that the Malays are already influenced by Indonesia."

"All the defendants," said Counsel, "admit that there is no foundation for any of these disgraceful allegations and they are here today, by their respective Counsel, to apologize to Lee Kuan Yew for having made them, and unreservedly to withdraw all imputations upon him and thus upon the office which he holds. They have in addition agreed to indemnify Lee Kuan Yew fully in respect of the whole of his costs of these proceedings.

"*Utusan Melayu* have also undertaken to give the fullest publicity to this apology and withdrawal, by publishing in two separate issues of *Utusan Melayu,* circulating in all the areas in which that paper is normally available, in a prominent position on the front page of each issue, the whole of the text of this statement and of any statements made by Counsel for the defendants in Court this morning.

"As Lee Kuan Yew brought these proceedings for the sole purpose of clearing his name and establishing, as is now admitted, that there is not and never has been any truth in the allegations made against him, he is willing to accept the amends now offered by the defendants."

Counsel for Tan Sri Syed Jaafar Albar, and *Utusan Melayu* and Inche Melan, the editor of *Utusan Melayu,* associated themselves with these remarks.

Tan Sri Syed Jaafar Albar, *Utusan Melayu* and Inche Melan acknowledged that the allegations were unfounded, and they were unreservedly withdrawn. They also expressed their sincere regrets to Lee Kuan Yew for publishing the statements containing the allegations, and they apologized to him for the distress and embarrassment caused to him by such publication.

III

Early in March, Lee Kuan Yew accepted invitations from the two Governments to visit New Zealand and Australia. He extensively toured both countries, and spoke frankly about Malaysia. At Auckland University on 7 March, Lee discussed Southeast Asia in turmoil. It was, he said, a subject which was geographically still remote from New Zealand, but he reminded the students that, just as he was able to get to Auckland from Singapore in a flying time of less than twelve hours, so events in Southeast Asia would catch up with them in a much more significant way than events had done in the past hundred-odd years. Lee dealt with the past. And then peered into the future.

"What is to happen in 1975? How will it present Southeast Asia to the world? If you look back over the past thirty years, one thing everybody must agree—that the rate of change has gone at a speed which no one anticipated. And I think it is a fair assumption that this rate of change will certainly not slow down. I do not know exactly what the impact of China as a major industrial, later commercial, and a military power will be on the whole region. I do believe, however, that unless the countries in Southeast Asia learn quickly enough to act in their own collective interests, first as nations in themselves, and then in concert with each other, to prevent an erosion of their national interests in the next ten to twenty years, a very different picture will emerge.

"The most marked single distinction between Southeast Asia and the more established nations of Europe is not only that these nations are new in most cases, but that, worse, even where they are old and established nations with a history and background of their own, they tend to be inward-looking, and, for some reason, have not been able to act in concert with each other in their collective interest.

"It does seem, looking back now over the past eighteen years since India became independent, to be almost incredible that such a vast nation with such vast potentials should have allowed herself to think that the world would believe in world order, that the rule of law would prevail, that international rights would be respected, and that force, as a means of settlement of international disagreement and disputes, would never be resorted to. I think one of the most tragic personal events was when Mr Nehru faced the agony of disillusionment in his basic, fundamental belief. That, in fact, power politics in Asia is as old as the first tribes that emerged, and that, whether we like it or not, if we are to survive and maintain our separate identities, it is necessary that we should learn what is in the joint interest at any single time of a group of nations...

"Very few doubt that, whatever the miseries of South Vietnam, if the Americans had not intervened in 1954, if in fact the Geneva

Agreement of 1954 had been honoured solidly in the spirit and the letter, South Vietnam would have been reunified with North Vietnam and would now be under a national front government, or probably by now a completely communist government. And, strangely enough, even in that situation, you find Thailand quarrelling with its neighbour Cambodia, and Cambodia more frightened of Thailand and South Vietnam than of anything else. India is in deep conflict with Pakistan over Kashmir, the Ceylonese have not yet settled the problem of the Tamil non-citizens of Ceylon in the tea and rubber plantations—some three-quarters of a million of them—the Indonesians for some incredible reason find themselves completely in accord with China to crush Malaysia. The Philippines are in conflict with Malaysia through their claim to sovereignty over Sabah, based on the titular right of some ancient Sultan of Sulu. And you cannot find a nation, a set of nations, in a more vital region of the world, more in disarray... Southeast Asia is in discord...

"What is to happen, I think, depends very much, first, upon whether the leadership in these countries matures rapidly enough to identify these common interests and act in concert, and, secondly, upon the intentions and policies of the two big potential industrial powers in Asia: China and India. And the third, Japan. Now, for the first time, after an abstention of twenty years, the Japanese have, not without Western encouragement, probably from the Americans, made a bid to play a role again in Asian politics. They knew that they were in bad odour for a long while in South Asia, and they made no attempt at exercising the influence which a nation of their capacity, their industrial capacity, would normally do. We are now witnessing the beginnings of Japan's re-entry onto the world stage.

"In the midst of all this, if I were a New Zealander, I could adopt one of two attitudes. One, to watch it with dispassionate disinterest, and, as long as the Australians had not been overrun, life could go on just as usual. Or, second, to begin to identify where in this kaleidoscope of power conflicts New Zealand's ultimate interests lie. You are not yet put into the acute position of the Cambodians. But, nevertheless, when the Prime Minister of Australia said that he had taken certain decisions—military conscription amongst others, and the decision to send one regiment for active service in Sabah—he rounded off his remarks by saying that he had to live with the Indonesians as neighbours for two or three hundred years. Well, I was surprised, because I would have thought that the Indonesians might well endure for more than three hundred years.

"I do not intend to arrogate to myself what I think is New Zealand's interest in this matter. But I do suggest that, whatever the dilemma in wanting to be friends with a potentially powerful and intractable neighbour, it is in the interests of everyone in Southeast

246

Asia to see that Indonesia's attempt at resolving nationalist ambition and national frontiers by a combination of diplomatic and military pressure should not succeed. If it does, then forces will have been let loose which must ultimately end with great disaster for all those around the region.

"But I advance a further reason why I believe Malaysia's survival is also in the interests not only of Australia and New Zealand, because of communications and because of other reasons, and of having to defend themselves in depth, but also of countries like India, who may otherwise find themselves later in a more difficult position. The Indians face an even more acute dilemma. The whole object of confrontation, the first object of confrontation, is to remove a Western presence in the region. This is the first step. Before anything can be done, before one can readjust national boundaries at will and if not absorb one's neighbour, at least assert authority over its policies, the presence of Western powers must be removed, as represented by military bases—in the Philippines and in Malaysia. President Sukarno has clearly stated this. The Indians are committed to non-alignment, and in over seventeen years of neutralism they have committed themselves to a fixed posture against military, foreign, European bases on Asian or African territory... If these regions develop by themselves, make progress, strike roots, in two decades (by the time a nuclear stalemate is reached and wars on the Asian mainland may well no longer be resolved by nuclear deterrent but by foot-soldiers), the position by then may be already pre-empted, so far as they are concerned. Non-communist systems of government may have taken root in South Asia, found sustenance, and become self-generating.

"But if these countries are perpetually embroiled in internal conflict, and conflict with each other, and their energies are dissipated in futile strife, and the governments are unable to satisfy the material aspirations of the people they led to freedom, then revolutionary doctrines will still have their attractions for these people. And I think this is the most important single factor one must remember. Only history will prove whether the Americans are right in believing that China is an aggressive, expansionist power; or whether this is a very self-possessed, supremely confident nation, absolutely believing in the doctrines of revolution, selling ideas, equipping those who believe in their philosophy, in their ideology, to fight their own revolution.

"I believe that so long as this present leadership in China continues, they are sufficiently steeled in the processes of revolution to understand that if a Chinese army begins to liberate or to bring freedom or communism to any non-Chinese territory, then communism will be equated to Chinese imperialism. And that is a mistake that they will never commit. The real revolutionary force they pose to

South Asia is their fervent belief that revolutionary situations already exist in these territories because of unsatisfied aspirations of the people. And that all that is needed is the assistance given, both ideologically and otherwise, to revolutionary groups and movements within these territories. And therefore the Americans have found themselves in a dilemma in South Vietnam, not because Chinese soldiers are confronting South Vietnamese or American troops, but because Chinese example and sustenance have brought about a situation in which both North Vietnam and South Vietnamese trained revolutionary digits are able to bring the whole economic life of the country to a halt and leave the regime completely dependent on American sustenance. . .

"So, at the end of all this one is left with the abiding impression that if the nations and states that have been allowed to emerge in South and Southeast Asia are to find their own identities and survive, and then grow, these factors must operate: they, each and every one of them, recognize and act in terms of their collective interests as a people. They recognize their inter-group interest between nations in order that there shall be a balance maintained, as the European powers once maintained a balance. When the Russians got too powerful, the British and the French got together. When the Germans got too powerful, the French and the Russians and the British got together. And, in that way, whether for good or for evil, they were able to maintain their separate national identities.

"I do not say that this is necessarily a good thing. But, having emerged with definite boundaries of our own in Malaysia, we have an irresistible urge to see that those boundaries are not altered, that we are in fact masters of our own destiny within our boundaries and that we can, in concert with others in the region, see that there shall not be an imbalance of power in the region. I think this is important, that you must first have a people who want to save themselves. If you don't have that, then no amount of external help, either military or economic, can prevail. . ."

In Wellington, at Victoria University, on 11 March, Lee Kuan Yew dealt sweepingly with Southeast Asia, discussed how Malaysia fitted into the modern scene, and again spoke of the future. "Today, we face a world in which the ancient civilizations, the Chinese, the Indian, the Arabic, have been aroused and are wanting to reassert themselves on the world scene. Accompanying them are a vast majority of smaller groups of people, broadly grouped together as the Afro-Asian nations. India is in it, the Arabs, as represented by the UAR, Algeria, Morocco, Tunisia, Syria—so are the Chinese. But one thing still remains as it was—for how long, I do not know—the supremacy of the European peoples in the scientific techniques of conducting war and, more important, in the industrial capacity to sustain modern warfare.

"So it is unlikely, in my view, whatever one may believe of the wickedness of the communists and the Chinese communists, that they will seek war. They know that under the present circumstances it is not in their interests to seek war. But I think they also know that, given time in which to consolidate their gains, given time in which to consummate their system, perhaps in another twenty, thirty or more years, the odds will not be that unequal, and then brinkmanship from their point of view need not be a one-sided thing.

"What is the meaning of all this? The past twenty years, since 1945, have seen the early idealism of the rule of law, international morality, a counting of heads in the United Nations, a try to bring about majority rule of some sort in relations between nations, provided of course that in the things that really matter to the big powers, the veto can be exercised...

"From an Asian viewpoint, I see this as a period in which the European world begins to learn to readjust its attitudes to the non-European world... old civilizations, China, India, the Arab world and ultimately, how these old civilizations, non-European civilizations, together with the Europeans, decide to deal with the lesser groups of human societies scattered throughout the rest of the world.

"For twenty years we have played—or there has been either a pretence, if one is cynical, or a genuine attempt, if one is sincere—at bringing morality and civilized standards into international relations, without the over-riding force and sanction of ultimate authority. Deference has always been paid to majority opinion, the world view, the Afro-Asian view, the emergent nations, the under-developed nations. There are many of them. And playing within that limited cosmos, short of large-scale war, it was useful for the major contenders, who were world powers, to be able to present this facade—if one were cynical—or the solid mass support of the righteous indignation of right-thinking people—if one were sincere. But, nevertheless, because neither of the two contending military powers saw it in their interests to put their might to the test, for the minor skirmishes it was in their interest to try to line up the votes in the United Nations.

"I now say we are at the watershed of history because, I think, we are nearing the time when it is possible that the big powers will again begin to think in terms not of just counting heads, but of real ultimate capacity to survive conflict... The second half of the twentieth century will witness first, in my view, the reassertion of the ancient civilizations. And next, after that, assuming that the world still has not destroyed itself, it will witness how they collectively view the less sophisticated civilizations that exist...

"I have no doubts whatsoever that in the ancient civilizations, the Chinese, the Indian, the Arab people, not only with the cultural techniques with which to galvanize and mobilize human nature, but with a calculated sense of greatness, not only of their past but in their renaissance—in them is the first challenge to European domination and supremacy...

"The fact that the capacity for reassertion varied amongst these different groups was a matter which was glossed over in the initial stages. Now, perforce, it has become more prominent. And, because it has, schisms have developed on the broad anti-European front. And the events of the next, second half of this century depend upon whether the Europeans... intend to act collectively as one group of human beings against the rest, or whether their ideological and other compelling interests will blur and confuse and make more complex the lines of conflict...

"And that brings us to the problem of Southeast Asia. It is a confused and complicated situation in which the various parts, some of them old ancient civilizations like Cambodia, or even the Vietnamese, or the Thais, or new ones like Malaysia, are unable as yet to identify their collective group interests, and to see how to gather strength by getting together with those who share, if not common interests, at least common fears. And in this very confused milieu you have the fascinating spectacle of the Indonesians, determined that they shall become a great power...

"Speaking as one who comes from a country which is destined for a very long while to be a very small digit in Southeast Asia, however fast and hard we multiply, I am resigned to accept the arbiter of the power-interests. If in fact Malaysia, if in fact Singapore, and its important geographic position are of no value to the West, or if in fact the Western presence is not desired by the West in Southeast Asia, then nobody will be interested really to expend all this money, to expend all this effort, divert their resources, in defence of freedom. But it so happens that these things do matter, that whether we perish or we survive does affect the course of events for the big powers. And our capacity to survive is related to our capacity to discern where big power interests must collide, and how in this conflict of power-interests we are to find a coincidence of interests for ourselves.

"If today I believed that a Western presence in Southeast Asia were inimical to the advancement of eleven million people in Malaysia, then we would advance a different set of reasons why in fact all this is wrong...

"The tragedy of Southeast Asia is not only the tragedy of its lack of mature appreciation of Southeast Asia's own national interests, but lack of wisdom and mature policies of those who had the physical wherewithal which gave them the right to world leadership. The only reason why Malaysia emerged from very near chaos, from the early days of the 1950s to the peace and tranquillity and progress of the 1960s before confrontation, was because, first, the British had the wisdom to recognize what was irresistible, and therefore not to resist it; and secondly, having decided that freedom movements were irresistible, to try, in so far as they could, to make sure, if they could not get anti-communist groups to emerge as the dominant force in a territory they had to abandon, at least that the leadership was non-communist...

"Behind all this play of the small powers seeking shelter within the conflicts of big powers, behind the cynicism of the approach, there is a genuine and sincere identity of interests of groups of people in similarly placed circumstances. Slowly I would want to convince people in Malaysia that, whatever the past, the British are not rapacious colonialists now, whatever their economic and other interests are in Malaysia; that the Australians and the New Zealanders, however unaltruistic their motivations may be in coming to our defence, nevertheless make a real and positive contribution to our survival. And when we get our own people understanding that, and a large mass of other similarly small people in Afro-Asia appreciating, accepting and sympathizing with that attitude, then the ground can be more firmly held, and the flexibility of the military response can be much more subtle and much more immediate. This is a continuing battle which I hope will not be fought in vain."

At Canterbury University on 15 March, Lee Kuan Yew described Malaysia as an accident of history, of the activities of Dutch, Portuguese and British navigators in the eighteenth centuries, and the merchants who followed them, and the subsequent colonial administrators who followed in the wake of the merchants to establish the political structure under which the exploitation of the natural resources, which the metropolitan powers lacked, could be carried out with the least interference possible from the local inhabitants.

"In this process a considerable distortion of what would otherwise have happened was inevitable. Unlike the Dutch in what was then known as the Netherlands East Indies, the British found it necessary in order to exploit the mineral, agricultural resources, tin and rubber, to bring in considerable quantities of disciplined and cheap labour, principally from South China and South India. The indigenous people who were there, principally Malays and a few of the original tribes in Malaya, the Semang and Sakais, Negritos and others, never took to the regimentation of the plantations and of the tin mines. The idea of a money economy where a man applied himself in dull, repetitious jobs, found no attraction for them. Fishing, farming was their way of life, and therefore considerable numbers of Chinese and Indians came in, first as workers and plantation tappers, later to become the shopkeepers, the bankers, the entrepreneurs, the technicians and the professional men, and now also the politicians in the area.

"So you have in Malaysia a curious imbalance in economic and social development between the original communities and the people of immigrant stock...Power was never in the hands of the immigrant community, and when it was handed over from the colonial raj, it was handed back, by and large, to the people of indigenous stock.

"This presents Malaysia with a fascinating problem of how it is to adjust itself and seek accommodation and balance between the indigenous and the immigrant peoples: the indigenous being left in control of the apparatus of the state—the police, the army, the administration—the immigrants in charge of industry, finance and generally working the modern mechanics of a civilized community—the sewers, the water mains, the electricity and all the other mundane things in life, which are very important if we are to continue to enjoy one of the highest standards of living in South Asia.

"Malaysia is many things to many people. The British would like to present what they have done in the region as a pattern of orderly decolonization, an example of how power is handed back to once subject peoples. To the Indonesians it is a neo-colonialist plot designed to threaten the progressive forces which Indonesia represents, the new emerging forces which will spread and conquer the world. To Malaysians, I would like to believe without exception, it represents the only coherent, rational way in which we can preserve the majority of the benefits we got out of being one unit under the British colonial administration, and avoid the grievous perils which surround us...

"New Zealand and Australia will, more and more, have to take more active and positive interest in this region. I do not think it is possible to have Malaysia stand on her own feet and withstand a big and aggressive neighbour without some Commonwealth assistance. But the problem which New Zealanders and Australians face is one of really making sure that they have not jeopardized their own interests in choosing to assist Malaysia as against Indonesia...

"In the long run, whatever the temporary respite may be, we shall have to accept the fact that all political groups in Indonesia, whether they are members of the Indonesian Communist Party, or followers of the Murba or the PNI or PSI, believe in Greater Indonesia, or Indonesia Raya. If you go back to the records which were kept before they proclaimed their independence on 17 August, 1945, when the Japanese were still in occupation of Indonesia, you will see that they seriously contemplated proclaiming independence over the whole of the archipelago.

"In the words of the President, if I may paraphrase him: 'God has ordained that this group of islands stretching between the Indian Ocean and the Pacific, straddling the Northern and the Southern hemispheres, should be one nation.' And Malaya, as it then was, should be part of this nation. For then, whoever controls Malaya and Sumatra would control the Straits of Malacca, the Sunda Straits, and would be at the crossroads of the world. This is the kind of geo-politics which we must expect from the Indonesians until such time as they understand that their smaller neighbours are not necessarily weaker neighbours...

"I am sufficiently sanguine about the future because if you look at the history of the region you will find that these were not cultures which created societies capable of intense discipline, concentrated effort, over sustained periods. Climate, the effects of relatively abundant society, and the tropical conditions produced a people largely extrovert, easy-going and leisurely... And I think that is a source of considerable comfort to us, because we are much smaller than they are."

IV

By the second week of March, Lee Kuan Yew was in Australia. At the National Press Club on 16 March he spoke of how smaller nations, such as Malaysia with an eleven-million population, and Australia, could find their separate identification and fulfilment without being absorbed or otherwise becoming satellites or vassals of bigger powers.

"This is a subject which must interest you as it passionately concerns us. For, in the long run, as we face the realities of big-power conflicts—not just ideological conflicts, but big-power conflicts, sometimes ideological and at other times not so ideological—where do the smaller nations find their own fulfilment?"

Lee said that, at Bandung in 1955, the solidarity of Afro-Asia, of India and the smaller countries of Asia with China and the states as yet to emerge in Africa, was demonstrated in resounding terms. Panchasila was Afro-Asia's new code of international ethics. Afro-Asians affirmed their belief in peace, non-aggression and the solution of all problems on the basis of mutual respect and esteem. "All these hopes of a brave new world based on justice and moral right have somewhat faded away...

"It is clear now that Afro-Asian solidarity was founded on a common antipathy to European domination. They had also proclaimed their solidarity for the virtues of peace, non-aggression, non-interference, mutual respect, regardless of the size and power of all the newly independent nations which have and are yet to emerge from European colonial rule. But in less than a decade, many conflicts, some old, some new, between the different peoples of Afro-Asia led to disillusionment, as Asians fought Asians over the Himalayas, and Africans fought Africans in Algeria and Morocco, Somalia and Kenya and Ethiopia.

"And so a new mood is emerging, not only in Afro-Asia, but also amongst the European powers. All are conscious that the great divisions in the world need no longer be between Europeans and the rest. That would have been too simple, too dangerous for the Europeans and too easy for the Afro-Asians. Nor is the division simply between communist and non-communist powers. Instead, the picture is a complicated one, for in any given instance there is an overlap of many divisions of interest. There is the division between the communist revisionists, who want peaceful competition with the non-communist world, and the communist revolutionaries, who despise non-communists. Then we are told by the leaders of Indonesia that the great division is between the new emerging forces and the old dying forces. And, from the way Indonesians treat their neighbours, not only Malaysia, but also young and bustling Australia is in danger of being classified under old dying forces.

"One of the divisions which interest Australia and Malaysia is that between big powers and small powers. Malaysia shares a common problem with Australia. Both have small populations. How are they to survive, seek their legitimate national aspirations without being destroyed or made vassals or satellites of big powers? Now whatever the reasons for great power, besides a large population and abundant natural resources, there would appear to be a fairly limited number of national groups in this world capable of achieving great power—the Americans, the Russians, the Europeans, the Japanese, and amongst those likely to emerge from the under-developed countries of Afro-Asia and join the ranks of the great are the Chinese, the Indians and the Arabs. These are peoples with an ancient past. Their past history indicates that they were, once upon a time, capable of intense endeavour and sustained effort to give them a pre-eminent position amongst nations. Given the right leadership and the opportunity, they will undoubtedly again vie for a leading place.

"As nations, Australia and Malaysia, however well off they may be in natural resources, and however advanced their citizens may be as human beings, are unlikely in the immediate future to achieve great power status on their own. So they must seek some shelter with one or more of these big powers. It is against this sombre background of big power politics that Australia's relations with Malaysia can be seen, I hope, in some fair perspective. . .

"Malaysians can understand Australia's approach to the problems of Indonesia. Like Australia, we are aware of Indonesia's size, her potential for advancement of her own people if her leaders choose to bend their energies on constructive and economic progress, and her equally great potential for mischief if her leaders, for a diversity of reasons, prefer external diversion to internal construction. And worse, if one or more of the big powers exploit Indonesian restlessness for other revolutionary ends the situation can become complicated and dangerous. . .

"Malaysia is fortunate that both Australia and New Zealand, though not big powers, are sufficiently alive to their interests in peace and stability in Southeast Asia to have committed themselves to helping to uphold Malaysia's integrity. We know that military and economic aid cannot guarantee us our ultimate success, but at least it will buy us time.

"We can use that time which is being bought, to greater advantage than it has been used in South Vietnam. And I hope historians will never say that, in spite of the bitter lessons of South Vietnam, Malaysia and her allies never learned to do better. There, eleven precious years bought at enormous expense in economic and human resources, were frittered away. This experience showed that, however massive the military cadre, however enormous the economic assistance, if the leaders of the people who are to be saved do not set out to secure their own salvation, the end result is still perdition, both for the helper and the helped. If the exercise this time in Malaysia is to be successful, Malaysia's leaders must use the time they are given to consolidate the economy. And a political system sufficiently sensitive to popular feelings and aspirations must be evolved to make resistance to subversion and infiltration an enduring one. Only then is external military and economic aid worthwhile. For then it can be reduced and eventually be dispensed with. Afro-Asian countries are only worth the saving it they can save themselves. . ."

Five days later, on 24 March, Lee Kuan Yew was the guest of honour on the Australian Broadcasting Commission's network. He recalled that some twenty years before, the Japanese armies had overrun Singapore and some 90,000 Commonwealth troops, British, Indians and Australians, had tramped into captivity. "I saw them tramping along the road in front of my house in Singapore for three solid days —an endless stream of bewildered men who did not know what had happened, why it had happened, or what they were doing there in Singapore in any case. I was bewildered too. We were all unprepared for this. We thought Singapore was an impregnable fortress and the British Navy was supreme. No one expected the Japanese to march down Southeast Asia and capture us. Nobody had warned us of this. It was a shock. For myself, as perhaps for those Australians who marched wearily in front of my house to three and a half years of near hell on earth, that was an experience not easily forgotten.

"Looking back over these twenty years, reading the memoirs of the generals on both sides who fought that battle, I thought that if only we had known what was coming and had been prepared for it, we should all have given a much better account of ourselves and avoided the miseries of defeat. We must never let this sort of thing happen again, either to you or to me. We must know what are the

255

perils around us, where our troubles are likely to come from, and how we can prevent unpleasant things happening to us. . ."

At the Institute of International Affairs in Melbourne, on 24 March, Lee Kuan Yew said that international affairs was a subject "as old as man". Motivations for human behaviour had always existed, and whether these motivations were greed, envy, ambition, greatness, generosity, charity, inevitably "they end in a conflict of power positions". How the conflict was resolved depended upon the accident of the individuals in charge of the tribes or nations at that given time. What had changed was the facility with which men could now communicate, and transport not only ideas but also man himself and his weapons. Therefore, into a very old situation had been introduced a very alarming possibility, which put the whole problem of international relations in a very different perspective. . . Conflict of two absolute powers meant the destruction of all.

"How does this affect us in the Pacific region? The same human ingenuity that discovered these modern means of communication, which make it possible for us to communicate with each other so rapidly, to transport human beings from one place to another rapidly, and to deliver weapons of destruction instantaneously should enable us to find, if not a final solution, at least some way to stave off the inevitability of complete destruction, if we pursue power, and play with the mechanics of power, in the way nations of Europe and of Asia have been accustomed to do for so many thousands of years.

"More immediately of concern to us is the question of the ideological conflict between East and West, between communism and anti-communism, with a large mass of Afro-Asia still non-communist, in the sense that they do not want communism but are not convinced that the answer to communism is anti-communism and Western capitalism. In this situation, how are we to find some accommodation to prevent calamity? If not to find a solution, at least to be able to win some time in which accommodation is possible while some final solution is being worked out?. . ."

Tracing developments in Afro-Asia since the end of the Second World War, Lee said: "The most spectacular things about 1945 to 1965 in Southeast Asia—the age of Nehru, I would call it, because he set the pace, the idealism, the belief in great principles—was the absence of cynicism, to a point where vast numbers of otherwise cynical people were led to believe that, because Asians have gone through a common tribulation and common humiliation at the hands of the European powers, therefore thereafter they would always be brothers in a common struggle. Which was not true, unfortunately. . . none of these powers were able to exercise an influence outside their own region in aid of their own interests. I think this is the most spectacular single fact of Asia in the two decades since the Second World War. . .

"I think the first admission we have to make is that not only is it possible, but it was inevitable, that the idealism which generated so much hope of a brave, new Afro-Asian world had to go through this phase of disillusion before man discovered that Afro-Asians were men, human beings just like the others, as much prisoners of their past as apostles of their future.

"I have said that there is nothing new in human relationships, in human situations, in the permutations and combinations of any given situation between two groups of men, either as tribes or as nation states, but that the big difference is that the capacity for quick transportation of ideas, men and weapons has created a new problem. And Malaysia is, in a way, a very special manifestation of this problem. . .

"The Malays and the Indonesians, under the beneficence of tropical sunshine and tropical rainfall, are, by and large, a leisurely people, not intense, with no tendency to gastric ulcers, no desire to accumulate fortunes, leading lives as satisfying as any other human beings anywhere in the world. They would be quite happy, but for the impact of Western civilization which brought Chinese and Indians into their milieu. The Chinese, products of floods, pestilence, famine, an intense people, not better or worse, but different because of that experience—a different climate, a different situation, produced a different type of culture. They went south to make fortunes. That is why they left their homes. . . Similarly, to a lesser extent, the Indians: they were also migrants seeking a better life, many with the intention at the time they left their country to return when they had made good. But, for various reasons, they lived on in the leisurely climate of Malaysia because life was good.

"What is it that keeps Malaysia together? For over a hundred-odd years, that same British raj governed the whole of these territories. They divided it into little protectorates and had little potentates whom they installed and regularly removed whenever it was inconvenient, and installed another cousin or uncle, or aunt twice removed. And the business of extracting wealth from these regions continued with unremitting efficiency until the Japanese came in 1942 and the whole system collapsed.

"And when they returned in 1945 I think it redounds to the credit of the British that they were able to see that this was the end of Empire. . . there was a conscious effort to try and go along with history. They knew that to re-establish the old dominance was no longer possible.

"They tried in many diverse ways to keep a foothold in the region, and one of the biggest mistakes they made, not with malice, was to divide Singapore from Malaya and allow the development to go on in the two territories, one more or less Malay, in which Malays were

257

predominant, and the other with Chinese predominance. For eighteen years it went on—1945 to 1963—until the two territories were brought together again. And the problems we are facing today are problems which need never have arisen if that artificial political division had never taken place..."

V

There was no doubt that Lee Kuan Yew left a very favourable impression on thinking people in New Zealand and Australia. The *Sydney Morning Herald* described Lee as "a man who can fairly be ranked as the most able political figure in all Southeast Asia, shrewd, tough-minded and supremely a realist". Nobody was better fitted to put Malaysia's case.

This was not the belief of the ultras in Malaysia. Exchanges between them and the PAP became more bitter, more personal. Inche Mohammed Ghazali, Political Liaison Secretary at the Singapore Ministry of Culture, issued a statement complaining that "certain leaders" had become "so hysterical" about the PAP's influence outside Singapore that they were saying that the PAP is now "a bigger threat to Malaysia than even Indonesia".

Inche Ghazali said that hardly a day passed without some Alliance leader "declaring that the PAP is out to destroy the Malay race", that it was spreading teachings "contrary to Islam". Tuan Haji Othman, an important UMNO official, warned in a speech: "If Lee Kuan Yew maintained his present attitude it would spell death for him, and his own political aspirations." According to *Utusan Melayu,* Jaafar Albar urged the Malaysian Government "to take firm and practical action against those people who, under the mask of non-communism, were really the most dangerous enemies of Malaysia". "*Utusan Melayu,*" said Inche Ghazali, "made it clear that this reference was to Lee Kuan Yew and other Singapore Government leaders."

Lee Kuan Yew plunged straight into the domestic political scene upon his return. Opening the sixth annual National Language Month on 23 April, he said, "Although we have escaped from the excesses of language fanatics in getting Malay accepted as our national language six years ago, and before the establishment of Malaysia, we must be careful that we are practical and realistic in the way it is gradually implemented. It is not easy for the present generation of adults to change their habits of thinking in the language with which they grew up either at home or in school. For the non-Malay adult, when he speaks Malay, however diligent he may be, is consciously translating from the language of his youth to the language that he learned in adult life. This always is an effort. The future lies with our children now in school. They can grow up with this common language as part of their mental equipment. . .

"If Malaysia is to progress, a common language is necessary. But equally necessary for our progress, is the acquisition of knowledge to be able to build a modern industrial society. . . We will only acquire these skills and techniques if we keep on seeking a knowledge of the languages that will open up this scientific and technological data in the applied sciences, particularly the languages of the nations which have established themselves as modern industrial societies. . . "

Relations between Kuala Lumpur and Singapore were rapidly getting worse. Lee Kuan Yew felt that the time had come for some direct speech. In Hokkien, on 25 April, he said that the crux of the problem was not the difference between the Central Government and the Singapore State Government, nor the administrative difficulties between the two governments, but lay in fundamentals. These were "the relations between the races in Malaysia, and the long-term objective of a Malaysian Malaysia".

Lee said that certain political leaders in Malaya still believed that in Malaysia one race could dominate the other politically, and that they could continue to be in power by gaining the support of this particular race.

He said: "This is absolutely wrong, because the political situation in Malaya before the formation of Malaysia was entirely different from the present situation in Malaysia. The sooner these leaders realize there must be accommodation and adjustments between the major races, the better it will be for Malaysia. . . "

Lee understood the gravity of the situation but he said it was wrong to shout, at this stage, for Singapore's secession. "We must be patient and allow Malaysia more time to prove its worth. From my observations I see that some of the people in Malaya are beginning to see the light in Malaysia. They are beginning to realize that the peaceful and democratic way of accommodation and adjustment towards a Malaysian Malaysia is the way out. Therefore we must be patient. We must be prepared to wait fifteen or twenty years. . . "

Lee sounded another grave warning on May Day. "The problems of Malaysia," he reiterated, "cannot be resolved by force; they must be resolved peacefully, democratically, a process of adjustment and accommodation: the average which will give the maximum benefit to the maximum number of people regardless of race, religion and language. . . try and enforce the advantage of one group, whether the group is based on ideology or on race or on language, then I say the whole basis of the prosperity and well-being of Malaysia will collapse. . ."

VI

In spite of the internal tension, Lee Kuan Yew went to Bombay to open the Asian Socialist Leaders' Conference organized by the International Union of Socialist Youth. He said on 6 May: "There was a time, not so long ago, at the end of the Second World War, when people expected the whole world to go socialist. Throughout the world there seemed to be an inevitable trend towards a more egalitarian society. When a socialist government in Britain, shortly after it assumed office in 1945, decided to liquidate its empire in Asia, there were hopes that the future would mean a more just and equal world where governments of socialist leaning, varying from progressive liberal, social democrat, or democratic socialist to communist, would soon take charge of the destinies of mankind in nearly all countries of the world.

"Today, two decades later, we have a much more sober realization, that automatic progress towards an equal and just world is not something that can be taken for granted... The world consists of more classifications and permutations than just the capitalists, the communists and the socialists. Throughout the world, national survival, the advancement of purely sectional interests within a nation, have confused the course of development.

"It is not only in emergent nations that nationalism has found its strong expression. Even between the industrially advanced nations of Europe and America, mostly all capitalist in their economic system, there is a clear divergence of interests and of views. And, at the other end of the spectrum, we have discovered that even with communism, whatever its ideological claims to international brotherhood, the working class is riven by even deeper schisms, as national communist groups attack each other in ferocious dialectical ritual to justify the pursuit of their own separate national interests.

"But, however disappointing it has been to those who seek the ideal world where all men are brothers, these developments have given corroboration to the major premises of democratic socialism. For decades the communists have maligned the democratic socialists, or social democrats, as betrayers of their working classes because of their petty bourgeois shortcoming...

"It is twelve years since the first Asian Socialist Conference in Rangoon in 1953. They have been twelve years of many disappointments and few successes for democratic socialists. Many of the leaders who forgathered on that occasion are now no longer able to lead their countries towards socialism. Quite a number are in gaols, put there by governments that assert themselves as equally, if not more, socialist and nationalist than the people they have displaced. Why have these things happened? Why have the hopes of inevitable

260

progress towards a socialist world so lamentably failed to materialize in Asia?

"How is it that some manifestly non-socialist governments in the region have made more economic progress and increased their gross national product more rapidly than countries in Southeast Asia with socialist governments?

"True, the capitalists, and in particular the Americans, have poured in aid and investments, and perhaps a part of this massive economic transfusion has to some degree benefited the workers. And for a long while Americans preferred to support only anti-communist governments. Indeed, they used to find it difficult to distinguish between socialists and communists. Why, then, did not the advanced countries in Europe with socialist governments give corresponding assistance to their counterparts in Asia? We knew that the communists would never help the democratic socialists. But what of the democratic socialist governments in Europe? Perhaps they did not have the abundance of resources to help the enormous populations of South Asia to any appreciable degree. But the fault really was nearer home. The democratic socialists who were in charge of some of these governments in South Asia lacked the organizational drive, managerial and technical expertise in administration and management, and the technological and industrial skills to be able to realize their plans for economic transformation. The lack of these instruments of policy implementation could have been made up by borrowing expertise from abroad. This could have helped these countries tide over the period of transition when local men were under training and acquiring new skills. . . But the most grievous indictment against the democratic socialists for their failure to put up a better showing is that, in preaching individual human liberties and human freedoms, they forgot to insist, as the communists and the capitalists did, on the individual human duty to work hard and give his utmost. For in the last analysis the better life is produced only by continued and sustained intense effort.

"As democratic socialists we should uphold all individual human liberties. Perhaps we have underestimated the human problems in finding the techniques of organizing men for production, and in persuading men to accept the disciplines of modern agricultural and industrial production if we are to fulfil their dreams. If we want to mobilize human resources, to pitchfork our countries and backward economies into an industrial and technological era, then no person has the right to slack. The capitalists make people work through monetary incentives which we call sweated and exploited labour. The communists do it by regimentation and exhortation and a systematically induced state of semi-hysteria for work, using both the stick and the carrot. The democratic socialist is less ruthless and consequently less efficient, torn between his loathing for regimentation and mass coercion and his inhibition in making more effective use of the carrot by his desire to distribute the rewards more fairly and equally too soon.

"I am an unrepentant socialist. But in my own state I have to concede that, because it takes a long time to inculcate the high values of public duty and sense of service to the community, performance has been best only when workers were offered high incentives for high performance. . .

"We have had to recognize these faults. It has not changed our belief in the basic tenet that no man should exploit his fellow-man. We believe it is immoral that the ownership of property should allow some to exploit others. But in order to get economic growth we have had to base our policies on the principle 'From each his economic best, to each his economic worth'. The ultimate ideal 'From each his best, to each his need' can only be relevant after we have moved away from ignorance, illiteracy, poverty, and economic backwardness.

"Reflecting on the past decade of few achievements and many omissions is a sobering exercise. But the fact that we are today gathered in Bombay to discuss these problems is in a small way a tribute to the tenacity of the democratic socialist. If we re-evaluate and reformulate our thinking and policy to make a more effective contribution in the next decade we can still make a contribution to Asia's and Africa's advance. The biggest contribution we can make, of course, is to the peace, progress and prosperity of the people of Afro-Asia. Democratic socialists in the advanced countries are fortunate in that the relatively comfortable state of their societies makes it possible for them to maintain their tenets of a tolerant but progressive society against more totalitarian creeds.

"For us in Asia, and even more so in Africa, the acute despair and, worse, the obscene and often also the ostentatious display of individual wealth in the midst of grinding poverty are a constant incitement to sudden and violent revolution. Those who want a social revolution without destroying individual human values find this setting makes the task an intensely difficult and delicate effort. And if we approach Asian problems of poverty and under-development through the rosy spectacles of the western European socialists we are sure to fail.

"It is no use talking of the ideals of democratic socialism when the situation has denegerated into naked brutality between competing power blocs as in South Vietnam, with both sides engaged in brutality and cruelty all in the name of the highest ideals for the freedom and liberty of man. Even here in Bombay the shadow of what is going on in that corner of South Asia casts a gloom over all of us. We know that what is happening is wrong. We know that if the communists are able to advance their frontiers to envelop South Vietnam it will be only a matter of time before the same process of emasculation by military and political techniques will overtake the neighbouring countries.

"On the other hand, we know that any extension or escalation of the war is dangerous and contrary to the ideals we claim to espouse. We have been unable to advance a more constructive alternative than to talk of unconditional negotiations, hoping that negotiations could lead to a neutral South Vietnam. However, we know that this is hardly likely to be the end result of negotiations. For what is required to keep the rest of Southeast Asia free from going through similar tribulations is not just a neutral South Vietnam, but also a non-communist South Vietnam.

"As Asians we must uphold the right of the Vietnamese people to self-determination and to be free from any hint of European domination. As democratic socialists we must insist that the South Vietnamese have the right not to be pressured through armed might and organized terror and finally overwhelmed by communism. So we must seek a formula that will first make it possible for the South Vietnamese to recover their freedom of choice, which at the moment is limited to either communist capture cr perpetual American military operations. Then, after the South Vietnamese are able to exercise their collective will without duress from either side, ultimately, be it after five, ten or twenty years, they must have the right to decide their final destiny, whether or not they choose to be re-united with North Vietnam, and, if so, on what terms. . . "

Upon his return to Singapore, Lee on 22 May told reporters that he thought it unlikely that a common form of socialism would emerge in Southeast Asia because similar conditions did not exist. He said: "One of the most significant aspects of Asian socialism has been its preoccupation with the theory of democratic, parliamentary practice and, at the same time, with the welfare state, with the result that the mechanics of power and the problems of development in a very poor region were overlooked, because democratic socialism, basing its emphasis on human values, and democratic socialist leaders wanting to give immediate results in spreading the benefits of national production to workers too quickly, were unable to maintain the momentum required for progress. The nett result is the curious phenomena of manifestly unsocialist countries with unsocialist regimes, as a result of intense American aid, making more visible progress, particularly in the towns, than countries which have had democratic socialist governments for long periods. I think we have got to have a more realistic approach to these things; and unless we do that, I do not think we have got a future."

VII

Relations between Singapore and Kuala Lumpur were now near breaking point. In this atmosphere of tension, on 27 May, Lee Kuan Yew spoke in the Malaysian Parliament on the motion of thanks to the Yang di-Pertuan Agong for his speech from the throne.

"With the formal opening of this second session of the Parliament of Malaysia we open a new chapter in the drama of Malaysia. Parliamentary democracy makes the joining of political issues in the open debate often a dramatic and vivid way in which alternative programmes, policies, can be presented to the people, and it is therefore with special significance, after what has happened in the past ten months, that we listened to the Address of His Majesty the Yang di-Pertuan Agong. The issues are being clarified, they are being joined.

"It was timely for us—a brief, succinct, if somewhat equivocal address in parts, and in particular I would like, if I may, to read to the House first the last paragraph of this Address:

" 'We,' (said His Majesty), 'are now facing threats to our security from outside,' (and he defined it, i.e. from Indonesia). 'In addition we are also facing threats from within the country.' (There is no definition of where this threat from within the country is coming.) 'But' (he went on) 'both these threats are designed to create trouble. If those concerned achieve their objective, it will mean chaos for us and an end to democracy.'

"And it ends up with an incantation to Almighty God to give us 'strength and determination to face these threats'. "

Lee Kuan Yew submitted that no useful purpose was served by pretending "that we do not know what was intended".

While His Majesty was making his speech, said Lee, *Utusan Melayu* was printing a story headlined: "Lee is an Enemy of the People of Malaysia". Dato Harun, Mentri Besar of Selangor, was reported by *Utusan Melayu* to have described Lee Kuan Yew as an enemy of the people of Malaysia, who was endangering the peace of Malaysia. *Berita Harian* the same day reported the Mentri Besar of Perak as calling upon the Malays to note that "Lee Kuan Yew is not only our enemy, but he is also the most dangerous threat to the security of Malaysia".

Lee Kuan Yew reminded the House that as a Member of Parliament he had sworn on oath to "bear true faith and allegiance to Malaysia and to preserve, protect and defend its Constitution. What have I or my colleagues done to deserve this denunciation as an 'enemy of the people'?"

Lee said he still supported the Constitution. He said that what he feared was the hint in His Majesty's speech that there would be an end to democracy, that the Constitution might be suspended or brushed aside.

Lee's argument was that "every act carries a penalty and I say the penalty for not playing in accordance with the rules so far as Malaysia is concerned is disintegration. . . either a Malaysian Malaysia or nothing. . . we cannot agree to anything but a Malaysian Malaysia . . . we are prepared to play in accordance with the rules for five, ten or fifteen years, but ideas we represent must come true. . . "

Lee added: "We will honour the Constitution because we believe it can provide a solution to the problems of a multiracial society in Malaysia. . . "

At the end of his long speech Lee Kuan Yew moved an amendment to the motion of thanks, the following words to be added: 'but regrets the Address by His Majesty the Yang di-Pertuan Agong did not reassure the nation that Malaysia will continue to progress in accord with its democratic Constitution towards a Malaysian Malaysia, but that on the contrary the Address has added to the doubts over the intentions of the present Alliance Government and over the measures it will adopt when faced with a loss of majority popular support.'

"I would like to make this one observation in moving this amendment. Loyalty to Malaysia is not equal to and not the same as loyalty to the Alliance party or the Alliance Government. I am under no constitutional obligation to be loyal to the Alliance party or the Government, but I must be loyal to the Constitution of Malaysia and I must obey the dicta of a democratically elected government of Malaysia: I accept it. But don't confuse these two things, as I fear His Majesty was somewhat confused by this: that we are facing threats from within the country. Threats to the security of the nation, an end to democracy, because unions want to strike for better conditions, wages; because we speak our minds and propound a better policy for Malaysia; because we exercise our prerogative in accordance with this Constitution to pose to Malaysia an alternative way in which it can become a prosperous, happy nation, give honest, effective government and dynamic ideas to propel it? It is because we know that time is on our side, Mr Speaker, that we will always be loyal, always act in accordance with the rules of this Constitution and with the decisions of the Government which are made and taken constitutionally."

May was not out when Jaafar Albar, the Secretary-General of UMNO, made a speech in which he again urged the Malays to unite, and never forget they were Malays. "What is all this about?" demanded Lee Kuan Yew. "I thought the Constitution said we were all Malaysians? I say we had better decide now," added Lee in a speech on 30 May. "Are we Malaysians or are we Malays? Because I cannot be a Malay. I can be a Malaysian and sixty-one per cent

265

of the people of Malaysia can be Malaysians, can be loyal to Malaysia, accept the concept of Malaysia."

Lee went on to point out that Albar said there was no harm in calling for the Malays to unite. The Chinese could also unite. "He hasn't spent his time calculating the significance of what he is doing. The Chinese will never unite under the MCA because they are political eunuchs. . . but supposing we real, virile Chinese stood up and shouted 'Chinese, unite!' there would be real trouble in five or ten years. . . because there are five million Chinese. . . forty-two per cent of the population."

Lee said it was necessary to decide the issue now. It would be easier to make alternative arrangements. "And the alternative arrangements? Well, we don't want to talk too much about it. But if really it is necessary, then I say, 'Look, all those states that want a Malaysian Malaysia can come together.' I can think of three straightaway: Sabah, Sarawak, Singapore. I can think of a few others like Penang and Malacca. I can even believe that Johore. . ."

Lee insisted that Malaysia as originally conceived was "best of all, Malaysian Malaysia; let us all stick to the Constitution; honour each other; accommodate, make adjustments, live happily in a multi-racial society, with everybody equal, Malaysian citizens regardless of race, language, religion. This is the message I want to give. It is not just in Singapore that people are not accustomed to Malay rule." That is what Dr Mahathir an Alliance MP had said in Parliament.

"Let me tell him this," said Lee. "When we joined Malaysia, we never agreed to Malay rule; we agreed to Malaysian rule; never Malay rule. This is all bunkum. Somebody has made a grave error of judgment if they believe that we agreed to Malay rule. We never agreed to it. The Constitution means democratic rule by representatives of the people on the basis of adult franchise: one man, one vote, one citizen, one vote, which means Malaysia is ruled by Malaysians. And we want to make that clear now. That is the only kind of rule that we will agree to. . . "

VIII

On Singapore's National Day, 3 June, Lee Kuan Yew reminded Singaporeans—and Kuala Lumpur—of the significant contribution Singapore could make to the future of Malaysia.

"Without Singapore and her bases Malaysia cannot be defended. Whatever mutual defence pacts there may be, if tomorrow we were to obliterate Singapore from the map of Malaysia, then the sinews with which Malaysia can be defended would be destroyed.

"We have a contribution to make, not only in dollars or percentages of our revenue, but also a contribution to the rapid industrial growth of Malaysia, the building up of technical skills and managerial talent that can bring a better life to all in Malaysia, from people in the towns to those in the kampongs. If these potentials are utilized, then not only will Singapore prosper, but the rest of Malaysia will also prosper. For when official attitudes of the Central Government change and they accept that these economic potentials must be used, then it is our duty to share our prosperity with all the other states, so that all can develop and prosper.

"There is another field where we in Singapore can make a significant contribution to the future of Malaysia. Ours is a politically sophisticated urban society. Through the turbulent years of the last decade, we have been nurtured in the democratic practice. We have learnt to abjure communal issues and communal politics...

"Singapore as a military, economic and political asset, is something precious to us and to others in Malaysia. We must never allow assets to be frittered away by racialism or communism. Both racialists and anti-national elements preach a society where one group dominates the others either by virtue of its race or by virtue of its ideology. We must check both, for both creeds preach the use of violence and the betrayal of the nation to achieve their objectives..."

IX

Lee Kuan Yew believed it was the success of the Malaysian Solidarity Convention, held in Singapore on 6 June, which decided the extremists in Kuala Lumpur that Lee must be stopped. Representatives from Malaya, Singapore, Sabah and Sarawak—the four components of Malaysia—attended. This gathering was, in effect, a mostly Chinese protest against a definite and deliberate tendency, they thought, to move away from the original multiracial concept of Malaysia.

Lee made a fighting speech. It was not one of his best. Dr Toh Chin Chye, the Deputy Prime Minister and Chairman of the People's Action Party was clearer, more forceful, less emotional. Lee described the occasion as the "beginning of a new tide in the affairs of the people of Malaysia. It took a long time for us all to come to the same conclusions despite our differing experience in Malaya, Singapore, Sabah and Sarawak. There is no doubt about it that it took us a long time to reach the inevitable conclusion that these people were up to no good. You know the line they were taking;

the growing truculence with a heavy racial accent, the intimidatory postures, and the snarling guttural notes on which they sent out their signals to their followers on the basis of race, lead us to only one conclusion—that if this goes on, Malaysia will not belong to Malaysians. And since there are so many Malaysians, we decided that the time has come for us to speak our minds. The technique is quite a subtle one. They speak on two different wave-lengths—one for multilingual, multiracial consumption, the other meant for their followers. The good men, multiracial men, the top leaders, from time to time completely dissociate themselves from this special wave-length, but the wild men keep up the pressure. All nice things have been said in Parliament—'Yes, of course, Malaysia is a Malaysian nation', that in fact it was their idea. Well, it does not matter. If in fact it was their idea—so much the better. But it disturbs us that, even after all this had been said, today *Utusan Zaman* continues the crude, communal approach...

"We have a vested interest in democratic constitutional methods of change," insisted Lee. "We are a loyal Opposition group because the Constitution offers us, in the long term, a way out towards a Malaysian Malaysia... but we cannot afford to be intimidated... we have not the slightest intention of breaking Malaysia up... we have not the slightest intention of seceding and obliging their ultras, leaving our friends, our fellow countrymen, to the tender mercies of the ultras..."

This, much abridged, was the tenor of the speech responsible persons in high places in Kuala Lumpur considered subversive and sufficient grounds for throwing Lee Kuan Yew into gaol.

I wrote about "Malaysia's racial war of words" in an Australian magazine, *The Bulletin*, on 19 June. I said it had been going on, in some form or another, almost since the formation of Malaysia.

"Mutual suspicion of intent is the basic cause. Both sides, the Alliance Government in Kuala Lumpur, and Mr Lee Kuan Yew and his State Government in Singapore, now openly accuse each other of communalism. Mr Lee's complaint is that UMNO (the United Malays National Organization), which provides most of the Central Government's Ministers, is out to create a Malay-dominated Malaysia. UMNO's Secretary-General, Dato Syed Jaafar Albar, makes fiery speeches in which he sometimes calls Mr Lee a communist, a traitor to Malaysia, or an enemy of the Malays, and never fails to call upon the Malays to unite. Mr Lee says a Malaysian Malaysia cannot be created this way.

"Dato (Dr) Ismail, Malaysia's pipe-smoking Minister for Home Affairs, a typically kind and considerate Malay intellectual, offered what was, presumably, the Alliance Government's explanation of the wordy battle, the deep suspicion. Dr Ismail told Parliament there were two ways of establishing Malaysia. One, the platform of the PAP, 'which wants to impose non-communalism right away'. The other, the Alliance method, which requires two steps: first, inter-racial harmony between racially organized groups, such as the United Malays National Organization, the Malayan Chinese Association, and the Malayan Indian Congress: second, the ultimate stage of non-communalism.

" 'Thus,' declared Dato Ismail, 'as can be seen, both the Alliance and the PAP subscribe to the concept of a Malaysian Malaysia, but they differ in their approach to make it a living entity. It is this difference in approach which generates a great deal of heat, and which disturbs the hitherto comparatively tranquil political scene in Malaysia.'

"The PAP had no experience of politics in a multiracial society, he argued, because Singapore was a 'homogeneous society with some racial minorities'. Probably, he went on, 'like mediaeval men, it is easier for them to destroy than to understand a phenomenon which is strange to them'.

"Mr Lee Kuan Yew welcomed Dato Ismail's two-step plan for non-communalism. 'If Dato Ismail is sincerely supported by the Alliance, then we have the solution,' he said. 'But, for a year and a half, the Malay *ra'ayat* in the kampongs have been pumped with communal propaganda.' This had to be stopped if they were to go ahead with Malaysia. The open squabble in Parliament lasted five days and was interrupted by the King's official birthday when the Sovereign took the opportunity (being a constitutional monarch, this upon the advice of the Prime Minister) to call for calm.

"Unfortunately, it was a vague remark in the King's speech in Parliament which had set some of the hard words in motion. Not even the Cabinet, at one time, seemed to be agreed upon their true meaning. These were the words, in the Royal Address: 'We are now facing threats to our security from outside—from Indonesia. In addition, we are also facing threats from within the country. Both those threats are designed to create trouble. If those concerned achieve their objective it will mean chaos for us, and an end to democracy. . .'

" 'Do you mean us?' demanded Mr Lee. An Alliance back-bencher yelled, 'Yes.' Nobody on the ministerial benches corrected him. Other Government speakers made it clear they considered Mr Lee and the PAP the enemies within. Dato Sambanthan spelled it out when he said: 'Malaysia is being externally threatened by Indonesia, and internally by Mr Lee Kuan Yew and his brand of politics.'

"On the final day of the debate, which was wound up by the Deputy Prime Minister, Tun Razak ('the Prime Minister feels there is nothing of any importance left for him to speak about') corrected Dato Sambanthan and chided Mr Lee. Malaysia's threat from within

269

were the communists. They were the traitors. It was 'sheer deceit' for Mr Lee to imagine he and his colleagues were the threat. Lee knew full well what the Government meant. 'The Prime Minister has never thought of Mr Lee Kuan Yew or his party as the enemy from within,' declared Tun Razak.

"Several times during the debate, Mr Lee was invited to give proof of his belief that UMNO were working for a Malay-dominated Malaysia. He said he would be glad to do this. Mr Lee notified the Speaker of his desire to make clarifications and the Speaker agreed to allocate Mr Lee forty-five minutes at 8.15 on Thursday evening. On Thursday evening, the Speaker told Mr Lee that two ministers wished to speak before him. They held the floor until the House adjourned. When the House assembled on Friday morning, Mr Lee rose, expecting to be then allowed to make his reply. He was at once informed by the Speaker that he had lost his chance. When Mr Lee protested, the Speaker ruled that this was not the 'proper time' for him to address the House.

"Denied the opportunity to speak in the House, Mr Lee hurriedly summoned a press conference in another part of the House. It went on for two hours while Mr Lee, after explaining the background to the Speaker's original arrangement for him to speak, produced the evidence he presumably would have given. He produced little that the Singapore Government had not already published over the past year. It consisted mostly of translations from *Utusan Melayu's* editorials, and reports of Dato Syed Jaafar Albar's speeches.

" 'This is the sort of communal propaganda being pumped into the Malay villages. Malays are called upon to unite.' He said seriously that 'here, in *Utusan Melayu*, is where the real message is given by UMNO leaders.' In Parliament they just paid lip-service to multiracialism. Lee claimed that the extracts he produced proved the existence of a clear intention and systematic policy to build up an atmosphere of communalism and racialism. 'Are we inflaming passions by pointing out what they are saying? Are we the communalists? We have never said: Chinese, unite! or Indians, unite!'

"As expected, Lee's amendment to the King's speech regretting that the Government did not 'reassure the nation that Malaysia will continue to progress in accord with its democratic constitution to a Malaysian Malaysia...' was heavily defeated by the powerful Alliance majority. A *Straits Times* editorial strongly urged, 'a period of reflection while the lessons of this debate are digested and a resolve is born to strengthen Malaysia, not weaken it, an effort to heal, not destroy'.

"Lee Kuan Yew looked jaunty and confident as usual when he returned to Singapore. He told reporters that the Parliamentary session had been breezy, and all to the good because 'it has blown open cupboard doors to disclose some musty skeletons'. He felt it was a good beginning to a new phase to consolidate Malaysia. He reckoned that the important point had been made that all Malaysians were co-owners of Malaysia and not guests. Lee said he was confident foolish things would not happen if good sense prevailed all round.

"That, then, is the present situation of the verbal war. Throughout the parliamentary battle the Tunku remained silent. Many unofficial explanations were offered. Lee's friends claim that, in this way, the Tunku indicated his disapproval of UMNO extremism. One explanation is probably as good as the other. Most observers felt the Tunku lost nothing politically by keeping out of what was a rather bitter debate. What is of rather more immediate concern is whether the ultras, the zealots, the extremists, the racists, the wild men, can keep silent, at least during the Tunku's absence in London for the Prime Ministers' Conference, and later, perhaps, at Algiers. Malaysia's international image at this time is of special importance."

This article was used by Jaafar Albar and *Utusan Melayu* as proof that I was anti-Malay and guilty of interfering in Malaysia's political activities. Tunku Abdul Rahman was away in Europe. During his absence the campaign against Lee Kuan Yew increased in volume and intensity. After separation Lee said he had anticipated being arrested during the Tunku's absence from Malaysia.

X

In the midst of the gathering tension, Ong Eng Guan, leader of the United People's Party, dramatically resigned from the Singapore Assembly. He announced on 16 June that he had decided to renounce politics for ever. The Singapore Government later described this as "a surprise move to embarrass and weaken the Singapore Government in its fight against the extremists in Malaysia". Ong's decision at that time to quit politics provided an opportunity for a potentially dangerous by-election. Later in the year, on 13 September, Lee Kuan Yew said publicly that he suspected there were "some very good reasons of a cogent and probably attractive character" which caused Ong to bring about a political contest between the Barisan Sosialis, with their cry of "Crush Malaysia", and the PAP, with Ong and the whole weight of the Alliance pitted against the PAP.

Lee Kuan Yew believed that the plot was to bring about a PAP defeat by the communists. He argued that the Alliance knew they could not beat them in a by-election, (the Alliance did not in fact put up a candidate), but they could help the Barisan "cut us down to size". Having been cut down to size, unable to defend Malaysia in the by-election, then, said Lee Kuan Yew, the intention was "*kaput*".

During a Press interview, on 12 August, Lee again spoke of schemes to "devour Singapore leaders". He recalled the visits to Singapore late in July of Tun Razak and Tan Siew Sin, Malaysia's Acting Prime Minister and Finance Minister. He described these visits as "their final test". He was implying that these two Ministers were then making a final effort to capture Malay support in Singapore. "Their original intention," he said, "was to make use of the Hong Lim by-election to hit at the PAP. They themselves did not have the capacity, so they worked hand in glove with Ong Eng Guan. Ong Eng Guan conveniently resigned in order to allow the Barisan Sosialis to fight it out with us. They thought that through Barisan they could repeat the setback of 1961, when the PAP lost. They wanted to see us lose in the Hong Lim by-election in July this year, to lower our prestige internationally, and then they would have dealt with us thoroughly and finished us off." That failed. Sixty per cent of the electorate returned the PAP candidate Lee Khoon Choy.

Ong Eng Guan, former Treasurer of the People's Action Party, and ex-Mayor of Singapore, won the 1959 Hong Lim general election with the biggest majority of the day. In 1961, after his expulsion from the PAP, he again won in a straight fight by-election against his former party. He had resigned his seat and challenged the PAP. In the 1963 general elections, as leader of the tiny United People's Party, Ong held Hong Lim but with a majority which had slipped to 1,277, less than a fifth of his majority of four years before.

In 1965, Right-wing forces joined the extreme Left in what Lee Kuan Yew called a "concerted but futile attempt to check and undermine the progress and confidence of the Singapore Government. The Alliance Party and *Utusan Melayu* openly backed the Barisan candidate Ong Chang Sam... the PAP victory was clearly a victory for the leadership of the People's Action Party and its concept of a Malaysian Malaysia. It was a staggering blow to the sectarian and racial politicking of the ultras in the Alliance, who wanted to see the defeat of the PAP at Hong Lim, in order to vindicate their policy of communalism, and to use the defeat as an excuse to carry out repressive measures against Singapore."

XI

Election fever (in the Hong Lim by-election) was mounting when, unexpectedly, I was banished from Malaysia. I was given fourteen days to leave Singapore where I had lived since 1948. I was to be out of Malaysia by 20 July, and "to remain outside Malaysia".

In London, a spokesman for the Malaysian Prime Minister told the United Press International that the Tunku did not have anything to say regarding "the Kuala Lumpur Government's decision to expel British journalist Alex Josey". The spokesman added: "The decision was made in the Malaysian capital during the Tunku's absence and so it would not be right for the Tunku to make any comment."

That same evening, on 8 July, Lee Kuan Yew spoke at a by-election rally. "In the middle of an election campaign," he declared, "the mailed fist is shown". Singapore's Prime Minister said the real reason for my expulsion "is what Syed Nasir said in today's *Berita Harian* and *Utusan Melayu*. He said Alex Josey twisted the true facts about Malaysia by reporting what I had said." Lee added: "We know this was a deliberate move made during election time with full significance to me and to my colleagues."

In an editorial headed "Clumsy and Weak", *The Times* of London on 8 July said: "The expulsion by the Malaysian Government of Mr Alex Josey, a British freelance journalist, who has been living in the country for over sixteen years, will be read as a sign of weakness and ill-temper. Mr Josey has been told to go within fourteen days because his going will be 'conducive to the good of the Federation'. Such mumbling reasons carry no weight at all. Arriving during the Emergency as a British official, Mr Josey lost his employment for being too critical of the Establishment. In common with Englishmen in other imperial territories he had been an active supporter of independence and was well known in political circles. But he became identified with Mr Lee Kuan Yew's People's Action Party and was made the object of attack. Two years ago a campaign was mounted against him by the Malay Press in Kuala Lumpur because he had compared Malays unfavourably with Chinese in an article in an Australian newspaper. The matter was treated as if it were a national insult and as if Mr Josey as a British journalist had no right to express such an opinion. Other complaints were that he often travelled abroad with missions from Singapore and acted as a public relations officer. As the atmosphere between Kuala Lumpur and Singapore has become worse, even to the point of angry quarrelling in recent months, Mr Josey's involvement with the Singapore Government may have been embarrassing. Tun Abdul Razak's statement yesterday touches on this without making the charges any more specific. But the irritation could have been ventilated and the matter resolved by the Federal Government in Kuala Lumpur without recourse to the clumsy and unjustifiable act of expelling him."

While the Tunku, in London, on 8 July, was handing out a prepared statement to London editors (some of them personally protesting the

273

allegations made against me), Dr Toh Chin Chye, Singapore's Deputy Prime Minister, was holding a press conference at the City Hall "to explain the Singapore Government's stand on the expulsion of Mr Alex Josey and attempts by extremists in the Alliance, particularly the UMNO, to have Lee arrested". With Dr Toh were the Minister for Finance, Dr Goh Keng Swee, the Minister for Law, Mr E. W. Barker, and the Minister for National Development, Mr Lim Kim San. Dr Toh opened his conference with the announcement that the Singapore Cabinet was solidly united on this matter. He read from a prepared statement.

But first, the Tunku's statement: "The Central Government of Malaysia has taken action to expel Mr Alex Josey because he has interfered in the internal politics of Malaysia and has indulged in activities aimed at disrupting inter-racial harmony, thereby abusing the privileges he has enjoyed as a foreign correspondent. The first occasion Mr Josey came under the Government's attention was when he wrote in the Australian *Bulletin* stressing differences in leadership between Mr Lee Kuan Yew and myself. While projecting the image of Mr Lee Kuan Yew as the ablest leader in that region of Asia, he unwisely belittled me and suggested that I belong to the race of people who have no tradition other than piracy while Mr Lee Kuan Yew belongs to a race with thousands of years of culture.

"I passed this off good humouredly saying I was proud of my ancestors in as much as the British made heroes of their pirates such as Sir Francis Drake and others. But Mr Josey went further and in the various publications to which he contributes articles from time to time, we noticed signs of a definite bias against the Central Government of Malaysia. On one occasion I had to take the matter up with the Australian Government with regard to an article which appeared in *The Bulletin* which finally led to a visit of its editor to Malaysia, during which time he expressed regret for the article that appeared in his publication as he had not been rightly informed. We know who the informer was and he was none other than Mr Alex Josey. Mr Josey passes off as a freelance journalist while in actual fact he is more than a press relations man to the Prime Minister of Singapore. Recently he travelled with Mr Lee to Australia, New Zealand, India, Cambodia and Burma. In Burma there was some trouble over the presence of Mr Josey in the party as he had been banned from entering the country.

"What I am concerned about is Mr Josey's deliberate and persistent attempts at disrupting the inter-racial harmony which has been built up and achieved over the period of years since independence, and which I consider as the greatest achievement of the Alliance Government and the people of the country. There have been incorrect reports by various foreign correspondents from time to time in the past but we were content to overlook these mistakes because we saw no ulterior motives behind their writings other than sheer carelessness or lack of information. In the case of Mr Alex Josey, however, he is not a freelance in the proper sense of the word. He has persisted in his attempts to stir up trouble among the races in a very subtle manner in keeping with his background as an expert in psychological warfare. He came to Malaya during the colonial regime as its Director of Psychological Warfare."

There are errors of fact, as well as faulty reasoning and wrong conclusions, in this statement prepared partly by Inche Mohammed Sopiee, then Minister at the Malaysian Embassy in London in charge of Press matters. I had never been banned from entering Burma. There was no trouble over my presence in the party: this was the second time I had accompanied Lee Kuan Yew to Rangoon. Both times all members of the party including myself were received with every courtesy.

The Tunku's statement was given front page prominence in Friday's *Straits Times*, but Dr Toh Chin Chye's press conference, and statement, reported on the same page, claimed the headlines with his disclosure of a scheme to arrest Lee Kuan Yew. The paper said Dr Toh revealed that "instructions had been issued for a case to be made out for the detention of Mr Lee Kuan Yew. But Dr Toh would not say who had issued the instructions, and to whom they had been issued." Dr Toh was quoted as saying: "I personally do not wish to enlarge on the matter but I say those in the Central Government who are responsible for such matters know that we know." Dr Toh said that the expulsion of Mr Josey was only the first step towards the suppression of liberalism in Malaysia's political field. It was a step the Central Government had taken in response to pressure "from communal extremists designed to cow and silence all those who persist in reporting or espousing views contrary to certain UMNO leaders". Referring to the Central Government's "justification" of the expulsion, the "cryptic remark" that it will be "conducive to the common good", and the Acting Prime Minister's further comment that I had interfered in internal politics, Dr Toh said that what these remarks really meant was contained in the inspired leaks to the pro-Alliance *Malayan Times* and in *Utusan Melayu* reports and editorials preceding and following the expulsion order. The *Malayan Times* on 6 July claimed it had learnt the real reasons from "reliable sources": "Malay circles are highly incensed with Mr Josey for the anti-Malay propaganda he has been conducting on behalf of the PAP in magazines and newspapers abroad."

Dr Toh told his Press conference it was "completely untrue" that the PAP had conducted any anti-Malay propaganda either at home or abroad. He argued that I could not therefore have reported any

275

such "non-existent propaganda". Dr Toh added: "that these 'Malay circles' have no basis for being incensed at factual reporting of the Malaysian situation appears to make no difference. It is enough for these 'Malay circles' to declare they are incensed for the Central Government to comply."

Dr Toh said the move had serious implications not just for foreign correspondents, journalists and others whose task it is to observe and report. "It has graver implications for all those in Malaysia who hold views contrary to those held by the extremists." If it was not conducive to the interests of Malaysia for a foreign correspondent to report factually what leaders in Malaysia were saying, to readers abroad, then obviously these extremists would want equally stringent action against those who actively mobilized opinion for a Malaysian Malaysia. "Several resolutions were recently submitted by the UMNO Youth Movement to Tunku Abdul Rahman and Tun Razak and reported in *Utusan Melayu*. One was for the expulsion of Mr Alex Josey from Malaysia at once. The Central Government has acted on this resolution." If, warned Dr Toh, "the Central Government continues to placate these extremist elements, further repressive measures must be taken which must lead eventually to the break up of Malaysia. For another demand was for the arrest and detention of Mr Lee Kuan Yew."

Dr Toh said "we know" that soon after the recent meeting of Parliament, and the first public rally of the Malaysian Solidarity Convention in Singapore on 6 June, "instructions were given to make a case for Mr Lee's arrest." Dr Toh urged the Central Government not to believe that "with Mr Lee out of the way" the PAP Government would quietly acquiesce to his detention. "The Alliance leaders must realize that Malaysia will break up if any such repressive action is taken." He urged the Central Government to consider carefully the consequence of yielding to the course advocated by "these extremist circles". By acceding to extremist demands overnight the Central Government leaders had damaged their image abroad as tolerant liberal men. "The world press will now find it hard to depict Malaysia to their readers as a growing democracy. In countries which are committed to the defence of Malaysia, the question will inevitably be asked: what is it that is being defended in Malaysia—democratic freedom or a repressive ruling group?"

Dr Toh said some people might think that because banishment was a prerogative of the Government, it had nothing to do with the Singapore Government. "But our contention is that the expulsion of Mr Alex Josey cannot be treated as simply involving him, who is neither a citizen of Singapore or Malaysia. It must be seen in the light of development which has been taking place during the past few months, and in the context of statements made by extremist leaders in the Alliance, in UMNO... the expulsion of Alex Josey is only the first step towards the suppression of liberalism in the political field in Malaysia."

Saturday, 10 July, was polling day in Hong Lim. The fight was between the People's Action Party and the Barisan Sosialis, between those anxious to create a Malaysian Malaysia and those supporting President Sukarno's slogan "Crush Malaysia". That morning's *Straits Times* carried a front page denial by Tun Razak of Dr Toh's "detain Lee" allegation. Malaysia's Acting Prime Minister, said the paper, described as "wild and mischievous" Dr Toh's statement that the Central Government has issued instructions for a case to be made out for the detention of Mr Lee Kuan Yew. Tun Razak said the statement was too wild and mischievous to merit any comment. He added: "The people of this country know that the Alliance Government is a responsible, just and fair government. We do not go about arresting people without sufficient grounds or reason. We believe and uphold the principle of parliamentary democracy and the rule of law. Only those who act contrary to the law of the country will have to suffer the consequences." He added that the Alliance Government had a clear mandate from the people to govern the country and defend its independence and sovereignty. "We shall not shirk our responsibilities and will not hesitate to take any action under the Constitution and under our law in the discharge of our responsibilties. At the last meeting of Parliament I warned political leaders, in particular Mr Lee Kuan Yew, that they should not make use of communal issues that might disrupt harmony and the goodwill of our people. If, as a result of their speeches and activities, they endanger the peace and security of our country, they would be held responsible." Tun Razak did not specifically deny Dr Toh's charge that the Central Government had given instructions that a case for Lee's arrest was to be prepared.

Lee Kuan Yew was addressing a rally winding up the PAP's by-election campaign when he was told about the statement put out that evening by Tun Razak. Lee said that instead of replying directly to Dr Toh's charge, Tun Razak had beaten around the bush with talks about compliance with the law. "We know all about the law. You don't have to tell us that," declared Lee. "Did the Federal Government order the case for the arrest of me or not? Why don't they answer that?" Lee told the voters that the expulsion "is a warning to us, to show us how strong they are. The whole world knows it is pressure against us, even if the local newspapers dare not say so." The previous day Inche Senu had told the *Malay Mail* that Dr Toh's allegation was "utter rubbish". It was a "preposterous statement". Dr Toh had "invented a ludicrous allegation against the Central Government."

277

Commenting on Dr Toh's statement that the expulsion order was aimed more at the PAP than me, Inche Senu said: "It appears from Dr Toh's statement that Mr Josey is not only a symbol of power behind the PAP but also a power behind the concept of Malaysian Malaysia."

The PAP claimed their success in Hong Lim marked "a turning point in the mechanics of power in Kuala Lumpur. Unable to undermine the political base of the PAP and fearful of the grave consequences of repressive actions contemplated against Singapore leaders, Kuala Lumpur in its dilemma increasingly toyed with the idea of expelling Singapore from Malaysia."

Ten thousand Hong Lim voters went to the polls on 10 July, the Prophet's Birthday. The year before, on that day, bloody racial riots broke out, the first ever in the 140 years' history of Singapore. They followed months of intense communal agitation in *Utusan Melayu*. For months the Central Government refused to set up a Commission of Inquiry, and not until the Singapore Government threatened to make their own inquiries did the Central Government move. No Commission ever met.

Three days later, in London, the Tunku came out with a statement that so far as he knew there was no evidence against Lee Kuan Yew to warrant his arrest. He said that had there been plans to arrest Lee the matter would have been discussed with him. "The Central Government has never acted arbitrarily or wilfully," he said. "Whatever is done is done with the full knowledge and consent of the members of the Cabinet. On the question of arrest of any individual the Government has first to be fair with all the evidence against the persons concerned, and must be convinced that his freedom is a great security risk to the country. It is only then that the Government will consult the full Cabinet with all the evidence before it and an action will be taken on its decision." Nowhere in his statement did the Tunku deny Dr Toh's charge that instructions had been given to the police to make out a case for Lee's arrest. What Malaysia's Prime Minister did do was to advise the State Ministers of Singapore "not to make wild guesses which could produce unhealthy relations between the State and parent Governments. Malaysia has enjoyed peace and harmony. Let us keep it like that. If we have to quarrel among ourselves let it be on an issue that is worth quarrelling about. But let it not be on Mr Alex Josey, who is not a citizen of the country."

Referring to Dr Toh's charges that there were ultras in UMNO responsible for much of the political troubles, the Tunku said "There are ultras in every party and UMNO is not free of them. Without ultras the party will have no life. It will be devoid of all political spirit. All members of UMNO have been loyal to the headquarters and to me. They have their views and are free to have them, but it would be wrong to put the blame at their doors. To me the UMNO Youth have been a great help to the party and their loyalty is something of which I am proud."

In a statement put out the following day, on 14 July, the Singapore Government noted "with appreciation" the Tunku's remarks that so far as he knew there was no evidence to warrant Lee Kuan Yew's arrest, and said this was the first comment by any Central Government Minister on Dr Toh's challenge of 8 July that the Singapore Government knew that instructions had in fact been given after the Malaysian Solidarity Convention held in Singapore on 6 June.

The Singapore Government statement continued: "On many an occasion, and recently with increasing frequency, demands have been made by senior UMNO leaders for Mr Lee's arrest. It was in the same way that they agitated for Mr Alex Josey's expulsion. After Mr Josey's first article in *The Bulletin*, in October, 1963, both the Tunku and Dr Ismail, refusing to yield to demands for Mr Josey's expulsion, said that this was a free country and correspondents could report what they liked. Now Mr Josey has been expelled and the reason advanced publicly was his article in *The Bulletin* of October, 1963."

The Singapore Government statement referred to a meeting held shortly before the Tunku left for London on 11 June. "A few Ministers of the Central Government were together at this meeting in which Mr Lee's proposed arrest was discussed with certain other persons."

Back in Singapore on 6 August, on his way to Kuala Lumpur, Malaysia's Prime Minister said: "Whether it is in internal politics or international politics there is no need for us to have any drastic changes. There may be minor points here and there, which I will discuss with my colleagues." In Kuala Lumpur he was asked if he would be meeting Mr Lee. He replied: "As soon as I have settled down, I shall ask Mr Lee Kuan Yew to come and meet me to discuss some of the things he has been shouting about." Four days later, the Tunku was telling Parliament, during his speech announcing Singapore's separation from Malaysia, that he had reached the conclusion that Singapore must leave Malaysia, whilst he was "lying in bed in London".

According to an interview the Tunku later gave to Felix Abisheganadan, a veteran Malaysian journalist, published in *The Straits Times* on 10 August, 1965, "the whole plan started on 25 June when the Tunku was in the London Clinic for treatment for shingles." On 29 June, the Tunku reached his decision on separation. "If there could be no agreement with the PAP to call off the heavy politicking which he feared would lead to racial bloodshed", Singapore must go.

That day, the Tunku wrote to Tun Razak telling him to talk to Lee. On 22 July, when the Tunku was in France, he received a reply from Razak saying that "all the senior Cabinet Ministers" were agreed that no agreement with Singapore could be reached. Parliament was convened for 9 August to enable a Separation Law to be passed. On 2 August, three days before the Tunku's return, Tun Razak instructed the Attorney-General to draft the bill to amend the Constitution.

Was it a coincidence that the Tunku reached his decision three days after the Central Executive of the UMNO Youth Movement met in Inche Senu's house and passed four resolutions? One of the resolutions called upon the Prime Minister and his Deputy to refuse to hold discussions with Lee Kuan Yew until he had openly apologized to the Malays "for insulting them". Another strongly condemned Lee, the PAP, and the PAP organ *Petir*. The third called for my expulsion. The fourth called upon UMNO Youth "to be on the alert and keep calm", await instructions, and not take any action outside discipline.

On 29 June, Tun Razak did meet Lee Kuan Yew: two days later seven delegates from UMNO Youth called upon Razak and demanded an explanation. A Government statement was put out assuring them that "Tun Razak's meeting with Mr Lee was an official meeting and that was the reason it was held in the office of the Acting Prime Minister. Tun Razak reviewed at length the political situation in the country and he called on UMNO Youth to be calm and prepared, because the problems faced by the Government are not only great but also delicate. They should not have any doubts, for the Government is closely watching the political development in the country and carefully facing the problems." Inche Senu headed the delegation. *The Straits Times* quoted him as saying "We are happy to hear Tun Razak's statement." Dato Syed Jaafar Albar, Secretary-General of UMNO, also attended the meeting.

At a farewell dinner given by the Minister of Culture (which was attended by the Prime Minister, the Minister for Finance, and the Minister for Law), Mr S. Rajaratnam, then Minister for Culture, later to become Singapore's first Foreign Minister, said there was nothing Singapore could do about my expulsion. "Alex Josey will make history as being the first foreign correspondent to be expelled from either colonial Malaya or from an independent democratic Malaysia." Yet there was a great deal they intended to do about this detention order which certain UMNO extremists were publicly agitating should be conferred on Singapore's Prime Minister. "We know," Mr Rajaratnam said, "that Alex Josey's expulsion was a sort of *makan kechil* (small eats) to whet the appetite of the extremists for the main dish— the arrest of Mr Lee." The logical outcome of this, the Minister believed, "must be the arrest and detention of other PAP leaders," and eventually "all those who do not supinely accept the kind of Malaysia the extremists have in mind." Mr Rajaratnam said that Inche Senu betrayed what was in the back of his mind when he said (the day before) that there were two kinds of Malaysians: those in Malaysia as of right, and those who should be grateful for being allowed "to enjoy this right given them by what Inche Senu calls 'the natives'." The Minister said it was "in this context of the battle for a Malaysian Malaysia that the expulsion should be seen. Alex Josey did not so much interfere in local politics as local politics interfered with him. The extremists chose him as their target for three reasons:

(1) Because he was a personal friend of long standing of some of the PAP Ministers.

(2) Because his reading of the Malaysian situation was not the sort of thing that the ultras liked to read.

(3) It was safe to take him on because he was one man, and a non-citizen to boot."

The object of the exercise was "to see what would be the effects of clobbering Alex Josey. Would the PAP leaders duck for cover? What would be the impact of foreign correspondents writing about Malaysia even after Alex Josey has gone? How would the local newspapers react to this first move towards Inche Senu's concept of One Voice?" In Mr Rajaratnam's view the opposite had in fact been achieved. PAP leaders had not been intimidated: the movement for a Malaysian Malaysia had been given added impetus. And, by accepting the advice of the ultras, the image of the more responsible leaders in the Alliance—of themselves as liberal men—had been badly damaged by one foolish act. "Some of their apologists are trying very hard to present the expulsion of Alex Josey as a victory against desperate odds. Alex Josey has been presented in some Malay journals as the representative of forces bigger and stronger than him. He menaced Islam, the Malay race, language and culture, the integrity and independence of Malaysia, and the well-being of Malaysia's eleven million multiracial population." Added the Minister: "Judging from some of these articles the victory over Alex Josey may even go down in our history books as the Day when the Nation was saved from a fate worse than Death." Chuckled Mr Rajaratnam: "I look at Alex Josey and wonder whether Malaysia is all that wonky that his articles in journals abroad could have brought it down." Mr Rajaratnam ended on a friendly personal note. "He tried to be objective as a journalist, but he was not indifferent to the fate of Malaysia because he believes in Malaysia. In pre-independent Malaysia he was branded by big business and big planters as a communist. He was branded by some of his fellow Britishers as anti-British. He was branded by pro-communists as a reactionary. And now he is being packed off by Alliance extremists as a colonial agent, as anti-Malay, anti-Chinese, a race-monger and an anti-Malaysian.

All this is quite a record for one man... many Central Government Ministers and officials know that without compromising his objectivity as a journalist he has done more than they would care to admit now to help in combating anti-Malaysia propaganda abroad."

It is interesting, if nothing else, to recall that the Tunku sent the following message to the Commonwealth Correspondents Association Silver Jubilee Dinner in London on 7 January, 1965, some six short months before Malaysia expelled its first foreign correspondent: "Facts, opinions, trends," said the Tunku, "these are your daily concern. To maintain consistent standards of accuracy in this age of ultra-swift communications is indeed a great responsibility, as your reports, analyses or judgments can and do exert great influence. I may say from my experience that no one is more conscious of the importance of this duty and responsibility than the correspondents themselves. On this happy and eventful anniversary, I would like to pay a special tribute to the general all round performance and sense of service shown by Commonwealth correspondents in the exacting demands of their profession."

On 20 July, I flew to England. Tunku Abdul Rahman returned to Malaysia on 5 August. Parliament had already been convened for 9 August to pass the law which the Tunku had instructed the Attorney-General to prepare, to separate Singapore from Malaysia in accordance with the decision the Tunku had reached in hospital in London, in June. Messages from Kuala Lumpur had convinced him that there was no other way to avoid bloodshed. And at this late stage the Tunku was probably right.

The tragedy was not so much that politicians had been allowed to exploit racialism and religion in a plural society, though this was dangerous enough, but that leaders in Singapore and Malaysia at the onset must have had entirely different mental concepts of what Malaysia was to mean. To Lee Kuan Yew it could mean nothing other than a Malaysian, multiracial Malaysia in ten or fifteen years, perhaps longer. That was not how Jaafar Albar saw it. And not until Singapore was separated from Malaysia was Albar removed from high office in UMNO. By then the damage had been done.

XII

In a hushed House, on 9 August, the Tunku told of events which led to his decision. He said the news he was to give them would be "a big surprise and shock". It was painful and heartbreaking news, and he considered it a "misfortune" that he should have to make the announcement. In ten years of leadership in the House never had a duty been so unpleasant to perform. He said he could not find any way out except the course he was forced to take. "We have tried everything possible to avoid separation of Singapore from the rest of Malaysia. In the end we find there are only two courses of action open to us." One was to take repressive measures against the Singapore Government "for the behaviour of some of their leaders". The other was to sever all connections with the State Government "that has ceased to give even a measure of loyalty to the Central Government". The position of the Central Government, not only at home but worse still, abroad, "has been mocked on many instances. It was clear some action must be taken. It is odious for us to take repressive measures against the Singapore Government, for such action is repulsive to our concept of parliamentary democracy. Even then, it would not solve the problem because there is not one problem but many, and one that gives us the most concern is the communal issue... we feel that this repressive action against a few would not therefore solve the problem..."

Just what sort of "behaviour" some of the Singapore leaders were guilty of to justify "repressive measures", presumably in accordance with the law of the land, has never been revealed. It is unthinkable that anyone in the Central Government could have even contemplated illegal action: yet there is evidence and admission that the arrest of Lee Kuan Yew and others was seriously considered, presumably because of their "behaviour".

The Tunku said it would have been odious to have taken repressive measures "for such action is repulsive to our concept of parliamentary democracy". But if the behaviour of the Singapore leaders was in fact damaging to Malaysia, if they were deliberately creating communal mischief, then surely, far from being odious, legal action against them would have been more than justified? In the eyes of the extremists, legal action would have meant the Central Government arresting Singapore Government leaders under the Preservation of Public Security Ordinance, and tossing them into gaol without trial. Dato Albar and the editors of *Utusan Melayu* knew this is what happened to political opponents, and annoying journalists, in the Congo and Indonesia and elsewhere, and they approved and envied and sought to bring this rough and effective justice to Malaysia. Malaysian law officers must have known this would have been a most dangerous path to tread. In an interview published in *Malaya Merdeka*, UMNO's official organ, in the August 1965 issue, the Tunku confessed that ultra pressure groups within the ruling Alliance had demanded "totalitarian methods to force the 'rebellious' State of Singapore into submission". He said: "I was exposed to this temptation, but doing a thing like that is against my conscience, and I accordingly resisted it." But "things had gone so much out of hand that my colleagues and I were left with no alternative but to legislate Singapore out of the Federation."

In his speech in Parliament on 9 August, the Tunku went out of his way to say that wherever he went foreign correspondents in articles and reports were giving the world "an entirely wrong picture, about events in Malaysia". They were reporting, he said, stories of Malay domination.

Malaysia's Prime Minister, better versed in world affairs than all his colleagues, knew what the world Press would have said about Malaysian leaders had Lee's government been toppled by an outrageous detention order against Lee and Lee's Cabinet. The Tunku saved the day. He did all he could. Mr Rajaratnam, independent Singapore's Foreign Minister, described the separation at that final stage as an act of statesmanship. Bloodshed was averted.

At five o'clock that evening on Monday, 9 August, the Tunku put out the following statement at a Press conference: "I have thought about the problems of Singapore very thoroughly during my period of convalescence in Europe and have come to the conclusion that the only answer lies in allowing Mr Lee Kuan Yew what he wants—to be the Prime Minister of an independent Singapore. Now he will have the burden of responsibilities to maintain peace and security in Singapore. We wish him well and will continue to assist and co-operate with him whenever possible.

"It is feared among certain quarters that Singapore may resort to a course of action detrimental to our allies and the Commonwealth, but I feel sure Mr Lee Kuan Yew will not do anything which will jeopardize our mutual interests. Singapore is free to make friends and establish diplomatic relations with any country it chooses but it is mutually agreed that this should not mean that it should enter into treaty with any country detrimental to our interests.

"We would wish to continue to be on good terms and friendship with Singapore. We will establish a High Commission in Singapore and appoint a High Commissioner. We will also sponsor Singapore's entry into the United Nations and the Commonwealth."

That same day Lee Kuan Yew issued a proclamation which began: "Whereas it is the inalienable right of a people to be free and independent" and ended with the following: "Now I, Lee Kuan Yew, Prime Minister of Singapore, do hereby proclaim and declare on behalf of the people and the Government of Singapore that as from today the ninth day of August in the year one thousand nine hundred and sixty-five Singapore shall be forever a sovereign democratic and independent nation, founded upon the principles of liberty and justice and ever seeking the welfare and happiness of her people in a more just and equal society."

XIII

At noon, Lee Kuan Yew met the Press, and was televised, weeping in anguish for the collapse of an ideal for which he had struggled all his adult life.

Earlier he had spoken of his hopes of economic co-operation. He recalled what the Tunku, the day before, had said to him when he took his departure after their historic meeting in Kuala Lumpur. The Tunku said: "Tomorrow when you are no longer in Malaysia and we are no longer quarrelling either in Parliament or in the constituencies, we'll be friends again, and we'll need each other, and we'll co-operate." Lee said it was his "earnest desire that this should be so".

Asked if he could outline the train of events that led to the proclamation which separated Singapore from Malaysia and established Singapore as an independent state, Lee said: "When I first met the Tunku at 12.30 on Saturday morning, I was still not convinced that in spite of everything Dr Goh had told me (because he had been for a few days in discussion with Malaysian Ministers), there was no other way. I believed then that I could still convince the Tunku that there were a number of other ways of reducing communal tensions in Malaysia, such as a looser federation. Even at the time when I was just beginning my discussions with him, I found it hard to believe that there was no other way. But, after my talk with the Tunku—and with the Tunku alone—there was no other way than what he thought was the solution; that we had to leave Malaysia. And I knew from what he said, and he has an intuition about these matters, that we would all be in for big communal trouble if Singapore, or if I and my colleagues, insisted on going on with Malaysia as it is. And, I'll be quite frank—any other kind of Malaysia than a Malaysian Malaysia is unacceptable. Well, perhaps now, with Singapore out, there could be a Malaysia, because the process would be much slower, will be much more gradual. The impetus of a highly-urbanized and a politically sophisticated city and two million people in it maybe set a pace which was too— well, which they thought was too fierce, too rapid. I didn't think so myself, but . . . unless a stand was taken about all these outpourings every day in the Jawi newspapers, everything would be lost. The Tunku convinced me that he could not go on holding the situation much longer; he could see real trouble in Malaysia if Singapore continued to be in it. I met the Tunku again yesterday morning because a number of my colleagues felt very strongly against this. And I told the Tunku so. Everybody knows that a good number of my colleagues were born, bred in Malaya. They feel passionately about what they consider to be their homeland. They settled here, they got jobs, they became Singapore citizens, they have become Singapore Ministers. They are basically Malaysians, or Malayans. I think Dr Toh would not have signed, unless the Tunku convinced him that there was no other way ... every time we look back on this moment when we signed this agreement which severed Singapore from Malaysia, it will be a moment of anguish. For me it is a moment of anguish. For me it is a moment of anguish because all my adult life... I have believed in the merger and unity of these two territories. It's a people connected by geography, economics, and ties of kinship..." At this point the interview had to be suspended to allow the Prime Minister to regain his composure.

Not until later was it possible to piece together the story of what had happened. Lee told a group of journalists in Singapore on 11 August, that he had met the Tunku in Kuala Lumpur on the Saturday, 7 August, after the Tunku had told Dr Goh Keng Swee of his plans the day before. Lee told the journalists that he asked the Tunku: "Couldn't we loosen a bit the ties between the State and the Central Government, and the component States of Malaysia?" Lee said he recommended to the Tunku a political truce: clashes did not occur so often in the field of administration as in the political arena. There could be an agreement between government and parties not to clash. *Utusan Melayu*, Lee suggested, should cease publishing inflammatory stuff, and then Singapore would remain silent. The Tunku rejected the proposal, Lee Kuan Yew told Malay journalists: the Tunku believed it was too late. That day the Tunku sent a handwritten message to Dr Toh Chin Chye, Chairman of the People's Action Party, confessing that he had lost control. The Tunku's letter was not dated. It read as follows:

"My dear Chin Chye,
I am writing to tell you that I have given the matter of our break with Singapore my utmost consideration and I find that in the interest of our friendship and the security and peace of Malaysia as a whole there is absolutely no other way out. If I were strong enough and able to exercise complete control of the situation I might perhaps have delayed action, but I am not, and so while I am able to counsel tolerance and patience I think the amiable settlement of our differences in this way is the only possible way out. I request you most urgently to agree. Kind Regards, Yours sincerely, Abdul Rahman."

Dr Toh Chin Chye replied on 8 August thanking him "for your undated letter which I received yesterday. It is indeed sad that in your view our problems can be solved only by asking Singapore to quit Malaysia and this barely two years from the day Malaysia was inaugurated.

"My colleagues and I would prefer that Singapore remain in Malaysia and we felt that there could be other solutions to the present impasse. However, as you have indicated that the situation does not lend itself to any other workable settlement, and as you have impressed upon me that Singapore remaining in Malaysia will lead to a situation you may not be able to control, we have no alternative but to be resigned to your wish that Singapore leaves the Federation of Malaysia.

"I and my colleagues had rejoiced at the reunification of Singapore with Malaya in September 1963. It has come as a blow to us that the peace and security of Malaysia can only be secured by the expulsion of Singapore from Malaysia. If this is the price for peace in Malaya and Singapore then we must accept it however agonizing our inner feelings may be. Although lasting unification of Singapore and Malaya has not been achieved this time, nevertheless it is my profound belief that future generations will succeed where we have failed... With kind regards, Yours sincerely, Toh Chin Chye."

Later the same day, Lee Kuan Yew told other journalists that he believed that bloodshed could have been avoided with a looser Federation. "Smack down six people. Six people, smack them down. Stop this poison in the Jawi Press... They run this Press. Smack down six people. Have a looser federation and this thing will tick. Now it is over..."

Lee Kuan Yew repeated this assertion the following day, on 12 August, when he was interviewed by Neville Peterson of the Australian Broadcasting Commission. He told Peterson, "It is just six men, six wild men, ultras, who caused this. They squeezed the Tunku; and last year, after the riots, I told the Tunku it was all up to him; anything he said. He should have smacked Jaafar Albar down then. He waited one year: it is one year too late."

Fred Emery of *The Times* of London interviewed Lee Kuan Yew the same day. Lee said that in Kuala Lumpur one of the versions of the trouble was that he wanted to be Prime Minister of Malaysia, and was therefore a man with overweening ambition who wanted to oust the Tunku and take over, and so on.

"Didn't you want to be Prime Minister of Malaysia one day?" asked Emery. Prime Minister replied, "One day, perhaps, but not for a very long time. We want to bring the races and the States together. It takes time, for the thing to happen. And we were quite prepared to help them in a secondary capacity. But they didn't want it."

XIV

Gradually the rest of the story emerged. On 14 August, Lee told

287

Richard Croll of Channel Seven in Sydney, Sam Lipski of *The Bulletin*, Gavin Young of *The Observer* and Rene McColl of *The Daily Express* of London, that the PAP had been prepared to set up a government in exile in Cambodia, if necessary.

Lee Kuan Yew made the admission when he was asked if it was not a fact that Jaafar Albar wanted the Constitution to be suspended, Lee to be gaoled, and Singapore ruled by edict. "In fact," said Croll, "the alternative was that you resigned or Singapore separated?" Lee denied those were the alternatives, but he agreed that Albar wanted him in gaol. As for taking over the Singapore Government and ruling by edict, Lee said they were prepared for that. "Prince Sihanouk is a very personal friend of mine and Phnom Penh is very close to Malaysia. I would be in gaol because I cannot run away... But quite a number of my colleagues who have got international contacts could run a much more effective campaign than the Indonesians or the communists ever can." Lee went on to say that the idea was abandoned because of the realization that a government in exile, if it ever came to that, could lead to race conflict.

But what if he had personally resigned? Lee said he had been prepared to do that, to serve under Dr Toh. "But my colleagues could not accept it because they would be in a worse position. Mr Tan Siew Sin openly said in Parliament that there could be no co-operation with Singapore so long as I am the Prime Minister of Singapore. Do you think if I resigned, Singapore would believe there would be co-operation, or that the Malaysian Government had got its own way?" Lee argued that his successor would have to take an even firmer line than he took to avoid being dubbed a Malaysian stooge.

Sam Lipski wrote an article in the 21 August issue of *The Bulletin* in which he said: "One of the last solutions which was suggested, and which some people believe might have worked, was a plan whereby the Kuala Lumpur Government would have accepted two PAP Ministers, Dr Goh Keng Swee and Lim Kim San, into the Alliance Government, in return for Lee Kuan Yew's accepting the Malaysian ambassadorship at the United Nations. Although this plan was not exactly hailed by the Alliance leadership because it feared that Lee would be making his own foreign policy, it might have worked if Lee had not stipulated that he would accept the job but only for two years. This left the Alliance leaders fearing the return of a Lee firmly established as a world figure just in time for the 1967 Federal elections. This hitherto well-kept secret proposal had the indirect blessing of Britain, Australia and New Zealand."

The proposal was one of several conceived by the British High Commissioner, Lord Head, none of which were ever seriously considered by the Alliance Government—or by Lee Kuan Yew.

XV

Utusan Melayu continued to follow a narrow racial line, and began to print stories that Christians were trying to get Muslims to change their faith. They printed interviews with Muslims prepared to say that Christian priests had offered them women and money to adopt Christianity. None of these stories was true. Each was proved to be false. The Prime Minister said the intention of *Utusan Melayu* was to incite. Their purpose, he declared publicly on 26 September, was to create racial and religious conflict. Many Afro-Asian countries such as the United Arab Republic and Algeria were Muslim countries. "If *Utusan Melayu* succeeds in its attempt to cause friction," added Lee Kuan Yew, "we will be in trouble."

Five days later, Lee Kuan Yew summoned religious leaders and members of the Inter-Religious Council to his office. "You all know," he told them, "that there is an active, vicious campaign which is working up into a crescendo. The allegation is that the Catholics are going around, looking for Muslims; and then when they find a Muslim, a young boy preferably, they ply him with a beautiful female Christian and with $500 and the promise of a job. Then they convert him into a Christian. And a special kind of Christian: a Roman Catholic. That is as I read the translations of the *Utusan Melayu*, our well-known if not so well-loved newspaper: this is what Catholics and Christians do. They have got nothing better to do, they go around looking for nice Muslim youths to do this to them. This is religious agit-prop but, I think, not without political objectives.

"If, for instance, trouble were to break out between Muslims and Christians in Singapore, regardless of who gets the worst of it, my position with the Muslim leaders of Africa would be somewhat embarrassed... This, maybe, is one of the objects of the exercise— one of the political objects.

"It could be that there are multifarious objects. You have one bullet and it ricochets and it knocks a few other objects down. One of the other objects is, of course, to get the Muslim community outside Singapore, in Southeast Asia, excited into a very bellicose frame of mind with the result that the non-Muslims, particularly in the other parts of Southeast Asia, may be suitably reduced to a state of mild and submissive docility. And this is one of the ricochets of this kind of exercise.

"Now, I have no jurisdiction over what happens outside Singapore. But I am responsible for what happens *in* Singapore, and I have the advantage and privilege this morning of discussing this problem with the Christian leaders first separately, and next with the Inter-Religious Council, and now with the Christian leaders and the Inter-Religious Council which also has Christian representatives.

"Now gentlemen, I would like to leave it to you, if I may, in the next hour, to deliberate amongst yourselves and to come out with a clear, crisp statement of facts and intention. The facts are fairly reasonably clear: this is a worked-up synthetic campaign. Synthetic froth is being generated. But, if I could get from you—after your deliberation—a statement of your intentions, that you understand what I have said: that this is a multiracial, multilingual, multireligious society, and that tolerance between racial groups, linguistic groups and religious groups, is of the essence for our survival; and if you could give that assurance not to me—because you have already given it to me—but give that assurance to the people of Singapore in general, then you would have done a service to all the people of Singapore, to all religious beliefs; and even done service to the heathens and the animists and the idol-worshippers and so on...

"I have assured the Christians that Singapore has many people with no religious beliefs whatsoever... I would say more than seventy per cent are either vaguely agnostic or iconoclasts... And there is a very wide field of operation. I see no need for going around looking for the twelve per cent Muslims to try and convert them because I think there are sixty to seventy per cent of people who are in need of some form of religious and moral guidance..."

XVI

When Sri Dinesh Singh, the Indian Deputy Minister for External Affairs, came to Singapore on 8 October the Prime Minister, at a dinner in his honour, spoke of Singapore's debt to India, of India's friendship and help. "And it didn't start yesterday," Lee added. He said that it "started many years ago when the Indian Congress Movement knocked the bottom out of the British Empire and set the world free... whether we liked it or not we have so many things, so many problems in common—multiracialism, multilingualism, multireligion. Furthermore, we are trying to solve these problems on the basis of a secular, scientific, modern state. We do not believe in obscurantism. We are not a theocratic state, nor is India. So we share so many attitudes in common...

"I take pride in the fact that here, in this corner of Southeast Asia, and in some neighbouring territories which are no longer part of us, four great civilizations met in confluence: the Malay, the Indian, the Chinese and the European—and did not just meet yesterday. It met over centuries. The Portuguese came, the Dutch came, the British came and stayed for 140 years and we took over from them.

"We inherited this. But, we inherited more than this. Like you, we inherited a set of values: right and wrong, good and bad, friend and foe. And our tragedy is that we know that if our foe wins we will die, and die painfully, but that when we win our foes live comfortably even in prison with butter and eggs and meat according to special rations which the rules of the game lay down upon us. This is in part an unequal conflict because, on the one side is terror which is absolute, on the other side is terror which is not really terror. It is just a deterrent, and often no more than a soporific. You put a man in, you feed him, he studies, he writes memoirs, he comes out, he fights. The other side, he pulls your finger-nails out and you are dead—and that is real terror.

"But, alas, we have not found a solution that will resolve this imbalance of deterrents without ourselves losing what we believe we are fighting for: a just, equal, and a humane society. And we hope that over the years, slowly around Southeast Asia as we get closer to one another—because we must, if we are to survive, support one another's independence and integrity—we will find some means of preventing this seepage of terror. And eventually, I hope, as I am sure you would wish to see too, the Indian, the Chinese, the Malay, and what was given to us of the European in Southeast Asia, fused and integrated into one tolerant, peaceful, peace-loving nation. India has only that path to travel if she is to survive. And so also with Singapore. We have some neighbours who believe that they've got other options. We think that they have not, but they are determined to try. We do not think that the theocratic state can solve these problems of multiracialism, multireligion, and multilingualism, multi-cultures. And we can only cross our fingers and hope that in the process of trying they would not destroy whatever chance there is left of redeeming what was good in our past.

"We are really ancient peoples stranded in the part of the world which the ancient Hindus used to pass by... the climate was so inhospitable, the soil was so infertile, they passed us by and they went on to Java and they built Borobudur. There are no ruins because there wasn't anything worth building on until they discovered rubber and tin. And that's where my great-grandfather came in. And that's where I am now. Having built this Singapore we are determined to keep it. This is mine. This is every Singaporean's, regardless of race, religion, culture, language. We built this together, and I say we will live here together, peacefully if we may..."

XVII

Towards the end of the year, Dr Subandrio, Indonesia's Foreign

Minister, proposed that there should be bilateral negotiations over confrontation with Singapore, and Malaya, and with the Borneo states, all separately.

Lee Kuan Yew discussed this proposal during a televised interview with four foreign correspondents on 11 December. The correspondents were Dennis Bloodworth of *The Observer*, Arthur Cook of the *Daily Mail*, Bill Gasson of Reuters, and Patrick Killen of UPI. Dennis Bloodworth said there were indications from Kuala Lumpur that they regarded the whole proposition with suspicion. He asked how Lee felt about it.

The Prime Minister said he thought it was up to the people in Sabah and Sarawak to show their solidarity with Malaysia, if they felt that way inclined. "If we were still a component state of Malaysia, were doing well in Malaysia, and were progressing towards the kind of society we wanted, and the Indonesians made us this offer, we would be outraged at the provocativeness of it. But we are out of Malaysia and we have to look at our own little sector."

Arthur Cook asked if Singapore would set up diplomatic relations with an Indonesia that was still at variance with Malaysia. The Prime Minister replied: "We want to be friends with Malaysia, but that does not mean that we have to be unfriendly with all the people who are unfriendly to Malaysia. Malaysia's friends may be our friends, but Malaysia's enemies need not be our enemies. In fact, as you will have noticed from the policy statement delivered by the Head of State recently, we have made it quite clear that we want the maximum number of friends and the minimum number of hostile or unfriendly states . . ."

Bill Gasson wanted to know if Lee would be prepared to mediate between Malaysia and Indonesia "if you do meet up with the Indonesians, somewhere, at some time". Lee said that Singapore had always been a kind of middleman, but he thought that sort of transaction a bit too heavy, "and we will leave it to bigger and more competent nations . . ." Lee added, however, that "the overriding interest of the people of Singapore demands that they should never let down the people of Malaysia." As for Dr Subandrio's proposal, Singapore was open to all propositions. "They will be carefully looked into and seriously considered. And the decisions we will arrive at will be based on the long-term considerations which we can never afford to forget, and of course, on the short-term benefits which may be worthwhile pursuing in certain circumstances."

Arthur Cook asked if the Prime Minister was thinking of trade benefits or politics. Lee Kuan Yew replied that he was thinking in terms of survival. "I mean, trade is valuable in so far as it feeds our people and increases our national income. But if we take steps which end up with the Malaysian side of the one people coming to grief, then I think this is part of the implication behind the Head of State's recent address: that if Singapore is unwise and shortsighted and plays with opportunist policies, Singapore may find itself surrounded by a hostile sea of obscurantist and xenophobic forces which will necessitate very drastic measures for survival. This situation should be prevented; it should never be allowed to arise. We must never forget our abiding destiny as part of the continent of Asia."

Patrick Killen asked Lee under what conditions he would be prepared to meet with the Indonesian Government.

Prime Minister: "Conditions? I will meet anybody any time any place to seek peace."

What would be the next step? Dennis Bloodworth asked that question. The Prime Minister in his reply revealed that the Indonesians had been making overtures from time to time, and from time to time Singapore responded to those overtures. "And no doubt, if they wish to pursue the matter further, an overture will be made. And I have already indicated that our response will be one of sincerely desiring peace without jeopardizing our security, our integrity, and the survival of the one people now in two countries."

Asked by Arthur Cook if he intended to consult the British at the same time, the Prime Minister said that before any decision was made which would affect Britain's interests, or would jeopardize the interests of the people of Malaysia, "I think we would be very unwise not to consult Britain ... it would certainly be criminal folly if we allowed the Malaysians to go down the drain ... I think the Government in Jakarta knows our stand on these basic long-term factors of survival, and within that framework it may still be worthwhile to make certain adjustments."

Bill Gasson wanted to know if Lee expected Indonesia formally to recognize Singapore as an independent state before meeting with any Indonesian. The Prime Minister said that Singapore did not really mind whether people recognized them or not. "We are here to stay! The majority of the world recognizes us, and those who don't, well, it is up to them ... China has existed as a communist republic for sixteen years. China has not been hindered by the fact that a large part of the world does not recognize her ... We are here to stay and we have every intention of staying here for the next thousand years."

In another question, Bill Gasson asked if Singapore had decided when to resume barter trade with Indonesia.

Lee Kuan Yew replied: "I would say that we have decided on the fact of barter trade long ago." Pressed for a date, the Prime Minister said he had no intention of prejudicing "what is going on at the moment. We would like to bear in mind the interwoven nature of our defence arrangements. We would be loath to do anything which anybody could say might upset the defence structure ... "

Replying to further questions, Lee answered: "We have said:

293

'Defence and security are closely interwoven between Singapore and Malaysia.' That is premise number one. Premise number two: 'Defence and security are indivisible from trade and industry.' But premise number two will have to be left over for some time until the meaning percolates through. We would hate to do anything to upset premise number one, or to do anything which would go against that premise. So long as there is any way in which we can live, we are viable, we are sound — well, we'll carry on. But, to be viable, and to be sound, we've got to live and to live we've got to have markets and trade with all the world — not just with Indonesia. The Indonesian trade was 8·7 per cent of our national income. And we have made that up. But that is not the point. There is a bigger principle at stake. Can somebody tell my people that they will not trade with Russia, for instance? It may well come to that if we concede one small point..." Later in the interview the Prime Minister revealed that the Soviet Union and Eastern European countries would be sending trade missions to Singapore.

This prompted Arthur Cook to ask if it was Singapore's policy to put some accent on friendship with the communist side of the world.

Lee Kuan Yew said he did not think there was any necessity to change attitudes. "Our attitudes were formulated in the early fifties, on the basis of being friendly to all; on the basis that Russia is there to stay, and China is there to stay, and so is North Korea and North Vietnam, and lots of other parts of the world, and we are going to live with them. It is not within our dispensation to decide whether they are to survive or they are to go under. We assume they will be there for the next thousand years and we will live with them. Similarly with Britain, the West — they are there. We want to trade with them. We want to live with them. But we want to stay out of either the East or the West. We want to be ourselves. And I think we are in that particular phase of history... we have gone through the dullest phase, when non-alignment was an immoral act. I think the Americans now realize that in certain parts of the world non-alignment may be a jolly good thing for them, because it saves them the cost of involvement. And it is not all that far-fetched that the Russians, and eventually others as well, may decide that non-involvement of countries like Singapore, and even Malaysia, may be in their long-term interests. And that will suit us fine."

Asked by Patrick Killen about his views on the Vietnam conflict, Lee Kuan Yew said they were exactly what they were six months earlier. "I think it is a very grim situation because the will to resist is largely imported, the capacity to resist is also largely imported. But what alternative is there for the time being?" The Prime Minister felt that whether the South Vietnamese wanted to come together with the North Vietnamese, or whether they wanted to stay distinct and separate, South Vietnam, he hoped, would determine. "But the first prerequisite

At a concert in Budapest

At Invercargil, New Zealand

In Egypt, at the Great Dam

On a visit to the United Arab Republic, Lee visited the famed Temple of Abul Simbel

A windy day in San Francisco. With Professor Oppenheimer, Singapore's Ambassador in Washington

Relaxing in Greece

Lee Kuan Yew in Moscow, in 1962

In Tokyo, with the Emperor and Empress of Japan

Receiving an honorary doctorate from the Governor of Hong Kong, Sir David Trench

In Bulgaria. Climbing to the top of the monument to the Russian armies

In 1969, Lee Kuan Yew was made an honorary bencher of the Inner Temple

With the youngsters in Cambodia

is that nobody should impose a solution on South Vietnam."

Dennis Bloodworth wound up the interview by asking the Prin Minister about the "rather interesting developments on the Left-wir front in Singapore". The Barisan seemed to be taking a pro-Chine line and Lim Chin Siong, in prison, appeared to be taking a pro-Sovi line, "in other words, one of peaceful co-existence rather than acti revolution". How did Lee Kuan Yew assess the two rather divergei events?

The Prime Minister described this as a schism that was inevitabl It was in the making fairly early on, even in the 1960-1961 phas "They were at that time pursuing the soft line, hoping thereby t capture the PAP, and then the Legislative Assembly, and then go o to capture the Government. Well, that didn't work. And the questio then arose for them whether they should go back to revolution. An I think those who were outside gaol decided they would go on wit the revolution and treat this constitutionalism just as a side-line. An there were some, like Lim Chin Siong, who believed that this wa futile and would lead to more unhappiness for them. History wil decide who is right and who is wrong. I am quite sure that both side are wrong: that in this part of the world neither brand of Marxist Leninism is going to succeed. I think it is just who is more wrong Fortunately for us, the chaps who are outside peddling this hard lin — that Singapore's independence is phoney, its existence is phoney its policies are fascist, that it should recognize and exchange diplomati representation with Indonesia and China to the exclusion of all other — fortunately, I say, these hardliners are probably less sane than th other side."

XVIII

A sober and dispassionate account of all that led up to Singapore's eviction from Malaysia was presented by Lee Kuan Yew to Parliament on 14 December. No members of the Opposition were present. The Barisan Sosialis decided to boycott Parliament. Later they all resigned. By 1967, after by-elections, the PAP occupied forty-nine of the fifty-one seats. The other two were held by Barisan Sosialis members who went underground. In the 1968 elections the PAP won all 58 seats in the new Parliament.

Lee said it was not often that a people achieved independence the way Singaporeans did. There were a number of unusual features about Singapore and its geographic, economic and demographic nexus with Malaya. There have been cases in history where nations have fallen apart into independent halves—like Syria and Egypt. But then

Syria was already an independent nation before she went into voluntary federation with Egypt. There have been federations like the Central African Federation or the West Indian Federation which did not succeed and component parts of the federated whole then became sovereign as in the case of Zambia, Malawi, Jamaica, Trinidad and Tobago.

"But," said Lee, "I think in the annals of nation-making, Singapore must occupy a unique place. For one of the most strategic islands in the whole world acquired sovereignty over its Western, European bases without violent revolution.

"For the price of about $70 million in loss of revenue over two years, an excess of payment over actual federal expenditure in Singapore of $25 million per annum making approximately $50 million for two years, and the loss of two years of currency profits at $10 million a year, we acquired sovereignty without bloodshed. If we could put things in pecuniary terms, that was the price we paid in place of blood—not that the British would have taken that price, for I think they knew the value of this real estate in Singapore...

"But there was another price which we paid besides the $70 million: two years in which we came face to face very rapidly with the stark realities of conflict over race, over language, over religion. Very quickly all the cliches of inter-communal co-operation were shorn off as we found ourselves confronted with a somewhat crude and blatant attempt to subdue us as a submissive member of a federation, the inner workings of which we were not so conversant with before Malaysia. Whilst we laid the emphasis on the constitutional framework and good faith, intending to bring the territories and the peoples closer together as they operated within one national unit, sharing one economic system, irrevocably wedded together by ties of common experience and the fact that their destinies have been so closely interwoven in the past, we found that there were certain inarticulate major premises upon which others had based their calculations. And the Constitution which was written, and the inarticulate major premises of race, language and religion which were unwritten, were irreconcilable.

"All that is over for us for the time being. Not that the problem has been solved; but that for us, the problem does not immediately arise. What we wish to do now is to get into a new working relationship with our former partners in Malaysia...

"Before a new working relationship is established, we must first dispel the illusion that because we wanted merger in Malaysia, therefore we were vulnerable without merger. Whilst politically an independent Singapore holds hazards in the longterm, not just for ourselves but for all in Southeast Asia, economically it does not follow that it is within the dispensation of our neighbours to decide our economic destiny... Eventually, I am reasonably confident that we can reach a rational relationship—not one in which the bigger assumes automatically that he must get the greater benefit, but a relationship in which each and every step is weighed in accordance as to whether it is of value to them and to us..."

The Prime Minister reminded the House why the Opposition decided to absent itself. On the day Parliament assembled on 8 December, the Barisan Sosialis issued a special edition of its party publication called *Shih Chen Pau*. In this publication the Barisan explained why it boycotted Parliament, and why it was not going to participate. They attributed three reasons why Parliament was convened. "First, to give legal seal to our departure from Malaysia which was a neo-colonialist plot to divide and rule. Second, to get legal cover for our abuse of public funds. Third, to use this session of Parliament as a platform for propaganda to cheat the people and confuse them." They therefore came to these conclusions: "Under these circumstances to attend Parliament and to lend support and credence to the mockery enacted by the PAP, either intentionally or otherwise, is to help the PAP to cheat the people with regard to Singapore's false independence. And the final conclusion is: therefore, if we are to oppose them, we must resolutely expose the PAP, the falseness of their parliamentary democracy and their anti-the-people views. Also, we must go a step further and expose the falseness of Singapore's independence..."

Lee concluded from this that the Barisan Sosialis were now anti the Parliamentary system. "This is a challenge to the whole system of government. They consider that system to be the handmaid—to put it in orthodox Marxist-Leninist verse—the handmaid of the capitalist monopoly. And whether it is the Parliament of Singapore or whether it is the Parliament of Westminster, it is the instrument of repression of the revolutionary working-class which the communists say they represent.

"Logically, arising from those attitudes, not only must they boycott formal sessions of this House—since this is a ruse and guise to confuse the populace with the false independence that we have acquired to get legal sanctions and respectability for votes on public expenditure which we are seeking—but they have to carry the battle one step further: wreck it. The question is how?

"For all these years, we strenuously sought to prove that, in fact, they were operating on the twin premises of (1) work the system and shake it and rock it, (2) undermine it altogether. In other words, use constitutional forms of struggle which the bourgeois enemy is foolish enough to afford the communists, use the public forum, not to work it better but to denounce the system and break it, shake public confidence in it. And the other: the armed revolution, where state power is wrested from the hands of the monopoly capitalists and vested in the hands of the vanguards of the proletariat—the communist party.

"I am not quite sure whether the present leaders of the Barisan Sosialis intend to pursue this to its logical conclusion or whether they intend to go back to the much more subtle line which they used to follow of pretending to be a constitutional party whilst at the same time operating on directives issued by illegal and unconstitutional parties seeking to usurp power by violent means. But I think it is useful for us to remember that whatever the shifts and turns of policy or tactics, from time to time, their objective never changes. . ."

Lee then went on to deal with "the danger of a major catastrophe which we can precipitate if we are not conscious of the problems of finding a new balance in Southeast Asia to take the place of a balance which was maintained by the European empires before the war." Lee argued that the multiracial character of the population of Singapore and the states of Malaysia created the probabilities of two different trends. As long as British rule put everybody in place, multiracialism, or the problems of having a multiplicity of communities of different races, languages, religions, never gave rise to any problems of law and order. The British Raj decided who should do what and who fulfilled what roles in their system. The disappearance of direct political control brought about the necessity of finding an authority indigenous to the peoples now residing in those territories, and a compromise was found in certain forms of elected representation weighted to hold the balance between people who were supposed to be indigenous, and those who were supposed to be more recent immigrants.

"As long as we were one, Singapore and Malaysia, the danger of multiracial communities going their separate ways was less than it is now. If we are not conscious of this and we each play only to our own immediate electorate, then having two halves of one whole —and not very equal halves of one whole—one in Singapore, people of migrant stock, the other, in Malaya, peoples of indigenous stock, will bring about a polarization of policies and attitudes which, in the end, may well bring major calamity for all in Southeast Asia, with repercussions throughout the whole of Asia. . .

"If, on the Singapore half, account is taken only of the Singapore sector of this one people, then the solution that will be derived out of that one sector will be very different from the solution which will be derived if we took into account the whole. And the very different solution attempted here, based on the demographic features of Singapore, will in turn act as a spur to contrary measures being taken on the other side. And so it could go on until inevitable conflict. Conflict, not only between two independent and sovereign nations but between two independent and sovereign nations both with plural societies.

"We are no longer in a position to decide, or in any way to influence, the course of political events in Malaysia. That was the price of independence for Singapore. But I think we would be dishonest to ourselves if we did not express a profound interest in the policies and the consequences of such policies upon the relationship between the communities in Malaysia which would, in turn, help to influence attitudes and relationships between communities in Singapore. . .

"But whilst we have no control over events there, independence has given us a unique opportunity to order our way of life, and I would like to believe that the two years we spent in Malaysia are years which will not be easily forgotten, years in which the people of migrant stock here—who are a majority—learnt of the terrors and the follies and the bitterness which is generated when one group tries to assert its dominance over the other on the basis of one race, one language, one religion. It is because I am fortified by this that my colleagues and I were determined, as from the moment of separation, that this lesson will never be forgotten. So it is that into the Constitution of the Republic of Singapore will be built-in safeguards in so far as the human mind can devise means whereby the conglomeration of numbers, of likeness—as a result of affinities of race or language or culture—shall never work to the detriment of those who, by the accident of history, find themselves in minority groups in Singapore. . .

"Mr Speaker, we have a vested interest in multiracialism and the secular state, for the antithesis of multiracialism and the antithesis of secularism holds perils of enormous magnitude not just for the people living here in Southeast Asia but dangers of involvement by bigger powers who see in such a conflict fertile ground for exploitation of either the ideological or other power interests.

"The future is not ours to see, but we can safely conclude that there are two possible trends in which events can unfold themselves. One, the emergence in one half of a tolerant society not based on the concepts of exclusiveness of race, language, religion; which means an ultimate reassociation, a political reassociation, of the parts which form the one larger federation of which we were a number until so recently; and the other, a trend towards a bias and emphasis on exclusiveness of race, language, religion, which must have fissiparous effects, divisive effects on the other.

"There is an element of urgency in this; and we are reassured to see an air of more confidence in dealing with problems of language and culture now that we are out of Malaysia. This in turn helps us in our solution of the problems on this side and, for us, we can only hope that ultimately our policies will also be able to help our

299

neighbours in reaching similar rational adjustments in their own domestic arrangements. . .

"We are here in Southeast Asia for better or for worse and we are here to stay, and our policies are designed to ensure that we stay peacefully in Southeast Asia in accord and amity with our neighbours but with a right to decide how we order our own lives in our own homes. And every action, every policy must be decided by this yard-stick. Any policy which endangers our long-term interests as a separate and distinct community in this region must be eschewed; and any act, any programme, and decision which will help to secure a more enduring future for ourselves and our progeny in this region must be pursued whatever the sacrifice.

"We have not sought this particular formula of survival, but it is now the basis on which we move forward; and with independence comes an independence of action in policy and planning which can help establish that enduring basis for ourselves in Southeast Asia. It is with confidence—a confidence born out of the past performance of our people—that we feel we can overcome problems of economic development, problems of unemployment.

"But in the other wider fields of inter-racial harmony, tolerance, there are so many other factors that even though we are independent, we have not got an exclusive prerogative to decide what is to be that relationship, even between our own citizens. For as I have said, there are other factors, factors outside our dispensation which can affect our own position. But whatever the result will be, I think we would like those who come after us to believe—and to have grounds for believing—that we did not leave a stone unturned in seeking a just and enduring future for all the people who made up the society—those who were here when the British were in control and those who are now rooted in this corner of Southeast Asia and whose destinies are interwoven—whatever we would have wished it to be."

CHAPTER TWENTY

The Year of Power 1966

THROUGHOUT 1966, the Barisan Sosialis continued its boycott of Parliament (inaugurated in December, 1965), and towards the end of the year ordered its remaining nine Members of Parliament to resign. This was in accordance with pro-communist assertions that neither national independence, nor parliamentary democracy, existed in Singapore. The Barisan Sosialis decided to "carry on outside Parliament the struggle against imperialist oppression". PAP candidates were elected to all their places bringing the total PAP membership of Parliament to forty-nine. The remaining seats were considered to be occupied by Barisan Sosialis MPs. They went underground in 1963, and are believed to be in Indonesia.

During the year, Indonesia ended its confrontation of Malaysia and Singapore, and trade between Singapore and Indonesia was resumed. Private traders in Singapore agreed to a $150,000,000 credit for trade in rubber and tin.

To dispel "any false image of Singapore as an anti-communist bastion and armed stronghold of British imperialism", Lee Kuan Yew, accompanied by the

Foreign Minister, S. Rajaratnam, toured five East European countries after visiting Cambodia, Thailand, the United Arab Republic, Britain and Sweden, where Lee spoke at the Socialist International. Later, Lee and the Foreign Minister paid an official visit to India.

At the Commonwealth Prime Ministers' Conference in London Lee Kuan Yew played a crucial role in helping to reach agreement on the Rhodesia issue.

During the year Singapore signed trade agreements with the Soviet Union, Bulgaria, Poland, Hungary and North Korea. More factories were opened in Jurong. Singapore now had 2,500 factories. Total import and export trade increased to $7,097·8 million, but, in spite of an annual creation of over 10,000 jobs a year, ten per cent of the economically available population remained unemployed.

Pro-communist elements were active among students and in trade unions, but they failed to obtain popular support for the issues they tried to exploit.

Relations with Malaysia continued to be correct but not close.

302

I

IN his New Year Message for 1966, Lee Kuan Yew said that Singapore would concentrate upon two tasks: the strengthening of ties "with those closest to us in identity of interests, to expand trade, and to establish assured markets for our industries", and at home "to create the pre-conditions for rapid industrial growth", by which Lee meant "a sound, stable, and predictable political situation". Lee said he believed that a nation could be bound together "without coercion, all into one race, or one language, or one religion".

Hari Raya Puasa fell on 21 January, and in his message to the Malays the Prime Minister reminded them that in independent Singapore all men were brothers. "All men are equal citizens and their cultural, religious and linguistic heritage will be respected. On this Hari Raya Puasa, I send my good wishes to all Muslim citizens and wish them security, progress and happiness in the years ahead.

"We are a people of many communities. The happiness of all communities depends upon our ability to be tolerant of each other, of our different habits of life and of religion. No one community will be allowed by virtue of its larger number to impose its way of life on the others, either in matters of religion, language or culture. Slowly, over the years, we must raise and equalize the opportunities of education and employment so that all will have an equal chance for a good job and a decent life. . ."

Chinese New Year was celebrated shortly afterwards. "This," said Lee Kuan Yew, "is the first Chinese New Year we celebrate as our own masters. It is cause for rejoicing. The Year of the Horse will bring us strength to defend what we have got and to build a better future for our people. We must plan and work for this. We must be conscious of our rights as joint owners of our country. We must together protect these rights and repel any pressure to prevent us from exercising our sovereignty. We must instil into our children that sense of endeavour to greater purpose which alone can secure our place in Southeast Asia.

"But in the midst of these rejoicings, abundance of good food and good clothes, and free from the stifling shroud of silent intimidation and the threat of oppression, let us remember our friends and relatives who are struggling to achieve the ideals of human equality and justice which guide our own society. For in the end our destinies cannot be separated. Let us renew our resolve that in co-operation with like-minded peoples in Southeast Asia we shall build a better and more just society."

February started badly. There was a riot with strong racial undertones at a military training depot, sparked off by misunderstanding over an order. Lee handled this himself, and the danger passed. There was more tension a few days later when the Tunku refused to move his Malaysian troops from barracks needed by Singapore soldiers back from a tour of duty on the jungle frontier in Sabah. They were looking forward to getting into their own barracks again. Instead, they were told to pitch their tents in a park because the Malaysians would not move out. The Tunku insisted that under the Independence of Singapore Agreement the Singapore Government was responsible for providing Malaysian troops with suitable accommodation. Lee disagreed and offered to take the issue to an independent Commonwealth or international tribunal for a ruling. The offer was not accepted, and to avoid trouble Lee found the Malaysians alternative accommodation. The Malaysian troops vacated this in 1968 and returned to Malaysia.

II

Every developing state must define the status and the purpose of its universities. Lee Kuan Yew's stand is that education must serve the people in their plans and their hopes to develop the nation's economy. In Singapore Lee faced additional problems created by Chinese chauvinists, and the exploitation of the Nanyang University, founded to perpetuate Chinese language and culture.

"What is the value of a university to the targets, or the objectives, which I would like to achieve? What does it cost? Could I achieve the same targets by sending men abroad at perhaps less cost?"

Those were questions Lee Kuan Yew asked himself when he opened a seminar on the role of universities in economic and social development, at the University of Singapore on 7 February. Lee said that before he answered the questions, which involved the value of the University of Singapore, Nanyang University, the Polytechnic, and other institutions, he wanted to say what he thought was the milieu in which these values were determined.

"We are," he said, "talking of newly-independent countries in Asia, in Africa. Almost without exception, all the leaders who have emerged in the first generation of leaders have been people who received a university education, usually abroad—whether you take Jawaharlal Nehru, Mohamed Ali Jinnah, Don Senanayake of Ceylon, Tunku Abdul Rahman of Malaysia, Kwame Nkrumah, Jomo Kenyatta, Dr Hastings Banda, Julius Nyerere or Milton Obote. They have all been through universities.

"The net result is that the acquisition of a university degree is deemed a status symbol of immense political magnitude in all these newly-independent countries. The argument is: 'If my leader is what

304

he is, it must have been because he went and imbibed knowlege; and if I can similarly imbibe knowledge, I can therefore similarly emerge.' Hence, the great desire of all institutions of tertiary education in all these newly-independent countries to award university degrees.

"This presents us with our first problem. Is the university degree a symbol or proof that a man has imbibed knowledge? Or is it a certificate that the man has gone through certain disciplines which will enable him to do critical analysis in search of the truth and which will enable him to be capable of creative thought? And the biggest problem faced by all universities in newly-independent nations is that, with a very few exceptions, the university degree is only a proof that a certain amount of knowledge has been imbibed, that the graduate has gone through a test which indicates that he has imbibed a mini-mum amount of knowledge within a certain fixed space of time. . .

"I would like to propound what I think is the role of universities in such situations: how a university can best reach a position where it can discharge its role. With the exception of Japan, seventy-five per cent of the universities in Afro-Asia were established after inde-pendence. The faculties that have been established invariably are the easier faculties to establish—the arts and the humanities. Very few have had science and technology faculties. So they all inherit more or less a situation such as ours, where we have established a more or less educated elite in the sense that they can write, they can read, they can compose their thoughts, they can perhaps become administrators, they can alleviate suffering as doctors or help discharge the administration of justice as lawyers; they can, in fact, increase our population and our capacity to consume, but they are unable to increase the things that the people want to consume. Our men who can produce our modern industrial society—our industrial chemists, our technocrats—are missing. So, in so far as the first stage is con-cerned, our problem is accentuated, and not solved. I think there is considerable truth in the proposition that the more you persist in pro-ducing men who are educated, but unable to increase productive capa-city, the more you are heading for an unstable situation.

"I think what we must at the same time remember is that this is a position not easily remedied; not *quickly* remedied. For you do not produce a technocrat in the tertiary stage. You begin by producing him in the secondary stage. And unless you are first able to remedy *that* lack, it is unlikely that your university can fulfil its function of produc-ing the man who can produce for you the industrial society.

"But I think the biggest dearth of talent in the university in a situation such as ours is not just a lack in the skills in the technologies required for a developed society or an industrial community, but, even more important and more urgent, the corps of informed thinking to lead, formulate and guide national thought on constructive lines. It is when this is lacking that military leaders can take over. If a population, like ours, revere people who have learning and scholarship, and if the people of learning and scholarship can give an informed lead on· these matters, it is very unlikely that obscurantist theories can find popular acceptance. It is when that is lacking that you find your ground beginning to accept xenophobic, obscurantist, absurd policies which are in no way related to their economic problems.

"In the countries of Afro-Asia the one that has emerged as an industrial state is Japan. And I therefore look with considerable interest at the teacher-to-student ratios and the subjects they teach. With a population of about ninety million the Japanese have a student-to-teacher ratio of 10:2. I then look at the other big country in Asia, India. With a student population of 1,107,000 in fifty universities, India has a student-to-teacher ratio of a 100:3, and even more interesting is the division of the students between the arts and the humanities, and science and technology. Again it is a reminder to me that the solution does not begin at the tertiary stage, but in the secondary stage; and that if you do not have your secondary pupils sufficiently equipped to go into science and technology in the tertiary stage, then your universities are unable yet to begin that function.

"The other country which is of relevance, because it faces a situation not unlike ours, is China. I have not been able to fathom the sum total figures of students. But I have discovered that there are fifteen universities for arts and sciences, and 125 engineering, technological, medical, agricultural and other specialized institutes or colleges. Surely the key to their industrial growth and their determination to emerge as an industrial power is the 125 engineering, technological and other specialized institutes or colleges?"

III

Five days later, Lee Kuan Yew made a speech in Mandarin to the Nanyang University graduates. He examined Singapore's position: the situation in Southeast Asia was increasingly critical, particularly the war in Vietnam, which was worrying the whole world. What· was happening in Indonesia was unclear. Developments in Malaysia were not easily foreseen. Singapore, it would appear, could ensure its own survival and consolidation. How long could this be maintained? "Let us," Lee continued, "suppose the British decide to pull out from Southeast Asia and from Singapore, and to leave the countries in Southeast Asia to decide the relationships between ourselves. What will happen to us then, with our present defence capacity? The Indonesians have an army of 400,000 and other neighbouring countries are much more powerful than us. We must calculate carefully, taking everything into consideration. All must understand that this is no longer a matter of survival of the individual, but a matter of the survival of a large group of people—of millions! What are the prospects of our survival?

"First of all, we must understand that, whether the Chinese in Burma, Thailand, Cambodia or Vietnam can or cannot be, have or have not been, completely assimilated with the indigenous peoples, in Singapore, Malaya, Sabah, Sarawak and Indonesia the descendants of the Chinese will be identifiable from the other races even a hundred years from now. They find it very, very difficult to be assimilated completely with the indigenous peoples. This is not because of language and culture, but more because of religion, a very important factor. And this will probably give rise, in the future, to a grave problem for the several millions of Chinese descendants in the region, because there are many people who think that, because you are a Chinese, you will one day become an agent of China or subversive element. It is not easy to dispel this sort of thinking. In the circumstances, do you not think you should quickly make up your minds how to defend your own interests?

"It has been said that, if the military might of China today were able to stand up to that of the United States, the problems which are being faced by the overseas Chinese—the Chinese in Southeast Asia—would be completely different. I cannot say how much merit there is in this view. But I have always felt that we are not so much overseas Chinese (that is to say Chinese who sojourn in the South Seas and then return to China), as descendants of Chinese. Nobody can change this: China is China, and we are ourselves. However, we must nevertheless sometimes take note of what others are thinking. . .

"I have been asked this question very often: how can the few millions of Chinese in this part of Southeast Asia survive, regarded as they are with suspicion by various quarters? And my answer is: establish a multiracial society where one community helps and respects the other.

"What some people dread most is the eventual establishment of such an equal and multiracial society. What they dread most is our being able to solve the problems of the Malays and our then being able to join hands with them. Why did they force us to leave Malaysia? If we were able to mobilize only the Chinese they would not have cared. But because we are also capable of helping the Malays, and of winning the Malays to our cause, they felt that it endangered their position. They then created contradictions and then exploited them without considering the outcome.

"If you want a Chinese chauvinistic society, failure is assured. Singapore will surely be isolated. . . We must firmly hold on to our

307

corner of Southeast Asia. It is not negotiable. But we must also try our best to establish a model, multiracial society based on the principle of equality..."

IV

At a Rotary Conference, on 19 March, the Prime Minister discussed the implication of the Rotarian principle "Service before Self" and wondered how he would interpret and implement that manifestly sound and humane principle in the circumstances in which Singapore found itself.

"I ask myself: 'Service before Self' means service to whom?—to my little community, to my nation or to humanity at large, the whole world? For there are different answers as you apply these different questions... ultimately the answer is: 'Service to man'. Mind you, if one seeks to implement this high ideal prematurely, disastrous consequences may well be brought upon one's own national head!

"As survival for the individual becomes more and more complex and not the simple business of a Robinson Crusoe with a knife and gun seeking shelter and food for survival, so it becomes increasingly difficult to define when selfishness becomes self-defeating. In a complex human society, individual and unrestrained selfishness is self-defeating because it destroys the community prosperity and security on which the individual comfort and prosperity are based. One must therefore move one step forward to enlightened unselfishness to one's own community, and from there, move eventually to service to mankind—if the human being is to survive with the ever more powerful weapons that he has shaped for himself in the conquest of this planet.

"In every community you have people who, for reasons of conscience or temperament, do more for their fellow men than the average person. And the 'do-gooder'—regardless of his motivations—*is* a valuable asset in any community, whether he is a Rotarian or a Seventh Day Adventist. Whether he seeks to save souls or bodies, he does do more than just ensure his own survival. He can, therefore, contribute to the survival of the whole community. But, unorganized individual unselfishness is often futile. And so, whether it is with Rotarians or with other charitable organizations or with governments, unselfishness to be effective must be organized.

"In the end, one reaches a situation where nations in pursuit of their own national interests have to be unselfish. Even if the Americans had known in the early years after the war that Gaullist France one day would spurn the hand that gave them back their industrial sinews with the Marshall Plan, their group survival would have demanded that Western Europe be resuscitated and strengthened in order that basic American national interests could be preserved.

"The Russian response to the Atlantic Alliance in the Warsaw Pact, the Russian response to the European Economic Community in the Comecom arrangements with Eastern Europe, are taking the same problem of, first, individual, then, community, and from thence national, then international, survival, one step further. And the problem which is being faced by the west and by Russia in Asia today is the problem of identifying their wider interests in a smaller world.

"If, apart from differences in infrastructure and capacity for industrial development between the Asian nations and Europe, the Americans had embarked in non-communist Asia on a rescue operation of dimensions commensurate with those upon which they embarked in Europe immediately after the war, perhaps today they would not be so bogged down in South Vietnam. But then, the Americans are not the only people who find it difficult to take this further step of recognizing the ever-widening identification of the group. For the Russians too, when confronted with problems of co-operation with another large power, withdrew technicians and economic and industrial assistance in the late 1950s as the Chinese Government insisted on its own ideological policies. But that does not mean that the Russians were able to opt out of Asia. Their interests as a communist power demand that the solution of the Vietnamese problem is brought about in a way which does not sacrifice their own collective interests as a communist group of nations.

"It is with these thoughts that I console myself when I find Singapore and her neighbour Malaysia increasingly unable to identify their overriding common interests. Service before Self: I must serve Singapore before I serve myself... Yet I am confronted with the wider and the higher contradiction that if, in fact, Malaysia—or, more important, Malaya—goes under, and goes either to the extreme Right or to the extreme Left, then my survival as a separate and independent entity at the tip of the Malayan peninsula becomes problematical.

"So you see, Mr President, that whilst you have only three words for your motto, it can raise a whole host of problems! In the end... those individuals, those communities, those nations, that group of nations survive who are more accurately able to discern with sagacity where their immediate interest commands their service to be, and who are able to undertake that service in such a way that they do not jeopardize their long-term chances of survival within a wider community.

"Coming back to my own national terms: it means, for me, being able, first, to define and to discern for the immediate present what is

309

necessary for the continued survival, prosperity and well-being of Singapore; and, next, being able to do it in such a way that developments around us will, in turn, be encouraged to move in a direction which ensures a larger and wider area of security, well-being and prosperity, and this, in turn, within the power conflicts taking place in Asia, creating an ever-widening area of security and stability within which, ultimately, the individual can serve his interest best by serving his community, then his nation, then the group of nations whose interests go together with his own. So that, ultimately, you reach a position where the other group of nations realizes that its interests also demand co-existence first and, ultimately, co-operation. . ."

V

Lee Kuan Yew's admiration for hard work and thrift, and his abiding interest in migrant communities, permitted him to make some friendly remarks on 27 March at a gathering of the Punjabi-speaking people. Like the Chinese, they came to Singapore with next to nothing. Now they owned valuable property which reflected their desire to build something permanent for themselves. "It is natural," said Lee, "for every human being to want to keep something of himself which he recognizes. But I am hoping that apart from that conservative instinct—the instinct to conserve what you believe to be good and which is part of yourself, part of your history, part of your heritage—there is always the capacity to innovate, to move forward, to progress to a better future. This innovation in which we are engaged—the multiracial, multireligious society—is one which is fraught with difficulties, and it demands a great deal of tolerance of each other and of our different habits and customs. But we can take heart from this one fact: that because sometimes we abandon the old milieu which has become conscribing, inhibitive of change and progress, so we can advance the more. From my own observations, there is much more ferment, more social change and rapid rise from the bottom to the top of the social ladder among the Chinese and the Indian communities here in Singapore than in our countries of origin.

"If my great-grandfather had never come to Singapore and I had been born in China, it is very unlikely that my relatives and I would have moved so freely up and down the social ladder. We would have had our place in China, our own little niche in society. But then, even China—which my grandfathers left—has changed. And similarly the India which some of you here personally have left and, in other cases, which some of your fathers left, is undergoing a change. Whether

310

that change will influence the course of events in Singapore, Malaya or Malaysia is something which is too difficult to answer—just as it is impossible to say whether the changes that will take place in Indonesia will have their impact on our society here. But we must have faith that, in the process of innovating, we can keep that little part of us which belongs to the past and which, at the same time, does not destroy what we have got together with each other in the present.

"In the old days, rows between Chinese districts in South China had repercussions here. And, indeed, a lot of the history of our secret societies and the triad societies was connected with the history of China. But, over the past thirty to forty years, and particularly since the war—when the links became more sentimental and less direct—all these cultural and civic patterns in Singapore have begun to assume more meaning locally. They are tuned, geared, to local aspirations. Similarly, I hope that, as the years go by, the Sikh community, together with the other Indian communities, will also become more rooted here in Singapore, here in Southeast Asia. For, in the end, that is our way out. To try and duplicate, for over two dozen communities, the conditions, the milieu, the atmosphere of two dozen different homelands would be to seek disaster. You belong here. It is my business and that of every government that wants Singapore to continue to thrive and to prosper, to make every community feel that it belongs... This is important. You should have not only in law the right to belong—you are part of Singapore—but it behoves the Government and the other communities to make you feel that you belong. Then the process of taking root becomes easier and better for us all."

VI

How to build a nation? "How to get our society, with its different cultural values, to adjust itself to modern needs and modern conditions?" Presenting medals to blood-donors, on 2 April, the Prime Minister said that the idea of having blood drawn off was one "which is quite frightening" to large numbers of Singaporeans. It was difficult to overcome the almost traditional concept that the drawing of blood must weaken.

"How do we solve this? Basically, we can do so by re-educating our people into values which are consonant with our modern needs. In other words, we have to debunk old phobias and implant new attitudes—attitudes which are useful to the survival of the community. This process of modifying and, in some cases, of eradicating old values and old beliefs and planting new ones is a very long and a very difficult one. Superstitions, the passage of ideas from mother to child, the family milieu, they can defeat the best of the propaganda pamphlets and radio and television broadcasts any group of advertisers or public relations officers can think of. Because you have first to break through the cultural and social cocoon that human beings build around themselves as they are brought up...

"But we are now trying to save life using a technique with which the cultural values of our population do not form a congruous whole. And so, we shall plod on with our propaganda and educational efforts, one after another, until finally we shall have bred, I hope, a new generation of citizens with values, attitudes and aptitudes which are consonant with the needs of a modern community.

"What struck me most when I looked up the data regarding blood donations and blood transfusions is the disparity in the different cultural groups between the donor and the acceptor. There is no inhibition here in anybody against the acceptance of blood... We have a population with a great desire to acquire—whether it is wealth, blood, health, anything. If you give them something, they will take it. And, if you look at all the cultural groups, you will find not one single group that says, 'No; accepting blood is against my belief; it will harm me.' And the acceptance of blood in percentage terms coincides with our cultural and communal percentage of population.

"What is interesting is the donor. Twelve point six per cent of all blood donated comes from Europeans, and the European community makes use of only one point six per cent... It is going to be some time before we get the same unemotional or completely uninhibited approach to blood donations which has been responsible for this very high percentage of blood donations from Europeans for use by the rest of our community..."

VII

Soon after Singapore separated from Malaysia the Indonesians began to make friendly moves towards Singapore, thus creating suspicion among the leaders in Malaysia. Unknown to Lee and his colleagues, Indonesia was also in secret contact with Malaysian officials, discussing the possibility of ending Indonesia's confrontation. Lee handled the situation with care. While emphasizing that Singapore was now an independent sovereign state, he also made public statements assuring Malaysia that nothing would be done that was harmful to

312

Malaysia's security or interests. This did little to relieve Malaysia's suspicions, and the Tunku angrily insisted that "Singapore must choose her friends". Malaysian Foreign Office officials at this time were meeting Indonesian army officers in Bangkok and in Kuala Lumpur, but did not inform Singapore.

This was the atmosphere in April when Lee Kuan Yew left to attend the Socialist International Congress in Stockholm, and to proceed afterwards on a rapid and comprehensive tour of East Europe. He first went to Cambodia, Thailand, the United Arab Republic and London. Lee intended to put the Republic of Singapore on the map and to seek trade with everyone.

In Cambodia, at a banquet in the Royal Palace in Phnom-Penh, on 12 April, Lee Kuan Yew told Prince Sihanouk, the Head of State, that he had come to Cambodia to pay his compliments, his esteem, to express the gratitude of the Government and people of Singapore for the warm support that Prince Sihanouk had given them in their hour of need. "We value friendship most when we are in need of it. Some time last year, due to forces beyond our control, we needed friendship to be expressed publicly from countries which could and did put us into the right perspective for the rest of Afro-Asia. I have always believed that perhaps with the end of the colonial era, we should try and reassert ourselves, not as masters, but as equals with the rest of the world. I have always held the policy pursued by the Royal Government of Cambodia as laudable in its objectives and admirable in its methods. In a very difficult situation you have been able to uphold the integrity, the honour and independence, both of the thinking and the action of your Government. I now find myself placed in a position not dissimilar to yours. I have bigger neighbours than you have. I would like to be friends with all of them, as no doubt, Monseigneur, you yourself would like to be friends with your neighbours. The problem is: can we succeed?

"I envy Cambodia in a number of respects. You have inherited something which has endured over the centuries, defined geographic boundaries, even though attenuated through the ages, and a people conscious of its long history. I have inherited a boundary line drawn by cartographers at various conferences in Europe. The history of the people of Singapore in Southeast Asia is in association with the period of a colonial rule. But their determination to endure in that part of Southeast Asia is boundless, and as abiding as that of Cambodia wanting to remain Cambodian forever after."

Prince Sihanouk, in his speech of welcome, had suggested that perhaps Lee Kuan Yew could be a go-between in the Vietnam war. Lee said, "It is against this background of flux and change that I listen with some trepidation to your proposal that perhaps I could be a go-between. Those who go in between stand in danger of being

313

crushed in between. It is not without significance that, when two of the bigger powers in Asia very unhappily came into conflict some time last year, it was a very much bigger power both in Asia and Europe that attempted not without success to bring about a detente. I wonder what we small nations can do when confronted with problems of divided nations, divided; as in the case of North and South Vietnam, North and South Korea, by neat geographic lines and regimes of opposing ideologies. But all of us who owe a duty to ourselves, to Asia and to mankind, try to achieve first a detente in South Vietnam. What is happening there is a crime against humanity. But to say who is committing the crime would be taking sides. Yet we cannot afford to be neutral when humanity and the survival of smaller nations in Southeast Asia are at stake.

"I do not altogether believe that the problem of South Vietnam can be solved in South Vietnam. And the manner of the solution of the conflict will in turn influence the destinies of countries beyond the boundaries of South Vietnam. If all the other countries in Southeast Asia were as adamant and vehement in their neutrality in the conflict of big powers in Southeast Asia as Cambodia then perhaps we might achieve a peaceful settlement.

"It may be a long time coming. But I would hope that eventually the smaller countries would be left alone to decide their destinies in their own way. If, however, we begin—as indeed there is a very great temptation to do—to take sides on the basis of who is winning, there will be great tribulation for the whole of Southeast Asia. I do not propose to opt for the prospective winner. I do not propose to put my fortunes on the gambling table. I propose simply to hold what I have got and build on it, just as many other governments in Southeast Asia wish to do."

In Thailand, Lee Kuan Yew had long conversations with Thai Ministers about regional co-operation. Kuala Lumpur thought he was secretly meeting Indonesian envoys, and, to quieten fears, Lee sent the Tunku a cable once again promising that Singapore would do nothing to injure Malaysia's interests. The Tunku insisted that the cable be made public. Lee at once agreed. He had not, of course, met any Indonesians in Thailand, except a news agency man in an open Press conference.

VIII

In Sweden, at Upsala University, before the Socialist International held their Congress in Stockholm, Lee in April spoke for Asian emerging nations in a seminar organized for new states by the International, with the help of the Swedish Social Democratic Party.

The Prime Minister observed that Sweden was one of the few nations in Europe without a colonial past, "yet in spite of that, and without having exceptional wealth in natural resources in a rigorous climate, they have been able to establish very high standards of life. We meet here as democratic socialists from many parts of the world, Asia, Africa, Latin America, Europe, to compare our various experiences and to find an answer to fit our own particular circumstances.

"One of the problems the new countries face is the result of too many facile assumptions—that political freedom would bring an end to poverty and economic exploitation of the subject peoples; that they would no longer be merely the producers of raw materials and the markets for the manufacturers of the industries of their metropolitan powers; that naturally and easily all could become as wealthy and as prosperous as the colonial powers that had governed them. These fallacies not only prevailed in the minds of many of the poor people who sought quick and instantaneous relief from poverty, but were encouraged in the minds of some of the leaders of former subject peoples. These leaders erroneously believed that, because the transfer of political power from a European metropolitan power to local indigenous leaders was followed by a rapid change in standards of life for the leaders and the elite of the subject peoples, therefore it followed that a rise in standards of life for the population at large would be similarly easy to bring about. It has come as a painful disillusionment that this is not so: that there are certain limitations unconnected with European domination or colonial exploitation which determine and inhibit the rate of growth towards a prosperous society.

"In a recent meeting of ECAFE there was a report by a team of experts—by and large Asian experts—that, if the rate of economic growth which was taking place in Malaysia last year when Singapore was a part of it were to continue at its present speed, then it would take Malaysia fifty years to reach the standard Japan now enjoys and a hundred and twenty years to reach the standard that New Zealand now enjoys. In other words, in fifty years, when the Japanese with their rate of growth have broken through to another stage of prosperity, Malaysia would just arrive at their present position. This not unnaturally has led to some basic rethinking, a re-examination of the fundamentals of the problems that have beset men in social groups from the beginning of time.

"The basic factors for wealth and growth have remained unaltered through the centuries. First, natural resources, second, human resources, and, third, the technological skills and capital equipment which are available to the human resources, to exploit the natural resources. In other words, the creation of goods and of services, which today is popularly known as the gross national product of a particular country, is determined by these three factors. . .

"Even more difficult is the problem of capital accumulation. . . The poorer one is the more difficult it is to accumulate capital, because the less there is to put away. So it is a vicious cycle which we must break through if we are to stop using the hoe and go on to the pneumatic drill and the combine harvester. But, unlike the first and second factors, natural resources and human resources, the third, technological skills and capital equipment, can either be loaned or be given, and if the receiver is not inhibited by charges of being thereby made effete as a result of being loaned the technological talents which he has not yet produced, or the capital equipment which he has not yet accumulated, then he will be able to make more rapid and effective use of his natural and human resources.

"It is with these as the basic digits that I discuss the differences between the different modes of human organization to exploit the natural and human resources. Feudalism, capitalism, socialism, communism. What difference does it make whether we choose one or the other of these paths? I would suggest that the difference lies in the manner in which these different systems mobilize human resources, mobilize the talent, energy and creative capacity of human beings in large groups for collective effort, in order to create a better life for all. For the manner of the mobilization of the human resources determines the speed with which we can acquire the different technical skills and can also determine the rate of capital accumulation.

"I believe in socialism because I believe it is one of the most effective ways of mobilizing human resources. Give equal opportunities to all, regardless of rank, race, religion, sex, in a given nation and you are likely to draw the best from each of your nationals. Give him the best opportunity to educate himself in order to use his talents and, if you throw your net wide enough to cover your whole population, the chances are you will have ever so much more talent that will emerge at the top. And in a society based on equal opportunity, if rewards are correlated to the effort and output of the man and not to his possession of wealth or status, then it is likely that you will give your people the incentive to strive for themselves and for their community.

"But it does not mean that if you have a socialist society it must inevitably lead you to become like the other socialist countries in the world. Or if you choose communism, it does not mean that you will all become like Soviet Russia, and indeed China has shown how different she is. And in the course of time, North Vietnam in turn will show how different she is from China. Further, let us never forget that two big industrial powers travelled the road to the industrial society in very different ways: Russia and Japan. Japan emerged as

316

an industrial power with a society whose pattern was still reeking with feudalism. Their leaders were determined that their people should acquire all the technological skills, and they used the capitalist method to sweat their workers in order to accumulate their capital. And in the Meiji era of less than a hundred years, they emerged as one of the major powers of the world at the outbreak of the Second World War.

"On the other hand Russia, whilst it was not altogether a feudal backward society, was able by its techniques of social mobilization and human organization to emerge from what was largely an agricultural nation in 1917 into a major industrial power by 1966.

"I would suggest that the differences in natural resources and perhaps the cultural and ethnic factors in their populations, and not just ideological differences, predetermined their different rates of growth.

"Finally may I draw your attention to a phenomenon which has emerged in the two decades since the end of the Second World War. It is becoming increasingly obvious that when human beings are in large numbers with vast land areas together with highly developed communication systems then a super-power emerges, as in the United States of America, and in Russia, and most likely in China. And so it is that European countries, fragmented by years of feuding and the futility of historic differences, are searching for ways and means to pool their resources in order that together as one bloc they may become another of the super-powers. Against this sombre background South Asia and Africa are being fragmented into small and often non-viable nation states, to seek parity and equality of status and form, but perhaps never equality in substance in an age of super-powers.

"I would like by way of illustration to recall what has happened in some of the countries in South and Southeast Asia. There have been democratic socialist governments in some of them: in Burma, in Ceylon, in Indonesia, and also, in a muted way, in India, where for seventeen years under Pandit Nehru's leadership there was a socialist government. But only in India was there any appreciable progress towards the industrial society, with the erection of steel mills, hydro-electric dams, as the infrastructure of the modern industrial state. But unfortunately, even in spite of central planning and outside aid, both technological and by way of capital equipment, the increase in economic wealth has been more than obliterated by the increase in population. In the other countries, such little advances as have been made have often resulted in literally a setback by the growth of population made possible by new standards of public health. In many instances serious setbacks have taken place in economic development through sheer lack of appreciation of the working of their own economies and the factors required for economic prosperity. In Burma for instance, a strong nationalist and a socialist government, now under a military council, also avowed to follow the socialist path. Economic advance has not been what it could have been because of the dismantling of the skills for collection and distribution in the economic network which were run largely by Indian merchants. Nationalist sentiment demanded that they should take over the collection and distribution system, but unfortunately it was done before there had emerged a group of Burmese sufficiently responsive to economic and profit incentives. The net result has been a setback in the rate of economic growth.

"In Ceylon this same problem was bedevilled by a plural society of indigenous Sinhalese with migrant Indians from South India, some of whom may have been there for a thousand years.

"In Indonesia the first Prime Minister, a socialist, recently died in Geneva and his body was taken back to Indonesia for a state funeral in his own capital—very little consolation for twenty years of wasted economic opportunities, in one of the greatest island empires in the world with vast mineral and agricultural resources.

"Curiously enough, we find some very unsocialist governments in South Asia—Thailand, Malaysia, Laos, the Philippines, Pakistan— where there has been more economic growth than in some of the countries which have had socialist governments. There are diverse reasons for it: in Thailand, for instance, injections of American aid and massive aid expenditure. Then there is an intermediate country like Cambodia, a kingdom with a government, led by a king turned into a popularly elected leader, based on socialism. Cambodia works in close harmony with the communist countries, but is determinedly non-communist in its own internal policies.

"We should not take history for granted. It was inevitable, the emancipation of man from slavery. It was inevitable, the emancipation of nations from colonialism. But it is not inevitable that we shall all progress towards a more prosperous, a more equal and a more just society. We cannot take that for granted. For in several parts of the world societies have moved backwards, not forward to freedom, equality and justice, but backwards to tyranny, to greater injustice between human beings in one community, and to greater poverty for all.

"I would like to believe that, as democratic socialists, and by the co-ordination of our thinking and co-operation in economic and social fields, both on a regional and on a world basis, we can help the realization of a satisfying life for all.

"For the new countries, I would like to end on an optimistic note. Feudalism, I think, is untenable, for it means standstill in an era where, even without formal education, the mass of the populations are already aroused. They may not be aware of what it is they want or what they have to do to get what they want. But their expectations have been aroused, expectations of a better and a more just society. So it is impossible for feudalism to continue, for it means standstill in an era where the populations want change.

"Capitalism appears too slow and too wasteful a process for the transition from the agricultural backward society to the modern industrial society. Our problem as democratic socialists is the challenge which communism poses in all these new countries, for they plan, they mobilize human resources, although in a somewhat stern and ruthless way. They are producing examples of how relatively underdeveloped backward societies, not just in big nations like China, but in smaller ones like North Korea and North Vietnam, with tight organization for the maximum utilization of human and natural resources, can, at a price, eliminate backwardness.

"As democratic socialists we lack ruthlessness in the pursuit of the interests of the state which represents all the citizens. Often we are unable to use methods which compel a higher rate of capital accumulation. India, using democratic forms, considers herself lucky if she can save anywhere between eight to twelve per cent of her gross national product as capital. China is estimated to be putting back anywhere between twenty and thirty per cent of her GNP per annum. I am not suggesting that the Indians lack the capacity to withstand the same hardship. But the nature of the political organization makes it impossible for any democratically elected Indian government to employ methods which produce an accumulation of capital and savings at the rate the Chinese do.

"But there is already a developed and prosperous non-communist world. So the chances of democratic socialism succeeding in these under-developed countries should not be that slender. It is possible, through trade and the borrowing of technological and capital resources, for democratic socialism with less ruthless methods of human organization to match and even outpace the rate of economic change which communist systems can bring about in under-developed countries."

As rapporteur of the Upsala Conference, Lee Kuan Yew spoke on 7 May at the Congress of the Socialist International in Stockholm. Lee said that Dag Hammarskjold "whose remains lie in the University grounds of Upsala would have approved of what the Socialist International, with the help of the Swedish Social Democratic Party, did in three days of a special conference there. Some fifty people representing different racial and cultural communities met to discuss democratic socialist thought and action in the new countries, to see whether it was possible to crystallize their thinking and co-ordinate their action for common benefit. Representatives from Latin America, Africa and Asia talked of their problems and their aspirations, whilst representatives from Europe listened, sometimes in sympathy, sometimes in bewilderment, at the different emphasis and values of the non-European socialist. . .

"On the third day of the Special Conference a full session was devoted to settling a statement to reaffirm our belief that the tenets of democratic socialism are still relevant in the world today. There was nothing new in the proposals contained in this statement on the problems of development, of trade and aid, of loans and technical assistance, matters which have been discussed and debated at great length in conferences held under the auspices of the United Nations and at Afro-Asian gatherings. The proposals are expected to help solve the economic problems of under-development. If only the have nations would help the have-not nations to do for themselves in one or two decades what the have nations took several centuries to do for themselves! Euphemisms abound in these discussions, to glide over the sensitivities of the new countries and soothe the consciences of the not-new countries. To be new is to be developing, but to be developing is often not to be developing. And not to be developed is to be under-developed. And to be under-developed is to be poor. Now the opposite of poor is rich. To be rich, unless a nation has struck oil, it must be developed. If a nation is developed then it is not 'new', whether or not it is 'old'.

"Nobody seriously expects these problems to be solved as a result of the proposals of the Special Conference being adopted by this Tenth Congress of the Socialist International. Why should developed nations give two per cent or even one per cent of their gross national product to aid the development of under-developed countries, many of whom are politically awkward to the West, some of whom have corrupt regimes, and nearly all of whom are not publicly grateful for assistance which they have come to expect as of right? It was suggested by a representative of a socialist party from a developed nation that because disease and pestilence knows no boundaries, so for their own health they must preserve the good health of their poor neighbours in an ever shrinking world. Another reason he gave was that the lesser the inequalities of wealth between nations, the lesser the tensions in the world. But the misfortune of the under-developed countries was, as a comrade from Turkey pointed out, that they have no sanctions they can apply against the developed nations for refusing to help either in trade or aid, loans or technical assistance. . .

"Once upon a time, before the word 'revisionism' became fashionable in the vocabulary of communism, there was at least the fear of an ever growing monolithic communist world absorbing large poor areas, isolating the rich countries, and eventually engulfing them in the poverty of the large whole. This was a real threat. And it increased the capacity of the poor countries to extract concessions from the West. But this fear has now receded.

"Then there was a time before 1962 when the spectacle of an aroused and united Afro-Asia pulling themselves up by their boot-straps to seek revenge for all the indignities and extortions they had suffered at the hands of the West made it prudent for the West to win friends amongst their former colonies. But since the winter of 1962, when conflict broke out between China and India over their border regions, this spectre has been dispelled. A relieved West is subsiding into complacency, confident that to ancient quarrels will be added new frictions to keep Asians and Africans and Latin Americans sufficiently preoccupied so as never to be able to unite to pose a massive threat for revenge. But, just as positions have changed so rapidly and dramatically in the past ten years when the West was freed from these two obsessions, first, a monolithic expanding communist world, and second, a united massive coloured front seeking revenge and retribution, so the positions may again change if in the next two decades the poor nations get poorer and the rich nations get richer, for the line between rich and poor countries coincides with the line between white and non-white peoples, between developed and under-developed . . .

"As democratic socialists, within our own countries we reject the proposition that the rich should get richer and the poor should get poorer. We fight economic and social injustice, eradicate unfair prac-tices and create more equal opportunities for all. So, internationally, if we are to be sincere to our own beliefs as democratic socialists, we cannot allow rich nations to get richer, and poor nations to get poorer. If it is wrong that a man should exploit his fellow men, so it is wrong that a rich nation or a group of rich nations should exploit a poorer group of nations. If it is unjust and economically backward and old-fashioned to allow a man, through his possession of property or status, to exploit his less fortunate fellow men, then, by the same token, no nation or group of nations should be allowed, through their possession of industrial capital and technological skills and scientific knowledge, to exploit other groups of nations, who, through the accid-ents of history, have not got these essentials for development.

"Surely, if all nations become developed and rich, then everyone will be richer and the world will be better off. Seen in this context, the demands for commodity price agreements to ensure stable and fair prices for the produce which the poorer countries sell to the richer countries, for the reduction of tariffs which bar the entry of the simple manufactures of the developing countries, and for technical assistance, training, and loans without onerous conditions—these demands become as meaningful as the socialist struggle against economic and social injustice committed against their own people within their own national frontiers.

"Democratic socialism cannot make a poor man into a rich man. But it has offered to the poor man opportunities for good health, good

321

education, training and purposeful employment which carries a reward commensurate with his contribution to society. And all that we democratic socialists of the under-developed countries ask for, whether it is in aid, loans, training, technical expertise, are the opportunities to make our own way to a developed society... in the final analysis, whether a people organized together as a nation in a defined geographic area make the grade or otherwise must depend upon the quality of the people themselves and the mettle of their leadership..."

Before he left Sweden Lee Kuan Yew was asked by a reporter what he thought the small neutral countries could contribute to security and peace in Southeast Asia. What were his views about the possibility of the creation of a demilitarized zone in the region?

Lee replied that the best way to maintain peace and security in Southeast Asia would be for the major powers to agree to leave Southeast Asia as a neutral area in which no major power would use any of the smaller countries in the area as an extension of its own might, and at the same time to guarantee the integrity of each of these smaller nations against encroachments by the others.

He said that the urgent problem of all the countries in Southeast Asia was economic development and the modernization of their societies. Unless this happened and the aroused expectations for a better life of the peoples of Southeast Asia were met, or at least showed a promise of being met in the foreseeable future, then the attractions of doing it the communist way would eventually be too strong to resist.

Singapore, he said, hoped to develop mutually beneficial social and economic ties with Indonesia and China. But these ties would only be tolerable if there were at the same time a firm undertaking of non-interference in the internal affairs of each other.

IX

On 26 May, Tun Abdul Razak, Malaysia's Deputy Prime Minister, announced that unofficially Indonesia's confrontation was over. There were displays of great jubilation in Kuala Lumpur, where Indonesian Army officers were greeted by high-ranking officials of the Malaysian Foreign Office as "blood-brothers".

Lee Kuan Yew returned to Singapore from East Europe on 1 June. On 4 June Indonesia announced the recognition of Singapore "on the basis of equal standing and mutual respect for each other's national integrity and sovereignty". Four days later Lee Kuan Yew saw the Malaysian Prime Minister and assured him that Singapore would establish diplomatic relations with Indonesia only if Indonesia established simultaneous relations with Malaysia.

The end of confrontation was, of course, welcomed by Lee Kuan Yew. Singapore had lost lives and trade as the result of Sukarno's criminal aggression. Lee publicly welcomed an end to it and the resumption of normal relations. At the same time, he was disturbed that the newspaper presentation of jubilation, the way in which peace was greeted, with heavy emphasis upon the racial links between the Malays and the Indonesians, created a certain amount of nervousness, "because people for the first time began to doubt and question the possibilities and problems that may arise in this new situation".

X

Opening the new Science Tower at the University of Singapore, on 1 July, the Prime Minister contended that there were three factors which determine the well-being of any nation. First, the natural resources at its disposal; second, the human resources it can marshal, and third, the technological and scientific skills it can exploit in order to bring out the best in its natural and human resources. Lee said "Short of wars, the natural resources of a country is a fixed factor. From time to time, people do extend their natural resources and the temptation to do so is always a very great one. And occasionally we have troubles about the extension of the territorial waters of countries from three miles—which was the length of the first effective gunshot or cannon-shot from the shore—to fifteen miles; and, in some cases, it is many more miles as human being discover that valuable gases and oils and other things can be discovered on the off-shore of their continental shelf.

"Our human resources are also limited; therefore for us the way forward is to exploit the virtues that we have. Both in actual size and in actual numbers of population, we may be the smallest nation in Asia. But there is one thing for which we need not be apologetic; the quality of our people. But quality alone, without the training and the disciplines which are relevant, will have no significance for our future well-being.

"I would like those who, from time to time, doubt the capacity of a people of about two million to survive under arduous and perilous circumstances to remember that two million New Zealanders were able to produce men who pioneered the world in science. The first atom and its mysteries were discovered by a man called Rutherford, a New Zealander.

"Our own population is near two million. I am not suggesting that we should go and pilot the fields of unexplored science. But I would like today to remind our scientists of the need to emphasize what can be made relevant in our situation...

"Great Power status is not for us. But a verve and quality that can help the growth and development in the whole of the region—through the peculiar circumstances in which we are placed—will be the strongest guarantees of our long-term security and prosperity.

"We are not land-locked. We are a centre of great communications, the crossroads between the northern and southern hemispheres of the world; between the East and the West, the Indian Ocean and the Pacific, and all centres of great traffic become centres of great culture, learning and civilization. And it is this factor which we must exploit to our utmost...

"How many people have we who have had twelve years of schooling? At a rough computation—if we leave the over forty-fives out of our computation—today, we have about ten in a thousand, which means ten times more than Nigeria, which has one in a thousand. And our average per capita income at about $1,400 to $1,500 per annum—this means somewhere about five hundred US dollars, approximately eight times that of Nigeria which is about sixty-four US dollars.

"We are all agreed that we have certain natural factors which are working for us. If we took the island of Singapore and put it in the Caribbean—or, if you like, in the South Pacific—we could live much more peaceful and tranquil lives. But I doubt whether we would end up as a people with a more satisfying life, with the stimulus of an awakening society making a contribution to levels of civilization and life in this part of the world...

"So, let us draw up a list of all these things which we cannot do as well as the big powers—rocketry, astro-physics, nuclear-physics, and let us put our sights on the things which can really matter to us, the things which will make the difference to our economic development. This requires a great deal of careful scrutiny of our possibilities. But let me, by way of illustration, explain how our inability at an earlier stage to assess our possibilities and our needs led to an imbalance. We are in the centre of a great archipelago of islands, and sea communications is of the essence of life. We have, on this island today, three big dockyards: one at the naval base, one we run at Tanjong Pagar, another we are building in Jurong. And we have not a single naval engineer or naval architect—an amazing situation which has arisen through sheer oversight. The first moves were made to rectify this only in 1961—with the result that it will be well into the late 1970s before we can take over completely the whole of our own dockyard in Tanjong Pagar... And we must bear in mind, if not the probability, definitely the possibility of taking over the enormous installations in Seletar, Sembawang, and the naval base!

"I don't want to sound pessimistic, but with everybody becoming very national-minded and wanting to stand on their own, we must make provision for all kinds of contingencies. And this is one contingency which is very real and one for which we have poorly equipped ourselves. . .

"I believe our future depends upon our ability to mobilize the qualities in our population to maximum advantage. It is the one thing we have which makes up for our lack of size and numbers, and it is of the utmost importance that, in the field of science and technology, we should lead the field in this part of the world. So long as we are able to take better advantage of the resources at our disposal than the bulk of the populations in the region can, it is likely that we shall always be able to make a contribution to improving general standards in the whole area so that it is worth their while—and more, it is vital to their own continued prosperity—that we should survive.

"If you were to take Singapore away from where it is and park it in the South Pacific. . . not only would we ourselves lead less satisfying existences, but the impact on the whole region in economic and social terms must be retrogressive. . . the skill and the services which we offer to the region mean a quickening of their pace of economic growth. And it is absolutely vital for us to preserve that pre-eminence in modern science and technology, and stable economic, social and political conditions which will make possible long-term planning."

XI

Lee Kuan Yew's extensive tour in Europe caused him to think a great deal about the problem of changing values in a shrinking world—how quickly ideas had moved "not just in our midst but all around us". He spoke about this at the Political Study Centre on 13 July.

He recalled that in the past fifteen years, two of the cardinal axioms of the international scene had disappeared, axioms on which everybody made his prognosis of the future. The first axiom was of a monolithic communist world, ever-growing and ever-expanding—a solid, monolithic force. And that was no longer true.

"Equally so, it is no longer true that Afro-Asian solidarity—the unity, the sense of togetherness—of all the subject peoples who suffered at the hands of white European colonizers would last for a long time and provide a rallying force on a broad world-scale against the former colonial powers. Too quickly have people become disillusioned and discovered that with the end of European empires, you do not go back to an idyllic, romantic past where all was happy and all was well before the white man came and colonized. In fact, there was much feuding, intriguing and a constant process of contest for power between tribes, between nation-groups.

"I was impressed, most of all, by this one thought: that there is no danger of it ever being said in the last third of the twentieth century that we have become frozen in our past. This is very important.

"It has been said of many of the leaders in Asia, particularly of the Indians who led the anti-colonial revolution, that they were steeped in ideas thirty to forty years before their time. When they were students in Europe, they imbibed a few ideas—basic radicalism —and whilst the world moved on their ideas, their basic references stayed put. And so it was that the Indian Congress government attempted to implement the philosophy, the ideas, the political theories of what democratic socialism espoused in the early 1920s or even before the first World War, when Nehru and his generation were being educated in Europe. But now, with constant travel (you can take your breakfast in Singapore and have your dinner in London) there is no danger of that happening.

"I had never been to Eastern Europe before... But, what was interesting was to find how much of the contemporary world Eastern Europe is. There is none of the rigidity of the Stalin era and there is a lot of 'aliveness' and ferment. What struck me most was that the same ferment was going on amongst the West European countries, many of whose Left-wing leaders I had the opportunity to meet and talk with, for about a week, in Stockholm before I journeyed on.

"I am not saying the world is moving towards a common point. This theory is that the communists are becoming less rigid, becoming more pragmatic, decentralizing and handing over power to their technocrats and their managerial class—the 'meritocracy' as against the party stalwarts... the pressure of modern techniques of production makes it necessary. At the same time, the Poles are getting more democratic; the Czechs are doing some heart-searching; the Hungarians have gone through a lot of problems and are trying to build a less Russian-type society. On the other hand, you have your West European democratic socialist groups moving from the doctrinaire policies and beliefs of the early 1920s and 1930s—even of the early 1940s and the late 1940s—and moving towards a more incentive-based system. And right at the other end of the spectrum, are the Americans who are supposed to be the most wicked of all the capitalists. But even they talk of 'Medicare' and some form of state responsibility for basic needs like health and housing and so on.

"How much of this is the result of changes of techniques of production which require certain forms to be followed if you are to exploit these new techniques of production for the things that the human being requires; and how much of it is really basic philosophy? There is first, the realization that nobody knows really—not even the topmost men in these countries—what the world will be like at the end of this century. Nobody can say because, first, you cannot evaluate or give correctly the right valuation to each factor which is at play in influencing events; and, secondly, nobody really knows what new factors may enter the situation and change the course of events.

"Take the monolithic communist world. Who would have said, ten years ago, in 1956, that, in fact, the first beginnings of a split in this monolithic structure—the ever-expanding, completely unified communist world—was going to come asunder? And come asunder it has. Nobody pretends that there are no problems. Everybody pays lip-service to the principles of communism and the solidarity of the socialist camp. But what is interesting is this: each is a nation-group with a nation-interest. They are all communists and let there be no mistake about it: they believe in the doctrine. But the doctrine has not been able to resolve the eternal conflicts of race, culture, religion, history. They understand the dogma, the doctrine, the vocabulary. But the starting-point is: where do I go from here? And of course, where does the world go? But the attitude is: the world is of interest in so far as I have a reasonable place under the sun: which is a very far cry from what the starry-eyed communists that I met in my youth in London and subsequently here, believe communism to be—although even with them, it is slowly percolating that the monolithic structure really is gone.

"The other pillar which has disappeared and to which, I think, we must get accustomed, is Afro-Asian solidarity. Nobody really believes any more that the black, brown, yellow—all the coloured peoples of the world—belong to one band and that their whole purpose in this next stage of human evolution is to square their accounts of all the injustices done in the past. Only too acutely are they conscious that the moment European powers are removed, the old indigenous forces that had bidden for power come back into play. And nowhere is this more apparent than in the relationship of Cambodia and Thailand. I am a friend of both the Cambodians and of the Thais, and I hope it will be possible—because we are, at least, one neighbour removed—to be able to maintain this position.

"The strangest thing about countries is: your best friends are never your immediate neighbours! They get too close and your neighbour's hedge grows and infringes on your part of the garden and the branch of his fruit tree covers your grass and your roses do not get enough sunshine and so many things happen! And therefore our best friends, as has happened with so many other countries, are those who are far-

ther afield and with whom we can talk objectively... There are countries in Asia which are new, which had never existed before in this
form and shape. But there are countries whose entity goes back to
hundreds of years. And it is so with the Cambodians, with the Thais
and with the Burmese.

"There is Afro-Asian solidarity yes, on certain limited issues like
Southern Rhodesia, and South Africa. But how does Afro-Asian
solidarity resolve problems between Cambodia and Thailand, or the
problem of Arab unity? And nobody really believes that you can
go back to Bandung in 1955. That was the highwater-mark of that
age and it is finished. There are changing values, just like styles. It
is as if you suddenly realize that a style is not good, that it doesn't
work and is not comfortable.

"What I would like to try to assess is: what does this mean for
us? How does this affect our eternal interests?" Lee said, "We must
never believe that the happy situation we are in will go on for ever,
that the Americans consider South Vietnam fundamental to their prestige
and to the security of the whole Southeast Asia, and that the British
are a necessary back-stop in the region from allowing the whole area to
be undermined militarily and otherwise, and that therefore they will
just do this for ever and ever.

"First, we must never assume that they want to do this for ever
and ever. They tell you now they want to do this for ever and ever.
But there may come a time when their mood may also change and
they may say, 'No, no, this is not in my interest.' If you get a shift,
a major shift of policy after the present struggles in China, the whole
spectrum may change. South Vietnam no longer becomes important.
New forms to secure big-power interests can be arrived at, and big-
power interests do not necessarily coincide with your and my interests.
At the present moment, it so happens that there is a coincidence of
interests. But we must not assume that this can go on for evermore.
You might well get into a situation where big-power interests make
it irrelevant whether or not we are engulfed in a bigger whole, and
that is the only circumstance in which we can be engulfed, in a
bigger whole. And in that contingency, we must have the capacity
to make it extremely painful and expensive for ever after because
history is an unending process.

"This requires first, no closing of the options. There are a series
of possibilities which could happen in the next ten, fifteen, twenty
years. In none of these possibilities must we foreclose and say, 'I
abjure this particular alternative.' The whole position will have to be
reviewed probably by a new generation of leaders when the time
comes. But it is not for us to close these options. And in fact, it is
our duty to consolidate to make quite sure that more options are at our
disposal. And never believe that because you have a geographically

small area and a numerically limited number of people, we therefore do not count. History has not been made that way. There are any number of very small states which, because mainly of the quality of human organization vis-a-vis their neighbours, and secondly, by the accident of geography, have played key roles in the development of the whole region.

"For the next one, two or perhaps three years, this will be the burden of my message: we must learn to adapt, to adjust. The world is changing, values are changing, the basic assumptions on which all these prognostications have been made are constantly undergoing shifts in evaluation of the factors involved. Singapore cannot live just on the basis of doing what it did before. That is not good enough. The things we did which secured our position between the 1950s up till now will not be enough. What did we do? Eradicate injustices. We gave a stake to everybody so that he now begins to feel this is his home, this is his country and he is prepared to fight for it. He doesn't riot any more. But this is not good enough, just building more flats, more schools, more hospitals. We must keep on doing that, but we must also improve.

"I tell you the things which we must do. They trouble me. A population which is good at the acquisition of wealth, which this community is, is necessarily selfish, and it is. Your forefathers and my forefathers came here in order to make their fortune, and they worked hard for it. They had that spirit of adventure. Ninety-five to ninety-eight per cent of Singapore's people came from outside.

"In that situation, there was a free-for-all. You had your clan association to buffer you against unemployment and sickness. The government did the minimum. Therefore there were Chinese clan associations, Indian associations, this, that and the other. All those were meant really to be the minimum buffer for what a government did not do. Every man was out for himself. This is the dominant characteristic of Singapore. And this must be changed. There must be a change from a trading migrant community to a rooted community in a hazardous region. Can you make that change in attitudes and values?

"Your incentives, your motivations must change because the situation with which you are confronted has changed... The next five years, perhaps ten years are reasonably secure. Vast changes however are taking place, changes in values, in concepts, that affect us, because they not only affect the mood and the style of doing things, they also affect the projection planning of the super-powers who are interested, in the last resort, mainly in their super-power interests and, of course, the general welfare and happiness of mankind—if that is also achievable. But if that is not achievable, then the general happiness and welfare of their super-nationals.

329

"How do we ensure our interests are not prejudiced in this situation? I would say that our best chances lie in a very tightly-organized society. There is no other way. Many other small societies like ours have survived...

"The second important objective which we must achieve is an ability to mobilize the maximum that we are capable of. Societies like ours have no fat to spare. They are either lean and healthy or they die. You have not got much to spare. If you run a large army, you will run yourself bankrupt. If you do not have an army, you will always be exposed to perils when bases are run down and many problems arise.

"How have other people done it in other parts of the world? You calculate and you say, 'This is the way it can be done.' And this means new values. And that is the whole purpose of life! He who survives is the man who is able to adapt to changing situations. But in the end it really amount to this: nobody is in a position to say for sure what could happen by the end of this century. Who knows what factors will come into play? What is definitely certain is that those found in our situation, with higher standards of life in a tightly-organized, economic community like Singapore, who do not at the same time acquire the capacity to stand up for themselves, on their own if needs be, must perish. It is as simple as that...

"The lesson of all this is: those societies survive and prosper who are able to make the adjustments to meet the changing circumstances in which they find themselves. That really is the challenge for Singapore... My assessment is that we have about five to ten years; the options will have closed and if when the time comes you are weak and feeble, then you have to take what others dispense to you. But if you are not weak, you are not enfeebled, then you are in a position to use, to a very considerable extent, the various forces which are at work in this area, and which will be at work ten years from now. There is a manoeuvrability and a flexibility which can ensure not only our survival. I do not think if we consolidate in these ten years, that survival is a question at all. The question is—how well can we survive?

"What future our offspring will have here really depends upon how quickly we can adjust to these new circumstances. The human being is a creature of habit in his values. He learns, he reacts, he responds. But there are some habits which must change, which will not help us. By all means, strive; by all means, be successful; by all means, make a success of your life which is natural, particularly in a young migrant community. But if a 'soft' society is developed then we cannot survive. If you are easily rattled and panicked and if it is manifest to others that this is a population that can be rattled, that can be panicked, then the options at my disposal are limited. If people know that if they do certain things, the population will quake, then life becomes very difficult. But, if they know that this is a pretty rugged population, not just the leadership but the population, which cannot be threatened, then my options immediately widen.

"What is required is a rugged, resolute, highly trained, highly disciplined community. Create such a community and you will survive and prosper here for thousands of years."

XII

"We are fortunate in Singapore," Lee Kuan Yew told the Tamil Muslim Union at their Holy Qu'aran Conference on 17 July "in that throughout our recent history of over a hundred and forty years, religion has always been a cohesive, not a divisive, force in our community. Unlike many other parts of Southeast Asia collisions on religious lines have been singularly absent. Whether Buddhists, Catholics, Presbyterians, Methodist, Hindus or Muslims, we have avoided the excesses which in other parts of the world have made not only governments unhappy, but have also made the people miserable.

"Even a pacifist, humane, religious philosophy which Buddhism represents and which advocates that not even an insect should be destroyed, such is the love for living things, if given the wrong interpretation and in wrong situations, can lead to a lot of unhappiness—as has happened when a Ceylonese Prime Minister was assassinated; as is happening in a very unhappy part of Southeast Asia where Buddhist monks, far from confining the interpretation of their Holy Book to the spiritual values of men, have taken to the streets to contest the temporal power of the state...

"I am not a Muslim. But that does not mean that I do not understand how passionately and fervently quite a number of our citizens feel about the Muslim faith. Nor am I a Catholic but, in the same way, I hope I understand how important a very small but a very vigorous section of our community feels about Catholicism. I was late this morning for your symposium because I had to attend the rehearsal of some parades which will take place on the anniversary of our independence. And I was cheered to see how the different religious groups have made a positive contribution to our social structure—whether it be the Muslims, or the Catholics who run quite a number of our secondary schools, or the Presbysterians who run some

331

other schools, and so on. And I hope that the leaders of the Muslim community in Singapore will—as you have suggested, Mr President—interpret Islam in a way which will be to the benefit of its followers, and to the general good of the community. . ."

XIII

Probably nobody will ever know just how much Lee Kuan Yew and his colleagues grimly sweated through the first year of independence. It was a period of tension and anxiety: so much could have gone wrong, the pressure was constant, and the situation demanded a confident relaxed Prime Minister. There were times when Lee felt far from confident, but outwardly he endeavoured to convey the impression that everything was going well and firmly under control.

On the eve of National Day (the anniversary of Singapore's complete independence), on 8 August, Lee went to the television studio. "Tomorrow," he said, "we begin our second year on our own. The first year has been valuable experience of what we can do to thrive and prosper and to build a permanent future for ourselves in this part of the world. Our position now is much better than this time last year. We have consolidated our internal and our international position—made new friends and strengthened ties with old ones. Meanwhile, our economy continues to move ahead. Figures for trade, for industry, for cargo handled in our port, the increases in revenue through increased incomes being spent—they are cause for satisfaction. . . Meanwhile, construction went on with more roads, bridges, schools, houses, and fountains. We did not stagnate. They speak well of the capacity of a resilient and vigorous community always forging ahead to greater effort and fresh achievements. At home, our ground organizations: the Citizens' Consultative Committees, Community Centres and their management committees, the Vigilante Corps—have tightened the organization, put in leaders who have been trained in our Youth Training Institute to help in the administration and bring better coordination between the administration, the Government and the people. Most important of all, the effectiveness of our security forces—the police and the army—is much better. And the response of volunteers to our People's Defence Forces has been very good.

"We have, however, to reassess our plans for the kind of society we have to build. The emphasis must be on a rugged society. We are providing many amenities free or heavily subsidized, like housing, hospitals, clinics, schools, universities and public assistance. From now onwards, we must concentrate our expenditure on the areas which will help directly to increase productivity and accelerate our economic growth. For instance, take education. Expenditure on this is a necessity. In a highly urbanized society, our future lies in a well-educated population, trained in the many disciplines and techniques of a modern industrial society. On the other hand, in the more stringent circumstances we find ourselves in, on our own, paying for our own defence and our own foreign affairs, we have to be more prudent on the purely welfare projects which do not increase our economic growth. And in this field we have to bring in more public participation for charitable projects. For we must remember that, in the end, everything we enjoy must be paid for through the taxes we all pay.

"Another matter on which we must change our attitudes is the system of wages and salaries which we pay. We must make it worth while for everyone to work his best. In an easier situation—part of a broader economic base, part of Malaysia—we could have carried passengers. Unfortunately, we often did pay the hard-working and the not-so-hardworking the same wage, and we just cannot afford to continue this. Our system of incentives must change and rewards must be equated to results, and not just to time. High incentives for high performance will build the kind of society which will guarantee us our pre-eminence as a centre of orderly growth and progress in an otherwise troublesome region. . ."

Two days later, at a community centre, Lee Kuan Yew explained in more detail his reasons for insisting upon a new sort of education. They had to produce a multiracial generation which made up in quality what it lacked in numbers. . .

"It depends on the education we give them; the training they receive; the values that they are taught—what is good, what is bad; what should be done; what should not be done; whether we should have a soft society, fun-loving, pleasure-loving, weak, effete or whether we should have a rugged, robust, disciplined effective society, a hard society, a tough, rugged society. . . We want to live our lives as free men in an open society, not as sycophants or, worse, as serfs doing other people's bidding. . . If you want to live your own life, then you must be well organized and you must have a tough society. And everybody must know that small though we may be, this place is not a digestible morsel.

"Every year, we must use our time better than the average person uses it in this part of the world. And we can. What we have done in the past, we can improve and do better in the future. I do not think there is anything more important than to breed a generation that is conscious of what it has and what it must do to preserve and improve upon what it has. . .

"The system that we inherited from the British was lop-sided. Too much emphasis was laid on the examination and the paper qualification. We were, therefore, rearing a whole generation of softies, who were clever, who wore spectacles, who were weak from want of enough exercise, enough sunshine, and with not enough guts in them. That was all right for a British colony, because the officers came from England, who had the necessary brawn and toughness. It was they who gave the orders and our people just executed them.

"That is not good enough. We have to give our own people the orders. And you have to throw up a whole generation capable of that leadership, conscious of its responsibilities, jealous of its rights, not allowing anyone to bully it and push it around, prepared to stand up and fight and die. That kind of a generation will endure till the end of time. And that is what we can do and will do...

"The way we solve our multiracial situation here, our multiracial problems, will influence what happens in the rest of the countries in Southeast Asia which are faced with similar multiracial problems. And if we make a success, and in ten, fifteen years' time throw up a generation of leaders, men trained with a modern scientific outlook, and not only Chinese and Indians but also Malays and others, then we would have pointed the way to the future. And others must inevitably pick up the lessons from us..."

XIV

Lee Kuan Yew's official visit to India, in early September, on his way to London for the Commonwealth Prime Ministers' Conference, was a personal success. At the end of his stay, during which he spent many hours with Mrs Indira Gandhi, India's Prime Minister, and Sardar Swaren Singh, then the Foreign Minister, the two Prime Ministers issued a communique. This summarized in official terms what had been achieved by Lee's visit. The two Prime Ministers exchanged views on the international situation with special reference to the problems of Asia. They reiterated their faith in the policy of non-alignment. They recognized that the world must be made secure for each nation to develop according to its own genius and its own chosen political and economic system. They reaffirmed their adherence to the policy of peace and peaceful co-existence. They agreed upon the need to abjure subversion and interference in the internal affairs of other states and the use, and the threat of use of force, as a means of settling international affairs.

The two Prime Ministers affirmed their faith in the principles of secularism and multiracial integration. They felt this provided a just and harmonious approach to the economic, social and political problems of a pluralistic society. They discussed Vietnam. And they expressed their great concern over the danger to the world in general and Southeast Asia in particular, arising from a prolongation of the Vietnam conflict. But they offered no solution.

They discussed economic matters. And they agreed that the countries of South and Southeast Asia, as indeed all countries of Asia and Africa, must increase their economic co-operation in order to raise their living standards and give greater substance to their political independence. They felt satisfied that strong links in the field of science, education, culture and trade were being forged between India and Singapore. They expressed their determination to strengthen these relations in every possible way.

Singapore's Prime Minister spoke frankly, and enthusiastically, in private conversation, and in the speeches he made in Delhi. The Indian Press liked what he said. In the *Hindustan Times Weekly*, the commentator 'Recorder' wrote that Singapore "might well be called the most notable city-state of our day".

'Recorder' went to to say: "Known for tenacity of purpose and clarity of vision, Mr Lee has set out to persuade fellow Asians to create and strengthen as many common links as possible with a view to arriving later at a common agreed arrangement in which one would be for all and all for one."

The article was illustrated by a four-column cartoon at the top of the page. It showed a tiny Lee Kuan Yew standing on the belly of a sleeping giant Indian. Lee is prodding the giant with his pencil. He is shouting into the giant's ear. The caption to the cartoon said: "Stand Up!"

India's Prime Minister, in her speech at a dinner given in Lee's honour in New Delhi, acknowledged the identity of ideals and visions which animated India and Singapore. "Your ideals and visions," remarked Mrs Indira Gandhi, "are those which we also value: the vision of a composite society of many races and languages, committed to the ideals of democracy and peace. Like you," she told Lee "we cherish the exercise of independence in international affairs..." Singapore was one of the youngest states in the world. "But," Mrs Indira Gandhi added, "Singapore is a dynamic young state, and it is blessed with the dynamic leadership of a distinguished statesman."

Mrs Gandhi spoke of India's antiquity, and how it gave roots and a balanced outlook for the future. At the same time, history could be a burden. Today, India's task was not to do away with old traditions, but to break free from some in order to move ahead. "In that sense," she told Lee Kuan Yew, "you are fortunate. You start with

335

nothing to hold you back. You have only a bright future to beckon you forward."

In his reply, Lee Kuan Yew spoke of India as a special friend of Singapore. "We borrowed our name from one of the ancient languages of India," he told Mrs Gandhi. "And we have borrowed many other things—the secular state, the multiracial society, the multilingual community, all bound together in pursuit of a more equal and just society." Singapore's leadership, declared Lee, shared some of the special characteristics of India's leaders. Singapore, like India, was socialist by conviction, and pragmatic in practice. Both leaderships operated the system of rule which required a great deal of tolerance, patience and effort in political affairs. India pioneered the struggle for freedom of the subject people of Asia and Africa.

"Many of us," acknowledged Lee Kuan Yew, "owe a great debt to Indian freedom workers, not least of whom was Mr Nehru."

At a Press conference in New Delhi, Lee elaborated his idea of some sort of grouping among Asian nations. The Prime Minister said that any scheme for co-operation among Asian countries must cut across political prejudices and attitudes. Answering another question, Lee Kuan Yew said that Asian countries must pledge the preservation of each other's integrity, and also the integrity of the entire region. "The integrity of Southeast Asia should be preserved from whosoever wants to destroy it: communism of any variety, straightforward imperialism, or expansionism."

At the Commonwealth Conference in London, Lee Kuan Yew, conscious of his own youth, and of the fact that Singapore is Asia's newest and smallest sovereign state and among the Commonwealth's newest members, purposely kept in the background as much as possible. Even so, Lee did contribute, and his backroom efforts among Afro-Asian members were thought by many, including the Canadian Prime Minister, to have been of considerable importance in bringing about a consensus on the Rhodesia issue.

The Observer, of 11 September, said that "Lester Pearson emerged ... as the key bridge-builder between the old and the new Commonwealth at Marlborough House, but it was Lee Kuan Yew, the Prime Minister of Singapore, who made the deepest impression. His masterly television performance last week helped. His appearance is as tough and wiry as his politics, and his exits from Marlborough House between sessions were characteristic. He would stroll out with his hands in his pockets and a faint swagger as if he had just felled fellow-delegates with a few neat karate blows. While other prime ministers were being hustled into their beflagged limousines, he walked back to his hotel pursued by his two security guards. Lee has had a rugged political training and it has not been easy for him since he took Singapore out of the Malaysian Federation last year. His socialism is Western. . ."

A gossip writer in the London *Evening Standard* compared Lee with Harold Wilson, the British Prime Minister. The paragraph was headed: "Quick Brain"; and said: "The man who seemed to have created the biggest impression in a quiet way this week is Singapore's Mr Lee Kuan Yew. His quick brain makes him a match for Mr Wilson any day. Happily the two men are on good personal terms. . ."

Many times in London and elsewhere, Singapore's Prime Minister was asked what Singapore got out of the Commonwealth. Lee Kuan Yew's reply, in effect, was that it was not a bad club to belong to. An Australian commentator asked him what he thought the Commonwealth could do in Southeast Asia, and Asia generally. Lee believed that the African members, and the members from the Caribbean, could do little except provide understanding, moral support, and some little trade.

What could Britain do? Lee thought Britain could do a great deal. Britain was the pivot of the whole Commonwealth concept. Britain could contribute by not abandoning Singapore, New Zealand and Australia.

What could the Commonwealth members in the region do? Referring to India, Pakistan, Ceylon, Malaysia, Singapore, Australia and New Zealand, Lee Kuan Yew thought they could do a lot for each other, by bilateral and multiracial arrangements for trade, and economic development, exchange of experts and technicians, providing training and expertise for those in need. "It's a convenient club for getting these things going," Lee added. "Eventually, policies should be initiated which would bring about a more coherent and co-ordinated development of all the countries in Southeast Asia, some of which, by world standards, are just not viable."

The commentator asked Lee if he thought it would be wise to hold the next Commonwealth Prime Minister's Conference in Singapore. The commentator said it had been suggested that it would be useful to take some of the African delegates into Southeast Asia. Lee Kuan Yew said he doubted whether sustained interest could be maintained just by getting people to meet in a particular part of the world. More than that was required. All members would have to discern where their interests lie, and this meant a long process of educating each other. To some extent, Asians were being educated on African problems. What had to be brought home to Africans was that African hopes of rapid progress could fade away if, in Southeast Asia, say, the big nations—the Soviet Union, America, Britain and Europe—poured their resources into a contest of wills and strength. When this was realized by the Africans, their interest in Asia could be sustained.

Lee was asked how healthy he thought the Commonwealth was, particularly in view of the fact that eight and a half days out of the ten days were devoted to one subject. Lee said he wouldn't like to believe that every Conference would spend eight and a half days discussing Rhodesia. But this had been unusual, and he did not think it would be the pattern for future conferences.

Lee was questioned about the Afro-Asian caucus. Did he think this was a good thing? No, Lee on principle did not think it was a good thing. This, in effect, meant the drawing of a white and non-white colour line, and this should not happen in Commonwealth affairs. "But," insisted Lee, "on this occasion, and in these circumstances, at this time, an Afro-Asian caucus did contribute to the production of a solution. Privately, the Afro-Asians were able to speak very freely without embarrassment."

Lee Kuan Yew played an important part behind the scenes. He was trusted by the Africans. He was on excellent terms with the Indian representatives. Lee Kuan Yew's sincerity was never in doubt. When he argued realistically and firmly, his colleagues from Africa listened. A compromise was reached: some kind of formula, which expressed a consensus while noting certain points of dissent, was found.

Lee Kuan Yew played no part in the creation of an Afro-Asian bloc within the Conference, but once the Africans decided to meet informally to discuss Mr Wilson's proposals for dealing with the Rhodesian problem, and invited the Asians to join them, Singapore's Prime Minister accepted their invitation. Tunku Abdul Rahman, Prime Minister of Malaysia, decided not to accept. Malaysia did not attend any Afro-Asian caucus meeting. Singapore's High Commissioner, Mr A. P. Rajah, was at the first meeting where India played the role of the mediator. Lee had another important engagement and did not arrive at the meeting until later. He was at once asked to present the Conference with the Afro-Asian counter-proposals. "Be our advocate," he was asked. Lee had already spoken in the conference itself, and his demands for effective sanctions against Rhodesia had impressed the Africans. Lee had made it clear that he favoured the use of force, if necessary, to make sanctions effective. Later, over BBC television, Lee Kuan Yew made his comments about the need for a Vietcong-type of organization in Rhodesia. He was at once attacked by the Right-wing Press, and by others. Back in Singapore, Lee Kuan Yew explained just what he meant. He was, in fact, over-emphasizing his firm belief that a man must first help himself before calling for help. Lee said that at the conference he was dismayed with the sense of helplessness which he saw among the Africans, because they did not have the military power to take on two hundred thousand whites. Here were the leaders of black Africa. Some of them represented as many as forty million people. Yet none of them had the capacity, neither did they collectively have that capacity, to take on two hundred thousand whites. Lee recalled that at the conference somebody

338

said that sanctions were supposed to bite. "Yes," said the Foreign Minister of Zambia, "but when are they expected to kill?" Lee said that remark put his mind on a different train of thought. And he said: "Look, if you want to kill, and there are situations where it becomes necessary to use force because there is just no other way, then you must be prepared to do your own killing. Killing is a messy business: it is a nasty business. But you cannot ask the British Government to send troops to kill white Rhodesians because it goes against the grain. And so," explained Lee, "I said that the tragedy of Rhodesia was, and is, the fact that the black Rhodesians have not been able to organize themselves in a way that would attract world attention and create an acute situation. And I said that if they only had two battalions of people trained to the level of the Vietcong, the problem of white minority rule in Rhodesia would be settled very quickly." Stuart Hood, the well-known critic, described Lee's appearance on television as "agile, charming and tough".

Asked about Singapore's relations with Britain, Lee Kuan Yew said they were more than good. They were based on Singapore's long-term interests, and on the long-term interests of Britain and the British people. "These are the facts of life, and that is why the Commonwealth continues."

XV

At the Law Society, on 7 October, the Prime Minister discussed political leadership in developing countries. The president of the society had given Lee Kuan Yew the impression, in his speech, that the law qualified its disciples for political leadership. Lee disagreed. That was once true. "That was a British-type society in which the Parliamentarian, the man who legislated, had knowledge of the law, and the practice of the law afforded a man the leisure and the finesse which enabled him to lead his society. That is no longer true. It is true that Nehru was a barrister. It is also true that Tunku Abdul Rahman Al-haj is a barrister; and so am I. Law means language. Without language, the instruments of thought, how do you have the precision of the legislator?"

Law means a committal to a set of values, and those values mean politics, and politics is something fundamental, deep in the interstices of an individual and a people. "Law means language; language means politics; politics means a whole background of ideas, values, the kind of life you want your children to have and the kind of society in which you want them to live. This is where you come very near the bone."

Lee did not believe neighbours could be influenced by producing an eminent law school. "That is the last thing, if I may say so with humility. It is the last instrument I would suggest we use. If you want to influence your neighbours, you show them the carrot, and you say, 'That way lies gold, the jack-pot at the bottom of the rainbow. Multilingualism, tolerance, multiculturalism, a successful economic booster to prosperity.'

"You produce a law school and lawyers to prove the guilt of individuals for corruption, for nepotism, for all the stupidities and inadequacies of a political system, and you believe you are going to influence your neighbours to follow you? That is not on..."

Lee told the lawyers that if they were thinking of becoming leaders they would have to be more contemporary than he was. He said: "There are two types of individuals who emerge in positions of leadership. If your country is developed, then inevitably the people who emerge in positions of leadership are people with a very firm grasp of the bolts and nuts of life, of standards of living and the economics of life. And so Mr Wilson is an economist of some repute, and Mr Holt of Australia has spent many years as Treasurer or as Finance Minister of Australia. So too, with Chancellor Erhard; so too with Mr Sato of Japan.

"As I looked around the conference table at Marlborough House recently, I saw emerging the other kind of leadership—a new one; not one which we represent, the Tunku and I. I looked at two young colonels present, representing the governments of Nigeria and Ghana. And I say to all law students: pray that my successor will be an economist. Then you have a future. If my successor is a young colonel, then yours is the ignominious role of a mercenary, literally a mercenary, a paid hack of a prosecutor in some unfortunate tribunal in which the leaders of the previous government will be in the dock; or, worse for you, the state-paid hack as counsel for the defence.

"I demand the right, and I do not care whether the United Nations or the Charter of Human Rights guarantee me this, which I think I have and you have, that we should live in peace to be able to develop ourselves to the maximum of our capacity. And any one who sets about to destroy that right, I will resist either quietly and surreptitiously, or overtly and boisterously.

"How do we ensure that this society will always offer all its citizens a meaningful, purposeful existence? That is what should engage your minds. I am not interested in ideas as ideas themselves, however much of an esoteric thrill these can give you by way of intellectual stimulation. I am interested in ideas in so far as they can galvanize both our society, which means you and I, in a way which will enable us eventually to move our neighbours, or those of our neighbours who matter to us, in the right direction. And to do that

340

you need the law; you need the panoply of justice; you need the free play of ideas. But, most important of all, you need a very strong referee who, in this case, must have a gun because the contestants are often prone to using the gun. And the referee must not only have a gun but must know when judiciously to use it. If he does well, then the pianist will never be shot and you will always hear some music!"

XVI

There were, Lee Kuan Yew argued during a seminar on International Relations at the University of Singapore, on 9 October, two things which had to be kept in mind when talking about the foreign policy of a particular country. "First, that the foreign policy pursued at any one time is designed primarily for the long-term national interests of a group of people organized into a nation. And second, that the policy is designed for the specific and special interests of the type of regime, or the type of political leadership which for the time being is in charge of the destiny of that country.

"If you confuse one for the other, then you will make grave mis-judgments as to what are likely to be the power situations in various parts of the world from time to time. This particular aspect is very pertinent to us.

"In the past fifteen months, I have had to re-scan all the various steps we took, not by way of post-mortem to find out where we went wrong, for that is neither here nor there, but to discover what are the relevant factors that will determine our future in this part of the world.

"First, why did we attempt Malaysia? Was it an impossible thing to have brought together, into one national context, people of diverse racial, linguistic and cultural and religious origins? I do not think it was. I don't think—and I never did think—that race or ethnic affinity was a fundamental basis of any national unity. And, perhaps, it is because I am the product of my generation. . .

"If I believed all Chinese are brothers all over the world and that they are more brothers than they are with the Indians and the Malays, then we would never have attempted Malaysia. But I want to qualify this with a very strong proviso: that if you insist on treating a person as a political liability on the basis of race, then eventually he must coalesce in self-defence. . .

"Here in Singapore we are now presented with a segment of the Malaysian whole—not an equal segment nor, in texture, of the same kind, because the proportions are different. But I believe that it is

341

possible to nurture and inculcate the multiracial tolerant outlook, provided there are no extraneous forces let loose which will influence our internal situation and cause a reaction against these policies. Why do I advocate these policies? Because I believe they will lead to the maximum amount of happiness for the maximum number of people, not only in Singapore but for a large number of others who live near us."

Lee said there were two other factors that should always be borne in mind when talking about the foreign policy of Singapore. "There is something peculiar which we share with certain island-bases which have emerged as a result of European decolonization over the past hundred and twenty years. These are Malta, Cyprus, Gibraltar and a few others. There was a reason why all of them were chosen as strategic points. It was not just geography; it was also a juxtaposition of power-interests in a particular region. Malta was crucial in the 19th century and even as recently as the Second World War. But unfortunately for the Maltese, in the political texture of Cold War politics in Europe and the possibilities of the lines of conflict in another hot war in Europe, Malta no longer counts as a strategic point. In contrast, Cyprus still counts as a staging-post, and parts of Cyprus are held by the British in sovereignty for their base purposes. So far as I can see into the foreseeable future, both the geographic and the socio-political factors make this part of the world in Southeast Asia a crucial point.

"The other factor is the effect of human migration over the face of this world over the centuries...

"In four hundred years, led largely by English-speaking Anglo-Saxons, the Caucasian peoples—which means people ethnically from that particular part of the Eurasian steppes—moved westwards, and occupied and populated whole continents. All this in the space of less than five hundred years—a remarkable thing. Man is supposed to have existed for a million years. The history of recorded civilization goes back some six or seven thousand years. And yet, in this very brief space of time of five hundred years one particular group suddenly fanned out. Why? How?

"Are we safe in assuming that it was because of their technological skills, their break-through into the scientific store of knowledge and technical expertise which made it possible for them to do this, and that they will always set the pattern of things? We must ask ourselves this. This is crucial.

"Will somebody else, some other ethnic group or combination of ethnic groups reverse this process? Because if that is going to happen, then obviously our foreign policies and our attitudes must be different... The future is not pre-destined... But I am quite convinced on one point: man has migrated from the beginning of time and will migrate till the end of time...

"But out of this, I give you three conclusions. First, nothing is pre-destined. The second is: whilst your geographic and natural resources and other factors are by and large unchanging, your human factor is capable of change and it does change—with very important and significant consequences... That means for us the very real danger that in the same way as we see salvation through innovation —with new skills, new techniques, new methods of seeking a livelihood —in this type of situation, so others will consider us a threat. For our very resourcefulness poses a challenge to the type of society which they believe should be there for all time...

"The foreign policy of Singapore must ensure, regardless of the nature of the government it has from time to time, that this migrant community that brought in life, vitality, enterprise from many parts of the world should always find an oasis here whatever happens in the surrounding environment. When you talk about foreign policy, unless you are a big power, an inter-continental power, like Russia, United States, China, you are really talking about your neighbours. Your neighbours are not your best friends, wherever you are...

"I would say this: that a foreign policy for Singapore must be one as to encourage first, the major powers in this world to find it— if not in their interests to help us—at least in their interests not to have us get worse. This is important. If you do not like me as I am, then just think of what a nasty business it could be if I am not what I am! This is the first point. The second point is: we must always offer to the rest of the world a continuing interest in the type of society we project.

"If we can identify ourselves with the mass of new nations that have emerged with their ideals and their ideas of what a new modern forward-looking nation of the twentieth century should be, then the risk we run of being used as a pawn and destroyed is that much diminished. But, in the last resort, it is power which decides what happens and, therefore, it behoves us to ensure that we always have overwhelming power on our side...

"We want to be ourselves. Those who want to thwart us and prevent us from being ourselves must necessarily be not our friends. Therefore, we seek the maximum number of friends with the maximum capacity to uphold what our friends and ourselves have decided to uphold. That is the beginning and the end of any foreign policy for a situation like Singapore's.

"We have no aspirations, no ambitions to exercise and influence —in the sense of exercise of authority—beyond persuasive moral authority on others. But it must be our constant endeavour to ensure first, the political climate in which the force which can be lent to us can be exercised.

343

"Let me explain this. If we did not have force on our side when we were under confrontation, then the end result would not have been a solution in which Asians found an Asian solution to Asian problems. It would have been the case of one Asian finding a solution for the other Asians' problems! But there was a severe limitation in the way in which that force was deployed and exercised. It was unable to be used effectively without grave political consequences...

"So, my foreign policy must achieve these two objectives. One, the right political climate. The other: power. For you can have the best of political climates, but if the power to sustain your position is not there, you must lose..."

XVII

Because social problems in a plural society are often problems affecting communal matters, they must be handled with delicate touch and tact. On one occasion Lee Kuan Yew was invited to a Sikh dinner (on 13 October), when, unexpectedly, he was asked a favour regarding a Sikh shrine...

In his reply, Lee paid the Sikhs a compliment. He said they were a brave and physically courageous and very determined people. They had thrust: they struggle to better themselves, and this was a characteristic, he said, that he admired. "Good luck to you. That is the way we want our communities to be: always striving for a better future."

Lee waited for the applause to die away before going on to say how unhappy he felt when he had been asked about a Sikh shrine in the grounds of the General Hospital. He told them that eleven shrines, not all of them Sikh shrines, had been removed from various parts of the city: they had been growing up in road circuses and at busy junctions. "I am not against people seeking solace from spiritual sources... but it is impossible to govern this place with its teeming population without taking some firm and even unpleasant measures ... your shrine can go to wherever you can find another place to put it. But it's not possible to have it right in the middle of the General Hospital's grounds. It is not within my dispensation to take public property and give it to a particular set of devotees. It cannot be done ... In some parts of the world I have seen people born and bred on pavements. I have no intention of allowing that to happen in Singapore. And I'm quite sure that the Sikh community have got the verve, the thrift, and the dynamism to ensure that they are a prosperous part of our community."

Lee Kuan Yew was much more direct when he rebuffed the Chinese Chamber of Commerce, earlier that same month. He summoned them to his office to talk to them about reports in the newspapers quoting spokesmen of the Chamber as advocating a special place in Singapore for the Chinese language. He told them, without preliminary, what was in his mind. "You know," he said, "I have been expecting this... I thought that somebody would be fool enough to pipe up and say... I expected little boys who went to primary schools and never to secondary schools to say this... but I was deeply grieved when I saw that the intellectuals from the Chinese Chamber of Trade, men responsible for the commerce and industry of Singapore, said these very unwise things... Constitutionally Malaysia and Singapore may be separate, but as Dr Ismail (Malaysia's Home Minister) himself said: 'The human bond remains.' "

Lee urged them to think of the future, wider perspectives and not consider Singapore a little self-contained world. "Now, gentlemen, I hope we have made the position clear, and that we will hear no more of this." He dismissed them.

XVIII

Lee Kuan Yew returned to the "real and abiding problem" of the survival of a migrant people in Southeast Asia, when he spoke at Nanyang University on 29 October. He was particularly worried about the emphasis many Nanyang students put upon Chinese language and culture, and an article in the Malaysian Journal of Education, on the question of Chinese education in Singapore and Malaya, by Professor Wolfgang Franck, made a deep impression on him. During his speech, the Prime Minister, speaking partly in English and partly in Mandarin, read extracts from the article... The Professor pointed out that the main result of English education (if it is not coupled with a fairly thorough Chinese education at home or elsewhere) is the uprooting of the Chinese humanistic tradition. The English education, even if it lasted thirty years, usually remained superficial. Professor Franck went on: " 'Only a small number of outstanding students in a few eminent schools are able to penetrate to the basic values of Western culture and to acquire a genuine Western humanistic education to replace the lost Chinese one. The majority, however, remains satisfied with their superficial English education which offers them good professional opportunities and an income high enough to allow them to enjoy the comforts of life.

" 'There are, however, not a few of them who become sooner or later aware of their uprooted floating position. They realize their lack of cultural identification and some even reproach their parents for their failure to give them an adequate Chinese education. They may, under continuing favourable social conditions, be loyal Malaysian Chinese citizens and successful in their professional work. Physically and emotionally they are Chinese, but culturally and spiritually they are neither Chinese nor English nor Malay. They do not know themselves what they are... As long as there is no homogeneous Malaysian culture, there can be no ad-culturation but only de-culturation. A large scale positive assimilation of the Chinese into the Malay Muslims seems out of the question due to religious barriers. The common English education of Chinese, Indians and Malays together may further some positive aspects of adjustment. But a negative aspect of de-culturation seems to dominate. The integrated schools in Singapore seem so far to be the only positive steps towards mutual ad-culturation without the detrimental effects of de-culturation.' "

Lee believed there was something in the Chinese culture which was crucial for survival. He told the Nanyang students: "My colleagues and I are concerned with the survival of our society... of sixty thousand students each year, and on the free choice of their parents, two-thirds are going to English schools for plain bread and butter reasons; one-third to Chinese schools. And, if we are going to produce anaemic, up-rooted floating citizens without the social cohesiveness and the cultural impetus that gives the people the drive and the will to succeed as a group, then I think we will perish. And this is a situation which has troubled my colleagues and me for some time... The future of Chinese education rests primarily with the local Chinese. And they must be willing and able to integrate their new Malaysian political identity with their traditional Chinese cultural heritage and make use of the existing opportunities to give their children, even in non-Chinese medium schools, at least a partial Chinese education..."

XIX

On 20 November, Lee Kuan Yew told the Third Asia Teachers' Seminar what he thought about teacher-pupil relationship. He spoke of "the values which we must create in our next generation which can come about only if a person in whom we have entrusted the future of our children first agrees with those values, and second is prepared to give of himself or herself. For I can think of no closer an association than that of teacher and pupil...

"Any human society in this technological age, if it is to enter into the garden, in which people live happy and healthy lives, of the have nations of the world, must have their broad stratum of educated and knowledgeable men and women. This can only come about with a large spread of average knowledge imparted often by people with slightly more than average ability, but certainly with a great deal of more than average love and affection for the pupil put in his charge. For it is when you get them young and malleable that you can sharpen and discipline their minds. It is an influence upon our future generation which is excelled or exceeded only by the parent at home, and not always even by the parent. For when you have a society in which large numbers of parents are less educated than their children, it is inevitable that as the children acquire knowledge and literacy the respect for the teacher, who is better equipped, better educated than the pupil, must be greater than that which the pupil has for his parents.

"This is not a parochial problem, for I believe that these must be the kind of difficulties which countries and societies which want to expand their educational facilities at great speed must encounter. . .

"But it has to be paid at a tremendous price. The intimacy between teacher and pupil, the individual characteristic of a particular teaching institution, this has all been lost. Schools do two sessions—morning and afternoon. Two different schools are occupying the same building, same classrooms, same playing-fields. Different teachers have the same principal—a very tenuous nexus. . . The school buildings are all the same in design, to make for cheap and efficient building. There is no difference between school 'A' and school 'B', and there are so many schools that you name them after the streets: Upper Thomson Road Secondary School, Bartley Road Secondary School. You might as well call it the 42nd Street Secondary School.

"When I went to school, the school meant something to me. It had a name. It had a history. It had a roll of illustrious products. It had great teachers. It had principals who were proud of the school and grew up with the school. We belonged to that school, all those who wore a certain badge. And in the afternoons, it was still our school. We went back and played games there. But this is not so now. The school is a convenience. You go, it is not yours, because you have to clear the desk by one o'clock before the afternoon occupant comes in. The teacher also clears his desk, because he also has an afternoon teacher coming in. The living institution is lost.

"But this is not half as bad as what has happened with the mass-production of teachers. Men and women have been induced into the teaching profession on the basis of monetary reward. Now I have said that I believe that if I have to choose one profession in which you give the most for the least it is probably teaching—if you take it seriously. You have to have the temperament for it to coax, to stimulate, to cajole, to discipline a young mind into good habits. You must have an aptitude.

"The people I remember most in my life were the people who made the greatest impact on me as a student. Not that they were the best-equipped, qualified teachers in their line but because they really gave of themselves and took a personal and particular interest in all their pupils and in me personally, which was the part which I remembered. And so it was when I went on to university. I have heard many a brilliant lecture. But it is the man with whom I sat in a tutorial afterwards and discussed the problems, and in particular one who in bouts of asthmatic fits used to take out his apparatus, inhale deeply and then back into the intricacies of Roman Law, who made an impression on me which is indelible. He gave of himself.

"We have produced teachers as anonymous, faceless, and as listless in some cases as the institutions which now house them. The nett result is that now we are producing a literate but not an educated population. They can read, they can write, they can go to the cinemas, they understand the television programmes, they can pass examinations. But if you go around some of the community centres and you see the complete absence of social discipline, then you will know that somewhere something went wrong. . .

"I believe that this is an inevitable price which rapid expansion demands that we pay. But it is not one which I intend to continue paying. . . Our population is under control. . . the birth-rate figures are down from four point one per cent ten years ago to two point four per cent, and they are going down and will probably stabilize at one point five or one point four per cent. If the economy surges forward as it has been doing, then in another ten years a large majority of the schools, probably all the secondary schools, will only run one session. These schools must acquire character of their own. True, we cannot pull down all the school buildings and make them look different. But we can give them additional characteristics—halls, gymnasia and all the other things which make for a living institution. These things can be put right; the science equipment can be put in, calisthenics, all the paraphenalia—libraries, modern equipment. But, eventually, you come back to the principal digit: the man who sits in the classroom, the form master. If he is only thinking in terms of this as just a job, as a factory worker thinks of his work as just a job watching the bottles go by and the stoppers being put on each bottle, and he fills each boy's mind the same way as the machines pour in mellifluous liquid into the bottles as they go by, then we have failed."

Lee Kuan Yew concluded by referring to the four major streams of civilization in Singapore. He said the British came, and for a

348

hundred and fifty years they stayed, and there was an overlay of Western values, the language, culture. "But they neither smothered nor destroyed what was here, brought in by the Chinese, by the Indians, and the Malays, many of whom came from neighbouring islands. We are not hoping to put them through a sausage-machine, mince them up, and make them come out regular lengths at the end of it. You might do that with meat and sausages. You cannot do that with human beings without irreparable damage to human personality. So, to each, what he originally had—his culture, his language, a link with his past, his heritage. And to each something added, so that they can meet and talk and understand, laugh at the same things, be pained and disturbed by the same things, and eventually integrate into one society... I am not sure when this process can be said to have been completed, but I feel that if we go a long way towards success, it does hold out some hopes of a peaceful co-existing world."

XX

In October, the Barisan Sosialis walked out of Parliament: nine of them resigned "in protest against undemocratic acts of the Government". They had, in fact, boycotted Parliament since Singapore's separation from Malaysia. The Barisan said they would continue their struggle in the streets. Lee said they had degenerated slowly "into a gang of street fighters" and were no longer a political party, but a gang to be handled as a police problem.

Noisy demonstrations, engineered by the Barisan Sosialis, were held by students at Ngee Ann College and at Nanyang University. Some of the student leaders were from Malaysia. In November there were clashes with the police. On the Government's specific instructions the police acted with considerable restraint and some suffered injuries as a consequence. Several policemen were admitted to hospital. After warnings, demonstrations continued, and the Government then acted swiftly and strongly. More than sixty students were arrested and jailed and most of them were banished to Malaysia.

On 24 November, Lee Kuan Yew went to Singapore University to explain the Government's attitude towards academic freedom. He told them it was because they continued to lie in their own little cocoon "divorced and unaware of the realities of life, that you continually lend yourself as cover (sometimes consciously and knowingly, at other times unwittingly) for people who cynically talk about academic freedom when their examples of freedom are those from climates which would not suit you, such as Peking and the Red

Guards, but who are skilful and cynical enough to know that academic freedom means nothing to the masses, and spice it up with popular issues like the elimination of Chinese cultures, and a mobilization of mass action."

Lee asked: "What is a university? What are its relations to society? How did this phrase 'academic freedom' come to mean what it means to you? When British people talk about academic freedom they refer to a system of education that grew up in Britain...

"The first thing I want to bring in your focus is the fact that this is a peculiarly British concept—that a university is something sacrosanct. Not even in American social systems does it occupy the same place. And any scientist, any astro-physicist, will tell you that the quality of the work that is being done in Russian universities is equal to that which is being done in British and American universities. Even in Peking where the Red Guards are rampaging, those who are in charge of China's nuclear physics and guided missiles are left quietly outside the cultural revolution.

"So, do not believe that you are quoting a universal truth when you say, 'university autonomy, academic freedom'. It is not. It is a peculiarly British concept and one which has been followed in varying degrees throughout the English-speaking world—in Australia, New Zealand, America, Canada and, in lesser degree, in the non-white parts of the Commonwealth such as Malaysia, Singapore and Africa.

"How did this system arise?... this is a peculiar evolution between state and church, between scholarship and administration, which grew up in a British society. They were given charters; they were ancient monasteries. Colleges in Oxford and Cambridge were originally built as monasteries, with walled colleges, closed gates, no women inside; with wine in the cellar, celibates living in quadrangles, churches for prayers, libraries. The university, having got its charter, gave its own degrees to which the state either chose to give heavy or lesser consideration. Eventually, a system developed in which the English gentry found that this was one way of breeding an elite. From private schools which they called 'public schools', where they are carefully tutored and nurtured, they sent their children to the great universities in Britain to be educated and then to be inducted into the civil service, the foreign service, public life, the army, the navy and so on.

"So you have a whole social system interwoven into these universities. They are not distinct and separate from their society. And as part of a great centre of empire, they take in a few students from India, Ceylon, Burma, Malaya, Singapore and latterly, after the war, from Africa. They bred an elite designed to serve a British society, inculcated when you are there with traditions and values to make you a commander of men.

"It was not designed to create a breed of scholars who are going to spend their time studying the universe and searching after truth. Of course, there is the Cavendish Laboratory; of course, Russian nuclear physicists also studied in the Cavendish Laboratories. But they were nurtured and cultivated because they bred successive generations of rulers. And their teachers—of course, you have the odd ones, the very brilliant Jew who ran away from Hitlerite Germany or Austria—but they are all Englishmen determined to nurture British tradition. And you don't need to tell the Vice-Chancellor of Oxford what he has to do to ensure that these traditions are maintained. He knows! You do not have to tell him!"

To support his general thesis, Lee Kuan Yew quoted from the *Encyclopaedia of Social Sciences*: "'It is the freedom of the teacher or research worker in higher institutions of learning to investigate and discuss the problems of his science and to express his conclusions whether through publication or in the instruction of students without interference from political or ecclesiastical authority or from the administrative officials of the institution in which he is employed, unless his methods are found by qualified bodies of his own profession to be clearly incompetent on contrary to professional ethics. The freedom of opinion, speech and publication claimed for the university teacher is not in extent significantly different from that usually accorded to other citizens in modern, liberal states. And the reasons for maintaining it are, in part, the same. It is peculiar chiefly in that the teacher is, in his economic status, a salaried employee and that the freedom claimed for him implies a denial of the right of those who provide or administer the funds from which he is paid to control the content of his teachings.'

"Now that is what 'academic freedom' really means... What does it, in fact, imply? Does it imply that your university is above the state?" The Prime Minister believed that it was not. "Research, teaching, is big business—the business of governments..."

For argument's sake Lee wondered if it would not be better to close down the university and send bright students abroad to be educated. "It is cheaper really, to do it that way: to send them abroad, pay their passages, their fees. Why have we not done that? Because surely, like all other countries, we have that pride in self. We want to create an institution which will be self-perpetuating, which can constantly and continuously produce a stream of trained and disciplined minds which are imbued with the values of our society, keenly alive to its problems and able to respond to them..."

Lee Kuan Yew next dealt with the question of security. The Academic Staff Association argued that security was a matter entirely for the Government. The University should be concerned only with academic freedom. Lee told them this was an unrealistic attitude. "To say that a man's political loyalty and inclinations

351

are irrelevant is akin to saying it was irrelevant what Professor Pontecorvo's loyalty was as long as he was academically good... If this purist's attitude is persisted in, there is bound to be growing difficulty between the Government in charge of security and the University giving cover to communist activities under the banner of academic freedom..."

Lee said that the University's answer was that any security objection was a matter entirely for the Government and the responsibility of the Government. And if action on security grounds was to be taken, it should be by the Government, and the University should not be asked to act on its behalf by terminating, or by not renewing, the appointment of a member of the academic staff.

"What they said in effect," continued Lee Kuan Yew, "was: 'We are not saying that security has got nothing to do with academic staff; but we will promote or do anything according to just purely academic merits and we will put a man in charge of nuclear physics even if we know that he is going to study all about the secrets of nuclear physics, whip across to the other side, manufacture the bomb and deliver it back to you. Nothing to do with us; but, of course, as the Government, you can arrest and banish him.'

"That is what I get. I do not think any British Prime Minister would have got that from the Vice-Chancellor and the academic staff, of Oxford and Cambridge, or Red Brick. They would not have written that. Because they are Englishmen to their core and their primary responsibility is to their society. They are not searching after truth in vacuo..."

XXI

When the International Labour Organization held its first Asian conference in Singapore, on 28 November, the Prime Minister again returned to the question of Singapore's specific labour problems. Lee said that every Asian state had to face the drift from the countryside to the towns. This was happening throughout the world in underdeveloped areas, and it meant a growing pressure on all governments to find some economically useful activity for the mass of unemployed and under-developed people who gathered in shanty areas around all urban centres.

Lee said that in Singapore they had been able to do a lot of the things which they otherwise could not have afforded, because of a freak situation. "We give free medical services, free hospitalization for everybody who is prepared to take third class treatment. We give unemployment benefits, sickness and disability benefits which sometimes aggravate our own social problems. All this was possible because for many decades our population was a migrant one. It came fully adult, trained or untrained. They were not a drain on the community. They did their stint, earned their money, got their gratuity and left, leaving us with a minimum of old age problems." Today, the Singapore Government paid $4.55 per day to every unskilled worker employed in any government or government statutory authority: treble pay on twelve days a year which were declared public holidays (which very often were made compulsory working days in order that they should have the treble pay); double pay on Sunday; forty-two days sick leave a year ("and about forty per cent of all workers invariably fall ill for nearly the greater part of the forty-two days per year"). In almost all government departments and statutory authorities, where the profit motive was not the driving factor, overtime payments of up to as much as forty per cent of the normal wage bill was a regular occurrence in all branches of the administration.

Said Lee Kuan Yew: "In a way, we created these problems. For in the pre-independence phase our unions were part of the political mass movements. The legitimate trade unionism became a useful omnibus cover for the carrot you must offer the masses if you want them to join you in driving the colonial power out...

"Trade unionism became a systematic recruitment of people for organized mass indiscipline. Strikes, go-slows, protests, demands for wages, fringe benefits, were all mounted on the basis of similar patterns to those which are prevalent in other places. We have dirt allowance, obnoxious allowance and every conceivable kind of allowances which the British Trade Union Congress had thought up. And they were dutifully reproduced here, for this was the carrot without which the lowly-paid workers would not have joined in a mass movement. And in the process of trade unionism in which both supervisor and supervisee joined the same movement, the same union, discipline broke down. Now the problem arises of post-independence.

"The carrot that you had offered—'Come with me to freedom and I will give you what the British employer gives his British workman'—that promise must now be redeemed. And the first thing that we have got to do in this situation is to identify what were deliberately created problems and what were a legacy, in any case, of the past.

"First, there must be a restoration of working efficiency. We all joined one mass movement to get rid of the British, for otherwise how could we have self-government? But self-government and independence having been established? The army, which whilst in rebellion had no ranks, all were comrades, slowly finds itself becoming more orthodox. Inevitably, supervision, discipline, working norms have to be established. But in the peculiar context of Singapore there are a certain number of problems which cannot be resolved just by forcing the situation to the status quo ante.

"For in the process of the quest for freedom we have aroused and sparked off in the hearts of all our population, and all the young, a desire for a better life and a better future. Mass education: every boy, every girl, in school; mass literacy and a raising of the expectations of the parents—which is often more telling in its effects than the raising of the expectations of the boys and the girls whom we have sent to school.

"It is no longer possible to go back to when labour could be sweated because they were migrants and they came from countries worse off; they were not rooted, and were not particularly concerned as to what would be happening to the country after they had done their little stint and moved away. Our old-age problems are now with us. People are no longer going back to China, going back to India or Indonesia. They are born here; they are going to stay here. Can we maintain these standards? Worse, can we meet the rising expectations? Unless we can establish sufficiently stable industrial conditions to justify confidence, both internally and internationally, there will not be the economic expansion which will meet this rising expectation. But if we can meet that, and produce a highly skilled, highly educated, and a highly paid working population, then, within two decades—maybe less—we could move into a situation of self-sustaining growth, have an economy that could generate prosperity, a meaningful life, not only for all our citizens, but at the same time stimulate similar economic activity amongst those who by proximity of geography and the complementary nature of their economics could be geared in to our own industrial growth.

"But the biggest problem which we have created for ourselves, more so than the British did for us, was to have educated a population which now will never go back to the low levels of rewards of the past. One of the by-products of a migrant community is that it produces a population of triers; whatever else they may lack, the off-springs of migrants are prepared to try anything to improve themselves. Having left tradition, their history, their past behind, they have only the future to go in quest of . . . And so we grope forward trying to find solutions to problems, some of which in any case would have come upon us even if the British had continued their colonial system, even if we had never been allowed to raise expectations and ambitions. But when you complicate this with the political aspirations for self-fulfilment, then a great deal of heart-searching, clear thinking and social discipline becomes the pre-requisite to any self-sustaining group. Having educated our population, we can no longer go back upon the targets with which we lighted up their minds. Having had a highly organized labour situation, we can never take recession in our economy by spreading the load on all the working population. Any slackness in industrial

354

growth would be carried by an ever-growing body of unemployed or under-employed. And therein lies the real rub of the problem that all urbanized cities in Asia will inevitably go through. Eventually, however good your management-labour relationship may be, however good your social security and insurance arrangements, if the general level of economic activity is unable to give gainful and meaningful employment to an ever-growing body of educated men and women, then the time must come when they want to make a bid for some other system which they believe would give them a place in the sun.

"I would like to believe that having embarked on this road, fired by idealism and faith in ourselves as equal human beings, able to run our own communities as good as any other in the world, that we have enough iron in our souls to brace up our population to the problems that confront us. The same unions that I egged on to industrial protest actions I now have to face, to explain why a repetition of the habits learned in the pre-independence era must mean the disintegration of the whole of the society as the economy ceases to keep pace with growing demands of an educated population."

Lee now advocated a system in which employers, whether local or foreign, get their returns, or else their capital must go elsewhere to stimulate other industrial activity in some other place where there are governments less moved by these considerations, with unions led by men who understand just how far they can go without really crippling or killing the goose whose eggs they want. It is only in these conditions that urbanized situations like Singapore can continue to thrive and prosper.

"In other words, it requires the greatest amount of sophistication in labour machinery, economic policies, an understanding of this on the part of the management, and a grasp of realities on the part of the union leaders that ultimately more pay, more fringe benefits, more security can only come with higher productivity and greater economic growth. . ."

CHAPTER TWENTY-ONE

The Year of Power 1967

SUBSTANTIAL economic progress marked 1967. Trade increased by eight per cent, building construction by sixty-six per cent. To meet the demands of Hong Kong industrialists, a crash programme was instituted to build more factories. Labour-employer relationship was good: in five months of the year there were no stoppages of work. By and large, Lee Kuan Yew's new trade union policy was accepted. One trade union, however, decided to challenge Lee when the Government moved to create a more efficient public cleansing service. Against TUC advice, they called an illegal strike. Fifteen trade union leaders were arrested, tried in open court and fined.

The Barisan Sosialis continued their "mass struggle outside Parliament"—an exercise in futility—with mass demonstrations, which were followed by mass arrests and mass trials. There was no public support for these demonstrations.

Lee Kuan Yew went to London to discuss Britain's military withdrawal from Singapore, and in July the British published a White Paper which stated Britain would withdraw completely by the mid-1970s. Lee at once began to make his own defence plans. Later, the British advanced their withdrawal date to 1971. Singapore's first batch of army officers trained in Singapore were commissioned. National Servicemen began their two-years training.

In August, Singapore helped to form the Association of Southeast Asian Nations, "to accelerate the economic growth... and to strengthen the foundations for a prosperous and equal community of Southeast Asian Nations".

In September, the Republic of Singapore played host to the Prime Minister of Japan. At a state banquet, Lee Kuan Yew referred to. Singapore's bitter experiences during World War Two. "That chapter is closed," said Lee, "but not forgotten."

In October, Lee Kuan Yew left for a five-weeks journey which took him to Malta, Britain, Ireland, Switzerland and the United States. He attended the British Labour Party Conference at Scarborough, and the Socialist International Congress at Geneva. In Washington, President Johnson described Lee Kuan Yew as "a patriot, a brilliant political leader and a statesman of the new Asia". Shortly afterwards, Lee Kuan Yew went to Cambodia to talk with his old friend, Prince Sihanouk.

The Singapore-Malaysia relationship improved, and the two Governments agreed upon the interchangeability of their currencies. Both countries independently decided not to devalue the dollar. It was revealed that Singapore's reserves were sufficient to back the Singapore dollar four times over.

In November, Parliament unanimously elected President Yusof bin Ishak for another four-year term of office. Later in December, the Prime Minister flew to Australia to attend the memorial service to Mr Harold Holt, the Australian Prime Minister drowned at sea.

The Finance Minister introduced a budget which contained not a single tax increase. He made no effort to play down the formidable tasks facing the republic. Possibly nine per cent of the work-force of just over half a million were unemployed. In the next three years Singapore had to (1) generate an additional $80 million expenditure each year to offset the reduction of British military expenditure, (2) create 18,000 additional jobs a year to absorb current unemployment and base workers retrenched, and (3) create a further 25,000 new jobs a year to cope with school-leavers. "Our future", declared Lee Kuan Yew, "is in our own hands."

On 14 January, the Prime Minister dined with the management and workers of Jurong Shipyard Ltd. He congratulated both the union and the management of the shipyard "for having reminded us of the possibilities that our position in Southeast Asia offers us. We have had a big shipyard all these years for building small ships and repairing big ones in Keppel. We have another large shipyard in Sembawang. But it needed the Economic Development Board and a Japanese concern to remind us of the potential we have got. Many people believe that because we are a small place, we therefore owe our prosperity to others; that we owe our living to other people's hinterland. This is not altogether true. Slowly, as we are forced to rethink our problems, opportunities will open up. And one of our greatest assets is our location—just being at the southernmost tip of Asia. If you want to go from the Indian Ocean to the Pacific; from the west to the east or the east to the west; if you want to go from Australia to Europe or to Japan, the sea-routes and the air-routes make us a logical point of intersection.

"We are an island-nation and there have been other island-nations in recent history, and they were always great shipbuilders and great sea-faring people—for instance, the British and the Japanese... I think we can take a leaf out of their history. We are a people never too proud to learn from others. We are not ashamed of learning. What you do, I will learn and try to be better. That is what has made Singapore survive. We will repair ships, build ships, sail them; and fish the oceans. The oceans and the seas are international. They are for everybody and they are singularly open to those who have access to good harbours as we have..."

II

The development of a migrant society into a nation-building society was the theme of a talk given by Lee Kuan Yew (on 19 January) to residents of a constituency in which Lee himself had lived for twenty years.

"If you ask me today, just as a citizen, what is the difference between the River Valley that exists today and the one that existed twenty years ago. I would say this—there is a sense of participation; a sense of ownership and of belonging; of feeling, and of being, a community. This was not present twenty years ago. We were then tenants, licensees. Somebody else owned the place and ran the machine. You came like the washerwoman or the charwoman to clean, to get your little benefit. There was no sense of building upon ownership. If you were lucky and were either a shopkeeper, a pawn-broker or an owner of a chain of stores, then you owned more than the rest of the community. And you tried to make more, and paid homage to Caesar, and Caesar was represented by the Governor who lived down the road. There was no participation. Today, not only does everyone believe, but absolutely demands, as of right, that he should have his chance in life as a member of the community and as a citizen, to be educated, to get a job befitting his ability and train-ing, and to make a contribution to the well-being of the community. And this sense of participation, more than any other single factor, has taken out the bitterness and the frustration that used to fester in the old society..."

"You know, a battle goes on all the time in some of the schools in Singapore for the hearts and minds of our younger generation. All the time, this battle is relentlessly fought between the communists who established their cells in some of the Chinese Middle Schools thirty to forty years ago and who are trying to bring in more recruits and involve them in a communist movement, and us, we who are trying to get the community to build an open, democratic society with free and equal chances for everybody. And as the communists find their breeding-grounds shrinking, they begin to use force and terror, in order that teachers and principals may acquiesce, just do nothing to stop them, acquiesce in their continued evil. And evil does not need active co-operation. All evil needs, to succeed, is quiescence; abstention on the part of good men who watch evil, feel it is wrong but do nothing about it. And they then succeed. And over the past eight years, we have managed to stiffen the will and resolve in a small but growing body of teachers, principals and educationists to get together and take a stand and fight this."

Not until the 1960s was Lee Kuan Yew able to cripple, though not completely to eradicate, the influence of some of these schools wherein communist cadres, under the guise of teaching history, were able to deal with modern development in China while discussing Mao Tse-tung's interpretation of Marxism-Leninism. In this situation it was not difficult for these Maoists to urge the application of com-munist theories to Singapore and Malaysia. When principals resisted, the communists sent strong-arm students to beat them up. An indica-tion of Lee Kuan Yew's success in gaining public support for the removal of the communist menace from the schools was when, early in 1967, non-communist students intervened in one of these assaults, while on another occasion the public came forward to assist the police in arresting a gang which attacked a non-communist principal with iron bars. For the first time communist propagandists met direct and active opposition from members of the public. Hitherto, passivity and non-involvement had been the common attitude, even of those who disapproved strongly of the teaching of communism in schools.

III

At a dinner given by the United Kingdom Manufacturers Association and the Confederation of British Industries, on 7 February, Lee Kuan Yew spoke of the long-term relationship between Britain and Singapore. When Raffles landed on 29 February, 1819 there were 120 Malays and thirty Chinese. From a minor fishing village of 150 souls Singapore had become the biggest metropolis two degrees north of the Equator. "There is only one other civilization near the Equator that ever produced anything worthy of the name. That was in the Yucatan Peninsula of South America—the Mayan civilization. There is no other place where human beings were able to surmount the problems of a soporific equatorial climate." Singapore was also different in that the British dispossessed nobody. "I cannot claim like Julius Nyerere or Tunku Abdul Rahman that you dispossessed me... my great grandfather came here with nothing. He made something and he decided to get out while the going was good. My tragedy started when he left his son behind who was my grandfather; and here I am. I inherited what you have left me. In a way, it was not all created by you because my great grandfather did play a subsidiary role and so did my father and so did I myself. So we have left Stamford Raffles standing on his pinnacle outside the Victoria Memorial Hall. But for him, Singapore would still be a mudflat. Let us not pretend it was anything else. We brought in the skills and gave the reason for what is now here... The British deliberately, as a matter of policy, encouraged an inflow of entrepreneurial skill—even to a point where it competed with their own wholesale and retail trade. The Dutch in the Netherlands East Indies did not want that. They wanted the wholesale and retail business—everything excepting tax collection. Because of the nastiness of it, get the Chinese: they will go out and squeeze the Indonesians and make them pay all their taxes. The net result was that they never succeeded in building the human infrastructure that was necessary to by-pass Singapore and they never did by-pass Singapore.

"What lesson is there in it for me? I say to myself—looking not just towards tomorrow, or the next decade, but to the longer-term future—that perhaps there was some affinity of soul. There was a reason why we came together in Singapore... My colleagues and I have weighed the odds very carefully. We say: here is a connection worth the keeping. There was reason why the two groups got on. Both had a very keen sense of property; both desired, with an almost irresistible impulse, the acquisition of more property. And both had an overweening conceit in their civilized standards of human behaviour. This makes me rather chary about changing my patrons.

"Having said all those things—let me tell you why I think a greater effort must be made, and my fears of why the greater effort may not be forthcoming in a sufficiently aggressive intensity to make it worth your and my while. A lot depends upon your assessment, British assessment, of the kind of role Singapore will play in Southeast Asia in the 1970s and 1980s. If you think, that at the end of the century, this is all going to be overwhelmed, enveloped either by nations with 700 million or by nations with at least 100 million, then you will make your calculations accordingly. But if I were an Englishman with a pragmatic approach, then I would keep on making something through Singapore probably indefinitely. There is a new kind of role which Singapore could offer you—the British entrepreneur, the British industrialist—a special role which no other place in Southeast Asia can offer you. In all the other places—and this is not just sentiment, but just the hard facts of life—in all the other places, they need not put up with you. But here, for our own reasons, we have decided that it is better this way, keeping this relationship we have all got used to.

"The next question, if your role can fit in with mine, is: whether we together have a role in Southeast Asia. My frank answer to you is yes but I do not know if we will be allowed to play it. But, if we are not, then it will be a mess. I have tried to weigh it quite dispassionately. Let us assume first, that xenophobic, irrational and extremist tendencies gain ascendancy. Then this whole area is going to go into a crescendo of increasing conflicts, leading to unhappiness all round. But we can take the optimistic view: that the Americans with their enormous material resources... could make it worth everyone's while to do what they think is right, namely, try and make it a co-operative effort to prevent further expansion of the communist heartland which today stops at the seventeenth parallel in Vietnam. If that is the trend, then again Singapore has a very big role. Either we act as a dynamo, a sparking plug, generating the ignition for all this development or... conflict and poverty. This alternative will lead to policies which will end up with Singapore as a Cuba in Southeast Asia and a very different Cuba...

"If you decide that Singapore will be playing the dynamo role, then you may remember that it has also the social organism that can play the role well. My worry is: can you, the British, exploit this?

362

The problem is, can you suddenly become as aggressive as the Japanese or the Germans — the West Germans? For the problem is your capacity to adjust and to adapt your attitudes from that of privileged trader within an empire, to this fierce competition outside a sheltered harbour. We will offer you a sheltered harbour for such length of time as we can. But even Nigeria has opted to go and get associated status in the European Common Market. You will have to face more rugged competition. You know what has happened to Commonwealth preferences elsewhere. Whether in or outside Europe, you have a role in Southeast Asia. Singapore has a role in Southeast Asia, and here is an opportunity for the British with a people in spirit after your own heart . . .

"We are out for a good living. That is what makes Singapore tick. If you understand that, and think that Singapore can offer you a role, we are determined as a Government to facilitate and give you every opportunity to play that special role here. The alternative I prefer is the one which would carry on this partnership, a partnership which built a thriving metropolis out of a fishing village of 120 Malays and thirty Chinese. When we are counted in the roll-call of history, never let it be said we did not know what opportunities we missed."

IV

"There is tranquillity, poise and confidence in Singapore," the Prime Minister declared in his Chinese New Year Message on 8 February, "and it is a confidence born out of the knowledge that there are very few problems which we cannot overcome, given the framework of honest and effective administration. For in this framework our people's natural industry and talent will continue to blossom and flourish and generate prosperity for all."

V

On 15 February Lee unveiled the tall concrete memorial to the civilian victims of the Japanese occupation. It contained the bones of thousands of unidentified Chinese. Lee said: "We have come together this morning, twenty-five years after the Japanese capture of Singapore, to dedicate this memorial. We meet not to rekindle old fires of hatred, nor to seek settlements for blood debts. We meet to remember

363

the men and women who were the hapless victims of one of the fires of history. This monument will remind those of us who were here twenty-five years ago, when the Japanese forces swept down Malaya into Singapore, of what can happen to people caught completely unaware and unprepared for what was in store for them. It will help our children understand and remember what we have to tell them of this lesson we paid so bitterly to learn.

"This monument is not intended to alert us to another imminent invasion from the Japanese. For the balance of world power has altered radically in the past twenty-five years. And it is because it has so altered that we should be aware of the new dangers in the region, indeed in the world. It should spur us on to pursue policies which will cultivate for us the largest number of reliable and strong friends. We must resolve that if in spite of every insurance we cannot avoid being caught in a major catastrophe, then unlike the previous time, we will not be unprepared for the trials and tribulations that will follow, nor left prostrate and suppliant in the face of terror. This piece of concrete commemorates an experience which, in spite of its horrors, served as a catalyst in building a nation out of the young and unestablished community of diverse immigrants. We suffered together. It told us that we share a common destiny. And it is through sharing such common experiences that the feeling of living and being one community is established. If today as we remember these lessons of the past, we strengthen our resolve and determination to make our future more secure, then these men and women for whom we mourn would not have died in vain."

VI

On 21 February, on the eve of the introduction of the National Service Bill, which made every fit man and woman elegible for compulsory service in the citizen's defence forces, the Prime Minister explained to a gathering of youngsters just what this meant. "I think seventy per cent of the little boys and girls who are present here tonight are going to English schools because that is what the figures in the Education Ministry indicate. But I want the little boys and girls who are present here tonight to know this: go to English schools, learn English. But at the same time, never forget that you are not an Englishman, and I am not an Englishman. English is a language we learn and we use it. But we must keep a part of ourselves—the part that leads us back to our histories, to our cultures, to our civilizations from whence we came and out of that, the past, and together we will create a present and a future worthy of a people who have come from very ancient cultures and civilizations. We are pioneers in this region. . .

"Nowhere in Asia are people living the way we are, and discarding the past—the wooden hut with the attap roof going on to the modern, multi-storey homes with car parks, wide roads, squares, playing fields; and planning, planning to make you live in beautiful surroundings and planning so that all of you, when you grow up, will find jobs which will give you a meaningful life. We, who have lived and been brought up in a past generation under the British, understand the meaning of this difference. You will never quite understand what it is to live your own lives in a free society because you will never know, you will never have experienced, what it is to be a subject people. Today, you stand up free men, equal to me, to anybody. And you take it for granted. But twenty years ago, if you were not a white man, you were considered inferior and you were treated as an inferior. And the net result was that many people became mentally and psychologically inferior, suffering from an inferiority complex. But all that is the past. We do not want to try to refight old battles. But we must train our young children in a way that will make them fit to face up to the new problems that are coming.

"Singapore is an oasis in Southeast Asia. No other place in Southeast Asia offers you the kind of life which you are having. And I often try to think of ways and means whereby I can send young people to visit some places in Southeast Asia. Why? Because when they come back, they will kiss the ground and say, 'How lucky we are to come from Singapore!' Because nowhere else have a people organized themselves to look after their own interests—not the interests of a few people, but the interests of the whole of the people in Singapore. Nobody here dies of starvation. Nobody is allowed to beg in the streets. When we find someone begging, we put him into a home and feed him. And, in two or three years, with all our cleansing services reorganized, we will make this one of the cleanest and most beautiful cities in Asia with trees, flowers and shrubs in all the public places.

"But, behind it all, remember this: if you who are growing up do not understand that you have to defend this, then in the end, we will lose. Other people will come, smack you down, and take it over. And therefore we have decided, after very careful consideration—one and a half years of careful consideration—that every boy and girl will learn what it is to be a citizen and what is necessary to defend this country. Next Monday, we are going to introduce a National Service Bill in our Parliament. That will make it possible for us to train every boy and every girl as they grow up from our schools, to learn not just to be clever at reading and writing and earning a living but also to learn to stand up and be able to acquit himself or herself, if ever it becomes necessary, with honour and valour. Not all of you will have the opportunity or will have the privilege of serving in our army, navy or air force because we want only a small force.

"Many will get the basic training for the People's Defence Forces, and for the Special Constabulary and the Vigilante Corps. But every boy and girl will learn how to be useful. And those who are chosen —and it is an honour to be chosen—the ten per cent who are chosen for full-time duty for two years will be men who will be an elite. After they have served their two years, they are guaranteed jobs either in the Government or in the Statutory Boards or in the private sector.

"I will tell you why we do not want professional soldiers. This place must learn to live and work for a living. And if you are only a soldier, you do not contribute to the productivity of the place. So we train... Every man who is chosen becomes a soldier or sailor for two years. Then he goes back to earn a living in a factory, in an office and, for the next ten to fifteen years, he is part of a reservoir of people who understand discipline, who know the mechanics of self-defence, and who can in an emergency help to defend their own country. It will take many years—perhaps five, perhaps seven, perhaps ten years—before we can get the whole machine into gear. But in the end, every boy and girl here will understand that what he or she has in Singapore, he or she must be prepared to fight for and defend. Otherwise, it will be lost."

VII

At the Advocates and Solicitors Society on 18 March, Lee Kuan Yew dealt with some of the anxieties which occasionally assailed him and his colleagues about the continuance of the rule of law in newly-emergent countries... "First of all, the fact that today the rule of law is reasonably established—no one doubts that anyone will be executed at the whim and fancy of somebody else—is cause for quiet congratulations. For it might so very easily have been otherwise...

"It might be good fortune, perhaps, that not just I alone but some of my colleagues were brought up in fairly liberal traditions. We don't have to be lawyers to understand right, wrong, good, evil. This is basic and fundamental in the values of a people. And I think even if the Minister for Law and myself were to go wrong, you will have some consolation, Mr President, in the knowledge that quite a number of my colleagues are men imbued with some of the values, some of the traditions of an open, of an equal, of a tolerant society. You cannot maintain that kind of a society unless you are prepared to practise it yourself. In other words, your style must be open. You must yourself be tolerant. And most important of all, you must be able to ensure, in so far as you can, that your successors—even though they may not be of the same political colour as you are—are imbued with this value.

"Let us not deceive ourselves that we can do all these things because we just believe in democracy, the rule of law and the certainty of the law. We have paid a very heavy price." Lee referred to the persons detained in Singapore gaols without trial. To let them out would be "to run the very grave risk of undermining your whole social fabric. We have had to adjust, to temporarily deviate from, ideals and norms. This is a heavy price... I would like, therefore, to appeal to your conscience this evening since it is, as your President has said, 'a conscientious Bar'. I appeal to your conscience to try and help us find the answers to some of these problems. First of all, the Bar: the courts, the administration of justice. If we continue as in the past, it will fail..."

Lee agreed there must be certain ideals, certain standards, certain norms which are desirable and which should be striven for. "Then relate that to your existing society, your existing circumstances: what is achievable in this given situation. The crucial thing is: do not be afraid to innovate. I will give you an illustration of where I am at the moment thinking of real innovations. This is in regard to the problem of bribery and corruption. We live in an area where to be corrupt is a way of life. And there are scales... There are rates for the job... What is most important really for us is that because it is a way of life for others around us, it has to be understood.

"What is your answer? I say unless we give our Civil Servants pride in their standards, and reward them for being able to maintain those standards, the standards in the end will be undermined... I am seriously contemplating an innovation in the law because corruption is one of our key problems. Singapore's progress, its verve, its vitality is assured because the administrative machine works. There is no grit. You don't have to grease somebody to crank up the machine. We must keep it that way. To ensure this I am thinking of an amendment to the law. The innovation is: if any official is found with wealth which cannot be explained and there is uncorroborative evidence of corruption, his whole property can be sequestered. There must be some punishment or they get away. And I have not the slightest doubt that there will be an uproar from a lot of people, not least of all from members practising in the criminal law.

"You have done me the great compliment, Mr President, of reminding those present how long we have been in office. But I think the deepest compliment we could pay to ourselves is to remember that there must come a time—and not so very long—when the torch must be passed on. And there is no greater compliment that a man

367

can pay to himself and to his group, than to pass the torch on to like-minded people, fired by the same ideals, but younger, more vigorous, more capable to meet a more contemporary situation. I would like to believe that, as with me, so with you: as you pass the torch on to the next generation, you pass it on not only to capable hands but to good minds and good hearts."

VIII

Lee was invited by the German Socialist Foundation, the Friedrich-Ebert Stiftung to take part in an international forum in Tokyo, on 22 March. He spoke on the role of developing countries in world politics and began by saying that the subject was antithesis in itself. "For, if politics is concerned with the exercise of power, then the developing countries which are hoping to develop this power cannot by definition have much of a positive role. For until you have acquired the power you cannot take initiatives on your own. Not having the power to shape and determine events, the role that is thrust upon the under-developed countries is to arrange their relationship with the developed countries in order to exercise some influence. And this can come about in one of two ways—first, by the policies of the developed countries in wishing to expand their influence, power and support amongst potential adherents; second, by the developing countries coming together to increase their capacity to influence events.

"So long as there was keen competition between the monolithic communist world on the one side and the west on the other, between Russia and her allies and America and her allies, there was this great wooing of the emerging world. At the same time the emerging world, led by first-generation leaders who assumed authority in their respective countries in the post-colonial era, forgathered to try and exert a greater influence on the policies of the developed nations—Bandung and Afro-Asian solidarity marking that phase of the politics of the developing world.

"Two developments have taken place which determine our present phase: first, the break-up of this monolithic structure in the communist world; second, conflicts within Afro-Asian ranks, both of which worked to the disadvantage of the developing nations. Once there is no longer that same acute anxiety of the communists acquiring more and more populations and territories on to their side, the West is in a position to take a more dispassionate view about aid to developing nations. There is no longer the same urgency to forestall communist policies designed to win large sections of the world population—India, Indonesia—over to the communist side. It is not for us to apportion the blame for the breakdown in Afro-Asian solidarity. Whatever the inherent causes of conflict, when this great brotherhood of have-not nations are unable to find sufficient congealing factors to bind them for some concerted action to bring forth more favourable policies, stability of commodity prices, soft loans, technical aid and co-operation programmes, then is it realistic to hope for enlightened and disinterested help from technologically advanced nations to help the backward nations to join their ranks?

"We have a lot to learn, by hind-sight, from the experiences of the few non-European nations who have striven to make the grade into the ranks in that order. First let us recognize that no nation in the world ever gives away a technological advantage for reasons of 'charity. Whether it is the Russians refusing to help the People's Republic of China to become a nuclear power, which from all accounts is one of the main factors which caused the rift between Moscow and Peking, or whether it is the widening technological gap between America and Western European nations, the fact remains that no nation ever gives away its hard-earned technological secrets... There is a great deal of unease in the Western capitals of Europe over the ever increasing gap in computer technology, electronics, space rocketry and space communications... There are certain lessons which we must draw from this. Whilst American, British and generally European technologists were reluctant to share their technological know-how with non-European groups for reasons of self-interest, they were less reluctant to extend such co-operation to similar European groups who are less likely to become cut throat competitors. This accounts for the rapid development of the industrial potential of Australia since the war.

"All we can reasonably hope for is some assistance in the basic training of personnel, managers, administrators, professionals, technologists and also capital equipment on favourable terms for simple manufacturers.

"And, indeed, this was all that the countries of Japan, China, India and Indonesia have obtained from the advanced countries. The results vary, depending upon their capacity to exploit what assistance they were able to get for their development. The Japanese worked within the framework of an intense patriotism woven around the feudal fabric, working on capitalist incentives. This gave them the impetus required for sustained effort with great sacrifices in low wages of the workers until very recently. In China, it was the strict discipline and organization of a communist system, the vision of the great millenium spurring people, all enveloped in great patriotism. They accounted for such industrial progress as has been made.

"I venture to suggest that it is the absence of severe controls over human activity, the abstinence from the use of the spur or the whip on the working class in the public sector, plus the checks on outright exploitation of the working class in the private sector, which explains why, in spite of external help in investment in heavy industry, there has been no spectacular break-through as yet in India. One of the other factors is the absence of jingoism which has marked the policies of rational democratic government in India. So much so, that now it is reported that there are about 10,000 Indian Ph.D.s working abroad for either foreign agencies or enterprises. Nearer to Singapore is the experience of Indonesia. If the experience of our Indonesian neighbours proves anything, it is that there are certain pre-requisites necessary for any planned economic growth. The absence of a trained cadre of administrators (which India had), the absence of any systematic training in the professions and technology, made it difficult for successive governments to implement plans which were basically sound in the context of the great resources, both human and natural, with which the Indonesian people are endowed.

"What lessons are there for us as democratic socialists in Asia? First, that there is no one single simple highway to travel to the technological age. You, Comrade Chairman, spoke of plurality of means in the developed world. So there are plurality of means which we must investigate in the undeveloped world. Whatever your political ideology, and this is hind-sight after twenty years of the experience of developing nations, there are certain basic ingredients necessary for any economic and technological progress. There must first be the willingness to work and learn, and to reshape the social structure of one's society to fit in with the needs of the industrial technology. Second, there must be capital, either through enforced accumulation or massive loans. If I am to sum up these two ingredients in one phrase, it is the will and capacity. There must first be the will to want to be developed, so passionate that no effort is too strenuous. Then only will borrowed capacity in loans and technical aid be put to full advantage... There are certain other lessons which Asia can learn from others. To provide large masses of untrained and unskilled peasants with the incentive for prolonged effort and sacrifice as industrial workers at privation levels, you must offer them the goals of a great future, that vision of a better life which alone makes suffering bearable.

"Communism and socialism offer this to the people who are asked to pay the price of rapid industrial growth. The problem democratic socialists face is not only to offer this vision of a great future but, because they are democratic, to be able to make this vision credible by periodic boosters in the standards of life of the people who are asked to make this sacrifice for future generations. This in turn makes it vital to have a leadership which can give them confidence

370

that the sacrifice would not be in vain. There must be high standards of integrity, if not dedication, amongst those entrusted with the power. If democratic socialists have not got this quality to match communist zeal and fanaticism, then they cannot provide that alternative to communist methods of rapid industrialization. In fact, without these qualities, it is easier to try and do it the capitalist way. For then at least you have efficient exploitation, ruthless but efficient, of cheap labour and large natural resources which have marked the early history of the capitalist nations of Western Europe and America.

"I have refrained from drawing any conclusions as to the possible trends in Asia. For the first lesson is that there are too many imponderables among the factors which will determine the course of events. No trend, however clear and distinct, continues to its logical conclusion, be it Afro-Asian solidarity, or the monolithic communist world movement. However, one constant theme recurs again and again in the history of tribes and nations. The desire amongst the bigger to compete to become bigger, to extend their influence, their power and to win support. And this is why Asia has more attention from the contestants for super-power status, compared to the other undeveloped worlds of Africa and Latin America. First, the vast geographic area. Second, the enormous populations. And third, these populations have shown in the course of the past few thousand years, not few hundred years, that given the right social, administrative framework and the political leadership, they are societies capable of high endeavour. Relics and monuments throughout India, Cambodia and Indonesia bear evidence to this. Therefore, the contest for accretion of these large groups of people, on one side or the other, will be much keener in Asia than elsewhere. And so it is that our African friends find the developed world not overwrought over the problems of racial discrimination or oppression in Rhodesia and South Africa. But there is already a whole hive of activity, with a great potential for good, bringing benefits to the nations in South and Southeast Asia, to take account of the day when competition is resumed for the hearts and minds of South and Southeast Asia. So we have the stirrings for regional co-operation, none of them disinterested.

"And it is against this background that we as democratic socialists must seek to make a contribution to the growth of the kind of open democratic societies which offer a meaningful life, meaningful intellectually, culturally and materially. This challenge for change will be answered not by democratic socialists alone. The power structure of nation states in South and Southeast Asia has undergone several mutations since the first generation postwar leadership took over. Socialists have come and gone out of power in a number of countries. In some, military rulers have emerged, often fired by similar, if less defined, ideals of the equal and just society. For these military leaders are also part of the generation that emerged from colonialism, fired by the same ideals of a more just and equitable society. But all are caught in the contradiction of having to demand greater sacrifice from their people in order to have the kind of society which gives them a meaningful life. In the end, success or failure for each of the nation groups must depend upon its own capacity to use the advantages offered by competition for extensions of power and influence by the larger industrial nations of South and Southeast Asia.

"Our task is not made easier by the thought that the next decade can see changes as dramatic as the decade that has gone by. The conflicts that have taken place within the communist world to the advantage of the capitalist world, the conflicts that have taken place within the undeveloped Afro-Asian countries to the disadvantage of the underdeveloped, do not mean that new patterns or alignments for extensions of power blocs cannot rapidly be redrawn. Schisms will be healed and new competitive groups will emerge. It is this probability which has motivated much of the creative planning in the capitals of Europe and America—the planning for the next decade in Asia when the race will be recommenced. Inevitably we all see this in the context of our own immediate position in Asia. When Japan talks of regional co-operation, she means Japan, East and Southeast Asia and Oceana, including Australia and New Zealand. For this is an area in which Japan can play a role. When America and the West talk of countervailing forces, they mean that large crescent stretching from Pakistan, India, Indonesia, up eastwards on to Japan. When our Indonesian neighbours talk about regional co-operation, they mean Indonesia, and the smaller countries of South and Southeast Asia, not including India or Pakistan to the west, nor Japan to the north or Australia and New Zealand to the south. If democratic socialists are to make a contribution to the course of events, they must cease to think in terms of abstractions. They must give meaning to socialist ideals in pragmatic and realistic policies to produce changes for the better in the daily lives of their peoples."

IX

Lee had something to say about "the lean and rugged society" he aimed to create, when he addressed the Singapore Employers Federation (31 May). The Government, he said, had been stressing this for two years, with a purpose "to create that mood in our people to be prepared to sacrifice, to make the effort to respond to a harsher situation. It is not just physical and psychological ruggedness alone which is required. . .

"When we talk of leanness, it means that we carry no passengers. Every single person in Singapore now, whatever the past policies or principles of government, must either pull his weight or he deserves what he will get. If we do not measure up to the challenge we deserve to perish either as individuals or together as a community. I am sanguine enough to believe that there are enough of us prepared to pull our weight and able to make this community prosper and to offer some encouragement to those around us who are faced with not dissimilar problems. . ."

Lee reminded the employers that Singapore was a community of two million people on an area of 224 square miles with some outer islands. "If the economy sags they must starve; particularly with a Currency Board because there are no means by which you can generate economic activity by the issue of bank notes which are not backed by equal assets held here and abroad. The basic problem which we have already begun to solve is to get rid of this attitude that: You owe me a living. I was born here. According to the Charter of Human Rights, I am entitled to the following things: minimum wage, holidays with pay, education and so on. It is this attitude which we have set out to dispel. Unless you dispel this belief that the world owes us a living, then none of our other problems will even begin to be solved. I take comfort from the fact that, after two years, our people are in a mood of grim determination, with a keenness to adjust ourselves to the new situation, to gird ourselves to make the grade. We will get what we can earn and earn what we strive for. This must mean correlating rewards to performance. . . Very simply, it means a revamping of the methods and values by which we get high performance. No two persons are equal, not even identical twins. No two persons will give of their best if you pay them equally for unequal work. This is one of the basic problems of man. How is this to be translated into actual dollars and cents in payment for services rendered? I hope the National Productivity Centre will find some formulae to fit the different industries. But if you measure a man's reward by time, you can be sure it is the most inefficient and unrewarding of all the measurements. . .

"It is not by accident that our building trade is probably the most successful. Supervision is at a minimum, problems of discipline do not arise. A man is paid for performance. I am not suggesting that we could do this for all the complicated mechanical operations of modern industry. But we must recognize this urge, the instinct in our people to perform and give of his best only if he is rewarded better than the other who did not do as well. More and more we must make this a cornerstone of our drive for high performance. It is not just the capitalist or free enterprise world that has had to recognize this hard fact. One of the most instructive journeys I had was the one to Eastern Europe in May last year. They understood that uniformity must mean a lcwering of the effort. And in the many factories that I went to the wages were not equal. They were paid in accordance with their performance...

"I do not wish to exonerate myself from many of the aberrations which were inevitable in the early stages of the trade union movement in Singapore. It was so tied up and rolled up with the whole anticolonial movement. It became a protest movement. In the nature of things, it broke down two things: discipline and efficiency. Fourteen years ago, a number of my colleagues and I organized the Government workers and others in a movement of protest to challenge authority, and trade unionism became a banner behind which we challenged the whole system. Now we have to re-educate not only our trade union leaders but, even more important, the workers that this can no longer be. They have got a Government which they can change at will and this Government could dispossess all the employers if it so decides and distribute the loot to all workers if thereby we increase the sum total of human happiness. Slowly we have educated a whole generation to understand this will not increase their wealth or well-being and what has happened in other countries has helped in the education. So there is support for the rational policies: better wages with better results and all the social privileges and opportunities which they never had before—Housing Board homes, an assured place in society, health service, schools for their children, community centres, and recreation facilities which never existed before.

"I would like to believe that employers on their part are able to recognize this new mood and to respond in a creative way. Nothing is more soul-destroying than to have to repeat this whole process all over again, for employers to believe that 'ah, now, we have taught these workers a lesson, the Government understands our importance: we, employers, are giving jobs'. Then we will have to go round the awful cycle of teaching everybody again an unnecessary and painful lesson already learnt by all. We have a willing population. We have a set of unions prepared to make adjustment on all the fundamental practices whether it is retrenchment, or the method in which they get their rewards. A creative and a sensitive response from the employers could make a positive contribution to the kind of relationship which we as a Government want to see established: a partnership in enterprise, ever increasing output at ever lower costs...

"In the long run, whether this island with the second highest per capita income in Asia thrusts forward and upwards or whether it gets bogged down in a morass like so many newly independent countries depends upon three simple factors: the first is effective government; the second is a willingness of the people to work and pay for what it wants, never something for nothing; and third, whether it has amongst its people that quality of enterprise, that drive, that capacity to anticipate and take intelligent and calculated risks. These three factors are crucial to Singapore's future..."

X

On 18 July, the British Government announced that by the mid-seventies they intended to leave their bases in Singapore and Malaysia. By coincidence, that day 114 officer cadets, the first graduates of the Israel-assisted Singapore Armed Forces Training Institute, were commissioned. At a ceremony, the Prime Minister remarked that this was taking place "at a time when we have just received formal notice of the changes that will be necessary in the structure of the security and defence of our part of the world... We must build, together with such friends and allies as have an interest in the security and future of the Singapore-Malaysia area, sufficient forces for our security. And the defence assistance we can expect in the long run from Britain may be in the nature of mobile forces, both aircraft and naval vessels. There are five years to go before 1973, the earliest of the middle-70s, or ten years to go before 1977, the latest part of the middle-70s. The British Government says that the precise time will depend upon the circumstances. In this time we have to build all the sinews we can so that we will not just be passengers in any defence alliance. The more self-reliant and effective we become, the more desirable and reliable a partner we make in any defence arrangement. What we lack in numbers we will make up for in quality in the standards of discipline, training, dedication and leadership. There is no reason why we should not, by the middle-70s, achieve an equally secure arrangement against external aggression. For we can safely assume that we need make provision against the possibility of only a middling, not a big, power attack.

"Those of you who were in Singapore in 1942 when the Japanese Imperial Army swept into Singapore will know that there were vast differences between the capacity and quality of the different soldiers we saw. The Japanese Imperial Guards were accompanied by Koreans and Formosans. The British had Australians, Indians and Gurkhas on their side. Everybody knew that one Japanese soldier was worth more than one of the others in tenacity and doggedness. Everybody also knew that some of the British contingents were made of sterner stuff, and they were not related to the physical size of the soldiers of the various Commonwealth contingents... What is the conversion rate between the various armed forces? In other words, how many Koreans and Formosans in the last war equalled one Japanese soldier? Or to bring the example more up to date, how many South Vietnamese soldiers equal one Vietminh soldier from the north or vice-versa?... Upon your performance in the years ahead, people will assess if one Singaporean equals one Gurkha as foot soldiers. But that is not good enough, for, unlike the British officered Gurkhas, we must form our own officer cadre. As we go up the scale in sophisticated weaponry, the Singaporeans must match themselves against the best in the world. For only then will our survival rate be high and secure.

"Remember, if knowledgeable people, like military attaches in foreign embassies, trained to observe and report on these matters, regard us as unequal in discipline or perseverance and, under adverse conditions, to be wanting in courage, or that we lack in intelligence to develop the skills which can come only after intense application to sophisticated weapons, then it will not be long before others pick up this contempt for our capacity to stand up for ourselves. This is one of the surest ways to invite an attack to subjugate us and turn us into economic serfs, or worker ants, for the welfare and well-being of others. We in Singapore have established our reputation as a resourceful and ingenious community of merchants, manufacturers, workers and technicians. We have ample time up till the middle '70s for you and those who will follow you in SAFTI to establish a reputation for us as a hardy and well-organized people. We must transform a rootless society of migrant stock into a closely knit community determined to dig our toes in into our own corner of Asia."

In a statement put out the same day (18 July) the Prime Minister said he had "acquainted the unions with the dimensions of the problems involved between now and 1971 and the further reductions between 1971 and the middle '70s. I have discussed the matter frankly with all the leaders concerned. I do not think glossing over the severity of the cuts will do anyone any good. Both the Government and the unions are agreed that this problem must be faced intelligently and sensibly to minimize dislocation and maximize the opportunities for conversion to civilian use of the base facilities as they become redundant. There will be close consultations between the unions and the Labour Ministry to ensure that the principles on which redundancy has been agreed are faithfully and impartially administered. Our future depends upon our capacity to discipline and organize our community so that they can make the adjustments required. We must brace our people up to meet the changes that are coming. Our paramount duty is to protect the collective interests of all those who have nowhere but Singapore to look to for their future. If in 1971 a sane, stable and secure position is achieved, the chances of our successfully overcoming the second half of the problem will be assured. The

Government will make every effort to ensure that Singapore citizens who become redundant as a result of defence cuts are given every opportunity to be retrained for civilian jobs. But I have explained to the unions that it is not easy to convert a 45-year-old clerical worker into a 46-year-old skilled tradesman."

XI

At a cadet corps parade (26 July), Lee Kuan Yew spoke of the content, the purpose, the direction "of what our education and our training is supposed to do for our young citizens. . .

"If we live in a different society and grow rice or rubber or pineapples for a living, then all this complex training would not have been necessary. All you have to know is the simple things: about when you grow rice, just before the rains come, transplant immediately after the rains and so on; and when you reap, how you prevent rats from eating up your grain. But we do not live in that kind of a society. This was a centre of great trading. People lived as a result of great skills developed on how to collect the kind of goods from the surrounding area which other parts of the world want, and to import and redistribute the kind of goods which other people in the region want. That kind of a world, which made possible a great trading centre like Singapore, has already changed and will continue to change. And the world in which you, ten years from now as adult citizens, will live in, will work in and learn to run, will be one in which more and more our livelihoods will depend upon technological and industrial skills to be the kind of community that acts as a kind of workshop for ourselves and for the region. Therefore, the whole purpose of your training is to prepare you to meet these problems. But there is one problem which every boy and girl in Singapore faces, and this is a function which everybody must be able to discharge, whether he is to be a scientist or whether he is going to be just a plain skilled worker. This is to be able to stand up for yourself as an effective digit in a security arrangement with such allies who have an interest in this region, to ensure that what we have built, what our forefathers have handed to us and on which we are building is not brought to ruin. Small communities like ours must be either rugged and tough or they must perish. Whatever the specialization you may do in life, there is one thing we ask and we must ask of every one of our citizens: the capacity for group discipline, group activity, specialized skills and training to perform the minimal functions for our security and our continued peace and prosperity. . . "

On the eve of National Day (8 August), Lee Kuan Yew faced the television cameras. "Tonight we complete the second year as a republic on our own. We have more than maintained the pace of progress that we achieved in the first year. The figures for the past twelve months, as against the twelve months before that, show that our imports went up eight per cent and our exports nine per cent... On the industrial front our net output for manufacturing industries increased eighteen per cent. Our exports of manufactured goods also increased eighteen per cent. If we take the exports of only the new or pioneer industries, the exports increased by seventy per cent. In the meanwhile, our foreign exchange reserves moved up by $136 million to $1,174 million from November, when the Finance Minister made his Budget Speech, to May this year—an increase of over twelve per cent... At the same time, construction progressed. The Housing and Development Board spent more than $70 million, an increase of seven per cent... In the private sector, the value of houses built was more than $40 million, an increase of twenty-nine per cent. And all other construction increased forty-four per cent.

"But, in the long run, it is the quality of our youths that will determine our future. And we have to invest in them more than any other sector. Changes are taking place in the schools. The emphasis is now on content and quality. We want our schools to produce citizens who are healthy and hardy, with a sense of social purpose and group discipline, prepared to work and to pay for what they want, never expecting something for nothing. Our schools will train students in the classrooms and in the playing fields to make them healthy and robust. But even more important, they will teach our students high standards of personal behaviour, social norms of good and bad, right and wrong. Without these values, a literate generation may be more dangerous than a completely uneducated one... From this year, with National Service, every boy—and later on, we hope every girl—will undergo some form of national service, not just to be a fighter but to learn to be a good citizen... Without good administration it is impossible to live in comfort and security in a crowded and densely populated island republic. The Labour Ministry has registered all those above twelve years, given them new identity cards which cannot be easily forged. One million two hundred thousand people were given red cards. They are Singapore citizens, members of the club, entitled to all the care, the training, the assistance, the job-opportunities which we can provide for ourselves. We have also issued 160,000 people with blue cards. They are not citizens...

"But as we solve old problems—and the year that has passed has been a year of considerable progress—new ones, however, have appeared. The British Government has decided to cut down their force in the Singapore-Malaysia area by half in four years, by 1971. By the middle seventies, i.e. some time between 1973 and 1977, depending upon conditions in this region, the British will leave their bases. Thereafter they will maintain only a military capability. This will consist of a strategic reserve in Britain, and sophisticated weapons, chiefly ships and aircraft. This presents us with a grave challenge, almost a change of life, a new and different way of living. We shall have to arrange new means to secure our defence with old friends and allies. These defence cuts will also create immediate problems. 15,000 civilian employees will lose their jobs by 1971. About half of them will be our citizens. And as the British Service families leave, so about 5,000 women, now earning their keep as domestic helps, will also lose their jobs. The problem is this: that while we can and we will maintain our economic growth, we have not been able, and may not for some time be able, to solve the problem of unemployment. We must create between 7,000 to 10,000 new jobs in manufacturing industry every year... we have a working population of 550,000. Of them, 59,000 are on work permits. They are non-citizens... 43,000 of our citizens are unemployed... Now our birth rate, with family planning and better housing and living standards, has gone down from forty per thousand of population in 1959 to twenty-nine per thousand this year. And it is still going down, and, in about seven years' time, it will be about twenty per thousand...

"But, meanwhile, Barisan Sosialis and all the other communist front organizations keep on their senseless hit and run demonstrations. We will counter them. Political protests will not create more jobs. On the other hand, they will discourage investment, check the growth of industries and restrict the number of new jobs. And so we have got to be firm and effective in dealing with these problems. And only such an administration can maintain that public order and confidence, with which alone new factories will be built and new jobs created. This requires an efficient administrative framework, without which no effective government is possible. Given time, there are very few things we cannot do in Singapore. For we have got a young, active, adaptable and striving community prepared to look for new answers, sometimes well tried solutions, sometimes imaginative innovations, to meet our problems... From our past performance, not just over the past two years but over the past eight years, I say we have the capacity to make the grade. If we gird ourselves to meet these problems we shall carve out a better and a more secure future for ourselves and our children in this corner of Asia."

At a community centre National Day celebration on 15 August, Lee Kuan Yew said he thought that in the midst of festivities "we should sit back and ask ourselves what kind of future we will be giving to the young children we have brought into this world. What will happen in 1975? What kind of Asia will it be, what kind of world will it be in 1985, twenty years from now? And the answer very frankly, is: nobody knows because there are too many factors, too many imponderables. But one thing I can tell you for certain: that if we don't organize ourselves and anticipate quite a number of the problems which we know are coming, then whatever else may happen to the rest of the world, there will be a lot of unhappiness for the children that we have brought into Singapore. There are very few countries in Asia and probably fewer in Africa that have got independence since the War who, as a people, have done better than they were doing before, when they were governed by the white man, whether it was the British, the Dutch, the French or the Belgians. Why is this so? I have asked myself this many times. And as I travel through parts of Africa and Asia, I try to formulate the reasons why this has happened. There are many reasons. The simplest one is this: because somebody with a superior organization structure, a superior civilization, a superior technology came, whether to Asia or Africa, and built up the apparatus of a modern state—the government, governors, officers all down the line, tax gatherers, laws to see that you can order your activities accordingly, law courts, police enforcement, public cleansing, some form of education—it does not mean that therefore you can automatically just take over, that when the colonial governor goes out, you can walk in and put on all the plumes and uniforms and things will go on just as before. It is not true.

"First, the people together must have the will to be a nation. And what has happened in the Congo and in parts of Africa goes to show that when a superior group captures a chunk of territory with many races and many tribes and many cultures, and sets up one administration, it does not mean that the people comprised in that territory can just take over. This is our first problem: the will to be a people. That we must have. If you and I are so many individuals, here just because our forefathers came here to make money and we got left behind, and we continue to be just so many individuals without the will, the collective will to assert our right to be ourselves, then we must perish. Somebody will come in, smack us down in the face, take over and say, 'Well, I like your house, you had better put up an attap shed; I will take this over.' That is what happened when the Japanese Imperial Army came here. And we must never assume that these things cannot happen again. How do we express this will? How does a nation express this will? In some countries there is no such thing as the will of a people because it is confused. There is no means of expressing that will. It is just one chaotic mess...

"I tell you what happens in an established country, whether it is Japan, China, Britain, France, Russia or America. There is always a hard core of people who represent that will, people whose instinctive reflexes are those of the national interests. You must have that... America, in 200 years, has thrown up a leadership, a hard core. I am not saying it is good or bad. But the fact is they have such a group... The Japanese have it, too... They ran big empires up in Korea, Manchuria, down in Taiwan and stretched into Southeast Asia. They were defeated but they have come up. And deep down inside, there is a hard will in all Japanese to be a strong nation. This is the first thing we must have..."

Lee said that at the top in Singapore there were probably about 200 people. And at grass roots another 2,000. "If you can kill the 200 on top and the 2,000 on the ground in one blow, you will have destroyed Singapore. It is, therefore, a very fragile foundation. Over the years, we must consolidate this will and the mechanics by which this will is able to express itself: we must institutionalize the various organs of leadership. If we have that leadership and that will in our community to be a nation, there is no problem which we cannot overcome... However far Singapore may be from the ideal, it is a good deal better than anything you can get elsewhere in the region..."

Lee said that what was required all the time was "that push, that thrust to counter the natural sluggishness which this climate tends to build into our physical system, and, all that while, we must have an awareness of the realities of life. We can build the industries. We have what sociologists call a highly 'achievement-orientated' type of society. For every boy, every girl here, tonight, there are fathers and mothers egging them on to perform better than the other pupils in school. Not all societies have this. In many societies, they are quite happy just to sit down under the banyan tree and contemplate their navel. So when there is famine they just die quietly. Here, they will not die quietly... To reduce the argument to the bone for a lot of people whose reflexes have always been that of individual survival: the migrant community suffers from this one disadvantage, that having moved once from their ancestral homes, they are ready to move again if things get too difficult here. But the boys and girls who have been born here have nowhere to go to. Therefore, they have to stand up and fight. I think we will succeed because they have no choice but to succeed."

XIII

In old Japan the soldier had an honoured place in society. Neighbours sent him off to battle, and in due course received him (or his

381

body) back again, covered with glory. Lee Kuan Yew decided to follow that principle. For in old China, the soldier had figured low in the pattern of society. Hardly anyone was lower than a soldier. With the introduction of national service in Singapore it was urgently necessary to modernize ancient attitude. Youths were told it was an honour and a privilege to serve the state as a soldier. Groups of young men called up were sent off to do their national service with a community dinner. Speaking at the first dinner held in his own parliamentary constituency (29 August) Lee Kuan Yew reminded them that Singapore was a young community with a short history.

"Tonight is a special event in our lives. It marks a significant beginning which, if pursued successfully, will ensure a permanent chapter for ourselves in the history of Asia. For over 150 years, four great cultures have met here in confluence. The British held sway and left their imprint. The Chinese, Indians and others came and settled. Now we have to look after ourselves. We have no tradition to guide us. But instinct tells us what we must do. We must build into our young that spirit of togetherness. Through common training and common experience we must inculcate the qualities of valour, comradeship, discipline, common social purpose, pride in themselves and their community. Only then will all that we have built be safe for posterity, a relatively advanced urban community with one of the highest standards of living in the region. If we do not have this we will be brought down to the filth and squalor, the degradation and corruption, the poverty and misery, which prevails in large parts of the newly independent countries.

"The young men we honour tonight have been chosen for full-time National Service, a special responsibility, and also a great privilege. They are the ten per cent of their generation who, if they make the grade, will serve a full period of two years and then go on into Reserve Service. Those who make the stern standards we require, at the end of their two years will be assured of a job. We are creating a tradition tonight by gathering here the elders and leaders of the community to do them honour in the presence of their families and friends. It will remind them of the need for perseverance, grit and effort to achieve the high standards we ask of our armed forces. For on this will depend the security and happiness of all of us. Soldiers and uniforms of any type used to have unhappy memories for us. We were a people governed by others; the British, then the Japanese. Even in the course of riots after independence within Malaysia, there was never a sense of being at one with those in uniform who held the bayonet and enforced compliance. These memories, coupled with the Chinese tradition that good sons do not become soldiers, plus the factor that most of our Indian community are from non-warrior castes, are a disadvantage. This means a special effort must be made to honour and respect those of our citizens in uniforms, those who carry the guns that will protect us.

"It also requires that those we put in uniform shall always have high standards of moral rectitude and personal courtesy to win the respect and affection of the people. Too often with the new armies of new countries, the soldier becomes a brigand. From his original role as protector of the people, he degenerates into their tormentor and preys on them in the midst of growing chaos. Our soldier must and will be different. To all of you called up for National Service, let me remind you: You are citizens first and last. Remember that the more the authority the community invests in you, the more it expects you to be of exceptional discipline and keep a high code of honour. Never sully the good name of the unit you will join. Finally, when you leave tomorrow from the community centres, remember that your family and your friends, your whole neighbourhood, will watch your training and follow your progress with deep interest. They will visit you from time to time in your camps to applaud your achievements and to cheer you on in the hard training awaiting you. You cannot let them down. However hard, however rigorous, however trying the tasks that you will be asked to undertake, you must never give up. When we welcome you back as a fully trained warrior, you will be a better and a stronger citizen. I wish you well in your careers."

XIV

The Prime Minister on 8 September told Parliament that the British had decided to reach a reduction of about half the forces deployed in Singapore and Malaysia during 1970-71, and to withdraw altogether in the middle 1970s.

Lee said that this meant that right up till the middle seventies, a period of between six years at the earliest and ten years at the latest, there would be an actual presence in the area consisting mainly of aircraft and naval vessels. The British Government also planned to maintain a military capability for use, if required, in the area, even when the British no longer had forces permanently based there. This capability would be largely drawn from the forces of all three Services which would be stationed in Britain as a strategic reserve. They would probably keep in the Far East some naval and amphibious forces.

"These decisions have now been made public. They require reappraisal and readjustment in the foreign and defence policies of all the governments that have planned their previous policies on the basis of a continuing British military presence in the region into the indefinite future. Before the 1970s, rearrangements will have been made in the pattern of defence in which we must seek our own security.

"But whilst our problems of defence are those of the middle term and beyond, the economic impact of the defence cuts will be immediate. Total British base expenditure constitutes roughly twenty per cent of Singapore's GNP They provide direct employment for some 30,000 civilian employees in the armed forces and another 10,000 women and girls as domestic helps for the service families. About 15,000 of these civilians employees and 5,000 of domestic helpers will be out of jobs by 1971, adding to our already large pool of unemployed. Our problem is to lessen the dislocation of our economy. In this connection, it will be useful to recall that from 1819 right up to the 1930s there was a thriving and prosperous Singapore without either a British naval or air base. The naval base in Sembawang and the air base in Seletar were built in the 1930s. And it was only the introduction of the practice of allowing serving officers and other ranks to be accompanied by their wives and children in the 1950s, that British base expenditure began to constitute so sizable a percentage of our GNP. Over a period of about a decade, this figure will tail back to zero. We shall be back in the position of the thirties, where the British base expenditure constituted a negligible proportion of the economy of Singapore. There was a thriving Singapore before the bases were built and manned, and if we set about it intelligently and in good heart, there will be a bigger and economically more self-reliant Singapore, after the bases have been run down and the uniformed personnel withdrawn.

"The problems arising out of this process are of considerable magnitude and complexity. What to do with this vast military complex, one naval base and dockyard, three military airfields and a vast army complex of workshops, supply depots and other supporting services? Whilst we will inherit all the fixtures which have been built over the years on lands made available by the Singapore Government to the British armed services, we will also inherit more than 40,000 bread-winners and their families who have come to Singapore from India, West Malaysia, as far off as Hongkong and even Weihaiwei. With their families, they now comprise some 500,000 persons. About three-quarters are now our citizens. Both in their public statements and in discussions and communications between British Ministers and ourselves, the British have made it plain that they shared our interests in maintaining confidence in the continued stability and prosperity of Singapore and were anxious to assist in meeting economic problems which the rundown of their bases according to programme will cause. They have stated that they would be ready to consider with us the most effective and productive uses of the economic and technical resources they could provide... But, however significant the aid, the future of Singapore depends upon our capacity to maintain orderly and stable economic and social conditions as we go through the pangs of withdrawal of British Base expenditure. The success of this operation depends upon three factors. First, the ability to maintain that climate of quiet confidence and the establishment of labour attitudes and social conditions which will assure investors, local and overseas, of the certainty of their planning assumptions for the establishment and expansion of their industries. Second, the capacity of our population to adapt and adjust, without any whimpering or wringing of hands, as a way of life to which they have been accustomed over thirty years comes to an end... The third factor is whether the economic aid that we have been promised will be substantial enough and utilized intelligently enough to create the maximum number of jobs. Whether British performance will be equal to their promises will in part depend upon the performance of Britain's own economy.

"But it will be foolish to believe that others can do for us what we as a people and organized as a representative government must do for ourselves. From our past performance, given no ill-fortune, it is more than likely that we can, and will, make up for the loss of this twenty per cent GNP which will take place over the next decade. Our economy has grown at the rate of six per cent to nine per cent per annum, except for the first full year of confrontation, 1964, when the increase was only two per cent. But what we may not be able to do unless our performance is better than that of the past eight years is to create meaningful jobs as the annual 15,000—20,000 young boys and girls who now come into the labour market, are joined by another 40,000 workers, about 30,000 of them our citizens, who will be put out of employment. All the family planning and other methods of controlling population which we may have to use will be of great benefit to whoever is the Government in the late seventies and eighties. But we are already saddled with the baby boom of the post-war years of the 1940s and early 1950s.

"We have assured the British Government of our co-operation to ensure the orderly withdrawal of their forces and the rundown of the bases according to programme. The civilian employees unions leaders have reacted in a rational way in the best interests of their members and of Singapore. Consultations and discussions will go on between our officers and the officers of the three services to work out intelligently and in a friendly way how their redundant base facilities can be put to some economic use. It is our intention that the changeover be done in a quiet and orderly manner and with goodwill."

Replying to a question Lee said "This is an unhappy disengagement which has come earlier than either they or we expected. The best way of meeting the problem is to go about it quietly and intelligently, discussing our problems in a low key, and with as little fuss and bother as possible."

XV

On 23 September, the Singapore newspapers printed the news that the libel suit brought by Lee Kuan Yew against the former Secretary-General of UMNO, Tan Sri Syed Jaafar Albar, and the Utusan Melayu Press Ltd., and its editor Inche Melan bin Abdullah, was discontinued before the Chief Justice Mr Justice Wee Chong Jin, in the High Court, all the defendants admitting that "there is no foundation for any of the disgraceful allegations" they made against the Prime Minister, and agreeing to apologise to him. In addition, they also agreed to idemnify him for the whole costs of the proceedings. They were believed to have amounted to more than $80,000. *Utusan Melayu* undertook also to give the fullest publicity to the apology and withdrawal of the libellous statements by giving a prominent front-page position for two days of the text of the statement made before the Court. Mr R. C. Hoffman, on behalf of Albar, acknowledged that the allegations made by Albar "are unfounded and he unreservedly withdraws them. He also expresses his sincere regrets to the plaintiff for publishing the statements containing the allegations, and he apologises to him for the distress and embarrassment caused to him by such publication."

XVI

On the eve of his departure for Britain, Zurich and the United States, (25 September) the Prime Minister gave a banquet for the Prime Minister of Japan, Mr Sato. Lee told the Japanese statesman that his visit came at a time of "significant change" in the thinking and planning of the nations concerned with Asia and the Pacific. "It is twenty-two years since the Second World War ended. But we are still searching for a formula to establish an enduring framework to secure the peace of Asia and the integrity of the many new and several old nations that the continent comprises. Twenty-five years ago, it would have been impossible to imagine the circumstances which have enabled my colleagues and me to welcome you to Singapore today. How it happened is the history of the past twenty-five years. Perhaps everyone has grown a little wiser in the meantime. But there are times when one doubts if the lessons of the past have been learned by new aspirants to new forms of supremacy and hegemony, either through the power of a super economy or through ideological and doctrinal disciplines. The age of European domination of Asia has passed. Japan contributed in some measure to the hastening of that end. Her own Asian domination of a large chunk of Asia was short-lived and thwarted by the combined might of American and British power. But it has left Asians with no illusions as to the nature of hegemony. The nearness of colour and affinity of ethnic origins do not make hegemony any the better.

"We are in a state of flux and change. What is to happen to Asia? Have we learnt from the past? Can we passively co-exist, or better still, actively co-operate, the big with the small, the hardy with the gentle, the intense and the easy going, and let time and circumstance slowly re-shape these communities and nation groups into viable societies each moving at a tempo which suits the temperament, character and aspirations of each particular society? Or is it impossible for the big to resist the temptation of doing in the small? Will the hardy always acquire a bigger share of the resources available as against the gentle? Must the intense inevitably out-pace and eventually out-do the easy-going? These are riders, the answers to which I do not know. But I do know that whilst we can learn from the past, it will be a mistake to allow our policies and our thinking to be prisoners of the past. The old balance of power in Asia and the Pacific is gone. The present balance is too directly dependent on an American intervention on so prodigious a scale that it cannot go on indefinitely. It depends so much on outside bolstering that it must become tiresome to those who have to do the bolstering, and debilitating to those being bolstered.

"Let us hope that all countries will persevere and strive for a fair solution to this tragic conflict in Vietnam, so that the enormous sacrifices that have been and are still being made, will be worthwhile—namely by securing a more peaceful Asia, where both the non-communist and communist parts of it learn to live with each other, and to leave each other's political systems alone, allowing every country to devote all its resources to economic and social development. And so this search for regional groupings, ASPAC, ASEAN, the Asian Development Bank, and other proposals for a Pacific Basin grouping of developed and not so developed countries. They all represent this search for a framework of neighbourliness to ensure steady economic growth, and sufficient collective strength to provide mutual security for all the lesser nations in Asia placed in varying degrees of proximity to Asia's potential super-power.

"But whilst the political structure of Asia has changed, the basic characteristics of the ethnic groups, their cultures, their values, their philosophies, their way of life, the passions that move them to greater effort, have not changed. And so we marvel at the miraculous recovery of Japan from the ashes of defeat in less than a quarter of a century only because we have forgotten that it was this same Japanese grit and stamina, industry and discipline, ingenuity and inventiveness that made Japan the only non-European military and industrial power in the world before the Second World War. Slowly all the new nations will learn that it requires more than just the purchase or, worse, the free gift of industrial machinery, technological equipment and training scholarships to create a modern industrial society. But whilst they are learning this, the industrial nations, and in particular Japan, could help those in Asia who want to progress and have both the will and capacity to make the grade.

"We in Singapore have no inhibitions as a result of our experiences in the Second World War. That chapter is closed, although not forgotten. We have no fear that Japanese capital, technological skills and management expertise will end up with our losing our own identity or freedom. Perhaps, as people see demonstrated how regional economic co-operation can be mutually beneficial for the industrialized and the not yet industrialized countries, so they will be less reluctant to enter into bigger and bolder arrangements for mutual prosperity and security which an imaginative interlocking across the Pacific Basin can provide.

"Whatever the result of the present bustle of activity for regional and sub-regional groupings, associations and compacts, Japan is likely to continue as Asia's most industrialized and technologically sophisticated society for quite a while, and, if potential super-powers are excluded, for the indefinite future. So it is that we in Singapore welcome your initiative in coming to visit the smaller capitals of Asia. Singapore is keen to learn and equip its people with the attitudes, aptitudes, training and discipline to lift itself into the modern world community. We are not shy to ask about what we do not know. We are not afraid to try new ways of making our economy bigger and better. We make no apologies for maintaining antiseptic conditions of public administration to keep the endemic disease of corruption down. We are not unhopeful that in quiet collaboration with industrial powers in Asia, around the Pacific Basin and beyond, we can make a contribution to our own well-being and, by giving a little stimulus to the economies of those around us, consolidate our security. We have welcomed your nationals participating in· our plans to industrialize. It has been a promising start, mutually profitable and holding out promise of wider fields for joint endeavour. May your own distinguished presence in Singapore give impetus and gathering momentum to this process. With these thoughts and sentiments, we wish Your Excellency every success in your journey around the Southeastern rim of the continent of Asia."

In a joint statement, the two Prime Ministers the same day "welcomed the growing trend among the countries of Asia and the Pacific basin towards closer regional co-operation. This trend is closely reflected in the inauguration and activities of the Ministerial Conference for Economic Development of Southeast Asia, the Asian Development Bank, the ASEAN and other regional organizations. The Prime Ministers agreed that the two Governments should closely co-operate to ensure that these organizations will function in a mutually complementary manner so as to contribute more effectively towards the social and economic development of this region. In this connection, Prime Minster Sato extended his best wishes for the success of the Third Ministerial Conference for Economic Development of Southeast Asia to be held in Singapore in 1968."

XVII

On 26 September, the Prime Minister left for Europe and the United States. In a television interview taped the previous afternoon, Lee Kuan Yew was asked what kind of role he thought the Americans should play in Asia. He replied that not being an American he would not know what the compulsions on a big, or super-power were.

"But I would like to see an Asia, particularly my immediate part of Asia—South and Southeast Asia—largely self-sustaining, interlocked with each other in trade, commerce, industrialization programmes, economic growth and mutual security with the minimum of direct support or intervention from outside—whether it be America or Russia or China. They are the three super-powers whose attitudes and policies will determine the shape of Asia in the middle 1970s. Britain has decided that this is really not her crucial sphere of influence, and we have got to live with that fact."

Questioned whether he would still want some support from other countries, perhaps Australia or New Zealand, Lee replied: "Yes, of course, our connections with the Commonwealth are close and intimate and from a purely selfish Singapore, and I should imagine also a Commonwealth, point of view we ought to try and maintain this link for as long as we can."

What about Japan's role in Southeast Asia? "I think it is unrealistic to believe that a thrusting nation like Japan will forever be penitent for its misdemeanours in the last war and just produce transistors and scooters and little cars for the rest of Southeast Asia. There is a certain inevitable dynamism about the progress in the growth of nations. And I think we have got to learn to live with the kind of nations that have emerged in Asia: China, India, Pakistan, Japan, all the other nations here, including the smaller ones that have had enough of hegemony and like to live their own lives. I think the ideal, really, is to have an Asia the non-communist half of which is accepted by the communists as being there for all time and impervious to subversion or invasion... I think if we dig our toes in and slog it through, eventually they will accept this fact."

By "slogging it through", did he mean fighting?

"Fighting if there is an actual invasion, yes, with help from outside," · Lee answered. "By slogging through, building up the kind of society which feels that it wants to be what it is... growth, meaningful lives, representative government—the kind of community which feels that it is not completely so despairing as to be willing to try anything, any regimentation whether communist or fascist. And if you get that kind of a society which feels that it has got something worth building on, then I think we have already begun on the road at least to the kind of balance which has been established between Western and Eastern Europe... Each country must find its own form, its own style, its own idiom of nationhood. But if any society wants to be impervious to communist subversion and manipulations it must carry the bulk of its own population with it..." Asked the purpose of Singapore's military training, the Prime Minister said: "What we want really is, first, to establish our right to be ourselves so that nobody will be tempted to believe that all he has to do is brandish a gun and we will hold our hands up in fright and hand over all that we have got. I think for the immediate future and the middle-term future what we want is a kind of arrangement among the present Commonwealth partners to build up a creditable force that can protect the integrity and security of the interests of Singapore, perhaps Malaysia and Australia and New Zealand, and I hope Britain wouldn't have lost that interest."

"Have you any plans to invite the Americans to station any troops in the Republic here?"

"No, I don't think that is profitable, either from their point of view or from mine. I think it is much better to try and work towards a long-term ideal situation, a healthy situation, one which is tolerable and definitely enduring. If I have got to have American troops to prop up my regime, my Government, my kind of society physically, I think it is hopeless: it is not worth the carrying on."

The Prime Minister was asked about the chances for a communist take-over of Singapore either by constitutional or unconstitutional means.

"Well, regarding constitutional means I think they have fairly successfully blocked all their chances for a decade because, according to them, Singapore does not exist; it is not a republic; it is part of Malaya, and Malaysia does not exist and only Malaya exists which includes Singapore. So if you start off on that basis, which is completely false and spurious, nobody is going to believe that your way is going to solve the economic and political problems." Lee said the other way was a combination of open mass demonstrations and destruction, and at the same time eventually half coup half terror, linked possibly with outside support. "I think the dangers are there and one of the contingency plans we have to make will be how to deal with an unconstitutional attempt at power... an attempt at a coup—assassination plus a military take-over—is not something which we can afford to rule out." Lee told the reporters that he thought there were probably about twenty-five to thirty "key communist digits" operating in Singapore and probably in the nearby Indonesian Rhio Islands, and probably in Johore.

Asked if he was going to do anything in Washington to encourage American investment in Singapore, the Prime Minister said there was no immediate urgency. "So far as my United States tour is concerned I am now interested in the middle and long terms, not the immediate terms. In the immediate terms, my ties are with Britain and the Commonwealth and if it can go on as planned till the middle 1970s, better the late middle 1970s, that is a very long time. It is a good decade. And perhaps it may be up to my successor to make arrangements for the security and welfare of Singapore in the late 1970s and beyond."

Did that mean he was thinking of retiring?

"No, but this is an open democratic society and ten years is a very long time. We have been in office already nine years and in another ten years we would have been in for nineteen years. I would think that would be a good reason to have a fresh young team with new ideas taking fresh stock of the world situation and how Singapore can fit in."

XVIII

In Britain, at an eve of conference rally on 1 October, Lee Kuan Yew told the British Labour Party that theirs was the "movement from whose experience we in Singapore have profited. Half the members of the Singapore Cabinet of ten were students in a Labour Britain immediately after the last war. We imbibed the values and ideals

391

which moved Britain towards a more just and equal society. They were ideals which the then British Labour Government put into practice, not just in Britain, but throughout the then Empire. In the decades after the war, these beliefs in freedom, social justice and fair play led to a systematic dismantling of the Empire.

"One has only to look and see what is happening in Vietnam to know how different the lives of the people of Singapore and Malaysia could have been. In 1945, both in Vietnam and in Singapore and Malaya, resistance movements against the Japanese led by indigenous communists were poised for a bid at power. The French, in a succession of coalition governments in which French socialists participated, were unable to extricate themselves from the web of empire and so communist leadership by the Vietminh took over the whole of the nationalist anti-colonial movements. Final defeat at Dien Bien Phu in 1954 was unavoidable. It was followed by more strife and tribulation in the southern half of Vietnam, until today there are some half a million Americans, and some Australians and New Zealanders, South Koreans and Filipinos, all embroiled in a messy, nasty, vicious war of attrition.

"This same process could so easily have happened in Singapore and in Malaya. The Malayan Communist Party was as determined and ruthless as the Vietminh. But a combination of firm response to armed insurrection, plus intelligent policies allowing political advance, made it unnecessary for nationalists to make common cause with the communists. Non-communist leaderships grew in strength and ascendency both in Singapore and in Malaya, and eventually they were capable of taking over power from the British without being undermined or routed by the communists. The communist insurrection failed as their ground support melted away. Today, unlike Vietnam, there is peace in Singapore and Malaysia. Some forty to fifty thousand British troops are there not to engage the local people in conflict but to help the growing strength of indigenous armed forces to protect the integrity of the new countries from external aggression, which the former Indonesian President, Dr Sukarno, called 'confrontation'. I am reminded by Denis Healey that the British do not do these things in order to gain gratitude. However, we in Singapore are not unmindful of the fact that but for intelligent policies to advance the enlightened self-interest of the British, we would not have inherited an administration which worked, and an economy which we built upon to provide a standard of living in Asia second only to Japan.

"I have not come to seek reprieve from the execution of the decisions that were announced only recently in Parliament on Britain's role East of Suez. No one has the right to ask the British Government or the British people to expend their resources to protect the interests and sustain the economies of some other country which is no longer part of British responsibility. But our long association with the British over a period of 150 years emboldens me to hope that the disengagement can take place in a way to give us the best chance of continuing security and stability. I am not unoptimistic that given a little time and no little effort, we will make the adjustments and live as well in the middle seventies without British base expenditure as we are doing now. After all, there was a thriving and prosperous Singapore for over 100 years from 1819 to the 1930s, before the bases were built—a naval base, then an air base. These were intended to keep a check on the growing Japanese strength. And it was only after the war, when British servicemen were accompanied by their families, that base expenditure rose to twenty per cent of the G.N.P. of Singapore. Quietly and intelligently we can sort these problems out as we face the changed circumstances of the world in the seventies. And British troops in Singapore, unlike the French in Vietnam, can depart with ceremonial style and with good wishes and goodwill. This area of relative stability and security is testimony to the wisdom of the policies which were initiated by the Labour Government of 1945.

"We are living through a difficult and dangerous period, particularly those of us whose homes are in Southeast Asia. For this tragic conflict in Vietnam could have the most grievous consequences for all of us, should there be any miscalculation on the possible consequences of either escalation or, equally dangerous, sudden evacuation.

"I do not want to sound either like a hawk or a dove. If I have to choose a metaphor from the aviary, I would like to think of the owl. Anyone looking at what is happening in Vietnam must have baleful eyes. It need never have been thus. And perhaps it was not the wisest place, nor the safest ground, in Asia to have made a stand. But enormous sacrifices have already been expended, and in blood, both Vietnamese and non-Vietnamese. One can only hope that all countries and all parties will persevere and strive for some rational solution, so that the non-communist countries in Asia can avoid the same dreadful ordeal, and that eventually the communist states of Asia will accept the existence of non-communist countries of Asia as a fact of life. These are crucial and critical issues that cannot be willed away by wishful thinking. And non-communist Asia must show that they have the same tenacity of purpose and unflinching will to be themselves. And eventually we shall achieve the kind of detente that has been established in Europe, where the western and eastern parts accept the right of the other to order its own life in its own way, and with no illusions that easy victories can be won either through armed intervention or subversion. . ."

Speaking of Singapore, Lee Kuan Yew said: "I do not pretend that we are an idyllic socialist community in Southeast Asia. We still have the highest number of millionaries per ten thousand of population in South Asia. But we are one of a few places in Asia where there are no beggars, where nobody, old or young, dies of neglect and starvation. True they are modest achievements, but nonetheless precious to us. As we move into a different world of the 1970s, mutual and intelligent accommodation as Britain cuts down on East of Suez and, perhaps more important, American patience and prudence in Vietnam, could leave us in peace to improve on the small advances we have made to civilized living in a turbulent part of the world."

XIX

In Zurich for the Socialist International meeting on 10 October, Lee Kuan Yew said that when Singapore was asked to leave Malaysia in 1965, "we made a study of what smaller countries surrounded by large neighbours with big populations do for their own survival. The study eventually led us us to compare three such tightly knit communities: Switzerland, Finland and Israel. As a result of this study, there are quite a number of Asians in Singapore who know what a tough and rugged process every Swiss male goes through for more than twenty-two years in the service of his nation. In the end, Singapore opted for the Israeli pattern, for in our situation it appears necessary not only to train every boy, but also every girl, to be a disciplined and effective digit in the defence of their country."

Lee said he was sorry there were not more democratic socialist comrades at the conference from other countries of Southeast Asia. "For it may help their parties project an image in greater depth of the meaning of social democracy. It is not just a simple business of taking from the haves and giving it to the have-nots, so that everybody, or the majority of the people 'who are have-nots will have more, without doing anything more for it." It was an over-simplified view of democratic socialism, to say that all a socialist had to do was to take over power from the colonialists, take over all the big houses, big cars, big offices, the chairs and tables and the few factories of the capitalists and distribute them amongst the poorer people, and the problems of poverty would disappear." It was believed since poverty is caused by exploitation, when exploitation is ended so will poverty. When several democratic socialist parties were given the chance to govern after the Second World War, in Indonesia, in Burma and in Ceylon, they failed pitifully. For to eradicate poverty, one had to eradicate ignorance and banish obscurantism. People, mainly have-nots, had to be educated, trained,

394

disciplined and made into useful digits of the modern industrial society. When they failed social democrats were thrown into jail by successor military regimes.

"Socialism, indeed all ideology, is being discounted generally in Asia, and perhaps throughout the world, including the communist states of Europe. It is only in the communist states of Asia that there are people who still believe that pristine faith in dogma and fervour can solve all the problems of modernisation and industrial development. In the past years, democratic socialists in Asia and the Pacific have lost national elections in Japan, India, Australia and New Zealand. In all cases, they lost to the Right. It appears the younger generation in Asia is no longer stirred by the simple slogans of an egalitarian society. More and more, the young are showing that they want to be equal in order that they can strive to be unequal. What they want is not to be equal throughout life, but to have equal opportunities, so that those whose ability and whose application are better than the average can become more equal than the others.

"Without a realistic appraisal of human motivations with which alone we can frame the incentives to bring forth high performance from each and every one, the road to self-sustained economic growth is long and tortuous. But whilst it is true that ideology and dogma is no longer the simple divider between East and West, yet I view the contemporary fashion to reduce human effort and organization for human happiness to technical economic terms an unhappy and unhealthy trend. We are being fed with scientific economic idiom, talking in terms of G.N.P., productivity, unit cost, management expertise, balance of payments, bank rate, deflation, reflation (never inflation) until we dehydrate and dessicate the blood and sweat out of the human formula for achievement, which alone makes politics and political movements a meaningful and satisfying experience. This new politico-socio-economic idiom leads the mass of have-nots to believe that the answer to their aspiration for a life of plenty lies in getting some magic formula for the application of science and technology to industry, and a prosperous leisurely society is the inevitable effortless road to the golden age, where they all sit back and watch the meters and press buttons for only part of the time, but are paid enough for all the time. Perhaps this may be possible in highly developed industrial communities.

"Bertrand Russell used to talk about the problems of leisure some twenty years ago, wondering what man would do with himself when, because of his technological and scientific progress, he is not required to work to keep himself and his family in comfort. The communist system was supposed to do this naturally and inevitably, until the State would wither away. There was a time not so long ago when some American economists propounded the theme that the self-sustained growth of American affluence can provide for the Vietnam war and also bring forth the Great Society. Now we know that even America's prodigious wealth, accumulated capital, technological know-how, management techniques and an achievement-orientated society, cannot provide the enormous additional resources required for two stupendous projects simultaneously. And it is so easy to give up the one that appears less likely to be immediately successful.

"The future of a large chunk of the world may be decided by the manner in which the bitter conflict in Vietnam is brought to an end. As socialists, we all would like the sufferings of the Vietnamese, both South and North, to cease as soon as possible. But let us not be unmindful of the even greater misery that may befall so many more millions of other South and Southeast Asians if this costly effort were to end in circumstances which did not lessen the dangers of similar trials by ordeal on other adjacent non-communist states of Asia.

"I do not know whether in the next world conflict Switzerland will be a haven of neutrality and refuge as it was in two world wars. I have the feeling that in the smaller conflicts Singapore's best policy is to adopt the posture of the Swiss, in avoiding committal and engagement, or being used by one side to do in the other. But I have more than an apprehension that in a bigger conflict, there is no opting out."

XX

In Washington, on 17 October on the South Lawn of the White House, President Johnson greeted Lee Kuan Yew as "a patriot, a brilliant political leader and a statesman of the New Asia". He said Singapore was a "very bright example of what can be accomplished not only in Asia, but in Africa and Latin America, wherever men work for a life of freedom and dignity". President Johnson said he knew that Lee was looking ahead, beyond the Asia of today, to the Asia of the 1970s. "You want and deserve to know what will be America's interest in the new Asia. I trust that your visit here will give you these answers. You will find an America that looks beyond the conflict of today, to an Asia that realizes its promise, that lives at peace with itself and with others. All that we have done and all that we shall do is intended to help bring that Asia into being."

Lee Kuan Yew said that for better or for worse ("and we in Singapore must hope they will be for the better"), the decisions of the

American people next fall would strengthen the capacity and the already known resolve of their government to create the peaceful and stable conditions in which alone trade, industry, and construction would be possible. "We in Singapore, like others, want to build this brave new world of modern science and technology, and the great life that they can provide when these disciplines are applied to industry. Most other countries in Asia also want this—to find equal excite- ment and fulfilment in building, instead of destroying. But some find it difficult to be brave all by themselves, particularly when old friends from Western Europe are leaving and no new and strong patrons are willing to take over. A few have even suggested that they would give up, and immediately, rather than put up a futile fight against big and massive intruders. In the end, Mr President, his- torians will acclaim and applaud the super-powers, if after all the harsh trials they demonstrate that not only they, the leaders, but more important the people, can show patience and perseverance and prudence, can demonstrate that firmness for a fair peace, which can make the world a safer and better place for all—Asians, Africans, Americans, Europeans... That Americans are powerful, all the world is too painfully aware, and of the fact that they are brave—or perhaps a better word, courageous—morally, no one doubts. But do they see it in their interests that this courage and this power should be con- trolled? For, in a world full of bears and dragons, that is the best way to ensure that a peaceful future is not unduly threatened. Do enough Americans believe that their progeny will inherit this brave new world that they have built, only if they make the effort now? That, Mr Presi- dent, is what I have come to find out. I hope I will leave reassured of the future of mankind, of their progress to a better life in a better world."

Shortly after the ceremonials were over the President and the Prime Minister talked together privately for eighty minutes, about Vietnam and Southeast Asia. They met again that evening at the White House at a small dinner in Lee's honour. In his toast, Presid- ent Johnson remarked that Lee Kuan Yew represented a small nation whose influence in the world belied its size. He represented a new nation, whose people were endowed with four thousand years of Chinese civilization. He was a young man, but he had already earned a formidable reputation as a lawyer, a thinker, legislator, and party leader, as the architect of his nation's future, as a spokesman for his new generation in Asia. In short, Lee Kuan Yew was what Asian philosophy would call a "superior man", a man not confined to the ivory tower, a man who combined thought and action in a life of public service. President Johnson declared that Lee's administra- tion was one of the most honest, efficient and successful in Asia.

Answering Lee Kuan Yew's question, posed on the lawn in the morning, President Johnson said America had the resolution and the restraint to see the struggle through in Vietnam. "We are fighting now to secure the future of the New Asia... our interest and our friendship in Asia will remain long after the guns have fallen silent..."

In his reply, the Prime Minister said: "We will still be good friends with the British even after they have left, because at the end of the day, there is abiding mutual respect. That is what I would like to believe Singaporeans and Americans can achieve. You are big and you are powerful, but unless we and others like us in the region can also learn to trust your judgment and to respect it, then I think you will have continuing problems in Asia."

Referring to the President's remarks that Lee represented a "nation whose people were endowed with 4,000 years of Chinese civilization", the Prime Minister said he represented more than the Chinese in Singapore. "We also have Malays, Indians, Pakistanis, Ceylonese, Eurasians, British and others. I think if I, or my successor, begin to want to represent only Chinese, then we have put the clock back not only for Southeast Asia, but for what we must try to achieve in this world, ever growing smaller, and therefore ever demanding, if not love and understanding, at least tolerance and forbearance."

Lee went on to say that he thought the next few months would impose enormous strains on all those in charge of the destiny of mankind—large parts of it if not the whole of it—and that, in fact "we are approaching a watershed in history". The Prime Minister spoke of his belief that the centre of gravity of the world was moving towards the Pacific. "For on this ocean you have three super-powers —or two super-powers and one potential—all sharing coastlines on the same basin." Lee said there were people in every one of the communities in Asia "who want to feel that sense of achievement, self respect, to try to catch up with the modern world". He did not believe that with a little time and no little effort the United States could not discern, identify, the modernizing groups, and these various communities, and stimulate, help propel, those forces that want to bring their communities into the twentieth century, into the direction they want to go.

Lee raised his glass to a "probably much misunderstood and much misrepresented man in the world Press". He described President Johnson as a man "whose policies, if persisted in prudently and patiently, can establish a winning line and may bring a great deal of peace and security to my part of the world, and indeed to other oceans and countries beyond."

In a joint statement put out on 18 October, President Johnson and the Prime Minister said they had a frank and useful exchange of views covering a broad range of topics of common interest. Their talks reflected the cordial relations existing between Singapore and

398

the United States and were directed towards enhancing mutual understanding.

"The President and the Prime Minister agreed that the security and welfare of the entire Pacific community is dependent upon the countries of Southeast Asia being able to maintain their independence and accelerate their economic growth in an atmosphere of self-reliance and mutual co-operation. The President expressed the hope that Singapore would continue to make her contribution to the growth of regional co-operation in Southeast Asia. The Prime Minister expressed Singapore's readiness to play her part in constructing a regional framework for common prosperity and mutual security.

"The President and the Prime Minister agreed that mutual respect, non-interference and equality among all nations are essential principles underlying the creation of a stable, peaceful, international order. The leaders agreed that every nation should have the right to select its own political, economic and social system and its own way of life free from any outside interference or pressure.

"The two leaders reviewed recent developments in East Asia in the context of the universal desire of all peoples of the world to achieve a peace that respects liberty, human dignity and provides more equal opportunities for all peoples to achieve better and higher standards of life which the application of science and technology to industry has now made possible. The President expressed his deep and abiding interest in the achievement of peace and stability in East Asia which would permit the countries of the area to devote all of their energies to economic development and the enrichment of the lives of their peoples.

"The Prime Minister expressed his hope that a settlement would be reached in Vietnam which would enhance the prospects of peace and security for the rest of South and Southeast Asia.

"The two leaders expressed the support of their countries for the United Nations and stressed the need for it to develop into an increasingly effective instrument of international peace and security, and for the promotion of friendly relations and co-operation among nations and peoples for their economic and social advancement."

On 18 October, before he left Washington, Lee lunched with the Overseas Writers. He told them he was not seeking American aid, nor was he in receipt of any. He did not have an American guarantee for Singapore's security, nor did he seek any. He was worried about the changes that were going to take place in South and Southeast Asia. He was, he said, concerned with the kind of problems which Singapore would have to face, both in economic and in security terms, in the seventies and beyond. Lee said he had come to the United States to try and make an assessment for himself of the kind of situation Singapore will have to face in the middle seventies when the British leave their bases.

Lee developed his theory that the centre of gravity of the world will shift to the Pacific. He reminded them that when people talked about Asia they talked about a vast continent, and when they talked about Asians they talked about diverse peoples. The East Asians especially, he believed, intended to take their place in this modern world. Southeast Asia was slightly different, in climate, culture and religion. It was not an achievement-orientated society. There was nothing wrong with them. They had bright men, great scholars, but achievement and the acquisition of wealth were not admired. What was admired was leisurely living.

The Prime Minister said he did not consider China a "yellow peril". The Chinese are human beings: they consider themselves to have been the centre of civilization for a long time. They feel a deep sense of grievance, bitterness: they want to restore their dignity, their stature, their sense of importance as the central kingdom. Lee said he did not believe they were going to come down to Southeast Asia with their armies. But the whole region could be lost if the United States misplayed Vietnam, and backed the wrong forces in the rest of the area. What had happened in Singapore can be done in other parts of Asia provided the United States backed the modernizing forces, not the obscurantists, the reactionaries, the ones who want to go backward not forward.

Asked about the future defence of Southeast Asia, the Prime Minister spoke of a situation where there was confidence that the territorial boundaries of South and Southeast Asia would not be changed by the use of force, "and you get them to jell together and co-operate economically on sub-regional and then wider regional bases". This situation could lead to the Japanese conception of the great Pacific Basin Scheme, which interlocked developed nations like Canada, the United States and Australia with the underdeveloped parts of Asia. Lee Kuan Yew thought this could lead to a very prosperous and peaceful world community in the 1990s, "and this is what I hope will happen".

In a speech to the Far East American Council in New York, on 20 October, the Prime Minister called upon the United States to form a new relationship with Southeast Asia based on equality. He said sudden United States withdrawal from the area would be disastrous. "Three great powers, the United States, the Soviet Union and China, border on the Pacific and it is in the nature of big powers, just like big companies, to want to grow bigger. If you don't win over the Southeast Asian people someone else will, and you are going to have very few friends. These are a people who want to be friends with you if you treat them as equals in trade and investment and, as friends, form a new kind of relationship."

Lee described Singapore as a nation of immigrants with a short history, no natural resources, but plenty of hustle and determination.

"All I can give you today is a flavour of the kind of men you will deal with in Singapore. We've got nothing but two million highly-motivated, achievement-orientated, relatively intelligent human beings, and we are going to be there a thousand years from now."

Lee said that he and his fellow socialists in power in Singapore still sought to bring their people equal opportunities and a fruitful, meaningful life, but have abandoned youthful illusions of creating a luxuriant paradise on earth. "We gave that up a long time ago. We cannot afford it. We work, or die... basic beliefs don't change, but methods do. You have to take human beings for what they are. If you want high performance you must give high pay."

At Harvard the following day, Lee Kuan Yew expressed the view that Hanoi will come to the negotiating table if the United States Government and people demonstrate determination to "stick out the Vietnam war until the end of time if necessary".

Lee elaborated his themes in a speech to the Asia Society later the same day. He warned the United States that if America turned its back on the Pacific it would be at its own peril. China might then achieve in Asia the very thing that Japan tried for in World War Two but failed to get. The Chinese, he said tend to look down on the Japanese as having borrowed their laws, customs, language, even chopsticks from China. "They have not the slightest doubt that what Japan can do, China can do better." Lee claimed that Singapore "is the one place in Southeast Asia where the communists were defeated by ballots, not bullets. This should give heart to those who would write off Asia." Lee cautioned against underestimating the capacity of China in the years ahead.

The *Honolulu Advertiser*, on 28 October, in an editorial headed "Lee, the Tiger and Us", referred to Lee Kuan Yew as "one of Asia's most remarkable leaders", the man President Johnson toasted for successfully riding the tiger of communism. The paper said that the essential point was that Lee was still riding. "Moreover he is riding with us, and a stranger set of partners is hard to imagine. Lee, now 44, is a combination of influences that do not make him a fawning admirer of Americans. These influences include a British education, strong ethnic nationalism and a socialist viewpoint. Both his achievement and his views command respect far beyond his vibrant island city-state in the heart of Southeast Asia." The *Honolulu Advertiser* went on to say that Lee Kuan Yew had made the best of a very tough, often nasty, proposition. "Many shared the view of Denis Warner, the Australian writer who wrote in *The Reporter:* 'If there have been times in the past when Lee's impetuosity, rashness and excessive ambition seemed to negate his intellectual and political brilliance, and he seemed too often a debater and too rarely a diplomat, the superbly-run Singapore Government is a tribute to his skill and his now evident sense of responsibility.' " The *Honolulu Advertiser* described Lee Kuan Yew as a pragmatic Prime Minister. "He has managed to talk socialism and take major steps in social welfare while further promoting Singapore's touchy capitalist economy. He is proudly Chinese, but understands that Singapore and neighbour Malaysia must become truly multiracial states. If he is hardly pro-American in the usual sense, he understands reality that escapes many others."

Before leaving Los Angeles, Lee Kuan Yew sent President Johnson a message of thanks "for your warm reception and, more meaningful, the considerable time and attention you gave me". Referring to the "political battle positions already taken by so many of your own opinion formulators", Lee said he reacted instantly "and with an immediate urge to give them the truth as I saw it. I am for a policy of great resolution and immense restraint. Such a policy can and will win in the end, if the American people show indomitable determination, infinite patience and prove that their feeling for the fate of Asians is no less than for their fellow Americans." Lee Kuan Yew told President Johnson he did not now believe, having spoken to so many in executive positions in Washington, "that it is the arrogance of power which makes the American administration do what it is doing. In fact I fear the problem is that there is arrogance, alas so natural, with ancient peoples, but without power to match yours yet. This gives us time. We in non-communist Asia must use this time to consolidate our positions. The relative peace and security your effort in Vietnam provides, as a by-product to us, must be turned to our advantage so as to avoid us being churned up by similar techniques of terror, subversion and international propaganda, as in Vietnam." Lee explained that this message was being dictated in haste before leaving Los Angeles. "Perhaps, because it is hurried it is more candid than the carefully weighed, polished and repolished composition. What it lacks in literary style I hope is made up for by being unequivocal."

On arrival at Honolulu, the Prime Minister was handed a message from the President. Mr Johnson said he wanted Lee to know "how delighted I am that you were able to make this visit to the United States. I profited greatly from our conversation, and I know that you have been a strong and articulate voice throughout the country for your own nation and for Southeast Asia as a whole."

Lee rested for five days in Hawaii. The pace in the United States had been gruelling, and had included thousands of miles of travelling, sometimes three speaking engagements a day, as well as Press conferences and private discussions with political leaders and businessmen.

As he was leaving Hawaii he summed up his journey through the United States as "instructive and meaningful". He had been exposed "to a full range of what is the equivalent of the American Establishment: people in power, people in the corridors of power, and most important of all, the rising young generation of American youth in the universities. It is their emotive attitudes now being set towards Asia and Asians which will make or mar American relationships with Asia. The future of mankind depends upon our acceptance of each other for what we are, different though we may appear to be. But however different we look, or talk, or write, we all have very much the same human feelings for ourselves, our own society, our cultures, and our progeny. If we want our children to inherit and improve on the great civilizations that man has created from time to time in his wanderings over the hospitable parts of the world, then we must get the Vietnam conflict settled in a way that will diminish, or extinguish, the dangers of similar confrontations thereafter. This will require restraint and forbearance on the part of the Americans. Several of the men I met around the President were men with fine minds and sensitive souls. I feel less pessimistic about the future after meeting them. I am not convinced, having had some time with the President and his principal executives, that it is the arrogance of power which makes the American administration do what it is doing in Vietnam."

XXI

Forty-four journalists representing thirteen European countries interviewed the Prime Minister on Television Singapore on 8 November. Lee was asked about the Bill then being discussed in Parliament which provided severe penalties for rioting. Did he not think that too severe penalties for free assembly could damage Singapore's image as a democratic state?

Lee said he was just as concerned about Singapore's young boys and girls, as he was with the image of the Singapore Government. It was the youngsters the communists used.

"You can mar a young teenager's mind for life the way you mishandle it. What we are trying to do is to tell the communists, the people who are manipulating these boys and girls, that they are not going to get away with this. We will collect all these boys and girls, feed them well, look after them, teach them good manners, and one day slowly but relentlessly we will find where the leads are to the adults who manipulate them. Then we will deal with the adults the way that I think they deserve..."

Asked what form of economic interdependence he would like to see as a prelude to any future arrangement in Southeast Asia, Lee replied: "We have to recognize that Southeast Asia will not be decided by Southeast Asians alone. This is the first major premise. There are many other powers outside Southeast Asia that will decide which way the smaller countries or even the middling countries in Southeast Asia will go. There is America, with the world's greatest industrial potential and military capacity... There is Russia with more and more interests in the Pacific... And in the next ten, perhaps less, perhaps more, years, there will be a fairly meaningful capacity from the People's Republic of China. It is within that context that the smaller countries in Southeast Asia must accommodate each other because the worst thing that can happen is for each to get a backer. It will be a very dangerous world. What happened in the Balkan Peninsula between the First and the Second World Wars is nothing to what can happen to the rest of the world because of Southeast Asia.

"We want to get that lesson home first: that the boundaries in Southeast Asia inherited from cartographers in Europe... I am not saying they are unchanging, permanent, there for all time. But they should not be changed by force. By plebiscite by all means, by consent of the people, genuine consent, but not a bogus one. But horse-trading between the bigger powers or the middling powers or the smaller powers will lead to a lot of unhappiness. The moment that point is understood by the middling powers they will come to the conclusion that it is best to leave each other as we are, and to co-operate economically first..."

A question suggested it was absurd to expect a joint guarantee by China and America. Lee replied:

"I will not rule that out. I would say you could easily get, first, a situation where the Southeast Asian countries guarantee in a credible way each other's sovereignty and independence and then economically assist each other and not try and do each other in, and ensure that each other's boundaries will not be changed by force and the Americans can underwrite that. They have the Seventh Fleet. It is conceivable that even the Russians may find it in their interests to underwrite this and say: 'Right, hands off. No change of boundary lines by use of force.' And I can envisage that in the 1980s a new generation will emerge in the People's Republic of China that has had quite a lot of the trials and tribulations of building up a great industrial society from nothing and is not very anxious to see it all go back to the Stone Age by pursuing policies which must provoke or run the danger of provoking a nuclear conflict. When a pragmatic, realistic and hard-headed younger generation emerges as it must, whether it is in the late 1970s or in the 1980s, I can well imagine such a group of men saying: 'All right, let us keep what we have and build on it.' But this is a slow process and we have to be very patient."

On 10 November, Lee Kuan Yew spoke to the American Association. The American Ambassador, F. J. Galbraith, who accompanied the Prime Minister on his journey through the United States was among the audience. The speech was televised. Lee said that he had to repeat "more audibly in Singapore" some of the things he had said in America in a low key.

"You know, I was most concerned not only about Vietnam but also about American policies to the whole of Southeast Asia—in particular my peaceful neighbour in Malaysia and my peace-loving neighbour in Indonesia... My concern was and is, that you, unlike the Russians, should not make the grave error of providing attack weapons, as distinct from defence weapons, for they were in fact used against the very people whose interests the provider of weapons wanted to advance. I have read with interest that an Indonesian Army newspaper has said that they have nothing against ethnic Chinese as such, but only against Chinese communists. I sincerely hope that the Chinese communist in Indonesia looks so very different from the Chinese Indonesian national... in the Indonesian soldier's gun sights. But I would be happier still if nobody took any chances with anybody else's life by supplying attack weapons of offensive destruction, which can so unpredictably change hands from apparently pro-West to anti-West forces.

"Having underlined the dangers, may I say to you that as a trading community, we in Singapore have learnt over 150 years that if we are not constant and consistent, if our words are not our bond, then we shall do very little business with each other. I have explained to your leaders in Washington that it is more the long-term trust and confidence, than the effusive but sometimes ephemeral friendship, which Singapore seeks. I would like to believe that my journey to your great country has been a step forward towards a more abiding relationship of mutual respect, which can come only after we trust each other's good intentions and have confidence in each other's sound judgment..."

Lee, speaking of Vietnam, said he suspected the Americans did not want to see Southeast Asia "become communist because if Southeast Asia goes, then in the course of the next decade or two, the whole of South Asia right up to Iran, could go communist. All will have indigenous fraternal communist parties, all friendly and receiving help from China or Russia. And then all the wealth and resources of oil and minerals and human energy, harnessed through the help of communist cadres and technologists lent from the Eurasian communist heartland to the north will be enormous. And if this industrial strength is geared into the industrialized communist countries of the north the

405

effect on American present predominance and affluence may be somewhat discomforting. Americans may find the world a less congenial
place to live in. And if and when the Asian Communist grid
were to gear into the Russian and the Eastern European, then in the
twenty-first century Americans may find that it is they who will be
embargoed against, in the export of strategic materials, in order
that Americans will be kept one down, not the other way round as
at present."

Lee said that he and his colleagues in the Government were all
committed to an independent, democratic, non-communist Singapore.
"In any competition, or conflict between the power blocs, we would
prefer to stay out or be non-aligned. But where Singapore's survival is
at stake, where our right to be ourselves is endangered, we cannot
be neutral. And a non-communist progressive South Vietnam will
add to the stability of the whole of South and Southeast Asia. It
will also enhance the prospects of peace and security, and greater
economic strength and prosperity as we establish regional co-operation
between the smaller nations in Southeast Asia...

"There will be fierce competition in the Pacific between the three
super-powers who share parts of the rim of this Pacific Basin—
America, Russia, and last, most numerous and not least, China. They
will all compete for the friendship, loyalty and support of the other
countries around the Pacific. But the problem is more easily posed
than answered... you must know in each nation who are the people
worth making friends with. The status quo cannot be maintained
for long and making friends with those who are for the status quo
may be a costly waste of time. Man's inventiveness, his creativity,
his application of science and technology to comfortable and graceful living, and to rapid transportation, a field in which Americans
have made a major contribution, all these developments make it impossible for the people of Asia to sit back contentedly in their villages,
as their ancestors have done for centuries before them. They can
see the jets flying over them. They are receiving, on little transistorized
sets, broadcasts from all over the world, many urging revolution, wars
of national liberation, and the settlement of old scores, the reviving
of past grievances, real and imaginary. The villagers are drifting
into the big towns and cities. And your jets not only carry all your
newspapers and glossy magazines, but also your television features.
They depict the attractive kind of life which Asians think it is not
unreasonable that they should have for themselves. And since they
do not think themselves inferior to Europeans or Americans or Russians for that matter, they want this better life now. In fact, if we
want to talk about arrogance, I think there is as much arrogance in
the Asian as in the American. The only difference is that American
arrogance is for the present backed by enormous fire power. But

406

one day, and not too far ahead, some Asians are going to prove that they can more than equal American industrial and military capability. . .

"Just as you Americans have become so completely a different nation group so we in Southeast Asia are becoming more and more Southeast Asian, and we doubt whether the Chinese in China will want to invite nuclear devastation for the sake of a few millions of their cousins in Southeast Asia. The long-term answer to our problem of an ever shrinking world is patience and prudence, resolution and restraint. If the American people can show indomitable determination, infinite patience and demonstrate that their feeling for the fate of Asians is no less than that for their own fellow Americans, then you will find that you have friends on the western side of the Pacific on Continental Asia, and not just Caucasian friends in the islands of Australia and New Zealand.

"A generation is growing up in all the new countries of Asia no longer interested in the slogans of the old generation about anti-colonialism, the white versus the yellow, or the brown, or the black. More and more of the thinking ones are no longer convinced that the way to a prosperous and peaceful future lies in nationalism, which ends up in chauvinism and communalism. Slowly, and with some help more surely, a generation will emerge, educated and aware that it is their own efforts in a dynamic education, economic and social policy which alone can bring their people forward with the rest of the industrial world into the great technological age we may have in the twenty-first century. If you resolve this conflict in Vietnam in a way that makes it the last of the great confrontations between the communists and the anti-communist forces, as you did in Berlin, then in the end the boundary lines will hold. But in doing so you must have some consideration for other peoples' anxieties, in particular those who live near Vietnam, and who cannot view with equanimity the prospect of their being blown up in an enlarged conflict or, worse, destroyed in an exchange of nuclear compliments."

Lee Kuan Yew's remarks about his Indonesian fears produced reaction in Washington and in Indonesia. In Washington, on 15 October, United States officials stated there was no solid basis for Lee's fears that the United States will rearm Indonesia with offensive weapons. The United States was providing Indonesia with road-building and other heavy equipment for its civic action programme. No offensive weapons were involved in the programme.

Passing through Singapore the same evening, Adam Malik, the Indonesian Foreign Minister, said at the airport that the Indonesian Government had no intention of dominating Singapore. He said that with the establishment of ASEAN, member countries should dispel fears that the bigger partner harbours intentions of dominating the smaller ones. He said: "The objectives of ASEAN are to co-operate and if member countries unite they can repel any outside force that may threaten the organization."

Adam Malik said that if Singapore feared the Partai Kommunist Indonesia might stage a comeback and threaten Singapore's security, likewise Indonesia too, would be afraid that communists might take over Singapore and thus threaten Indonesia's security. These fears should be dispelled, and the immediate task was to get ASEAN on its feet and give it a chance.

The following afternoon Singapore's Foreign Minister, Mr S. Rajaratnam, said Mr Malik's airport statement was welcome re-assurance. "I have met Mr Malik and other leaders now in control of Indonesia. I am satisfied that they, representing the progressive and modernizing forces in their country, have a vested interest in peace and prosperity in the area. Our fears relate to those obscur-antist and expansionist elements in Indonesian life, who not so long ago, under the guise of confrontation, made manifest their ambition to dominate Singapore and Malaysia through armed intervention and subversion. Like Adam Malik and his colleagues, the Singapore leaders are aware that the aggressive and obscurantist forces latent in every society are best contained and conscribed through regional co-operation designed to strengthen the peaceful, constructive and forward looking elements in our respective countries. I agree with Mr Malik that, if this spirit of ASEAN is sincerely adhered to, all will be well."

XXII

The *Far Eastern Economic Review* (12 October) reported their im-pression that Lee Kuan Yew was, as a result of his visit to the United States, "sitting pretty on the bamboo fence. The cult of the bamboo is a wellknown Asian pastime: to bend with the wind, to reserve positions of maximum flexibility, to leave all escape hatches well open, to sidestep commitments already made." The *Review* thought it dis-appointing to find such "obvious dedication to expediency" in some-one of Mr Lee's calibre. "Expediency is no crime, but it makes an uncomfortable bedmate with a penchant for preaching. Mr Lee... now exhorts the Americans to resolution while he himself waits in the wings... He admits that without the United States shield he would have from 'five to seven years'. But he refuses to reciprocate with any endorsement, even verbal. In his rhetoric, generally, one detects increasing symptoms of more myth and less reality. 'I' and 'my people' indicate growing paternalism. He would like to be bracketed with Prince Sihanouk. In recent interviews he sidestepped awkward questions and left conclusions undrawn... The American tour has therefore failed to achieve any clarification of his position. It may have encouraged some marginal investors in the United States to look more favourably at Singapore. It has certainly established Mr Lee's reputation as articulate and intelligent (so is Harold Wilson). But on such a basis he can make no claim to be the 'Kennedy of the East': only the conventional head of a 'bamboo' republic."

Life (30 October) thought that Lee Kuan Yew talked like President Johnson. Reporting an interview in London, Thomas A. Dozier called Lee bumptious and voluble. He had a "nimble brain" and a "quick tongue". At times his "articulatory skill seems to enmesh him in contradictions, but Lee has a remarkable capacity for making sense even while appearing to talk out of two sides of his mouth at once." Dozier also thought Lee "obviously enjoys phrase-coining".

Dozier reported that Lee "with some justice" observed that he knew Asian communists very well and they always believed they had more resolution than their opponents. "I think we have to disillusion them on that." Assuming peace came about in Vietnam, what did the Prime Minister think about the future of the non-communist states of Asia?

"I think it varies from non-communist state to non-communist state, because there are varying degrees of rapport between the governments and the people they represent. The greater the rapport, the better the chances of a permanent, or more or less permanent, non-communist and relatively democratic form of life and government. Much depends upon the way the United States disengages itself from Vietnam. A scuttle disguised as an honourable withdrawal would be disastrous. But the future for Asia will be bright if an eventual settlement in Vietnam constitutes a lesson which both sides have learned: that force does not pay. That the integrity and independence of the nation-states, however small and fragile, will not be allowed to be destroyed, or to be undermined, or to be emasculated by political methods, or by a combination of political and military methods."

Dozier said that Lee's vision for the future of non-communist Asia and "the only justification for the kind of intervention America is engaged in in his part of the world, is a 'healthy community of viable nation-states with governments having the support of a majority of the people... something akin to what has happened in Western Europe with the Marshall aid programme'. He does not think this will come about very rapidly. Asia will take longer than Europe 'because it has not got the infrastructure of industrialized skills and experience which could rapidly use the assistance offered it'. For the long run, Lee is eloquently optimistic that freedom and representative government will triumph in Asia, although the believers in these ideals may have to stand up and fight for them." Dozier concluded his piece with the comment: "Except for the polished British accent, it could have been Lyndon Johnson himself talking."

XXIII

Perhaps to prove that he was still at heart a neutral, and that he had not deserted his old friends, Lee Kuan Yew went to Cambodia, with his family, soon after his return from the United States. Prince Sihanouk at the airport said it was "a great joy" to welcome him. "Despite the friendly ties which his country maintains with powers and countries hostile to us", added Cambodia's Head of State, Lee Kuan Yew insisted on "proclaiming to the world that Khmer policy, both in its external and internal aspect, is exemplary." Prince Sihanouk described Lee as "one of the most dynamic Prime Ministers in Asia".

At a banquet given in Lee Kuan Yew's honour (7 December), Prince Sihanouk accused the United States "and their mercenaries" of trying to destroy Vietnam and its people "in the name of democracy and Christianity".

The Charge d'Affaire of China did not accept Prince Sihanouk's invitation to the banquet, but the rest of the diplomatic corps attended, including ambassadors from North Vietnam, North Korea and Cuba. Representatives from the National Liberation Front, the political arm of the Vietcong, were also present to hear Lee Kuan Yew's response. He had brought his family to Cambodia, he said, to broaden their education. "The ruins at Angkor are silent witness to the glories of a great civilization the Khmers sustained for 800 years from the 7th to the 15th century. They could only have been created by a great people. But they underline a cruel truth, that no one can take for granted peace, security and continued prosperity... I leave conscious that it is not just Angkor that a visitor must see. For the buildings in Phnom Penh, although the more functional, are no less monuments to Khmer creativity. It was a lesson of what is possible, given a united people, led by a patriot of great verve and vitality. And its future has been made more secure by a policy which is as consistent as it is sincere. Throughout all the changes of circumstances in the world, your non-aligned policy has never altered its fundamental principle, that the destiny of Cambodia and the Khmers is your paramount consideration."

Lee made a delicate reference to Cambodia's trouble with China (Cambodia accused China of interference in Cambodia's domestic affairs), when he remarked that "I cannot tell you how grateful I was, that my forebears decided to sail a thousand miles further south, beyond the Indo-Chinese Peninsula. I noticed that some of your officials who greeted me wore badges. I was startled. But I was pleasantly relieved on closer scrutiny to find that they bore your likeness. The greater distance that fortuitously my forebears had travelled has made it possible, for the present, for me not to have to compete with the thoughts of others in Asia...

"An eminent statesman, a distinguished jurist, and a great friend of Cambodia." That was how the Cambodian Minister of National Education, Mr Vann Molyvann, described Lee Kuan Yew at the conferment upon him of the degree of Doctor of Law *(honoris causa)* of the Royal University. But practice of the law, added the Minister, was to prove too limited and arid a field for such a dynamic personality, passionately interested in political, economic and social problems. Lee became a politician. And, in due course Lee assumed responsibility for the government of Singapore, a development which occurred in strict conformity with established democratic practices: "a fairly rare phenomenon in an age of military dictatorships".

The Cambodian Minister felt that the ceremony was an appropriate occasion for "reaffirming our shared belief in the sanctity of international law". He condemned "the leading Western power for opting for the law of the jungle" in Vietnam. "In the tribulations and trials with which Cambodia and all states in Southeast Asia are at present threatened, there will be at least some voices raised to plead the case for a return to the reign of international law. And amid these voices that of Lee Kuan Yew will certainly be clearly audible."

Lee, in his response, paraphrased the Justinian definition of law. "Justinian stated that law is the will of superior and enforceable authority. There have been a spate of definitions in hundreds of languages, before and since Justinian. But through all these definitions, two elements are common. First, law is laid down in certain and precise terms; second, it is backed by the sanction of superior power, whether in criminal or in civil cases. Hence the significance of one thought of Chairman Mao, that power springs out of the rifle barrel."

Turning to the economic problems of developing countries, Lee Kuan Yew said that economics, industrialization, and technological development "are the bolts and nuts of industrial strength. And industrial strength is what the military capacity and well-being of each nation is built on. Whatever the ideology, the thoughts, the beliefs, which can enthuse, stimulate, and galvanize a people, we have still to count the hard units that make up industrial strength and growth;

411

that is to say the technological capacity and skills and sophisticated capital equipment which is economically feasible only if there is a vast market to serve. Further, there is a correlation between the educated and skilled digits of a community, and its gross national product...

"The dismantling of empires has not altered the hard facts which determine a nation's capacity. The Africans seek solidarity on their continent to acquire greater economic strength through unity in a wider whole. So the contemporary trend towards wider opportunities in co-ordination and co-operation, in Latin America and in Asia. Hence the Asian Development Bank. Hence the interests of the Japanese to achieve wider co-operation between the nations around the Pacific Basin. They do not have a large continental land mass and have only a middle-sized population of ninety millions. They have to seek their future, like us, the smaller non-communist countries of Asia, in a wider whole, through regional co-operation.

"May I add that a grouping of industrially developed nations makes for very great industrial strength and added prosperity for each. But a grouping of countries all industrially undeveloped, economically not affluent, and technologically backward only means greater poverty to share the little prosperity co-operation can create. That is why Singapore seeks association and co-operation with technologically advanced and industrially developed partners. We welcome the Japanese, Australians, British, Americans, Germans and Russians to Singapore, whether as ship-builders, ship-repairers, tyre-manufacturers, assemblers of transistor radios, television sets, steel tubes, motor scooters, motor cars and so on. In non-communist Asia, Japan alone has the capacity to supply us with what we lack, the manufacturing skills, the technological and management expertise without which we may be back in the rice-fields, and planting bananas or waiting for the coconuts to drop... Two qualities, the capability, knowledge and skills of the population, and the quality of their leadership, determine the efficacy of their social, economic and political organizations. For only then can they utilize to the maximum the limited human and natural resources available. Hence the super-powers are recognizing the fallacy of the 'numbers game'. It does not mean that because a country has a large population and land area, therefore they are better off than a country with a smaller population and less land area... Those who watch with baleful eyes what is going in Vietnam, know that one South Vietnam government soldier is not the same as one Vietcong. The motivation is different, hence the difference in discipline and effectiveness.

"It is my hope that eventually all in non-industrialized Asia will work out the arithmetic of the technological age and rapidly acquire the skills, knowledge and expertise and accumulate and acquire the

capital equipment. Then in co-operation and collaboration, we can
moved forward with both the Western and the Eastern blocs. If we
learn this lesson in time, perhaps we might hold up our heads and
move at more or less the same tempo with them into the space age
of the twenty-first century. Given the continued solidarity of the
Khmers and the wise leadership of His Royal Highness Prince Sihanouk
and I hope in collaboration and co-operation with us, Cambodia and
Singapore I hope can keep up with the rest of the developed world.
For let no one forget that whilst the White Americans were not even
in America 1300 years ago, and their forebears were living in caves
in Europe, you and I, our ancestors, had already discovered and developed methods of production that made possible cultivated and civilized
ways of living. Let us hold our heads up with some pride and renew
our determination that what we have lost in the past 1300 years, we
will make up for in less than the next 1300 years."

XXIV

Lee Kuan Yew peered into the future during his speech in Parliament
(30 November) proposing the election of President Yusof bin Ishak for
a further term of four years. He felt confident his government could
continue to "encounter and checkmate" communists and communalists.
"But at the same time we must all be constantly alive to the dangers of
being the same persons too long in the same office. We are all creatures
of habit, and the creative and imaginative parts in the human being are
stifled by the repetition of the same thought or speech patterns.
In the long run, as a Government, we shall be judged not just by our
own performance, but by whether we have provided for continuity in the
quality and verve of political leadership for our society... Younger
talent there is and always will be. And we must pass on to that
talent, the knowledge, the know-how, the tried and proven methods
of good government. Only then can new ability, dedication and sincerity of purpose find expression and relevance in the necessarily different mood of a younger generation. Whilst perhaps, for the present,
Singapore may not do better for itself by electing some other team,
the same need not be said for the middle seventies and beyond. For
it will be a very different world. And it may require a different style
to carry off, with good grace and sustained strength, a different posture
and a revised and up-to-date set of political, economic and social policies,
which the continued survival and increasing prosperity of our multiracial society may require of its leadership...

"It is among the men and women of disciplined talent and ability,
with the freshness, enthusiasm, and idealism which every new generation

brings to its tasks, people now in their twenties and early thirties, that we must seek the possible leaders of a robust and rugged generation. It is not in the nature of things, in an open competitive society, such as ours, to nominate one's heirs and successors. But it is within our capacity to ensure that long before that time comes, there is available a whole cohort of younger people who have been equipped and steeled for tasks of political leadership. To them we should have passed on the valuable experiences of the past two decades, the esoteric knowledge of men and the affairs of men to which we have gained an insight in this strange corner of Asia. . ."

XXV

On the last day of 1967, the Prime Minister put out his New Year Message. Lee Kuan Yew claimed that "the stars were shining on Singapore in 1967. We did even better than 1966." To prove it Lee quoted statistics. From January to October, 1967, total imports and exports went up from $6,138 million in 1966 to $6,624 million. Cargo discharged and handled for the same period in 1967 went up fifteen point seven per cent to twenty-five point three million. The number of ships using the Singapore harbour increased more than eleven per cent, tonnage by fourteen per cent. Bank deposits for the first eleven months of 1967 increased thirty-two per cent over 1966. Building and construction statistics increased by twenty-three per cent. "But," added Lee, "God helps only those who help themselves. And to help ourselves, we have to be trim, healthy and alert, ready to tackle every problem and seize every opportunity that comes our way . . . Next year we face a fresh challenge to our capacity to adjust and adapt. Changes are going to take place in our economy and the pattern of employment as the British Armed Services begin their rundown. Britain has promised to help. But they can help only as much as their economy will allow them. More important is that we help ourselves . . ."

Lee Kuan Yew's belief, based upon British promises, that he had five years in which to prepare for massive unemployment consequent upon the British withdrawal, was shattered on January 16, 1968, when Mr Harold Wilson told the House of Commons that British forces would be withdrawn by the end of 1971.

Shocked, Lee Kuan Yew responded positively. "This is no time to wring our hands." He decided to dissolve Parliament and to seek a fresh mandate from the people. He needed, he said, their full support for harsh measures in the "crucial years that lie ahead". In the general election the PAP won all 58 seats. Arguing that they intended to do nothing to help make parliamentary democracy work, the Barisan Sosialis ignored the elections.

As soon as the new Parliament convened, new laws, covering worker-employer relations (laying down a 44-hour working week for all), national savings, technological education, and the encouragement of tourists and industrialists, were publicly debated and passed. Singapore was getting ready to meet the new challenge.

CHAPTER TWENTY-TWO

The Year of Power 1968

ALL fifty-eight seats in Parliament were won by the People's Action Party, the party-in-power, in a general elections held early in the year. This demonstrated the voters' support for the policies proposed by Lee Kuan Yew and his Cabinet to meet the new situation caused by Britain's new decision to withdraw militarily from Singapore by 1971.

Discussions between the five Commonwealth countries (Britain, Australia, New Zealand, Malaysia and Singapore) affected by the British withdrawal, went on throughout the year. Singapore and Malaysia agreed that the defence of the two countries was indivisible.

By the end of 1968 twenty men were undergoing training with the Royal Air Force in Britain. They were the pioneers of the Singapore Air Force. A Navy Training School was set up, and six patrol boats ordered. Before the year was out, the Singapore Army had five Infantry Battalions, and the sixth was being formed. Preparations for an armoured unit were at an advanced stage. Tanks and armoured cars were on their way.

To retrain some 40,000 civilian workers who would

become redundant as British troops left, the Government set up a Bases Economic Conversion Department. The British Naval Base Dockyard was put on a commercial basis with the formation by the Government of Sembawang Shipyards Ltd. The Government took formal possession of the dock-yard, an historic event, on December 8.

Singapore's economic progress during 1968 was reflected by a twelve per cent increase in gross national product. The port, now on a twenty-four-hour service basis, remained the core of the national economy, although considerable advance was made in the nation's industrial programme. More than 66,000 ships (180 a day), of 127 million registered tons, entered and cleared the port in 1968, record figures, a sixfold increase since 1967.

More than half a million children attended 590 schools, twenty-nine per cent at secondary schools.

Towards the end of the year, the Prime Minister took six weeks' leave for study and contemplation in Cambridge University, and in Harvard. He had now been continuously in office for almost ten years.

I

IN his Hari Raya Puasa Message, on 1 January, Lee Kuan Yew extended his greetings to all Muslims. All great religions of the world, he said, preached universal brotherhood regardless of race, language and culture. In a world growing ever smaller by man's conquest of air and space, in travel and communications, no religion or ideology can ignore the diversity in the social mores, the habits and custom, the different histories of the many peoples of the world.

"When", added the Prime Minister, "the super-powers have learned to co-exist and sometimes even to co-operate in fields like research in Antarctia, and in the formulation of a just nuclear non-proliferation treaty, it is not too much to hope that the smaller countries in Southeast Asia will learn, before it is too late, that there is much to be gained by co-existence and co-operation ... co-operation of a realistic basis of mutual benefit and the common good."

Two weeks later, Britain, faced with financial and other difficulties, suddenly announced that the date of withdrawal of its forces from Singapore would be advanced. Lee Kuan Yew decided to fly to London to talk to the British Prime Minister. Lee had already accepted the fact that Britain would pull out, but he had been told in 1967 that this would be in the mid-1970s, and he had made arrangements accordingly. Now, unexpectedly, the date was to be advanced by several years. Lee went to London to counsel delay, and to make provisions for speeding up Singapore's own defence plans. He persuaded the British Government to delay their accelerated withdrawal at least until the end of 1971.

Back in Singapore, Lee Kuan Yew made a statement in Parliament on 24 January and read extracts from a speech made by the British Prime Minister in the House of Commons on 16 January, in which Mr Harold Wilson spoke of the withdrawal of British forces from Malaysia and Singapore, and Britain's intention to retain a general capability based in Europe which can be deployed overseas.

Lee Kuan Yew's message on Chinese New Year, on 29 January, surveyed the current situation. Lee recalled that Singapore had made considerable economic progress over the previous twelve months, despite three major events "not calculated to help". These had been first, the announcement in July 1968 that British forces would be run down to half by 1971; then the devaluation of the pound in November; and third, "a fortnight ago, the decision of an accelerated withdrawal of all British forces by 31 December, 1971".

Lee said that economic progress and security were closely inter-related. The volume of bank deposits in Singapore went up by thirty-two per cent by the end of December, 1967, an indicator of confidence in the management of economy and currency. "No one doubts our ability to surge ahead at a higher rate of economic growth, provided there is continuing security. It is in this field that the challenge has become more intense. Some say that perhaps the Conservative Party will be returned to office before March, 1971. But it will be foolish indeed reckless, to bank on contingencies such as these. We must proceed forthwith with the proposals for joint aerial defence which the British Government have offered to set up for the Singapore-Malaysia area. If we arrive at credible alternative security arrangements, then the mild boom we are enjoying will continue for several years."

But there would be the problem of considerable unemployment by 1970, unless citizens took and tried every opportunity for retraining for new jobs as they become redundant to the British Armed Services.

Lee believed that so long as Singapore had the will to work, to adapt and to adjust to changing circumstances, the Republic would continue to remain a haven of peace and plenty, a place of refuge for all who sought relatively greater security for their fortunes and themselves.

Nine days later, the Prime Minister advised the President to dissolve Parliament on 8 February. Under Article 50 of the Constitution a general election then became necessary within three months. Lee and his colleagues had decided to seek a fresh mandate from the people before embarking upon a policy based upon detailed planning, close-community endeavour, a great deal of hard work and perhaps sacrifices as well. There was, Lee thought, no other way of solving the serious problems that lay ahead.

The Prime Minister dealt with some aspects of these problems when he opened a seminar on economic co-operation between Southeast Asian nations at the University of Singapore on 15 February. Any discussion, he said, of economic and political co-operation in South and Southeast Asia, as in any other region of the world, must include an evaluation of the stability and security of that region. "Without stability and security, economic co-operation is an exercise in collective soliciting for aid from the developed countries." It was only after several hundred years of warring had proved the futility of advancing nationalist interests through force of arms, that the six in the European Economic Community got together. They had to overcome deep-seated national prejudices. They were encouraged in this direction by America; and massive American investments, particularly in war-ravaged Germany, was a push towards EEC. Moreover, the Marshal Plan that rehabilitated the ruined economies of Western Europe had preceded the EEC. Then the presence of powerful communist armed forces in Eastern Europe and Russia, threatening to close the corridor to Berlin. All these factors helped to bring about the Treaty of Rome.

Lee Kuan Yew reminded the seminar that as recently as 1962, when a British Conservative Government first applied to join the EEC, there was no unanimity of opinion that it was in Britain's long-term interest. "Only recently have the realities of the new technological

419

age become obvious to more than the experts. Economies of scale require mass production for mass markets. Today, it is universally accepted that America and Russia are super-powers because each has a central government with authority over a large continent with good road, rail, river, sea and air communications, each with large populations of over 200 million and 220 million respectively, with high standards of education particularly in the applied sciences. Without a vast pool of manpower, disciplined in the scientific and industrial techniques of the space age, they could not hope to conquer space. In 1945, there were five big powers. Their special status was recognized in the United Nations by their being given the right of the veto. They are still the only five that have exploded the atom. But Britain and France both know that the trends are not in their favour. Only three of the Big Five of the last world war have each one central authority over a large ethnocentric population and a continental land mass, to provide the industrial base for the race to the moon and the stars beyond."

Lee went on to point out that economic and political co-operation in South and Southeast Asia had been slow because the leaders had been preoccupied with their own problems in the post-independence era. Most of these leaders led their people to independence accompanied by strong nationalist sentiments. Their values were those of the inter-war years, when they were at universities in the metropolitan capitals of Europe. The ideas of that age made them intensely nationalistic. Then national self-sufficiency was the ideal aimed at by all European nation states. Each sought out its own empire. "It is emotionally and psychologically difficult to rid themselves of the values of their youth, adopt new values and adjust policies to meet the different conditions of the technological age. The developed countries acknowledge that inter-dependence and co-operation is the way towards ever higher standards of life for all. Even the present two super-powers co-operate in searching for a just formula to prevent the spread or proliferation of nuclear weapons, and to a lesser extent exchange information in their space probes. Although the second-generation leaders in South and Southeast Asia realize these hard facts of new technological age, co-operation in economic and political matters has been slow. Fear that such economic and political co-operation may lead to subversion and absorption of the smaller partners by the larger is one reason. The sluggish pace of advance in meaningful economic regional co-operation reflects the suspicions, sometimes justified but more often ill-founded, that such co-operation may lead to subjugation. And even when subjugation is not likely, the larger country may be not too willing to co-operate with smaller countries because the smaller partners, being more efficient, may get more out of it."

Lee said it helped to remember that several countries in the region had never before existed in their present form of nation states. Their boundaries and population, often not homogeneous, were inherited from

420

European empires. Decolonization led to the re-emergence of some old states like Burma and Ceylon. But never before in her history did India have the boundaries it now shared with Pakistan, both in the east and the west. Indonesia included half of New Guinea, divided longitude-wise between the Dutch and the Australians, and half of Timor, divided between the Dutch and the Portuguese. Malaysia, with its capital in Kuala Lumpur governing Sabah and Sarawak across the South China Sea, was new. So too was the Republic of Singapore. "Even if we could restore the position to what it was before the Europeans came, the *status quo ante* is no longer tenable. Modern science and technology, particularly in transportation and communications, have made the historic barriers of mountain ranges and rivers no longer the natural buffers to conflict. This was vividly demonstrated in the winter of 1962 when the timeless Himalayas which had prevented the Hindu and Chinese civilizations from colliding was proved to be not as impassable as it had been. Only the sea is still difficult to cross. So the German army stopped on the other side of the English Channel, and Britons lived to win the war, with Americans as allies. But for the super-powers even the sea is no barrier to their influence. Large American and Russian fleets are in the Mediterranean, and in the Sea of Japan."

The events of the last 300 years were irreversible. Four hundred years ago Red Indians hunted buffaloes across the whole North American continent. Today a largely ethno-centric, English-speaking people of European stock, with a ten per cent black African minority, had emerged as the world's greatest industrial power, the United States of America. Nothing could bring back the Red Indians and buffaloes. About 150 years ago aborigines were still hunting small animals in Australia with the boomerang. Now an English-speaking people, predominantly of British stock, had created the beginnings of what could be a considerable industrial power in the South Pacific, given a few more decades. "One hundred and fifty years ago, when Stamford Raffles came to Singapore on 19 February, 1819, the archives of the East India Company bear evidence to 120 Malays and some 30 Chinese living in what was a fishing village. Today Singapore sustains two million people, highly urbanized, and increasingly industrialized to provide a standard of living second in Asia, second only to Japan. A hundred years ago the Japanese were a feudal community. But 100 years after the Meiji restoration, Japan is moving from fourth to perhaps third position in the world in industrial production and strength. Up to 1949, China was one chaotic conglomeration of war-lording provinces. In 1964 she exploded the atomic bomb. In 1966-67 she had fathomed the mysteries of the hydrogen bomb." Nothing could reverse this.

"What of the future? Living in Singapore, one gateway opening into the Pacific and the other into the Indian Ocean, we are deeply conscious of the vastly changed balance of world forces. This was

421

underlined by the recent decision of the British Government to accelerate the withdrawal of her forces in Asia. In the next hundred years we shall have to live with the fact that at present two, and later three, super-powers will contend, in the Pacific and Indian Oceans, to so order the political and economic life in the region to the maximum national advantage of each super-power. The first conclusion to draw is that the eventual fate of South and Southeast Asia is dependent more upon the resultant policy decisions of America, China and Russia (put in alphabetical order and not their respective order of influence) than in the decisions of the dozen or more governments in the region. There are other nations with power potential in the area. Individually, and combined, they may constitute another force to work between and around the three super-powers. First, there is Japan. Her industrial capacity and military skills were forcibly demonstrated in the last war. If America considered it in her long-term national interest so to do, Japan could very rapidly become a force in the Pacific. If this were to happen, we must hope that she will be a factor for stability. However, the Japanese Constitution is a pacifist one. And there are psychological difficulties both in Japan and in South and Southeast Asia to be overcome."

Lee said that India was the second great potential power. British India was a power house, an enormous sub-continent for industrial production and military might Britain tapped and mobilized in both world wars. Unfortunately since then India had become two nation states, India and Pakistan, with Kashmir a permanent source of unhappiness for both, negating the potentially great contribution they could have made. Then there was Indonesia, 100 million people in 30,000 islands. Unfortunately the Dutch legacy to Indonesia was meagre, unlike the British legacy to her Commonwealth partners. At independence they were left with no core of trained administrators, no broad strata of educated men with the professional skills for a modern industrial community.

Lee felt that the prospect for economic and political co-operation in South and Southeast Asia would be much brighter if there were more stability and security. For then each of the nation states would feel more secure and so be more confident of co-operating economically and politically, without nagging doubts that it might lead to their dismemberment or disintegration.

One factor that tended to optimism was that none of the countries in the region were self-supporting in the weaponry of the technological age. Even India and Pakistan, relatively big and advanced compared to other countries in the region, discovered during their last armed conflict that if the super-powers who supplied them the weapons did not supply spares and replacements, their military capacity could be severely restricted. India and Pakistan may in time achieve, like the Japanese and the Chinese, the capacity to duplicate and then improve on the techniques and weaponry of the West. "However, there are no other countries in the region likely to be able to do this in the foreseeable future. Even the Australians—a people with all the skills and know-how brought over from Britain and Europe—have to buy their Mirage Supersonics from the French, and the F.111s from the Americans. So if the major powers who are the only manufacturers of these weapons decide that it is in their own interests not to have South and Southeast Asia embroiled in constant conflict, peace and stability can be easily established. Unfortunately, hitherto the major powers have pursued policies to the contrary. Vast quantities of modern weapons have already been introduced into the region as the suppliers sought to advance their interests and diminish those of their opponents. These arms cannot be removed by wishful thinking. Hence the need of continuing the joint defence arrangements between Singapore, Malaysia and those of the Commonwealth who consider they have a more than sentimental interest in continuing stability in the Singapore-Malaysia area."

The Prime Minister said that a modest series of beginnings had been made. The Asian Development Bank and ASEAN were two recent advances. The results had yet to be seen and felt. "We must not forget that co-operation between developed, industrialized and affluent nations like those in the EEC means greater wealth and prosperity to be divided amongst already prosperous communities. But co-operation between educationally not advanced and industrially under-developed countries can only produce miniscule economic gains to be divided between large numbers of poor and hungry people. So up till now, co-operative arrangements that have been established in South and Southeast Asia have been arrangements to please developed donor nations, so that gifts, or aid, may be more generously given to the co-operators."

Lee said that to make real progress there must be a hard-headed appraisal of the economic potentials each and every member could make in a co-operative effort. Such appraisal must take many factors into consideration: population, natural wealth of the countries, the educational standards of the people, the industrial skills and capital equipment, the infrastructure of industry and commerce that each community already had, the purchasing power of each of the communities in the region, the motivations of their people, which in turn depended upon the cultural and social value patterns, and their past history. "Only a practical approach will provide the step-by-step advancement, first in economic co-operation, then into political fields, and finally on to collective security. To make progress, which can be more quickly felt by the people, the under-developed countries of South and Southeast Asia must be associated with the more industrially advanced and prosperous, to borrow on fairly generous terms not only the capital and equipment, but also the expertise in management, technological and industrial techniques, education and training methods."

There was a correlation between the educated and skilled digits of a community and its gross national product. America had a gross national product of US$790,000 million for 1966. It had a per capita income of about US$4,000. Three hundred out of every 1,000 Americans had had more than twelve years of education, up to at least high school level and to university level. Nigeria, black Africa's biggest and potentially richest country—with oil, power, mineral resources—had 40 million people. But Nigeria had a per capita income of only US$64 per annum. Less than one person in 1,000 Nigerians had had an education of 12 years or more. In 1966, the GNP of America increased by more than the total GNP of the African continent, which was hardly changing at all.

Recapitulating, Lee Kuan Yew stressed that stability and security must first be established. This could be done if two or more of the super-powers agreed that it was in their separate national interests to do this. It could also be done if one super-power had the strength to support all the smaller countries who wanted to get on with economic construction together and excluded super-power rivalries from their region. Slowly it could then be demonstrated that economic and political co-operation would lead to greater prosperity and security, not subversion or disintegration of smaller members. Eventually, like the European Economic Community, all partners would develop a vested interest in continuing and expanding co-operation. "This situation can be achieved, given intelligent inducement by the developed countries, and hard work between the economic planners of the countries seeking development. Then the wasteful and contra-productive military plans will be abjured." The Prime Minister concluded with the remark that all this presupposed that wars of national liberation, or so-called people's wars, would not continue beyond Vietnam. "It is a major assumption. If this assumption turns out to be over-optimistic, then the whole course of events will be different, and the consequences unpleasant for all of us gathered here."

II

Two days later (on 17 February) the Prime Minister announced that the Government had decided to give the Opposition candidates the maximum time under the law before polling. This was eight weeks. Polling day would be on 13 April. There were fifty-eight seats in the new Parliament and fifty-one PAP candidates had already been returned unopposed. The Prime Minister said that eight weeks would allow the seven Opposition candidates time to get organized. Nobody need complain that they did not have sufficient time to put across their views. The Barisan Sosialis boycotted the elections.

Lee Kuan Yew admitted he would have preferred many more contests, particularly from pro-communist organizations. He said that neither in 1959, nor in 1963, had a new government been elected to face the kind of problems of the dimensions that Singapore now faced. "Our continued defence and security is a precondition to continuing confidence for continuing investment and expanding industries. A robust economy will in turn provide the revenues that will enable Singapore to carry more and more of its own defence and enable it to make its common defence with Malaysia even more secure."

Lee finished up by warning that the problems of redundancy, following the withdrawal of the British bases, would probably mean new and imaginative policies, and some would require new legislation. Singapore had 75,000 registered unemployed and people seeking better employment: and yet 60,000 permits had been issued to non-citizens. In a humane way, he said, steps would have to be taken to put citizens in jobs in the unskilled and semi-skilled categories. All those with industrial skills, management expertise, or trained in the professions, would however always be welcomed to Singapore.

On 20 March, the Prime Minister spoke to the second batch of a hundred newly trained army officers at a commissioning ceremony. He reminded them that by 1972 "we must demonstrate that we have the wherewithal to make it extremely unpleasant for anybody contemplating taking liberties with us". He said Singapore welcomed co-operation "with all our Commonwealth partners" in common defence arrangements. But most importantly, everyone must know that "we are not passengers" in such an arrangement. "Our survival must not depend only on the charitable disposition of our friends and neighbours". ˙

Lee Kuan Yew urged the new officers to be of good heart. There were not many communities that could start from scratch and in two and a half years build up the infrastructure, the administrative network, and the organizational institutions to produce an unending stream of officers and soldiers, men who "besides being trained for combat will, after their two-year national service is completed, contribute to the developing of our economy". Events around Singapore constantly underlined "the lessons of weakness, the terrible price those, who are caught in positions of weakness not of strength, must pay when they are the wealthier sections of the populace. And we happen to be the wealthiest community per capita of population in South Asia."

Launching a series of radio and television election campaign talks, Lee Kuan Yew said on 22 March that there had never before been so decisive and so quiet a general election. The reasons were to be found in the history of the past nine years. "Today, people take for granted the stability, the social cohesion, the orderliness, the willingness to work, the awareness of the problems of our people. These are the factors which determine our economic progress. And in 1959, when my colleagues and I first took office, these factors were not much in evidence."

Lee Kuan Yew outlined the past and sketched in what he thought the future held for Singapore. He said that in 1959 many doubted whether the non-communist leaders in the party would be able to withstand capture by the communists: they appeared overpowering. They held mass rallies at every conceivable excuse to intimidate the Government and the people by their demonstration of massive strength. Now they had become hit-and-run gangs, exposed as a vicious minority. "We had", Lee continued, "gone into Malaysia seeking independence and security upon a wider base. But within nine months, in June, 1964, inter-communal riots broke out for the first time in the history of Singapore. We refused to be intimidated. Within fifteen months Singapore became independent on its own. People doubted whether we could survive—two million people, all migrants, or descendants of migrants. Most political scientists, economists, the experts in newspapers, magazines and scholarly journals predicted we would collapse. We had no natural resources, no viability, no future. Yet, two and a half years later, these critics agree that we have succeeded. They were confounded because they did not give adequate weight to one vital factor: the human drive, that verve in a determined and a resourceful people who know the terrible consequence of failure ... "

The Prime Minister reminded his audience that Singapore had the highest population density of any nation state in the world. Only Hong Kong, run as a colony by British officials, surpassed Singapore's population density of over 8,000 persons per square mile. This population concentration emphasized the magnitude of the task. "If we were a soft society", declared the Prime Minister, "we would already have perished, for a soft people would not be able to take their problems in their stride, nor support a government that takes measures requiring stiffer effort and greater sacrifice to ensure collective survival. A soft people will vote for those who promise a soft way out, when in truth, there is none. This has happened in several Afro-Asian countries, newly independent. A soft people faced with tough problems, electing a soft government, soon find themselves in chaos and confusion, which in turn inevitably lead to the imposition of military rule. There is nothing Singapore gets for free. Even our water we pay for. And if you want to improve the air you breathe by air-conditioning, that costs money. True, our children go to school free, they get dental and medical attention free. But you and I are paying for it. What of the future? By the end of 1971, the British would have withdrawn from

426

their bases. One-fifth of our GNP is what the British bases have been contributing to our economy. Thirty thousand direct jobs would have gone, probably another 10,000 to 15,000 indirect jobs. More crucial, we shall no longer have the British Army, Royal Navy and Royal Air Force to defend us. This is the final chapter in the making of a nation. From a protected trading centre of a vast empire, we must become a self-reliant industrialized nation state responsible for our own security."

Lee Kuan Yew claimed that there were not many communities in the equatorial belt that had attained Singapore's standards of organized and cultivated living. But then there were very few communities that had demonstrated their stamina, vigour and vitality in spite of an enervating climate. "There was a prosperous and thriving Singapore before the British built their naval and air bases. There will be a throbbing and humming industrial, commercial and communications centre long after the British bases have gone. But for the first time, we must fight for ourselves. This is the acid test. Have we the will to be a nation? Have we the grit? It will be folly to minimize the size of our problems. But having had the privilege of leading a team of able, dedicated and hard-headed men; and watching the response for nine years from a rugged and robust society, I have no doubts that we shall make the grade. We will not flinch from the unpleasant, and we will not yield to the temptation of a soft solution when this this is no way out. Together, we shall build a more secure and better future for our children."

III

Lee Kuan Yew talked to the port workers on 28 March when he laid the foundation stone of the Singapore Port Authority Union premises. He spoke to them frankly about the need to cut out what he called "fantastic overtime earnings", sometimes 200 per cent of substantive pay, which certain port workers were taking home. "This has to stop. We have tens of thousands of Singapore citizens knocking at the door of the Labour Ministry wanting jobs."

Lee reminded the workers of what happens when unions do foolish things. Britain, one of the richest, most advanced and industrialized countries in the world, with 400 years of the accumulated savings of Empire, in two decades of prodigal living and very unwise trade union practices, had to devalue the pound. Not because of lack of brain-power or managerial skill, but because of unwise trade union practices. These restrictive practices resulted in workers believing that the whole purpose in life was to work less for more pay. "Perhaps", said Lee Kuan Yew, "wealthy, industrialized nations can get away with this. But if countries like Singapore do this, they go bankrupt; they do not just devalue the dollar; they literally starve. And, so long as my colleagues and I are entrusted with your fate, our duty is to see that you do not starve. One of the ways to make sure that we don't starve is to see that everybody does a good forty-four-hour week, with perhaps two hours overtime per day. Work fifty-six hours per week, and conserve your strength so that you will live long and healthy. Don't try to work eighty hours a week. You will either be bluffing the management, or bluffing yourself, and in the end, the country will come to no good."

Lee told the dock workers that their task as a union "for the next few years" is not just to jump around, holding mass rallies for more pay, without showing first increased productivity. "We have to move away from outmoded practices. With this new union building you have to reach out for new targets." During the next four or five years, Singapore trade unions would face this problem: how to keep union morale and memberships up while "there is no agitation for more pay without showing increased productivity. We need a lot of rethinking on how to have better organization, high productivity, and more modern methods of work. So you have to provide other activities, meaningful to your members, to keep them together. You have to grow up, just as Singapore has to grow up. We live in a dangerous part of the world and if we don't grow up, your children never will ... You are moving into an age where modern technology is altering the whole landscape of international transportation, whether it is jumbo-jets or containerized cargo. Any port that is slack and slow is not going to be a big containerized centre. If we are going to be that, we have to have up-to-date expertise, an open, keen mind, and a willingness to learn new ways of doing the job."

Lee Kuan Yew spoke with similar candour at the NTUC Delegates Conference on 7 April. He said the 1970s were crucial years for Singapore—for the people, for the Government and for the NTUC. The challenge was basically unchanged. How could an enterprising, resourceful, energetic and industrious if acquisitive people—two million human beings of migrant stock inheriting one of the most developed cities in Southeast Asia and on the equatorial belt—survive and create a stable, industrial, commercial and communications centre?

"This was the problem", Lee said, "we have faced from 9 August, 1965. If we then thought we did not stand a chance, we would have packed up a long time ago, and the course of history would have been different. But I believed then, as I believe now, that we have it in us to respond to this challenge. The response of our population to the difficulties that we have faced over the last decade has been a source of constant inspiration: the ability to adjust, to adapt and to change. It is this collective sense of endeavour which will carry us through. In

Singapore, we have to be a tough people in order to accept stern measures for collective survival. Otherwise the Government cannot govern by consent. If you elect people who offer soft solutions to tough problems, there will be no solution and bankruptcy and chaos will result."

Two illustrations of the recovery of nations from the wreckage of defeat in World War Two, said the Prime Minister, showed how, given certain basic elements and the right conditions, a smaller territory with a larger population could still achieve miracles. Germany lost the war. She shrank to less than two-thirds her pre-war size. Her population increased because of all the German refugees from East Germany, Czechoslovakia and Poland. Similarly, when Japan struck in the Pacific in 1941, she had Manchuria, Korea, Formosa and large parts of China. She lost the war. Millions of Japanese had to go home to a much smaller Japan. She had more population. But today, next to America and Russia, Germany and Japan are the world's third- and fourth-ranking industrial powers. In Japan and Germany, the skills were there as well as the sense of national purpose. The Germans and the Japanese were determined to get back to the top of the league again. So entrepreneurs, industrialists, politicians, workers and unionists worked together to reconstruct their country. The Americans helped. But the miracles of Germany and Japan happened because the Germans and the Japanese used this aid to maximum advantage.

Contrast this with Britain. She won the war, but she lost her empire. Her industries were relatively untouched, compared to the ruins of Japanese and German factories. Why did she lose her pre-eminent position? Lee Kuan Yew said that what really held them back was not the lack of brain power or of industrial or technological skills, or lack of cultural or ethnic drive and stamina. The workers were carrying on a relentless class war against employers. There was no sense of national purpose as was the case with the defeated Germans and Japanese. The British won the war and the workers asked for the fruits of peace. More and more for less and less became a way of life. So the British ran through all their savings. "And then the London dockyard workers decided to go on strike . . . Let me be frank. If that happens here at our harbour I will declare this high treason. I will move against the strike leaders. Charges can be brought in court later. I would get the port going straightaway. The Singapore dollar will never be devalued. And I think the people of Singapore expect this of their Government."

Lee Kuan Yew referred to some of the problems facing the trade unions. One was the brake on the expansion of jobs. "It is the selfishness of established labour." He described the overtime racket as "a grotesque distortion of our society". He said: If we maintain our economic growth rate at eight to nine per cent, as we probably will, and increase job opportunities, say at the rate of four per cent, it will go a long way towards solving our unemployment problem. What we must seek to achieve is high morale at home and international confidence in us abroad. Some 40,000 people will be losing their jobs by 1971. The simplest way for the Government is to let this problem solve itself through a free and open labour market. Organized labour would be broken by the sheer impact of this massive unemployment. Management-union agreements will fall apart. My colleagues and I could fold our arms, take a deep breath and look the other way, when the impact of redundancies from the military bases become heavy. But the political price we will have to pay is that we go back again to the kind of situation in the early 1950s, when we had such a bad labour reputation internationally. The communists can move back and easily exploit frustrated, ignorant and unorganized workers ... Hence the importance of intelligent co-operation between the labour, management and government. We must have the sense of national purpose."

What is this purpose? "The purpose is national security and a better life for all. What can pay for this security and higher standards of life? Higher productivity, greater economic growth, better distribution of employment opportunities. Higher wages as productivity increases, and workers educated by their own leaders in the realities of our economic position will, by the 1980s, produce a solid and secure situation which the communists cannot easily exploit. Can you, the unions, together with management and government, achieve this? Can we, together, create that confidence in our continued stability? Without confidence there will be no investment in industrial enterprises, because industry, unlike commerce or speculation, means long-term planning."

Today, Lee continued, confidence in Singapore was based on the political leadership continuing for the next decade. But Singapore was going to live for more than just one decade. Therefore, in this one decade the basis on which confidence is based must be extended so that it will be more enduring. "Similarly in the trade unions you must produce a continuous flow of capable and practical leadership. I am a realist. I am asking you to lick the labour movement into shape, cutting out restrictive practices which are no longer relevant and stopping abuse of fringe benefits which leads to lower productivity. You and I know that an average of thirty-two days' sick leave being taken by a daily-rated worker in the public sector just means malingering. The average worker cannot be sick for thirty-two days every year. Look at our workers: are they sickly and underfed? Yet the records show that, since they are entitled to forty-four days' sick leave for a year, they are sick for thirty-two days. Cut all these evils off, jack up productivity. Cut out abuse of privileges and create a new image of a thinking, hard-headed labour movement—high morale at home and confidence abroad—and we will boom."

IV

Late in the evening of 13 April the results of the seven seats contested in the elections were announced. The People's Action Party won them all. In a statement the Prime Minister said that the results comprised a fair example of what would have happened if all the fifty-eight seats had been contested. "People in Singapore", he said, "know what is at stake—their lives and the future of their children." He was confident that a vigorous and resourceful people, given a determined and dynamic lead, would overcome the problems which they know are ahead in the 1970s.

V

On 24 April, in a discussion on student leadership in a developing Southeast Asia, the Prime Minister said there were many explanations for student unrest in various parts of the world. Each country had its own peculiar set of circumstances. There was a common feature in all of them: students never achieve power. "The unrest, demonstrations and agitations inevitably end up with the adults, the 40-plus, in authority, and, in the end, asserting their will." However, out of this broad category of those who are better equipped mentally, or have that high glandular activity that make them activists, or drive or push or interest—out of this broad category some would go on to be adult leaders. "Therefore I want to encourage student movements. But I want the widest participation. I am not altogether convinced that out of the activist of our student movement will come the next generation of leaders for Singapore, or for any part of South and Southeast Asia. Was Mao a student leader? He was a librarian at Peking University. He spent a lot of time thinking problems out. Was Kennedy a student leader? Was Khrushchev? Was de Gaulle? Can you imagine him leading students down Champs-Elysees."

Lee ended with a word of encouragement: "You must take yourself seriously. If you don't, what is the purpose of all this? But do not take yourself too seriously. You are young. In ten to twenty years, when you have developed the canniness and an understanding of the crafty ways of men struggling to get into power positions, you would have become much more worldly wise. But I hope you will still be inspired by the ideals of equality, equal opportunity, the ideals of the brotherhood of all human beings, particularly those within your own community, and the ideals of a better life for all. If you can retain these ideals—one to two decades from now—and acquire in the meantime a lot of the other attributes that make up for national leadership, then my visit this evening would not have been in vain."

431

VI

In his May Day message to the trade unionists, the Prime Minister said that a way of life, "to which we have been long accustomed, sheltered by a big power", was passing. "We used to be subject peoples. In the past two decades, as imperial power waned, we began to assert our right to freedom. Sometimes we took liberties with ourselves and with the imperial power who protected us. In part good fortune, but in the main good analysis, planning and execution, have enabled us to carve out a stake for ourselves out of the remnants of Empire. We are one of the few exceptions where freedom has brought the better life, with higher standards of education, social amenities, health services. We will move upwards and be part of the developed world, if all are conscious of the contribution each one of us, leaders and members, must take towards the rugged and robust society."

In spite of the complications of compounding the trade union movement with a political freedom movement, work discipline had been maintained. Workers found their new dignity in freedom, and were able to look the employer and the whole world in the eye, without cringing and fawning. At the same time excesses had been avoided which could have led to insubordination and a breakdown in discipline and order in the work force, which would have brought poverty and chaos.

The price of failure was terrible. The price for success was more effort and efficiency, the expunging of excessive fringe benefits and their abuse. "The overriding consideration is for greater economic growth and more job opportunities. Government, and unions and enterprise together can achieve this. However, if the trade union movement opts out and leaves it all to the Government, then the movement will not grow and develop in sophistication and strength of leadership. Then we would not have educated our workers to the facts of life, and they would not know how a protected trading community transformed itself into a self-supporting industrial, commercial and communications centre. And if our society is that ignorant and gullible, then the ground will always be susceptible to communist and anarchist blandishments. We are a young community with no deep social or class divisions. Whether coolie or millionaire, our children go to the same schools, with equal opportunities for advancement to higher education, to leadership roles. Rewards correspond to merit and performance. We must keep it that way, and prevent the divisive influences of class hatred and class exploitation. From worker to trade union leader, from union leader to executive and management promotions, this social mobility must be encouraged."

Lee Kuan Yew warned that the union leader who could only feel strongly about the needs of his workers and who was anti-bosses, but without comprehending the economic realities on which his fellow workers' livelihood depends, would become as outdated as the dinosaur. "Our trade union leaders must be as up to date in thinking, methods and techniques as the best on the management side. It is the intention of the Government to provide the opportunities to develop this quality of leadership. It is up to the unions and their leaders to seize these opportunities and go on to higher standards and greater sophistication, but without losing the inner fire, the zeal to create a more equal and just society, where no man should be able to exploit his fellow men."

VII

When Parliament reassembled on 6 May, the Prime Minister congratulated the Speaker Mr Punch Coomaraswamy on his re-election to the Chair. He said that his experience as Speaker must be unique. In two successive Parliaments Mr Coomaraswamy had presided over a House without an Opposition. In the first, the Opposition had boycotted the House. Now they boycotted the general elections. "But", continued Lee Kuan Yew, "in spite of the extraordinary circumstances, a legislative chamber without the stimulus of provocative criticism, those of us who were in the last Parliament are confident that under your guidance, this House will keep the parliamentary machine in good shape, and also sustain and cultivate the attitude of tolerance and calculated deference to opposing views. Those of us who are natural optimists, or not long acquainted with the social science of psephology, may believe that the return of all fifty-eight members from the PAP reflects the unanimity of views amongst people outside. My colleagues and I, who have gone through more harrowing times, cannot afford to be so naive, or so ingenuous. In 1963, the pro-communist groups, under the banner of the Barisan Sosialis, collected over thirty per cent of the vote and thirteen out of fifty-one seats. True, their fortunes have declined. This is partly the result of our social and economic policies, partly the result of higher political sophistication amongst the voters. But it is mainly because of their own irrational rigid orthodoxy, their obsequious subservience to directives from outside. They have mechanically chanted ridiculous slogans and asserted incredible untruths—that Malaysia does not exist, that 'Malaya' includes Singapore, and that the Republic does not exist. Even so, had the communists decided to contest the election through Barisan Sosialis, or other front organizations, like the communist-led trade unions, or the old boys' associations and the cultural groups, I would not have been surprised if they had collected over fifteen per cent of the votes, which would have ensured them some six to eight seats in this House. If they persist in orthodoxy, and their orders continue to be as unrelated to the realities of the situation in and around Singapore as they have been in the past five years, and more important, if our economic and social policies make the progress they have made over the past five years, by 1973 then their electoral support may further sink down, perhaps to below ten per cent. But I doubt if I can give as cheerful an estimate in the corresponding decline of their cadre strength. One of the subsidiary reasons why their electoral support has declined is that they have withdrawn their trained and experienced cadres from open front activity to conserve their strength for future deployment."

Of the fifty-eight Members in this House, twenty-six Members had never known what it was to be in a Parliament with an Opposition. Indeed, sixteen of them had been returned unopposed, and had never known the rough and tumble of a contested election. To them, Lee commended *Hansard,* the report of the proceedings of the House since May, 1955. He particularly recommended the years 1955, '56, '59, and '61-3. In 1955, the governors stopped presiding over sessions of the Legislative Council. A mainly elected Legislative Assembly of thirty-two members, of whom twenty-five were elected, was allowed to meet under an independent Speaker. Three were from the PAP. Lee Kuan Yew was the sole survivor of that first Assembly.

Some of the clerks of Parliament and Lee had personal knowledge of the boisterous and rumbustious past of the House. There was no dearth of differences of opinions, or independence of views, sometimes sincerely and often vehemently, held. *Hansard* recorded this clash of minds, the exchange of retorts courteous and not so courteous, the conflict of ideas and ideologies, and the face-to-face confrontation of the exponents of different ideologies. They revealed all the bounce, the abrasiveness and the self-confidence that Singapore had had and still had. They made for lively meetings. Debates were often bitter and vicious. "The fact that we now have such a homogeneous group in fifty-eight Members does not mean that it will remain so hereafter. Opposition in this Chamber will, and must, inevitably return. But the Opposition will not be individuals claiming to act as the conscience of the people, or offering themselves as the necessary accoutrements of parliamentary democracy on the spurious argument that because there is no Opposition, therefore there is no parliamentary democracy. Singapore is not that gullible and credulous. The Opposition, when it returns, will comprise a group offering an alternative policy, and offering themselves as a credible alternative government to implement the policies they expound. This can come about in one of two ways, one less desirable than the other. First, it could come as a result of severe economic setbacks, the failure to meet and overcome the problems coming upon us in 1970s. Then the Opposition that emerges will be extreme, either orthodox communist, or revisionist, or Trotskyite. The divisions will be sharp and angry, and the country the worse for it. Second, the more desirable alternative, economic success and enhanced social stability, and further reduction in electoral support for communist or extremist policies. With stability and prosperity, the sense of national urgency and unity, which binds together a people faced with a common danger, will slacken and more relaxed mood will set in. A new restlessness will bestir the people, a desire for improvement and change, or just change for change's sake, will appeal to a younger generation. The emergence of a party or parties either to the Left or Right of the PAP must result. But they would be constitutional alternatives, willing to work the system, prepared to compete and attain power within the system, and to surrender it by the same rules through which they came into office."

But, Lee thought, for the crucial '70s, it is as well that in the PAP "we hold together in national consensus a wide cross-section of our society, from semi-skilled and skilled workers like the Members for Kampong Kembangan and Geylang Serai, both former employees of the Singapore Telephone Board and leaders of its union; clerical groups represented by the Members for Kallang and Toa Payoh; teachers and principals like the Members for Telok Blangah and Moulmein; university lecturers and professors like the Members for Katong, Joo Chiat and Alexandra; to professional men and business executives like the Members for Bukit Panjang, River Valley and Jalan Kayu."

The Prime Minister told the Speaker, that their task was to help him ensure that the parliamentary machine was well maintained and tuned to meet the new circumstances that would evolve in the 1970s. He was confident that Members of Parliament would debate matters before them frankly and freely. They would have to learn and practise, as much outside as inside Parliament, the cut and thrust of debate, the retort and rejoinder, the rebuttal and ripost.

Lee recalled that from 1955 to 1959 he was a Member of the Chamber occupying the seat, if not the title, of Leader of the Opposition. "At every crisis, crowds thronged the Gallery to watch the Government being castigated and whipped for its many misdemeanours. I changed places and became Leader of the Government from 1959 onwards. It was our turn to be pulverized. From 1961 to '63 crowds were drawn like a magnet to this Chamber, some waiting outside to hear, if they could not see, the pack of Barisan wolves come in for the kill of the PAP lamb. I do not believe that these large numbers of pro-communist sympathizers and supporters have all vanished or been converted just because they left disappointed as the Barisan wolves were chastised in the encounter."

Whilst this would not be a Parliament with the suspense and excitement of earlier years, nevertheless there would be momentous times ahead and the House would have enough drama if not anxiety in the next crucial years ahead. Lee urged Members to speak their minds freely and forcefully. "Our future is at stake and we must give the lead in thinking and feeling in the country. If the new Members, we now welcome to our fraternity, learn and drill themselves, there is no reason why, when actual blood is drawn in a subsequent Parliament, it should not be from the other side."

Later the same evening, in his speech setting out the broad outlines of policy of the newly elected Government, President Yusof bin Ishak remarked that this was a Parliament faced with problems of more than usual magnitude. Not only because Britain would be withdrawing her forces from Singapore by the end of 1971. The whole security and political situation in South and Southeast Asia was in the process of change. The balance of forces was now poised for a possible major shift. The President said that in the next five to ten years, issues would be determined more by factors around rather than within Singapore. Optimum use of the time available would be made in conjunction with Malaysia and other Commonwealth partners to ensure continuing security. "This must be done at a minimum cost, so that most of our resources will go into economic development." The President stressed the need for greater economic growth, "higher productivity with the elimination of restrictive practices, abuses of fringe benefits, and more efficient management. With ever lower costs we must reach out for more export markets."

Three days later, speaking on the Motion to thank the President for his Address, the Prime Minister said that the People's Action Party had been given a mandate as great as the responsibility that went with the task. He was confident that if the people maintained group discipline, if everyone contributed his fullest share of physical and intellectual effort to the fulfilment of plans, "we shall not fail". He was confident that Singapore could, and would, build up an adequate defence force before 1972.

"We can counter recession, expand our economy, train and educate the artisans, technicians and the technocrats for our growing industrial and servicing sectors. In the next few years, as British forces withdraw and leave Singapore and Malaysia to make their own arrangements for security, we shall find out whether, as a community, we are like a creeper or a sapling. Both need support. But unlike a creeper, a sapling does not need support as it grows older and stronger. It will grow into a tree and dispense with the supporting stake. No amount of aid and assistance, grants and loans, technical assistance and training, can do the job that we must do for ourselves. A people who by nature are creepers must, when the stake they are leaning on is removed, fall and crawl on the ground. If we are that sort of a society, then all the brave talk by leaders and encouraging noises by observers, and all the fine words of comfort and promise of aid, will find us still crawling on the ground. However, the manifestations of the last decade point to a sapling growing sturdier and stronger as it matures into an upright tree. The stake, which the British presence provided, has enabled sapling Singapore to grow straight and tall without being too buffetted by the winds while it is still young and fragile. We must have that spirit of self-reliance and self-respect as a community if we are to be compared to a tree. To join the growing number of countries, who beg for alms from the developed countries, will destroy our pride and undermine our self-confidence."

Lee Kuan Yew said that quite a number of countries, after gaining independence, had failed economically and collapsed socially. They lacked one essential quality: self-discipline, either in their leaders, or, more often, both in their leaders and their people. It required self-discipline "to budget and live within your means, when you can just print more money". It required self-discipline to sustain the integrity and efficiency of government, and to punish and keep down corruption, especially in high places. Self-indulgence soon led to personal wealth and security for the few, the political leaders, the military chieftains, and the principal administrators. "Whatever the evils of British, or French, or Dutch colonial administrations, they provided firm, rigid frameworks within which constructive endeavour was rewarded. Seldom were colonial budgets ever in deficit. They invariably spent less than what they got out of each colony, for colonies were intended to provide profits, not incur losses. They kept stern discipline and stable conditions, sound currencies, good sanitation and healthy conditions. It is sad to see how in many countries national heroes have let their country slide down the drain to filth and squalor, corruption and degradation, where the kick-back and the rake-off is a way of life, and the whole country sinks in self-debasement and despair."

If the political leadership ever allowed Singapore to degenerate into these conditions, "then we shall perish". For Singapore did not have that agricultural base, "where you can scatter seed on the ground, and the soil, the sun and the rain will produce the rice, the corn and the fruits with which to feed yourselves. On the other hand, with imagina-tive and intelligent leadership and stiff standards of honest and just administration, we can make maximum use of our not slender resources. We have not often underlined these valuable resources." Lee enumerated them: first, the more-than-average human intelligence, diligence, skills, knowledge and expertise; second, Singapore's superb geographic location at the southernmost tip of the continent of Asia, straddling the route between the Indian and Pacific Oceans, the northern and southern hemispheres. "We have been important for 150 years as a great sea junction. And for the last twenty years we have also grown in importance as a great air junction."

Singapore's third asset was the accumulated total of 150 years of infrastructure and experience in commerce, industry and com-munications. This did not merely mean the physical buildings, the ports, airports, warehouses, roads, banks, shops, power stations, water works, telephones and cables. Most important were the in-visibles, the accumulation of knowledge and expertise: how to run the port economically and efficiently; how to keep up to date with containerized ships and jumbo-jets; what banking, money, finance, stocks and shares, bills of lading, and insurance were all about; how and what to buy in bulk from the industrial countries and how to break down bulk to retail in the area, and conversely to buy retail and package in bulk for export to industrial countries. This required a well-trained professional, managerial and executive elite, supported by a well-educated, skilled and industrious working population.

"These assets", contended Lee Kuan Yew, "constitute our inheritance. We must maintain and improve upon what we have inherited. Bustling commercial and administrative centres have been known to sink into disrepair for lack of self-discipline, often starting with the leaders, but invariably infecting the whole population. We have a stable economic and political situation. We maintain sane, orderly and healthy conditions. There was a time in the last few years, particularly in 1964 and '65 after the riots, when discipline broke down, when it looked as if we might slither down the slippery slope. Organization and administration became tangled and discipline slackened amongst our workers. Cows roamed the streets in the city leaving dung all over the place. Some people died driving cars into cows, before they could die through disease as a result of the filth. Stray dogs, sick, mangy, and wild, were becoming a menace. We had the laws changed and enforced. Cows found in city limits provided food for our welfare homes. Stray dogs were eliminated as efficiently and humanely as possible. We shall not just maintain standards of public health and cleanliness. We shall go further and make this the cleanest and greenest city in South Asia. If we want high morale, we must have high standards. If we want high standards, the law must be enforced fairly and firmly. There will be no squatters and no beggars sleeping on our pavements doing their ablutions in our drains. People will be housed and cared for. Hawkers will not clog up the main streets. There will be thorough and proper cleansing every day of the year. Law will have to be passed to help rid us of malpractices that have crept into our work force. Only the year before last, malingering and shirking and sabotage to create the overtime and treble time for public holidays was a way of life. Discipline and efficiency must be re-established.

"Our children will grow up in healthy and clean homes, with adequate ventilation and sunlight, water, electricity and modern sanitation. Many will go to kindergarten even before they begin primary education. All will have at least six years of primary plus another two years of vocational training. Of the total number admitted to Primary I every year, over fifty per cent go on to complete four years of academic or technical secondary education, over ten per cent reach university entrance standards; over five per cent of the best go on to university and other tertiary institutions. No other community in South Asia offers its people these standards. Nobody believed that

Singapore could make it, except Singaporeans. And we are proud of being Singaporeans. And that pride and patriotism will grow over the years as we add to our inheritance: improved and higher efficiency in our harbours and airports, modernization in containerized facilities and landing aids for longer runways to take the jumbo-jets; better housing and more home ownership for our workers, better schools, clinics, community centres, gardens, libraries, for their children; more factories and better jobs. We shall build up our defence capacity. We should be able to make arrangements for continuing security in conjunction with those with similar interests. There are possibilities for greater economic growth. The sea offers limitless prosperity, some of which we have already grasped in ship repairing and shipbuilding. They will grow and expand as we develop our skills and expertise, and as our reputation spreads. We shall build and run a merchant fleet. We shall go for deep-sea fishing and eventually save about $30 million we spend every year in buying fish from abroad.

"Our economic growth will be accelerated if we provide ideal conditions for the siting of the headquarters of international industrial, commercial and servicing enterprises. But the quickest way to reduce unemployment is the greater inflow of tourists, for tourism is labour intensive. With Singapore clean and green, exotic and efficient, with good and courteous service, and shops filled with the good things of life, the tourists will flow in from America, Japan, Australia, New Zealand, and even Europe, as they do the circuit: Hong Kong, Angkor, Bangkok, Singapore, Bali and beyond."

The Prime Minister was confident that if the momentum was kept up, far from going down in the next five to ten years, Singapore would not only provide jobs for their own unemployed, but would also be able to take in a controlled flow of the professionally and technologically trained, the skilled and even those unskilled workers prepared to do the hard and heavy jobs. "We shall have a prosperous, thriving, multiracial Singapore. And nothing is more infectious than success. In the longer run, Singapore will be the light that radiates hope, throughout the region, for similar successes of other multiracial communities not unlike us. By example and precept, our success will influence the formulae others are seeking to transform old-fashioned communities into modern, industrialized and affluent societies.

History is a long and unending process. History bears witness to the ascendancy of the more fit and more adaptable. But no one could predict what will happen in the region. "No one knows what will be the world balance of power in the late '70s and '80s, or whose influence will prevail in Southeast Asia. But whatever happens in Southeast Asia and in the wider world beyond, we must use the time given us to grow sturdy and strong. Our people have in abundance the capacity to learn and to adjust to changing circumstances. The future belongs to the

most adaptable, the most intelligent, and the best organized. We can
be counted amongst them."

VIII

Lee Kuan Yew spoke to the employers' federation on 10 May. He
said that if the clock were switched back nine years and people in
Singapore were back in the mood they were in then, and if the occasion
were to be televised, he could have lost the last election. This was the
measure of the change in Singapore's physical and emotional environment. "We have all learnt. I have not changed my views on fundamentals. I have always believed that no man has the right to exploit his
fellow men by virtue of this possession of greater wealth or higher
status. These are fundamental beliefs.

"Unlike ten years ago, I have taken considerable opportunities to
see where theory has not been fulfilled by performance. I am a great
believer in the positivist school of logic. Never mind what the theory
is, what happens when it is put into practice? If it doesn't happen in
accordance with theory, then either the theory is wrong, or you try
again. Nine years ago, many thought the way to the great millennium
was by way of collective farms, communes, a great equalizer of a communist society where distinction is in accordance with party hierarchy
as against the property ownership. In the nine years the communist
world changed, because they also had to face the test of performance.
This has been of great advantage to us. Then during the years 1959
to 1963 we were reacting to a situation, which in part we helped to
complicate. The communists held the initiative. They sent their first
agents from Shanghai to Singapore in the year I was born—1923.
And as we went into the ground to organize the workers for a political
purpose—to get rid of British imperialism and run the place ourselves
—we crossed lines with them. How to get in charge? We combined
forces with them. It was a logical, hard-headed tactic which we knew
would land us in difficulties. But we knew what we were doing. In
1958-59 we feared that, if we made a bid for power and obtained the
right to govern, we might not be strong enough to meet communist
pressure. They were well organized, well disciplined. In the early
months of 1959 we decided that if we allowed the incipient graft and
maladministration to continue, by the time we became strong enough to
take on the communists, the administrative machine would have broken down. Then we would not have any chance at all, because unlike
the communists, we did not run a party that we could substitute for
the government and administration. So we took our chances. And
from 1959 to 1963 we reacted to communist pressures. This led to

competition at trade union level. We were conscious of what we were doing. We held it within bounds, prevented the polity from breaking and splintering, introduced innovations, the Industrial Arbitration Court, and new legislation. We tried to isolate those unions that went on political strikes, and punished them, demonstrating to their followers that political strikes did not pay. Only in 1963—after we had beaten them in the 1962 referendum and the 1963 general elections—were we in a position to sit back and reassess the situation. Unfortunately, in 1964-65 we came under heavy communal pressure, and were kept too busy to put things right.

"Now in 1968, we have no doubts in our minds what must be done, not just in the short term or in the intermediate term; but to do it in such a way that in the longer term we create a healthy equilibrium that can maintain itself indefinitely. The longer term is most important for we cannot be sure that there will be a political leadership that could assert its ascendancy and will, and implement unpleasant policies without losing the ground. This is crucial: without losing the ground ... First, let me say what we do not want: sluggish, ineffective labour, because that is ruinous, whether you are in a communist, capitalist or mixed economy. When you read articles about the state of the economy of the various nations in the world, America, Britain, France or China or Russia, they always talk about increase in production, and rise in wages, balance of payments and productivity. They never tell you about the crucial item: how good is the human digit, how hard does he work, what is his motivation, how good is the management that uses him, how hard is the organization, how up to date is the thinking, the planning and the machinery. At international conferences they use fine words about the application of science and technology to industry, but seldom about sheer sweat and elbow-grease. That is what makes Singapore work. Whatever the shortcomings, people do work. Secondly, we do not want ineffective management on an old-boy or father-to-son basis. We learn from other people's experiences. Modern management is almost a science in itself and is being taught as such in good universities. The third factor which helps us is that we have not got deep class divisions. Social mobility is half the secret of Singapore's success: from rags to riches, from riches down the ladder. When you have social mobility, then you haven't that animosity and antagonism. Looking back over the last decade, one of the reasons why the communists failed was that they worked on a class hatred which was not there.

"Let me put in a positive way what we want. First, a striving acquisitive community. You cannot have people just striving for a nebulous ideal. They must have that desire to improve, whether it is the scooter, the mini car, the flat, the fridge, the washing machine, the television set, better shoes, better clothes or better homes. You must equate rewards to performance because no two persons want to be the same. They want equal chances in order that they can show how one is better than the other. This is a fact of life, which even the communists have had to admit. The constitution of Rumania, a socialist country, says that each man shall be rewarded in accordance with what he contributes, not "to each in accordance with his needs". Next, we want forward-looking good management. The old family business is one of the problems in Singapore. It is not so with European or foreign enterprise. One of the reasons for our floating an industrial development bank is because of the sluggishness with which people change habits. They are accustomed to buying and selling. And business is kept in the family. They have done this for hundreds of years. And the idea of sinking money into an anonymous corporation run by professionals over whom they have no direct personal control is foreign to them. They are loath to make this change. So we have to accelerate this process. Business management is a professional's job and we need professionals to run our business effectively. And third, easy social mobility. One of the reasons contributing to Japanese and German recovery was that their defeated capitalists, managers, executives, engineers and their defeated workers, all suffered defeat and they were fired with a singleness of purpose: to put their country back on its feet. That made the miracle of recovery. If the Japanese worker and the German worker had felt that his job in life was to defeat his employer and deny him that profit because he was being kept one down by the employer's son going to a public school and acquiring all those graces in life which was denied the worker's son, then he was bound to go sluggish and inefficient. With these long-term aims in view, we have formulated a Bill designed to achieve certain immediate targets. But it is no use achieving these targets if we are to lose the longer-term objective.

"In the late '70s or the early '80s, a new generation will take charge: the products of our education policy. We must ensure that the political leadership will find an already institutionalized and stable system to run. It must not depend upon the accident of a prime minister who has a long association with the workers and their trade unions. It also should not depend upon the accident of just a few good trade union leaders. It must be a stability on a broader institutionalized base. Patterns of relationship between worker, employer and government, the rewards, the easy moving up of the social ladder, must be a way of life. One advantage is we are compact. There are many disadvantages of only having 224 square miles and two dozen outer islands. But one great advantage is that there is no union leader or worker that we cannot personally get into physical communication with within a matter of minutes. This makes understanding a lively and cohesive factor in policy implementation.

"In this period of industrial tranquility we must rethink our policies, and reshape our instruments to implement those policies. As of now,

442

the communist unions are absolutely inert. The initiative is with us. This may not be so in ten years' time. But if we do the right things now, in ten years' time, they will not have a chance to create mischief. What is the target? Rapid economic growth. What for? For you, higher profits. I concede that. I was happy to hear your president talk about sacrifice. But to be frank and honest, if you don't make profits, you won't be here. That is the basis on which I do my negotiations with the unions and with the employers. I want the greatest economic expansion to produce two things: a higher GNP, and so higher revenue and next more jobs. New laws will be passed. Do not believe that this is done for the benefit of just more profits. I want to ensure your profits in order that Singapore will have a good reputation, and investment accelerated, more capital, more machinery, higher economic growth, more jobs, more revenue. What we do with revenue by way of defence, education, health, social amenities to equalize opportunities is another matter. First we must have higher revenues. Any practice, any agreement which hinders this objective will have to be unscrambled.

"Employers want more profits for the purpose, I hope, of expanding their industries to make further profits. The workers must respond in the knowledge that unless this happens there will not be enough revenue, and therefore not enough security and in turn not enough further investments, and no more jobs. Our interests are different, but at least we appreciate what it is we want out of each other. You want maximum effort from the workers to produce you the goods at lowest cost which you can sell for maximum profits. The worker sometimes believes that what he wants is to give the minimum of work for the maximum of returns. However, that has been proven in many parts of the world to be ruinous for the country as a whole. And so it cannot be good for Singapore. The worker must put in the maximum effort in order to get the maximum possible in the circumstances. And what he can't get by way of direct reward in wages, we as a government will ensure that he gets by way of housing, health, education, social benefits and so on. That is the purpose of the Government.

"In the next three more months, but before this year is out, after this debate, argument and reassessment, we will reach a new pattern of relationship. If we are honest in our dealings with each other, we shall get this done. The unions are prepared to accept this because they understand that these adjustments have to be done and their advisers have told them so. I hope you understand that it is in your longer-term interest to meet this opportunity and grasp it in the spirit which will give us a more lasting solution. Remember that in ten years' time you will be dealing with a population which is 100 per cent literate and educated, and nearly all in two languages. You are going to meet a different kind of Singaporean. He will be able to talk your language of costs, profits and losses, productivity and price and wage increases. And I would consider this evening's effort worthwhile if as a result of

443

this discussion you leave more convinced that we are determined to and will make a go of this place."

IX

The many reasons why regional economic co-operation had been limited and slow were discussed by Lee Kuan Yew in a talk he gave to a group of businessmen on 12 May. He enumerated them. First, the background and the thinking of the first-generation independence leaders: the Nehrus, Jinnahs, Aung Sans, Sukarnos. Most were educated in the metropolitan centres of Europe between the two world wars and some even before the First World War. They absorbed the political thinking and philosophy of the 1920s and the 1930s. Every European metropolitan power wanted to be a self-sufficient unit unto itself. So political and economic autarchy was a goal desirable in itself. Next, modern industrial technology and what it means in massive research, and massive markets to justify the massive research, had not become so obvious. The facts of modern technology and mass production for mass markets were just beginning to dawn on the second-generation independence leaders. India was the first colony to obtain its freedom after the war. Many assumed that this huge land mass with a large population would enable it to become a second USSR. There were many reasons why this did not happen. The belief in national self-sufficiency influenced the thinking and the attitudes of a whole generation of freedom fighters. "Now, twenty-three years after World War Two, the second-generation leaders, though intellectually convinced of the need for a large base for economies of scale, are emotionally still caught by the thinking of the 1920s and the 1930s."

The Prime Minister said: "From our own limited experience we have come to the conclusion that it is best to make haste slowly. Logic and reason told us that the way for Singapore to blossom and flourish, as well as for the peoples who comprised one political and administrative unit under the British in Southeast Asia, was to hold it together as one unit. We went into Malaysia, with the promise of a common market. We never got it. Instead we were turned out. The lesson very simply is this: that there are many emotional factors unrelated to the economic realities which are too dominant. As a result of our experience, we are persuaded that our contribution to regional economic co-operation is to make haste slowly. First of all, this is Southeast Asia. It is tropical and equatorial, and before air-conditioners, there was only a half-working day. This has had its effect upon the habits of successive generations. One of the habits is not to put something by. People do not save for the winter, because there is no winter. So capital accumulation

444

is slow. When the Portuguese, Spanish, Dutch, British, French and Americans moved into this region they later brought in people who knew how to save for the winter. So the Indians went with the British into Burma. The Indians came with the British into Singapore and Malaya. The Dutch made use of the Chinese as tax collectors. And Chinese were encouraged to come to Singapore and Malaya. The Spaniards after two successive massacres of the Chinese still brought them back to the Philippines . . . We have in Singapore a fair sample of the various types in Northeast, South and Southeast Asia, and of the wider world beyond. To the untutored eye we were just so many Chinese, Indians and Malays. But not to a Singaporean. The Chinese could be classified distinctly in the past, though less so now. Hokkiens are the majority of the labourers and the small shopkeepers; the rice merchants are Teochews because they have organized the rice wholesale trade in Bangkok, and Teochews also do the textile wholesale and retail trade. The Cantonese are goldsmiths, and the Hakkas own the jewellers, pawnshops, and Chinese medicine shops. The Hainanese originally ran coffee shops but now are in charge of the whole of the catering business. So with the Indians. The Tamils are small shop-keepers and labourers. The Malayalees with a high level of education and inadequate opportunities voted in the communist state government in Kerala. They are clerks and artisans in Singapore. The Punjabis, the Sikhs, are a remarkable people. There are only about 10,000 in Singapore. But if you watch a passing out parade of our officer cadets, you might think that Singapore comprised about fifteen to twenty per cent of Sikhs, because the people with turbans are distinctive. They were brought in as burly watchmen. They turned to money-lending at keen rates of interest. They educated their children to be high court judges, surgeons, and to fill the other professions."

Lee continued: "We have Singapore Malays. To those not from this part of the world, they are all Malays. But Singaporeans know that there is a big difference between a Rhio or a Johore Malay, or a Sumatran, and between a Menangkabau and an Achinese or a Batak, all from Sumatra, a Boyanese or a Javanese. We know that the Boyanese are the most thrifty of the Malay groups. However there has been a great deal of inter-marriage within the ethnic groups. Hokkiens marry Hakkas, Teochews, Cantonese, Hainanese; the Tamils marry Malayalees, or Bengalis, or Punjabis. There is much less of those who marry across ethnic groups. But all groups have in common that desire to make good. They are migrants who have left their past behind them. They are determined to make good, and have a passion for education and learning. There is a zealous striving which did not exist in the original societies from whence they sprung. One of the problems which has worried me is the uneven rate of development within the community, because the Chinese, Indians, Ceylonese and Eurasians progress at a faster rate than our Malays. If we do not correct this imbalance then in another ten to twenty years, we will have a Harlem, something not to be proud of."

Lee said that he turned from politics to anthropology and sociology to seek the reasons for this. He was not sure whether this was the final explanation, but his tentative reading on the subject was that the cultural-ethnic factors had a decisive influence on performance. He quoted several authorities who dealt with the different cultural values of the Chinese and Singapore Malays. One said that the Singapore Chinese, on the whole, considered the acquisition of wealth to be one of the most important aims in life, almost an end in itself; they were indefatigable workers and keen businessmen. Singapore Malays, on the other hand, attached great importance to easy and graceful living.

Lee Kuan Yew said that this posed an extremely delicate problem. "We tried over the past nine years systematically to provide free education, from primary school right up to university, for any Singapore citizen who is a Malay. This we don't give to the majority ethnic group—the Chinese. They pay fees from secondary school onwards. We don't find it necessary to do it for the other ethnic minorities, because, broadly speaking, they are making similar progress as the Chinese. All are achievement-oriented, striving, acquisitive communities. The reluctant conclusion that we have come to after a decade of the free education policy is that learning does not begin in school. It starts in the home with the parents and the other members of the family. Certainly the adoption of values comes more from the home, the mother, than from the teacher. This means change will be a slow process. It can be accelerated in some cases by our judicious intermingling of the communities so that, thrown into a more multiracial milieu we have in our new housing estates, Malay children are becoming more competitive and more striving."

The Prime Minister asked the businessmen: "What does this kind of Singapore portend for Southeast Asia? Naturally, we would like to play our part, whether like a sparking plug or little dynamo, to help light up the surrounding area. Self-interest tells us that if our neighbours progress, the higher the purchasing power, the greater their economic growth, the better the spin-off for us. But at the same time I make one reservation, that the converse is not necessarily true. We don't have to go down. This is a fundamental point that must be recognized, and we have not the slightest intention of going down. You are hard-headed entrepreneurs and executives who have skill, enterprise and capital. You are not going to screw machinery into the ground just for purposes of charity. If you get this message across that all in this region can modernize their societies, that they can open up their windows and get fresh air to blow through bringing in that verve, vitality and vigour which new ideas and methods bring, then the future will be that much more comfortable for them."

X

Mrs Indira Gandhi, the Prime Minister of India, paid an official visit to the Republic in May. At a state banquet given in her honour on 19 May, the Prime Minister said that Mrs Gandhi was the head of a Government which represented a people who had given Singapore "a part of ourselves and more than a part our inspiration". He recounted some of the things that Singapore had borrowed, and for which Singapore was indebted to India, First, *Singapura* was a celebrated Sanskrit name. Next, Singapore's earliest public works and monuments were built by Indian labour and skills, albeit forcibly brought here by the British Raj. One hundred and forty-six years ago the British brought Indian convicts to build Government House, "where you are now staying. And woven into the fabric of Singapore society are many strands that come from India, mainly from the south, Madras and Kerala, but more than a few silken threads from Bengal, Punjab, Sindh and Bombay."

Lee Kuan Yew said that Singapore had been the confluence of three great Asian civilizations brought together under the aegis of a great European civilization. Here the British brought together the Chinese, the Indians and the Malays. The British had a few schools to produce English-speaking clerks and junior staff but otherwise the different ethnic groups were left to tend to their own languages and cultures. "By the time we achieved political power, we found our society permanently encrusted with several languages and their literatures —literature which carry memories of past glory, some history, part mythology. No community was willing to give up its rightful heritage, although all agreed that it was necessary to find a common ground. So about a decade ago, despite all the inevitable complications and tiresome duplications of multilingual and multicultural education, we allowed free choice and free competition to establish the common denominators. Every parent could and can choose whether to send his child to an English, Chinese, Malay, or Tamil medium government school. For these are our four official languages. Whichever school a child goes to, he or she is tutored in two languages, one of which must be the mother tongue. Now by common experience we find it convenient to continue English as the language of administration and as the channel into the scientific and technological era we hope to break into."

The Prime Minister said that without the contribution that Singapore had had from India, her rich and enduring past, her sagacious and enterprising people, Singapore would have been that much the poorer. For it was the continuous inflow of fresh blood that brought the stimulus of fresh ideas. These contributed to the verve of a busy trading, and now manufacturing, transportation and communications centre. "We have not kept everything of the old. You may find Singapore Indians look like Indians, speak like Indians, but those who were born and educated here, as you get to know them, you will find are no longer Indians. Caste and customs, rituals and taboos which inhibit innovation and modernization have been discarded under pressure of competing influence from other cultural and value patterns and religions, all seeking pre-eminence in the context of modernity. So too with the Chinese. We look Chinese. We speak Chinese. But if a man from China speaks to a Singapore Chinese, he will discover that the Singaporean is already a distinct and different type."

Lee Kuan Yew said that Mrs Gandhi had come to visit Singapore on the eve of momentous changes about to take place in the region. These changes India initiated when she achieved independence in 1947. The peoples of Asia wanted to be rid of Western domination. India's leaders played a consistent and significant role in influencing world opinion which in turn settled the mood and policies of the imperial powers of Europe. The earlier liberation of Asia and Africa was in large measure due to India. "Only recently we were all subject peoples of European empires. We now find, however, that our hopes of universal brotherhood among fellow Asians have faded as old feuds are resumed, and new ones are pursued. Worse, the traditional buffers to conflict between nations—the oceans, rivers, mountains, desert and jungle—are no longer impenetrable to armies equipped with modern means of transportation. Now over two decades later we have to adjust and adapt ourselves to the post-colonial era as we search for security and economic progress in rapidly changing conditions. There can be no going back to *status quo ante*. Whatever might have existed before the West came, Asia has to live with the present, irrevocably altered, after four centuries of Western domination. Like India, we are going through similar difficulties in modernizing and educating our multiracial, multilingual population into the secular values of a modern nation state. Like India, in the past decade, we have had many difficulties and some successes."

Singapore had had long trade ties with India. "But the pattern of economic relationship is altering as we proceed with our industrialization plans. We welcome India's participation in these industrial projects. For nothing reinforces sentiment and friendship better than bilateral economic advantages. We would like to multiply these ties to mutual advantage. It is the future that consumes all our attention and energy, as we seek continuing security and stability that will enable us to forge ahead with our economic and social plans."

Lee Kuan Yew referred to the recent visit of a flotilla from the Indian Navy. He hoped it was the first of many visits. "Our harbour will always be a friendly haven for Indian naval units. Placed as we are with one avenue looking westwards into the Indian Ocean and the other eastwards into the Pacific, not unnaturally we feel more relaxed and comfortable when there is no oppressive and overpowering hegemony by any single power."

XI

A month later, John Gorton, Prime Minister of Australia, visited Singapore. At a state banquet in his honour on 10 June, the Prime Minister spoke of changing times. Two hundred years ago, he said, there were no Australians or Singaporeans as they are known today. What had happened in between had irrevocably altered the physical and demographic landscape. Australia would not revert to the bush, nor would her great cities or her farms in the outback vanish. "And we are sanguine enough to believe that Singapore will not go back to the mud flats and the fishing village from whence she grew. What has happened is part of the history of man, his conquest of nature. Man's inventive capacity to improve means of transportation and communications has enabled him to migrate more and more freely over the face of this earth, and to take advantage of the scientific and industrial knowledge of the time to build a better life for himself. Britain was one of the greatest maritime powers, and the journeyings of the British have incidentally helped to create modern Australia and modern Singapore. Now Britain has served notice that she will soon withdraw her immediate presence. Hence the increased dialogue, as we all re-examine and reassess what this will mean to each of us."

Lee Kuan Yew said he had always found Australians a bluff and blunt people, characteristics he found agreeable. "I would not expect of you anything other than a hard-headed appraisal of where Australian interests lie. Your decisions may in some measure help to determine whether this area will subside from turbulence to stability. If, after a careful scrutiny of all the conceivable hazards, your Government decides that Australia's national interest is better served by considering the Singapore-Malaysia area as part of your neighbourhood, then you will find us a practical and realistic people to work with. And your association with us will be that much the more agreeable because, of the countries in the region, you may find us one of the not so difficult to understand. Like you, we are the result of a British maritime tradition. Like you, we have migrated into the region and built up through our own efforts and sheer hard work a higher level of life and living than ever existed before we came. Like you, having left behind a culturally richer and an emotionally more secure past, we are determined to secure and to enrich the future for our children.

"This is a crucial period in the history of the region. The decisions that you and other leaders in the region will be making will shape the course of events as irreversibly as what has gone before. There are doubts and uncertainties. What is to happen in Vietnam? Will it be decided in Paris? Who is to be the next American President to make the massive decisions on what his administration conceives as American interests on this side of the Pacific? To what lengths is he prepared to

go in furtherance of those interests? For the moment, these are imponderables. So perhaps it is best that we maintain our present postures
and positions and so keep all options open. It is not for ordinary
mortals to read the future. And since like Australia, the Singapore
Government has no vote for soothsayers in its budget, we can only
carefully test and probe our way forward. Needless to say, we welcome
partners to help ensure stability and security, without which constructive
or meaningful endeavour is not possible. If we could consolidate this
area of relative stability where economic and social progress is being
made, then we can slowly extend the boundaries of the area through
economic co-operation, so that the well-being and prosperity of all in
the region is advanced. Then peace in the area will be that much the
more enduring."

Lee hoped that over the years they could build up an understanding
and mutual confidence "for this could make a contribution to the rational
growth and development of a not unimportant sector of the world".

XII

On 9 July, the Prime Minister made public a message which he sent to
the Singapore Bank Employees' Union which was making demands
upon employers. It read as follows: "The recent unrest in France has
highlighted the price a whole nation has to pay when a section of the
community goes on the rampage. It started off with students demonstrating. Then workers stopped production. Finally, and fortunately,
a showdown came in general elections within the constitution. Meanwhile, French gold and foreign exchange reserves went down by a
reported US$1,500 million to US$2,000 million out of over US$7,000
million gold and foreign exchange reserves. The franc came under
pressure. So now foreign exchange controls, import restrictions, export
subsidies and all the paraphernalia of bureaucratic controls have to be
introduced to maintain the exchange rate of the franc.

"Though circumstances are different, the British pound in spite
of devaluation, has not made the recovery everyone expected it to have
made. The pound is still under pressure, hitting new lows. It is
because, amongst other things, British trade unions have put their
sectional interest first. A whole motor-car industry came to a halt because
a few hundred women demanding equal pay went on strike and eventually held up millions of pounds of export orders. BOAC pilots went
on strike. Railway workers went on a go-slow. Hence international
bankers, financiers and, thus, their customers, generally doubted the
future of the pound. Now a new loan scheme by Western and European central bankers is being negotiated to secure the pound against

450

the tendency to withdrawal of sterling reserves by holder countries.

"We must learn from the lessons of contemporary history. We enter the 1970s in the full knowledge that unless we have in ourselves the capacity for self-discipline and sustained effort to make the grade, we shall be down on our knees. Once down we shall have to crawl around on all fours for a long time. The closure of the British bases only underlines the urgent need for our trade unionists and workers to face the facts of life. All the hidden benefits, which so easily add to the cost of labour when they are abused, must be exorcised. Our workers must be keen and productive, giving of their best for the wage agreed. Every union leader I have spoken to agrees that this must be so—except when it comes to his union making the sacrifice. Either we learn to think in terms of the national interest instead of sectional interest or we are in trouble.

"I trust the Bank Employees' Union leaders agree that my recent discussions with them are worth repeating to their members both privately and publicly. The past, our successes and excesses are over and done with. The future can be won with quiet and determined implementation of our already outlined policies for accelerated economic growth. In this success our workers must make their contribution."

XIII

"One of the reasons why we called earlier general elections", explained the Prime Minister, speaking on the important Employment Bill, on 15 July, "was because we have to adjust our plans to meet the military and economic consequences of the British Government's decision to withdraw from her bases in Singapore and Malaysia, by the end of 1971. The overall objective is simple: to attract expertise, know-how, enterprise and capital, to use Singapore's domestic capital and her workers to greater advantage in the manufacturing, assembling and servicing sectors. We must also stimulate expansion of existing industries and enterprises and encourage them to new lines of business, all with the accent on export. We must get our young men and women trained and skilled in the techniques of modern industry, so that the quality and costs of our products are competitive on the export markets. This will increase the GNP to give us a higher standard of living, and to pay for the ever increasing cost of our own defence.

"There are ample funds in Singapore as every banker will tell. Every sound share issue put on the market has been oversubscribed sometimes by four and more times. But until we have enough industrial expertise, managerial talent and export promotion know-how, this capital will not be used effectively to give meaningful jobs to our ever

451

increasing numbers of educated but not technically trained workers."

Lee argued that Singapore's gross national product could treble "if our two million people were made up of people from the highly developed countries, like workers from Japan with their intensity of purpose and high skills, technicians and engineers from Germany with their efficient and specialized apprenticeship training, scientists and technologists from Britain with their sophistication and imaginative research, and executives from America with their well-developed disciplines in business administration and management and their hard-sell approaches". Such a two-million population would not be just repairing ships. They would be building ships. They would be running their own merchant fleets like the Norwegians, and their own deep-sea fishing fleets like the Japanese. They would be running a fully fledged, round-the-world international airline. They would be a centre for the maintenance of airframes and aircraft engines in the region. They would be a centre for computers and computer servicing in the region. The problem therefore was how to educate and train Singaporeans to reach the standards of these technologically advanced peoples as quickly as possible. "First we must ask if our people have it in them, for otherwise this will be a vain and futile exercise. From the record of the past nine years since we started to manage our own affairs, I believe nearly all our people have got the stuffing in them to make the grade. What they need are the opportunities and the training. One way to educate our young people to higher degrees of technical skill is to send them abroad. But this is only for a few, since it is costly. The more practical, economical and productive way is to import outside expertise to manufacture or assemble, or set up the servicing organizations for which there is a demand. With inservice training, our workers will develop higher and higher skills ... We must put to maximum advantage the capacity of our workers for intense effort and rapid acquisition of skills ... the final performance depends upon the ability, stamina, skills, knowledge, expertise and discipline of our population."

There were testing times ahead. Details of the British withdrawal plans had been revealed. They showed an ever increasing rate of redundancy of local civilian workers and repatriation of British uniformed personnel. The heaviest blow would fall in 1971. From the experience of the Economic Development Board it was known that it took two to three years from first discussions on a project, through its planning and construction stages, to the first production. Therefore, unless manufacturers were attracted to Singapore now, there would be neither the factories nor the jobs in 1970, '71 and '72 when the pressure of unemployment would be heaviest. The first major task of the new Parliament was to carry through the series of legislative amendments that would put the working population into trim. Lee described it as "a package which is fair and attractive". The amendments were designed to make everyone put in a greater effort for the higher performance to

452

bring in higher rewards and with the home-ownership scheme for the mass of workers and not only for the higher salaried groups, more and more of the working population would have a growing personal stake in the continuing prosperity and stability of the society.

There were some enterprises that could profitably work round the clock for every day of the 365 days in the year. They should do so. The harbour, the dockyards, the airports, and some factories, whose export orders make this worthwhile, would do this. "We must cut out unnecessary stoppages of work. Over the years, each cultural and religious group had holidays added onto the annual list. We were well on the way to having the highest number of public holidays per year for office workers in Asia. Now we shall go back to eleven public holidays a year which is what it has always been for industrial workers. In the essential services work will carry on, holidays and Sundays notwithstanding, providing more jobs for our unemployed. Singapore will be kept clean and green. Shops and restaurants can open on Sundays and public holidays—the whole year round if they find it profitable—so that they can better cater for their customers or for tourists. But workers will get one rest day per week, and double pay for a public holiday if the employer wants them to work. But if it is the employee who wants to work on a public holiday then he gets only single pay."

The Prime Minister stressed that the assumptions made in the '50s and '60s by the trade unions and their advisers, "of whom I was one", were that the workers wanted more leisure to enjoy their pay. These assumptions were based on British practices "which were and are completely irrelevant to our social conditions. Our workers want work, and more money for more work—not more leisure to spend the inadequate sums they earn." Lee said that for the vast majority of workers, over three-quarters of whom were not in any unions at all, the new legislation meant an improvement in their working conditions. It was only the minority, less than one-tenth of the work force, the better unionized clerical groups, who would have to make some adjustments in their working hours per week before being entitled to overtime. This was a helpful change for it would bring blue-collar workers into line with the white-collar workers. "And we need more blue- and less white-collar workers. This is a legacy of the education policies of the past when it was never envisaged that we would be other than a dependent people assisting in the lower ranks of a trading and administrative capital of one part of a vast empire."

The Prime Minister emphasized that *nobody would lose either in wages or fringe benefits. All existing agreements between unions and employers would continue until they expired.* But when these agreements expired, unless new jobs had been created, the redundancies that were taking place, plus the annual inflow into the labour market from the schools, would alter the supply and demand situation and determine the wages and other benefits to be renegotiated. So unions and their members had a vested interest in helping to create conditions under which more industries and enterprises were established creating a greater demand for workers. "We are also checking the tendency to increase labour costs, not by increases but by fringe benefits, hidden costs which can be easily abused, like casual sick leave which is taken whenever workers feel like a day off, often when they are not sick."

But the Government had *not* attempted to regulate agreements between unions and employers on the wages to be paid. Maximum or minimum wage levels had not been fixed. That wage would depend upon what a particular industry or enterprise could afford, taking into consideration the rate for the job, the performance of a particular company's workers and the profits of that enterprise. *In other words, with less hidden benefits and more open rewards, with higher incentives for higher performance when industries and enterprises prosper, so wages would go up. So would bonuses.* Legislation was also designed to help improve management discipline and establish a sensible relationship between unions and management.

It went without saying, Lee argued, that as new and better management techniques were introduced by subsidiaries of the large industrial concerns who go into partnership with Singapore citizens, so Singapore's own established enterprises must modernize and improve work methods, machinery, and organization for increased productivity, or they would go under.

The Prime Minister admitted that in the early stages of the labour movement, the trade union often became a place of refuge for the inefficient, the slack, the lazy and the antisocial. As happened elsewhere, these people were the first to join the union to seek protection against the natural tendency of any employer to be rid of bad workers. "When some Russian trade unionists were in Singapore several months ago they told our union leaders that Russian trade unionists report to and require of management the dismissal of inefficient workers and thereby increase productivity. I am not asking our union leaders, in an open society, to take on the role of management. But I do urge them, with the help of these new laws, to stop giving cover to those who do not pull their weight. *We must avoid slipping into a situation where trade unionism is the practice of protecting the weakest and the slowest worker and, with everybody being paid the same wage, no worker will have any incentive to work harder than the weakest and the slowest.*"

But just as there were bad workers, so too there were bad employers. From his discussions with the various employers' associations and chambers of commerce, the Prime Minister said it was clear that the old-fashioned, family-type businessman had no conception of the wider and longer-term relationships between management and labour in an age of educated and organized workers who were conscious of their indispensable role in the production of the wealth of the whole community. These employers would have to be educated and taught the facts of present-day industrial life. "We call upon everyone for improvement and effort. This is our duty as a government. No one is asked to sacrifice for the benefit of the privileged and the corrupt, nor will revenue go in wasteful and extravagant expenditure. With higher performance and greater output, there will be more industries, and more jobs, better trained artisans, technicians, engineers, and executives. From the higher GNP will come greater revenue. From this revenue will flow improved standards of education, health services, social amenities, and housing for all." Lee Kuan Yew said the Government did not expect workers to put in more effort for nothing. Employers would have to contribute more to the Central Provident Fund. "As a government", concluded the Prime Minister, "we shall be judged by results. These results depend, among other things, upon the morale and enthusiasm of the people, and the pace set by their leaders in the House and outside. If we were a soft community, then the temptation would be to leave things as they are, and hope for the best. Then, only good fortune can save us from unpleasantness which will be ahead. But we are not an easy-going people. We cannot help thinking, calculating and planning for tomorrow, for next year, for the next decade, for the next generation. And it is because we have restless minds, forever probing and testing, seeking new and better solutions to old and new problems, that we have never been, and I trust never shall be, tried and found wanting."

XIV

On 8 August, the eve of National Day, the Prime Minister, in his address to the nation, referring to the years of independence, said that they had been three remarkable years. "On our own, we have done better than in any three previous years of our history. The performance improved each year. They reflect the success of a community where high performance is admired and rewarded.

"In the past twelve months, industrial output went up 21 per cent, domestic exports up 7 per cent; external trade up 9 per cent; cargo handled up 15 per cent; income tax, at the same rates as last year's, up by 15 per cent; revenue from property tax up 7 per cent, liquor up 8 per cent, tobacco up 12 per cent. Public housing and construction up 16 per cent—14,500 units in the past 12 months, or 1 unit every 36 minutes; private construction up 27 per cent. Bank deposits as of June this year, against June last year, up 31 per cent. Ninety-four per cent of the total old currency circulating in Singapore, Malaysia and Brunei have been redeemed. We have got over 35 per cent of this,

455

namely 460 million Singapore dollars. Our rate of economic growth (increase in GNP) has exceeded 9 per cent per annum for the past three years. The natural population increase in 1967 was 2.1 per cent and will probably go down to about 1.6 per cent per annum. With economic growth kept above 9 per cent per annum, this means ever rising standards."

"You may ask", continued the Prime Minister, "why then this tighter work discipline? Why this insistence on higher productivity? Why the new Employment Bill? The answer is: because we are looking ahead into 1971 and beyond. We must accelerate our economic growth to meet the growing redundancies and the full cut of British service expenditure in the final phases of the rundown. Our main problem has been, and will continue to be, large unemployment in spite of favourable economic growth. Despite a growth rate of over 9 per cent last year, the number of new jobs in the industrial sector increased by only 5,700 compared with 5,200 the year before. We require at least 10,000 new jobs in industry to absorb our annual school leavers. In other words, the rate of expansion of industry must be doubled. And we have also to absorb the present heavy unemployment. 69,000 persons are registered with the Employment Exchange.

"We must encourage a growing inflow of capital and expertise. Industries will increase and expand if we combine the political stability we have with healthy and keen labour conditions. In 1961, seven years ago, we had 116 strikes and we lost 420,000 man-days. Last year, 1967, we had only 10 strikes, and a loss of 41,000 man-days, 10 per cent of the 1961 loss. This year, 1968 we have had only 2 strikes and a loss of only 700 man-days. Because of the changes we have made in the Port of Singapore Authority, cutting out excessive overtime and introducing a third shift to work round the clock, we have given jobs to over 500 citizens, an increase of 10 per cent in the wharf cargo work force. And the third shift has improved the economic attractiveness for ships calling on Singapore. So with Keppel Dockyard. Instead of one shift with excessive overtime, we shall be working two shifts. This will give jobs to 300 citizens to start with. Later, we may go on to a third shift. And in the public health division we shall give several hundreds of jobs by working in shifts right round the whole year, Sundays and public holidays included."

But more significant were the changed attitudes, and the positive outlook of the people. Singapore used to be a conglomeration of migrants with an each-man-for-himself attitude. If he cared for anybody else at all, it was for his own immediate family. Singaporeans now, particularly those born and educated there, were aware that personal survival was not enough. "What we have can be preserved only if we together defend the integrity of our country and secure the interests of the whole community."

The Prime Minister pointed out that a new generation was growing up, more united, better educated, and emotionally and psychologically prepared and equipped to meet the challenge of their time. "You can see them in the schools. You can see them in the younger students at our universities. You can see them in our completely multiracial National Service training centres. They are a different breed, self-reliant, bouncing with confidence, eager to learn, willing to work. They expect nothing for free. And there will be leaders amongst them able and strong enough to take the torch from us and to carry it forward to light up their future."

XV

What is a Singaporean? The Prime Minister discussed this question on 7 September. He said that all new countries faced the grave problem of identity, for they invariably embraced more than one race or tribe within the boundaries which they had inherited from a colonial power. "We ask ourselves: what is a Singaporean? In the first place, we did not want to be Singaporeans. We wanted to be Malayans. Then the idea was extended and we decided to become Malaysians. But twenty-three months of Malaysia—a traumatic experience for all parties in Malaysia—ended rather abruptly with our being Singaporeans. By legal definition the Singaporean is a citizen of Singapore. Under our citizenship legislation you will find various categories by which one becomes a citizen. A person born here in the pre-Malaysia days automatically became a Singapore citizen. Now he has to be born here with one parent at least a citizen. Why? Because we have so many non-citizens living and working here who may or may not belong, or want to belong. Then there are those who have resided here for more than ten years and can acquire citizenship. Then wives and children of such people, and so on. But my colleagues and I know that whilst this may be the legal definition, the acid test of who is a Singaporean is whether the person is so committed to Singapore that he is prepared to stand up and fight for Singapore. And emotive definition, a qualitative not quantitative test, of a Singaporean, is: a person who either by birth and upbringing or residence in Singapore feels commited to upholding this society as it is—multiracial, tolerant, accommodating, forward-looking—and prepared to stake his life for this community."

Lee said that strange though may seem, some of the people most willing to stake their lives for Singapore were those born and brought up outside Singapore and who had settled here. This was probably because they knew how unpleasant life could be in other societies neither tolerant nor accommodating. These were the people most prepared to fight for

457

Singapore, for a multiracial community that offered them a place under the sun.

What were the characteristics of a Singaporean? Lee Kuan Yew said these were difficult to define. "For it would be dishonest to say that the person who put one dollar on a scrap of paper in 1957-58 has acquired all the attributes that we require of him. But we already have a hard-core of people who know exactly what kind of attributes the Singaporean must have if he is to protect our collective interests. Whether we leave that impress, and build in the responses of group survival into the next generation, will depend upon how successful our schools transmit and nurture these attributes.

Schools like St Andrew's (the Prime Minister was speaking to a reunion of St Andrew Old Boys) made a contribution. So too now were schools as different from St Andrew's as the Chinese High School, or the Chung Cheng or Catholic High. These schools used to produce completely different types. "If we are to succeed in gelling the various ethnic, linguistic and cultural groups into a uniform distinctiveness, separate from the rest of Southeast Asia, then they must inculcate the same basic values and attitudes to life and proficiency in a common language. With the end of empires, new political elites emerge. Ethnic, religious, linguistic pulls become divisive when the levelling influence of superior authority is removed. A jostle takes place for ascendancy between the different ethnic, religious and linguistic groups. If you have the one-man-one-vote system, then the temptation to get votes on the basis of ethnic, linguistic or religious loyalties often becomes irresistible. And so the relentless process of economic decline sets in, because productive digits brought together to co-operate and complement each other under one authority are dislodged and disrupted in a contest for political ascendancy between the diverse groups."

Lee Kuan Yew said that one of the reasons for Singapore's relative success was that there had been no pretence that there were no differences in ethnic, linguistic or religious pulls and loyalties. "But having admitted these distinctions, we go on to provide each with his place under the sun in an open, competitive society, whilst ensuring that the collective group interests of all is not jeopardized by any sectional selfishness."

Lee congratulated the mission schools, including the Anglican Mission, for having adjusted and adapted to the changing political situation. They would continue to have a benevolent influence on the society. "It is a leavening influence, the opening in the minds of our young of more windows into other worlds—one of the factors for the thrusting, vigorous, forward-looking society we have. I am not a prophet. I do not know whether the process we have started will continue and progress uninterrupted into the end of the twentieth century. There are many extraneous factors which may decide the ultimate result. But of one thing I have no doubt—that whatever the vicissitudes of fate and fortune, the future favours those who are determined and firm enough to assert and secure their right to be here. If by the year 2000, St Andrew's School is still known by the same name, then the Singaporean has already been clearly defined—a fair percentage of Chinese ethnic descent, a good mixture of Indians, Ceylonese, Eurasians, Malays and others; each with a lifeline to his cultural and linguistic past and so some ballast in the traditional values of his own cultural heritage, but all seeking the widest common area of understanding in language, in values, in emotional attitudes, and most important in a common and undivided loyalty to the integrity of a society which affords them the maximum of personal freedom of choice compatible with the maximum of equal opportunities for economic advancement and fulfilment."

XVI

With the University of Singapore Democratic Socialist Club on 23 September the Prime Minister discussed "an Exercise in Political and Economic Modernization". He said that for most new countries, the transition from governor's rule to rule by elected legislature with elected cabinet ministers took less than twelve years. Then, in less than half that time, many countries changed over to presidential rule. Nowhere in Asia or Africa, except in Ceylon, had there been a complete circuit, where power was handed over from a constitutionally elected government to a constitutionally elected opposition and then back again. In the process, stresses and strains did considerable damage to the economy and the social fabric of Ceylon. In Sierra Leone, there had been a transfer of power to an opposition which won an election but only after two military *coups*. In India, Kerala once voted in a communist government. But Kerala was not sovereign, and power was handed over at a subsidiary level. Sovereignty resided in the Indian Union based in Delhi. Congress, the party that won independence, was still the Government. The exercise of representative government was not easy to sustain, not even, it was still feared by some, in Western European nations like Germany. "Even in France, a few months ago, there were again doubts."

For new countries, there were the added problems of making the inherited political system practicable and meaningful within the context of local conditions. The electorate must be politically educated, and must understand the economics of its national life. And most important in plural societies, contending political groups must be willing to mute the divisive pulls of race, language and religion. In some countries, like Singapore, the government must be able to devise safeguards which could prevent a communist party from using the rules of the

459

game to break the game itself. One of the communist methods was to operate within the rules of freedom of speech, freedom of assembly and freedom of political demonstration and participation, in order to break down the established order and, if possible, to attain authority through the process. But once in power the communists never handed over power by the process through which they were allowed to come into power.

The most difficult of all the problems was how to adapt, adjust and amend the system that was inherited from the British to meet changing circumstances. Even if the forms had to be altered, "we must try to maintain and uphold the fundamentals, namely, government by free choice of a people, by secret ballot, at periodic intervals". To do this successfully, there must be a sufficient sense of responsibility and self-discipline in the ruling party so that they kept up reasonable standards of administration and public finance, and could hand over a working administration to whoever subsequently commanded an electoral majority. "For many, like us, it is a test whether a nation state can exist within the boundaries of a former colony. Can a cohesive society, with group loyalties and group discipline, be moulded out of the various ethnic, linguistic and cultural groups, brought into one economic and political unity by an overriding European power?"

Lee said that nearly every transfer of power from European colonial governors to indigenous popular leaders had been accompanied by an economic decline. There were certain common factors which caused this. The new political leaders fought for and obtained power on the basis of indigenous ethnic nationalism. They then had to maintain economic unity and social order. But former colonial administrations, to better develop natural resources, had brought together different racial groups with complementary skills, expertise, managerial and professional talent to supplement and help colonial administrators and entrepreneurs, and so better develop the economy. In the course of decades, sometimes centuries, of colonial rule, originally primitive and backward economies were developed through technological, professional administrative expertise provided by Europeans, dependent at intermediate levels on non-European immigrant skills and labour. The Indians followed the British west to Africa and east to Burma and Malaya. They provided an intermediate group of entrepreneur skills and junior administrative talent and disciplined labour. Meanwhile, indigenous nationalist leaders, in order to wrest power, expounded to their followers the proposition that they were economically and socially down because they were being kept down. They promised that when political power was won, they, the leaders, would displace not only the European administrators, but all the intermediate non-indigenous groups and place their indigenous followers in economically and socially superior positions. Often this happened regardless of economic realities, with disastrous results. In Burma, as the Indians departed, the economy was affected. If the

Kenyans pursue their Africanization policy to its logical conclusion, displacing Indian professionals and shopkeepers, their economy must decline, unless the Kenyan people had exceptional qualities which could telescope two or three generations of the educational process into five or ten years.

Meanwhile, the whole pattern of world trade between the developed countries themselves, and between the developed and under-developed countries was undergoing constant change. This, more than any other single factor, was the cause for post-independence revolutions and upheavals. Preconceived ideas of what a political nationalist leadership could do to give the good life to its followers made things worse for the new nations. They tried to do what the colonial power had been seen doing, without understanding that different social values, attitudes and motivation (an achievement-oriented cultural pattern) must be inculcated into a people to equip them for the process of modernization.

At the same time, the developed countries between themselves had undergone a fantastic transformation into post-industrial society, into the age of computers, electronics and nuclear and space science. Economies of scale of modern technology gave the advantage to the vast continental land mass with good communications, vast populations of 200 million and above, all brought within one framework. "They, and it seems only they, can reach out for the moon and the stars."

Lee Kuan Yew said that the new post-industrial society trapped the commodity (raw material) producer. If the price of raw materials was low, the new countries would not get enough foreign exchange to buy the essentials for development. If it was too high, the advanced countries would turn to synthetics or devise ways of doing away with their dependence on expensive raw materials. So many popular beliefs were being exploded. One of them was that there is no difference in the capacity and intelligence of all human beings whatever the race; that all the differences in performance between ethnic, cultural, linguistic groups could be removed by giving equal opportunities for education and training. "This is true only up to a limited point. First, because we are dealing with people in the mass. Second, because it is a slow and painful process to catch up with the educational and technological levels of another society. There are fair numbers of black African students who have gone to universities in Britain and in France and done well. But this is a far cry from demonstrating that countries with low cultural levels have the capacity for group discipline, sustained application, high skills, intense concentration, all necessary for transforming a tribal rural community into a modern industrial community. The process, if properly and intelligently entered into, might take one, two or more decades. But unless intelligently attacked, it may take three or more generations, with disastrous consequences in the meantime on administrative efficacy, planning and economic development. To make full use of their natural and human resources for economic growth,

461

these new countries must be able to induce outside skills and expertise, scientists, technologists, managers and administrators, to come and help as catalysts in economic development. This depends upon the capacity of the political leadership in the new countries to create conditions which make it politically possible for them to employ such experts and professional digits, and upon the attractiveness of these new countries to these experts."

But instead of peaceful conditions and rational development, most new countries revived old feuds, or made new enemies. This led to rapid and costly expansion of their armed forces, and the build-up of an officer cadre with no tradition of constitutional government and acceptance of political leadership. Hence, the large numbers of generals now installed as presidents or revolutionary councils in Afro-Asia.

What is of special relevance to Singapore? "First, unlike most new countries, we have no rural base. Therefore, any economic decline, either because of political or social unrest, will be swift and spectacular. It will not be like the Indonesian way, where after over twenty years of misgovernment and mismanagement, most of the people can still live off the ground. However, the advantage Singapore has is the exact mirror image of this weakness, namely that we have no backward rural population, hidebound with superstition, religious practices and inhibited by traditional work methods. Instead, we have a compact, well-educated urban community, a migrant society keen on high performance, spurred on by the prospect of high rewards. That, combined with good administration and a sound infrastructure of harbours, airports, roads, banking and finance, makes rapid growth more than probable. And when man for man, skill for skill, enterprise for enterprise, the population is more than equal to any competition from the area, progress is likely to be rapid.

"The final factor, which gives the gloss on this human advantage, is the geographic location. We occupy the southernmost tip of the Asian continent, and this gives a competitive edge to a large range of our services and manufactures. But this exercise in political and economic modernization, representative government, the gelling of the community into a cohesive group with the capacity to think and act corporately and in unison, can only succeed if there is a strong streak of dedication and realism underlying our thinking and planning. Singapore needs to expand her economy rapidly enough to match the ambitions of a young and better educated population. From the very top, down to the lower echelons, every person invested with authority, whether in the Government or in a government agency, or in functional or professional organizations, or in the universities, must have that awareness that power is being exercised in the interests of a whole community, not of a few persons or sections of the population. In other words, there must be that capacity to make decisions other than on personal or sectional interests. Our young needs to be fired by idealism. But behind all the idealism there must be an awareness of the practicability of policies. It must never be forgotten that, whatever the declarations of human rights, whatever the ideals in any given situation, whatever the FAO or UNESCO can tell you about how many calories, what minerals, which vitamins, you ought to have every day, nobody tells you who is responsible for giving you two solid meals a day. Never forget that for each grain of rice you consume, you need foreign exchange, which brings us back to our balance of payments. This brings us back to the strength of the Singapore dollar, and this in turn brings us to the verve and vitality of our economy, to the need for high performance."

XVII

"If I had to be born a girl in Asia, where would I choose to be born?" Lee Kuan Yew posed this question during a speech at the tenth anniversary of the Eusoff College, Singapore University, on 5 October. He said that he would choose Singapore for two reasons. First in nearly all the other countries in Asia there were patriarchal societies where male ascendency was so complete that the female was almost an atrophied social version of the male. Next, they were mostly polygamous societies.

There were also other advantages for women in Singapore. "Ours is a society where the weight of tradition is least stifling and the debris of history can be more easily sloughed off. When the traditional social fabric of old societies do not offer the woman an equal place, it is extremely difficult to change this quickly. This is true not only of the unindustrialized Asian nations. It is true also of the Japanese. They are a highly industrialized nation. But the process of modernization has not altered the social relationships between their males and females. Then, as a centre of communications, exposed to almost all contemporary thinking via the newspaper, the cinema, the television screen, the contacts with visiting men and women and new ideas, our society is stimulated by what has been and is happening in all the main centres of human civilization. So we are the better prepared to meet the challenge of the modern world."

There were very few countries where women had equal educational opportunities, equal job opportunities, and equal pay. Singapore women paid separate income tax on their earned income. Recently when government servants had their salaries and salary scale revised, the Government decided that it would convert all women officers, like the men, to the new salary scales as if they were married with children. Now women in the government service had an advantage over the men — the men cannot have full-pay maternity leave. Lee Kuan Yew

463

wondered whether this would tend in the long run to leave most women graduates in the government service, as the private sector shied off the equal pay plus maternity benefit given to women.

What would happen in the next generation? What quality of men or women would they be? Much depended on what genetic qualities there were in the present generation. "I found when visiting our schools that most of the children in the not-so-good schools have brothers and sisters by the dozen, but in the better schools, children of educated parents have only one, or two or three in the family. So unless the better-educated and better-equipped stake out a bigger part of the future for their progeny, then the future will be that much the poorer for all. Educational experts, psychologists and physiologists agree that education begins almost from the day the mother communicates with the child, not from the day the child goes to kindergarten or school. There is a very big difference between having an educated and an uneducated mother."

Lee Kuan Yew held that there were almost no substitutes for the nurturing and nourishing which a child received from his or her parents, principally the mother. So he rejoiced when he read that nearly fifty per cent of Singapore's university undergraduates were women. For this augured well for the next generation. Later on, there would be other problems, such as the conflict between the home and work. The creche and kindergarten were inadequate substitutes for the home. "Perhaps we shall have to learn, like the advanced societies, that the investment a country puts into its women does not give the same kind of returns one expects to get from male citizens. For five to seven years after marriage there may be a hiatus in the economic returns as the woman devotes most of her time to rearing the family. The industrial societies, the advanced nations, particularly America and Russia, use their men and women power, their women's physical and brain power."

XVIII

At the end of September, the Prime Minister announced that he would be going to Japan for an official visit from 14 to 19 October. He said that during his visit he would have discussions with the Japanese Prime Minister on matters of mutual interest in economic and other fields. Later, Lee Kuan Yew stated that they had not discussed security.

A week before he left Singapore, Lee revealed that after his Japan visit, he would go to Canada for a three weeks' private visit to the University of British Columbia at Vancouver. He then planned to go on to Ottawa for two days at the invitation of the Canadian Prime Minister,

Mr Trudeau, and, after Ottawa, to Boston. He would be in Boston until the middle of December, at the Kennedy School of Government at the University of Harvard, an institute for Research Fellows with accommodation for visitors as Fellows. A statement from the Prime Minister's office said it would be a break for the Prime Minister of a few weeks away from "the ceaseless routine of administration" and an opportunity for reading and for meeting people. He had agreed to undertake several speaking engagements during his stay in the United States. It was arranged that Dr Goh Keng Swee, the Minister for Finance, would act as Prime Minister during the Prime Minister's absence.

On his way to Japan, the Prime Minister stopped over in Hong Kong, and there he spoke at the Foreign Correspondents' Club. He said that Singapore was indebted to Hong Kong. Three years ago, Singapore was suddenly faced with a future on her own. Correspondents had explained how, through good fortune, hard work or enterprise, these years were about Singapore's best in terms of economic performance. But no one had mentioned an important factor, namely, Singapore's knowledge of the example of Hong Kong. Hong Kong, with a population density of over 9,000 persons per square mile, no natural resources, negligible agriculture and a smallish population, had made the grade. This knowledge gave Singapore, with a population density of over 8,000 per square mile, that added confidence. If, however, Hong Kong had been overwhelmed by her teeming refugees, then doubts and hesitations might well have set in, and the result might have been different.

Lee Kuan Yew said he had watched with admiration the ceaseless bustle of Hong Kong, its resilience, bouncing back after each shock, each riot, each wave of refugees, each setback. He had read with interest that Hong Kong's external trade in 1967 went up 9 per cent over 1966, in spite of prolonged political disturbances in the middle of 1967. These disturbances were not dissimilar to the troubles that took place in Singapore in the 1950s and the early '60s. But despite all the difficulties which a few men contrived to put in the way of progress for the community, the Singapore economy surged forward. Now these troubles were part of the forgotten past. He ventured to suggest this phenomenon could only occur where there was that capacity for stoical application to the job in hand to the disregard of the turbulence around.

The immediate future appeared bright for both Hong Kong and Singapore. The long-term future, no one could foretell. "Who could have said, in the autumn of 1949, that Hong Kong could have taken in over a million refugees expanded its economy, rehoused and resettled its people, and prospered for twenty years? True, Singapore, placed in different circumstances by geography, is naturally calculating in different terms. Because the hazards are more manageable, people tend to plan for the longer term. Singapore is all freehold, not leasehold, all of it to be held in perpetuity. And given an elected government which has to reflect the mood and aspirations of the electorate, the tendency is to think and build in terms of the next generation. Singapore started to develop later than Hong Kong in the industrial sector. The deployment of the labour force between the trading and manufacturing sectors reflects this. Fifty-seven per cent of Singapore's labour force is in servicing and commerce, as against forty-one per cent of Hong Kong's. This is in part reflected by the higher per capita external trade figure for Singapore: S$4,000 per annum as against Hong Kong's S$2,500 per annum in 1967. But in manufacturing, Hong Kong has thirty-nine per cent of its labour force as against Singapore's eighteen per cent. It is an indicator of the ground Singapore has open before it. And Hong Kong industrialists are playing a valuable role accelerating this growth of industries. Hong Kong investments amount to five point two per cent of the total foreign investments in Singapore. There are in Singapore now a total of fifty firms with Hong Kong participation."

But the flow of capital and expertise was not one-way. Singapore capital and management in Hong Kong banking, entertainment, hotels, construction and even manufacture, like shirt-making, had been a long-established capital export from Singapore, bringing back valuable annual returns in foreign exchange. The per capita income for Singapore in 1967 was S$1,800, roughly twice that of Hong Kong. But this did not mean, as it used to mean, that the wage rates in Singapore were twice that of Hong Kong. "Over the years, we have watched with admiration how wages in Hong Kong have gone up, until in the skilled grades there is little difference between the Singapore and Hong Kong wage levels. In short, the performance of Hong Kong shows what is humanly possible, given industry, thrift and enterprise. The response of a people must equal the challenge. There is much good in Hong Kong's industrial progress for Singapore. Both were first founded in trade, then branched off into servicing and manufacturing. Singapore lost its trade with China in 1841 when Hong Kong was established. Singapore survived. Hong Kong may yet return some benefits to Singapore one of these days. Because in the longer run, there may well be a complementarity in the history and development of these two centres."

XIX

In Tokyo, at a state banquet on 15 October, replying to a speech by the Prime Minister of Japan, Lee Kuan Yew said that he was reminded as he landed in Tokyo that it was almost 100 years ago to the day on 13 October 1868 that the Meiji Emperor took formal possession of the Shogun's castle in Tokyo. It underlined the speed of the transformation that Japan went through to achieve her place in the top league of the industrialized societies of the world. A hundred years was a very short time in the long history of Asian civilization. However, it had been suggested that the longer the continuity in the history of a people, the deeper the traditional values, attitudes and modes of thinking and ways of doing things. This made it more difficult to shake off the debris of the past and to accept the necessary changes to catch up with science and technology, flowering in other contemporary civilizations.

The Prime Minister said he had reflected from time to time on the Japanese phenomenon wondering whether the Japanese transformation had any lessons relevant to Singapore. In so far as Japan's spectacular success was due to the innate qualities of her people, there was nothing others without these qualities could do about it. But perhaps there could have been other factors—the compactness and cohesiveness of the society; the intense sense of national and community purpose; the keen group desire not to be left behind on the lower rungs of civilized societies; the lack of natural resources which was compensated for by a keener human performance. Was there a lesson to be learned about the difference between what a Swedish social scientist called "soft societies" and their opposites, of which Japan was a distinguished example? "What makes some societies soft? Why are others more hardy? Is it the social organization and cultural values? What makes societies like Japan have that limitless capacity to endure hardship for future gains?"

Lee argued that the past was a valuable indication of future performance. Japanese research on nuclear physics and its peaceful uses, and on rocketry and space communications, were indicators of Japan's pre-eminent position in the technological post-industrial societies now emerging in the developed and affluent countries of the northern hemisphere. Add to this the restless search that Japan was making for new trading and economic arrangements in the Pacific basin, both for her prosperity and for her longer-term security, then few could doubt that Japan had both the intention and the wherewithal to stay in the top league. "I hope these attributes will bring not only greater progress to Japan, and prosperity, but that it will enable that prosperity to flake off on to the lesser-developed countries in Southeast Asia."

Lee Kuan Yew spoke of Mr Sato's references to the changes that had taken place and would yet take place in Southeast Asia. They were part of a tide of history. "Our connections with the British, who founded Singapore, are many and of mutual benefit. The departure of their forces at present planned for the end of 1971 does not mean the end of the many economic, educational and cultural links of value to both. However, it will mean a slowing of our rate of economic growth until the slack has been taken up. Last year some fourteen per cent of our gross national product was generated by expenditure of the British military bases. Fortunately, this was less by six per cent as against twenty per cent it generated in 1965, two years previously."

The Prime Minister said he found encouragement from what Mr Sato had said of Singapore's efforts, and from the example he had drawn of Japan's own experience of rebuilding from the wreckage of the past war. "Our confidence is reinforced by the fact that there was a prosperous and thriving centre of commerce and communications in Singapore before the British built their bases. Indeed, only after the Treaty of Washington in 1922 between America, Japan and Britain did the British move their principal naval base in the Far East from Hong Kong to a big one they built in Singapore in the 1930s. If, in the next three years, our economic growth can be sustained at over nine per cent per annum as it has done in the past three years, then all should be well. We are seeking, as you have suggested, increasing bilateral co-operation with such countries as can help us industrialize. We are conscious of the need for regional and sub-regional groupings to meet industrial and technological advances where economies of scale require mass production for mass markets. This can only be achieved if there is a pooling together of resources and markets to make economic development complementary and efficient, not duplicative and wasteful. At the same time, we are not unmindful of the political realities of the new nations and it may take some time and more than some patience to bring about meaningful economic regionalism."

XX

Members of the Japanese Federation of Economic Organizations gave Lee Kuan Yew a luncheon on 16 October. The Prime Minister said it was a privilege to meet a sample of the people who had led the economic and industrial recovery of Japan. Patterns of world trade and economic relationships were undergoing vast changes. The rapid development of trading blocs like the European Economic Community was an indication of the kind of problems countries like Singapore would face if they were unable to link themselves to a wider framework. Over the past five years EEC countries, in their intra-regional trade between themselves, increased somewhere over sixty per cent of their trade as against an increase of one per cent of their trade with the countries of Southeast Asia and Latin America. So it had been suggested that perhaps a Pacific free-trade area could be established between the countries of North America, Japan, Australia and New Zealand, giving special tariff concessions for the importation of raw materials and simple manufactures to the developing countries of Asia and Latin America.

British economists were also thinking along similar lines of a North Atlantic free-trade area. And it had been suggested that perhaps this could be related with Japan and the South Pacific in a North Atlantic and Pacific free-trade area. "But whether the United States, which is both a Pacific and an Atlantic power and interested in exercising its influence throughout the world, can go along with such a proposition is another matter. Meanwhile, in any case, the developing countries are caught in a dilemma. For whatever they produce, if the prices are high, the developed countries with their technologies can find substitutes. If their prices are low, then they can't afford to buy the machines, the technology and the expertise to pay for their development. And even soft loans from the World Bank, the IMF, the Asian Development Bank are getting harder and harder to obtain. It is in this context that I would like to refer to Singapore's association in trade and industry with Japan. It is against this sombre background that we seek to establish a realistic relationship. We do not expect you to come down and establish your industries in Singapore on the basis of charity or aid. Our greatest disadvantage for the establishment of industry is the small domestic market. Therefore, any industry must be export-orientated. And any industry that has either a wage or a freight advantage by being set up in Singapore is the kind of industry which will be mutually profitable."

Speaking from memory, Lee Kuan Yew said that the exports from Japan to Singapore were almost three times in value of the imports into Japan from Singapore. "But we are not disturbed by these figures. This is just a phase in the development of the relationship. You will find in us partners as realistic and practical as you are likely to find anywhere in the world. Nobody owes us a living. And every grain of rice we consume must be paid for in foreign exchange. And I am happy to tell you that the balance of payments over the past few years has always been favourable."

There were over thirty major enterprises with Japanese participation in Singapore. And Japanese investments comprised nearly ten per cent of the total foreign investments in industry in Singapore. Except for British investments which included massive investments in oil refineries, Japan's was the highest.

XXI

On 19 October, at the end of his official visit to Japan, Lee Kuan Yew flew to Canada. He spent two weeks in meditation at the University of British Columbia (and watched the American presidential election on television) and then journeyed to Toronto. Then, on 11 November, he went to Ottawa to meet the Prime Minister of Canada, Mr Pierre Trudeau.

This was a brief encounter, and on 4 December, at Harvard University, where he was accommodated as a Fellow, he gave the Jodidi Lecture. He spoke about Southeast Asia, past and present. He began by remarking that any member of a government in Asia who talked in public of Southeast Asia entered upon a hazardous exercise. "In today's world of instant communications, an indiscreet word, or an unhappy phrase, though uttered in Cambridge, Massachusetts, some 10,000 miles away from Singapore, could bring rapid rejoinders from sensitive souls in Southeast Asia. So, to avoid unnecessary controversy, an effort at subtlety and even sophistry is required. Although one has some knowledge of the subject, and is acquainted with the leaders of governments who determine the policies, one may be too close to the subject, and too involved in wanting to influence the course of events, to be able to discourse dispassionately on it. Then, whilst intellectual integrity demands that the untruth should never be uttered, active political involvement requires infinite tact. So, often the inclination is to gloss over the truth and, unwittingly, to suggest the false."

Lee Kuan Yew defined Southeast Asia as comprising those new nation states which emerged from American, British, Dutch and French empires (in alphabetical, not chronological order) on the south-eastern rim of the continent of Asia, and the archipelago surrounding it. By common usage, it included Burma, Thailand, Cambodia, Laos, Vietnam, on the southern-eastern borders of China, and Malaysia, Singapore, Indonesia and the Philippines. He said he always thought it a grave mistake to classify Vietnam as Southeast Asian. By its history, ethnic affinities and cultural patterns, Vietnam was East Asian, not Southeast Asian. And there were profound differences between these two groups of people. East Asia—Korea, Japan, China, Vietnam —consisted of people whose ethnic characteristics, cultures and religions were broadly similar. Their religions were more philosophies of life. So they were secular societies. They were, by and large, intense peoples, like the Zen Buddhists. Southeast Asia, broadly speaking, was a warm and humid, tropical and equatorial region. And until the advent of modern medicine, improved environmental health techniques and new drugs, life expectancy was very low. Even today, for most parts of the area, insurance companies based their actuarial computations on a life span as low as 33-37 years, although for some urban centres they were rated as high as 62-68 years. Until the introduction of effective climate control through air-conditioning in factories, offices, homes, cars and buses, the effective part of the working day was the cooler hours of the morning. The effect of climate and environment on the physical characteristics and culture of the peoples had been

470

considerable. Because it was more or less summer the whole year round, there had not been the necessity to put by part of the harvest for the winter. This could be one of the factors which explained the greater thrift of the immigrant groups, principally from India and China. And thrift was just an old-fashioned word to describe the process of capital formation, a necessary ingredient of economic development.

Southeast Asia, Lee said, could be divided into four main religious divisions. First, Hinayana or Theravada Buddhism stretches from Burma, across Thailand and Cambodia to Laos. Second, Vietnam, like the rest of East Asia, was Mahayana Buddhist. Third, south of this Buddhist belt, was the Malay peninsula, Indonesia, and part of the southern Philippines, mostly Muslim. These people were converts of the traders from the Yemen who brought Islam with the spice trade, and incidentally thereby ensured an elite status for Arab Muslims in these converted communities. These ethnic-religious demographies had undergone changes, as in the Philippines, the fourth religious grouping. There, after more than 300 years of Spanish and fifty years of American rule, the people of the main islands were today Catholic, many of them of mixed Malay-Spanish origins.

The traditional working dress for East Asians, both male and female, was trousers and jacket. That of the Southeast Asians, both male and female, was sarong and jacket. The sarong was naturally better suited to the warmer and more humid conditions of Southeast Asia. But what effect this better ventilated garment had on the physical freedom of movement, and on the speed and intensity of the work of the wearer, did not need research. However, research on the mental attitudes and psychological approach to sustained and intense work, and on the social mores and values between the wearers of the sarong as against the wearers of the trousers could be illuminating. "When the sarong wearer is also an orthodox Muslim, whose religion enjoins him against the receipt of interest as a mortal sin, the effect on economic performance and growth has been debilitating. This problem is aggravated because, whilst receiving interest is a sin, the payment of interest however is permitted, and therefore practised to the advantage of the non-Muslims in their midst. Hence problems of indebtedness, mortgage and eventually the landlessness of the peasantry become intractable."

Into each of these countries came several waves of immigrants: Indians into Burma; Indians, Ceylonese and trouser-wearing Chinese into Western Malaysia and Singapore; and before World War Two, some Japanese and Taiwanese into the main urban centres of all the countries in the region. Some of these immigrant groups pre-dated the arrival of the Europeans. More were encouraged to move in by the Europeans. As with the Indians in East Africa, they assisted the colonialists in the extraction of the natural resources and the governing of these territories. They provided administrative, technical and commercial expertise at a secondary level to assist the Europeans. In some cases,

471

they were the only source of disciplined and reliable labour for the opening of plantations and mines, the building of roads and railways. Frequently they became the shopkeepers of the country.

And shopkeepers in these circumstances were for practical purposes the village bankers. When from time to time these shopkeepers were forced out of business by rioting or legislation, or both, the villagers lost their banker. This local knowledge and expertise could be replaced neither by other villagers, by the administrators who introduced the laws to create native entrepreneurs, nor by substituting members of the Peace Corps. Southeast Asia today, its peoples and civilizations, was the outcome of the impact of European colonial administrations on the economy and culture of these territories, and the demographic alterations through migration encouraged by the administering colonial powers. "How and what the different political leaderships have inherited varied with the European empires they had been part of. What they have done with their inheritance since independence varies considerably from country to country, depending on the quality of their political leaderships and the cohesiveness, educational standards, drive and stamina of their peoples."

What were the reasons for the failure to realize the visions that the first-generation, anti-colonial nationalist leaders in Southeast Asia held out to rally their people in their quest for freedom? Why was it that European empires were able to extract considerable wealth from the areas under their control for the enrichment of their metropolitan bases in Europe, whilst at the same time building up the infrastructure of roads, railways, harbours, postal and telegraphic communications, and a network of law-enforcing and tax-collecting agencies? Why was it that these same areas after independence sometimes could not do as well?

Lee said that having observed this doleful subject over the years, he advanced the following reasons. First, the population explosion placed a sharply increased burden on the resources of these countries as modern medicine and improved environmental health techniques reduced both infant and adult mortality rates. Second, inter-ethnic peace, previously ensured by the colonial overlord, proved difficult to maintain after independence when power was often passed into the hands of the ethnic majority, since the European powers had created imperial boundaries of convenience. Third, power was handed over to those elite groups who had demonstrated that they commanded popular support. When these new governments attempted to demonstrate continuing legitimacy by holding on to their support after independence, they brought divisive forces to the surface. For political supremacy, competing political leaderships could not resist the temptation to appeal to ethnic, linguistic and religious loyalties. Fourth, the inadequate number of trained men, in the political leadership, government administration, professions, commerce and industry, retarded economic development. Fifth, a number of these states were handicapped by being what Gunnar

Myrdal termed "soft societies". With the withdrawal of the unrepresentative, and, probably for that reason, decisive rulers, and the introduction of elected governments, a softening took place in the firm framework of administration. Corruption set in, and became a way of life for all those invested with authority, from the highest to the lowest levels of bureaucratic power. By the nature of the people, their cultural values and social organization, they had not succeeded in getting their political elites to exercise self-discipline. Sixth, the educated were not put to best use. Wage differentials between the highly educated and the untrained were narrowed as politicians sought the popular votes of the masses, and sacrificed the interests of the few—those with professional and technological competence. Worse, educational opportunities for the children of these people became markedly inferior to those available in the developed countries where they could sell their training and skills. This is often the point when the pulls of social conscience, loyalty and patriotism snap and a further brain drain results, depleting limited resources and aggravating an already difficult situation. Lastly, attitudes toward free enterprise made a difference in terms of development performance. Almost concurrently with the ethnic and cultural divisions between East Asia and Southeast Asia had been the division between the areas where free enterprise had been allowed to flourish and those areas where government planning and controls stifled enterprise in the private sector. This happened either because state philosophy favoured state planning, or because the entrepreneurs were ethnically a minority and so had their activities conscribed and restricted for political reasons.

Most of the new governments pursued policies of economic self-sufficiency. It was free enterprise which accounted for the progress of Thailand, Malaysia and Singapore which, though in Southeast Asia, had considerable East Asian, or Chinese, enterprise which had been allowed to operate and flourish. Thailand was also fortunate in never having been incorporated into a European empire. So the Thais were aware that besides the removal of colonial exploitation, there were other positive factors needed, like enterprise, management know-how and technological skills and capital, before national wealth could be increased. Many governments in the region had tended, sometimes deliberately, to overlook the fact that it was free enterprise, and not state planning and planning agencies, which had achieved industrialization of the economies of Western Europe, America and Japan.

Was there a brighter side to this recital of unrelieved gloom? Lee Kuan Yew said that the main problem was that of ensuring a general climate of peace and security. Without security, constructive endeavour within each nation was difficult, and co-operation between nations impossible. Conflicts between these new countries, and interference by countries both inside and outside the region through subversion and through economic and political pressure and manipulation, made for

473

unnecessary turbulence. They resulted in a frittering away of precious resources and energy. Southeast Asia had been an unsettled area. Yet the basic environment of security could only spring from the policies of the major world powers. The manner in which the war in Vietnam will be resolved might well prove crucial to the development of other countries in the region. One of the objectives of the war had been to try and prevent this same kind of internecine strife from engulfing the other countries adjacent to Vietnam. The enormous expenditure of American resources would only have been worthwhile if this was at least partially achieved, if the solution achieved in Vietnam bought time for these other countries to make the economic, social and political changes for their own survival. "For, in the longer term, the only way to peace and progress is through the modernizing of these societies and through rational economic and social policies providing the political stability. Only economic and social change will remove the latest internal pressures for violent revolutionary change."

There were, Lee Kuan Yew thought, a number of hopeful signs. Although the problem of high birth rates with net population increases of between three to four per cent per annum was already with these countries, and might continue with diminishing virulence for another decade, there were hopeful signs in the urban centres, and perhaps later, as communications improve, in the rural areas, for a dramatic slowing down of the population growth. By the spring of 1968, all governments in South, Southeast and East Asia were on record (in a United Nations' document) as supporting population control. "And if the policies pronounced by the new President of the World Bank are implemented rigorously, namely that aid will be inversely correlated to population growth, then the leaders of those countries will have a real incentive to put the brakes on."

Next, as xenophobia wore thin, the need for trained men as administrators, managers, executives, and technologists was openly acknowledged. It was becoming possible for the second-generation leaders to borrow or hire expertise from the manpower of the developed nations to help plan and implement development programmes in the economic and social fields. Assuming the continued good health of the world economy, it was safe to predict continued progress for the economies of South Korea, Japan and Taiwan for the next five years. It might not be easy to be equally optimistic of developments in Southeast Asia. But it was reasonable to assume that those governments which had allowed free enterprise to play its part in the development of their countries, whether the entrepreneurs be indigenous or immigrant groups, are the ones that would make the most progress.

Power in many of these new countries was in the process of being passed to second-generation leaders. The lessons of the last two decades had been privately learnt, even if not publicly admitted. True, in some cases, the damage which their predecessors had inflicted on the

474

economy and on the social fabric of their societies had been grievous. It would take considerable time, effort and resources to repair the harm done. The unwisdom of economic policies based on national self-sufficiency had been quietly acknowledged, if not completely abandoned. There was now an acknowledgement that economic progress and improved living conditions could be better realized through economic co-operation in regional and sub-regional groupings, to create broader markets, and so to complement development, avoiding duplication of capital equipment and a waste of scarce resources.

Now that the reasons for poor economic performance were understood, and steps could be taken to overcome them, development funds such as could be mustered could be put to more effective use. If expenditure was supervised into economic projects assessed and approved beforehand, and if the intelligence and skills of the various peoples could be better utilized through education and incentives to higher performance, then guarded optimism would replace the present dreary outlook. There were cautious beginnings. New acronyms have been coined to describe these new groupings. Hitherto regional co-operation had been no more than a thinly disguised exercise in collective soliciting of aid from the wealthy nations. Now, they represented at least the desire, if not yet fruition, of practical co-operation for mutual benefit. The ADB for Asian Development Bank, the Southeast Asian Ministerial Conference on Economic Development, ASEAN for Association of Southeast Asian Nations, and ASPAC for Asian and Pacific Council: they were the result of indigenous initiatives within the region, compared to two early efforts, the Colombo Plan and ECAFE or Economic Council for Asia and the Far East. If these promising trends continued, then economic progress would be made. But, whatever the economic progress, none of these countries in Southeast Asia had the potential, either immediately, or in the long-term future, or were likely to become even a medium-sized power in the modern day sense of the term. As the European powers, who knew these countries and their peoples well, withdrew from the region, the super-powers, at present America and Russia, who knew less about these places, had been drawn in, testing the limits of their power. Russian naval units in the Pacific were on the increase and perhaps, late in the next decade, if China industrializes, the position may be further complicated as three major powers, instead of the present two, test the limits of their influence in the area.

The Prime Minister concluded: "The long-term future of Southeast Asia will be determined as much by the policies of the major powers outside the region, as by the initiatives of the governments within the region. It is an area which could produce great wealth as the European powers proved during the centuries they were in control. If helped, these new national governments could learn to build that firm framework of effective administration, sound currency, orderly social conditions and work discipline, so making labour productive, enterprise profitable, and revenue more or less equal to the budgetary needs of a developing economy." There were two views one could take of the future of the region. One was a pessimistic view. Projecting the dismal record of the past two decades into the next two, one was reluctantly forced to the view that in very few places in the region were people being welded into viable nation groups, and nowhere had freedom realized its promise. Democracy was preached, but not practised. On the other hand, old feuds had been revived, and new ones were being conjured up and pursued. Barely submerged animosities against the migrant groups, Chinese and Indians, had surfaced, and new schisms were being added to badly fragmented societies. The other was a cautiously optimistic view. "For, although this is not a well-demarcated area of contest like that between the communist and non-communist world in Western and Eastern Europe, nevertheless, from the lessons of Vietnam, all contending parties may recognize the dangers of wars of national liberation enlarging themselves into far more perilous conflicts. Nations may learn to sublimate their irresistible impulses to ascendency and an expansion of their influence, by a competition on the economic and ideological planes. This would give time to the second-generation leaders of Southeast Asia who have learnt from the mistakes of the past—time to put things back on a constructive track, to modernize their societies, and through regional co-operation between themselves and with the developed countries, achieve economic growth and a better quality of life for their peoples. Then there would be greater social stability, making for more security in the area, leading to higher investment flows, more economic growth, and so a climb up the face of the cliff to higher levels of civilization. Not unnaturally, as a practitioner, I must take the more optimistic view."

XXII

Lee Kuan Yew dealt with the same topic when he gave the Gabriel Silver Memorial lecture at Columbia University, New York, on 12 December. The day before, Lee Kuan Yew paid a private visit to President Johnson. They discussed in general the security situation in Southeast Asia. No statement was issued: the visit was strictly unofficial at the Prime Minister's request, the White House spokesman said.

Before he left New York to return to Singapore, the Prime Minister met newsmen at his hotel on 14 December. He said he now had a better feel for undercurrents of American policies and politics. He said he hoped to arrange similar breaks in routine for other members of his Cabinet as a refresher from "the conveyer belt of daily decisions".

Lee said that although a new isolationism was one of the strands in the complex pattern of American politics, he did not expect it to gain ascendancy. "I see no new isolationism in trade. I would say the outlook under the Nixon administration is at least pretty fair," he said. "I would be surprised if trade policies, which are the first and most crucial thing, were reversed, with trade walls erected, and so forth."

Asked about Vietnam the Prime Minister said that in America the "bulk of the young people and a good deal of the older generation would like to see the Vietnam war ended".

Asked how he viewed suggestions that Japan should assume a greater share of security arrangements in Asia, Lee said it appeared that Japanese leaders were not anxious to do so. "We would like to see a friendly naval presence all around Southeast Asia," he said. "It keeps the trade routes open."

Asked about neighbouring reactions to Singapore's employment of Israeli instructors to train its defence forces, he said: "We are not very particular where other people get their advice. We turn to those whose experience is relevant to ours. We don't want a large standing air force." He had looked into the Swiss and Finnish patterns for a military structure which, without draining away needed productive workers, would still enable large numbers to be mobilized for national defence. "The Israeli model offered us a better pattern to go by."

Lee said he was looking forward to the January meeting of Commonwealth Prime Ministers in London and stressed that his relations with Mr Wilson were "most cordial". He added: "Britain is far from written off in world affairs. People who do so make a mistake. It is only a matter of time for them to right their balance of payments problem and to set their trade unions straight."

Lee Kuan Yew estimated his two months abroad well worthwhile in that he could better assess what would happen in the US in the Nixon administration. He hesistated to stay abroad longer "only because if I stay away too long Singapore might find it can do without me," he joked.

The previous day he paid a thirty-minute call on the UN Secretary-General, U Thant.

Back in Singapore, Lee Kuan Yew met the Press on 21 December.

Ray Herndon of UPI said that in the United States Lee had given the impression that he did not have a very high regard for America, or things American. Had the trip changed his views? The Prime Minister replied that, on the contrary, he had a very high regard for American technology, gadgetery, drive, marketing, management skills and so many other things connected with the industrial and technological society in which we live. "I have a great admiration for the space programme which you are running in friendly competition with the Russians. Where

477

I feel, perhaps, more years of history would give wisdom and judgement, is in the dealings of American governments of human situations, particularly human situations abroad—such as in Southeast Asia and Vietnam in particular. That is a human problem, not just a technological problem. It is not just the business of finding out a ray detector to catch a guerilla fighter in the dark to shoot him down or to defoliate the countryside. I think the problem is deep down in Vietnamese hearts and in what the South Vietnamese is thinking."

Asked by Lewis Simons of Associated Press if he believed that the new President may have new plans for the broader aspects of US foreign policy in Southeast Asia, Lee said he doubted whether Mr Nixon and his Cabinet themselves had made up their minds. "Everybody starts off with his own personal set of major premises and then they have to mesh in with one another. But I should hardly believe that an administration keen on cutting down Federal expenditure and checking unnecessary inflation would want to spend a billion dollars on the Mekong."

Ray Herndon wanted to know if Lee believed that Nixon had the resolve to carry through with the effort in Vietnam and Southeast Asia in general?

The Prime Minister replied that he did not think it was Mr Nixon's resolve that was going to determine the outcome or the manner in which the South Vietnamese involvement was ended. "I think it is the mood in America, particularly the younger generation. They are completely disenchanted with what they think is not a worthwhile cause in South Vietnam. They are impatient with what they consider to be an inefficient and a corrupt regime and they believe that if South Vietnam is to remain non-communist, then South Vietnamese who are non-communist must fight for it. And I must say that I am not altogether unsympathetic to that point of view that if South Vietnam is to survive as a non-communist state, then there must be enough South Vietnamese to rally around a dedicated and an effective leadership."

Answering other questions the Prime Minister said that he thought that the only kind of solution, peaceful solution, to the Vietnam conflict was a peaceful political competition for the support of the majority of the people of South Vietnam. "And you have got, in so far as is possible, having ravished the country with all the latest inventions in terror and destructiveness, to try and restore some semblance of stability and security and peace and allow the different political groups to compete and vie with each other for political support. And if it decides to go non-communist, then good luck to South Vietnam and I think the rest of Southeast Asia will cheer and will be greatly relieved. If it decides to go communist and to rejoin the North, then the American President can very honestly say that he did his best on behalf of the free world and that he enabled the South Vietnamese to do their best for themselves and the South Vietnamese just didn't believe that the non-communist South Vietnamese leadership was good enough for them."

Lee Kuan Yew went on to say that speaking as a Singaporean, he hoped that "the others" around Singapore, "particularly to the north of us", would not lose their nerve. He did not believe that Thailand, for instance, the constituted authority, the monarchy and the Government, the generals and the advisers around the monarchy, could be subverted and destroyed by the same processes which undermined South Vietnam because basically they were a different type of people. They were Thais and they had a history of their own, a culture of their own. It was a culture which did not lend itself to guerilla fanaticism which was what was required for a successful guerilla insurrection. "And so, if we all don't lose our nerve, and the United States leaves enough behind in Thailand so that the Thais don't lose their nerve and believe that they have been over-extended, then I think the rest of Southeast Asia will stick and will gel and I hope common sense will prevail and we will all co-operate and help each other, flourish and prosper and grow stronger, and more secure."

Fred Emery of *The Times*, of London, said that one of the greatest problems in the peninsula of Malaysia, Indonesia, Singapore and perhaps the Philippines as well, was racial tension, "fears between the different races that inhabit this part of the world and obviously have to live together; otherwise, disaster. What can ASEAN do to help this racial tension to be kept at a reasonable level? Your assessment on the wider question: the racial tension?"

The Prime Minister said that on the wider question of racial or inter-ethnic co-operation everybody had to solve his problems his own way. "I can't tell my neighbours how they should solve their minority or other problems just as I think they have no business telling me how I solve mine. I prefer to solve mine by sinking a lot of investment into education, into housing, to give the people who are less competitive a chance to keep up with progress. And I would like to believe that, in the long run, because it is successful in lessening friction between ethnic groups this may point the way to similar solutions elsewhere. But the last thing we want to do is to give advice."

Asked about Japan, Lee Kuan Yew said that American experts believed that Japan would play a bigger and bigger role in both the economic and security fields of East and Southeast Asia. He thought that if this, in part, reflected the wishes or the anticipation of the American elite who, in turn, reflected or shared the thinking of the American administration, "then Mr Sato and his Government or whoever is the Prime Minister of Japan will find himself gently pushed forward. But as you yourself have read in the newspapers recently: Mr Sato says Japan can't undertake these very expensive responsibilities. But I am told that this is very Japanese. You know, one says that this is very much the way of going forward slowly."

CHAPTER TWENTY-THREE

The Year of Power 1969

AT the end of the year (the 150th anniversary of the found-ing of modern Singapore by Raffles), the Prime Minister reported that in ten years, from 1959 to 1969, Singapore had doubled its per capita income, and increased the gross na-tional product two and a half times.

The defence build-up continued satisfactorily. By 1979, Singapore would be able to mobilize immediately a well-trained army of 45,000 troops.

Lee Kuan Yew went to London for the Commonwealth Prime Ministers' Conference. The Middle Temple took the opportunity to make him an Honorary Bencher.

Lee was in Washington for talks with President Nixon when race riots broke out in Kuala Lumpur. There were repercussions in Singapore but firm and impartial security measures soon restored the situation.

Princess Alexandra, and Fred Peart MP, Leader of the British House of Commons, came to Singapore for the National Day and 150th anniversary celebrations. There were eighteen tanks and some armoured cars on parade during the National Day procession.

New laws were introduced abolishing the jury system and legalizing abortion in certain circumstances.

United States golfers won the World Cup, held in Singa-pore for the first time.

I

"NINETEEN hundred and sixty-eight was an historic year for Singapore," Lee Kuan Yew claimed in his New Year Message. "On 6 February, 1968, we commenced the 150th year of our history." Just before that, at the beginning of January, the British broke the "grave news" of a change in the British Government's defence policy East of Suez. Instead of half their forces out by 31 March they were planned for a total withdrawal by that date. By mid-January the British Government, relenting a little, extended the date by nine months—half out by 31 March, 1971, the rest out by 31 December, 1971. "So we began our 150th year with a shock. But we turned adversity to advantage. What could have been a fatal shock became shock therapy. Looking back over the past year, we can be proud of the way our people responded."

Lee reminded Singaporeans that 6 February, 1961, would be the 150th anniversary of the day Stamford Raffles came ashore and founded modern Singapore. Students of history knew that the destiny of a people was not pre-ordained. "It is not pre-determination but determination which decides what happens to a people. When the figures for 1968 are complete, they are likely to show that our economic growth was even higher than 1967, which was an eleven point nine per cent growth, at current prices, of 1967 over 1966. And this was in spite of British military expenditure being reduced from twenty per cent of our GNP in 1965 to fourteen per cent in 1967. British military contribution was three to four per cent less for 1968, yet we recorded another successful year."

As the United Nations Development decade for the '60s draws to its close, development economists were discovering that the crucial factor was the quality of human resources which decided the pace at which poor backward, agricultural, illiterate or semi-educated communities were propelled into thriving industrial communities of well-educated, skilled and trained professionals, technocrats and technicians. They had been perplexed at the wide differences and discrepancies in the development rate of the LDCs (less developed countries), "a euphemism for backward communities". The irresistible conclusion was that whilst material resources, capital investment, mineral, oil, timber, fertility of soil and abundance of water supply, determined the population density per square mile, or what a country could sustain in an agricultural economy, the uneven economic growth rates could only be explained by the differences in human endowment and the cultural values and patterns through which these innate qualities were nurtured, cultivated, and groomed to best advantage. The conclusion was that it was social values and social organizations which determined total group performance, that some of the most important factors for rapid growth are the efficacy of the administrative machine, the number of professionally and technologically trained digits, and the mettle or quality of the political leadership.

The Prime Minister contended that some of the less developed countries, at the rate they were going, "will not, even in a thousand years, achieve the present standards of America, Western Europe or Russia—unless they change the cultural and educational milieu through which alone they can bring forth the best of the innate qualities in their peoples". He clearly did not put Singapore in that category.

But he felt constrained to utter a word of caution. "That we have done well under circumstances which would have crushed lesser spirits, does not mean we can afford to slack. We cannot afford to carry passengers. Whether brains or brawn, whether university student or unskilled labourer, we expect, and we will exact, from each his best. No one is privileged to ask somebody else to carry the burden of making secure the quality of life which we have achieved. A New Year resolution for 1969—'I will give of my best', and judging from the figures of 1968, our best will be good enough."

II

On 3 January, the Prime Minister, accompanied by the Minister for Foreign Affairs, left for the Commonwealth Prime Ministers' Conference in London. Lee Kuan Yew was away almost a month.

In London on 9 January, he addressed the Royal Commonwealth Society and spoke of the usefulness of the Commonwealth. He referred to the vastly different mood in Britain. He said it was reflected in the Press, on the television and even in statements in the House of Commons. It showed a deepening disenchantment with the Commonwealth; and the problems of colour in Britain, in Rhodesia, and the failure of some black African governments after independence to maintain British standards of government—they had made their contribution to this. They reflected a change of life. As Britain and the British Labour Government discovered (even though the Labour Party said in the autumn of 1964 that they wanted to revive the Commonwealth), the transition from Empire to Commonwealth was accompanied by the loss of economic worth of the Commonwealth to Britain as other industrial countries with more pressures to rebuild their damaged economies—Germany, Italy, France, Japan and even America—moved in, into each independent Commonwealth territory with great alacrity.

"I sometimes think that *The Times* or *The Economist*, with each special supplement on the independence of a former dependent territory, besides quite rightfully congratulating the British Government and those that they had governed for making peaceful progress towards disengagement from colonization and nationhood, could perhaps," said the Prime Minister, "also have put in the obverse side—how much British manufacture was sold per annum, what the tariff walls were, and how important it was that British exporters must meet delivery dates, must meet competition from hungrier and keener workers and entrepreneurs and industrialists from countries like Japan and Germany." Lee went on to speak of the strength of the pound, the unpopular prices and incomes policy; the attempts at rationalizing and making management more efficient by mergers and vertical and horizontal integration; the proposal to make unofficial strikes illegal and punishable—they all represented a preoccupation with Britain's domestic problems as she tried to re-structure her economy and her society to meet the very different circumstances in the aftermath of Empire.

The Prime Minister feared that the frustrations at the attitudes of European countries Britain helped to save in the last war, and at the querulous colonies she nurtured to independence and after independence, poured aid into, and in return received churlishness and sometimes abuse—all these had not made a contribution either to Britain's future role or the welfare of these new independent Commonwealth members. "But then I recall that when a British minister was asked in Parliament not so long ago why it was that action was taken by an independent Commonwealth government against Britain when she had only recently poured a great deal of her resources to safeguard that country's sovereignty and integrity, he replied that Britain did not do these things in expectation of gratitude."

Lee Kuan Yew said it was at that moment difficult to take an optimistic view of the future of the Commonwealth if one concerned oneself only with the immediate present. "But if, and as I have attempted to do, one looks forward a few decades ahead and looks backwards a few centuries to see what indications this can give from past performance of future expectations, then I think the past 400 years have given an indication of the capacity and quality of a unique island civilization, and this is not an exercise in nostalgia. I have no desire, in recounting these events, to try and revive a sensation of past grandeur. But the fact remains that no island-nation has ever before in history created an empire overseas so vast and so powerful that at the end of Empire, are created centres of civilization in North America —the United States and Canada combined—five to six times bigger in population than Britain, six to seven times larger in industrial capacity; centres in Australia and New Zealand, potentially civilizations which could grow as big; and, but for a change in the tide of history, a civilization in the south, the central and the temperate highlands of Africa."

But it was Britain's very success in Empire and in creating civilizations overseas which now threatened her economic position and sapped trade and influence. Because, unlike the French and their empire, British brains could more easily drain to wealthy, affluent English-speaking communities in America, in Australia, in New Zealand. It was true Europeans too migrated to America, and some Germans migrated involuntarily to help the American space programmes. But there was for the French, and for other Europeans, a difficulty of jumping over a language hurdle and then the uncongenial thought of living in a culture not one they were accustomed to and which they found alien. This was not so with the Englishman.

The Prime Minister argued that the probabilities were that if Britain did not re-establish the soundness of her economy, maintain and sustain the creativity of her research projects and keep abreast in technology, then Commonwealth members now linked through Britain and through Britain to each other—a link now radiating from the centre outwards—would forge new links. "And, if I may borrow a phrase from another context, polycentralism will be the inevitable consequence, as the advanced English-speaking countries—the Americans, the Canadians and the Australians—take over the ready-made markets that Britain leaves behind. All Commonwealth members, however, with the exception of Canada, Australia and New Zealand, had lower standards of living and a lower level of technology than Britain. It would take them a very long time, some if ever, to get to the present levels of science and technology in Britain. But if Britain could get back into the top league of the industrialized and technological nations, either through a bigger base in the European Economic Community, or an Atlantic free-trade area, and perhaps an Atlantic free-trade area linked with a Pacific free-trade area, in place of a common market, then the links with London in trade, industry, education, technology would be re-established, renewed and reinforced.

Lee Kuan Yew thought that even though many members of the Commonwealth today might not realize this, they might find hitching on to some other technological wagon a little more exacting and stifling. "Americans and Russians may be generous peoples, but their Governments expect total and unqualified commitment and unquestioning support, and when American proteges or former proteges, like China or Cuba, turn ungrateful, then reactions and sanctions from the Americans are sharp and angry. So too Russian displeasure with Czechoslovakia."

At the moment, Britain was bedevilled with the problem of colour. But it was not a British problem, not even that of Rhodesia. "It is a world problem: white and non-white. And when the non-whites are Africans, the problem becomes particularly awkward and sensitive. For reasons of history, it is erroneously believed that the Negro is always inferior for he has no relics in stone, no written language, no literature. And centuries of deep prejudice, slavery of the Negro with the Arabs as masters long before slavery in the New World, have all accentuated this deep prejudice and led to irrational animosities between black and white. But I think it is useful to remember that to make penance it was Britain that led the crusade to abolish slavery. It is also useful to remember that this prejudice is not just a prejudice of the Americans or the Western Europeans. Slav-African riots in Lumumba University are worth mention. And even the Asiatic is inflicted with this irrational prejudice. Fifty thousand Negro GI babies are a psychological and pathological problem because they are not accepted into Japanese society, and many of them have gone to Brazil. And Red Guardism notwithstanding, I think African leaders should do well to remember that if they have African students in large numbers, not just African leaders being banqueted, in Peking, the same problems will arise."

All this was part of history. Lee Kuan Yew felt that cautious optimism on the future of the Commonwealth was not misplaced. The French resisted freedom movements. Now they had excellent relations with the former Francophobe states—not only in Africa where they gave over the reins of power without conflict, but more strikingly so in Indo-China. After a decade of bitter, cruel and vicious war, the North Vietnamese Government were on excellent terms with General de Gaulle and his Government.

Referring to the Commonwealth Prime Ministers' Conference, Lee Kuan Yew said that he had seen and heard signs of a growing realization —unlike in the Conference in September 1966—that it was not just the problem of the moment "that should decide our relationships with Britain". A more sober reassessment of the value of these ties, and not just sentimental values, was being made. One advantage was that of not being overwhelmed in an unequal partnership or association with Americans or Russians. "And Commonwealth members may find it less stifling if, despite their proximity to the gravitational pulls of these countries with very big GNPs, they have at the same time some connections with the British in their economic, their educational and their social fields. But the danger is that by the time this realization sinks in, it may be too late, because Britain may have either dropped out of the top technological league or, because disgusted with the excesses of language and postures of Commonwealth members, she may have allowed the special knowledge and expertise of former administrators, merchants, bankers, technicians to be lost as they age and pass away."

Lee said that one of the most remarkable things that had happened in Asia was that the Indonesians, who after 350 years of Dutch exploitation and twenty years of hatred and suppression of Dutch enterprise, today find themselves more at ease with Dutchmen than anyone else. The moral, both for Commonwealth members and for Britain, was that, whatever the present disputes and quarrels, the former dependencies might in the end find the British and their technological and industrial power the most valuable and the most comfortable to make use of provided, as the Russians and the Americans race to Mars, to the moon and beyond, Britain is able to keep abreast with these new frontiers of science and technology. For it would be a great pity if and when the moment of truth arrives, Britain had already dismantled the organization and lost the expert knowledge and skills acquired through decades and sometimes centuries of association. Many people would then be that much the poorer off if the knowledge and expertise, now in the files of the colonial office and in the memories of former colonial administrators, engineers, technicians, merchants and bankers, were allowed to be lost.

III

At Marlborough House the following day, at the Commonwealth Prime Ministers' Conference, Lee again referred to the changed mood and thinking of the British people about their role and responsibilities in world affairs, including Rhodesia. He said that since the unilateral declaration of independence by Ian Smith, successive Commonwealth Conferences had approached the Rhodesian problem as primarily a British responsibility, to be solved by the British after the pattern of peaceful progress to independence of other colonies. Tactics and strategy were based on this assumption. Perhaps those assumptions had been valid three years ago. Today they were not. Many things had happened since the autumn of 1965. And one of the results had been the changed mood and thinking of the British people—not just their Government—about their role and responsibilities in world affairs, including Rhodesia. This mood of disenchantment and withdrawal from centuries of the responsibilities of Empire was all-pervasive. "Some of us may be of the view that this disillusionment with what is happening in their former colonial territories is based on too shallow and short-term a view of the future of Britain's former dependencies. The African case for ending the illegal Smith regime is irrefutable on moral and political grounds. Neither the British Government nor the British public denies the cogency of the moral argument."

Lee revealed that a few weeks earlier he had written to the President of Zambia in reply to a letter from him. Lee quoted some paragraphs from his letter to the President:

"I delayed replying in order to have more time to reflect not just on the immediate question of tactics and strategy at the coming Prime Ministers' Conference in London, beginning on 7 January, but more on the long-term implications of colour prejudices particularly against the black peoples of Africa. These irrational feelings of unease, amounting often to hatred and fear, exist not only among white peoples in

486

Rhodesia, South Africa, Mozambique and Angola, but here in the United States, in Britain and other parts of the European world, and even some non-white countries. For they too have been influenced by centuries of prejudice and bigotry which have associated the black African peoples with slavery, first by the Arabs, and then by the Europeans who transported them by the hundreds of thousands across the Atlantic to help cultivate the New World in North America, the Caribbean and parts of the northern half of the South American continent.

"The immediate problem of Rhodesia that you have raised requires the mobilization of opinion against the tendency to apathy and a dulling of the conscience as the issue is pushed into the less prominent parts of newspapers throughout the urban centres of the world. In particular, we must re-arouse the initial feelings of outrage at the time of the illegal declaration of independence, and re-focus attention on the iniquities being committed against over four million black Rhodesians, and even more millions of blacks in South Africa, Angola and Mozambique. We must do this within the Commonwealth and in the United Nations. We have to prevent it from becoming a perfunctory passing of a resolution as meetings are held periodically to discuss the problem.

"However, unhappy events have involved black African governments, like the tragedy still being enacted in the Ibo territories of Nigeria. They do great damage to the cause of the black peoples. In spite of the danger of being accused of preaching a sermon on a subject I am unqualified to do, I shall be dishonest in my dialogue with you if I do not express my concern at the harm that is being done to this crusade against prejudice, bigotry and injustice to the black and coloured peoples in South Africa, America, Britain and elsewhere by such instances of an African's inhumanity to his fellow-African. I understand the desire of the Federal Government of Nigeria to preserve its territorial integrity. But I cannot help sensing the grievous harm this is doing, as the white backlash in Britain and America exploits these happenings to shore up their theories justifying racial discrimination.

"The course of future events will be determined as much by the mobilization of public opinion against the racist regime in Rhodesia, and probably the use of revolutionary methods of guerilla warfare, as by the example of high standards of political maturity, sophistication and multiracial tolerance by black African governments."

The Prime Minister said that those, who believed that politics should not be just the art of the possible, must regret the fact that the British Government had not held fast to fundamental principles regardless of changes in prevailing conditions. The British Prime Minister, Lee added, had become an uncomfortable prisoner of his earlier optimism.

Lee went on to say that after the end of World War Two, when Britain embarked on decolonization, it was in the expectation that the

487

transformation of Empire into a Commonwealth, a political and economic association of free nations, would be a source of strength and pride to Britain. The British people and their leaders then believed that this transformed Empire would enable Britain and each of the Commonwealth members to wield influence in world affairs more substantially than each could have done separately. Also they had hoped that after independence their former dependencies would be thriving, dynamic democracies with which Britain would be proud to associate for mutual benefit. So, during the first two decades of decolonization there was considerable enthusiasm in Britain for rendering aid, educational, technological, economic and military, to help her former dependencies to grow into thriving democracies.

But the post-independence phase had been one of growing disillusionment. In many new countries British concepts of democracy were abandoned for forms of government alien to British tradition and beliefs. They saw some of the former dependencies rent and torn apart by unbelievably cruel civil wars, fought ferociously on racial, tribal, religious or linguistic loyalties. Day by day the British public, and the rest of the world, had been given regular doses of atrocities and *coup d'etat* in some part or other of Africa or Asia or Latin America, murders and assassinations of prime ministers and presidents, the arrest and detention of a prime minister in the midst of being sworn in after having won an election lawfully and legally. All this had been part of Britain's daily breakfast reading. "So we rejoice when the Prime Minister of Sierra Leone, illegally arrested even as he was sworn into office, has now rightfully assumed his responsibilities and can join us at this Conference."

Lee said that the British saw themselves ousted economically and even politically as new patrons were courted, some of them Britain's keenest political and economic rivals. They found themselves caught in the cross-fires of internal conflicts and rivalries. Accommodating the demands or yielding to the sentiments of former wards had become for Britain an unprofitable and irritating exercise in futility. So decolonization of Rhodesia was taking place under different circumstances in a vastly changed world. In the first phase from middle 1940s to the early '60s, the handing over of power was to broadly representative majority governments. The belief then was that Britain's newly independent former colonies had been set on the path of democracy. "In the case of Rhodesia, it is how to be rid of an unnecessary problem, a political and economic embarrassment and a source of conflict within Britain—a Britain which has decided, for the time being, that it pays to openly put Britain's interests first."

This had happened not only in the case of Rhodesia but also in Southeast Asia. Undertakings solemnly given in June and July, 1967, regarding the phasing and timing of the scaling down of British defence contributions were unilaterally abjured within the space of six months, in January 1968. "For me and some other members in that part of the world, this sudden devaluation of her previous pledges was a disappointment. But unfortunately the devaluation of the pound in November '67 was as sudden as it was unexpected."

Lee Kuan Yew thought that a British solution to the Rhodesian problem would not and could not be what Africans or Asians would like. "This is not to say that we should not press the British Government to go as far as they can, if only to facilitate the pursuit of other possible solutions to which the Africans will have to give increasing attention." A solution of the Rhodesian problem that would satisfy black Africans could only be achieved if Africans themselves were prepared to pay the price. "In Southeast Asia the Vietcong have demonstrated that, given the tenacity, the capacity, the will to slog it out to the very end of time, even the world's mightiest military and technological power can be persuaded to negotiate a settlement. One hundred and fifty thousand Rhodesians, even backed by four million white South Africans, cannot constitute an invincible force for all time, but Africans must develop the discipline and the durability which a war of attrition demands. And when white Rhodesians are convinced that an African solution to the Rhodesian problem is a distinct reality, not just oratory, then a settlement just to black Africans will be the more readily negotiated and achieved."

IV

President Kenneth Kaunda of Zambia, Prime Minister Pierre Trudeau of Canada and Lee Kuan Yew discussed the question of Rhodesia in a colour television interview recorded by the Canadian Broadcasting Corporation, on 12 January, in a London studio.

Lee Kuan Yew said that he thought everybody knew that if Rhodesia was settled the following day, in the sense that Governor's Rule, or indirect rule, was re-established and gradually over a period of years democratic government—that is to say, majority government of all the peoples living in Rhodesia—were established, that still would not solve the problem in southern Africa, because there was still Angola, Mozambique and South Africa. This was a deeper and a wider problem which would have to be lived with for a very long time and to be solved somehow because the world had become very small. "It is so quick now—the contact between different types, different ethnic groups, cultural groups, and this makes it imperative that we find some way to mute the antipathies, the animosities, and find some way to bring people together in harmony. And this will take time."

Lee Kuan Yew was reminded that he had been quoted in the Press as advocating something "pretty drastic"—that there should be something more of the spirit of the Vietcong, so far as the African guerilla movement was concerned. The Prime Minister replied that "one of these facts of life that you have to prove, or a particular group of people have to prove", is that they "had what it takes", before others would treat them as equals. Lee said: "I think it is a tragedy that people thought the Japanese were funny, short-legged human beings, not to be taken seriously, until they smacked right down into Southeast Asia and demonstrated that they were not funny men. Similarly, the Chinese armies were thought to be a ragged, rag-tagged and bob-tailed group of looters and pillagers until they smacked the American forces down from the Yalu to the tip of Korea, and now they are not thought to be funny men. The same way, I think, with the Africans in Africa. And I hope they will demonstrate in a more intelligent way, because you don't have to demonstrate the whole thing from A to Z. You can just establish your credentials, so to speak, that you are not jokers and people will begin to take you seriously. I believe that this is, unfortunately, a fact of contemporary life."

Dr Kaunda said he was afraid that there was a great deal of truth in what Lee Kuan Yew and the others said. "Until the African people, we ourselves," he said, "make ourselves strong and therefore able to pressurize, in Angola, or Mozambique or Rhodesia, or even South Africa, or Southwest Africa, what we are calling for will remain outside the agendas of important meetings. I'm afraid that is just the truth. And only when those people have, perhaps, lost more of their numbers on the battlefields is it going to be possible for their case to be put on the agenda of the world conferences. That is the truth of the matter."

The discussion between the three statesmen turned on Britain's attitude towards immigration, towards letting Africans and Asians in. Britain's policy had been attacked. Asked for his views, Lee Kuan Yew replied that he thought that one of the values of a "more intimate" meeting like the Commonwealth Prime Ministers' meeting was that they could talk to each other not only because they spoke the same language, but because they had similar terms of reference. A lot of the humbug and hypocrisy could be shrugged off. "Let us not pretend", Lee Kuan Yew said, "that there isn't colour prejudice deep down in the middle strata of every population. I am not going to absolve myself or my population from this. We have a multiracial community and we still suffer from this difficulty of getting the overseas Chinese and the Indian migrants and the Malays to accept each other completely and without reservation. I think it is going to take a very long time. Let us not pretend that twenty or more million Negroes in America are being treated as equals of the white Americans. True, adjustments have been made in the immigration laws of Canada and the United States itself.

You know, you find a measure which does not define race but which excludes the group you do not want. And I think that is part of life. It makes it possible for us to sit around and pretend that we are civilized, equal human beings. But it is possible for us—three individuals—to sit down and do that. I wonder whether it is possible to get, say an unskilled labourer in Lusaka and an unskilled labourer in Singapore and an unskilled labourer in Ottawa to do so. Is there a common acceptance of the fact that we all *Homo sapiens* in one very small world? I don't think they have conceived of it. And this is going to take a very long time."

Mr Trudeau was asked what there was in the Commonwealth for Canada, and the Canadian Prime Minister promptly replied: "The same thing as what's in it for Britain or for any other country." Mr Trudeau agreed with President Kaunda that there were certain common characteristics which made the Commonwealth. But to him the number of differences were greater than the similarities. "The common thing in the Commonwealth is that we all, by historical accident, as the President said, happened to be issued from some common empire. It is only an accident that makes us part of the Commonwealth. This isn't a reason for rejecting it. But this, I think, is a reason for being realistic in stating its objectives with respect to the self-interest and fulfilment of each of the country participating in the Commonwealth. For some, it will be greater knowledge of such parts of the world; for others it will be better markets; for some it will be cultural advantages; for some it will merely be the exchange of information."

"But, for most of us, wouldn't you say, Prime Minister, it offers us a counter-gravitational pull?" asked Lee Kuan Yew.

Dr Kaunda referred to the point Lee Kuan Yew had made earlier —that the world was becoming smaller and smaller. "And, surely, what this means is that all of us are moving in the direction of a world government, whether we like it or not. We are being pulled in that direction."

President Kaunda was asked whether he wouldn't agree that nationalism was the force of the times. The President agreed. "But," he added, "when you look at the way in which tribal feelings have been narrowing, bigger groupings are getting more and more attractive for all human beings on earth." This was the point, he said, that was underlined when Prime Minister Lee Kuan Yew referred to science and technology defeating time and space. "I think", the President added, "we have to preserve any organization that has such advantages as the Commonwealth. That's one reason why we in Zambia are in it."

Lee Kuan Yew argued that this really meant that the Commonwealth countries were trying to find shelter behind the bi-polar pulls of the American GNP and Russian GNP. "This is the problem," he said, "It's like getting stuck around a very big planet without the power to get out of its gravitational pull. Hence the value of the Commonwealth."

Some of the gloomier sections of the British Press had been talking about the present Commonwealth Prime Ministers' meeting being the last. What did Lee think? The Prime Minister agreed that there had been a lot of deliberate working up to some climax. But now it was an anti-climax. The Commonwealth had not broken up and he did not think it would.

The Canadian Prime Minister was asked about the question of diplomatic relations with China. And then Lee Kuan Yew was asked whether he had any views about Western nations establishing diplomatic relations with Peking.

Lee Kuan Yew replied: "My answer is quite simple. I think China is there. There are 700 million Chinese. It just will continue to be there and probably one of these days, the excesses of Red Guardism will be over and the atomic warheads will increase in number and so will the ICBMs... And it is not world government we are moving towards, as I see it. I think it is some kind of world order in which the major powers agree that they shall keep the peace between each other and then they can prevent the smaller ones from scrapping. And this was the whole intention of the United Nations in San Francisco in 1945. There was the Big Five with the veto and if they agreed, then action could be taken. If they didn't, as in the case of the Congo—Dag Hammarskjold broke his heart, he failed. And I think you have to face up to the fact now that there are seven very Big Powers who have developed their muscle..."

At this point the television programme ran out of time.

V

In the Commonwealth Prime Ministers' Conference itself, Lee Kuan Yew contributed to the debate on the world economic situation and trends. He said that while he agreed generally with his colleague, the Prime Minister of Ceylon, who had complained of the niggardly attitude of the developed countries, at the risk, he said, of overstating the case, he wanted to underline the inadequacies of the less developed countries. For Lee said he saw no profit in "our seeking alibis for our failure to develop".

Present-day Southeast Asia, its people and civilization, was the outcome of the impact of European colonial administrations on the economy and culture of these territories, and the demographic alterations through migration encouraged by the administering colonial powers.

What the different political leaderships had inherited varied with the European empires they had been part of. What they had done with their inheritance since independence varied considerably from country to country, depending on the quality of their political leaderships and the cohesiveness, educational standards, drive and stamina of their peoples. Lee developed this theme along the lines of the lecture he delivered at Harvard University, in December 1968.

VI

An outspoken and severe critic of striking British dock-workers, Lee Kuan Yew came home to find that Singapore stevedores were handling less cargo per gang-hour. On 30 January he issued the following statement: "On the Prime Minister's return to Singapore, his attention was drawn to the fact that certain gangs in the first and second shifts of the Port of Singapore Authority have been deliberately going slow, and cargo handled had, on the average, dropped from fourteen and a half to eleven and a half tons per gang-hour. Investigations have disclosed that although the PSA union leaders have expressed their disapproval of these tactics, in some sections some workers and some gangs are deliberately going slow in order to work with contract labour on the third shift, which is the best paid per hour. The going slow is sometimes deliberately to create work for this third shift. The Prime Minister has discussed the matter with union leaders and management this afternoon. He has stressed the fact that Singapore was doing well economically and that employment figures having gone up, and unemployment down, did not, repeat *not*, mean that we could afford to slacken in our efforts to increase productivity. With the support of the union, he has instructed the Chairman of the PSA to discipline whole gangs, by dismissals if necessary, where they are caught out engaged in such malpractices. Dismissal will include their vacating PSA quarters. So those who choose to work with contractors for higher pay per hour on the third shift will have to look for their own accommodation. The Prime Minister takes a serious view of those gang leaders who believe that in this way they can increase their take-home pay. They are sabotaging Singapore's rating as the fourth biggest, and one of the most efficient ports in the world. He considers such activities high treason. Offenders who persist will meet their just deserts."

A few workers were disciplined. Later, the Prime Minister announced that cargo handled, on the average, exceeded fourteen and a half tons per gang-hour.

VII

On 6 February, exactly 150 years after the founding of modern Singapore by Sir Thomas Stamford Raffles, the 132-year-old Singapore International Chamber of Commerce organized a banquet "to celebrate and commemorate" that historic occasion. The Prime Minister was the guest of honour.

In a toast to the memory of Raffles, Mr R. G. Bennett, chairman of the International Chamber of Commerce, described him as an administrator, remarkable for speed and efficiency, an historian, a zoologist and a linguist and according to his devoted clerk, Abdullah, a man of infinite grace and charm. But Raffles' most outstanding characteristic was undoubtedly his appreciation not only of the needs of his day, but also of the possibilities of tomorrow. To an extraordinary degree he grasped and shaped the opportunities of the future for Singapore.

Mr Bennett would not say that the Prime Minister possessed every single one of the qualities and characteristics of Raffles. But he would say that he possessed many of them, "especially the vision of what Singapore can be, to a sharper degree than anyone else who has since walked this island in the past 150 years". The Prime Minister was fortunate in that he had a government that was 100 per cent behind him, and the population unanimous in their choice of government. Raffles, on the other hand, had considerable opposition, although some powerful names supported him.

Lee Kuan Yew said he was flattered, if a little apprehensive, by the generous comparison of the qualities of Sir Stamford Raffles with the attributes he was supposed to have. "If", he added, "fifty years from now, your successor would say of me some of the things you have just said, it would be of immense satisfaction to me, even if I should be in some other world. For no judgment can be as fair and as final, or as cruel and conclusive, as that of history. Only posterity can pass judgment objectively on the wisdom or otherwise of their forbears. Only with the advantage of hindsight can people accurately analyse and assess the rights or wrongs of important decisions. Often these decisions had to be taken hurriedly and under intense pressure. But once taken, they could not be easily undone." Clearly referring to the British Government's decision to withdraw from bases East of Suez, Lee continued: "And one particularly momentous decision changed the destiny of several millions, not all in Singapore."

Lee said that decolonization was usually supposed to mean the orderly dismantling of an empire. Conversely, viewed from the position of the subject peoples, it should mean a restoration to freedom and nationhood. But several hundred years of Empire had created civilized communities where none previously existed. When Stamford Raffles arrived 150 years ago, there was no organized human society in Singapore, unless a fishing village could be called a society. There were now over two million people with the second-highest standard of living in Asia. "We thought the rational and orderly way forward was to build a nation out of the conglomeration of British colonies and dependencies in Southeast Asia. So Singapore joined Malaya in Malaysia. But for a number of compulsive reasons, Singapore was asked to leave, suddenly and abruptly."

Lee said that historians record that five years after 1819, the disposition of Southeast Asia was settled in Europe, in a treaty on 17 March, 1824, between the British and the Dutch. That treaty gave the outer islands to the Dutch. Penang, Peninsular Malaya (including Malacca) and Singapore became British. One hundred and fifty years was a short span in the history of a people. But even so how vastly different was the world today. Europe could no longer decide the fate of Asia. Even America was shy of being embroiled ever again in guerilla insurrections on the Asian mainland. "How much, more different the world will be twenty years from now, after Vietnam, after Britain's military withdrawal East of Suez, after Japan's self-defence forces have started to pay more courtesy visits, after China's recovery from the excesses of her Cultural Revolution and her inexorable climb up the technological and military ladder.

One hundred and fifty years ago, there was no Suez Canal, and Raffles took four months to get from Bencoolen to London. Now, it took eighteen hours from Singapore to London by air, even before the super-sonics. But whilst technological and political changes had gone on at a geometrically increasing speed, it was a sobering thought that geography had remained unchanged, except where there had been the dredging of canals, the erosion of the coastline by tides or reclamation of foreshores by tractors. Almost as unchanging were the nature and character of ethnic-cultural-religious groups. "You spoke highly of Munshi Abdullah or Abdullah bin Abdul Kadir, his full and proper name. He was a shrewd teacher, an astute observer. Not only was he a chronicler who faithfully recorded the facts worth noting. He also commented on what might or should have been. In 1832, 137 years ago, whilst travelling to the north of Peninsular Malaya, he wrote in his book *Pelayaran Abdullah* of many things which, if I had carefully read and digested earlier in my political life, would have saved me much disappointment."

The Prime Minister remarked that the Chamber in its commemoration programme had thought it worth mentioning that on that memorable day in 1819, some thirty Chinese were present to witness the ceremony. How proud they would have been to know that their descendants would be amongst the Malays, Indians, Eurasians and others who by their hard work, thrift, resourcefulness and enterprise had built modern Singapore. And what satisfaction it would have given them to know that their progeny would be amongst those who came into their own inheritance.

And considering the contribution they made in converting a fishing village into a humming centre for commerce, communication and industry, it was only just that it should be so.

The Prime Minister said that the celebrations of Singapore's 150th year would reach a climax in August, the nation's fourth anniversary of independence. Anniversaries, he said, must not mean a harking back to some idyllic, romanticized past, though even such an exercise in nostalgia was not without its therapeutic value. "For us this anniversary is a significant and formal moment, for a brief pause, to study and scrutinize the record of the past 150 years, learn the lessons therefrom, and with confidence renewed surge forward to improve upon the past."

The past was a good indicia of innate ability. It was also a good teacher of future relationships. It underlined the close links Singapore had always had with West Malaysia. "Half my Cabinet colleagues still have their families in West Malaysia. The ties are close and, in several respects, inseparable. In the future, as it has been in the past, there will be an enduring community of interests despite differences of styles, methods and ways of life."

The past also recorded the mutual advantage found in joint adventure. British administration and enterprise, plus local sweat, drive, skills, and ingenuity, had created what Singapore now had. "We look forward to British industry and technology continuing to make a valuable contribution to our growth and progress in the next 150 years."

The Prime Minister asked: "Are we being sentimental over this continuing association? But it is worth noting that even sentiment has its worth in foreign exchange and helps to balance payments. For in the balance sheets of companies, when mergers take place, substantial sums are set against what is known as goodwill. And goodwill is but an old-fashioned word to denote the economic value of well-established ties, ties which enduring sentiment and continuing habit support and reinforce in newer forms of association."

What of the future? "Our future is what we make of it, and we will use to best advantage the factors in our favour. First, the strategic. As long as the balance of geo-political forces in South Southeast and East Asia remain as they are, then Singapore's strategic value will continue undiminished. Second, our contribution to world trading, shipping, and servicing will continue to grow and expand whilst we add an ever bigger industrial sector to our economic base. Third and most important, the ability and industry of our young people, willing and eager to learn, prepared to work hard and pay their way in the world, finding pride and pleasure in constructive endeavour. But in any case, they are also disciplined and determined to defend what their ingenuity and effort have created."

In a less serious tone the Prime Minister remarked that with the rapid advance in medicine and in surgical techniques, perhaps not just for transplants but also replants, it was not beyond belief that there would be many besides young students present that evening who, in the year 2019, would recall "this memorable occasion".

Lee said: "Those of us who will be present then can look back on 200 years and say how right it was that we worked and sweated on the assumption that no one owed us a living, that we strove so hard and nurtured so rugged and robust, so resilient and resourceful a generation. Without this physical and spiritual ruggedness, all the fruits, the results of our labour even in concrete and steel, could end literally in ruins—ruins for the delectation of tourists in the year 2019, as they rummage in the rubble and dustbins of Singapore's past. And they would wonder how under such adverse climatic conditions a thrusting and striving society built such a thriving city with all the grace of cultivated living. And they would be perplexed and saddened by the unexpected and unexplainable destruction, when a dogged defence could have saved it. But we are not going to let that happen. Your children, and grandchildren, and mine, will be here to welcome all visitors to Singapore and offer them more excitement in present and future achievement than by goggling at past glory in ruins. When visitors come in the twenty-first century they will find Singapore an open and hospitable city to all those who come as friends or visitors, a Singapore strong and confident and thus at ease in offering the traveller a warm, comfortable and memorable welcome. Singapore has been and will remain more than a place on the map. She will give cause for satisfaction to all those who chart man's progress and who will find corroboration in Singapore's performance that this climb up the face of the cliff to a higher level of civilization, to a better life in a more gracious world, depends on man's constant and ceaseless striving for new and higher goals, depends on man's restless, organized, and unending search for perfection."

VIII

Invited by the University of Cambridge to deliver the Smuts Memorial Lecture ("an opportunity for a distinguished member of the Commonwealth to express his views before an informed but non-political audience"), the Prime Minister journeyed to Britain in April. While in London he had informal talks on security with the British Prime Minister and other Ministers. After his stay in Cambridge, Lee planned to accept President de Gaulle's long-standing invitation officially to visit France. President de Gaulle's sudden fall from office caused the French Government to cancel the visit, and Lee Kuan Yew stayed on at Churchill College until, on 10 May, he flew to the United States to talk with President Nixon.

Previous Smuts Memorial Lectures had been given by Sir Robert Menzies, Sir Chintaman Deshmukh, Sir Keith Hancoke, Lord Caradon and H. F. Oppenheimer, all, apparently without incident. But Lee Kuan Yew's oration was delivered (on 24 April) at the time of Left-wing student agitation in London. This had repercussions in Cambridge, where while Lee was speaking students outside Senate House banged on windows and chanted the thoughts of Mao Tse-tung. Other students began to throw a ball about and accidentally a window was smashed and a shower of glass fell near Lee. He continued, amidst applause, after remarking that, from his experience he could judge this to be no more than a "synthetic revolution".

The title of Lee's talk was "Continuity of Association After Empire". He said that the spring of 1969 was not a particularly auspicious time to eulogize the Commonwealth. British publications, including *Hansard,* reflected the desire of a growing body of opinion for full membership of the European Economic Community. And because Britain must be manifestly "European" to improve her chances of early membership, there had been a conscious effort to play down the Commonwealth and to mute Britain's "special relationship" with America.

Throughout history, empires had waxed and waned. But the British Empire was remarkable in three respects. First, it was the greatest of the overseas empires. Second, it seeded civilizations like the one in North America which became bigger than the metropolitan centre. Third, it was dismantled as an act of conscious policy with the minimum of rancour and maximum of continuing association after Empire in the Commonwealth. The British Empire was the only one that had territories on all six continents. Because of her inability to expand on land, Britain had to go across the seas to seek new lands. Britain's naval supremacy had been assured after the Battle of Trafalgar in 1805. She had unimpeded access to all six continents, and so to their markets. This made possible her industrial revolution, and for a long time she was the leading industrial society. The old Commonwealth was settled and colonized in the classic Roman definition of the word "colonize". After losing the American colonies, Britain was more sensitive to demands for autonomy, and more liberal in granting representative government. In retrospect, perhaps it was inevitable that more and more autonomy to Britain's own white settlements would lead to independence. Even if the North American colonies had not rebelled in 1776, they would eventually have demanded greater and greater self-government ending with separate sovereignty. Even the non-white empire seemed destined for separate independence. When Britain, as an act of deliberate policy, sought separate membership for India in the League of Nations, she conceded autonomy in principle, and thereby made independence inevitable. And after India and Pakistan became independent, the other colonies and protectorates in

Asia, Africa, the Caribbean and the Pacific were bound to follow the protocol path to independence ceremonies.

The Prime Minister said that Britain's dilemma in the 1940s and the 1950s was that, unlike the war-devastated countries of Europe, she was victor, not vanquished. The vastly changed balance of power in the world was perceived early enough for European Union sentiments to be nurtured. Britain played a part in setting up the Council of Europe in 1949. However, she was then not so much a part of continental Europe, as the centre of a world-wide and far-flung empire. Though more rather than less European in her culture, akin but not completely alike, Britain's history, her language and her literature had always been distinctive. With the wisdom of hindsight, most people agreed it was unfortunate that Britain did not sign the Treaty of Rome in 1953. It would have been painful, especially for the old Commonwealth countries exporting temperate climate produce to Britain, because a common tariff wall would have had to be built around Britain and the EEC countries as from 1956. But the Commonwealth trade ties could have been adjusted, and growth resumed in a wider European context. British membership would also have made the EEC more outward-looking.

When India and Pakistan became independent in 1947, a feasible alternative could have been some economic arrangement between Britain, the old Commonwealth countries and the new Commonwealth countries, giving British industry the economies of scale necessary for expensive research, production and marketing in high-technology products. It could have given the Commonwealth countries the advantage of sharing in the benefits of research and getting their technologists trained. Then other members of the Commonwealth could have joined as they became independent. But in 1947 both old and new Commonwealth countries were keen to diversify their economic ties and were hoping thereby to accelerate their economic growth. In fact, in 1945 Canada left the sterling area and went with the US dollar. For the decade 1958-67 trade within the EEC countries increased 260 per cent. But it was an inward-looking Europe. EEC trade with the under-developed world increased by only forty-nine per cent. Trade within EFTA increased 254 per cent. But the volume of intra-EFTA trade (excluding Britain) was only one-seventh that of the EEC countries. And Britain's share was only thirteen per cent of this, although her population at fifty-five million was ten million more than that of all the other EFTA countries. However, trade within the Commonwealth, including Britain, increased only by twenty-two per cent. For the same period, Commonwealth trade with the rest of the world grew by 105 per cent. The volume of intra-Commonwealth trade was less than forty-five per cent that of the intra-EEC in 1967. Furthermore, the new Commonwealth countries did not develop as fast as the old Commonwealth countries. Ethnic, religious and linguistic strife tore whole sub-continents apart, like India

499

and Pakistan, and Ceylon. "Nor can we forget the tragedy in Nigeria." Then, encroachments on Commonwealth trade were made by American, European and Japanese manufacturers as Commonwealth preferences were lowered a few years after independence was gained. The services of Crown Agents were reduced as British colonial service officers retired.

Lee Kuan Yew thought that perhaps more grievous was the loss of exports of high-technology products to Canada and Australia, as their economies geared into that of the USA. Civilian jet aircraft, built in America and painted with the names of British and Commonwealth airlines, vividly carried this message at all British and Commonwealth airports. For the immediate future, EEC offered a wealthier and bigger market especially for commodities with a high technological content. The figures for 1967 were—EEC: population 182 million, GNP £124 thousand million. Commonwealth: population 849 million, GNP £96 thousand million. EFTA: excluding Britain, population 44 million, GNP £30 thousand million. Further, the Treaty of Rome meant free mobility of labour and capital. "Membership of the EEC would have stuck the spurs on British unions and management. It would have forced the unions to modernize their outlook, discard restrictive practices, and stop wild-cat strikes, to meet competition from keener, and in 1956, hungrier and lesser paid French, Italian and German workers. For management, 'the establishment', both old-school-tie and old-boy networks, would have to give way to a meritocracy. Whether in the '50s or in the '70s, membership of the EEC requires considerable structural changes in Britain's economy. It would not be a painless process. Courageous leadership from the Government will have to be matched by an enlightened and spirited response from unions and management."

However, apart from the advantages of a bigger market in the EEC, there were other special reasons for the spectacular performance of the Germans, and the recovery of the French and Italian economies. They had labour resources not available to Britain. It was the large number of idle workers which made capital investments in new growth industries profitable, and resulted in high growth rates. By contrast, Britain had full employment right from the immediate post-war years. At one stage, considerable immigration from the new Commonwealth countries took place to increase Britain's labour pool and so increase her GNP. But this was to lead to considerable domestic problems, particularly when the "freeze" and the "squeeze" led to increased unemployment. Unfortunately, by the time Britain decided, in the autumn of 1961, to take the preliminary steps to apply for membership of the EEC, she was blocked by the French veto. In January, 1963, Britain was not "European" enough.

Nearly five years later, in the autumn of 1967, Britain was still not "European" enough. This was in spite of moves making clear that she was loosening her links with the Commonwealth, ending her East-of-Suez responsibilities, and no longer pressing for special transitory terms for old or new Commonwealth countries. But the "overseas" links of the French, Dutch or Belgians did not seem to make them less "European". But then this privilege was only for founder members. French special links with French-speaking Africa entitled her to send paratroops to restore legitimate governments when they were deposed by military coups. And, despite devaluation in November, 1967, and the diminution of the role of sterling as a reserve currency, the French Government had not changed their views on Britain's inadequate "Europeanness".

Besides the many reasons that had been advanced across the Channel to show how inadequate were Britain's qualifications for membership, Lee thought there might be another, so far unexpressed, objection. "If the end objective of EEC is political integration leading to political unity, then language and culture are most important considerations." New France, as Quebec was once named, and again recently called by de Gaulle, had held on with tenacity to the French language and culture. They had resisted anglicization in a continent overwhelmingly English-speaking. Why then should old France be anglicized when its own language was until recently supreme as the language of Europe and of international diplomacy? Why should French culture be displaced or demoted? This was what might happen if the EEC six were to admit the EFTA eight under the present rules of the Treaty of Rome. The present EEC had a majority of Latin-speaking, French, Belgians (most of the Flemish-speaking also speak French), Luxembourg, and Italians, 112 million to 70 million Dutch and Germans. In practice, when the representatives of the EEC six met, four spoke or understood one another in French or Italian. So it was that proceedings were usually conducted in French. Add the EFTA eight, and the Latin group became a minority of 121 million to 160 million British-Scandinavian-German-Dutch. "In practice, if the fourteen representatives of an enlarged EEC were to meet under the present rules, English will be the language most understood and likely to be used. And if political unity is achieved, English will be the language best qualified to be the common language of any supra-national European Assembly or Parliament. Otherwise, the gathering will be like a smaller United Nations General Assembly. With a language goes the literature. And literature will pass on the history, ethos and culture of a people. The fact that Britain readily agreed to have 'Concorde' spelt with an 'e' only underlines British confidence in the growing strength of the English language. The 'e' in Concorde has been explained as standing for England, excellence, elegance and *entente*. But 'e' for the French stands especially for Europe."

Lee said that today, English-speaking governments represented over a third of the world population. The new Commonwealth countries all needed to learn one language that would give them access to scientific

501

and technological expertise. English offered the most advantage. It meant access to Britain, the developed Commonwealth countries, and America. This had led many countries, Japan, China, Thailand, Latin America, Belgium and Scandinavia, to adopt English as their second language. This was happening even in former European dependencies. The Dutch ruled the Indonesian Archipelago for about 350 years. The present elite was educated in the Dutch language. The next-generation elite would probably be at ease in English. For English was the second language taught in Indonesian schools. The present South Vietnamese elite was more French-speaking than English-speaking. But the next generation would be more English-speaking. As the world grew smaller through man's ingenuity and inventiveness in communications and transportation, the tendency was towards fewer but larger blocs. Russia and the Slav-speaking people of Eastern Europe formed one bloc. Latin-speaking Rumania wedged in the south-western Slav bloc was an accident of history. China, and what de Gaulle had referred to as her numerous millions, formed another bloc, more Chinese than communist.

Even as early as the 1940s, after India and Pakistan became independent, Churchill spoke of the English-speaking peoples, meaning those of European stock, Britain, America and the white Commonwealth. He conceived of a cohesive bloc on which British international influence could be sustained, now that the Empire was dismantled. Churchill's vision of the future was in the same lofty historic terms as de Gaulle's. Expressed in percentages of world population, France was one point five per cent to Britain's one point six per cent. France and Quebec was one point six per cent to Britain, Canada (minus Quebec), Australia, New Zealand and America's eight point five per cent. However, if there were a strong French- or Latin-led EEC there could be a "Latin" bloc of French-, Italian-, Spanish-, Portuguese-speaking, fifteen point seven per cent of the world population. There were forty-two "Latin" governments in the United Nations (twenty-one French-speaking, nineteen Spanish-speaking, two Portuguese-speaking) to thirty-one English-speaking governments.

Lee argued that if a larger economic grouping was to be created, then, for France, the present rules were not suitable. For the EEC would undergo a qualitative change. A directorate of the larger four—France, Germany, Italy and Britain—was one way of avoiding anglicization. It might be worth Britain's while to explore the implications of these proposals.

He predicted that if only full membership under the present rules of the Treaty of Rome was acceptable, then the British application was likely to remain on the table unconsidered for some time. The danger of such a policy was that it might lead to stop-gap measures whilst waiting for membership, when in fact Britain could recover her economic health without the EEC, provided she was prepared to make the effort, undertake the changes necessary, and pay the political price. The Japanese had done this. They were another island people, with almost the same land area, if more mountainous. They had nearly twice the population. They lost huge pieces of valuable real estate after the war —Korea, Manchuria, Formosa, and half of Sakhalin. Like the Germans, they had to take back large numbers of their ethnic kind expelled from their extended empire. This meant large unemployed labour reserves, to make investment give high returns. They had no common market, free-trade area, or even commonwealth preferences. But the Japanese, like the Germans, having gone through national humiliation in defeat, had that resolve to redeem their national pride, to make that greater effort to demonstrate that they were not down. And the Japanese had got around the problems of economies of scale by specializing in certain fields like electronics, and petro-chemicals. For instance, Japanese colour television production for 1969 was expected to be five million sets, three million for home consumption, as against Britain's 130,000 sets. They were doing this even though their per capita income was half that of the British. Britain unfortunately competed with America in very high and sophisticated technology like civilian and military aircraft and missiles. Whilst she was as imaginative and creative as the Americans, Britain did not have America's large domestic market to enable export prices to be reduced and competitive. The VC10 was technologically as good, if not superior to the Boeing, Douglas, or Lockheed jet aircraft. But, without a large domestic market for long haul aircraft, Britain's export prices could not be as competitive. Nor could she afford to invest in further expensive research and development to make the VC10 more economical in running cost, nor produce a comparable jumbo-jet version of it. Meanwhile, Russian Ilyushins and Tupolevs kept out all Western aircraft from the national airlines of Eastern Europe.

But the Concorde showed what was possible with European collaboration. So also the MRCA aircraft now under discussion. If EEC membership was not immediately possible, some other form of economic co-operation or association could be of mutual value especially in research and development production and marketing of products of very high technology. So long as Britain was strong and thriving, the English-speaking civilizations she had created overseas—North America, South Africa, Australia and New Zealand—were a source of added strength. In two World Wars they came to Britain's aid. Their "brains", like many of the Rhode scholars, including Americans, came to Britain to learn and many stayed on. But a Britain which had become less thrusting no longer offered fulfilment. These English-speaking centres of civilization had now become her competitors. The United States and Canada were five times bigger in population, had nine times Britain's wealth and industrial capacity, and an infinitely bigger multiple in potential growth. What began as a useful method of settling second and third sons in circumstances approximating that of the eldest who came into the inheritance under the rules of primogeniture, had now become a magnet drawing away frustrated brains and skills. They threatened to take over British influence and markets throughout the world, especially in the English-speaking new Commonwealth. It was ironic that those European countries, which failed to create comparable civilizations overseas, were placed in less hazard of being drained of their brains and their influence.

The old Commonwealth countries now wanted more British brains and brawn to populate their countries. English-speaking Canadians wanted to increase the ethnic British component of their population. So too with the Australians and the New Zealanders. From 1963-67 there was a net outflow of 616,800 Britons to the old Commonwealth, America and South Africa. More debilitating than the loss in sheer numbers was the loss in men of quality. In 1961 the brain drain into Britain equalled the flow out. The loss from Britain to America and the old Commonwealth started in 1962, with a net loss of 400. The total net loss for the five years 1962-66 was 7,800 scientists and technologists. Whilst Britain had always sent out the middle quality of her population to help build up the old Commonwealth, she could not afford to lose her best. It was not numbers, but quality and high performance, which gave and could again give Britain a pre-eminent place amongst the nations of the world. The quality of life, as distinct from standard of living, was higher in Britain than in North America, Australia, New Zealand or South Africa. Many Britons who had migrated to America found the violence and the problems of Negro-white relationships so disturbing that they had moved on to Canada or Australia. If, Lee continued, Britain's economy recovered, and her standard of living improved, then the present mood of depression would pass off; in place of frustration would be fulfilment in professional or artistic creativity. If high performance was given social and material recognition, the brain drain could be reversed. A thriving Britain had always attracted the best from the old Commonwealth and from America.

Britain could not and should not compete in the numbers game. There were more Commonwealth students in America than there were in Britain. In 1960, there were only 7,000 Commonwealth students in Britain as against 13,000 in the USA. In 1967 the numbers in Britain had increased to 10,000, by only thirty-four per cent, as against a 126 per cent or fourfold increase to 29,000 in America. America could offer more scholarships in more universities. Perhaps also some American colleges classified as tertiary educational institutions would not be so graded in Britain. "For Britain, the emphasis must be on excellence, both in her own institutions and in the scholars she takes in from the Commonwealth, and from America."

Meanwhile, new sub-groupings were formed, as links were formed by the lesser-developed, non-white English-speaking peoples with the

504

developed white peoples of America, Canada and Australia-New Zealand. Canada was developing a special interest with the Caribbean Commonwealth countries, and with both the English- and French-speaking countries of West Africa. Canadian economic assistance extended to India and Ceylon for reasons of sentiment, compassion and potential economic relationships. Malaysia and Singapore had as many of their students in Australia and New Zealand as in Britain. For security and economic reasons both were getting closer to Australia and New Zealand. But whatever centres of new sub-groupings might emerge, none would replace Britain as the hub of the Commonwealth. Britain would always have a special link with each one of the twenty-seven members of the Commonwealth. With growing maturity an adult relationship was being established. Old ties were valued, not just for economic advantage. Both for the old and new Commonwealth, continuity of association with Britain after Empire was a useful and valuable counter-weight to the new and more aggressive forces they all had to face in a world growing ever smaller. The Americans and the Russians, however generous and agreeable they might be as individuals, were demanding as governments. And bigger neighbours suspected of expansionist tendencies were always troublesome.

Trends do not continue indefinitely, said Lee Kuan Yew. Some historians had made the point that discontinuity, as much as continuity, marked the history of nations, peoples and empires. A cruel example of this was Smuts' vision of a continuing white Commonwealth of Nations, with South Africa a proud and leading member of it. He would never have believed that in 1962 South Africa would be officially refused continued membership in a multiracial Commonwealth. Perhaps in a decade for some, or more for others, the new Commonwealth countries would either sort out their problems themselves, or seek outside help to re-establish conditions which made economic and social progress possible. When stable conditions for constructive endeavour had been established, then investment would flow in and rapid growth will be achieved. Their present backwardness could be the very reason for high growth rates. Japan, Hong Kong and Taiwan had very high growth rates. One of the reasons Japan had been galloping at about fifteen per cent growth per annum from 1950, when the Korean war gave her a booster, was because she started from a relatively low base. For Britain, there could be no easy return to the comfortable past. The sooner adjustments were made, the sooner the recovery. The worst that could happen was a Britain with economic problems becoming chronic because her entry into the EEC or any other economic association was systematically blocked. "To aggravate the situation her trade unions and management do not see the economy as a joint responsibility but as that of the government of the day. Then the old Commonwealth will want to cream off British brains and brawn to build up their economies and populate their empty spaces. And the new Commonwealth countries will gravitate elsewhere for their development needs in education, expertise and high-technology equipment." The best was a Britain with her economy put in order because the Government inspired and carried her people and, more crucial, because her union leaders and her industrial managers accepted a joint responsibility to get the country moving forward and upwards to higher levels of technology and productivity. Then confidence would be restored, Britain's confidence in her role and future for the next hundred years. And more mundane, but no less valuable, was the restoration of the confidence of other peoples and their governments in Britain's economic strength. She would then add to the strength of Western Europe, the Commonwealth and America. To achieve this, some formula must be found with West European or North American Governments for joint research, production and marketing of products of very high technology. It also required excellence to be once more admired, nurtured and rewarded. Such a Britain could the better afford to care for her less fortunate, the old, the disabled and the unemployed. A Britain recovered in poise and prosperity, once again pushing outwards on the frontiers of discovery in the pure and applied sciences, would be the intellectual and cultural centre of all the English-speaking peoples.

Meanwhile, Lee concluded, it would be a pity if temporary irritations and frustrations with seemingly intractable economic and political difficulties were to lead to false economies, the abandonment of links, and the losing of expertise. As the old generation that knew the Commonwealth countries well passed on, a younger generation must keep up the expertise. The links Britain had with the Commonwealth countries, old and new, her special relationship with America, were part of her history. It might be prudent to maintain these Commonwealth links. They could be of considerable economic value in the next few decades. "The remarkable way in which the Empire was dismantled, consciously, and with the minimum of animosity and antipathy means goodwill." And goodwill, another way of describing trust and confidence as a result of long association, was not without economic value. But some theoreticians for the welfare state, accompanied by high personal taxes to pay for the welfare, had expounded that the British were not interested in the acquisition of wealth. Lee said: "Even if this were true, I would like to recount what a worldly-wise minister of a member of the EEC told me when he passed through Singapore recently. 'We thought', he said, 'that if all our people enjoyed high standards of life, with all the things needed to make them comfortable, then they would be happy. Now we have comfortable homes and the good life, but we are not happy. We have lost that sense of adventure when we travelled overseas and found fulfilment in this part of the world.' He added: 'I fear my British friends may discover what we already have, that without that challenge, life is not as meaningful, not as exciting, not as satisfying.' I would hope my British friends will never be without that challenge at home and overseas, which is where this island people have historically sought adventure and found fortune and fulfilment."

"If all Commonwealth leaders were as well-informed and unprejudiced as Lee Kuan Yew," declared *The Daily Telegraph* in an editorial comment the next day, headed "A Candid Friend", "the group would be in far better shape than it now is, and certainly command more loyalty and respect. In his Smuts Memorial Lecture, while giving Britain more credit than she usually receives nowadays for her colonizing and de-colonizing role, he also gave a frank and shrewd diagnosis of her present *malaise*. High on the list of defects he puts out-of-date trade unions, restrictive practices and wild-cat strikes: management also has not transformed itself as the fierceness of modern international competition demands. He is no opponent of the European Common Market, and deplores Britain's failure—through a preoccupation with the Commonwealth to which he pays tribute—to go in at the start. Britain would have exercised a liberalizing influence which would have benefited Commonwealth countries. But Britain seems to him to be prepared to sit moping indefinitely because entry is barred. The Japanese, he points out, also an island people who had lost an empire, overcame far greater difficulties than Britain has had to contend with. Mr Lee finds the Commonwealth an inspiring enterprise, and although aware of its practical limitations, hopes that false economies will not lead to the abandonment of links. The answer is surely that much depends on reciprocity. Both militarily and economically Singapore's case is a strong one."

Once again the name of Lee Kuan Yew was mentioned in London as a possible successor to U Thant at the United Nations. *The Times* on 18 April carried the following item: "Although U Thant's second five-year term as Secretary-General of the United Nations does not expire until December, 1971, there has already been some speculation about who might succeed him. One theory, strongly held in certain Commonwealth quarters, is that Singapore's brilliant Prime Minister, Lee Kuan Yew, might not be unhappy to tread the wider stage of the UN. It is an attractive theory, partly because he was one of the Afro-Asians suggested when U Thant was showing reluctance to take on another term; partly because his abilities are widely recognized. Lee reacted with characteristic crispness when we popped the question. With a shrug, and a touch of scornful exasperation of the man who has been asked the same question many times, he said: 'First, the job is not vacant. Secondly, it's not the sort of job that gets offered: and thirdly it's only for a man who has a certain philosophical approach towards life ... and is prepared for an endless series of disappointments and can be consoled by—well—contemplation. I mean, exchange, for a lifetime of frustration, what we have here—where it blossoms, and blooms? No, at the end of ten years you won't recognize this place . . . ' Lee is a man of action whose first consideration is the flourishing emergence of Singapore, where he exercises real and virtually full power. Ambition would have enticed his hopes, once, to be Prime Minister of Malaysia, but that hope seems extinct. Given a different UN in ten years' time, with Singapore safely launched, perhaps his view might change. He is, after all, only 45. Until then the jocular comment is likely to persist that the story is always started in Kuala Lumpur, in the hope that his removal from the scene would facilitate new links between Singapore and Malaysia."

Lee Kuan Yew declined to make any further comment on *The Times* report, but a spokesman said the Prime Minister wanted to devote all his energy to the development of Singapore "for the next ten years at least".

While Lee Kuan Yew was in England considerable feeling was being aroused in Malaysia by intemperate speeches during the general election campaign. In Penang, the Malaysian Prime Minister on 5 May made the astonishing allegation that the Peoples' Action Party was trying to destroy Malaysia. "That is why", Tunku Abdul Rahman was reported to have said, "it is pouring in money to help opposition parties here. The Singapore Government", the Tunku continued, "is working hand in glove with traitors of Malaysia who are bent upon destroying the Malays." A spokesman accompanying Lee Kuan Yew said that the suggestion was too extravagant for any serious comment. He added that Singapore's Prime Minister had engagements in London, Washington and Tokyo, and would not be returning to Singapore until 20 May. Further, to emphasize that Lee Kuan Yew was hardly the man "bent upon destroying Malaysia or the Malays", the spokesman said that the Prime Minister was that afternoon taking a seminar at the Centre for South Asian Studies in Cambridge, and on the morrow, would be lunching with Mr H. Hinsley, Reader in History of International Relations, and dining with Dr E. R. Leach, Provost of Kings College and Reader of Social Anthropology. The following day, Lee Kuan Yew was made an honorary Fellow of his old Cambridge College at Fitzwilliam. He dined that evening with the Master and Fellows at High Table.

Lee Kuan Yew's state visit to France abandoned, the Prime Minister remained in Cambridge, completing his "Sabbatical" until it was time for him to fly to the United States to see President Nixon. He was with the President at the White House for an hour on 12 May. A statement put out by the Prime Minister's staff said that Lee also met the Defence Secretary and Dr Henry Kissinger, the Security Affairs adviser. Later, the Prime Minister met Mr Marshall Green, Assistant Secretary of State for East Asian and Pacific Affairs, Mr Elliot Richardson, Under-Secretary of State, and Mr Alexis Johnson, Under-Secretary of State for Political Affairs. The statement said this was the first time Lee had met Mr Nixon since the President took office. He also took the opportunity to meet some of the President's Cabinet Ministers and the aides who help formulate policy towards East and Southeast Asia.

News came from Malaysia of riots in the capital and Lee Kuan Yew told the Press he was concerned over reports of communal clashes in West Malaysia. "Malaysia", he said, "is our closest neighbour. Her well-being or otherwise must affect us all in Singapore. I hope her present difficulties will be quickly resolved and reasonableness and tolerance become the order of things."

The *New York Times* on 14 May reported that Lee Kuan Yew told reporters that the United States should not withdraw too quickly from combat in South Vietnam "just because the burden has become too costly for you". A gradual disengagement, he said, could probably be carried out without serious repercussions across Southeast Asia— but only if the South Vietnamese were given adequate time to "get on their own feet and carry the burden themselves". The *New York Times* said that after talks with President Nixon and Secretary of Defence Melvin R. Laird, Lee spoke bluntly about the military and political tasks that lay ahead for the South Vietnamese—responsibilities, he said, that they should have taken upon themselves long ago.

Twelve hours before President Nixon's nation-wide television address on Vietnam, Lee said: "I am confident that Nixon will do the right thing—I like the deliberately thorough way in which he is approaching the problem." He expressed reservations about the intention to disengage American combat forces. "Every thinking person in Southeast Asia has already accepted this trend in United States policy," the Prime Minister said. "If this disengagement is gradual and orderly, then confidence in American commitments in the region can be maintained," he added.

To the astonishment of his aides, Lee Kuan Yew, said the report, assailed Vice-President Nguyen Cao Ky of South Vietnam in an interview with the Columbia Broadcasting System. He accused his Southeast Asian colleague of "extravagance and lack of sensitivity to his people".

"The South Vietnamese leadership must understand the mood in the United States. Unless they show the capacity—not just the willingness—the capacity to stand up for themselves and for what they believe, then this last chance will pass them by," the Prime Minister said. "Either they've got it by now or they'll never get it—they must be put to the test."

In his televised report on the war in Vietnam, President Nixon said that the United States had ruled out attempting to impose a purely military solution on the battlefield, and had also ruled out either a one-sided withdrawal from Vietnam, or the acceptance in Paris of terms which would amount to a disguised defeat. "If", he added, "we simply abandon our effort in Vietnam, the cause of peace might not survive the damage that would be done to other nations' confidence in our reliability."

In a comment to the Press on 15 May, the Prime Minister said that "if there is to be a negotiated settlement it has to be fair and honourable. It must be as fair to the National Liberation Front as to the South Vietnamese Government in Saigon, offering both an equal chance of achieving power through an expression of the popular will of the people of South Vietnam. This will also be an honourable way for the North Vietnamese and American Governments to withdraw their forces from South Vietnam." The problem now, the Prime Minister added, was how to establish conditions of stability and security, so that the people of South Vietnam could express their wishes in free elections, without intimidation or terror.

A month later, the *Washington Post* editorially referred to Lee's remarks in the United States. The paper said that the Prime Minister had a correct and realistic view of America's position in Vietnam. "This country has had no stronger supporter of its Vietnam effort over the years than Mr Lee Kuan Yew, the Prime Minister of Singapore, and yet when Mr Lee was here in town a while ago he was not asking as much of us, in his private conversations with old friends, as we have been asking of ourselves," the newspaper said. "He had read American public opinion rightly, and, while he was puzzled and dismayed, he was realistic. If the public would not see it through, it was time to begin a gradual withdrawal of our forces—to Vietnamize the war. And if the South Vietnamese prove incapable of handling the increased burden and succumb in time to communist control, what would the repercussions be elsewhere in Asia? They would not be serious—the American position would not collapse. Provided the South Vietnamese were seen to have been given a reasonable opportunity to save themselves, provided we were honest about it, and did not pull out precipitiously, provided it was plain that we had done as much as any outside power reasonably could be expected to do to foreclose a communist conquest by force. This was the hub of it, giving the South Vietnamese an honest, reasonable shot at their own salvation, and, while these are not easy measures to make, this is the test which must somehow be applied to the proposals for disengagement put forth by Mr Clark Clifford ... "

IX

Lee went back to his old school, Raffles Institution, on Speech Day, 6 June. Because of a traffic hold-up he was a few minutes late, and he took the opportunity to tell the scholars that this was not a good example. It was one he urged them never to follow. One hundred and fifty years, he said, was a very short time reckoning in the terms of the histories of the various civilizations which had existed in Asia. But 150 years was a very long time in the life of any community. It had seen the rise and fall of empires; it had seen the emergence in the past twenty years of over sixty new nation states, of which Singapore was one. "I do not pretend to be able to see the kind of world we will live in, or our progeny will live in, 150 years from now. Suffice to say that if we do our duty, five or ten years from now we will have a more thriving, more robust and a more secure Singapore and that much a more certain future for all of us."

Lee left the students in no doubt about what he thought their duty should be. "It is my intention, and that of my colleagues, that the University of Singapore is worthy of the young men and women we are producing from our schools, whom we are nurturing with the right values. And by right values I mean the values that will ensure you a reasonably secure, a relatively high standard of living which demands a disciplined community prepared to give of its best and ready to pay for what it wants, work and earn and pay for what it wants. Nothing is more disastrous than to be sucked up into the fads and fetishes that we read about and see on our television screens, the kinds of student protest, unrest, *malaise* in North America, in part of Western Europe and in Britain. They have their problems; we have ours. We share some problems in common, living in a world which has grown smaller as a result of man's inventiveness and his capacity for instant communication and rapid transportation. Ideas pass quickly from capital to capital and we happen to be on the jet route and on the satellite communication system besides the SEACOM communication system. So what happens in London, Washington, Paris, California, Tokyo, Canberra, Melbourne, Wellington, we know of in a matter of minutes or see on our television screen in a matter of hours. But always ask: is this relevant to me? Ask yourself that question. The American student is caught in his own problems, the dilemma of either being patriotic and dying for a war which seems endless and unwinnable or listening to some of his professors and teachers say that this is a wicked, vicious, inhuman war which he should dodge; of wondering how he is to solve the problems of black versus white, problems of poverty, lack of education, lack of educational and entertainment opportunities. They are different from the problems the British student faces. He has to ask himself what his country's role is, now that Empire is over. He is undergoing a period of *malaise* because his elders in government, in opposition, in industry, in the unions are themselves groping for answers to his future. I am not groping for answers to your future," said Lee Kuan Yew.

The Prime Minister said that he and his colleagues did their re-thinking as of 9 August, 1965 (when Singapore separated from Malaysia and became an independent nation). "We attempted the other way, the broader base, a place within a wider framework. It was not workable, not for reasons of personality, conflict of leadership, but for fundamental reasons; and we are determined, whatever people may have thought on 9 August, 1965, that we shall continue to thrive, to prosper and to uphold values which we consider critical to the survival of new nations which embrace within their frontiers more than one race, more than one language, more than one religion. In other words, giving and being seen to give equal opportunities to all to find fulfilment." And that could best be done in Singapore by each keeping his own links with his past, his language, his culture so that he would understand his parents, the fables, the folklore, the parables, but seeking common ground with all the other groups "because it is not in the past that we have to live. It is today and tomorrow that we have to prepare ourselves for; that means common ground, hence effective bilingualism."

Lee Kuan Yew said he believed in these things very profoundly and over the years he knew that they were absolutely fundamental to Singapore's future. "So much so, although I would like very much for my sons to have come to this school, I decided that because they would be effectively English-speaking, having an English-speaking environment at home, they went to a Chinese school; and they are completely at home in either culture, in either language and in more than just these two languages."

The Prime Minister reminded the students that their future was in his hands and those of his colleagues for the time being, but ultimately in theirs. "A generation passes on, a younger one takes over and I do not want to see what we have done over the past ten years go into fumbling, feeble hands. They must go into hands which are firm, minds which are just, free from muddle-headed thinking, which means that we will see to it that our universities and, most important, teachers in those universities, reflect the values which trial and error, plus theory, have shown to be important if we are to continue to prosper and to flourish."

Lee said it would be unrealistic if he did not advert their attention to what had been happening. "You know that there have been communal incidents. I returned on 20 May knowing that a Malay had been shot and killed by a group of thugs not very far from here. We held the ground. It erupted again last Saturday. When a situation like that happens, you first let everybody know that there will be just, fair, and firm government. We talk about goodwill, love, fraternity in one community after everybody knows that his life and his property are best secured by listening to reason and to what the Government through its police is urging him to do: not to take the law into his own hands, and not to believe that for reasons of sentiment he ought to beat another person up because of his race. That is a very foolish thing to do in Singapore. Those who take the law into their own

512

hands will be smacked down firmly and where the evidence justifies it, a criminal prosecution will go right through to the end."

When this sense of justice had been restored and everybody saw that justice was being done, "then we go back and then talk about long-term problems. For this is now a long-term problem, it's different from the riots in 1964. Then we had no control over the army and the police; this time we have. In 1964 the problems were not as deep and as abiding. They have become far more painful, far more difficult, because the magnitude of the problem has taken on a new dimension. From time to time we may have to face this little bit of fuss and bother but a population properly educated on what is best for itself should be emotionally inoculated from these irrational, communal, emotive outbursts."

It was in schools like Raffles where the different communities learnt to be one people that the future lay and eventually all schools in Singapore would comprise within their classroom more than just one ethnic group. This would take some time, but in the long run "we will not have any school where pupils are put together on the basis of just one race and one language. The monolinguist is a bigot because he does not know that there are other languages and other cultures as great if not greater than his own. A bilinguist has an aperture, a window open in his mind, into other worlds and when all of Singapore understand that and all of them have windows opening on to each other's worlds, then we will have a truly more tolerant, more understanding and for that reason a more peaceful and prosperous future."

X

In a long interview with *Time-Life* on 10 June, parts of which later appeared in *Time* magazine, the Prime Minister discussed, among other topics, the Asian Revolution.

What happened to it, he was asked. Lee Kuan Yew thought it got bogged down in a great deal of problems with which it started, namely, lack of trained administrators, technocrats and entrepreneurs with sufficient drive and creativity. Different ethnic groups, brought into one economic whole by a European overlord, did not hold together once power was handed over to indigenous majorities. They attempted to stay in office and prove legitimacy through the popular vote by making appeals to ethnic, religious and linguistic loyalties. These were some of the easiest of appeals to make. In short the Asian Revolution got bogged down with the mechanics of administration—or lack of it—and the plain facts of life, and economies of development.

Time-Life said that since the end of World War Two, the primary task of Southeast Asian leaders had been to harness the forces of nationalism to gain independence, and after that to forge a national identity. Had these tasks been completed? Lee did not think they had been completed—the forging of their national identities. None of these countries in Southeast Asia had completely established a new identity. What they must establish was an identity which comprised the various ethnic groups in the various territories which a colonial overlord brought together into one whole. One of the problems was that these things took a very long time.

Was forging a national identity the task of Southeast Asian leadership in the 1970s? Lee said it was one of the tasks of leadership. First to forge a people with a unity of purpose who found fulfilment by working together and giving each other a better life. They had to feel that they together belonged in one whole. "If you are making the effort for the prosperity and well-being of a group you do not consider a part of you, then people find it very difficult to make the effort."

What should be done to get the Asian Revolution going again? Lee thought there should be a move into a new phase. Not a revolution in the sense of sudden political change, of getting rid of one set of rulers and a system of government, to establish another set of rulers and another system. That had already been done. The question now was how to fulfil the expectations of a people that had been mobilized to get rid of European colonial regimes? They had been mobilized on the basis that once the white man was gone they would occupy all the big houses, the big desks, and the big motor-cars of the European. Well, that was fine. "But unless you know how to run the economy... You can get aid for some time. But in the long run you have got to pay for these things. And that means getting your economy going. From a purely agricultural to plantation-mining economics, to commercial economies, on to higher levels of industrial production and higher technology. This means educating the population into higher skills. Without discipline you cannot even begin the education and training. Once you have chaos, riots and civil commotion people do not go to school, and teacher training colleges close. So the teachers are not produced and so on. You can tie yourself up into a knot."

Time-Life turned to the outcome of the Vietnam war. Did Lee think that in the long run South Vietnam would come under the control of the communists? Lee Kuan Yew replied: "I would hope not. But nobody can predict that. It would depend upon what political leadership the South Vietnamese are given, or can produce. Militarily, American intervention has prevented the communists from winning. But politically, in order to win, the South Vietnamese have got to create a government which commands the loyalty and support of the bulk of the population in South Vietnam and galvanizes it into self-help. And that is something which only the South Vietnamese can do. I

514

hope that American troop withdrawals that have been announced, and undoubtedly will continue, will be at such a rate so as not to generate a sense of insecurity among the armed forces and the Government of South Vietnam. There must be sufficient time for the South Vietnamese to be trained and to stand up to fight for themselves. If they can't do that, well . . . that's that."

Time-Life said that some people felt that if South Vietnam did go communist this would put intolerable pressure on the rest of Southeast Asia in the form of continued insurgencies. Others believed that the main danger would not come from a wave of communist take-overs —that the real danger would come from the failure to solve the social and economic problems that confronted this region. "It is really two aspects of the same problem," replied Lee Kuan Yew. "If your country is moving to a higher level of achievement, of prosperity and the better life, then no one is going to listen to the rabble-rousers. The communists are going to find it extremely difficult to recruit people. If this is the case then what has happened in Vietnam will not be easily repeated elsewhere. But if you get more and more hungry and angry people, then communists will find it easier to recruit people as guerillas. Eventually, they will take over. In a chaotic situation, with the economy going downhill, a well-organized, tightly knit communist minority has a good chance to seize power. If South Vietnam is lost, then the chances are that whoever is the successor-government—whether it be North Vietnam or a combination of communists of North and South Vietnam—they will want to be the successors to French Indo-China, which included Laos and Cambodia. Whether they will be able to create a communist guerilla insurrection in Thailand is another matter. I feel that if the Thais do not let their will melt away at the thought of being on their own and having to fight for themselves, with American aid in arms and resources, but not in men, then Thailand will stay noncommunist. It is not a question of the Vietnamese taking over the Thais. That is not the method of People's Liberation Wars. And if Thailand sticks, then West Malaysia has a better chance, and so Singapore will stick."

Did this mean that he thought that the will of the Thais was somewhat in question? "Really, the will of the elite," replied Lee. "The mass of the people may or may not express that will periodically in some form." He thought it was absolutely crucial that the Thais did not over-react.

Time-Life said that it would appear that Southeast Asia in the 1970s would be more on its own than it had been for several hundred years. How would the region react to that situation? Much had been said about the need for regional co-operation in Southeast Asia. It seemed to be the great hope of the area. Yet so far the results had been quite disappointing, in that countries had been unwilling to put aside their own narrow national interests for the good of the whole. What did

515

Lee think were the chances for really meaningful regional co-operation in the 1970s? First of all, it depended, Lee said, whether things took a constructive turn, whether or not the different countries tried to make sense of themselves and of what they had inherited from former colonial empires. But the first thing to remember about regional co-operation for economic development was that geographic proximity did not mean that one formed a natural economic unit for advance into the industrial and technological society. If blind persons got together they were unlikely to get anywhere. Somebody was needed to lead the way, to blaze the trail. The Organization of African Unity, for example, expressed the desire for African Continental Unity. But after the past few years, all accepted the fact that the northern part of Africa, the Arab part, was very different from Africa south of the Sahara. East Africa was different from West Africa. Economic co-operation between, say, Kenya in the east and Sierra Leone in the west just did not make sense. There were no communications between them other than by sea around the Cape. How did they industrialize when neither had an industrial base? Putting this in a Southeast Asian context meant putting it into a more sensitive context. "Obviously we all need a more advanced economy to generate growth providing the capital and expertise. Who is more advanced? I accept the fact that Japan is an advanced industrial country. I accept the fact that although there are only twelve million Australians—they are also advanced in both the pure and applied sciences and in industry. Although not as far ahead as the Japanese, they can nevertheless make a contribution to education and training, industry and technology in Southeast Asia."

Asked his views on regional co-operation as far as defence was concerned, the Prime Minister replied: "Who are we going to defend ourselves against? When Americans talk about defence arrangements in Southeast Asia they usually mean defence against China. But is China going out on a predatory expansionist policy? I do not expect the Chinese People's Liberation Army fanning out through Southeast Asia. That is not their method. Their technique is through People's Liberation Wars. Vietnamese, not Chinese, have to die in Vietnam. And to counter that, the government of the country must give fulfilment to their people, isolating the ideologically convinced communists and preventing them from setting on fire the rest of the population."

Should the countries of Southeast Asia try for a better relationship with mainland China? Lee said that the whole world had to live with China. But the countries of Southeast Asia were not big enough to come to terms with China on their own. The major powers, America, Russia, Japan and the countries of Western Europe, must first come to some accommodation. Then the countries of Southeast Asia could, Lee hoped, find accommodation with China within the framework of the United Nations.

According to *Time-Life,* there was a feeling in the United States that the Americans had become over-involved in the affairs of Asia and should be less involved in the 1970s. What did Lee feel America's role in Asia should be during the 1970s? Lee's reply was that this was a question Americans had to answer for themselves. What kind of a world would they like to live in? Only they can answer that. "Your President has said that he is not a 'half-worlder'. By that I understand him to mean that he is not just interested in Europe alone. You look eastward towards Europe and Russia. You can look westward towards Asia and also Russia. The Russians claim to be both a European and an Asian nation. Distances mean less and less. So you must play the role you think is in your best interests. I would like to believe that you can discern your interests dispassionately so as not to have the pendulumn swing away from Asia because of your rather tiresome experiences in Vietnam. If you recognize that Vietnam was not the kind of war in which an army that is heavily dependent on conventional firepower and gadgetry is best equipped to fight, then you may discern that American national interests can be advanced congruently with the interests of the countries in Southeast Asia. The more there is a recognition of this, the easier it is for countries of this region to reach an accommodation with each other and with the bigger powers of the world."

Did he think America's role should be to lend economic and technical support rather than sending troops to Asia? Lee said he accepted the world as he found it. "One of the things I find is the disillusionment and even revulsion of the American people against the losses they have sustained in killed and maimed fighting this war in Vietnam. But at the same time what is not underlined, as much, is that you have prevented the communists from taking over."

Questioned about the future of Singapore's relations with Malaysia "after the present state of unrest is over", the Prime Minister said that much depended on what the position in West Malaysia actually was. The dust had got to settle. "Everyone, including us, will have to make his hard-headed assessment of what has happened and what the resultant position is. That it is very different from what it was before the afternoon of 13 May is obvious. Secondly, what will be the policy of the Malaysian Government when they have sorted things out? At some point the domestic emergency or crisis must end. Once it is ended officially what will be the policies of the Malaysian Government? Where we are concerned we are prepared to continue co-operation for mutual advantage, in defence and other fields."

Lee refused to discuss the recent riots in Malaysia. He said it was not proper, nor profitable to express his public views on this matter. As for racial tensions in Singapore, there had been some. But they were within manageable limits. They would continue to remain manageable so long as the Government, through its law enforcement instruments, the police, the courts, with the backing of the army ... remained completely impartial in the maintenance of law and order and the administration of justice. There could be no question of the Government being more partial on the side of the Chinese against the Malays because the majority in Singapore was ethnically Chinese. "If we get into that sort of position, we cannot solve the problem, because then we shall generate a sense of insecurity amongst the Malays and eventually bitterness and hatred against the Government."

As for Singapore's role in Southeast Asia in the 1970s, Lee said this depended on how Southeast Asia developed. "If it is constructive development, then we could play a useful role in speeding up development around us because we are a convenient source of expertise and a convenient channel through which these countries can get foreign exchange, which is important for the purchase of machinery and other capital equipment. Then, using a very broad metaphor, we can act as a spark plug for economic progress and development in the region. If it goes the other way, chaotic and nihilist, then, like Venice, I hope, we shall have enough wisdom and skill to isolate these forces of chaos and destruction. As the Dark Ages descended on Europe, places like Venice maintained relatively civilized standards of life in a very dark and gloomy chapter in European history. I would hope that such light from Singapore would eventually help to brighten up the area again."

XI

Considerable interest, in the Republic and abroad, was aroused when the Government announced its intention to abolish the jury system. Lee Kuan Yew, a practicing and successful lawyer for many years before he became a politician, spoke on this issue in Parliament on 12 June. He said the business of government was to ensure that the rule of law must be seen to prevail and not thwarted. This meant that the administration of justice must be carried out fairly and justly, and that the law did take its course. When making changes to existing practice, "we have to ask ourselves whether the change we are introducing will be for the better". Having spent a decade in the practice of the law, with some experience in the criminal courts, and another decade in government having to provide for the machinery of justice, the police and their investigations, public prosecutors and the courts, Lee said he had little doubt that this was a change which, in Singapore's circumstances, would ensure that justice was the more likely to be done, and seen to be done.

If, added the Prime Minister, three High Court judges could not decide on questions of fact better than seven random jurymen, then grievous harm was being done every day. Single judges and single magistrates had been, and were, deciding questions of fact, both in civil and in criminal cases. Every day single judges and single magistrates made decisions after findings on questions of fact on the evidence of witnesses under examination-in-chief and cross-examination. Sometimes they intervened to pose questions. Sometimes documents and exhibits were brought before them. "I have little doubt that they are the more likely to arrive at the truth as against a jury of laymen."

Lee thought that the jury system might work in Singapore, if jurors did not feel overwhelmed with the responsibility of having to find a man guilty, when they knew that this meant a death sentence. It also required judges who had complete command of their courts, and were sufficiently subtle and skilful to get juries to arrive at the right verdict through a judicious choice of words which could not be attacked on appeal. Even in England, the present Lord Chief Justice had occasion in recent years to make a number of caustic comments on the jury system. One could always fall back to Blackstone in the eighteenth century, and several English judges of this present century, to proclaim the virtues of the Anglo-Saxon method of jury trial. But, even in England, where once a unanimous verdict was required for a conviction, it was now only necessary to obtain a majority. Also not so long ago in England, juries were called upon to decide questions of fact even in civil cases, like actions for libel. Now they had been abolished. The administration of justice had to be kept apace and abreast with the times. And the reputation of the jury for divine discernment was now much tarnished.

"We have seen in Singapore several miscarriages of justice in the past few years," said Lee Kuan Yew. In one trial for murder recently, a trial that should have taken five days dragged on for over thirty days as judge and prosecutor leant over backwards to ensure the appearance of justice being manifestly done. "In my view, it was overdone." Every visiting psychiatrist was called to give evidence, ending with the majority of jurymen being so impressed or confused that a majority of the jury reduced the charge of murder to a conviction for culpable homicide. The time had come put this right. Western Europe was not uncivilized. They too had the rule of law, although more Roman law than Anglo-Saxon law. The French, Germans, Italians, and Dutch did not have juries for civil or criminal trials. No jurist or student of jurisprudence had been reckless enough to say that justice was not being done in these countries.

The question some lawyers unconsciously framed was: Before whom did an accused person, who could pay for a good advocate, stand a more sporting chance of being acquitted—three High Court judges or a jury of seven? "I suggest that as legislators concerned with the administration of justice, we are not interested in this question. The question that we in this House must ask is: Are three judges more likely to do justice than seven men chosen at random to serve on a jury? I think we know the answer to this."

Early in 1970, Parliament passed a law abolishing the jury system in Singapore. In future, two judges will decide murder cases.

XII

In the middle of June, Lee Kuan Yew flew to Australia to attend the Five Power defence talks in Canberra, between Britain, Australia, New Zealand, Malaysia and Singapore. He made it clear in a speech at the Australia-Malaysia-Singapore Association dinner in Sydney, on 18 June, that he intended to do nothing at the Canberra talks to jeopardize Singapore's future. He said he did not want to endanger Singapore's relations with other nations at the talks. He said: "I do not get into the permanent orbit of a major power so that I can't get out of it. Some big countries in our region have got into orbits of big powers, like the Soviet Union and the United States, and can't get out of them. But I put my cards on the table before going to Canberra. I have enough thrust: if I want to get out of orbit I do so."

Lee Kuan Yew went on to say that he preferred to be associated with Australia and its *Melbourne* (HMSA *Melbourne* collided with the US destroyer *Frank E. Evans* on 3 June with the loss of 74 American lives) than to be tied in with America and its nuclear-powered USS *Enterprise*. "If I get into that sort of orbit I stay in it until the end of time." However, if, after the British left, Australia and New Zealand decided to leave the region, too, "we've got to live and make other arrangements". But he thought there was more advantage for Australia and New Zealand to stay because of the minimum risk for maximum advantage. The friendship and goodwill these countries had established over a period of time were not without economic value. "But, when the chips are down, and this is for all governments when it comes to the crunch, it is up to what a government decides is in its national interests. I believe our national interests—and I don't know what Australia's are—are best served in an association with Malaysia, New Zealand, Australia, and I hope, the British."

The Prime Minister said that in the United States some six weeks earlier he had claimed that Singapore was a "more or less sheltered, secure and peaceful area". Having the tragic events of 13 May and after in his mind, the Prime Minister said there had been a lot of events reported since which denied this. "But I believe that to give up and say it is no longer secure, peaceful and law-abiding would be to invite more disaster. We must try as best we can to re-establish some sanity,

520

tolerance, reasonableness and accommodation, so that the Malaysia-Singapore area can become an area of relative prosperity, and perhaps this can spread outward and bring a slightly better life to others in the region. I hope the talks in Canberra are a step towards this end."

Lee Kuan Yew argued that the problems of the contemporary world were all inter-related. Even the super-powers had their problems, America with its "never-ending, almost unwinnable war in Vietnam", and the Soviet Union which was trying to "bash things out at the communist summit with no signal success". And a third world was also in turmoil. Ethnic, religious, and linguistic groups were brought together within boundary lines drawn by cartographers. When representative governments tried to sustain the myth of legitimacy by popular vote they found the temptation to appeal to localities and groups. The net result was Nigeria, Ceylon, a decade ago, India and Pakistan with the insoluble problem of Kashmir. All this affected Singapore by increasing tension, and Lee said he wondered whether ANZUS was a comprehensive insurance, or whether the United States might one day become more occupied with problems of its own.

The Australian papers made much of Lee's airport statement that if Australia and New Zealand withdrew from Singapore they would "never come back". He would like to think, he said, that "your Government, having done its sums carefully, will find a national interest, and not just sentiment, in not leaving the Singapore-Malaysia region. Because if you leave you will never come back, even if you want to, because a mutation takes place and people have to live. If the Australians leave and the New Zealanders leave, we will have to make other arrangements."

"Listen to Mr Lee," advised *The Sun*, in an editorial on 18 June, "He makes as much sense in Sydney as he does in Singapore." *The Age*, the same day, called attention to the fact that Lee Kuan Yew, in his speech, referred to the Soviet Union's invasion of Czechoslovakia as "an outrage". Lee had said that Russia had marched into Czechoslovakia not just to gain a buffer zone, but because failure to do so would have "unscrambled the whole of the East European States".

At a luncheon in Sydney shortly before flying on to Canberra, the Prime Minister again emphasized that if Australia and New Zealand withdrew from the region there could be no return to the *status quo*. But he reiterated that Singapore was not anxious to lose its alliance with the four nations represented at the Canberra talks. Lee Kuan Yew described the world as "bi-polar"—a world in which only two powers, the United States and Russia, had the capacity to destroy each other and the rest of mankind. "It is a problem that has arisen as a result of man's inventiveness and ingenious creative capacity, and leaves the lesser nations with a great problem. It would be foolish for us living in the Pacific not to recognize that moods change. The mood of the USA is of global interest with complete confidence. It has the

521

wealth and technology to influence the rest of the world. But what if the pendulum swings the other way, with the American people questioning their role of world policemen," he asked—and this at a time when Russia is increasing its range of nuclear weapons. "I would like to believe that between the competing forces of the major powers, Singapore, perhaps in consort with its neighbours and Australia and New Zealand, and maybe Japan, can find some area in which there could be relative security without being fully committed at the drop of the first bomb. This is what any national government of any nation must think about."

Lee Kuan Yew said that every age had its set of problems, "but our generation is having more than its fair share of trials and tribulations. Historians will tell us there were very few golden ages in the history of man. Perhaps the British Empire under Victoria, Germany under Bismarck and Japan before World War Two were golden ages for particular groups of people. But it didn't mean that everyone had a good life. Never before has there been this excruciating dilemma of having to live with ourselves in the knowledge that man can destroy himself completely."

The Prime Minister said Singapore was only a small, unsophisticated country in a world of "little planets revolving round bigger planets. And if you're an extremely small particle in orbit, you don't want to choose a planet with too great a gravitational pull," again referring to his desire for links with countries at the Canberra talks rather than with bigger powers. "I like to leave my successors with the option of putting thrust on and going to another planet," he added.

When he arrived at Canberra, the Prime Minister was asked by newsmen about the proposal to remove Australia's battalion of troops from Terendak Camp in Malacca to Singapore. He caused some astonishment by replying that he thought they could be "more effectively deployed" from Malacca than from Singapore. He reasoned that the views of Australia in Malaysia would then have been backed by Australia's firm intention to maintain forces of sanity and stability. But Lee stressed that the decision was one for the Australian Government alone and he would not presume now to try to persuade the Australian Government to reverse a decision made after very prolonged consideration and deliberation.

Lee said that Singapore welcomed aid from Australia and New Zealand, "and as far as defence against external aggression is concerned, we welcome more battalions from the Australians, the New Zealanders and perhaps even the British. And we certainly intend to have as many of our own troops as we can muster. Singapore welcomes all forces which contribute to the stability and security of the region."

Asked if this included Russia, he said: "It need not necessarily exclude them. It depends on the circumstances. They are already in the Indian Ocean."

Asked if relationship between Singapore and Malaysia had deteriorated over the past few weeks, Lee said: "I see no official change in the relationship." He had earlier referred to "the strategic consideration which made us consider defence as indivisible between Malaysia and Singapore—that stands."

On Singapore's internal security, Lee Kuan Yew said his country's educational and social programmes were aimed at denying "the communists the kind of ferment from which they can mount revolutionary methods of seizing power."

Lee Kuan Yew arrived in Canberra suffering from an eye infection —"only a slight infection", he said, "but it gets worse in a smokey room."

In an editorial on 19 June, *The Australian Financial Review* remarked that it would be a tragedy if Australians regarded Singapore Prime Minister Lee Kuan Yew's warning that he would have "to make other arrangements" if Australia withdrew from regional defence as merely the pressure tactics of a clever politician. "In the first place, there can be no doubt at all that other arrangements with the Soviet Union would be all too easy to make and might well be strongly in Singapore's interests (as distinct from those of the region as a whole). Secondly, and more importantly, what Mr Lee was really doing was stretching out the hand of friendship, collaboration and partnership to Australia. It should be grasped firmly. In a world rent by bitter racial divisions, by multinational suspicion and by isolationism born of affluence, the opportunities presented by a close working partnership between Australia and its Asian neighbours are astonishingly unique. But the time element is such that Australia now stands perilously poised between a leap into genuine, wholehearted multiracial regionalism or a backward fall into the abyss of racial isolationism. Industrially, economically and militarily Australia is ideally suited to a "special relationship" with Southeast Asian countries which do not want to fall into the clutches of either of the big power bloc or become latter-day members of a neo-coprosperity sphere. But it is idle to pretend that this country can selfishly hope to enjoy the benefits of close economic collaboration while shunning any regional military responsibilities . . . "

In spite of a digestive upset, which caused him to miss social events, and though still worried by his slight eye infection, the Prime Minister spoke at the conference as the head of the Singapore delegation. The Minister of Law and National Development, E. W. Barker, carried on in his place when he was absent. In his speech, Lee Kuan Yew referred to "recent events" in Malaysia and Singapore. He said, "We have had our little difficulties." Singapore's position was that what took place recently "does concern everyone sitting around the table. Singapore's position is unchanged. The strategic considerations of geography and demography were what they were before Singapore joined Malaysia: were the same while Singapore was part of Malaysia: they are the same today whether before or after race riots. Singapore's feelings are that it would be very sad indeed if we have to admit that human ingenuity and just plain self-interest cannot find a way around the difficulties." Singapore hoped that in the course of these deliberations the conference could come to some conclusions which would reassure all who were making a commitment to their joint interests.

"It is our contention", Lee said, "that we should muster such strength as we can and in conjunction with Malaysia, Australia, New Zealand and Britain, present those who do not wish us well with a credible deterrent." The Prime Minister referred to statements he had previously made about what would happen if Australian troops withdrew and their places filled up. He said: "My public statement was intended for those who subscribed to the theory that Australian ground forces should not be in the area. I think too much is at stake on this point. Australians may or may not decide it is in their interest to have ground forces in the Malaysia-Singapore area. But they should take this consideration into their calculations, that if they withdraw their forces, in the nature of things, a shift would take place and it is unlikely that the *status quo ante* would ever be restored."

The communique issued at the end of the conference said that the five nations affirmed their continuing interest in the peace and stability of the area and their "joint concern with practical questions" arising from the withdrawal of British forces from Malaysia and Singapore. The five nations expressed their intention to continue the practice of close consultation among themselves about the situation in the area, and about developments affecting the security of Malaysia and Singapore. The conference reaffirmed that the principle that the defence of Malaysia and Singapore was indivisible "constituted an essential basis for future defence co-operation". Malaysia, Singapore and the United Kingdom welcomed the announcements that had been made by Australia and New Zealand to continue stationing elements of their armed forces in Malaysia and Singapore after the British withdrawal in 1971. And Malaysia, Singapore and New Zealand welcomed the reaffirmation by the United Kingdom of its intention to continue exercising and training in the area. The conference also noted that the major combined exercise to be held in 1970 would, among other things, demonstrate the capability of the United Kingdom rapidly to deploy forces in the area.

Interviewed by the Australian Broadcasting Commission shortly after the communique had been made public, Lee Kuan Yew was asked if he felt after attending the conference, that Australia could be counted on as an effective ally. Lee replied, "As much before the meeting as after the meeting. As in most things, the real proof in this particular case will be when the chips are down." Did he think anything more could have been done to make Australia's position more credible? Lee said he wouldn't have thought so. And if the chips were down would

Australia be there? That depended, Lee thought, first of all, whether it was in Australia's interest, and how big the risks were, and, most important of all, whether it was manageable. "If it is a middling power, I think it's manageable. If it's a super-power . . . "

The question was put to Lee Kuan Yew as to whether he was concerned at all that Mr John Gorton, the Australian Prime Minister, did not lead the Australian delegation. Lee had journeyed to Canberra believing that it was to be a prime ministers' conference, but he replied: "That is a matter of form, entirely a matter for the Australian Government."

Lee was reminded that upon arrival he had said that Singapore might have to look to other countries for support. "You did not exclude the Soviet Union. Are you serious about inviting the Soviet Union?" The Prime Minister replied: "No." Then he added. "I don't think, you know, that one should just pick up a phrase. This is a kind of interpretation which, I think, does not put things in perspective. Somebody threw a question: 'What about the Soviet Union?' and my rejoinder was: 'In certain circumstances.' For instance, keeping the Straits of Malacca open as an international waterway. I think they are a force to the good because they want to keep the Straits of Malacca open for navigation. They like to be able to go from the Atlantic through the Straits of Malacca up to their maritime states; to that extent they are a positive force."

Was he satisfied with the conference? Lee Kuan Yew thought that the conference went as far as expected. The really serious commitment which we must have fairly clearly defined would be the one in 1971 after the British Government's position had been resolved, and when the Australians and New Zealanders knew what had happened to Vietnam, and could see what kind of problems would arise post-Vietnam."

XIII

Concerned that student unrest prevalent in the United States and Europe might spread to Singapore, the Prime Minister spoke to the Association of Nanyang University graduates on 19 July about "growth and development or decline and chaos". He referred to what he called the disinterest of developed countries in new countries that could "yield no great rewards", countries that would "suck up more aid than pay dividends". He said that even global powers like the Soviet Union and the United States were reaching the conclusion that, other than for militarily strategic areas, it did not matter, and would not affect their military or economic strength in the world, if these new countries went chactic, or even communist. Hence Americans and Russians had shown little interest in Africa south of the Sahara. It was only still ideologically motivated China which was spending a few hundred millions of dollars building railways in Tanzania and Zambia, and roads in South Yemen. Just over 100,000 white Rhodesians united, well armed, well trained, with the backing of South Africa and of Portugal, had been able to flout with impunity the feelings of 150 million disunited, poorly organized, poorly educated, poorly armed, and poorly trained black Africans. Britain, like the rest of Western Europe and America, was disillusioned at what had happened to most of the new countries. After independence they had been torn asunder by conflicts between tribes or races, over languages and religions, like Nigeria and Kenya. This had led hard-headed British and European businessmen to conclude that there were very few countries in the third world worth bothering about. The exceptions were a few countries where there were quick profits to be made through the extraction of soils, minerals or timber, and a few areas of stability and sanity.

"We must always remember", continued Lee Kuan Yew, "that the choice before Singapore is either an orderly, organized community, enabling long-term planning for growth and development, or a disintegrating society sinking into chaos and perdition. It takes time and effort to build up an efficient organization to administer to the needs of a community. But in a short while one can run things down. Water, power, homes, roads, transportation, harbours, airports, schools, polytechnics, universities, teachers, industrial estates, all require a climate of stability and security. Without them, planning for long-term production and profit is impossible. We have the highest density of population with an elected government in the whole world—8,855 per square mile. Only Hong Kong exceeds us—9,966 per square mile. But Hong Kong does not have an elected government which has to worry about governing with the consent of the majority. Hong Kong also has almost no subsidized educational, medical or social services. We can continue to meet the ever higher expectations of our universally educated younger generation only if we improve on our organization and produce a better disciplined and better educated generation, more skilled in the techniques of modern industry. Our people cannot afford not to be diligent. Our people cannot take things for granted, whether it be prosperity or security. We must maintain the maximum of security with the minimum of cost. So our citizen's Army-National Service which will, as the administrative and infrastructure expands, enable and require every man and woman to make a contribution to both our economy and our security."

Lee said it was only when hard-headed businessmen and industrialists believed that what Singapore was doing was sound and practical and would ensure orderly working conditions with workers trained well and emotionally geared to high productivity, "that we shall get the maximum of capital investments, giving the maximum of economic growth, leading to higher incomes, better homes, better schools and new levels of achievement". The alternative was to join the many broken-back states of Asia, Africa and Latin America, where arbitrary government and insecurity was part of a way of life. "The economy runs down in the midst of social disorder. Inevitably there is an exodus of brains, skill, expertise and capital. But the bulk of the people without professional training or money will have to remain." Instead of a rational thinking government, constantly looking and planning forward, substitute an irrational, impulsive and unthinking leadership, and the worst would happen to Singapore. Then those who could not emigrate would have to put up with grinding poverty, disease and squalor. But worse, "because we are in a militarily strategic position at the southern-most tip of Asia, in the middle of the Southeast Asian archipelago, astride one of the world's most important sea lanes, between the Indian and Pacific Oceans, the super-powers cannot afford to have Singapore go Maoist-communist. So they will use others, to try and hold down Singapore and prevent it from ever being used by the communists in China." This might sound like a nightmare. But any government in Singapore that did not think through the most horrendous of possibilities was guilty of a grave dereliction of its duties.

Lee said that one of the contemporary dilemmas facing Singapore was that, on the one hand, excellent communications with the rest of the world by sea, air, wireless, cables and, soon, satellite, were a great economic asset. "You can take an aircraft, or a ship, any day to any part of the world. You can telephone through to all the main centres of world commerce. You can watch television and read newspapers and magazines within hours of publication in the main centres of Eastern and Western Europe, North America, Japan and Australia." But, on the other hand, this exposed Singapore to the fads and fetishes of the contemporary permissive society of the West. Some people learnt easiest by imitation. "Because students in North America and Western Europe are in a state of disorder, for a variety of reasons, and free sex, drug-taking, long hair, and funny clothes are thought to be fashionable, so this affects Australian students although their problems are so very different. An anarchic protest for the sake of protest becomes fashionable. Some young students in Singapore, particularly that part of the English-educated, without a grounding in their own cultural values, want to be 'with it'." Whilst such student aberrations would not wreck America or Western Europe, they would surely ruin Singapore. "It is the business of a government to govern. It should do this in the interests of the majority, or better still, in the interests of everyone. And in the interest of all, we cannot and will not allow this permissive, escapist, drug-taking, self-indulgent, promiscuous society to infect our young. Those who try to introduce these habits do so at their own peril, for we shall take immediate antiseptic measures to prevent and

527

scotch any such infection, or affectation. The choice before us is constant vigilance or a complacent slide to perdition."

XIV

Speaking mostly to Malays at a PAP branch meeting on 22 July, Lee Kuan Yew said it was very necessary, particularly after the comparatively mild troubles in Singapore in May and June, to reaffirm that the Government in Singapore "will, and must, ensure security and fair play to all, regardless of race, religion or language". If, said the Prime Minister, "we had not acted with complete impartiality, but had allowed some vicious hooligans and gangsters of Chinese ethnic descent, for their own reasons, to get away with bullying and murdering some Malays, because Malays are a minority in Singapore, then today it would have become a different Singapore." Once basic trust in a government that it would act impartially and protect every citizen was destroyed it would never be the same again. "We meet tonight in a secure and relaxed atmosphere because people of all ethnic groups understand that the rule of law will be upheld. It will protect you, whether you are Malay, Indian, Ceylonese, Eurasian or Chinese. That you are a Chinese does not allow you to flout the law." Similarly, an injured party, whether from a majority or minority ethnic group, was not entitled to take the law into his own hands. There were policemen and National Servicemen to back up the law-enforcement agencies.

Lee said that he was naturally proud of the way in which the multiracial police force and the multiracial National Servicemen behaved: with discipline and propriety. "Our young men in the Special Constabulary or in the Vigilante Corps or in the uniform of our Armed Services are ordinary citizens. They share in your happiness and success, or your trials and tribulations. They must and will always conduct themselves with decorum and courtesy."

This was a troubled part of the world. It did no good to pretend that all was well. "We know that all may not be well." But all difficulties would be manageable and resolved if preparations were made and precautions taken to ensure that nothing was allowed to disturb the racial harmony or upset respect for law and order "so essential for our economic growth".

Lee concluded: "The future is what we make of it. And we must resolve, particularly after the unhappy events in May and June, that despite the misadventures, we in Singapore will continue on the path of sanity, a fair deal for everyone, and fair shares for all. That is our way forward to a better life."

528

XV

On 8 August, Singapore's National Day, Princess Alexandra represented Queen Elizabeth at a banquet held to celebrate the 150th anniversary of modern Singapore. Proposing a toast to President Yusof the Princess, in a short speech, said that it was one man, Stamford Raffles, who had the vision to realize the potentialities of what was, in 1819, a largely uninhabited, jungle-clad island, situated strategically at the cross-roads of the East; but on the foundations he laid then, successive generations of immigrants from many countries had combined to create the Singapore of 1969. "Out of their efforts has emerged a society which is proving every day its ability to adapt successfully to changing needs, and since independence your city state—small in size but great in spirit—has gone from strength to strength. Today it is a Commonwealth in miniature, where peoples of many different creeds and cultural traditions are bound together by common ideals and interests, working for the good of all. If the economic, industrial and social advances of recent years provide a guide for the future, then Singapore's star is bright indeed, and though there must of course be problems and dangers in the years ahead, it is not difficult in Singapore to feel confident in the ability and will of the Government and the people to foresee and overcome whatever obstacles they may have to face. There is an atmosphere of energy and enthusiasm here which it is a delight to encounter, and which has impressed me greatly."

The Princess read a message of congratulations and good wishes from the Queen to the people of Singapore.

In a toast to Queen Elizabeth, Lee Kuan Yew remarked that change was a companion of life; but in no period of human history had the changes been as spectacular as those in the past thirty years since the Second World War. And it had been going at a geometrically increasing speed, until two men set foot on the moon. Few events in life were inevitable. However, the declared policies of Britain to withdraw from East of Suez, the painful American experience in Vietnam, "and their President's pronouncement that there will be no further Vietnams" made it likely that there would be momentous changes in Southeast Asia. This made it all the more necessary, "in our mutual interest", to continue co-operation in matters of defence between Malaysia and Singapore. And the statements by the Australian and New Zealand Governments, that they would keep their forces in the Malaysia-Singapore area beyond 1971, had already helped to reinforce confidence. Without confidence economic development was not possible.

The shape of things to come was not pre-destined. They could be altered by many imponderables, "and by our own initiatives". What could not be changed was the past. "This evening, we deem ourselves amongst the fortunate few who can afford to be proud of their past, with no desire to rewrite or touch up the truth. It is a short history, 150 years, but long enough for us to value our association with the British people. British naval and maritime supremacy is the golden thread that has brought about the four nations of Australia, Malaysia, New Zealand and Singapore. With the passing of Empire, British naval supremacy is being displaced as more and more American and Russian naval vessels fill up the Pacific and the Indian Oceans. But this is nothing compared to the debris and litter in the skies from American and Russian space probes."

No one could foresee in what kind of Singapore, or indeed in what sort of world, Singaporeans would celebrate their 200th anniversary. The chances were that there would be no reassuring presence of a resident British Commander-in-Chief. "So we take particular pleasure in having with us tonight the British Commander-in-Chief Far East, and his Navy, Army and Air Commanders. Geography may lead us towards closer co-operation with our neighbours in East and Southeast Asia and Oceania. But on this evening, we may be forgiven a little nostalgia as we give credit to our founder, Sir Stamford Raffles, and to those who came after him. Without them modern Singapore would not have been."

XVI

"History", declared the Prime Minister in his National Day broadcast, "is valuable as a guide to the future. It provides insights into the nature and potentials of various peoples, because both the innate qualities and the cultural characteristics of a people do not change easily or quickly. A hundred and fifty years ago Raffles could not have prophesied what Singapore would be today, an independent nation state, a busy centre of trade, servicing and manufacturing. But he had foresight. He knew the value of Singapore's strategic location for trade and communications. Then by establishing the principle of free trade and free competition, he attracted the adventurous, the resourceful and the industrious. In less than three years a few thousand traders had left Bencoolen, Malacca and Penang to establish their business in Singapore. While it was not inevitable that Singapore would succeed, the ingredients for success were present almost from the beginning."

Lee said that Singapore had enjoyed another successful year. The economy had again surged forward. "I do not wish to dwell on our progress. I want to strike a note of caution. It is dangerous to be complacent and to take continuing progress and prosperity for granted. The fact that things have been getting better and better each year, since we turned the corner in 1961, does not mean that progress comes naturally.

Better jobs, better homes, better schools, better public services, the better life can come only after careful planning and hard work. If we had shirked the unpleasant, or postponed the painful changes required of our thinking and of our working habits, first in 1965 after separation, and again in January, 1968, after the British Government announced their accelerated military rundown, we could have slithered downhill rapidly."

Government, Lee said, did not consist only of making speeches. "Of course, we need communication and *rapport* between a people and their leaders. More important are good judgment and bold planning. But most important of all is the confidence, the trust between a people and their government. It is when a people are behind their government, and not at odds with it, that the best results are achieved. When everything looks simple and easy, it means either the gods are on our side, or that the decisions we have made were right. But we have made mistakes. Then they have to be remedied. Four years ago, when we agreed to separation from Malaysia, we admitted that the kind of Malaysia we envisaged when joining the federation in 1963 was not to be. So we accepted a separate Singapore. However, separation required a fundamental reassessment of our position, the kind of economy we must develop as a nation state on our own, and the security and defence arrangements we need. But the ties of history, geography, and family between the people in Singapore and in West Malaysia were not changed by separation. The destinies of the two countries will always be inter-related."

Referring to the "incidents of racial conflicts in May and June in Singapore" Lee said they vividly demonstrated what was always known: that what happened in Malaysia could have profound consequences for Singapore. The converse was also true. "In this instance we snuffed out the fires before they spread."

There were few problems facing Singapore that the Government had not foreseen. "Where we may have been wrong is in the timing. Things have happened sooner than we had expected. We will face quite a few hazards in the 1970s. If we are to overcome our problems we must reaffirm our determination not to allow any citizen to be persecuted because of his race, religion, language or culture. Four great civilizations have met in confluence here. The British, Malay, Indian and Chinese came and they built a metropolis out of a fishing village near the equator. Eventually, perhaps after several generations, a separate, distinct Singapore identity will emerge in which the differences of race, culture and religion will be more than made up for by similarities in values, attitudes, and a feeling of belonging to one whole."

Lee said he wanted to pay a tribute to "our workers and their unions". A year and a half ago, the Employment Act was passed. It was designed to stop abuses of fringe benefits and to make workers keener and more productive. "We demonstrated to hard-headed industrialists

531

both in Singapore and overseas in the developed countries, that we had the will to put our own house in order. Our workers and our unions have entered into the spirit of the Employment Act. There were few strikes last year. This year there have been none at all. Investments have flowed in." This "superb response" from workers and their union leaders, together with capital and enterprise, industrial expertise and management know-how, made it possible for Singapore to achieve its high economic rate of growth of about nine per cent last year. "Our workers must always be willing to give of their best. And because they are intelligent, dexterous and hard-working, they learn new skills quickly. They are willing to put in intense and sustained effort. So entrepreneurs have found it profitable to base their operations in Singapore. Our economic strength will grow as long as the Government, workers, and management are all pulling in the same direction, with the minimum of friction and the maximum of reasonableness and accommodation."

Lee added that he and his colleagues would also like to pay a tribute to those civil servants and other officers in the public services who helped in the rethinking and planning of Singapore's economic strategy. "We have had also to build up our armed forces from scratch four years ago. We have built more homes for our people, schools for our children, roads, reservoirs, power stations—all the infrastructure of a modern industrial society. To this group of dedicated officers and their teams, Singapore owes much. Behind the throb of success is the constant monitoring, the unceasing alert. At the first sign of anything not going right immediate corrective action is taken. Problems are never allowed to get out of hand. It is organization and teamwork that make success come our way as if it were in the nature of things."

The future was as full of promise as it was fraught with danger. "We cannot slacken in our efforts. Nor can we allow liberties to be taken with our stable and orderly society. Each generation has its own problems. Our generation has either to add greater strength and security to our society or watch all that we and our predecessors have built up over 150 years be lost or ruined. We cannot afford not to succeed."

In another National Day speech at a rally on 16 August, the Prime Minister again warned of hardships ahead. He said it was sound government to plan on the basis that the worst would happen. In fact, it was not often that the worst did happen. "So we find ourselves better off for having made the maximum effort to meet maximum difficulties when less than the maximum troubles us." Any government that made plans on the basis of "tomorrow being a sunny day" would soon find that it had led the people into dire difficulties. "For if it rains, and no wet-weather arrangements have been made, confusion and chaos must result."

Lee Kuan Yew was confident that economically Singapore would continue to do well, but only "if our workers and our unions accept the challenge that 1972 will be a very different world, with many imponderables, in matters of defence and security, and also the consequential repercussions when the world balance of power in East and Southeast Asia is profoundly altered."

It was foolish to plan on any basis other than that "only we may find it worthwhile to fight and die for our country and for our children's future". The Australians and New Zealanders had already made it clear that they were not stepping into the role of the British. Theirs would be a subsidiary role. "As the Australian Prime Minister put it, he will be a part of the posse, not the sheriff." It was only common sense that if and when the chips were down, "we must be prepared to play sheriff in our own domain. Otherwise all that we have built up over 150 years will be destroyed or captured."

The decisions which Singapore made four years ago on the build-up of defence forces might have appeared more than was necessary at that time. Many were grateful in May and June that full use had been made of the time. It could have been a very different situation had the past four years been wasted. So the two and a half years between now and the end of 1971 had to be used to the maximum. Defence and security arrangements were necessary to ensure that economic growth could take place. And without economic growth, defence costs would overwhelm and smother the economy.

Singapore must continue to be clean and green, spruce and well maintained. "It is that air of general well-being, of trees and shrubs, flowers and creepers, no flies or mosquitoes, the general cleanliness, and the appearance of well-manicured and well-kept city, with nothing in a derelict condition, this is the backdrop for success."

Lee said that one of the most crucial factors of a people's performance, whether in military or in civilian fields, was morale. When an army or a people was slovenly and disorderly, it was probably because of bad leadership. "Morale goes down and the army is easily defeated, or the people are overwhelmed by their problems. When an army has an officer cadre, or a people has a leadership which keeps everybody on his toes, things are kept smart and spruce, morale is never down, even under the most adverse of circumstances. Things are never allowed to sag. Whilst we congratulate ourselves for achievements up to our 150th year, let us raise our targets even higher for the 151st year."

The Prime Minister claimed that Singapore had never looked back since that day, 6 February, 1819. From a population of 150 in a small fishing village, it became three thousand in a matter of months, and to the two million today. Singapore had always attracted the ablest and the most competitive. It thrived on the basis of free competition with the best man going to the top. "So we have attracted the

533

highly skilled and the talented. Provided people are able and prepared to make the effort required in high performance, we can go on to a population of three to four million, without lowering standards of life. But it requires professional competence, technological know-how, industrial skills and work discipline. People with these qualities can always find a place in Singapore."

XVII

Opening an exhibition showing the development of education over the past 150 years, Lee Kuan Yew said on 19 August it was the future that counted. "We have to make the effort, to plan, to organize, so as to bring into being a more secure, more stable and more prosperous Singapore. If the preceding generation only had the foresight to see ahead and the courage to assert their rights, we would have had a much broader framework on which to build our future. But the past is the past. Fortunately, the present generation had the courage to face difficult situations. So we have Singapore, making it possible for us to organize ourselves to preserve and safeguard the values that we all cherish."

Singapore, he said, was a small country, and it was imperative that the emphasis must be quality, not quantity. "We must nurture, train and educate our people and so organize our society, to enable us—a nation of two million—to match the performance and capacity of countries larger than us. To achieve this, the key is education. Every school, primary, secondary or university, all must train and educate our youth to bring out their best, a rugged and robust generation. They must have the capacity to contribute to national security and social order, and help the growth and development of our economy."

XVIII

Singapore's brain-power potential was reviewed by Lee Kuan Yew in a speech to university graduates—the International Alumni—on 5 September. The Prime Minister said that 26,000 or two point nine per cent of those over twenty-one years of age in Singapore had received more than twelve years of primary and secondary education. Of this 26,000, about 2,300 were non-residents, that is to say neither from Singapore nor Malaysia. Nearly all those 2,300 persons were holders of current professional visit or employment passes and had gone through some form of tertiary education.

Lee proposing a toast in 1968. Mr Sato, the Japanese Prime Minister, is on Lee's right

Welcoming Mr Kang Ryang Wook, Vice-President of the Democratic People's Republic of Korea, to Singapore in 1968

With the Crown Prince of Japan, in Singapore

General Ne Win of Burma on a state visit to Singapore

Instructing Princess Alexandra how to use chopsticks

Lee said that by Afro-Asian standards, Singapore had a high percentage of the population going on to tertiary educational institutions. But it was not high compared to American, West European or Japanese standards. In America, over thirty-five per cent of the secondary level students go through to tertiary level, as against thirteen per cent for Singapore.

Lee argued that the total performance of any society depended mainly upon, first, the general level of its population as a whole, and second, the quality of its top one to two per cent. The general level of the average digits, their physical and mental attributes, was inherited and at any one time was relatively fixed. But it could be improved by careful nurturing. The physical capacity could be increased with good food, training, health and medical attention. As for the brain power, While an IQ was fixed, a good environment, education, the imparting of knowledge and skills, the inculcation of values and the forming of new habits, could raise performance. "Given the human attributes of a given population, and the training, skills, knowledge, education and discipline of a people, it is left to the one to two per cent of the population who are in positions of leadership, to make the population give of its best. "This means", said Lee Kuan Yew, "organizational coherence, and that spirit of keenness which is necessary for high performance. When this one to two per cent of a people in positions of leadership are completely committed to the whole community, to share in their successes and failures, in their triumphs or defeats, then, and only then, will this leadership have that moral strength to arouse in their people that enthusiasm and drive to excel and to achieve."

Only a small portion of those who had received tertiary education would assume positions of leadership. The majority had to play their part in the administrative or corporation machine. On the other hand, many who had not been to institutions of tertiary education would, in fact, play decisive leadership roles. But with universal education, it meant that the majority of the people in positions of leadership would have had tertiary education. The broader the base of people with twelve-plus years of education, naturally the better the quality of this one to two per cent. One of the problems of the newly independent countries like Singapore, was that independence was usually preceded by a mass movement in which everyone's expectations were raised. Independence was also usually accompanied by a system where one man was given one vote, regardless of his educational standard. This meant that after independence, the political leaders had to face pressures to level down and narrow the differentials in rewards between people with unequal qualifications and ability, people who made unequal contributions to the economy. This could result in a brain drain. Those with internationally recognized qualifications had the mobility to cross national frontiers in search of better jobs. So, when standards of education, medical, health and recreational facilities were lowered as a result of a rapid and vast expansion to cater for the needs of everybody, social and economic conditions might drop to a level where it was no longer possible for intelligent people to believe that these standards would ever go back to what they were, let alone to rise to what they are in the developed countries of the West. "When personal rewards, professional satisfaction, and expectations of a better life for their children cannot reinforce or sustain loyalty to the group, then considerations of personal or family survival override duty and obligation to the community."

Fortunately, Singapore had been able to go through this difficult post-independence phase without serious disruption of the social fabric. "On the other hand, we have been able to offer opportunities for positions of command, and so opportunities for fulfilment and satisfaction. Because we are a new society, largely of immigrant stock, with a short history, the future will be decided by whether this one to two per cent consists of 'stayers' or 'quitters'. With established societies, there is no question of quitting. People stay and fight for what they have inherited, if for no other reason than sheer force of habit. This generation, yours and mine, has got to start this habit. We must decide as a community that we will see our problems through. It is only when we stay and solve our problems, and not quit and so dodge unpleasantness, that we can make a better future for all. The mass of people everywhere has to stay and face whatever is coming. But in a new society, the determinants are those who can leave, but do not, and help make things better for the majority."

XIX

Lee Kuan Yew made a plea for more gracious living in a public speech on 25 October. He said that while people were busy striving to achieve greater economic growth, to offset British military expenditure which would be reduced to zero in 1972, (1965—twenty per cent of GNP, 1968—eleven point one per cent), and to create more rewarding jobs, sight must not be lost of social and cultural goals that were nearly as important. Otherwise life could become mean and ugly. While spectacular rates of growth (twelve per cent in 1968 at current prices) were achieved "there could be very little of the gracious or the beautiful in our lives". Lee believed that at the end of each day's toil one of the most important purposes of all the planning and effort was that life should be more than just existence, more than just the business of making a living.

The Prime Minister said that social objectives which could raise the quality of life must accompany the hard-headed pursuit of economic and security objectives. "Our surroundings, the home, the factory, the shops, the roads, the whole of our environment must be improved, not just for a few in their villas and bungalows in the more wooded sections of Singapore, but for everyone, whether in government-built flat or kampong. A pleasant city, clean and green, with parks and gardens, music and paintings, drama and light entertainment. With over fifty school bands of fifty players, ultimately nearly 130 bands, one for each secondary school, we should in five years' time get together between 150 and 200 instrumentalists for a symphony orchestra."

Lee Kuan Yew revealed that in the next five-year plan, beginning in 1970, the Government would build 100,000 housing units, 20,000 units per year. They would be better designed to live in and to look at, better spaced and sited, with amenities that made for gracious living —parks, swimming pools, playing fields, recreational centres, shopping arcades. Architects and administrators could achieve higher standards through more experience, greater efficiency and an allocation of more resources into these targets: but at the same time "we must educate the families who have left the slums to leave their old habits behind and adopt new social patterns of behaviour without which life cannot be agreeable for their neighbours in these new high-rise blocks."

He said that a consciousness of beauty and a desire to maintain and improve the beauty of the neighbourhood must be part of the new way of life. Committees would be formed to look after each block of flats. These committees would have representatives from each floor in a block. They would be able to improve the control of noise nuisance, the cleanliness of the public passages, corridors, lifts, staircases, and surrounding grounds of each block. For undertaking these social duties, committee members would be accorded certain privileges. "Gradually we should be able to re-educate the people into more considerate and cultivated living. And when they move out from the squatter huts into modern homes, they must leave their own inconsiderate ways behind. We can teach the children in the schools new habits more easily. The adults in the offices, factories, and hawker pitches, will have to be re-educated in their homes. Just as we have succeeded in eradicating hopelessness, ignorance, squalor and poverty, in the same way, so also we can create a more socially sensitive people, appreciative of beauty and the arts. It is these higher social and cultural standards which, when achieved, can improve the quality of our lives and make the toil and struggle worthwhile for ourselves in our own lifetime."

"Perhaps one of the first qualities necessary for progress", Lee Kuan Yew told the Science Council on 29 October, "is a willingness to face the truth. As individuals, Singapore scientists can be as good as any in the world. But their opportunities to get to the top in any of the frontiers of discovery is limited by the wealth, in men and resources, which Singapore society can put at their disposal. Modern technology, whether in space travel, space communications, or nuclear power, demands such vast investments that only the super-powers can afford them. When results of such research are applied for the enrichment of human life, there must be massive markets, so that the research and development cost can be so spread as not to exceed twenty per cent of the price of the commodity produced in order to be economically competitive between the researching giants. Even in established products, like civilian or military aircraft, the relatively smaller industrially advanced countries of Western Europe have had, for economies of scale, to go into consortium to develop supersonics, short-haul jet air-buses and for variable geometry military aircraft. The moral for all, other than the big and developed countries, is a salutary one: that it is madness to aspire to the esoteric heights of original research in the pure sciences, and then put these discoveries to application in manufacturing and marketing for human needs." However, because of its comparatively advanced position in education and social organization, Singapore was a useful centre for the marketing, distribution, and servicing of established innovations, those which could play an economic role in the development of the region. As the advanced post-industrial countries moved on to the sophistication of new discoveries and higher levels of technological expertise, so they must and would find it profitable to pass on or farm out the secondary expertise to countries like Singapore.

Whether it was in the repairing, building and navigation of ships, or aircraft, as the developed countries went on to building specialized high-technological-content ships (like container carriers or automated super-tankers) so they found it profitable to let countries like Singapore take over the building, first of small general-purpose freighters, pleasure craft, patrol boats, and later of even hydrofoils and eventually hovercrafts, as they in turn became older discoveries. Similarly, first aircraft and air-frames of the propellor aircraft were repaired and maintained, then turbo-props, then the old-generation jets. It was difficult to forecast what lines the advanced countries would pass on to secondary distributive centres, just as it was difficult for the technological pioneers to predict which particular areas of scientific research and technological application were the ones which would have the greatest break-through. Sometimes the best forecasts went awry, as with the development of nuclear power stations which had disappointed earlier expectations. Certain fields were obvious choices for Singapore: transportation and communications, electrical and electronic appliances, food processing, freezing and canning, extraction and processing of timber, oil and minerals.

Because the particular field which Singapore would find most profitable could not be accurately pre-determined, flexibility and versatility must be built into the teaching of sciences in schools, the polytechnics, and universities. "We must avoid narrow specialization. The esoteric specialists we shall always have to borrow. On the other hand, our scientists and engineers must be management-orientated." In spite of rapid expansion in the secondary schools and the universities, there was a shortage of executives and technologists in Singapore—men trained to analyse problems, investigate alternative solutions, assess the implications of each possible solution, and then make a decision. Lee said it used to be much worse. "In the old days, the few who went on to tertiary education were trained to be subordinates, never to take primary responsibility. Our early graduates in the administration were taught to marshall and refine facts and figures, to present them to their superiors, the British officers, who almost exclusively made the decisions. So, today, we have more jobs requiring people with judgment and decisiveness than there are the people with these attributes. So, the value for our scientists and engineers having business-management training."

The Prime Minister said he had read with interest a recent American Aircraft Corporation report which gave the breakdown in their work force of a high-technology product as five per cent engineers, seventy-five per cent production personnel, including technicians and unskilled workers, and twenty per cent business management, including clerical staff. The best of engineers in that five per cent, without the support of the disciplined, hard-working technicians and craftsmen, would still result in poor sales, unprofitability, and failure. But, for all the best trained technicians, craftsmen, and the most industrious of clerks and workers in the world, without the five per cent professionally competent engineers, production could not get off the ground. All would remain unemployed. In Singapore at present, there were more than 4,500 professional visit and employment passes. This did not include the visiting consultants, nor the Europeans who had taken out Singapore citizenship. For everyone of these passes, there was an average of twenty jobs, on the ratio of personnel employed in high-technology products. For low-technology products, the ratio could be one to fifty jobs. "It is unlikely that in the immediate future, we shall be able to produce enough men to take over these jobs. And by the time we do so, newer and higher technology products would have been developed and passed on to secondary centres, including us. But as we catch up with the old technology, the inflow of new technology will keep up the numbers of these professional visit and employment passes. Ideally, all men should be equal. But they are not. For this reason, some become scientists, many are just workers by hand. The differences between human societies are as great as differences between the humans within a society. So long as we are able to maintain the quality of our population, trained, disciplined, skilled workers, with scientists and executives to form the sharp cutting edge, so we shall always have that extra to maintain life at a comparatively higher level, with the amenities and services comparable to that of the most advanced societies."

XX

Opening the National TUC's seminar on 16 November, the Prime Minister said there was a school of thought that for rapid industrialization for an under-developed country it was better not to have trade unions. This school of thought cited Hong Kong, Taiwan and South Korea in support of this theory. But Singapore's objective was not just industrialization. The development of the economy was very important. "But equally important is the development of the nature of our society. We do not want our workers submissive, docile, toadying up to the foreman, the foreman to the supervisor and the supervisor to the boss for increments and promotions." Lee Kuan Yew added: "To survive as a separate and distinct community we have to be a proud and rugged people, or we fail. You can neither be proud nor rugged if you have not got self-respect. Self-respect is what our trade unions have and will give to our workers, that protection for a man's right to his own dignity, his dignity as a human being, as a citizen. He may be an unskilled worker, but he is one of us. He must be prepared to fight and die for Singapore. He will neither be able nor willing to do this if he is a cringing coward."

To understand the present, Lee Kuan Yew briefly recalled the past. "The NTUC, as we know it today, had its origins in 1952, two and half years before the PAP itself was founded. Some of us who later founded the PAP were already planning a mass base for the political struggle for independence. We worked first amongst the government and city council unions, then with the civilian employees of the armed services, then the shop and factory workers, and the bus workers. The rest is recent history. It was a highly politicized trade union leadership. The primary targets were political. Anti-colonialism, anti-exploitation by foreign capital. The basis was solidarity of all the oppressed to band together and fight for independence. Demands were issued accompanied by the threat of strike if demands were not met, and followed often by a strike even when demands were nearly all met. But with self-government and later independence things have changed. Independence gave us the power to take over whatever there was." But it was accompanied by the responsibility to make things work, to make life better for all. "Then", continued Lee Kuan Yew, "our moment of truth arrived. The British military forces were leaving. We wanted freedom. We have got it. Now we have to defend it, or be dominated and exploited all over again, probably much worse, for next time it will not be the British. So the mood was set for a fresh start."

The Employment Act eliminated bad practices which had crept into industrial relations from a previous phase of history. In July, 1969, a team from the World Bank assessed Singapore's economic position. They reported in October that "in 1968 Singapore entered a new phase of accelerated growth with boom conditions in private investment, a decline in unemployment, buoyancy of government revenues, the emergence of an overall surplus of savings over investments, and a significant build-up of external reserves". They attributed "the greater than expected success in Singapore's drive towards industrialization" to four factors. They placed the Employment Act as the second of the factors. The Prime Minister said that legislation could prohibit and punish abuses and malpractices. But it could not give "that positive urge to work and to achieve. This urge can come only from the conviction of a people that they must, and want to give of their best. It is the consciousness of our being co-owners of the new society we are creating, that provides the drive for fulfilment. In multiracial countries like ours, trade unions have a special role in building up this spirit of *camaraderie* amongst the workers. Whatever our race or religion, it is what we produce that entitle us to what we get, not our race or religion. Developing the economy, increasing productivity, increasing returns, these make sense only when fair play and fair shares make it worth everyone's while to put in his share of effort for group survival and group prosperity."

Lee Kuan Yew told the trade unionists: "We have five years of intense effort before us. We are doing well at present. But it does not mean our problems are behind us. The same World Bank Report warns that adverse factors, like the British military withdrawal, are still the factors accountable for an expected slowdown in Singapore's economic growth during the next three years and a resurgence of unemployment in 1972, but the size of the problem now appears much reduced and the maintenance of GDP growth of perhaps five per cent at the trough seems feasible." It would be 1974, at least, "before we have put these problems behind us. Last year, 1968, British military spending still contributed eleven point one per cent to our GNP. In terms of GNP, the spending has gone down by half since 1965. But in terms of employment, however, it has been reduced only by one third. Unless we keep up the effort and get more industries and enterprises launched and operating profitably, about 20,000 civilian employees still to be discharged by 1971, and thousands more, serving the needs of British service families, will not find new jobs. When the British Government announced that their forces will be out by 1971, there was considerable gloom and pessimism, particularly amongst the civilian employees of the armed services. Today, the pendulum has swung to the other end. Every employee about to be retrenched knows or believes that he can easily get another job."

Browsing through the working papers, the Prime Minister said he was struck by the buoyant and confident mood they exuded. This was as it should be provided that it was not forgotten that there was still some way to go. This was no time to talk about amendments to the Employment Act. Anomalies could be ironed out. But the principles which the Act embodied would have to be "part of our way of life". Simply, it meant that nobody could be a passenger, carried by a charitable employer, his shortcomings shielded by his union, and his well-being and security guaranteed by a benign government.

Lee said there were two recent lessons of what happened to a people, their economy, and their standard of life when workers and the unions took liberties with their country. The French unions went on the rampage in May 1968. A year later, the French franc was devalued. The French economy was still not out of trouble. The British unions with their unofficial and wild-cat strikes could not absolve themselves from blame for the devaluation of the pound in November 1967. On the other hand, it was because of the German workers and their unions that their industrial managers did such a magnificent job. The German mark was revalued by nine point three per cent, that is, the purchasing power of the mark, in terms of foreign goods, went up. There were pressures for the revaluation of the Japanese yen. If the Japanese workers and their unions were as destructive as Japanese students, the yen would not be in this happy position of being thought to be worth more than the official rate of exchange.

The Prime Minister concluded: "Before you discuss your future, remember how we got here—the past. You have a role to play in transforming a dependent under-developed community to an independent industrial society. It depends upon how successfully we can mobilize internal and international capital and expertise, get people to learn the skills and crafts, and acquire the managerial and marketing know-how. Only then can we produce goods and services efficiently and competitively for international customers. So whilst throwing your eye towards the far horizon, do not forget the harsh realities of today. Let us first negotiate and overcome these immediate hazards."

XXI

The Prime Minister again dealt with the human factors in economic development when he talked to the Economics Society of Nanyang University on 12 December. Why, he asked, are some countries industrialized and others not? "Why are only two countries able to send men out into space? Is it because America and Russia have vast natural resources and huge populations? But so have China and India. Meanwhile, medium-sized countries like West Germany and Japan are expected to advance the most, industrially, in science and technology. If it is natural resources that primarily determines development, why did the North American Red Indians not achieve the high levels of the Central and South American Indian civilizations? But how is it that after the Spanish arrived in Central and South America, and the British,

Dutch, French in North America, the pendulum has swung in favour of North America?"

Lee Kuan Yew said it was generally believed that a large territory with a large population meant automatic progress when exploitation by a colonial power was ended. "This is now known to be too facile a proposition in economic development. The attributes of different societies vary. Now it is reluctantly acknowledged that these attributes are a crucial factor in any transformation from backwardness to the modern technology. Moreover, it takes a long time to develop and transform an agricultural to an industrial economy, because it takes a long time to educate and train a whole population, and to adapt to the different styles of working and living in an industrial society. The Japanese have taken over 100 years from the Meiji era in 1868 to get where they now are. When they embarked on a war in 1941, after seventy-three years, they thought they had matched the technological weaponry and industrial capacity of the West. They were wrong. They were defeated not because they were deficient in the art of war, but because neither their industrial capacity, nor their military technology, was comparable to that of America. When communists point to the dramatic transformation of a feudal, agricultural, Tsarist Russia of 1917 to the powerful, industrialized, communist Russia of 1957, the year of Sputnik, they do not mention that even by 1917 Russia had developed a considerable industrial potential."

Lee thought that nothing brought out the importance of the human factors more vividly than when comparing the spectacular results of investment in the ruined economies of Western Europe, as against the negligible returns from aid and development in new countries. Then there was the phenomenal recovery of two defeated countries. After their defeat, both West Germany and Japan were shrunken in area and resources. But both had populations highly educated and skilled in industry and technology, an abundance of scientists, engineers, technicians, and managers, all disciplined and easily reorganized. The new countries on the other hand, had largely uneducated populations, most of peasant stock, unaccustomed to the discipline and skills required on the factory floor. The speed with which Hong Kong, a territory without natural resources, had industrialized was the result of the influx of refugee capital and expertise. A cadre of ready-trained engineers and technicians, the product of over thirty years of painful development in China since the 1911 Revolution, gave Hong Kong their start.

But this was not to say that it was not valuable to have natural resources. "The oil sheikhdoms of the Persian Gulf, like Kuwait, have a per capita income higher than that of the United States of America. But 100 years from now, the chances are their oil would have dried up. Then whilst Americans have advanced to higher levels of technology, and bountiful living, unless the subjects of these Sheikhs have been educated, become skilled and trained, they would have to go back to their camels and live on dates, travelling. from oasis to oasis. Worse, they would by then probably have forgotten how to ride on a camel or to make their tents, having got used to riding around in American cars and living in imported pre-fabricated houses. If Singapore were to strike oil, then our whole economic and security position will be enormously enhanced. Perhaps the knowledge that this is unlikely to happen makes us get on with the job of the lasting long-term transformation: the raising of our standards of education, upgrading the skills of our people and increasing the number and quality of engineers, technicians and managers. Developed countries can sell us their finished products on easy terms. But unless we learn to use them properly, to maintain them in serviceable condition, to make the components and fit them, we shall never make the grade."

As with civilian, so too with military technology. Modern weapons were difficult to handle not only because they were all that difficult to operate, but because they took considerable engineering professionalism and technical competence to maintain in operational condition. Armed forces no longer only needed healthy, brave soldiers. Without a larger army of mechanics, technicians, electricians, artisans, engineers and scientists to keep the electronic gadgetry and complex machines in tip-top operational condition, all the potential fire-power of modern armour could become damp squibs.

Since 1965, continued Lee, it had become increasingly necessary to build a defence capability. "Without adequate security forces of our own to make a significant contribution to joint security arrangement, investments may slow down. If people believe that we are weak and defenceless, even our own wealthy citizens will move part of their capital abroad. Participation of our ablest in our defence forces is a necessary part of the process of changing patterns of education and training to meet different circumstances. Those who have made the universities owe a more than average duty to enhance our security and enrich our future. As we move to more sophisticated equipment, so our armed forces will require and train more technologists and technicians. Military technology is often more exacting and advanced than its civilian counterpart. But this in turn will help our economic growth, as this will increase the reservoir of people trained in modern technology, essential for our industrialization." It was not easy to predict what particular manufacturing or servicing industries would become profitable in Singapore. Hence the importance of flexibility in the education and training of the young.

The pattern of change in Singapore's economy had already been set. In terms of percentage contribution to gross domestic product, entrepot trade had gone down from nineteen per cent in 1960 to sixteen per cent in 1968. Meanwhile, in the same period, industry had gone up from eleven per cent to nineteen per cent. In the eight years between 1960 and 1968, Singapore doubled its GDP, from $2,000 million to $4,000 million. In manufacture alone, the value was more than trebled from $148 million to $506 million. "The growing industrial sector is our future. The higher the skills and expertise, the greater the value that is added to the materials processed. The greater the 'added value', the higher the wages."

"Value added" the Prime Minister pointed out was very low when labour was used in industries, low in capital and technological content. An example was textiles. American, British, and West European textiles had such high labour costs that they had to be protected by heavy tariffs and quotas from competition of imported textiles from Asia. "Value added" was high in science-based industries with high capital and technological content. An example was aircraft, jumbo-jets or supersonics.

With the passage of time, what was once considered high technology could become low technology. An example was shipbuilding. At the beginning of the century, the research, development, and building of steel steam-ships was high technology done only by very advanced nations. Today, except for specialized ships, like automated super tankers and container ships, it had been relegated to low technology. Because shipbuilding was low technology compared to aircraft, American and even Canadian labour costs were too high for them to compete in the shipbuilding industry. Americans and Canadians had found it more economical to buy their ships from abroad. The Americans now considered this trend dangerous because, for national security considerations, they want to keep a work force practised in the technology of designing and building ships.

Lee Kuan Yew argued that, as a rule of thumb, the standard of living of a people could be equated with their standard of technological competence. Trade between countries reflected this difference in their standards of technological competence. When America and the West exported to Asia and Africa, they exported commodities of high technology, like machinery and sophisticated goods. When Asia and Africa exported to the West, they sent agricultural or mineral raw products, or simple manufacture, like textiles. "The moral of it all is that the relatively high standards of life Singaporeans enjoy can only be justified and continued if our standard of technological competence is comparatively high for the area. Then we are exporting to this area products with higher technological content than the products we are importing from them. Naturally, everybody wants to upgrade his skills. So we have to move on to ever higher standards, or be overtaken by our neighbours. The human qualities that made us a successful commercial centre should be nurtured, and preserved. This keen sense for the percentage return on investment will continue to serve us well, as we broaden our base with more and more industries, making products of ever higher technological content. "At the same time, other goals must also be pursued for well-balanced development. If we are not to coarsen the texture of our society, we must improve the cultural and recreational facilities, encourage appreciation of the arts and music, and create an agreeable environment that will stimulate our people for further advance up the hill seeking perfection."

XXII

In the parliamentary debate on the Abortion Bill, Lee Kuan Yew on 29 December said that one of the noticeable trends in developed countries was that parents with more education had much smaller families than those with less education. This trend was also discernible in urbanized though still under-developed societies like Singapore. If these trends continued to their logical conclusions then the quality of the population would go down.

The Prime Minister said that in all societies, there were the more intelligent and the less intelligent. And he quoted extracts from an article by Professor Richard Lynn (Member of the Economic and Social Research Institute, Dublin) in the *New Scientist* of 20 March 1969. The professor said that geneticists had come to the conclusion that intelligence was principally determined by heredity.

Lee said that it was not unlikely that many other attributes of mind and body were also inherited. "But whatever the inheritance, man, more than any other living creature, depends on nurturing and training for his capacity to mature and develop. Man needs to be reared for one-third of his life span in order to be productive for the next two-thirds. In highly developed societies, students are supported for twenty-five to twenty-seven years until they get their Ph. D.s, and then begin to repay their debt to society. His final performance is affected by diet, health and cultural, social and educational opportunities. When the less educated who are also in the lower income groups have large families, the problems they create for their children are compounded. Resources, time, attention and care, lavished on one or two children, can nurture and develop the endowments of the children to their fullest extent, when spread and frittered over six or more in the family, prevent any child from getting the chances he could have had in a smaller family. In urbanized Singapore, this can become an acute problem. Free prenatal care, post-natal health and almost free medical services have reduced infant mortality to the low rates of highly developed countries. Free education and subsidized housing lead to a situation where less economically productive people in the community are reproducing themselves at rates higher than the rest. This will increase the total proportion of less productive people. Our problem is how to devise a system of disincentives, so that the irresponsible, the social delinquents, do not believe that all they have to do is to produce their children and the Government then owes them and their children sufficient food, medicine, housing, education and jobs."

The Prime Minister said there were certain areas of activity over which control by any government was both difficult and repugnant. "One such area is the choice of the number of children a father and mother decide to rear. One day the pressure of circumstances may become so acute that attitudes must change. Until such time, when moral inhibitions disappear and legislative or administrative measures can be taken to regulate the size of families, we must try to induce people to limit their families and give their children a better chance. The quality of our population depends on raising not only the IQ level but also getting parents to care, nurture and educate their children and to develop all those other qualities so crucial to effective living summed up in the word 'character'. Every person, genius or moron, has a right to reproduce himself. So we assume that a married pair will want to be allowed two children to replace them. This is already the average-size family of the skilled industrial worker in Europe. In Singapore we still allow three for good measure. Beyond the three children, the costs of subsidized housing, socialized medicine and free education should be transferred to the parent. We have changed the priorities in public housing, by not awarding more points for more children. One day we may have to put disincentives or penalties on the other social services. By introducing this new abortion law together with the companion voluntary sterilization law, we are making possible the exercise of voluntary choice. But we must keep a close watch on the result of the new laws and the patterns of use which will emerge."

Lee Kuan Yew thought it not unlikely that the people who will want to restrict their families are the better educated parents in better paid jobs. "They are the people who already understand that their children's future depends on their being able to care for their health, education and upbringing. One of the crucial yardsticks by which we shall have to judge the results of the new abortion law combined with the voluntary sterilization law will be whether it tends to raise or lower the total quality of our population. We must encourage those who earn less than $200 per month and cannot afford to nurture and educate many children never to have more than two. Intelligent application of these laws can help reduce the distortion that has already set in. Until the less educated themselves are convinced and realize that they should concentrate their limited resources on one or two to give their children the maximum chance to climb up the educational ladder, their children will always be at the bottom of economic scale. It is unlikely that the results will be discernible before five years. Nor will the effect be felt before fifteen to twenty years. But we will regret the time lost, if we do not now take the first tentative steps towards correcting a trend which can leave our society with a large number of the physically, intellectually and culturally anaemic."

CHAPTER TWENTY-FOUR

The Year of Power 1970

SINGAPORE continued to make progress economically and industrially during 1970. The Republic strengthened its defences. Considerable headway was made in vocational education.

During the year, Lee Kuan Yew was absent from the State for ninety days while visiting Ceylon, India, Tanzania, Zambia, the United Arab Republic, the Soviet Union, France, West Germany, Britain, the United States, Japan and Hong Kong.

In November Singapore suffered a grievous loss by the death of President Yusof bin Ishak. Parliament elected Dr Benjamin Henry Sheares the new President.

IN his New Year Message, Lee said: "We enter the 1970s with confidence." As with individuals so with nations, confidence was the touchstone of success. The 1960s had shown how much could be achieved by an active, striving and practical people, despite prolonged periods of conflict, unrest and disruption.

In the ten years from 1959 to 1969, per capita income had been doubled and the GNP increased two and a half times. The wealth accumulated as a community was invested in roads, schools, hospitals, housing, power stations, water works, extended wharves, airports, telephones, industries and foreign exchange reserves. All this capital would provide faster growth and higher returns in the next ten years.

But material wealth was a relatively minor factor compared to the immense improvement in human resources. "Ten years ago, we were so many individuals, each seeking his personal or family salvation. Now there is social cohesiveness. We have learned to think and to act as a people, to protect and advance our group interests. We have trained and educated our young people. We have increased their ability to use the instruments of modern technology to create wealth. The '70s will be better than the '60s. This is our confident expectation, provided we do not become complacent."

The Prime Minister said that another valuable asset brought forward from the '60s was the confidence other people had in Singapore's viability, reliability, and capacity for intense effort. "If we do not allow anything to upset this assessment of our potentials, investments will continue to flow in, generating more and better jobs, and increasing revenue to pay for better social amenities."

Much had been done by organization, ingenuity and work discipline. Much more would be achieved. Investments, construction and progress had a habit of gathering momentum. "We deserve to succeed if we can match this progress by a similar effort in security and defence." From time to time, in the history of a people, events took place, which historians subsequently marked out as turning points. One such turning point was August 1965. Another was May 1969. "There were some anxious moments we shall not quickly forget." There could be a turning point in the 1970s. There certainly would be anxious moments. The unfinished problems of the '60s would be carried over into the '70s. "We shall remain on top of our problems only if we stay trim and alert, flexible but determined. Everyone wants a prosperous new year. Work for it and ours will be. The pre-conditions have already been set."

At a state banquet in honour of Mr Spiro T. Agnew, Vice-President of the United States of America, on 10 January, the Prime

Minister said he was privileged to have had the opportunity to know him, and to learn of his views on the political mood in America, and its possible effects on shaping policies which may influence the course of events in Southeast Asia. "In recent months, many American visitors have asked me about the future of this region 'after Vietnam'. I have been constrained to explain that what is likely to emerge 'after Vietnam' depended to a large extent upon the manner in which American disengagement was accomplished. I had hoped that this disengagement from the military conflict would be ordered at a pace which could be seen to have given the South Vietnamese the opportunity to decide their future for themselves."

Lee said that being Americans, his visitors were keenly interested in forecasting the future. They wanted to know what America could or should do to increase regional security, regional co-operation and regional economic progress. He said he found it difficult to answer these inquiries. Much of it depended upon American assessment of their national interests. It depended also on an assessment of the worthwhileness of pursuing these interests when the costs necessary to achieve them might tax the patience of the American people, because results might not be visible within two or four years. "I confess to a great admiration for American technology, the programming and methodology in research and development. Targets are defined and a time-table for achieving them is set. In space technology, this has brought forth maximum effort and maximum results. So the journey to the moon and back we defined as the target, and programmed for achievement by 1970. And achieved it was, to the acclamation of the whole world. By naming a date, Americans spurred themselves on to win in the race, albeit at a higher price in lives and resources. But for political goals in Southeast Asia, where success or failure is related to qualitative and not quantitative factors, the fixing of dates for achieving intermediate targets may not be the best way to achieving final goals." What Southeast Asia needed was a climate of confidence, continuing security and stability in which constructive endeavour could become rewarding. It also needed to have the spirit of success. This spirit could be generated as enthusiasm spread when their own efforts brought growth and progress. Time-tabling and fixing dates would negate both the climate of confidence and the spirit of success. The danger of forecasting the longer-term political future was that people might begin to act as if the future was already here.

"So also", continued Lee Kuan Yew, "I doubt if we can fix a date by which conflicts within the region will have been lessened or muted and co-operation established between the countries in the region. These targets do not lend themselves to programming and computerization. America, with other major powers, can help by providing the background of security and stability. America can even add a little stimulus for faster growth. But the transformation of conservative agricultural communities, working with old-fashioned tools, into thrusting mass-consumption industrial societies, depends finally upon indigenous effort and perseverance."

Singapore's future as a ship-repairing and shipbuilding centre was discussed by Lee Kuan Yew at the fourth annual dinner of Jurong Shipyard Ltd, the following week. He compared the average weekly earnings for shipbuilding and ship-repairing workers in Britain, Japan and Singapore. In 1962 it was $135 for Britain, $70 for Japan and $46 for Singapore: which meant that the Japanese earned half what the Britishers got, and Singapore seventy per cent of the Japanese. But by 1968, it was $64 Singapore and $113 Japan. In other words, from over two-thirds of the Japanese worker's wages in 1962, the Singapore worker was now getting just over half the wages of the Japanese worker. This was because the Japanese economy was stronger, the Japanese worker more productive and so better paid. If the Singapore worker could match the skills, work as hard, and equal the productivity of the Japanese, then, at half the costs of that of the Japanese, the success of Singapore's shipbuilding industry was guaranteed. True, shipbuilding was not as labour intensive as ship-repairing. Even so labour was a high component of the total cost of building a ship. Because Japanese workers had been getting about half the wages of the Britishers, Japan had now established itself as the biggest shipbuilding nation in the world.

Singapore had a long way to go before full advantage could be taken of its strategic position, the skills of the workers, and the competence of the marine engineers and naval architects, to establish itself as the biggest ship-repairing and shipbuilding centre east of Suez and south of Japan. The figures of growth in the years 1966 to 1968 showed how much leeway there was to be made up before a plateau could be reached. "We doubled the output in two years from $64 million in 1966, to $120 million in 1968. It indicated how much could have been accomplished if we had concentrated earlier on bringing up to date our ship-repairing and shipbuilding capacity and changing union and workers habits. But it is not too late. And one day the Suez Canal will be re-opened. Whilst the super tankers may still go around the Cape, the medium and smaller ships will again come through the Canal and increase the traffic through Singapore." The aeroplane might have taken over the bulk of passenger travel. But into the foreseeable future no technological breakthrough could replace ships as the most efficient and economic form of transportation of goods. "If we build up a reputation for fast work, of good quality, at fair prices, ship-repairing and shipbuilding will become one of our great industries."

In a speech on 24 January, the Prime Minister warned that in the next two to three years Singapore must make the most of her great opportunities. Progress must not falter through a shortage of skilled workers. The educational system was being brought up to date and students were being prepared with the skills required. Meanwhile, skilled workers must be allowed to come in and help Singapore take advantage of this spurt in industrial growth. Skilled artisans from Hong Kong or elsewhere were now being offered permanent residence and, on completion of five years of good work, the opportunity to obtain citizenship. This had been made the more necessary because of National Service. Defence would suck in a good number of these skilled technicians and artisans for the maintenance and logistic branches of the Ministry of Defence. The repair and maintenance of sophisticated equipment required high technical skills. This increased the demand and created a temporary shortage of skilled men. But after a few years the position would ease up. These trained men would go into the reserves and enter the market. Moreover, more skilled artisans would be passing out of training institutes and technical schools. "The chance we now have for spectacular industrial expansion does not come often to a people. If we exert ourselves, maintain social stability, improve skills, increase keenness and productivity, do not turn away industrial opportunities which are coming our way, by the end of the '70s Singapore will no longer be an under-developed country. Our way of making a living will change rapidly. But most rapid of all is the change from a dependent and disparate community to one with the will and spirit, the organization wherewithal, to look after itself in most things, and the defence arrangements of the Commonwealth Five, to make more than a token contribution."

II

When, on 18 February, Hong Kong University conferred an honorary doctorate on Lee Kuan Yew, the Prime Minister in an address spoke of the history of Hong Kong and Singapore. Both started as British island-colonies, founded over 100 years ago for the pursuit of trade with the East Indies and China. Features which were common to all British colonies had left their imprints on both territories: equality before the law, effective and honest administration. Both went through three and a half years of Japanese occupation. Both had large ethnic Chinese populations, mainly from South China. Both had successive inflows of refugees. Both were urbanized centres with high densities of population. Originally based on entrepot trade, both now had manufacturing as the main growth sectors of their economy. Both had high growth rates, with the highest per capita GNP in Asia outside Japan.

After the Second World War, many countries became independent. There were great expectations of social, educational and industrial progress in these countries. This was particularly so for the large countries. Their natural and human resources appeared so abundant as to make progress and prosperity seem a natural result when independence brought an end to colonial exploitation. At that time, the unpromising places for industrializing and modernizing seemed to be Hong Kong and Singapore. Today, it was recognized that some undetected influences were at work. Some factors prevented the successful transformation of the large countries into modern industrial nations. This was all the sadder and perplexing when one recalled their ancient history, and the great civilizations that they had nurtured in the past. ECAFE, the IMF and the World Bank made annual reports on the economic performance of these new countries. The "development decade" of the '60s had not lived up to its name. Only Japan had entered the technological league. Amongst those that have shown the most progress were Hong Kong, Singapore, Taiwan, South Korea, Malaysia and Thailand.

Western social scientists who travel the region have tried to fathom the reasons for these variations in performance. What made for these different responses to the challenge of modernization? Was it because some societies are the products of a harsher attrition with nature, resulting in human types with more intense cultures which enabled them to be more easily geared to industrial techniques and disciplines? Could it be that some religions inculcate a tougher spirit in their disciples and a willingness to strive and slog against the unfavourable dispensation of providence?

Lee thought it was more than probable that ethnic and cultural factors do affect the group performance of various communities. But if it was all due to ethnic factors, then the outlook or a narrowing of the performance gap between the different ethnic groups was bleak. "I do not take such a pessimistic view. By the nature of my work, I am inclined to be more optimistic of what is possible with a change in values and in cultural patterns, with improved diet and health conditions, with better education and training. It takes some time, perhaps decades or generations, for peasants to learn commercial and industrial habits. However, if a people have had to break with their past, they will also have shaken off the debris of past beliefs, habits and inhibitions. Then in a new environment, they can more easily adopt attitudes and values which enable speedier acquisition of industrial-technological knowledge, skills and techniques. If it were only ethnic factors which have made for faster progress in these countries, why is it, between similar ethnic types, economic growth and per capita incomes in Hong Kong and Singapore are better than in Taiwan, although Taiwan has greater natural resources?"

One reason was that Hong Kong and Singapore had made a head start over Taiwan. Both in Hong Kong and Singapore, the British started new communities from scratch. The Japanese took over an established province of China. Next, Hong Kong and Singapore have always been more exposed to Western influences than Taiwan. Exposure to new ideas and methods may be unpleasant and unsettling, but it forces the pace of change. Further, the Japanese took over Taiwan some sixty to eighty years after the British founded Hong Kong and Singapore. Japan herself was then engaged in the difficult task of her own industrialization. And she was developing Taiwan as an agricultural, not an industrial economy. Even so, fifty years of Japanese influence has helped Taiwan's subsequent industrial development when the mainlanders went over to Taiwan after 1949. With this influx of entrepreneurial and managerial expertise, Taiwan received a booster for her industrialization.

All governments today accepted the fact that in order to develop into a mass-consumption technological society, universal education was a pre-condition. Mass education enabled easy training, and simplicity of communications for accurate instructions to be passed on. But the Chinese script, with ideographs in place of phonetic alphabets, was one of the most difficult in the world. It was developed for a scholarly elite, designed to leave ordinary people illiterate and in awe of the mandarins. So since 1911 China had been simplifying the language. "A script which is mysterious and difficult to the masses of the people does not go with a technological society. In more recent times, Chinese characters have been abbreviated and simplified, and the written style now reads like the spoken form. However, over a century ago, through the introduction of the English language, the Chinese in Hong Kong and Singapore have had their ideographic blinkers removed."

Next, learning by rote, for about 2,000 years, was a system calculated to maintain stability and discourage innovation. Chinese imperial dynasties tried to head off revolutionary pressures by the systematic induction of all the best brains into the doctrines of obedience and conformity, as scholars competed in the imperial examinations for entry into the mandarinate. However, the price for stability was the exclusion of Imperial China from the great scientific and technological discoveries of the West, and the industrial revolution. "On the other hand, when you have left the ancestral home and are no longer governed by mandarins trained in the Analects, but by British administrators trained on General Orders which enjoin them to hold the ring fairly and honestly for all who live under their dispensation, it is that much easier to break out of the barren confines of the past."

Lee said that of all the leavening influences at work, the one most likely to leave the most lasting impact on the future was education.

The imparting, not only of knowledge, but, more important, of the spirit of curiosity and inquiry was what made for innovation and enabled science-based industries to grow. For the mass-consumption society of abundance, there must be ample numbers of competent engineers. They must be supported by large armies of technicians. Then production and marketing must be efficiently conducted by men trained in business management. This could come only with the education of the total population, from which a meritocracy could emerge.

Lee went on to say that the Japanese had been the one non-European nation that successfully propelled themselves into the industrial age. They succeeded in injecting science and industry into their way of life, whilst retaining their culture and way of life. Modern Japan was a reflection of this marrying of the old and the new. Hong Kong and Singapore, both with Chinese- and English-language universities, had the opportunities of preserving some of the best of the old, whilst acquiring the necessary techniques and styles of the new. He hoped Singapore, with Malay and Indian contributions to her heritage, set in Southeast Asia, could result in an attractive blend of the East and the West. The short-term future held promise of further progress for both Hong Kong and Singapore. If the rate of progress of the past ten years was extrapolated into the next five years, Hong Kong's progress would be faster than that of Singapore. In 1963, per capita income per annum in Hong Kong was barely more than half Singapore's. By last year, 1969, the estimates were that Hong Kong had already surpassed Singapore's per capita annual income of $2,437. The middle-term future, around the year 2000, was more difficult to predict. But beyond that, into the long-term future, the peoples of Hong Kong and Singapore might have significant, even exciting, roles to play. As pioneers in modernization of their regions, Hong Kong and Singapore could act as catalysts to accelerate the transforming of traditional agricultural societies around them. These two most improbable and unlikely of places could deserve a mention in the history of human progress as centres which helped spread new styles of working and living, which were part and parcel of the urbanized industrial technological society. "By design, Hong Kong and Singapore were chosen as trading beach-heads to a vaster hinterland. They performed valuable roles as re-distribution points for the manufactured goods of the West. By the accident of subsequent developments, they may become dissemination points, not simply of the sophisticated manufacture of the developed world, but more vital, of social values and disciplines, of skills and expertise."

Lee Kuan Yew spoke to the Foreign Correspondents Club, Hong Kong, the following day. He said a positive approach to Hong Kong-Singapore relations was to investigate how both could benefit from

GNP AND GNP PER CAPITA OF SELECTED COUNTRIES
(AT CURRENT PRICES)

		1960	1967	1968
Japan				
GNP at market prices	US$ mil.	43,053	119,553	141,922
GNP per capita	US$	462	1,197	1,405
Singapore				
GNP at market prices	US$ mil.	717	1,270	1,492
GNP per capita	US$	438	649	751
Hong Kong				
GNP at factor cost	US$ mil.	996	2,377	2,630(estimates)*
GNP per capita	US$	324	620	680 „
Malaysia				
GNP at market prices	US$ mil.	2,173	3,178	3,362
GNP per capita	US$	268	317	326
Taiwan				
GNP at market prices	US$ mil.	1,560	3,595	4,144
GNP per capita	US$	145	270	304
South Korea				
GNP at market prices	US$ mil.	1,898	4,612	5,815
GNP per capita	US$	77	154	191
Thailand				
GNP at market prices	US$ mil.	2,641	5,079	5,576(estimates)**
GNP per capita	US$	97	148	165 „

Sources

Hong Kong	*The National Accounts of Less Developed Countries 1950–66,* OECD *World Bank Atlas 1969,* published by IBRD. * *London Financial Times on Hong Kong Review,* 12 January 1970
Taiwan	*Taiwan Statistical Data Book 1969*
Korea	*Economic Statistical Year Book 1969*
Japan	*Monthly Statistics of Japan,* October 1969
Malaysia	*Bank Negara Malaysia Quarterly Economic Bulletin,* June 1969
Thailand	*Bank of Thailand Monthly Report,* January 1968 and September 1969 ** IMF Article XIV Consultations, Thailand, 1969 IMF International Financial Statistics, October 1969

Exchange Rates in Converting the GNP in National Currency to US Dollars

Singapore	$3.06 per US$	South Korea	Won 130 per US$ in 1960,
Hong Kong	$5.77 per US$		Won 270 in 1967 and 1968
Taiwan	NT$40.10 per US$	Malaysia	$3.06 per US$
Japan	Yen 360 per US$	Thailand	20.80 Baht per US$

the competitive and complementary features of the two economies. Could they gain by co-operating? The old-fashioned view was that when two countries competed for industrialization, what one gained in capital, expertise and export markets, the other lost. This was too simple an approach. Economists drawing lessons from the development of the European Economic Community, stressed how industrial progress in a member country stimulated growth and prosperity in the other members, even though they manufactured and sold to each other similar goods, like cars, refrigerators and washing machines. And EEC prosperity benefited even those outside the Common Market. When purchasing power increased, the EFTA countries exported more to EEC. When there was a recession, EFTA exports declined.

American economic expansion through their corporations investing in Europe, either through take-overs or mergers, aroused suspicions, and even resentment. Now it was generally acknowledged that these extensions of American giant conglomerates had injected new management skills and production techniques, forcing indigenous European companies to modernize their management and increase efficiency to survive, or be taken over. Even Japan, the most nationalistic of all industrial nations regarding the control of their economy, had recently agreed to loosen the restrictions on investment of foreign capital in her industries.

Lee Kuan Yew believed that Hong Kong and Singapore could reinforce and back each other to mutual advantage. Industrial expansion in one was not necessarily at the expense of the other. It could be beneficial for temporary shortages of capital, managerial, professional or technical skills, to be made up by borrowing without any detriment caused to the lender. Before and immediately after the war, Hong Kong University trained doctors for Singapore. Today, Singapore was happy to return the compliment and have Hong Kong recruit doctors from Singapore. Hong Kong had international marketing expertise for light industrial products. Singapore's network in Southeast Asia facilitated the distribution of these products. She also gathered the raw materials, like timber, rattan and tropical produce, which Hong Kong needed for her manufactures. The two could supplement each other's network

Of the 500 industrial enterprises in Singapore with a paid-up capital of nearly $860 million, Hong Kong's participation was in 109 firms with a capital of $44 million, or five per cent. They were concentrated in textiles and garments (25), chemicals (8), plastic (7), all Hong Kong's specialties. Singapore's contribution to Hong Kong's GNP was through banking, hotels, entertainment and films, and some manufacture.

Singapore was keen to acquire a special feature of Hong Kong's industrial activity. "There is a thrust and bustle that comes to a people who want to make the most of time. Singapore offers the more circumspect approach, suited for any industry with a longer gestation period and a deeper base. These two different ethos of entrepreneurial activity can be married to advantage. The two can co-operate and develop a special relationship. As a sovereign state, Singapore participates in many regional programmes. Hong Kong, technically a colony, cannot. But she can plug into these programmes via Singapore." Added Lee: "The two are developing a co-operative relationship. And capital and expertise, which may otherwise be irretrievably lost if they leap-frog to places like Canada or Australia, will more likely flow back and feed back if they move from Singapore to Hong Kong, and vice versa."

III

In February, the Crown Prince and Princess of Japan visited Singapore. At a state banquet in their honour, on 26 February, Lee Kuan Yew said that the Japanese and the Singaporeans had got to know each other and to work together. There were enough common and complementary factors to make joint ventures in industrial enterprise rewarding to both. Everybody knew of Japan's economic miracle. What was not so well publicized was the miracle of her social strength and cultural coherence. They were the basis for Japan's economic success. One example of this flexibility and resilience was the transformation of the Japanese monarchy. In Cambodia, to meet changed political conditions, a king of extraordinary energy and talent, submitted himself to the popular process, the better to lead his people as elected leader. Nepal, a decade ago, had a democratically elected government with a monarchy. But the government had to be temporarily suspended because the traditional and elected centres of power were unable to accommodate each other in the new framework.

Lee said that some years ago, Whitehead, the British mathematician and philosopher, pointed out that "those societies which cannot combine reverence for their symbols with freedom for their revision must ultimately decay, either from anarchy or the slow atrophy by useless shadows". Any social order that could not revise and reaffirm its aspirations and values, and continuously re-structure its institutions to achieve its purposes, would be beset by increasing unrest and disorder. New countries were faced with acute problems of change in their modes of life and in arranging new systems for settling their public affairs. Their models of representative governments borrowed from the West often ran into troubles. On the other hand, in the West itself, these models were considered out of date. Social scientists were questioning whether their systems of representative and collective decision-making were adequate for the new social situations that had been brought about by technological progress. New communications technology, the television relays through earth satellites, created simultaneous interaction between large numbers of people, not possible before. People expressed the need for greater participation in deciding the affairs of their country. An American social scientist, in a symposium on the year 2000, stressed the urgent need for a new political theory for Americans, to replace the one which they formulated in the eighteenth century, which he said, "has become cumulatively inadequate and frustrating for the present and an impediment for the future".

Added the Prime Minister: "This visit to Southeast Asia by Your Imperial Highnesses reflects the enduring character of the Japanese monarchy, changing social forms and diplomatic styles with changing transportation technology. I have a feeling that the future belongs more to those who are ever willing and ready to meet new problems, adjust, adapt and accommodate, and so overcome new situations created by innovation and progress. I hope Your Highnesses will carry back to Japan Singapore's regard for the capacity of the Japanese people to change with changing technology, and yet remain Japanese enough in their styles of life, and thus avoid problems of disorientation."

IV

Considerable damage to life and property was caused through firecrackers welcoming Chinese New Year, and at a celebrations gathering on 28 February attended by both Chinese and Malays, the Prime Minister reminded them that they had to cope with "new ways of life, new styles of living". Progress meant problems. "As we become more industrialized—more people per square mile, more houses going up, more factories going up—we face new problems." He noted with sadness and anger the five deaths and many injuries caused by firecrackers. "It is just madness. People who could have been productive for ten, twenty or thirty more years have died for no rhyme or reason." He told the gathering: "It is alright throwing crackers or hanging them on a bamboo when you are in a little village, but when you have houses of ten storeys, twenty storeys high, you must change."

He also touched on the problem of dust and smoke in the atmosphere as a result of industrialization. He said, "These are new problems for which we must find a solution."

Another point the Prime Minister referred to was that the Singapore boy or girl who comes out from school, even though he or she fails Primary Six, does not want to work in the City Cleansing Department, to be domestic servants, or to be gardeners. "And so, we have given work permits to people to come in to do all the jobs that Singaporeans consider below their dignity. All this is alright," he said, "but if the boys and girls are not able to do highly skilled jobs, work. machines, go to technical schools when they pass their primary schools, then there will be trouble, because we will have to get our skilled workers from abroad. They will have to do the unskilled jobs and they do not want to do them. So there will be social problems."

The Prime Minister dwelt on the problem of gracious living. He said, "You have to be considerate to each other. You cannot turn on your radio full volume. You may be playing the latest Beatle music, or whatever is the latest craze, but your neighbour may want to listen to something else. So you have to make some accommodation for him. Life is not just eating, drinking, television and cinema."

He told the gathering that he visited ten flats at Queenstown the previous evening and only in two of them did he see books and magazines. In every flat he saw hi-fi, television, radio, which were the signs of affluence. But only in two flats there were books, magazines and paintings.

The Prime Minister said, "in schools, we are trying to teach our boys and girls music, painting, art—a little culture, so that they can do more than just press a button, see a picture or hear a sound. This is absolutely crucial because in that way you may have a creative, imaginative society. You want invention, you want to progress. The human mind must be creative, must be self-generating: it cannot depend on just gadgets to amuse itself." Lee told the people that Singapore will see more material progress. But, he emphasized, there must be more social progress to match more material progress.

Lee Kuan Yew discussed the responsibility of non-political leaderships in sustaining a democratic system when he spoke at the annual dinner of the Singapore Advocates and Solicitors Society on 21 March. He said that recently, a former Indian commander-in-chief, speaking out from the anguish of his retirement, recommended that presidential rule be imposed and the army brought in to govern India. He proposed that even when democracy was re-established, it should be one literate man, one vote; and that there should be only a limited number of competing political parties. There were many reasons why the parliamentary system had failed in many new countries Lee said he proposed to touch on one of the factors. Democratic government required, *inter alia,* that the government alone should not have to carry the responsibility of influencing public attitudes and opinion. To work the democratic system, leaderships at all levels, in particular non-political, functional or professional group leaderships, should play their part in educating the people. They should help create a climate in which difficult problems arising from changing circumstances can be met with new solutions. For the time being, Singapore had a government which was able, on its own, to carry through crucial reforms in the face of opposition, either well-intentioned or misguided. But Singapore might not always have such a government. The parliamentary system could only work if people, who do not necessarily have to shoulder the responsibility for unpleasant and unpopular decisions, go out of their way to undertake such responsibilities. "When I made astringent comments about the Vice-Chancellor of the University of Singapore in 1963, there were howls of protest about academic freedom. I have never regretted pressing the Government's view that the University must conform with the national objectives of the Government's policy. A representative government votes it the money for its maintenance and development, and is responsible to the electorate for the results. Today, British vice-chancellors are under pressure by student unions." Both the Leader of the Opposition and Mr Enoch Powell had openly criticized and derided the unwillingness of British vice-chancellors to deal with organized disorder, and for being flabby in the face of insolence and indiscipline.

"Perhaps", added Lee Kuan Yew, "you may take comfort from the fact that lawyers are not the only ones lacking the will for self-discipline and the strength to shoulder their responsibilities, not only to their members, but to society as a whole. The Singapore Stock Exchange Committee is the saddest example of the weakness of functional group leadership. They have shown a singular lack of discipline, responsibility or strength. They have used the authority the Government has allowed them to exercise to protect their own sectional interest at the expense of the public investor. The result is that the Government may have to intervene."

Half of the problems stemmed from the past. For 140 years, a paternal colonial administration governed Singapore entirely on its own. The responsibility for the well-being of society was not that of the individual Singaporean. "We have had just over ten years of representative government. Unless we learn very quickly, as individuals and as functional and professional groups, to take the wider view and uphold first the public interest, and only next our own sectional interests, the democratic system cannot endure, let alone flourish."

561

Opening a branch library in a suburb on 30 April, the Prime Minister said that one sign of an educated society was the number of books read by the people. "We have had universal primary education for over a decade. Today we have a literate society. But a literate society is not necessarily an educated society. One test of an educated man is his ability to continue reading and learning throughout his life." In 1969 fifty-three point four per cent children passed the Primary Six examination to get to secondary school. This figure would improve with time with better trained teachers, improved teaching methods, and more facilities, like audio-visual aid. But parents were the most important of all the factors. If they did not have large families, and anything more than three is large, then they could spend more time and money in nurturing their children. "Education will begin even before the children go to school, as the children play in homes or kindergartens with educational toys and nursery books, and learn nursery rhymes."

Lee said that the branch library in Queenstown was a milestone in Singapore's rising standards of life. "We shall have similar branch libraries in every major area, like Toa Payoh, Katong, Jurong, Woodlands. First, they provide a convenient access to books which most people cannot afford to buy. Next, they are sanctuaries of peace and quiet where concentration and better work is possible, particularly when neighbours are inconsiderate. Unlike countries in the temperate climates, our homes have open windows. They let in noise. For some strange reason, most people insist that others in the neighbourhood should share their TV, radio, hi-fi, *mahjong*, or just loud conversation. Hence the need for a library. Slowly, but surely, we shall reduce the noise level of life in Singapore. High-density living in high-rise buildings requires considerate habits, low radio and television sounds, no honking of motor horns and no fixing of special gadgets to exhausts of cars and motor-cycles to amplify noise. In the next decade we should have an educated society, where the majority are considerate by habits nurtured in home and in the schools, ever conscious of the need not to invade their neighbours' privacy. This branch library marks one milestone along the road up the hill towards a more educated society."

"Our problems in the next three to five years will be more external than internal," declared the Prime Minister in a speech at the Hong Lim Community Centre on 29 May. He was announcing that Minister of State in the Prime Minister's Office, K.C. Lee, MP for Hong Lim, would go to Indonesia as ambassador. Lee said that through good organization and planning, high skills and hard work, "we have been able to resolve many internal difficulties. We were prepared to face the facts and we knew that there is no substitute for hard work. People get the government they deserve. If people are prepared to face their problems, and have a political leadership prepared to put before them realistically programmes and policies which, though involving work and sacrifice, can resolve the basic difficulties, you have the ingredients of progress and success. But if a people wish to escape from realities because the realities are unpleasant and painful to contemplate, and you have competing political party leaderships trying to outbid each other in offering sweet panaceas which cannot resolve the basic difficulties, then you have the ingredients of more trouble. People who believe that there is an easy way to prosperity and happiness, with little work and no effort, will find themselves in serious trouble."

This was true for an under-developed as for a fully developed country. "Our policies are based on simple and proven principles. A tightly-knit and organized society, hard-working, productive, striving for higher targets and higher goals, means ever-rising standards. Ten years from now, Hong Lim will be more beautiful than Outram Gardens, because our architects would have become more experienced, and will improve designs and styles, and the people can afford better homes and give their children a better life. We will have more industry, particularly those which will pay more wages because the value added is higher, through higher skills. Instead of simple things like textiles, we shall manufacture complicated products, repair aircraft and manufacture aircraft components, and so on. But as we progress, so the progress brings problems in its train unless we adopt policies which can help others to progress also. Today, we can give places in our schools for ASEAN students. We can give more scholarships for secondary schools, junior colleges, universities, the Polytechnic and Ngee Ann College. ASEAN students can go home after they have had their training, and be useful to their country. Some may stay. But what is important is this gesture of our friendship, of our goodwill and of our concern for them."

Referring to the new ambassador to Djakarta, the Prime Minister said the time had come when it might be valuable to Indonesians and to Singaporeans for them to see a Singaporean of Chinese descent who could speak, read and write Malay, Chinese and English. "We intend to be friendly to all. We have many friends. But, equally important, we intend to be ourselves, self-reliant, prosperous and, when we can afford it, generous."

The Prime Minister paid a tribute to mission schools when he spoke at the Christian Brothers' Old Boys Association dinner, celebrating the 118th anniversary of the founding of St Joseph's Institution on 6 June. He said: "I agree with the principal Brother Patrick, that a school is as good as the dedication of its teachers. All the best of buildings, classrooms and facilities: audio-visual aids, swimming pools, stadiums, race tracks—they may help impart knowledge and build a strong constitution, but they are not the most important of factors in making for a good school. The most crucial part of education is still the age-long teacher-pupil relationship. Several thousand years of human civilization and advances in the sciences and technology, and yet no substitute has been found for good tutor-pupil relationship in educating a pupil. We can have all the scientific aids, good books, educational television, but to nurture those qualities which will help a boy or a girl meet and overcome the problems of life, we need good teachers. The impersonality of the text-book or the moving image on the screen, accompanied by sound or pictographs, cannot provide the inspiration, the exhortation of a devoted tutor who cares for his pupils."

Lee Kuan Yew said that the mission schools and aided schools were going to meet a new challenge in the '70s. In the '50s and the '60s, the government schools dropped in standards as experienced teachers were spread out thin over the many new schools built to meet the growing school population. Promotions from senior masters to principals often meant a break-up of the hard core of senior masters around the principals. They set the standard and quality of a school. Now this proliferation of schools had stopped. Senior masters and principals of mission schools were men moved by deep religious convictions. They cared for the pupils under their care, as if they were their own children. "I am disappointed that the Catholic missions have been slow in raising funds for their junior college. If you do not press forward, you are going to be left behind. It is the government's intention that there should be fair competition between mission and aided schools and government schools. It helps to raise standards. For this reason, we have encouraged the missions and the Chinese clan associations to raise funds to help build their own junior colleges. Then we shall be able to have at least twelve of our best secondary schools become single-session schools as they used to be."

The quality of education would rise over the next decade. "We should be more generous now that we can afford it and open our schools, junior colleges, polytechnics and universities to students from ASEAN countries who seek a good education. In this the mission schools have a role to play. We have an exciting decade ahead. The mission schools will have to find the money to match the facilities of the government schools. The government schools must find more senior masters and principals dedicated to their profession and devoted to the physical, moral and intellectual advancement of their pupils."

V

When Mr Edward Heath was elected Prime Minister of Britain,

Lee Kuan Yew issued a statement on 22 June. He said that a Conservative Government in Britain, with Mr Heath as Prime Minister, would enhance security and stability in the area where British forces have been part of the landscape for over 150 years. This stability helped investment and development. "However, from my discussions with Mr Heath six months ago in January, and with Sir Alec Home three months ago in March, I learned that it was not their intention to keep any of the ordnance depots, or any of the paraphernalia in a base complex that adds so much to annual recurring costs. Local civilian employees of the British armed forces and their union leaders should be under no delusions that a Conservative victory means a reprieve. The British units that will be here after 1971 will be those operating sophisticated aircraft and naval vessels, and some ground forces. Unless the British Prime Minister and his colleagues change their minds, there will be some 'teeth' units without expensive 'tail' outfits to inflate costs. Moreover, it is in Singapore's interest to keep British military expenditure to an absolute minimum, and employment of local civilian personnel to almost nil. There is no better time than the present to reduce employment in British service establishments. The accelerating pace of economic expansion and industrialization can offer many local civilian employees in the British armed services a chance to retrain themselves for productive employment in the industrial and servicing sectors. Sooner or later employment in British military bases will not be a part of our economy. It is better that this be sooner."

Lee made another reference to the new British Government five days later. He said that Conservative policy was to continue to maintain a British presence in Singapore. "However small the forces may be, they give us added security for another three and a half to four and a half years before the next elections in Britain. Now we can readjust our plans and have thorough training for our air and naval forces, and go on to more sophisticated weapons. This means more sophisticated skill to maintain these weapons. And after their National Service, our National Servicemen can go on to more sophisticated industries which can pay higher wages because the value added in the manufacturing process is higher. But if we do not make the best use of the three and a half to four and a half years, then we may be sorry for ourselves. What I fear is complacency. When things always become better, people tend to want more for less work. Things will get better. There is a certain momentum about economic growth. You gather speed, just like a car, as you press the accelerator and get into higher gear. Our children today are getting better education than in the 1950s. But this creates new problems, unless we inculcate the right values and attitudes. We are short of skilled workers and semi-skilled workers. Worse, we are now short of workers for heavy manual work and certain jobs which are considered 'infra-dig'. Our primary-school leavers, especially those who do not get into secondary school, prefer to be idle, unemployed, than to work in the Public Health Department, or the cleansing services, or road building. So we have had to allow more liberal immigration. We allow people to come into Singapore for such jobs. As the years go by, this may create a situation which the British face today. The British brought in the West Indians, Africans and others to be dustmen and do other jobs their own nationals would not do. The net result now is over one million West Indians, Africans and others, and trouble in several cities in the Midlands. We can solve part of these problems by more mechanization. We can get machines to help lay the roads, tar them and even sweep them. But there are corners in the drains where no machine can get to. So we must get men to clean them with a stick and a broom. But our young, having had primary education, now look down on these jobs. This attitude, the soft life that our younger generation expects, is what I fear most."

Lee Kuan Yew continued: "That this community has the brains, the energy, the ingenuity, the stamina, to achieve ever-rising standards, nobody doubts. But we must also have that willingness to do the difficult and even unpleasant jobs. Without oil, minerals or other natural resources, other than a strategic position, we must have that ruggedness of mind and physique, the willingness and capacity to slog it out and create a better future for ourselves and our children."

The Prime Minister concluded with the statement that the People's Action Party intended, "and will probably" stay in office for a long time. He addressed those who sought to change society for the better to join the PAP and achieve this change from within the party, "and through the party being in office, re-shape policies for the '70s and '80s."

VI

At the sixteenth anniversary celebrations of the Tanjong Pagar branch of the People's Action Party, on 12 July, Lee Kuan Yew recalled the time when he first came to Tanjong Pagar to organize the party branch, and stood as a parliamentary candidate in the 1955 election. He said the past was important. "It enables us the better to understand the future. It reinforces our determination to overcome our problems, to build a more secure, a more rewarding future for our children. It is not only the changes in the physical landscape

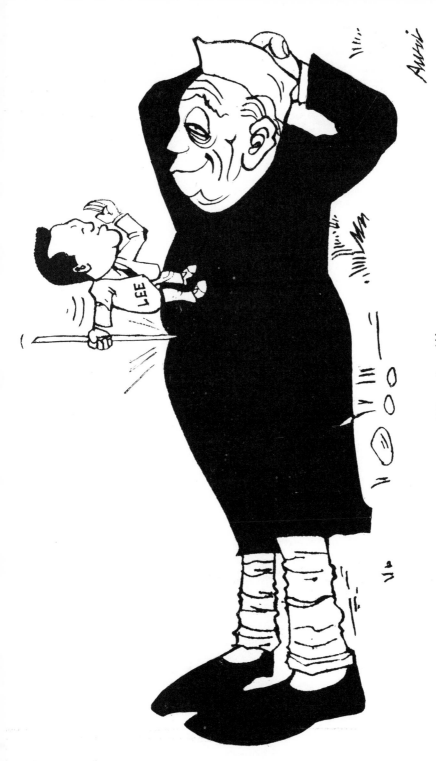

"Stand up!"

'National interest ? But that's us !'

—the new Tanjong Pagar which all of us can be proud of—the roads, the trees, the buildings, the schools. Behind all these changes, one quality is unchanged—the vitality of our people. Many in Tanjong Pagar live by the harbour, formerly called Singapore Harbour Board, now the Port of Singapore Authority. The natural harbour has remained the same. But the wharves have been improved and new wharves have been created by dredging and reclamation. Most important, the mechanization, the higher skills, the tighter organization, the introduction of the three-shift system: they have enabled an ever-faster turn-around of ships, and brought us from fifth to fourth busiest port in the world. Perhaps soon, the third busiest. This could not have been achieved without that verve of leadership in management, and that vitality of our workers, ever willing to acquire higher skills and higher work discipline."

Fifteen years ago, the children in Tanjong Pagar were not so well dressed, well shod or well fed. "We pay foreign exchange for every grain or rice we consume. Let us never forget that all this progress and prosperity is the result of a disciplined, organized and orderly way of life. The PAP has been the vehicle through which we have spread this spirit. PAP cadres have been the backbone of a not insignificant movement which has changed the history of Singapore and our lives. It is the future we must always probe and re-shape to our needs. No one can prophesy what is going to happen in this part of the world in the next few years. The bulk of American forces, probably even all, will withdraw from Vietnam before the end of 1972. The countries adjacent to Vietnam are likely to meet tremendous pressures. Whatever happens, we must be better equipped and trained by 1972. We must get stronger economically. We must have higher skills to be more productive. Moreover, modern military technology also requires higher skills in use and maintenance. Then we stand a good chance of overcoming many an awkward situation that may arise."

Lee said he hoped to join in celebrating the thirtieth anniversary of Tanjong Pagar PAP branch, fifteen years hence. Medical progress had enabled people to live longer and more effective lives. In many parts of South and Southeast Asia, actuarists put the life-span at between thirty-two and thirty-six years. In Singapore, actuarists for life insurance purposes estimated the life-span at sixty-six years. In other words, Singaporeans lived nearly more than twice as long as others who lived in the less healthy parts of the region. This was achieved by better public health, better medical facilities and better doctors. "Nobody in Singapore should find life uneventful. An exciting and challenging time in one of the most momentous periods of change in Southeast Asia is ahead of us. The past is being sloughed off quickly. The future is what we make of it."

567

VII

On behalf of Queen Elizabeth II, Sir Arthur de la Mare the British High Commissioner on 18 July presented the Prime Minister with the insignia of Companion of Honour. Referring to "the generous tribute" paid to him for the part he had played in making Singapore a better place to live in, Lee said that he and his colleagues had the advantage of building upon the firm foundations of sound and efficient administration bequeathed by the British. My generation grew up in the tranquillity of orderly and apparently unchanging colonial government in the years before the war. We took for granted that administrators were expected to be, and were, by and large, honest and efficient. Then came the shock of the war and horrors of Japanese occupation. Law and order were shattered as the Japanese shelled the city in February 1942. In several parts of Asia, law and order have never been restored. My generation was old enough to remember the nightmare of these three and a half years of Japanese military administration. Inflation, corruption, blackmarketing, the debasement of public and personal life—they were the order of things. But we were young, and proud enough, to believe that one day we could, and we would, govern Singapore better than either the Japanese or the British, if only because we cared and felt more passionately for our people. After the war, we got to know the British governors and their colonial administrators. Perhaps more important, we got to know their political masters in Whitehall. Several secretaries of state for the colonies left an abiding impression on us as men of great ability, enormous energy and penetrating vision. Members of parliament in Westminister, interested in colonial affairs, and moved by humanitarian and moral considerations, supported our struggle for freedom. They believed, in spite of the contrary interest of their officers in the colonial civil service, that power should be handed over. When the time came, the governor and his career officers, whose services were to be cut short by self-government, loyally carried out instructions from Whitehall. They arranged for the transfer of authority in an atmosphere of courtesy and goodwill, free from pettiness or rancour. So it was that we came to appreciate the strength and wisdom of our erstwhile adversaries. But it is the future to which we must cast our minds."

Lee said that the social and political milieu which produced his generation could not be repeated. Young men and women were growing up, who had no experience of the colonial past. More and more brighter and better students were going to universities in America, Canada, Australia and New Zealand. They would know little of Britain, of her great institutions, or the quality of her society. "The deepest compliment we can pay each other is to ensure that the esteem, in which we hold each other, is passed on to the next generation. British Colombo Plan experts in industry and technology, British Council visiting lecturers, Voluntary Service Overseas officers in our schools—they, and the managers who run British enterprises in Singapore, could help maintain British interest in Singapore." Singapore could ensure that a fair number of her more promising students, likely to play a not inconsiderable role in the leadership of Singapore, would study in Britain. There they could appreciate the texture of British society "which, despite some contemporary aberrations, is still one of the finest in the world".

If at the end of the century, the Prime Minister continued, "Her Britannic Majesty thinks well enough of the Prime Minister of Singapore to make him an honorary Companion of Honour, and he on his part finds that such an expression of British esteem does not subtract from his political credit with Singaporeans, then we would have done ourselves proud. For this can only happen if, despite increasingly changed conditions, we both make the effort to keep up our association, not only in trade and commerce, manufacturing and servicing, but also in culture and the arts, which our continuing use of the English language makes possible."

Lee said that Singapore valued its relationship with Britain. "We hope Britain may find it in her interests to preserve this association which dates back over more than 151 years. That we can be civil and courteous even when we have had disagreeable matters to dispose off, is a reflection of mutual regard and respect."

VIII

In recent years, Lee Kuan Yew reminded the Economic Society on 25 July, economists in Britain and America had watched with embarrassment as their predictions were proved wrong. It was not only with academics. Experts in government, in possession of all data, and formulating policies, had been making forecasts which had not come true. But, however unpredictable economic events might be, the business of present-day government required an understanding of the mechanics of economic forces and institutions, and of the methods and techniques to control and regulate these forces. If there was also an awareness that these forces operated differently in peoples of different culture, then economics need not be so frustrating an exercise of the art of interpreting cause and effect.

When the United Nations designated the 1960s as the "development decade", development economists believed that poor countries could be transformed into developed countries if the developed countries each gave one per cent of their GNP to supply capital and expertise to the undeveloped countries. They did not take into account the different cultural, social, and ethnic qualities. The results were frustrations which led to recriminations. Economics is concerned primarily with human beings working on the natural resources available. Many politicians overlooked the fact that economic and fiscal policies must take into consideration the cultural values and social habits of a people. Often under-developed countries uncritically followed the practices of highly developed Western countries in subsidizing food, providing free education, free health services and generous welfare and unemployment benefits. These Western countries had very small, if any, population growth. Some, like France, had their population static for several decades. Under these circumstances, generous tax concessions and even baby bonuses, free pre-natal, accouchement and health services, and free education, made sense. It was a policy designed, among other things, to encourage people to have larger families. But even in Britain, the Labour Party, which first introduced the National Health Scheme in the late 1940s, had to put up prescription charges in the late '60s in order to discourage indiscriminate over-use of the Health Service, and check rising costs. In developing countries, such subsidies could be ruinous. Most people had large families by force of habit, reinforced by religion and tradition. Such subsidies could only encourage social irresponsibility. There was nothing wrong about free health and education, if a society could afford it. But a developing country which wanted to develop could not afford a large increase in population.

Lee said: "We have to make a series of adjustments to make some people more aware of the real cost of large families. We must re-establish social responsibility. The ideal would be negative income tax (NIT), where the lowest-paid workers will have a sum of money paid to them by the government to bring their income up to a socially desirable minimum. Out of this, they will pay at least half the actual costs of the services each of their children uses. So they will have to make a choice between having another baby, or having the amenities of modern living: a flat with television, refrigerator, washing machine, scooter or mini-car. Fortunately, we never attempted to subsidize rice or other staple foodstuff. Those governments which have done so face grave problems, as more and more of their revenue goes into feeding more and more mouths at subsidized prices, generating over-population, under-education, low economic growth, massive unemployment and resulting social unrest. And this is what has happened because elected governments in several new countries have baulked at taking unpopular decisions."

He concluded his remarks with the observation that whilst economics would never become as exact as the physical sciences, analysis and anticipation could become more accurate, as the social sciences gave better insights into the group behaviour and responses of different peoples, and the character of their leaders.

IX

On 31 July, the Prime Minister made his first public response to the controversy over the sale of arms to the South Africans. He said: "A British presence East of Suez is to the advantage of Singapore. With the Suez Canal closed, the sea-route round the Cape is important. But we hope that neither France nor Britain, nor any other European arms manufacturer, will supply weapons to the South Africans with which South African whites can enforce apartheid. But, all said and done, in the last analysis, no weapons, however terrifying, can keep down a people determined to be free. Six hundred thousand American troops, at the height of their commitment in South Vietnam in 1968, equipped with all the latest in weapons technology and gadgetry, were still not able to crush the Vietcong. Only the South Vietnamese people themselves can do that. The day black Africans in Southern Africa are disciplined and determined enough to create their 'Black-cong', then all the automatic firearms, armoured personnel carriers, tanks and strike aircraft, equipped with rockets, anti-personnel bombs, and de-foliating agents—all these, and more, will not be able to prevent the black Africans from regaining their human dignity which apartheid has deprived them of."

At the beginning of his speech, made in Jurong, Lee Kuan Yew spoke of the development of the satellite town. He said there had been a transformation in Jurong since 1965. Then there were more houses than workers to move into them. Factory owners were not sure how and where their products were to be sold. The situation had now completely changed. Two factors brought about this trans-formation. First, an awareness in 1965 and the years that followed; Singaporeans faced a problem of life and death. "It was a change in our way of life. We knew that unless we developed into a tightly knit, cohesive and disciplined community, hard-working, willing to learn and acquire new skills and cut off the liberties we were taking with ourselves, we would go down the drain. The other factor was a climate of quiet determination which the government, management and unions exuded in a common search for lower costs, higher productivity, and wider markets. Today, the complaint is too much smoke,

571

soot, bad odours, from too many factories. Progress has brought in new problems. Jurong Town has 21,000 in population. Unfortunately, it represents only 8,200 of the workers and their families. Three-quarters of the 30,000 workers are still commuting. They are waiting for new housing blocks to go up."

Lee said that as industrial activities expanded, and a population of about 250,000 settled in Jurong, provisions would have to be made for the amenities for modern living. It was intended that Jurong would be a self-contained satellite town—better housing, better schools, shopping centres, recreational facilities, sports complexes, swimming pools and cinemas. "We are determined that Jurong shall be clean and green, a town that those who live and work in can be proud of. Anti-pollution measures will be relentlessly carried out. The plywood factories are burning their left-overs in the open. This should not be done. A month ago, I saw the ceramic factory belching black smoke from its chimney. The biggest offender is undoubtedly National Iron and Steel Mills, in which the Government owns a substantial share. National Iron and Steel is now preparing to set a good example by installing extractors to suck out the soot and dirt. All this and more must be done."

The Prime Minister added that what was important was good management-labour relations. He said he had been following a strike in Jurong with more than casual interest. The NTUC had given its support. "Where the unions are in the right, management will have to make changes. Employers must understand that good personnel relations are an asset. If you have supervisors who are rude and crude to Singaporeans, our self-respect demands that we put a stop to this. We can make our workers strive harder. But we will not allow them to be humiliated or brow-beaten. That said, let me tell the workers: don't make the strike a habit, like it was in the 1950s. If you recreate a reputation for being a strike-happy community, then the consequences are grievous. You can bargain for better wages, you can bargain for higher productivity bonuses. But once the bargain has been struck, then you must enter into the spirit of the agreement, and put in an honest day's work for an honest day's wages. There must be no looking around; work means discipline. Singapore's access depends on the spirit in which workers, management and government, all three, enter into the spirit of co-operation, necessary for prosperity.

In a National Day broadcast on 15 August the Prime Minister claimed that Singapore had made a promising start for the '70s. "Our economic growth for 1970 will probably be well over nine per cent. Unemployment is at an all-time low. We have been able to give work permits freely to workers from outside Singapore." This dramatic drop in unemployment was the result of two factors. First, rapid expansion in the industrial and servicing sectors. Second, National

Service. But after two to three years, National Servicemen would be re-cycled back into employment. Moreover, the rundown of British military bases would continue. Redundancies would be heaviest next year. "Therefore, we must continue to step on the economic accelerator. Wages must remain at sensible levels. Work discipline must be good. Productivity must be high. Otherwise unemployment problems will be back with us again in '72–'73." Over the next few years, expensive defence equipment would be delivered. Aircraft, fast patrol boats, and other sophisticated weapons were ordered some time ago. They had been paid for and the costs of manning and of maintaining them met without much increase in taxation. To continue to do this, growth rates would have to be maintained at over nine per cent.

Now the time had come to raise sights, to aim at a higher quality of life for all. In most towns in Southeast Asia, cleanliness and beauty began and ended in the homes of the wealthy. Outside the walls of these wealthy homes, the world was invariably ugly and filthy. "But we are succeeding in making all of Singapore our garden and our home: clean, green and gracious. Roads are being lined with trees. Road dividers will have palms, plants and flowering shrubs. Open spaces will be gardens or parks. Whether it is Bukit Ho Swee, or Geylang Serai, we shall improve our surroundings. Minimum standards of decent living will be achieved."

The Housing Board was building better flats, improving designs. They cost more, but they gave more privacy and more amenities. In this next five-year plan, the combined income limits would be raised to $1,500 a month, to let the middle-income groups buy larger and better-designed flats. Schools would have fewer students per class. Some secondary schools would revert to single-session schools, as more junior colleges were built. The University of Singapore would move to a beautiful new campus at Kent Ridge. Nanyang University would also be developed, particularly in engineering and the applied sciences. A new polytechnic for 10,000 students would be built off Dover Road. Beaches will be cleaned up. Open drains now running into the sea would go into underground sewers, and end up in treatment plants. A clean seaside was a recreational asset. Oil pollution by ship repairers or ships passing through, would be countered by heavy fines. The air would be kept clean. New legislation would require all vehicles and industries to reduce pollution. "We shall improve public transport. Then there will be fewer vehicles whizzing around endlessly, looking for passengers. And the roads will be safer for everyone. Our social standards will go up. Most parents now plan their families. But some do not. They have to, if their children are to make the grade. Social progress must be accompanied by social responsibility. The cost of maternity and general hospitals is rising. So is the cost of more facilities for extra-curricular activities in our schools. There will be gradual increases in the token payments now being charged. We owe each other the duty not to pull standards down."

Lee claimed that society was being made more just. Nobody was privileged because of his parents' status or wealth. Children all went to the same schools. All did National Service. They got into the universities on merit. They got jobs and promotions on merit. "And we shall give everyone a stake in our growing economy." However, there were some ominous clouds on the horizon. The communists were out to exploit racial and other conflicts. They were out for violence and terror. Their booby-trap bombs had killed an innocent child in Changi. They burnt community centres and buses. "We shall deal with them. In a turbulent corner of Asia, constant vigilance has become part of our way of life." But all said and done, the zest and zeal with which the twin objectives, security and prosperity, had been pursued had already given Singapore "that glow of success". If in the next five years Singapore worked as hard as. it had in the past five, and to as much purpose, Singaporeans would have that poise which came when endeavour and enterprise were justly rewarded.

X

At a ceremony concerned with the commissioning of officers for the armed forces, the Prime Minister on 18 August said that in the five years, the emphasis had been on speed in the build-up of the army. In the next five years, the emphasis would be on quality and maturity of officers, particularly for staff and command. Planning and strategy required more than just military knowledge. They required subtle, imaginative and creative minds. However tough and doughty soldiers were, poor leadership by officers in the field would lower morals and performance. But however good the field officers, keeping their men in high morale and discipline, poor staff work could lead to disaster.

Lee promised that schemes of service would be worked out in order to make a career in staff and command equivalent to what a very good graduate could get in the Civil Service, or in commerce and industry. Career opportunities would be worked out, so that a first-class officer would find it worth his while to take up a regular commission. And, when he left on retirement either at forty-five, fifty, or fifty-five, he would have enough managerial training and leadership experience to enable him to go straight into top management in the private sector, or into any of the growing number of enterprises the Government had a share in. Further, because Singapore's armed

574

forces were young, and expanding rapidly, promotion prospects were better in the services than in the Civil Service, or in commerce and industry. "Those of you who have confidence that you have got what it takes to make the grade, will not regret serving on as a regular service officer. We have no tradition to ensure a continuous supply of officers. Making a career in the armed forces is something new. But we can put together that mix of challenge, incentives, and status, to ensure that we recruit an officer cadre as good as that we have produced in the Civil Service, or in the professions. There are several charateristics common in men in top positions: strength of character and a mind able to take in the details and complexities of a problem quickly, seize hold of the essential elements, and act decisively to tackle the problem. I am sure there are a number amongst you with these qualities. With the induction of all HSC and university graduates, there will be more officers with the potential for staff and command responsibilities."

"Progress depends upon two factors: first, the pace at which a whole people decide to move forward, and the momentum they can maintain," the Prime Minister told residents of Kampong Kembangan at a dinner celebrating National Day on 22 August. "In a number of countries, millions of dollars of American aid, or millions of roubles of Russian aid, have been poured in. But little progress has been made. This is because the people, hide-bound by tradition, prefer to continue the way of life of their forefathers. They are not willing to change their pace of work to fit the needs of modern industry, but unfortunately they want to enjoy the fruits of industry. In such societies, foreigners can build the dams and hydro-electric power stations, the roads, the railways, but these investments would not be fully utilized."

The second factor, Lee said, was the leadership which propelled a people forward. It was not just the government. The government could plan and decide on the programmes. The leadership down the line at various levels was the crucial factor. "In any army, so also in a civilian population, you need leaders in each level to give the lead to take the group forward. Only then can a whole society move forward, and plans and programmes implemented effectively. Otherwise, there will be confusion and indiscipline, and the people cannot make the difficult climb up the industrial and technological ladder. In a democracy, people can argue over policies different political leaderships expound. But once the majority of the people has decided, everyone must go along with its implementation. The alternative is a free-for-all endless discussion, which leads to confusion and inaction. When economic and social plans have failed, a military dictatorship takes over. This is what had happened in many countries in Asia, Africa and Latin America."

At the end of August, the Prime Minister left Singapore to attend the non-aligned nations conference in Lusaka. On his way he paid an official visit to India and in New Delhi was the guest of honour at a dinner given by Mrs Indira Gandhi, the Prime Minister of India. In a speech Lee said that he was not a stranger to Delhi, and he was happy to say that each time he visited Delhi, he felt very much amongst friends and felt able to speak freely and frankly as one did amongst friends. "Not only because we share many ideals in common, but because we feel very much together in so many of the major issues in this world. Since my last visit in 1966, as the Americans would put it, the 'scenario' has vastly changed and we must find in this completely altered situation new relevance to policies which are designed to prevent us from becoming mere auxiliaries of either of the superpowers. Non-alignment must find new relevance in the vastly changed world and I look forward to sharing your thinking on these matters with both you and your colleagues in charge of foreign affairs.

Lee Kuan Yew said that as he flew in across the Deccan Plateau, he was struck by the greenness and the lusciousness of the crops below and he thought to himself how few could have predicted four years earlier that the green revolution would become a reality and open up new avenues for progress and growth in India.

"But," he added, addressing Mrs Gandhi, "as you have pointed out so vividly, material progress alone does not bring the fulfilment which human endeavour strives to give to its peoples. I would wish to believe that the ancient cultures can survive technological changes which bring about changes in ways of life and give fulfilment to our peoples, despite the materialistic, affluent, rather harsh, cold, hard-headed types of societies which today have emerged as the successful models for the developing countries. As one thing common about all those that have developed, they keep their profit and loss accounts very carefully and make sure that they are in the blank. I would wish that because our people in Singapore have descended from cultures which go back to the days before affluence is an end in itself, although we try and keep our books in the blank, we keep our souls very much warm and we keep our friendships more important than just our own self-interests. And in this regard, may I say how much I owe to you and before you, to your father, for the many valuable stays I had in Delhi and from which I have received so much friendliness and help."

XI

In Dar-es-Salaam, on his way to Lusaka, Lee Kuan Yew, on 5 September was entertained to dinner by President Julius Nyerere. He said that his friendship with President Nyerere was one he was privileged to have gained. President Nyerere in his speech referred to the 1969 Commonwealth Conference where, said the President, Lee Kuan Yew's "outstanding ability and devastating frankness made him a valuable ally and friend but a very dangerous opponent".

On the problem of South Africa, Lee Kuan Yew said this was a very difficult problem not only for Africans but for all those with any conscience at all. "But Mr President, I do not believe that these discussions we can have in Lusaka and all the resolutions we shall pass at Lusaka or at the United Nations can make up for that sustained build-up of a disciplined, dedicated, thrusting, organized fight for freedom by the peoples within these territories. Perhaps we are coloured by what happens in our own part of the world. I have had examples in Southeast Asia where all the latest of weaponry, gadgetry, military technology have been brought to naught by the ingenuity of man and his determination that he shall be free. The only successful counter to guerilla insurrections was accomplished by the British (Lee was referring to the communist revolt in Malaya and Singapore) but they had one great advantage. It was not just efficient communications and military competence: they had a political card to play. They gave independence and so it became unnecessary. If you can win by the ballot, why the bullet? And that's why I am alive and enjoying your hospitality and having the pleasure of meeting so many of my British friends, including the High Commissioner from Britain."

The next day, Lee Kuan Yew spoke at the University of Dar-es-Salaam about some dilemmas socialists face in slowly developing countries. He said the aphorism, "from each his best, to each his needs", was a slogan which enabled anti-colonial freedom movements to gather momentun—the sense of injustice, of inequality. Having achieved freedom and authority, they then faced the problem of "to each his needs" because these could not be met immediately. No country had developed and industrialized itself on the basis of universal franchise—not even Britain, the pioneer of industrial societies. They had to exploit their own labour and their colonies in order that they could become an industrialized society. Similarly, the Americans had a continuing flow of migrant expertise from Europe; and the vast open spaces—the new frontiers of the Wild West—enabled them to reach the degree of technology and competence which put them with the highest GNP in the world. And yet, newly independent countries were expected to run representative forms of government—one man one vote, not make their people give of their best, have minimum number of working hours per week, maximum paid holidays, maximun maternity, medical and other benefits, ending up with minimum productivity and no growth rate worth talking about.

The first dilemma to be faced was the thesis upon which freedom was achieved—that freedom must bring about a more equal, a more just society. And this could not be brought about immediately. For any development to take place, there must be capital accumulation; in other words, preferably consumption must be less than income, so that more could be ploughed back as capital and, in some cases, supplemented by soft loans at low rates of interest and, in very special instances, free grants for either ideological, political, strategic or other considerations from the more developed countries. The English-speaking part of the under-developed world faced a second dilemma: that as high-level manpower was trained the need arose to explain to the electorate that, in spite of belief in an egalitarian society, which was what had been preached pre-independence and post-independence, nevetherless a high-level technocrat commanded a world price. He could move across national frontiers, which an unskilled or semi-skilled or even a skilled labourer could not do. Trained, he had to be paid according to what he deserved in the context of an under-developed society. Unless he had a deep sense of dedication, which did not necessarily go with the investment the community made in him, he would leave. "And so the British are being creamed off by the Americans, and the British are creaming off the Indians and so on. What is the way out of this dilemma? Industrial and technological transformation requires two important factors amongst others. First, a highly disciplined work force, highly skilled, capable of intense effort over sustained periods. Second good managerial, engineering and administrative digits. The inequality, the wage differential, between an engineer and a factory foreman is less in a highly developed country than in an under-developed country—if that under-developed country is developing. Otherwise, it will lose the engineer and the whole factory will close down. This is one of the curious contradictions which we face in the contemporary world. A British engineer finds himself heavily taxed, subsidizing free education, extensive medical and social services, public housing, and his wage is not all that of a multiple over the foreman's. The under-developed country, on the other hand, in order to keep the engineer—in whom the state has invested considerable sums of money—has got to pay him not in money terms but in real terms, something comparable to what he can command in the world outside, in the English-speaking world."

The only countries that had avoided doing this, were those societies that were either closed, and therefore emigration was difficult, as the Russians and the Chinese, or where the cultural network was such that language and culture made emigration and a brain-drain very uncomfortable business. So with the Germans and the Japanese —both of them imbued with a deep sense of patriotism and a desire to rebuild their war-damaged, war-ravaged countries and to demostrate to the world that, despite the fact that they lost the war, they deserved to win the peace.

Lee said he did not believe that these problems were unsolvable. New patterns of trade, new methods of transferring technology enabled developing countries to seize hold of these opportunities and pull themselves up by their own boot-straps—preferably if there was a helping hand. If there was not, it just meant more effort. The old idea of import substitution, of a national frontier behind which the flow of manufactured goods from outside was cut off and these goods manufactured domestically, had been found to be of little help. The Americans, and now the Japanese, and even the West Europeans, and the Germans in particular, those whose labour costs are high, had now moved into a new type of export. They no longer exported just the finished commodity; they exported *whole* industries. All this meant that socialism in slowly developing countries was faced with several agonizing contradictions. The pledge was to create a more just, a more equal society. In order to develop the technology and the skills, the wage differentials had to be widened between the person who could emigrate—because he had professional skills—as against the unskilled, semi-skilled and skilled worker who could not emigrate. This unjust system had to be sustained for a considerable length of time before moving into a more developed situation which enabled a levelling out.

"And so, when we read of the problems of the under-developed world and the over-developed world, let us never forget that the development takes place under vastly changed conditions. The Russians and the Chinese close their societies. They pay an engineer what they think the engineer is worth, and the engineer cannot emigrate. He is sent to where his services are needed most. They pay their workers, their foremen in accordance not with their needs—which is the socialist ideal—but with their worth, and that worth is gauged by what they think is right. So, when we seek development in under-developed situations with very little or no education prior to independence, running a system of one man one vote in which popular appeals during election time must mean more to the mass of the unskilled and semi-skilled, and soaking the rich means really chasing out the few digits that you have, the system comes to a grinding halt, unless you are able to re-educate rapidly the whole population. I have seen it happen in several countries. I have seen adaptations, modifications attempted... And so, whilst we all seek our own separate roads to our socialist goal or Utopia—which is a very necessary ingredient of development, that enthusiasm and idealism that fires a people and makes them strive—let us never forget that these are the realities of the situation: that nobody gives you anything for free, that every arrangement an under-developed country comes into with a developed country is often an unequal arrangement."

Lee told the students he left them with some of these thoughts in order that they would the better understand what was happening in Singapore, and why it was that Singapore was developing painfully, unequally, often unjustly. "But the important fact is we *are* developing. It is a more equal and a more just society than the one we inherited from the British... perhaps, in the course of time, the wage differentials between the wealthy, the well-qualified and the not-so-wealthy and not-so-well-qualified may be narrowed. And it will be a very long time before we reach a situation where we say, 'From each his best, to each his needs'. "

At the third summit conference of non-aligned countries in Lusaka, Zambia, on 9 September, Lee Kuan Yew recalled that non-alignment was formulated in the late 1950s. It obtained growing support in the early 1960s. It was a method by which the new countries could ensure their security and make economic progress without military commitment or involvement with one of the two contending cold war blocs. At that time, the two super-powers and their principal allies were in a period of ideological evangelism. They considered it in their respective interests to increase and expand their political support amongst the new countries. So they were prepared to accord economic aid, technological assistance, and arms in this competition for support. Thus it was possible for some under-developed countries to play one super-power against another, getting aid from both blocs, sometimes more from one than the other, and with the minimum of constraints.

Before the end of the 1960s, the situation had altered. The monolithic communist world movement was showing signs of splintering. The anti-communist crusade of Foster Dulles, the US Secretary of State in the 1950s, was losing its relevance. The two super-powers had started a direct dialogue to resolve or lessen unnecessary tension or conflict between them. This led to the nuclear non-proliferation treaty and the SALT talks on limitation of nuclear missiles. How much the emergence of China as a growing power, soon with a credible nuclear capability, helped to bring this about, might never be known. But the American-Russian dialogue, and their loss of interest in winning converts to their different systems, had changed the context against which non-alignment must work. Neither super-power actively sought more political or military allegiance, except where they considered crucial strategic interests to be at stake. On the contrary, the American Congress was reported as wanting to cut down and even write off their military commitments in Southeast Asia. They were also reported as wanting to reduce their troops in Western Europe committed to NATO. They appeared preoccupied with America's own economic and social ills, and not with a US global role.

Polycentralism in the communist world, the independent policies of General de Gaulle, the re-emergence of an industrially strong Germany and Japan, each pursuing its own economic and political goals—all these had changed prevailing moods and attitudes. Russian enthusiasm for investments in high dams, engineering projects, and the arming of new countries, had shown a similar decline. They were interested only in areas which fitted into their global strategy. An application for association with the Warsaw Pact from a revolutionary government in the American hemisphere was viewed with a jaundiced eye.

Neither the Americans, nor the Russians, nor Japanese or West Europeans, had yet found it necessary to actively compete in winning the support of black African countries, and helping the African liberation movements to overthrow the white minority regimes in Southern Africa. Only China, still in the evangelistic phase, was interested in African liberation movements in Southern Africa. When China appeared likely to develop political and economic influence as a result of her active role in urging and helping insurgency, then competition would start. Then pressure would be exerted in earnest on the white regimes in Southern Africa. "We can feel the anguish and anger of the African peoples at this cynical approach to their problems. In a strange way, this is not without its benefits for Africa. The animosities and hatreds against the evil apartheid policies of the white government of South Africa have, but for some odd exceptions, united all African states."

The problems which bedevilled Southeast Asia were not quite the same. There had not been the same unity amongst Southeast Asian and South Asian countries in their reactions to the horrors of the war in Indo-China. Perhaps it was because neighbouring countries did not see this as a straightforward fight against colonialism, either British, French or Dutch. Nor did they see it as simple American neo-colonialism. The issues were clouded by competing ideologies within the countries. And more to the point, victory for one side might pose dangers of contagion and the spread of revolutionary guerilla insurgencies in adjacent countries. "If the Indo-Chinese peoples are to exercise their right to self-determination, then all interventionist forces must withdraw from South Vietnam, Cambodia and Laos."

Lee Kuan Yew said there was need to redefine the needs and problems of new countries in search of security and development. "We must find a new relevance for non-alignment, a new validity in altered circumstances." In several ways, this conference underlined the dilemma. "We were able to get to Lusaka to attend this conference because of the transportation technology of the developed states, either America, Western Europe or Russia. Nobody else builds commercial jet aircraft that could have taken us from our far-flung countries to Lusaka. We are able for a few days to re-awaken the conscience of mankind to the iniquities taking place in Southern Africa, the sufferings of the peoples in the Middle East, and of Southeast Asia, because of the communications technology of the developed countries. At the opening session, I was reminded vividly of our dependence on this communications technology, as I watched not only cameras and cinecameras made by the developed countries, the personnel who manned them. More important, I remembered the communications satellites which were to enable the speeches made, and the pictures taken here, to be transmitted swiftly to all the main centres of population in the world."

It was fortunate that there were a few amongst them in the conference who had reached the middle levels of technology. Their expertise had helped to make possible the conference at such short notice. And the Zambian Minister in charge had generously acknowledged this on page 3 of the beautiful booklet entitled, *The Building of a Conference*. This was an illustration of one way in which one nation could help another. Those with relatively higher technology could pass on their know-how and capital equipment in return for something they required from those who had developed the capacity to use the technology, and could give something in return. But by itself this would not be adequate. The high levels of technological competence which the Americans, Russians, West Europeans, several East Europeans and the Japanese had already reached, made co-operation amongst the developing nations a pitifully slow way of catching up with them. "Co-operation between developing nations which, with a few exceptions, have low or no technology is unlikely to bring about a rapid transformation of our backward role as producers of raw materials, oil, minerals, timber or agricultural commodities."

Another illustration of the way forward was the East African Community. Such combinations could broaden the avenues of economic co-operation. They might be able collectively to offer one of the competing developed countries sufficient of an attraction for the transfer of heavier industries requiring a broader base to support them, like iron and steel mills, shipbuilding, motor vehicles, tractors and engineering products. "The galloping pace of technological change confronts us with an acute challenge. Twenty-five years ago, the Germans and the Japanese were prostrate, their industries in ruins after the Second World War. Today, their GNPs are third and fourth in the world. It is a spectacular recovery, made possible first by their infrastructure of knowledge and skills, and second by the rapid transfer, by way of American loans and investments, of capital equipment and new expertise under patent and licensing. It had little to do with ideology. And in the case of Japan, it was a miracle accomplished with no basic material resources like iron or oil. It had a great deal to do with human resources, a hard-working and disciplined people with high skills, technological competence, managerial

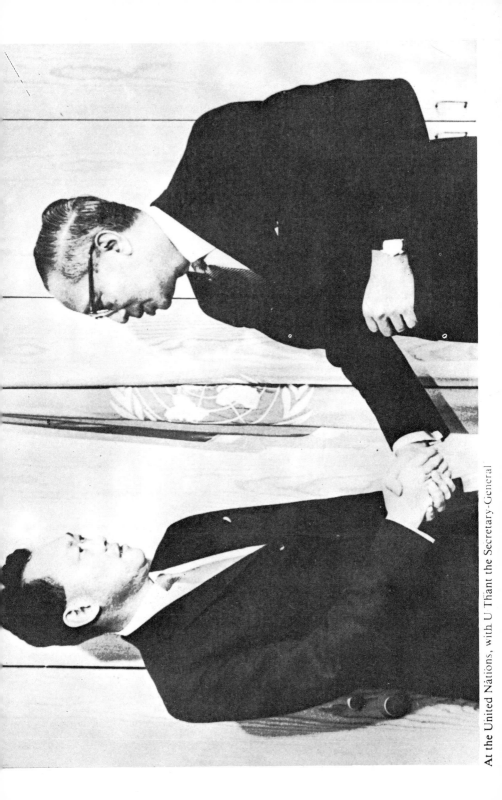

At the United Nations, with U Thant the Secretary-General

The Foreign Minister of Japan, Mr Miki, calls upon Lee

Outside No. 10 Downing Street. The Singapore High Commissioner Mr A. P. Rajah is between Lee and Harold Wilson, then British Prime Minister.

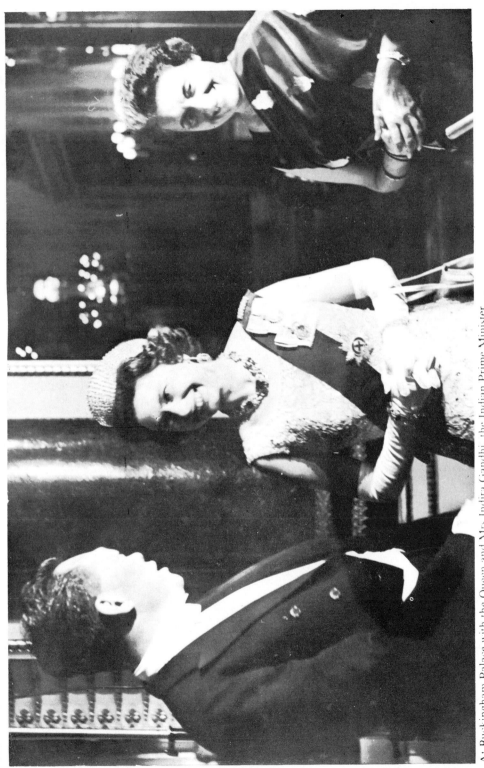

At Buckingham Palace with the Queen and Mrs Indira Gandhi, the Indian Prime Minister

In Malta, greeted by Dr Borg Olivier, the **Prime Minister**

Edward Heath in Singapore in 1969 discussing Singapore's defences

In Ethiopia with King Haile Selassie

Willy Brandt, Chancellor of West Germany

With Ben Bella of Algiers in 1964

Two Socialists. The late Sir Walter Nash, former Prime Minister of New Zealand, with Lee, outside Sir Walter's house

With Dr Subandrio, former Foreign Minister of Indonesia

Joking with Dr Luns, the Dutch Foreign Minister.

With Ambassador Averill Harriman, the famous American diplomat

At the White House. President Nixon, Lee Kuan Yew and Singapore Ambassador, Professor Monteiro

The late Harold Holt, then Prime Minister of Australia, Lee and John Gorton, until recently the Prime Minister of Australia

In Lagos, in 1964, with Sir Abubakar Tafewa Balewa, Prime Minister of Nigeria from 1957 until his death by assassination in 1966

Golf with Dr Thanat Khoman, Foreign Minister of Thailand

In Hawaii; golf with Governor Burns (centre)

With President Nyerere of Tanzania

With Mrs Golda Meir, Prime Minister of Israel at the Geneva Socialist Conference in 1968

With President Jomo Kenyatta

With the Tunku in 1963 when Singapore was part of Malaysia

With the late President

Nehru was a good friend of Lee

Lee met Marshall Tito in Belgrade

The thirty-two presidents, prime ministers and representatives of heads of government at the Singapore Commonwealth Heads of Government Conference, January 1971. Lee, the chairman, is ninth from left. On his left is Arnold Smith, secretary-general of the secretariat. On Lee's right is John Gorton, then Prime Minister of Australia ability, and marketing know-how. In Lusaka, just as in Singapore, Japanese motor-cycles and West German cars have made themselves inescapably seen and heard. We too have it in ourselves to make the grade. Economic progress amongst the less developed countries may be uneven. It will vary with the level of education and skills which our peoples have reached or can acquire. But given vigorous leadership, our peoples can be stirred to action and their enthusiasm and energies mobilized for economic and social advance."

Lee reminded the conference that over 1,000 years ago, one of the highest technology was the Arab sailing ship. And one of the highest of sciences was Arab algebra and astronomy. The Arabs sailed the Arabian Sea and the Indian Ocean and reached places as far away as the Celebes in the South Pacific. They spread their culture, their religion, their language, and their goods. Today, the most sophisticated manufacture was not the subsonic jet that carried delegates to Lusaka. It was not even the supersonic transport aircraft in which the Russians, the British and the French in collaboration, and the Americans, were competing. It was the rocket that sent space vehicles off into space, to get round the moon and come back to earth. "We have to make our own decisions on how we can keep up with these technological and scientific breakthroughs resulting from the inventiveness and creativity of men in the advanced countries. These researches were often aided by exceptional brains drained from the less developed. If we can get effectively together, in constant consultation and co-operation, we can work out a strategy to make less onerous the terms on which we can get from the developed countries high-technology equipment, expertise and skills."

For the time being, the major powers saw no urgency in seeking the support of the new and under-developed countries, except in certain strategic areas. In fact, they were learning to do away with the commodities that plantation economies produce, by synthetic substitutes, creating problems for the commodity producers. It might be, as one distinguished delegate had pointed out, that the countries represented at Lusaka owned more than half the world's natural resources. But natural resources often required capital equipment of high technology and considerable expertise before they were extracted from the bowels of the earth. Next, having extracted and refined them, the commodity was used mainly by the developed countries. Super-powers and major powers made hard-headed assessments of a less developed country's position today, and compared it against what it was yesterday. They then made tough-minded projections of what it would be in the next ten, twenty, thirty years. "If we can leave them with a clear impression that we shall develop, and rapidly, that we have the determination, the stamina and the organizational ability to make the most of our own natural and human resources, then they will take us seriously. In fact, they will immediately react on the assumption that sooner rather than later we shall be developed. Then, even before we are fully developed, they will cease to deal with us as if we shall never develop."

Lee thought that the conference might temporarily re-awaken the conscience of the people in the developed countries. Their advanced development had been achieved, in part, at the expense of the peoples in the colonies they exploited. But moral obligations and humane considerations were not compulsions to positive action. "We must create the organizations and institutions to enable more effective, realistic and practical co-ordination amongst us, the less developed. More and more, the advanced countries will compete against each other in exporting their older technology and skills. Our co-ordination can turn this natural rivalry to better advantage. The ending of colonialism does not in itself result in social and economic progress. It provides the opportunities for it. We must learn to make better use of them."

XII

From Lusaka the Prime Minister went to Cairo, to see President Nasser (he was greeted at the airport by Vice-President Sadat, later to become President upon the death of President Nasser), and then to the Soviet Union, France, West Germany, Britain, the United States, Japan and Hong Kong. In Cairo on 15 September Lee was asked by Reuters whether he saw any contradiction between the British military presence in Singapore and the stand of Singapore as a "so-called non-aligned country". Lee replied: "None whatsoever. I am less dependent on British arms and armaments, less in tow, than quite a number of the others present. I think 'non-alignment' has acquired a new definition. It means the desire not to be automatically aligned or committed to fight on one side regardless of its rights and wrongs, of being on one side."

The Prime Minister, when questioned the same day by Miss Safaa Sadik of Cairo Radio, said that Singapore had always taken the view that enduring peace in the Middle East might be achieved if the November 1967 resolution of the Security Council was implemented.

In the Soviet Union, the Prime Minister was asked by reporters on 18 September whether he thought that a long distance was an impediment to friendship. Lee Kuan Yew replied that he had been told that it was always easier to be friends if nations were not immediate neighbours. Therefore Singapore and the Soviet Union ought to be very good friends indeed because there were many intervening countries. In reply to another question the Prime Minister said that many countries in the world believed that just by calling themselves socialist or communist meant progress. "But that is not so. One has to work: that is the beginning of progress."

Lee was asked about his talk with Soviet leaders. He said the face-to-face discussions had given him an opportunity to get the feel of thinking. "I found", Lee Kuan Yew said, "in your Prime Minister, Mr Kosygin, a very quiet-spoken, but a very determined, mind of great ability and application. In spite of his many other duties and interests, I was agreeably surprised to find that he knew a lot about Southeast Asia and was keen to know more about it. I hope, in elucidating the subject, he also gets to understand what kind of people we are."

In Leningrad, on the eve of his departure to Paris, on 22 September, Lee Kuan Yew, replying to a question, said that his brief impression of the Soviet Union is "one of construction and progress in which a considerable amount of sacrifice has been made in order that the present standard of accomplishment has been achieved, and in order that the future will achieve even higher goals".

Asked about the developments of relations between the Soviet Union and Singapore, the Prime Minister said he thought there would be growing economic ties for mutual benefit. "As the world gets smaller, both by the frequency of air travel and passenger and cargo sea travel, we are bound to develop not only closer trade links but also better appreciation of each other's points of view and culture and ways of life. This is going to be, in spite of the fact that there is a huge land mass between the frontiers of the Soviet Union and Singapore, and there is a very long sea route before one can get either from the Black Sea or from the Baltic Sea to Singapore, with the Suez Canal closed. And that only reflects the growing air and sea transportation capabilities of the Soviet Union and the number of things that you have to export and the number of things you are prepared to import. Let me explain this. For instance, East Africa is much closer to us than Moscow or Leningrad, where we are speaking today. But because they have not got the technological capacity for communications and transportation and the ability to absorb our exports, to give us in their exports what we may find useful, so the links are much farther apart. So it is an indicator of your industrial and technological progress that despite these vast distances, you have got the ability to maintain the contact and you have the capability to make the contacts worth maintaining."

Finally, Lee was asked what he thought about the idea of the establishment of a collective security system in Asia, "as expressed by Soviet leadership". Lee replied, "We have always expressed a positive interest in this proposal, and would welcome further elaboration of the way in which peace and security can be consolidated for the countries of Southeast Asia."

In Germany, at a Press conference in Bonn, on 29 September, Lee Kuan Yew was asked about a report that in the Soviet Union he had said Singapore would be prepared to service Russian warships. The Prime Minister replied that he had stated publicly before that "we will repair any vessel from any country because we provide a service to the ships of all the world. We happen to be situated at a convenient sea junction and, whether it is a Russian trawler fishing in the South Pacific or whether it is a Russian scientific boat studying the marine biology, or sea life, we are quite happy to repair, just as we repair German ships and Japanese ships and even Indonesian naval vessels which come to Singapore for repairs. Mind you, I may just as well add that this, of course, obtains during peaceful conditions."

In London, on 2 October, the Prime Minister was interviewed by Peter Snow of ITN. Lee was asked if he thought the Russians were moving in, in a big way, in Southeast Asia? He said he thought they were going to move in a big way in shipping. "They are great chess players. If you think they just move from square one to two or three and it means nothing, then you are making a very great mistake. The Minister who accompanied me around the Soviet Union was in charge of sea transportation. And I welcome that because it is a peaceful economic approach to a greater co-operation. We already have a joint shipping line... Now they want to complete the circle, from the Baltic Sea round the Cape to Singapore and from Singapore up to Vladivostock and vice versa. And that would mean more trade, more ship repair, more supplies to ships and so on, and, I think, more prosperity undoubtedly for the Russians."

Peter Snow asked if he feared that this extension of Russian maritime influence was also an extension of their political influence? Was he frightened of this? Lee said it was no use being frightened. "I accept it as a fact of life that over the next five, ten years, there is going to be a fairly considerable Russian naval presence. There already is one. I think the Japanese are very concerned about their supply routes to the Gulf for oil, their energy. Ninety-five per cent of it comes through the Straits of Malacca. They have been charting it, probably wanting to put buoys, lights and dredge the bottom so that bigger tankers can go through. I don't think they are going to just leave their tankers floating around without any support, if support became necessary for protection against piracy and things like that. And so we accept the US Seventh Fleet, the Russians, the Japanese, and we hope a continuing British, Australian, New Zealand, Malaysian, and a very small Singapore contribution, would generally help maintain good traffic arrangement, you know. The sea is getting a bit crowded."

In another interview, just before leaving for the United States, on 7 October, the Prime Minister was asked if he saw the Commonwealth continuing, Lee replied, "I would like to see it making an effort to get on to a positive, constructive track, moving upwards, not just picking faults with each other, which is a sterile and futile business."

In the United States, the Prime Minister "switched off" for a fortnight in Harvard before attending, for the first time, a session of the United Nations General Assembly. Later, he saw President Nixon. He also spent a few days at Yale University.

On 11 November, Lee Kuan Yew delivered the Dillingham Lecture at the East-West Centre, at the University of Hawaii. He called it "The Twain Have Met". He argued that East and West have met, albeit unequally, in one society, in Britain and France, where thousands of Africans and West Indians had now settled. Lee said that as individuals there were many Asians whose ability and competence in their professional fields excelled and were equal to the best of the Europeans and Americans. But that, he said, was not the point. "More relevant is the question why, in group performance as nation states, most of the East, so far, have not been able to organize themselves, maintain effective administration, ensure political stability, provide proper sanitation, clean potable water, constant electric supply, control population growth, and widen the base and raise the levels of education, training and expertise." Only then, he added, can they, by the use of machinery and equipment they can buy from the West, make the technological, economic and social progress to equal the West.

After referring to the progress made by Japan, the Prime Minister said that theoretically it should now be easier for the less developed to develop. New countries should be able to sell more of their products for more foreign exchange, and buy more capital machinery for further industrialization. World Bank loans, United Nations agencies, bilateral and multi-lateral aid programmes, were designed to ease the painful and difficult process of industrialization, to make it less strenuous and exacting an effort. In theory these concessions should also shorten the time taken for industrial transformation. But first there were some harsh realities which had to be recognized. The first was how to reconcile, how to regear value systems and culture patterns to meet the needs of an industrial society, based on the higher sciences. "It is not possible to move from the agricultural economies of Asia, somewhere at the level of fifteenth- and sixteenth-century Western Europe, into the technetronic era the Americans have entered, without jettisoning those parts of the value systems and culture patterns of the traditional past which inhibit or impede the acquisition of scientific knowledge, engineering techniques and work discipline. Industrialized status can be achieved only if new value systems and behaviour patterns are grafted on the old."

Lee said it required courageous leadership to eradicate those values which hampered the advance of a people into the higher sciences and to inculcate new values and attitudes which would quicken the pace of change. Rapid acquisition of knowledge in the sciences and technology, higher manipulative skills, management expertise and marketing know-how, were not congruent with a relaxed culture. The second major contradiction which was to be resolved was that of language.

"Pride in one's past is necessary for self-confidence and morale. These are essential ingredients of success. With independence comes a revivalist, romanticist streak. The native language, modes of dress, even manners and mannerisms, are resurrected and given pre-eminence. Often they are the external manifestations of a supposedly glorious past. It is a phenomenon to be found not only in older civilizations. The pre-occupation of the American Negroes with Afro-American studies, new hair and dress styles, this may be an assertion of their right to a dignified and not inferior past. It is worth remembering that the Japanese preserved as much of themselves as was compatible with the industrial society. In order to get access to this new knowledge, especially in the applied sciences, men must be prepared and sent abroad to study in developed countries. This requires the learning of the languages of these developed countries: English, Russian, German or French. The easiest course would be to continue using the language of the former metropolitan power, particularly where this happens to be English or French. The contradiction between pride in one's own language and the mastery of a foreign language can be reconciled. The foreign language the less developed have inherited can continue to be taught and used, whilst the indigenous language, over the decades, can be modernized and enriched by extensively borrowing ideas and words, and eventually developing its own modern literature. Only in this way can scholars be sent abroad to learn new knowledge. More important, the textbooks, journals and publications of the developed countries can be imported, enabling more students to acquire scientific knowledge. The best reason for keeping up the learning and use of English or French is that professors and experts from advanced countries can visit the universities and institutions of the less developed, and instruct much larger numbers of students than can be sent abroad."

Lee Kuan Yew said that the assiduous learning of the language of an advanced country, and the fostering of one's own language, were complementary, not inconsistent policies. "On the other hand, the deliberate stifling of a language which gives access to superior technology can be damaging beyond repair. Sometimes this is done, not so much to elevate the status of the indigenous language, as to take away a supposed advantage a minority in the society is deemed to have, because that minority has already gained a greater competence in the foreign language. This can be most damaging. It is tantamount to blinding the next generation to the knowledge of the advanced countries. Worse, it leads to an exodus of the bright and the promising who do not intend themselves or their children to be blinded from new knowledge. No matter how good the translation from the English, Russian, French or German text can be, it will often be three to five editions behind by the time it has been translated, sent to the printer, and finally published and available in the bookshops. And the range of books or journals that can be translated can never equal the access to direct sources, nor enable direct communication and a dialogue with specialists in the advanced countries. Whilst national pride requires that the indigenous language be revived and expanded for modern-day use, to deliberately drop the teaching and use of English or French, and depend upon translations of scientific materials into an, as yet, inadequate language, is unnecessarily to maim themselves in their search for new knowledge."

Another major problem for many of the less developed countries was that they had to raise not only levels of knowledge and skills, but levels of intelligence, ability and dexterity. "The controversy over whether ethnic differences correlate with low or high IQ levels and manipulative skills, may never be resolved either for academic or political considerations. But whether it is nature or nurture, one problem more acute in new, than in old, societies is that the abler and more educated segments of their population tend to have much smaller families than the less able and less educated, whose families are often five or more times larger than the more educated. Even if genetics have no bearing on ability, and it were the environment, the opportunities, the diet, the care and attention which determines performance, this still poses a grave problem. But if it turns out that nature as much as nurture decides the level of achievement, then some system of incentives and disincentives must be found to make sure that, with each succeeding generation, standards of education and skill, levels of performance and achievement, will rise both as a result of nature and nurture. Whether it is the genes, or the environment, or both—to catch up with technology and capital accumulation of the developed, this problem must be faced by the political leadership of the less developed, then alternative solutions defined, explained to the people and vigorously implemented. Then the quality of life will rise as levels of education and performance are raised."

589

XIII

"If," declared Lee Kuan Yew in a speech on 26 December, "we achieve as much progress in 1971 as we have done in 1970, then we shall be able to absorb the loss of spending by some 30,000 British service families, the retrenchment of 16,500 civilian employees, and the disbandment of over 3,000 locally enlisted uniformed personnel. It is estimated that British military expenditure contributed somewhere around $350 million for 1970. It will tail down to neglible proportions after September 1971. But our performance for 1965–70 shows that we have the capacity to ward off a sudden drop in our economic growth in 1972, or a high rise in unemployment, as a result of a precipitate drop in military base expenditure".

Lee promised that when this danger had been safely overcome "we will spend more time and resources in upgrading the skills and increasing the earnings of our workers. We must move into the middle brackets of technology. Then the average take-home pay will go up because value-added in the manufacturing processes is increased." Lee went on to argue that achievement must follow upon success. "If we lose our vitality and our thrust then we will slowly go down. This was what happened to some countries after the Second World War. The once imperial powers of Britain, France and Holland suffered a temporary decline after Empire was dissolved. But the Dutch and the French have been able to overcome the debilitating effects of this slide downhill by new economic opportunities in the European Economic Community. The British are grappling hard to reverse this process of slowly going soft and sliding downhill. It will depend upon the will of their leadership, and upon the national pride of their workers, who must accept the discipline necessary in modern industrial relations, before there can be a restoration of national strength and prestige. We are part of a vastly changed world. We have to meet rapid changes and the problems this creates. But if we stay trim and fit, we shall stay on top of our problems."

In November, the Republic suffered a great loss by the death of President Yusof bin Ishak. In Parliament on 30 December, the Prime Minister said that President Yusof stood for Singapore's multiracial policies. "He believed in our multiracial approach to solving the problems of our multiracial society. At the same time he was keen that in the multiracial milieu, our Singapore Malays should break out from the bounds of customs which were preventing them from making the same progress as the other communities. He believed in policies to modernize our society, including our Malays. He believed that all men should be equal, or at least given equal opportunities to advance themselves through their own efforts."

The First Commonwealth
Heads of Government Conference
in Asia, 1971

A new level of achievement in Lee Kuan Yew's career was reached in January 1971 when he presided over the first Commonwealth Conference to be held in Asia. Most of the Western news media commented favourably on his chairmanship, and upon the Government's hospitality and efficient general arrangements.

In his address of welcome on 14 January, Lee Kuan Yew said that from small informal gatherings of five prime ministers "we have thirty-one presidents, prime ministers and senior ministers". There had been a change of style and format. Nevertheless, he hoped the delegates could still speak more frankly and freely than at other international gatherings. A wide spectrum of political views reflected the different economic, social and cultural characteristics of thirty-one nation states. "We all seek a better future for our people. But, given the different circumstances of natural and human resources, agricultural or industrial backgrounds, and industrial and technological competence, we have to chart different courses towards this goal."

Lee referred to the controversy over the proposed sale of arms by Britain to South Africa. On the one hand, it was seen as a decision which, on principle, must be that of the British Government's alone. On the other hand, it was seen to be an unprincipled act in support of South Africa and her apartheid policies, and against the interests of the independent African states north of the Zambesi. He knew how strongly both views were held. "My work, as chairman," he said, "will be made easier if we do each other the courtesy of being frank and trenchant, and polite, if only coldly so." He reminded delegates that there had been sharp differences of views about the use of force in Rhodesia. Many African governments felt that it was the duty of the British Government to bring Rhodesia back to constitutional rule by the use of force. Over five years, despite breaches of economic sanctions by several countries, besides South Africa and Portugal helping the illegal regime to carry on, most had come to accept the reality that the use of force never was, and still was not, politically possible for the British. There might be a sharper division on the proposed arms sales than over the use of force on Rhodesia. "We have gathered to listen to each other's point of view, and to seek common ground if that is possible. However, if, in the end, concensus is not possible, we shall have to decide whether we can agree to disagree. If we cannot contain our present differences over the proposed arms sales, then it is unlikely that the Commonwealth, as at present constituted, can long endure."

For, in the next few years, they would be faced by graver differences on vital world issues. Most associations of nation states were held together by a formal framework of rules which promoted some common national interests. In the United Nations, the communists and the anti-communists, the Arabs and the Israelis, all had found it necessary to sit in the same Assembly, however bitter their conflicts, because they all were in search of peace. They were also in search of solutions to common problems, one of which was the ever-widening rift between the rich and the poor nations, between the more and the less developed.

Other associations like the European Economic Community had tight rules. These rules bound them closer together with the passage of time. Over the 1960s, these rules had brought them into a common economic mould. Further agreements among them in the 1970s might make the EEC countries have a greater say in the joint defence of Western Europe. Eventually some European union might emerge to help them chart a common destiny. The Commonwealth had no such rules.

Successive Kennedy rounds, Lee Kuan Yew continued, had sought to lower tariff barriers to liberalize trade. But there was now a grave danger that the United States Congress might go through with legislation to slap quotas upon any import which was more than fifteen per cent of the consumption of any product which was produced domestically. "If this trigger mechanism of the Mills Bill is re-introduced and passed in the 1971 Congress, it may lead to tariff wars between economic blocs. In this event, the concessions agreed to in principle at the UNCTAD meeting in Geneva in October last year will become derisory." But issues of such gravity as the Mills Bill did not catch Press headlines. Perhaps the reader of a popular newspaper did not understand the consequences of these events to his job or to his cost of living. "We should not leave the impression that thirty-one Commonwealth heads of government failed to take this opportunity to underline this threat to all our economies. If world trade shrinks as a result of protectionist tendencies in the United States or the EEC, we all stand to lose. Our interests are best served by getting more liberal trade policies pursued by the United States and the EEC. This will become more important when the EEC enlarges its membership from six to ten."

The Prime Minister spoke of the new links all Commonwealth countries, the developed and the less developed countries, had forged in regional and international groupings. In addition to bilateral ties with Britain, all had developed multilateral ties with other developed countries, East and West. Caribbean members received more attention from Canada. Those from the South Pacific were especially closer to Australia and New Zealand, and in the long run may be closer to them than to Britain. Besides being members of the United Nations, participating in all her agencies, colleagues from Africa were members of the OAU. Singapore was trying to find a wider base in regional development in ASEAN with Malaysia, Indonesia, Thailand and the Philippines. At the same time, Singapore continued defence arrangements, in a Commonwealth Five, with Malaysia, Australia, New Zealand and Britain.

Australia and New Zealand were associated with Singapore's defence in the Second World War. They helped in the development of Singapore's defence capabilities since then. Singapore had as many of its students in Australian, Canadian, and New Zealand universities as in Britain. Nearly a third of the university graduates were from Commonwealth universities. "But we would be naive if we did not expect Australia and New Zealand, good friends though they are, from time to time to re-assess how best their resources can be re-deployed. It is in their interests, and ours too, that their nearer neighbour, Indonesia, is helped to greater stability and economic progress. For Indonesia can then become a stable and rich area for raw materials and, eventually, good markets for Australian and New Zealand exports."

Lee said that the developed Commonwealth nations might be prepared, for the present, to spread some of their external aid on Commonwealth countries for reasons of sentiment. Whether they continued to do so in the future would depend on whether such aid was likely to advance the economic, security, and other interests of the donor country. It was useful to have shared a common experience. But it was the future that concerns us more. "Seven presidents, a vice-president, seventeen prime ministers and five senior ministers in government leading their delegations, have not travelled thousands of miles to meet in Singapore if they did not believe in the Commonwealth. However, we must build up multiple mechanisms to increase our mutual interests in joint endeavour."

If Britain joined the EEC, as was not unlikely in the next few years, painful adjustments would have to be made by those Commonwealth countries that exported produce to Britain. Whether it was butter from New Zealand, grain from Canada and Australia, or sugar from the Caribbeans and Mauritius, all would be affected. In any case, regardless of British membership of the EEC, textiles from India, Pakistan, Singapore, and even Hong Kong would lose their UK quotas by January 1972. "How do we give a new content to this Commonwealth partnership in these circumstances? There are probably answers to this. But we shall not find them if we become so preoccupied with immediate issues that the broader picture is distorted or blurred. We shall then be the poorer for it. But if we can see the vistas on the horizon, further develop the many intangible ties born out of a common experience, and build on their foundations, we can all derive satisfaction and advantage from it... We all have different problems, not excluding Britain. But we live in one small world. If we can give the Commonwealth a new relevance, a fresh validity, it will be a more agreeable place for all of us. Our deliberations should strive to give the Commonwealth a framework for future development. If we evolve new patterns of economic and technological co-operation, making for more joint effort and mutual benefit, the Commonwealth could mean more to all of us."

In his closing comments, on 22 January, Lee Kuan Yew said after nine days the delegates had got to know each other better. That did not mean they had together changed their respective positions. But the possibility existed that there could be further adjustments and modifications of defence and economic policies. "Our attitudes to colour and other conflicts may shift, if only slightly, as a result of listening to the arguments expounded. But whether it is arms sales to South Africa, or the consequences of Britain's entry into the Common Market, or the financing of Commonwealth technical development and co-operation between the developed and the less developed countries, enlightened self-interest is tempered by a sincere desire to do what we can to improve the lot of the others, or at least make it more bearable."

Lee said there had been some thoughtful and constructive contributions from a good number of speakers on the world economic situation and trends, and the impact of Britain's membership of the EEC. He was grateful to his colleagues for their conscious moderation in the tone of their speeches. It stopped almost irreconcilable positions from becoming completely irreconcilable. Restraint and good manners prevented face-to-face encounter from degenerating into disorder, which characterized the French Assembly of the Fourth Republic. "I have tried to give every major item adequate time for discussion, and every participant his fair measure of attention. I was grateful that those being provoked stayed cool and calm."

The Prime Minister of Canada, Lee said, made an outstanding contribution in the private session. "He, of Caucasian stock, Prime Minister of a country with the highest per capita income of any Commonwealth country, felt that the stature of man himself would be diminished if we treat our fellow-humans the way South African whites are doing. But, emotion notwithstanding, his intellect probed the problem further. He has allowed me to paraphrase him. He said the problem would not be solved even if Britain did not sell arms to Africa. Others would. In any case, China or Russia would supply arms to the oppressed Africans in these territories. Bloodshed and suffering were inevitable. A logical step was that the liberals in the West should supply African freedom fighters with guns. He declared honestly that he could not contemplate this. But Canada could significantly help the economic transformation of Africa."

Singapore's position on this question was that Singapore stood with their African colleagues in the Commonwealth in combating "this evil of racism. We stand committed to the principle of human equality and dignity, in the struggle against racism, and towards this end we are prepared to help by way of education and finance. Contact and dialogue with South Africa was accepted in the Lusaka Manifesto. It may modify their attitudes. One delegate appropriately but inadvertently called them Boers. I do not believe that 'Boerish' behaviour can be wholly changed by dialogue. It was not contact or dialogue which made the white South Africans classify the Japanese as white for the purposes of apartheid. The Japanese used to be considered a strange, outlandish-looking people, with strange dress styles. But by World War One, they had demonstrated that they were more than the equals of the Afrikaners. I read recently that the Chinese in South Africa were to be allowed access to some white facilities. This is vicarious reward for the enormous sacrifices made by the toil and discipline which the People's Republic of China had to extract of their people. It demonstrated their capacity as a people to match the West in nuclear science and missile technology. White racist-supremist theories can only be demolished by clearly demonstrating that the whites are not superior. It is not from weakness that one commands respect. However desirable it may be to persuade white South Africans through contact, and not isolationism, to think and behave differently, I fear history will prove that it can only be done otherwise, more by force than by reason."

Lee continued: "We cannot despair either for the white, black, brown, or the yellow man. There are in every ethnic group the outstanding intellect, that percentage of high-flyers. Ralph Bunche or Arthur Lewis, in diplomacy or scholarship, or James Baldwin and Richard Wright in literature—many blacks have made outstanding contributions in open competition with a mainly white population. But the problem the less developed countries face is not that we' do not have the individuals with exceptional qualities. The problem is that we are judged by our performance as a group, not as individuals. And for group performance, more than a few men of outstanding qualities are required. The cultural ballast, the value patterns, the social discipline, the organizational framework of effective government within which individual endeavour is made rewarding and collective performance becomes a source of national pride—these are crucial ingredients. Then we will command equality, both as individuals, and as ethnic and social groups. History, deciphered from stone relics and parchments, has many instances of the rise and fall of many empires. Great civilizations have flourished and perished. Who would have believed when the Romans conquered Britain in the early years of the Christian era, that the barbarians they found there would, by the end of the nineteenth century, become the supreme naval and industrial power of the world? Who could have foreseen that this people, in the process of 300 years of naval supremacy, seeded colonies in the New World, which have overtaken them, both in technological supremacy and material wealth? But who can say what will happen to America if she does not solve her own problems of over-abundance, the listlessness which leads to drugs, permissiveness, the near break-down of civilized living in the urban ghettos as violence and organized disorder become a way of life? Some twenty-five million American Negroes are not going to disappear from the face of North America by the year 2000. Their problems of large families, poor education, poverty and deprivation of human dignity must be solved. But how? Unless the family unit is recreated after being destroyed in slavery, and family care and pride keep the numbers of children down to a few who can be nurtured and nourished, all the money, spent on the Vietnam war, diverted to black housing, education and job opportunities, cannot solve them."

The world had become too small for all. It would become even smaller with the jumbos, the super-sonics, the hydrofoils, and the hovercraft. It was becoming even more economically inter-dependent. "But we shall be disappointed if we believe that this dissolving of primeval prejudices will happen overnight. Behind the intellect is the primordial nervous system, reacting involuntarily with fear and pre-judice to the strange and the unaccustomed. Worse, this is reinforced in so many ways by the portraying of inferiority of certain ethnic groups in literature, on television, and even in dolls. In a multitude of ways, this conference has mirrored in miniature some of the irreconcilables the world community faces. They must be made less irreconcilable. It will become too costly and painful for mankind if these conflicts are not tempered by the spirit of common brotherhood."

The Prime Minister concluded his review with a tribute to the Secretary-General Mr Arnold Smith and his efficient secretariat staff: "Without their thorough preparation before this conference, their constant attendance upon our needs, their work at awkward hours, which we toss unexpectedly at them every now and again, our meeting would not have been so expeditious. But I must especially mention the energetic optimism of the Secretary-General. Without his zealous efforts to seek solutions to the most intractable puzzles, our meeting would have foundered."

Part Three

CHAPTER TWENTY-FIVE

How Much of a Chinese is Lee Kuan Yew?

I

LEE is his family name. Kuan Yew means "The Light that shines far and wide". His parents gave him these names to comfort him on his way through the dark patches in life. Lee was born in Singapore and has never been to China. "I have no links with China. I have no friends in China." His paternal grandfather, Lee Hoon Leong, was born in Singapore in 1873. His father Lee Chin Koon was also born in Singapore. Lee Kuan Yew's links with Singapore go back almost to the time of Raffles when his great grandfather came to Singapore to seek a fortune. Lee's grandfather decided that his grandson would be educated to become the equal of any Englishman.

Lee first attended a Chinese kindergarten, and then went on to an English government primary school. From there he went to Raffles Institution, and then to Raffles College (forerunner of the University of Singapore), and finally to Cambridge. Lee is thus "English educated". But he taught himself Mandarin in 1954 when the People's Action Party was formed because he realized that he must be able to communicate direct with the militant youth, many of whom were influenced by Mandarin-speaking schoolteachers. And he learned Hokkien in 1961 so that he might be able to talk with parents unable to speak Mandarin.

Professor Wolfgang Franke, then Visiting Professor of Chinese Studies at the University of Malaya, in an article in the *Malaysian*

Journal of Education (Vol. 2 No. 2, December, 1965), advanced the theory that the main result of English education in Singapore and Malaysia, if not coupled with a fairly thorough Chinese education at home or elsewhere, was the uprooting of the Chinese humanistic tradition: "The English education, even if it lasts thirteen years, usually remains superficial. Only a small number of outstanding students in a few eminent schools are able to penetrate to the basic values of Western culture and to acquire a genuine Western humanistic education to replace the lost Chinese one." But the majority, Professor Franke contended, were adrift spiritually "on the waves of material comfort without having any fixed cultural or moral standards... There are, however, not a few of them who become sooner or later aware of their uprooted, floating position. They realize their lack of cultural identification... Physically and emotionally they are Chinese, but culturally they are neither Chinese nor English or Malay. They do not know themselves what they are."

There is no doubt that Lee Kuan Yew is among "the small number of outstanding students" who did penetrate to the basic values of Western culture. Physically he is a Chinese. What is he intellectually, emotionally? Has his grasp of Western education and culture eliminated his Chineseism? Is Lee Kuan Yew more of a Westerner born in the East, than a Chinese, an overseas Chinese? Or is he, too, sometimes adrift, subject to contradictory pressures? How does he react to certain specific problems; for example, those in which the Chinese and the non-Chinese are involved? Does he always deal with them with his Western-trained mind, in an objective manner, or do his methods betray just a trace, perhaps, of hereditary Chinese influence? Lee's biological association with China is thinly stretched over more than a hundred years, though he has lived partly in an atmosphere of Chinese communalism which is inherent in all Chinese communities wherever they have settled in the East. To Lee, China is no more than a legend; and yet his doctors tell him that his body, his physical make-up, resents the hot and humid atmosphere of the tropics in which he was born, and in which his grandfather and his father were born. The climate of Singapore knows no seasons: the humidity is very high and the temperature varies between seventy and eighty-seven degrees Fahrenheit. It is a climate which Lee finds unpleasant because he dislikes feeling hot and sticky, because it renders him highly susceptible to colds. Lee's physical structure demands a climate which is cold and dry, as it is in those parts of China where the Hakkas live. In an endeavour to maintain his body temperature at the correct level for efficient working and thinking, Lee's office, bedroom and official cars are air-conditioned. He sleeps in a temperature of sixty-six degrees and works at seventy-two degrees Fahrenheit. He removes his office jacket when he walks along the corridor to the non-air-conditioned toilet. If it is correct to assume from all this that Lee Kuan Yew is still much of a Chinese physically, in spite of a gap of a century, is it not conceivable that Lee sometimes behaves as a Chinese without being conscious of the fact? "I am a Chinese by ethnic origin," he told an American audience in 1967, "I am not a Chinaman in the sense that I feel for what the Chinese Goverment in Peking wants, or does not want, to do."

Not only has Lee Kuan Yew never been to China (he has been to Hong Kong) there are times when he is acutely aware that he does not even feel like a real Chinese. This has happened when meeting Chinese from China with whom he has often felt less comfortable than with Malays and Indians and Chinese from Singapore and Malaysia. He is conscious of a much closer identity with Singaporeans and Malaysians than with people of his own race from China; they may speak the same language and they may look alike, but they react differently: they are foreigners.

"Lee Kuan Yew is an Englishman, an upper-class Englishman, with a Chinese name," a statesman whispered to me at the Prime Minister's Conference in London in 1966. "Basically Lee Kuan Yew is an Oriental," insisted an American in private conversation in 1967. "On the international political stage he is seen by the West as a man possessed of all the Western virtues. I say that when he is forced by circumstances, perhaps in the next five to ten years, to expose his inner self, he will stand revealed as a good Chinese, controlling a strategic island in the China Seas." Which, people ask, is the real Lee Kuan Yew?

These, and many other questions like them, are often debated by journalists and others, and a great deal of speculation is generated. What would happen, they asked, if, in a moment of truth, Lee was forced to make a choice: would Lee Kuan Yew, the modern Singaporean with the English education, prevail, or would he revert to the attitudes of his ancestors?

It is unlikely that Lee Kuan Yew himself could answer the question posed in this way. But it would probably be safe to say that he would never make a decision emotionally. All the relevant facts would be taken into consideration, and Lee would reach a conclusion which would best benefit Singapore. If this is what a modern Singaporean would be expected to do in these circumstances, then there is the answer. But that is not to say that Lee is not proud of his Chinese ancestry. Of course he is.

Lee is the first overseas Chinese to become a Prime Minister, and this has caused some writers to describe him as the leader of the thirteen million overseas Chinese in Southeast Asia. About half the population of Malaya is Chinese. In Thailand, one person in ten is Chinese. In Sabah, Sarawak and Brunei, one person in four is

Chinese. In Indonesia about one in thirty is Chinese. There are about a quarter of a million Chinese in the Kingdom of Cambodia, which has a population of four and a half million. In the Philippines about three hundred thousand out of a population of nearly twenty-three million are Chinese. In all these countries, the Chinese are directly involved as merchants or capitalists in the nation's economy. Most overseas Chinese know of Lee Kuan Yew, and they are proud of what he has achieved in the only state in the East outside China where the Chinese are in a majority; but each group of overseas Chinese is a community within the nation in which it has settled. There is no overall leader of these various groups; each is self-contained, owing loyalty to the countries in which they live, or to China.

In 1950, Dr Purcell wrote (*The Chinese in Southeast Asia*) that the Chinese were of the greatest political, economic and social significance in the region "and indirectly to the world as a whole". Whether or not this has ever been strictly accurate, it is not now. Most of the Chinese in Burma have been told to leave. Thousands have been sent from Indonesia, and thousands more were probably killed in the blood-bath which followed the abortive communist coup. The remainder have been instructed to stop behaving as Chinese and to become Indonesians in speech, dress and habit. Chinese newspapers have disappeared. Chinese schools are closed. No longer can a Chinese businessman in Indonesia put sign-boards in Chinese characters outside his shop.

In the Philippines, pressure continues to mount against merchants and traders. Chinese thrive quietly in Cambodia, to a limited extent in South Vietnam and Laos, and in Singapore, Malaya and Sarawak, and to a lesser extent in Sabah. In Malaysia, the Chinese still dominate the nation's economy. But only in the Republic of Singapore, where they have become Singaporeans, is it true to say in 1968 that the Chinese are of "great significance" politically, economically and socially.

To all the overseas Chinese communities, Lee Kuan Yew reacts as a Singaporean and not as a brother Chinese. Most of the countries in the East have their "Chinese problems". Whatever may be Lee Kuan Yew's private thoughts about them, as a person of Chinese origin, or as a humanitarian, he keeps them to himself. He is a Singaporean, with problems of his own. "Lee is no doctrinaire theoretician," wrote *The Observer*, in 1959. "While well-informed on world affairs, he is fundamentally parochial in outlook in that he studies events and trends principally in the light of their impact on Singapore and its future. It is perhaps to this that he owes his political flexibility, his immunity from ideological dogma."

The Chinese have never been assimilationists: wherever they settled in Southeast Asia they kept themselves in a group. They have always preferred to marry among themselves, although there were a number of Chinese-Malay marriages during the early days in Singapore and Malaya when Chinese women were in very short supply; but there were many difficulties, primarily religious (Muslims rarely marry non-Muslims). Lee Kuan Yew's grandfather was obliged to go to Sumatra to find his Chinese bride. In Malaya, at about that time, there were ten Chinese females to every thousand males.

In China, the Manchu citizenship law still obtained. This insisted that descendants of Chinese through the male line would be Chinese forever and this idea was adopted by Dr Sun Yat-sen. Dr Sun said: "China is the only country where 'race' and 'nation' are the same, with common blood, common language, and common customs—a 'single race'." Dr Sun's argument was that the Chinese were in danger from a white peril. His definition of a Chinese, as Dr Purcell pointed out in *The Chinese In Modern Malaya* is not supported by science, but it had considerable effect upon the Chinese in Singapore and Malaya: a person forever Chinese according to China's laws was not thereby encouraged to be a good loyal national of any other country. It is interesting to reflect that the Malay extremist, Jaafar Albar, was much later to shout "one race, one religion, one state" on behalf of the Malays when Tunku Abdul Rahman and Lee Kuan Yew were trying to build a multiracial Malaysia. Albar believed that Malays were in danger from a yellow peril.

Malay leaders encourage inter-marriage, and so do some Chinese, and they believe this could do much to create a Malay-Chinese society. Lee considers that most Chinese in Singapore are inclined to be rather conservative in this matter. Statistics show that the percentage of inter-racial marriages in Singapore is steadily declining: there were seven per cent in 1959, and three per cent in 1964. Most of these inter-marriages were between Europeans (mostly soldiers) and Chinese girls.

How does Lee Kuan Yew respond to the development of China as an industrial power? He believes, and his belief is based not upon emotion but upon reason, upon an examination of the facts, that China will emerge, perhaps within the next ten years, as an industrialized nation capable of waging limited nuclear warfare. As an Asian he may feel satisfied that Asia is thus giving further proof of its ability to make some technological progress—Japan is already among the world's industrial giants—and, though he may be highly aware of China's long history and achievements, it is doubtful whether he was excited when scientists in China produced their first atomic explosion in 1964.

Tunku Abdul Rahman, reacting as an Asian, remarked: "This is a great achievement for the Chinese." He went on, "They have shown the world that not only the West can achieve nuclear success, but that Asians are also capable of doing so." Tunku Abdul Rahman said that he was happy to note that Malaysian Chinese had not been particularly enthusiastic about the explosion. This reaction, he thought, showed not only that times had changed, "but the outlook among the people of Malaysia had changed, too".

Lee Kuan Yew issued no statement about China's nuclear tests, but privately he felt, as did many with interests in Southeast Asia, that the explosion marked the beginning of a new era which might result in a very different sort of Southeast Asia inside ten years. How would Malaysia and Singapore fit into the new situation created by an Asian nuclear power? Much, of course, depends upon China's real aims in the East. Lee Kuan Yew believes that China's foreign policy does not include the invasion of any part of Asia physically, but he does think it likely that China is determined to expand her influence throughout the region, either in the cause of international communism, or in China's own interest, or both. Within ten years there is almost certain to be a new leadership in what may then be a powerful industrialized China. Adjustments may have to be made all round; a great deal will depend upon events in Vietnam. "We will tackle these problems when the time comes," Lee is on record as saying. "Meanwhile we will follow a policy of making the maximum number of friends and the fewest number of enemies. We aim to be an island of neutrality in the region."

II

What must be remembered when we try to evaluate Lee Kuan Yew as a Chinese is that for two millennia and more Chinese loyalty has focused on the ruler rather than on the state, on Confucian culture rather than on the nation. The Chinese race-memory, declared Dennis Bloodworth, in his book, *The Chinese Looking Glass*, is restricted to a system in which an indoctrinated elite rules the country in accordance with an authoritarian ideology, which in turn is founded on a "universal truth". The Chinese, he argued, have an instinctive trust in the idea of a humanistic "reasonable" government.

Thus, none of the Chinese in Singapore (except the Barisan Sosialis communist-front organization) was concerned when the People's Action Party governed in 1967 without an Opposition, the Barisan Sosialis having withdrawn their Members of Parliament in order to continue their struggle in the streets, letting the by-elections go to the PAP unopposed. Lee provided a humanistic reasonable government, and that to most people was all that mattered. In the 1968 general elections the PAP won all fifty-eight seats.

Lee behaved as a Chinese in 1967, it might be argued, when he introduced National Service for a limited number of eighteen-year-olds and told them they would become an elite. The thought was left unspoken, but a Chinese mind could reason that an elite would serve the government, the rulers. Lee wanted them also to understand that primarily they would serve the State. In his speech of 21 February, 1967, he referred to the fact that seventy per cent of Singapore were going to English schools. That was all right, "but," he said, "never forget that you are not an Englishman, and I am not an Englishman. English is a language we learn and we use it. But we must keep a part of ourselves—the part that leads us back to our histories, to our cultures, to the civilizations from whence we came. And out of that, the past, we will together create a present and a future worthy of a people who have come from very ancient cultures and civilizations."

Precisely what form of government will finally emerge from these cultures, and histories, mostly of China, no one knows. "We are" confessed Dr Goh Keng Swee, then Minister for Defence, in 1967, "a complex, multiracial community with little sense of common history, with a group purpose which is yet to be properly articulated. We are in the process of rapid transition towards a destiny which we do not yet know." Parliamentary democracy anywhere in the East is a fragile plant which has failed to survive in most countries, and is much distorted in others. Singapore probably knows as much about democracy as any other state in Asia, since the city-state stands at an international cross-roads and has a relatively sophisticated urban population. Even so, in spite of this, and in spite of Lee Kuan Yew's ardent advocacy based upon his convictions and his fundamental belief in the rule of law equal to all, it would probably be more correct to say that most Singaporeans of Chinese descent are much less interested in democracy than they are in humanistic reasonable government by a leadership elite.

"In China," says Dennis Bloodworth, "The Chinese have long since resigned themselves to the fact that Confucian government-by-goodness is only practicable in a state which is liberally dosed with dictatorship ... they do not demand democracy, but a square deal." Neither do the Chinese in Singapore demand democracy: they accept the democracy Lee Kuan Yew has worked to give them, but they are more interested in Lee's constant assurance that his Government intends to create a more just and a more equal society. Lee is sufficiently a Chinese to know that Singaporeans prefer good government to chaotic lawlessness in which it is difficult to do business and live in reasonable safety; he knows they would prefer a square deal to liberalism; but the Westerner in him insists that they have both democracy and good government, including a square deal.

This has to be worked on constantly. Traditionally, the Chinese is accustomed to being governed. He had no sense of participation in China, and he had none until recently in Singapore, where for a hundred and fifty years the Chinese worked and lived more or less contentedly under benevolent British colonialism, until in 1942 the Japanese imperialists came with their fierce Asian nationalism and forced those Chinese in Singapore who were unable to return to China —and there were many—to begin to think of themselves as Singaporeans. Even then, in Singapore, there was no mass insistence that the British must leave; most of the Chinese were content to accept British good government, and it was events in China, where Mao Tse-tung was making every Chinese overseas again proud of being Chinese, which helped the Malayan Communist Party recruit youths and intellectuals to their ranks to launch the struggle to turn the Malayan Peninsula, including Singapore, into a communist republic. The revolt failed, though it lasted twelve years; but a different story might have been told if the communists had managed to obtain the support of Singapore, which they never did. The Singaporeans settled for good government.

The Chinese have always been accustomed to law which protects the state rather than the individual, and this probably mitigated against the communist revolt; it also helps to explain Chinese reaction to what they consider to be good government. When, for example, eighteen criminals were hanged in Changi Gaol in 1966 for killing two Singapore prison officials, not a single word of protest or criticism was publicly uttered by anyone. Lee Kuan Yew's view was that they were anti-social, unfit to live in Singapore society. Singaporeans of Chinese descent shared his view: in their opinion they were ruthless gangsters, extortioners, and unconvicted murderers: they had killed state servants, and destroyed state property by smashing and burning all the facilities and equipment of an island open-prison. In these circumstances the state was entitled to forfeits. Good governments rule firmly and demonstrate their ability to do so when occasion demands.

As a democrat, Lee Kuan Yew holds that every citizen must have the right to elect a government of his own choice. He hopes that parliamentary democracy based upon the British method, but adapted where necessary to fit Singapore requirements, will survive. To his legal mind, the democratic insistence upon all essential issues being openly discussed and voted upon in parliament, provides the "square deal" in government which citizens of Chinese and other descent demand. This ensures the continuance of the "open society" which is an important factor in Lee Kuan Yew's political thinking; but whether, in fact, Singapore can produce sufficient interest in democracy to provide the Government with an intelligent constructive Opposition is another matter.

Lee is a democrat by intellectual conviction. He does not believe that all men are intellectually equal, nor does he consider that all men should be treated equally by society, except in law and in so far as citizenship rights and responsibilities are concerned. Persons with initiative, drive and talent, energy and ability, in Lee's view, are entitled to higher rewards than those not so gifted. He is not an egalitarian. He believes a worker should be rewarded according to productivity. He believes strongly in social obligations.

Lee's dilemma is to wean Singaporeans away from their complacent attitude of leaving everything to the state, to the Government, and to replace this with a judgment which understands that, while good government must be supported, this still leaves a lot of community work for public-spirited citizens to organize for the good of the whole community. This is not easy in a community renowned for its individualism, and its basic belief that a good government provides the infrastructure and leaves the people to do the best they can for themselves.

An analysis of Lee Kuan Yew's speeches over the years, and a survey of his governmental decisions, show that Lee is no paternalist. He would probably accept without argument the contention that the traditional Chinese, even the overseas Chinese, focuses on the ruler rather than the state. He would not deny that to Singaporeans of Chinese descent, he is regarded primarily as leader, and only secondarily as the local embodiment of the Western concept of a Prime Minister. Nevertheless, he endeavours to create a closely-knit democratic society with a strong national consciousness because he knows that people in the process of creating a multiracial state must be activists, not observers. His task, therefore, is to infuse into migrant Chinese a feeling that they and their forefathers never knew in China, that of a powerful sense of nationalism. And this they must generate in an island most of them have known for less than seventy-five years, and which for less than a decade has been their ancestral home and the centre of their loyalty.

Lee is both Chinese and Western in his attitude towards leadership. He understands the feeling of the people, and their need for a leader. He abhors dictatorship, and believes fervently in the open society and the public argument. In the Cabinet, Lee Kuan Yew is the chairman and the first among equals: he considers himself to be a part of a collective leadership. · He does not always have his own way in the Cabinet, but he usually does, because his thinking, his arguments, have their own force of appeal. He believes that a government must govern, and that a Prime Minister must also be a leader in an Asian sense, in an Asian situation.

Dennis Bloodworth in *The Chinese Looking Glass* wrote that "Confucius had advocated the rules of ritual as a habit-forming discipline which would imbue men with the mystique of social sportsmanship. But he only succeeded in inspiring a split-level civilization in which the Chinese more often than not observed the rules to the letter in order to ignore the spirit of the game." Bloodworth goes on to say, referring to the real tears of professional mourners jerked out by the demands of filial piety, "It is dangerous to be cynical, for there is a point at which ritual and reality must meet. Chinese believe that tears are not mere manifestations of uncontrollable emotion. They are, legitimately, the recognized expression of patriotism, loyalty or filial piety."

As an example, Dennis Bloodworth mentioned the tears of Lee Kuan Yew at a Press conference recorded for television. "In August, 1965, the conservative, predominantly Malay Government in Kuala Lumpur ejected the small predominantly Chinese island-state of Singapore from the Federation of Malaysia. At the Press conference Lee Kuan Yew, Singapore's Chinese Prime Minister, broke down and wept so bitterly that proceedings had to be suspended for some twenty minutes. Lee's grief was sincere enough. Human defence mechanisms are traitors, however, and he was in danger of facing the Press with a quite deceptive and unbecoming composure if he failed to give way. But it was meet that he should weep, and the tears were there, requiring no bidding. Chinese crying by numbers, is like Christian church-going: laudable on the prescribed ritual occasion, if otherwise suspect." After the conference, Lee Kuan Yew said he had wept for the Chinese left behind in Malaysia.

III

Lee Kuan Yew is the first overseas Chinese to devote his life to politics. The Japanese newspaper *Asahi Shimbum*, in September, 1966 described him as a pragmatic politician, with a tremendous influence not only upon the overseas Chinese, but also on Southeast Asia as a whole. "In the past," remarked the paper, "the overseas Chinese were noted for their economic activities and their complete lack of interest in politics." This was true until the Japanese invaded the Malayan Peninsula, and Japanese soldiers began to bully young Lee Kuan Yew.

Lee Kuan Yew's complete involvement in politics is a measure of his non-Chineseism, for, as Victor Purcell explained in his monumental *The Chinese in Southeast Asia,* a strong feeling of non-involvement went right through Chinese society, at home and abroad. "Responsibility" was a far-reaching principle, a convention hostile to the growth of public spirit: it was a characteristic which has persevered down to the present day, "and, coupled with a willingness to pay for a quiet life, has been responsible for many Chinese difficulties". Their main concern is making a living. In Singapore, and more especially in Malaya, this is still very largely true, though a political and civic consciousness is slowly appearing in Singapore, mainly as the result of Lee Kuan Yew's constant warning that there will be no cow to milk unless every citizen does get involved. Participation is the word Lee Kuan Yew prefers to use. His own involvement, his participation in politics, stemmed partly from his absorption of English education and culture which enabled him to think like an Englishman, and to have English values, and partly because the Hakkas "are in some ways a people apart". Moreover, said Purcell, "they have a stubbornness of disposition which distinguishes them from their fellow Chinese."

Lee's complete dominance of the Singapore political scene can be attributed in part to the fact that the Chinese have never been supporters of lost causes, and the majority of the electorate, though led by English-educated leaders, still have a traditional view of the political world, "based", as Professor FitzGerald points out in his book, *The Third China*, "on the belief that a dynasty gained the 'Mandate of Heaven', by virtue of which it had the right to rule, so long as that rule was effective and strong". It would be interesting to know just how far Lee Kuan Yew would go in defending a lost cause which did not concern a basic principle. Multiracialism in Malaysia looked like being a lost cause almost before the ink was dry on the Merger Agreement, and Lee fought like a tiger to preserve this concept because he passionately believed in it, and because logic repudiated any other enduring solution to the problem of a plural society.

Put in its best possible light, there seems to have been a complete misunderstanding between Lee Kuan Yew and Tunku Abdul Rahman as to what Malaysia was to be. Lee accepted the words at their face value and believed that Malaysia meant multiracialism. This would be a gradual growth but nothing would purposely be erected to prevent that growth; on the contrary, growth would be encouraged and obstacles removed. Within a week of the creation of Malaysia, the Tunku was condemning Singapore voters for preferring PAP Malay candidates, (representing multiracialism), to UMNO Malay candidates, who represented conservatism. Important UMNO officials branded the Malay progressives as "traitors to their race and religion", and the Tunku uttered not one word of reprimand. Cynics thought Lee Kuan Yew, the smart politician, had been outwitted and deceived. Lee, they said, wanted Malaysia because the cunning Chinese could thus seize the Malays in a bear-hug, for on anything like equal terms the Malays would be no match for the crafty Chinese. Aware of this, and equally confident of their own ability to out-manoeuvre Lee because of their hold on the political and administrative machine, the Malays, the critics said, agreed to Malaysia to promote their own concept: which, the cynics said, was multiracialism in a Malay-dominated kingdom. If this was true, the Malays were right to resist an encroachment by the multiracial PAP upon their communal base.

Whatever the Tunku's real purpose behind Malaysia, Lee believed then that Singapore alone was not viable, was seriously threatened by a communist take-over, possibly through the ballot box, and could, if part of Malaysia, contribute a great deal towards multiracialism and to Malaysia's prosperity. But Lee could never accept a concept which visualized Malay domination: that was not multiracialism, and neither could Malay domination lead to multiracialism, because he did not believe it to be in the nature of any group to be willing to surrender dominance once power was in their hands. Lee thought the Malays understood what the population figures meant: that no race could dominate another, that it would be madness for any group to try.

What Lee Kuan Yew did not include in his calculations was the fact that in Malaya the Chinese were not so advanced politically as the Chinese in Singapore: they were, and in 1971 still are, more concerned with milking the cow than holding the cow's head. Purcell said this has been true of all purely mercantile communities since the dawn of history. Over the years in Malaya and in Singapore this had become less and less true, but not all Lee's skill and talent could move the Chinese in Malaya to abandon their attitude of non-involvement and they were content with things as they were. The Malays did not oppress them; they could make a living. Why get involved in politics? They could remember what happened to the young men shortly after the Second World War: they had become involved in the Malayan Communist Party's attempt to create a communist republic, and this had meant a great deal of trouble all round. The Chinese community in Malaya did not fear Tunku Abdul Rahman's concept of Malaysia. In this, of course, they behaved more like traditional Chinese than did the English-educated Lee Kuan Yew. Lee's own personal popularity in Malaya, among the Chinese, did not affect the issue. They were proud of him in a way, they respected him, but they were not sure that he was behaving as a Chinese was supposed to behave.

Lee himself never forgot his Chinese origin. "We in Singapore spring from four great civilizations, civilizations that go back thousands of years," Lee reminded a Tamil audience in December, 1966. "Three thousand years ago, there were no Anglo-Saxons because the Saxons had not yet gone over to Britain. One thousand years ago, they were still wearing animal-skins! Your people in the Deccan had by then already created a literature, and so had had my ancestors in China. But that is the past. It should only give us confidence that, given that same determination and will and collective endeavour, we should be able to succeed here."

Lee Kuan Yew also understands the resentment the very presence of the overseas Chinese creates among non-thinking indigenous people. The Chinese in Southeast Asia, he told *Time-Life* in 1965, presented something of a challenge to the indigenous people. Overseas Chinese were to be found in the capital cities of all the Southeast Asian countries; they migrated, not together with Chinese imperial or military strength, but under the cover of other European colonial systems. "Without political advantages of patronage they were able to take over the commercial and distributive processes, and they are the bankers and the importers and exporters and retailers. They are in charge of the retail trade, by and large, of all the countries in Southeast Asia." Lee believed they should be encouraged to become loyal nationalists, and not made to feel they were Chinese.

Not that he was ashamed of being Chinese. He was not. "I am very proud of the fact that my ancestors are Chinese and I am a product of thousands of years of written and continually recorded history, one of the longest periods of any civilization, of continuous evolution and revolutions unbroken, but I think our future lies in being part of Southeast Asia, not being just an excrescence of China. And whether we succeed depends, first, upon whether we try; and second, upon whether the others—the Malays and the other indigenous peoples here—want to accept us as part of Malaysia. It is a two-way process. We have to want to be part of Malaysia, not a part of irredentist China; and the peoples here must want us to be part of them."

IV

As a child, Lee Kuan Yew spoke Malay, English, and Cantonese, in his home and at school. Most of his education was in English and his Malay was always good because he had many Malay friends. When he became a politician, when he was about thirty years old, he realized that if he was to have direct contact with the majority of the young men in Singapore he must learn, also, to speak Mandarin.

At the time he was doing legal work, advising more than a hundred different trade unions, and was also the secretary-general of a busy political party. He applied himself to the task of learning Mandarin, with a teacher and with the aid of modern mechanical means. He persisted. The Chinese language is tonal: òne word may have four different tones—and the meaning of each can differ considerably. Pronounce a word one way and it means honourable; pronouce the same word differently and it means evil. Bursts of laughter sometimes greeted Lee Kuan Yew during his Mandarin speeches, at the beginning; but there were cheers too, for his doggedness, his determination to master this language. Today he speaks it well. Later, Lee decided to learn Hokkien so that he could speak direct to the older people, and to labourers. This was another agony of application.

To remain proficient in any language one must speak it constantly. This is especially true of the Chinese language. That is why Lee takes with him when he travels abroad someone with whom he can converse daily in Mandarin and Hokkien. Some Prime Ministers travel with their doctors, or their valet. Lee Kuan Yew takes a Chinese conversationalist. In his brief-case, always handy, Lee carries quotations in Chinese. Most speeches in Chinese are rounded off by appropriate quotations from the classics: listeners enjoy them, and a speaker's wisdom and humour, his humility (upon which the Chinese place great store) are often judged by their apt use. A good speaker, therefore, has many quotations in his repertoire ready for instant employment when occasion demands. In the aircraft, on the train, in the ship, Lee may suddenly pull out a page of Chinese characters and check his pronunciation with a Mandarin-speaking official. He looks upon this as another of life's many chores.

Lee's ability to make a speech in Malay and then repeat it in two Chinese dialects and English is accepted nowadays as being part of Lee Kuan Yew, as being something he has learnt to do rather well. Not all his friends realize the constant hard work needed to remain proficient in these languages. What does all this exercise, this memory-probing, do to a man's thinking processes?

Dr Klaus Mehnert, the German political scientist, dealt with the language question in his book *Peking and Moscow*. He compared the different demands made by language on the mental powers of Chinese and Westerners. He said the Chinese requires "thousands of hours (almost his whole lifetime if he is an intellectual or professional) just to become and remain proficient in reading and writing. On the one hand this learning process develops to an astonishing degree his memory, his visual powers of absorption for even minute details and his aesthetic sense, but on the other hand it does not encourage the faculty for logical, analytical thought which has become such a firm tradition in the West since Greek and Roman times."

Lee Kuan Yew is possessed of the industry, the endurance and the patience of a Chinese. He has profound respect, which every Chinese has, for education and higher learning. He is a Chinese aesthete. This is what makes him critical of American and Australian cultures. Both to him appear rough, unpolished, crude, lacking in finesse and depth. At the same time Lee is a logical thinker, and his talent for continuous analysis of a developing political situation is acknowledged wherever he speaks—at a Commonwealth Prime Ministers' Conference, a university, or a political rally. His thinking is naturally logical and analytical, and this is probaby because of his aptitude for Western learning. His weakness is that he believes everyone else uses the same mental processes which he employs, even when they are seized with emotional issues like race and religion. His critics say say that this inability to realize that there are times when logical analytical argument can be the worse possible weapon to use is among his lesser defects. To them, his inability to make concessions in advance to the possibility of passionate illogicality is a fault which can be attributed to the Chinese in him, that part of his subconscious, his endurance and his prodigious memory, which insists that reason (or anything else) must be pursued to a conclusion. On occasions, therefore, Lee Kuan Yew finds himself isolated, mentally playing chess, as it were, with someone playing draughts, or billiards, or with someone just screaming his head off. Purely Western thought would probably seek compromise. Lee's reluctance to bend like the bamboo in the wind, a Chinese trait, could be a manifestation of an inner contradiction which must be inherent in the make-up of any person subjected to the impact of two contrasting civilizations and cultures, one of which produces a logical analytical mind, the other endurance and patience: there must be times when they overlap. In addition to the contradictions thrown up by English learning, absorbed by a Chinese of unusual intelligence, Lee Kuan Yew also came into close contact with Malay culture, especially as a youth, and this must also have had some effect upon his thinking.

V

Dennis Bloodworth, writing about "face" in his book *The Chinese Looking Glass* explains that honour is an affair of conscience and reality. "A loss of honour is a blemish on the skin, while a loss of face is a smudge on the make-up ... A Chinese may perform an honourable action, not because it is dictated by his sense of honour, but because it will give him face. Conversely, when a man is sued for a discreditable action it is his loss of face not his guilt that worries his family. A gentleman, however, thinks not only of his own face, but of the face of others. He does not crush an opponent in public argument leaving him with nothing to say and looking very much of a fool. He is content to let the man know that he could do this if he chose."

Many Chinese in Singapore decided that Lee Kuan Yew was more of a European than a Chinese when he ruthlessly smashed a political opponent, the former Mayor of Singapore, Ong Eng Guan. Formerly a member of the PAP, and a Cabinet Minister, Ong foolishly accused Lee of nepotism. Lee set up a commission of inquiry headed by a judge and personally took part in the proceedings. He had Ong thoroughly exposed, politically and socially. He dragged out Ong's private life, accused him of bigamy to prove that Ong was a man of no principles and a liar. The commission branded Ong Eng Guan as a man not to be believed. "Chinese never do this sort of thing," an elderly Chinese friend told me. "This is the result of Lee's education. He is not behaving like a Chinese."

Ong's vague charges against Lee were dismissed by the commission as being reckless and without substance. There was not a word of truth in them. Lee's face was unblemished, Ong's, according to tradition, heavily smeared. Yet when Ong Eng Guan and Lee Kuan Yew's candidate met in a by-election shortly afterwards, Lee's man was defeated and Ong Eng Guan won the day. The election was not fought on that issue, but what the result did prove was that the mass of the Chinese voters in Ong's old constituency were not prepared to desert Ong just because he had got involved in what they considered to be a petty quarrel with the Prime Minister over an unimportant matter like nepotism. Bloodworth says a Chinese feels entitled to believe that his most precious possession is a sense of shame. But he has no sense of sin, for a sense of sin, the Chinese will say, is the product of laws. And Chinese have as little regard for man-made laws as they have for god-made morality. "Life is therefore lived at two layers, and for the Chinese the one that counts is the one underneath."

Lee is a materialist, an empiricist at times. He is not a religious man. He believes there are sound practical reasons why man must concern himself with the present and the foreseeable future If there is a hereafter, it will, no doubt, create problems of its own, but they will be dealt with when the time arrives. Until then, this world provides enough problems to merit the full and undivided attention of the average man, if the lot of the poor is to be made bearable. This is not to say that Lee Kuan Yew opposes religion, resists it, or does not have respect for those believing in religion: he takes the attitude that a man makes peace with himself, and that is his business and nobody else's. For the time being at any rate Lee is much more concerned with the task of wrestling with present-day difficulties, most of which are man-made and which, he believes, can also be unmade by man, than he is with celestial affairs.

Yet, materialist and pragmatist though he may be, Lee is prepared to believe that it is not always wise to seek a rationalization of everything.

As Victor Purcell explained in *The Chinese in Modern Malaya*, the Chinese have always been regarded as the most tolerant (or eclectic) of people in the matter of religion. "They have no scruples like Mohammedans or Jews: they have no caste system like the Hindus, no special restrictions about entry to their temples. Many of them adhere simultaneously to the tenets of Buddhism and Taoism. Confucianism is also professed by a cultivated minority and its principles form the basis of Chinese custom... The truth is that the majority of Malayan Chinese seem to be able to do without what is understood

614

Lee Kuan Yew in 1957

Lee golfs regularly. There is a private course in the grounds of the Istana, where he has his official residence.

Jim Callaghan, who became British Minister for Home Affairs with the Labour Government, with Lee in Singapore in 1950

Lecturing in America

At the grave of Dag Hammersksjold

Taking a constitutional in London with Mrs Lee and son, Lee Hsien Loong

Lee Kuan Yew in 1970

In London, Lee always stayed at the same hotel

Youthful lawyer

The mob orator

Lee, the party man, meets supporters

in the West as religion, and are satisfied with moral and social codes instead."

Purcell in 1956 predicted that left to themselves the several communities in Malaya and Singapore would evolve a common Malayan nationality. "If this happens the Malayan Chinese will continue to be an indispensable element in Malaysian society without losing the precious culture they have inherited from their ancestors of the Middle Kingdom. Their critics would do well to remember that without the Chinese Southeast Asia could never have been modernized and developed in the way it has been and that, moreover, they are in the region to stay."

Lee Kuan Yew has often been looked upon as a man with Christian virtues, in that he, an idealist, subscribes to the rule of law and order, despises corruption, believes in collective and mutual help, and will not compromise on what he considers is a basic principle affecting integrity. Lee is not a Christian and can separate virtues and morals from religion. Overseas Chinese, as a rule, still have a tendency to pay lip-service to the virtues while living an essentially practical life which, they say, demands a great deal of accommodation. Lee Kuan Yew is not prepared to accommodate and he will insist instead upon positive and conscious effort to "do things the right way", not the easy way. And if the right way means more work, the greater the reward of satisfaction.

That attitude does nothing to interfere with Lee's Chinese characteristic of asking, on behalf of his party, or the state, but never himself: "What is there in it for me?" Lee may be an idealist: but he is also a realist who understands power. He is not a do-gooder so much as an ardent reformist, and his aim in reform is to enable the individual to make the most of his talents and ability, to lead a full life according to circumstances. In that Lee could be a Confucian.

The Chinese in Singapore, seeking to arrange their future, go to the temple, buy Heavenly money and joss sticks, and pray to the appropriate gods; or, not knowing the religion, or even the language in which the services are conducted, and not caring, buy a candle and follow the crowd into a Christian church, and wish. This is happening all the time, for the Chinese are great gamblers and god-worshippers. Lee Kuan Yew's religion is his belief in the goodness of man and the need to plan and work hard.

VI

A real Chinese, in China, Bloodworth says, "has no tradition of alliances, for none could be the equal ally of the Middle Kingdom, and they have no outside loyalties for it has been the business of others to be loyal to them and not vice versa. China does not believe in international friendship for she knows that the only emotion shared between states is diplomatic cupboard love. She will join international groups, or fronts only when the profit for Peking is clearly marked on the tag, and she tolerates the companionship of neutrals and non-communists only as long as they accept her paternalistic leadership." Measured against this yardstick, how much of Lee Kuan Yew is a real Chinese, and how much the Western-trained lawyer? Is it worthwhile trying to make a useful comparison between Lee Kuan Yew, Prime Minister of Asia's tiniest state, and a Chinese born in the most populous nation on earth?

Lee does sometimes think like a Chinese. He believes in natural self-interest: Lee is not an altruist. He subscribes to the theory that "the only emotion shared between states is diplomatic cupboard love". This was the principle which guided his decision to invite friendship and trade treaties with the Soviet Union and Eastern Europe. Both China and Singapore understand why no steps are taken by either to formalize relations between them; there is nothing to be gained. On the contrary, any move to formalize relations could be fraught with difficulties. In no other independent state in Asia outside China, is there a tall, solid, Bank of China, complete with lions at the entrance except in Singapore and nowhere else in Asia has China such a vast market for China-made consumer goods as she has in Singapore.

What role Singapore is to play in the future, in world or Southeast Asian affairs, nobody in 1968 can foretell. The British have already given notice that they intend to reduce their military expenditure, and to withdraw their troops from Singapore and Malaysia by 1971. This may have considerable repercussion throughout the entire region. Instability in Malaysia would definitely affect Singapore, especially if this was brought about by communal strife.

What happens eventually in China could also have a considerable impact upon Southeast Asia as a whole. Professor FitzGerald, in his book, *The Third China*, predicted that if Singapore was "abandoned by the British and cast out by Malaya, its one hope and only refuge would be the protection of China. It was from these hard facts that the concept of Malaysia was born." Professor FitzGerald wrote this before Singapore was separated from Malaysia on 9 August, 1965. Malaya did cast out Singapore, and some thought this would mean the collapse of the People's Action Party and a take-over of the State by Chinese like Tan Siew Sin, in whom the Malay leaders have faith because they behave as overseas Chinese are expected by the Malays to behave. Others thought Singapore would crumble economically, that labour trouble would create chaos, and that Lee Kuan Yew would be overthrown by the communists.

Nothing of the sort happened. Not for a moment did Lee Kuan Yew and his colleagues lose their nerve, or their complete control of the situation. Neither did they look towards China. "We are not land-locked," observed Lee calmly. "We are a centre of great communications: the cross-roads between the northern and southern hemispheres, between the East and the West ... all centres of great traffic become centres of great cultures, learning and civilization. And it is this factor which we must exploit to our utmost." That is the role Lee Kuan Yew wants for Singapore: that of a centre for neutrality. He wants Singapore to be an Asian Geneva; not a refuge for persecuted overseas Chinese from the rest of Southeast Asia; not a protectorate of China, or of any foreign state; but an independent and neutral nation where all nations can meet. As Professor FitzGerald says, one of the great gifts of the Chinese is that of devising compromise. "It is inherent in a nation of bargainers, and particularly well developed in communities of merchants and businessmen."

Critics may suggest that Lee betrayed no evidence that he possessed this Chinese gift of compromise in his dealings with Tunku Abdul Rahman over Malaysia, and they would be right: Lee Kuan Yew is unable to compromise with basic principle or with a logical, inevitable conclusion. He believed multiracialism fundamental for the survival of Malaysia, and he was convinced that sooner or later anything other than multiracialism must end in racial conflict. On these matters he was not prepared to compromise. And Singapore and Malaysia in consequence separated. But that does not preclude Singapore as a neutralist republic from exercising the great Chinese gift of devising compromises, and of bargaining, especially bargaining, in wider fields in Southeast Asia.

Right from the beginning in 1949, the People's Republic of China has been indifferent, even contemptuous, of outside opinion. "The Chinese people," remarked Professor C. P. FitzGerald, in *Pacific Affairs* in 1963, "are among the most courteous in the world, but this often conceals the fact that they are also the most arrogant." FitzGerald said that for many years weakness imposed a restraint upon the expression of this characteristic. It nonetheless remained and was easily discerned. Foreigners were never popular, foreign countries were rarely esteemed. The conviction that China was the true and only centre of civilization, correct enough in the context of ancient times, remained unshaken in an age when it was no longer appropriate.

Most overseas Chinese are proud of being Chinese, but outside China they have no political cohesion: the China's-fifth-column-in-Southeast-Asia theory just does not hold up. "The overseas Chinese have become isolated communities, each seeking its own way out of the common dilemma," as Professor Wang Gungwu put it (*A Short History Of The Nanyang Chinese*, 1959). In the various nation-states of Southeast Asia they must assimilate, or live as aliens and return eventually to

617

China. Singapore is unlike any other state in that the Chinese are the largest of the communities. Here there is no difficulty over assimilation: Lee Kuan Yew's task is to persuade the Chinese (about eighty per cent were born in Singapore) to retain their pride in China, and to cherish the culture and the language, while embracing the many Western values and attributes in order that they may eventually emerge as multiracialists, as Singaporeans. Through education and environment Lee Kuan Yew is trying to make a new Chinese: a person capable of retaining all that is good in his remarkable past, but capable also of using modern technology, and of understanding that the centre of the world is not really in China.

Lee Kuan Yew's task would be easier if the large Chinese community in Singapore lived with other communities of similar size, for then multiracialism would be a practical necessity as well as an exercise in intellectualism. An advantage which tends to balance that drawback is Lee Kuan Yew's policy of an open society and an open door, and his line of neutralism and internationalism, his emphasis on a Singaporean, rather than a Chinese, outlook and attitude, in his approach to world affairs and to regional matters. In this Lee is helped enormously by Singapore's geography. Unlike China, which keeps the foreigner out, Singapore, on the cross-roads of East and West, welcomes the traveller, is prepared to do business with him, to listen to his arguments and to discuss, with polite interest, matters of moment concerning politics, economics, or anything else. What is good and useful from these foreign contacts Singaporeans will absorb. To survive as a separate entity, to resist being swallowed up by larger fish swimming in the areas, Lee Kuan Yew says Singapore must have a wide circle of friends and no enemies, and must be prepared to learn from anyone to achieve rapid progress.

In this, Lee has abandoned the traditional conservative attitude of his forefathers, convinced as they were that China was the centre of civilization. This is something which Mao Tse-tung refuses to do. There is, however, a further instance of Lee's repudiation of fundamental Chineseism which he does share with Mao Tse-tung, and that is the elevation of the social status of the soldier. Throughout China's long history, until the coming of the Red Army, the Chinese soldier was a person of no account. Mao changed that in the largest nation in Asia, and so has Lee Kuan Yew in the tiniest: this Mao and Lee have in common. The citizen soldier and the professional soldier now has an honoured place in society. Is it Chinese arrogance, or Western arrogance, which makes Lee Kuan Yew say defiantly, and seriously, that one Singaporean must be worth ten other Asians? Whatever it is, Lee is determined that Singapore will be a very prickly and unpleasant morsel should any greedy fish in the neighbourhood be tempted to try to swallow it.

VII

What sort of a man is Lee Kuan Yew when he is not the leader, when he is not a politician? How does he behave at home, with his family, with his friends? Is he as unsmiling, as intense, as strict, as he looks and sounds when he is "on duty"? Does he ever really relax?

There is only one Lee Kuan Yew. He does relax, he does smile and he can laugh as easily as the other man. But probably not as often because he does not find a great deal to laugh about. He relaxes almost exclusively with his family; from his political duties that is, not as head of the house. Family duties he carries out as seriously and as intensely as his other obligations. It is not in the man to do anything important lightheartedly. Besides, Lee places great store upon the family, as do most people of Chinese origin. To Lee the family is the unit which builds the nation, and upon which the nation is built. The family is where the child's character is formed, where education begins and is nurtured, where the child's values and judgments are created. Lee's family is a constant reminder to him of the practical purpose, the objective, of his political work.

Thus, when a group of medical students raided the women's hostel, stole the girls' underwear and wrote "dirty words" on the wall, Lee reacted angrily as a father as much as the Prime Minister. As the Prime Minister he told them that the university student owes it to the community (which spends thousands of dollars of public money on him each year), to be a decent, patriotic, hard-working, effective individual and not a rake and a flop. As a father he added: "And they thought it was funny. I did not think it was funny. If my son had been involved I would have been ashamed. And had my daugher lived in the hostel where these things happened I would have been very angry indeed." Ragging is now prohibited in the colleges and universities. Civil servants have been told to get their hair cut. Youths wearing long hair are not employed as caddies at the golf courses where Lee swings his clubs.

This is all part of Lee's determination that Singapore will not become one of the "so-called developing countries", as he describes them, "that every year sees further deterioration, officials becoming more corrupt, streets getting dirtier, flies more plentiful . . . And every anniversary is another sad remembrance of the days that used to be when things were better."

People had to make the effort, all the time. They had to maintain standards, improve them. There could be no slackening in any developing country. There would be none in Singapore.

On another occasion, calling upon the people to make Singapore the cleanest and greenest garden city anywhere, Lee said: "In other parts of the world they say: 'Let us be happy'. But happiness is a state of mind. You can generate it by pills: there are the hippies. I want a healthy and sound community, with happiness as the by-product of a satisfying life — a life of achievement and fulfilment."

He is constantly hammering this theme. His critics say this indicates his insecurity, a charge Lee will brush aside, impatiently. He is sure he is right. "If you slacken," he warns, "if you give up, then the drains will clog up, traffic will snarl up, there will be flies, plague and pestilence..." Lee has travelled extensively in Asia, and elsewhere. He knows what he is talking about. "This," he says, "is what is required of this community: all the time that push, that thrust, to counter the natural sluggishness which this climate tends to build into our physical system, and, all that while, we must have an awareness of the realities of life. We can build the industries. We have what sociologists call a highly 'achievement-oriented' type of society. We are a people with a compulsion to succeed."

In his 1968 May Day Message, Lee reminded them that they were "a young community with no deep social or class divisions. Whether coolie or millionaire, our children go to the same schools, with equal opportunities for advancement to higher education, to leadership roles. Rewards correspond to merit and performance. We must keep it that way, and prevent the divisive influences of class hatred and class exploitation."

Later, in Parliament, he again declared that Singaporeans "are a hard-headed people. If we maintain group discipline, if everyone contributes his fullest share of physical and intellectual effort to the fulfilment of our plans, we shall not fail. We can, and we shall, build up an adequate defence force before 1972. We can counter recession, expand our economy, train and educate the artisans, technicians and the technocrats for our growing industrial and servicing sectors... With imaginative and intelligent leadership and stiff standards of honest and just administration, we can make maximum use of our not slender resources... We shall have a prosperous, thriving, multiracial Singapore. And nothing is more infectious than success. In the longer run, Singapore will be the light that radiates hope throughout the region for similar successes of other multiracial communities not unlike us. By example and precept, our success will influence the formulae others are seeking to transform old-fashioned communities into modern, industrialized and efficient societies... The future belongs to the most adaptable, the most intelligent and the best organized. We can be counted amongst them."

Is this Lee Kuan Yew the Chinese speaking? Or is it Lee, the Singaporean of Chinese ethnic origin? "We look Chinese," Lee told Mrs Indira Gandhi, the Indian Prime Minister, when she came to Singapore on a state visit in 1968. "We speak Chinese. But if a man from China speaks to a Singapore Chinese he will discover that the Singaporean is already a distinct and different type."

What of the future? "Living in Singapore, one gateway opening into the Pacific and the other into the Indian Ocean, we are deeply conscious," he said in a speech early in 1968, "of the vastly changed balance of world forces." This was underlined by the decision of the British to accelerate the withdrawal of her forces in Asia. "In the next hundred years we shall have to live with the fact that two, probably three, super-powers (America, China and Russia put in alphabetical order and not in order of influence), will contend to so order the political and economic life in the region to the maximum national advantage of each super-power." The eventual fate of South and Southeast Asia will be more dependent upon their resultant policy decisions than on the decisions of the dozen or so governments in the region.

Lee Kuan Yew may be Prime Minister of Asia's smallest state for another decade. This should be sufficient time to test his theory that in spite of, or perhaps because of, the interests of the probably three super-powers in the region, development in Asia is possible with democracy: that it is not necessary or inevitable for developing countries to follow China's ideological example to achieve success.

Lee the humane realist, the pragmatist with the high ideals, will persist with his interpretation of "all the socialism that is practical in present circumstances" which means the encouragement of enlightened capitalism, including state participation in joint ventures with foreign investors, a relentless opposition to unfair treatment of workers, and the expansion of welfare services (including housing, education and medical care) commensurate with the wealth of the Republic.

And if this succeeds, if Lee Kuan Yew can persuade workers and employers to work in close sensible co-operation with the state for their mutual benefit, and if Singapore's status as Asia's great industrialized entrepot is maintained, then Lee, while still in his fifties, will have set an example for all developing states, in Asia and elsewhere. He will have proved that it is possible within twenty years to create a nation, and develop a nation, with democracy.

And that is something nobody yet has done.

Index

Abdullah bin Abdul Kadir, 495
Abisheganadan, Felix, 279
Abortion Bill, 546
Academic freedom, 350, 561
Advocates and Solicitors Society, 366
Age, The, 521
Al-Iman, 81
Albar, Syed Jaafar, 21, 80, 195, 201,
    231, 239, 242, 258, 265, 271, 280,
    282, 283, 287, 288; apologises to Lee
    in court, 386
Alexandra, Princess, 480
Alliance Party and Government, 21, 27,
    50, 68, 77, 83, 87, 199, 201, 236,
    258, 268, 272, 288
Anson by-election, 137
Asahi Shimbun, 608
ASEAN (Association of Southeast Asian
    Nations), 357, 389, 407
Asia Magazine, 78, 83, 85
Asian Revolution, 513
Asian Seminar on Urban Community
    Development, 163
Asian Socialist Conference (Rangoon),
    260
Asian Socialist Leaders' Conference
    (Bombay), 260
Attlee, Clement, 27, 184, 217
Australia, 449, 520, 522
Australian Financial Review, 523
Ayub Khan, 18
Azahari, Sheik, 163

Baldwin, James, 595

Bandung Conference (1956), 55, 206,
    253
Barisan Sosialis, 16, 19, 26, 66, 98, 130,
    146, 147, 153, 154, 159, 163, 178,
    179, 187, 188, 207, 271, 272, 295,
    297, 301, 349, 356, 379, 425, 433,
    603
Barker, E.W., 523
BBC, 68, 157, 338
Bennett, R.G., 494
Berita Harian, 269
Bloodworth, Dennis, 243, 244, 292,
    295, 604, 605, 607, 608, 613
Boy Scouts, 224
Brandt, Willy, 214
Britain, long-term relationship with Sin-
    gapore, 361
British Labour Party Conference (1967),
    391
British withdrawal, 356, 379, 383, 414,
    418, 451
Brunei revolt, 163, 169
Bulletin, The, 268, 274, 279, 288
Bunche, Ralph, 595
Burma, 27

Cairo, 584
Cambodia, 313, 327, 358, 410
Campos, 40
Canada, 464, 594
Canberra Defence Talks, 521
Canning, Earl of, 65
Canterbury University (New Zealand),
    251

623

Cantwell, John, 43, 53
Chan Chiaw Thor, 125
Changi Gaol, 27
China, 86, 103, 111, 182, 220, 247, 295, 310, 322, 369; "not a yellow peril", 400, 404, 407, 516, 595
Chinese chauvinism, 106
Chinese language, 56, 103, 304
Chinese Looking Glass, The, 604, 607, 613
Chinese in Modern Malaya, The, 603, 614
Chinese in Southeast Asia, 307
Chinese in Southeast Asia, The, 602, 608
Chou En-lai, 182, 206
Christian Brothers Old Boys Association, 563
Christians in Asia, 61
Chua Jim Neo, 4
Chua Kim Teng, 40
Churchill College, University of Cambridge, 497
Clifford, Clark, 510
Columbia University, New York, 476
Commonwealth, 184, 252, 375, 389
Commonwealth Prime Ministers Conference, 302, 337
Commonwealth Prime Ministers Conference (first in Asia), 591
Commonwealth Correspondents Association, 281
Communist cadres and cells, 360
Confucius, 607
Congregation of Buddhists from Asia, 62
Congress Party, Indian, 30, 32
Cook, Arthur, 292
Coomaraswamy, Punch, 433
Cooper, Derek, 68
Croll, Richard, 288

Daily Express, The, 288
Daily Telegraph, The, 507
Dar-es-Salaam, 576
Dillingham Lecture, 587
Dinesh Singh, Sri, 290
Djamour, Dr Judith, 74
Dozier, Thomas A., 409

Eden Hall, 141
Elitism, 234
Emery, Fred, 287, 479
Employment Bill (1968), 451
Encyclopedia of the Social Sciences, 351
Ends and Means of Malayan Socialism, The, 97
English language, 54, 102, 364
Enright, Professor D.N., 126
Eusoff College, University of Singapore, 463
Evening Standard, 337

Far East American Council, 400
Far Eastern Economic Review, 408
Firecrackers, 561
FitzGerald, Professor C.P., 609, 616, 617
Fitzwilliam College, University of Cambridge, 508
Five-Power Defence Arrangement, 6, 520
Fong Swee Guan, 141, 144, 169
Foreign Correspondents Association, 104, 156
Franck, Professor Wolfgang, 345, 599
Freedman, Dr Maurice, 73
Freidin, Seymour, 42
Friedrich, Ebert Stiftung, 368

Gabriel Silver Memorial Lecture, 476
Galbraith, Ambassador F.J., 405
Gandhi, Mrs Indira, 334, 447, 578
Gasson Bill (Reuters), 192
Gaulle, President de, 580
Germany, 429
Ghazali, Inche Mohamad, 258
Girton, 27
Goh Keng Swee, Dr, 28, 85, 152, 180, 285, 288, 465, 605
Goode, Sir William, 95
Gorton, John, 449, 525
Govind Singh, 330th birthday of Guru, 64

Hakkas, 3, 609
Hammarskjold, Dag, 319, 492
Hansard, 434, 498
Harvard University, 417
Head, Lord, 288
Heath, Edward, 564
Herndon, Ray, 478
Hindustan Times Weekly, 335
Ho Chi Minh, 216
Hodder, B.W., 68, 88
Hoffman, R.C., 386
Holt, Harold, 358
Hong Kong, 426, 465
Hong Kong Foreign Correspondents Club, 557
Hong Kong University, 552
Hong Lim by-elections, 134, 137
Honolulu Advertiser, 401
Hood, Stuart, 339
House of Commons, 26

Ibrahim, Rev. Adam, 74
Ideological struggle, Soviet Union and China, 38
Independence of Malaya Party, 79
India, 27, 86, 206, 317, 370, 447, 576
Indo-China, 105
Indonesia, 30, 33, 86, 96, 111, 119, 196,

252, 295, 301, 312, 314, 318, 407
Indonesian Communist Party (PKI), 153, 154, 157, 197, 252, 408
Indonesia's Confrontation, 68, 166, 189, 208, 221, 269, 293, 322, 323, 392
Institute of International Affairs (Melbourne), 256
Internal Security Council, 142, 168
International Labour Organization, 352
Ishak, Rahim, 76-8, 87
Ismail, Dato (later Tun) Dr, 268
Israel, 375

Japan and Japanese: 28, 52, 189, 306, 375; "blood debt" of, 179; and Lee's lunch with Federation of Economic Organizations, 468; gesture of contribution, 173; Lee unveils memorial, 363; occupation of Singapore, 7, 27, 102, 255; Lee's official visit to J., 464; recovery of, 429; Sato's visit to Singapore, 386; wartime massacre of, 172
Jodidi Lecture, 470
Johnson, President Lyndon, 45, 410 476
Josey, Alex: and article in *The Bulletin*, 268; banished from Malaysia, 272
Jurong, satellite town, 571
Jurong Shipyard Ltd, 551
Jury system, Lee's arguments on, 518

Kaunda, President Kenneth, 489
Kennedy, President John, 4
Kennedy, Robert, 45
Kennedy School of Government, University of Harvard, 465
Killen, Patrick, 292
Kim Il-Sung, 217
Khrushchev, 60, 216
Kwa Geok Choo, 5

Leadership, 57
Lee Bok Boon, 39
Lee Chin Koon, 4
Lee Hoon Leong, 39
Lee Hsien Loong, 5
Lee Khoon Choy, 272, 562
Lee Kuan Yew: ABC radio talk (1964) 255; on abortion and inherited intelligence, 546; and academic freedom, 127, 349; in seventeen African states, 194; and Afro-Asian solidarity, 253, 327, 368; Tan Sri Syed Jaafar Albar apologises to, 243; personal ambitions of, 43; and America in Asia, 47; "do enough Americans believe?", 397; and America's role in Asia, 389; and expectation of arrest, 271; and collective security system in Asia, 585; "had I been born a girl in Asia", 463; presides over first Asian Commonwealth Conference (1970), 591; and the Asian Revolution, 513; and future of non-Communist Asian states, 409; and young Asian leaders, 219; and relations with Australia, 520; and Australians, 17; "if I were in authority indefinitely", 70; and Barisan Sosialis formation, 16; in Belgrade, 156; basic beliefs of, 20; fortieth birthday (Malaysia Day) of, 20; born, 3; and long-term relationship between Britain and Singapore, 361; and British links with the Commonwealth, 506; a critic of British dock workers, 493; L.'s debt to British Labour Party, 391; and "the British plot", 140; in Cambodia, 410; at Cambridge, 1, 2, 17, 25-7, 41, 508; and capitalism, 319; and CBC television interview with President Kaunda and Pierre Trudeau, 489; Chatham House speech, 69; children of, 5; "had I been born in China", 310; "I am not a Chinaman", 601; "China not a yellow peril", 400; rebuffs Chinese Chamber of Commerce, 345; accused of Chinese chauvinism, 201; and Chinese Press, 103; L.'s letter to Chou En-lai, 182; and civil service, 99; first commissioned officers, 375; at Commonwealth Prime Ministers Conference (1962), 162; at Commonwealth Prime Ministers Conference (1966), 302, 324, 483; at Commonwealth Prime Ministers Conference (1969), 482; dangers of communalism, 104; on communal strife, 232; and communism, 28; and communist support, 14; and monolithic communist world, 327, 368; made Companion of Honour, 568; at University of Dar-es-Salaam (1970), 577; "defending ourselves?", 516; L.'s definition of democratic, 68; and democracy, 4; on tasks of democratic socialist party, 223; on role of developing countries in world politics, 368; and dilemmas, 577; Dillingham Lecture (1970), 587; and dock workers, 428; in Eastern Europe, 326; and human factors in economic development, 542; on education, 110, 535; early education of, 40; and purpose and direction of education, 377; and elitism, 234; and Emergency Regulations, 108; at Employers Federation, 440; and the Employment Bill (1968), 455; and the English-educated, 96, 100; and the English language, 54; "I am not an Englishman", 364;

"to be educated to become the equal of any Englishman", 39; and Professor Enright, 127; family association with Singapore of, 39; family name of, 599; as a father, 619; made honorary Fellow of Fitzwilliam College, 508; visit to France cancelled, 497; future of, 10, 391; and Mrs Gandhi's official visit, 447; and general election, 419; and general election victory (1963), 181; and golf, 5, 36; and John Gorton's official visit, 449; grandfather of, 39; maternal grandfather of, 40; great grandfather of, 39; habits of, 4, 5, 36; a Hakka, 3, 23; at Harvard, 401; in Hawaii, 402; and election of Mr Edward Heath, 564; and sense of history, 112; and Harold Holt, 358; and Hong Kong, 465; conferred with Hong Kong University degree, 552; and first year of independence, 332; and proclamation of independence, 284; in India (1966), 334; in Indonesia, 116,119; and Indonesian fears, 407; and Indonesia's Confrontation, 190, 323; and international relations, 341; and Israeli military instructors, 477; at banquet for Crown Prince of Japan, 558; and Japanese blood debt, 363; escape from Japanese of, 180; and Japanese Occupation, 27, 35,40,41; and Japanese wartime atrocities, 172, 180; L.-Johnson joint statement, 398; and President Johnson, 396, 402; and Justinian Law, 411; letter to President Kaunda, 486; and President Kennedy, 4; and Robert Kennedy, 45; addresses large crowd in Kuala Lumpur, 202; in Kuala Lumpur (1959), 96; and law, 1, 38, 519; and the rule of law, 366; a brilliant lawyer, 37; and leadership, 339; and continuing leadership, 57; and patterns of leadership, 183, 535; a legal adviser to 100 unions, 41; and why Lim Chin Siong was arrested, 168; in London School of Economics, 41; and murder of Patrice Lumumba, 131; at Lusaka (1970), 580; and Harold MacMillan, 11, 25; at the Malayan Forum, 28; on Malay chauvinism, 208; signs Malaysia Agreement, 166; on Malaysia being inevitable, 173; L.'s disappointment with Malaysian budget, 226; fought for Malaysia, 9, 149; and future relations with Malaysia, 517; and Malaysia general election (1964), 199; and motion for merger and Malaysia, 177; L.'s first speech to Malaysian Parliament, 191; at Malaysian Solidarity Convention, 267; and Malaysian troops in Singapore, 304; and turning point in Malaysia, 235; and Maphilindo, 197; married, 5; a materialist, 614; and Sir Robert Menzies, 10; visit to Moscow, 162; and multilingualism, 124; and multiracialism, 150, 307; with President Nasser (1970), 584; National Day speech (1967), 378; and National Service Bill, 364; at National Serviceman Community dinner (1967), 383; and nation building, 311, 359; on death of Nehru, 205; "neighbours not your best friends", 341; New Year Message (1962), 153; New Year Message (1968), 414; New Year Message (1970), 500; in New Zealand and Australia, 230, 245; "were I a New Zealander", 246; and President Nixon, 11; criticizes Vice-President Nguyen Cao Ky, 509; and NTUC, 428; and Ong Eng Guan, 15, 26, 118, 132; lunch with overseas writers (USA), 399; and Pacific Basin, 406; and parliamentary democracy, 202; on need for Parliamentary opposition, 434; no paternalist, 607; personality: aggressive – 24, "agile, charming and tough" – 339, "an owl" – 393; and political prisoners, 38; "my political views", 120; why he entered politics, 27; "arbiter of the power-interests", 250; and population control, 171; became Prime Minister, 95; as first Prime Minister of Singapore, 8; "the real and abiding problem", 345; pushed into drain, 23; on racial harmony, Chinese and Malays, 49; and Raffles College, 27, 40, 510; "a realist, a materialist", 4, 35; and regional associations, 47; and regional economic co-operation, 444; and religion, 62, 64; and religious tolerance, 107; offers resignation (1961), 129, 139; "patient revolutionary", 48; and Vietcong organization in Rhodesia, 338; and restriction of rights, 125; and riots, 209, 213; at Rotary Conference (1966), 308; on Russian influence in Southeast Asia, 586; and sale of arms to South Africa, 571; talk over Radio Sarawak, 148; and E. Sato, 386; and scouts, 233; and future of Singapore, 426, 496; at 150th anniversary of Singapore banquet, 530; and Singapore's 150th anniversary, 481, 495; opens Science Tower, University of Singapore, 323; socialism of, 34, 317; a socialist, 5; and socialism in Asia, 53, 261, 263; and implementation of socialism, 98; at Asian Socialist Leaders Conference (Bombay) 260; at Socialist Conference (1966), 314; at Socialist International 213, 217; at Socialist International

(1967), 394; L.'s belief in open society, 228; plea for "more gracious living", 536; on ideal society, 49; and "lean and rugged society", 372; "the nature of our society", 540; and long-term future of Southeast Asia, 475; in the Soviet Union (1970), 584; as student in England, 100; and danger of "student aberrations", 527; and student leadership, 431; and Dr Subandrio, 292; at Tamil Muslim Union, 331; and Tanjong Pagar PAP branch sixteenth anniversary, 566; and Tan Siew Sin, 177; and teacher-pupil relationship, 346; historic speech of 3 December 1959, 112; willing to serve under Dr Toh, 288; at Tokyo (1968), 466; and trade unions, 541; Tunku's accusation of, 85; and Tunku's sixtieth birthday, 22, 170; and United Nations Committee on Colonialism, 151, 159; and rumours about L. becoming Secretary-general of UN, 507; and universities, 304; accuses *Utusan Melayu*, 289; adviser to *Utusan Melayu*, 82; and changing values in a shrinking world, 325; and Vietnam, 45, 46, 246, 263, 294, 405, 510, 513; visit to Britain, Switzerland and USA (1967), 386; visit to Burma, India, UAR and Yugoslavia, 151; visit to Ceylon, India, Tanzania, Zambia, UAR, Soviet Union, France, West Germany, Britain, USA, Japan and Hong Kong, 544; in Washington meets President Nixon, 508; weight, height, diet of, 3; and Harold Wilson, 10, 337, 340; and worker-employer relations, 51, 355; admiration for hard work, 310; and youth, 403; tribute to President Yusof, 590
Lee Siew Choh, Dr, 129, 146, 159
Lee Wei Yew, 5
Leningrad, 585
Lewis, Sir Arthur, 595
Life, 409
Lim Chin Joo, 38
Lim Chin Siong, 38, 97, 124, 125, 129, 137, 139, 144, 166, 295
Lim Kim San, 288
Lim Lam San, 40
Lim Swee Aun, Dr, 232
Lim Tay Boh, 40, 41
Lim Yew Hock, 15, 24, 25, 93, 95, 133, 135, 140
Lipski, Sam, 288
London School of Economics, 41
Lumumba, Patrice, 131
Lusaka Non-aligned Conference, 575, 580

MacMillan, Harold, 11, 25, 95

Mahathir bin Mohamad, Dr, 266
Mahmud bin Awang, Inche, 139
Malay, definition of, 74
Malay Kinship and Marriage in Singapore, 74
Malay language, 8, 55
Malay Mail, 277
Malaya: A Political and Economic Appraisal, 67
Malaya Merdeka, 242, 283
Malayan Chinese Association, 14, 50, 83, 199, 202, 232, 236
Malayan Communist Party, 18, 22, 27, 67, 69, 105, 124, 126, 129, 140, 154, 158, 177, 179, 207, 392, 606
Malayan Forum, 28
Malayan Indian Congress, 20
Malayan Times, 275
Malays: basic character of, 89; growing chauvinism of, 208; economic backwardness of, 81, 87; in Singapore, 165
Malaysia: and Australia, 254; Lee's visit to Afro-Asian nations, 157, 169, 173, 174, 197, 251; Lee's warning of Malay chauvinism, 208; Lee weeps for Chinese left behind in, 608; M. elections (1964), 199; intemperate speeches at election (1969), 508; formation of, 8, 9; Lee worried about future of, 225; Malaysian M., 89; "to whom does it belong?", 229; Lee's insistence on multiracial M., 10; Was multiracial M. ever really possible?, 83; Lee's first speech in M. Parliament 191, 204; PAP's participation in M.'s general election (1964), 198; referendum, 153, 161; riots (1969), 509; Tunku blames Lee Kuan Yew for separation, 85; future relations with Singapore, 517; Singapore separated, 230, 295; bad start of, 20; Tunku's historic speech, 137
Malaysian Journal of Education, 600
Malaysian Solidarity Convention, 84, 267
Malays, The, 68
Malik, Adam, 407
Man in Malaya, 68
Mao Tsetung, 60, 71, 151, 217, 411, 498, 618
Maphilindo, 197
Mare, Sir Arthur de la, 568
Marlborough House, 486
Marshall, David: 15, 16, 133, 135, 139, 151, 159, 178; as first Chief Minister of Singapore, 10
McColl, Rene, 288
Mehnert, Dr Klaus, 612
Melan bin Abdullah, Inche, 244, 386
Menzies, Sir Robert, 10
Migrant people in Southeast Asia, 345
Mills, Lennox A., 67, 76
Mission schools, 458
Morse, Robert, 46
Multilingualism, 123

Muslim religion, 73

Nair, C.V.Devan, 97, 125
Nanyang University, 110, 117, 208, 304, 306, 542
Nasser, Abdul Gamal, 18, 162
National Press Club (Australia), 253
Nehru, 18, 60, 184, 205, 245, 317, 336
Ne Win, 18
New Scientist, 546
New Times, 163
New York Herald Tribune, 42
New York Times, 509
Nguyen Cao Ky, 509
Nichol, Sir John, 11
Nixon, President Richard, 11, 508
Non-political leadership, 560
Nyerere, President Julius, 576

Observer, The, 243, 288, 336, 602
Ong Chang Sam, 272
Ong Eng Guan, 15, 16, 26, 117, 124, 132, 137, 271, 272, 613
Onn bin Jaafar, Dato (later Sir), 79
Opposition (Parliamentary) in Asia, 133
Overseas Writers (USA), 399

Pacific Affairs, 617
Pacific basin, 406
Pan-Malayan Islamic Party, 202
Parliamentary democracy, Singapore and Malaysia, 65, 69
Party Raayat (Brunei), 163
Pearson, Lester, 336
Peart, Fred, MP, 480
Peking and Moscow, 612
People's Action Party: 3, 6, 11, 21, 25, 51, 55, 67, 68, 75, 79, 83, 97, 109, 115, 120, 124, 126, 137, 158, 167, 171, 175, 194, 201, 213, 232, 267, 269, 271, 295, 566; tenth anniversary, 48, 321; and by-elections (1961), 129, 134, 139; and Hong Lim by-election (1965), 272; and plans for government in exile in Cambodia, 288; breaks with communists, 118; wins election (1959), 95; and general elections (1963), 181; and Malaysian elections (1964), 198; finances, 19; formation, 8, 13; Ong Eng Guan expelled, 117, 132
People's Progressive Party, 66
Peterson, Neville, 287
Petir, 87, 280
Philippines, 184
Political prisoners, 38
Port of Singapore Authority, 567
Powell, Enoch, 561

Prince of Wales, 54
Prophet Mohamad's birthday, 107, 210, 278
Punjabi-speaking people, 310
Purcell, Dr Victor, 602, 603, 608, 611, 614

Quakers' Conference, 219
Quest, 50, 83

Raffles College (Institution), 5, 27, 40, 101
Raffles, Sir Stamford, 6, 39, 494
Rajah, A.P., 338
Rajaratnam, S., 78, 280, 284, 309, 408
Razak, Tun Abdul, 28, 75, 79, 89, 96, 102, 175, 198, 231, 269, 273, 277, 322
Reporter, The, 401
Reuters, 584
Revolution in Southeast Asia, 57
Rhodesian problem, 489
Riots, in Singapore, 210, 238
Rotary, 308
Royal Commonwealth Society, 482
Russell, Bertrand, 395
Rutherford, Ernest (later Lord), 323

Sabah, 8, 9
Sadat, Vice-President (later President), 584
Sambantham, Dato (later Tun), 269
Sandys, Duncan, 25
Sarawak, 8
Sato, E., 340, 386, 467
Selkirk, Earl of, 139
Senu, Inche, 277, 281
Sheares, Dr B.H., 8
Sheng Nam Chin, Dr, 146
Shih Chen Pau, 297
Short History of The Nanyang Chinese, A, 617
Sihanouk, Prince Norodom, 18, 162, 288, 313, 410
Sikhs, 344
Simons, Lewis, 478
Singapore: academic freedom, 127; Princess Alexandra represents Queen Elizabeth at 150th anniversary banquet, 529; Alliance, 159; Anson by-election, 139, 146; new assembly (1963), 186; brain-power potential, 534; relations with Britain, 569; per capita income (1966), 324; the real challenge, 330; chaos or progress?, 526; first Chief Minister, 7; first Chinese banker, 73; Chinese chauvinism, 106; Chinese Union of Journalists, 103; Civil Service Study Centre, 99; "clean and green", 533; damage by firecrackers (1970), 559; "defence indivisible be-

628

tween Malaysia and S.", 523; demonstrations, Ngee Ann College and Nanyang University, 349; Economic Development Board, 93; emergency regulations, 108; Employers Association, 372; family planning, 546; S. flag, 94; the future of, 426; general elections (1963), 181; general elections (1968), 416, 424; Sir William Goode, first Yang di-Pertuan Negara, 95; early history, 6, 72; relation with Hong Kong, 551, 555; Hong Lim by-election (1965), 272, 277; Hong Lim Community Centre, 562; S.'s debt to India, 290; India, S.'s special friend, 336; Industrial Arbitration Court established, 116; Inter-Religious Council, 289; visit of Crown Prince and Princess of Japan, 558; Japanese Occupation, 7, 27; state visit of Japanese Prime Minister, 387; Japanese surrender, 41; Jurong, 324; Jurong Shipyard, 359; abolition of jury system, 518; Labour Party, 66; labour problems, 352; Loyalty Week (1959), 114; Malays, 74, 405; Malays' inherent fears, 77; meeting of Malays (1964), 208; merger with Malaya, 104; becomes part of Malaysia, 9; relations with Malaysia, 517; separation from Malaysia, 8, 230; S.'s eviction from Malaysia, 295; Nanyang University, 110; National anthem, 94; National Day (1966), 332; National Productivity Centre, 373; first National Service officers, 357; National Theatre Fund, 94; National TUC, 51, 94, 147, 227; National TUC Jurong strike, 572; Lee at National TUC Seminar (1969), 540; National Union of Journalists, 173; declared a "sovereign democratic and independent nation", 231; and the Naval Base, 325; neutrality, 6; Sir John Nichol opens first Legislative Assembly, 11; 150th anniversary celebrations, 480, 495; parliamentary government, 8; Parliament House, 39; People's Defence Corps, 332; Pho Kark See Temple, 62; Political Study Centre, 325; Port Authority Union, 427; first president, 112; race riots, 90; Radio S., 114; referendum (1962), 153; freedom of religions, 63; riots, 210, 213, 303; Rotary Club, 120; Lee at Science Council (1969), 537; election of President Sheares, 8; shipbuilding and repairing, 551; S.Advocates and Solicitors Society (1970), 560; S. Armed Forces Training Institute, 375; S. Association of Trade Unions, 147; "S. is an oasis", 365; S. Stock Exchange Committee, 561; Sikhs, 64; St Andrew's School, 457;

cleansing staff strike, 356; "mild troubles" in 1969, 528, Union of Journalists, 100;
Singh, Sardar Swaren, 334
Smith, Arnold, 596
Smuts Memorial Lecture, 497
Snow, Peter, 586
Socialism in Singapore, 48
Socialist Conference (Bombay), 53
Socialist Front, 200, 202
Socialist International, 213, 313, 395
Sopiee, Inche Mohamed, 275
Southeast Asian nations, economic development, 419
Soviet Union, 309, 317, 525, 584
St Joseph's Institution, 118th anniversary of, 563
Straits of Malacca, "international waterway", 525, 586
Straits Times, The, 13, 127, 137, 162, 212, 270, 275, 277, 279
Subandrio, Dr, 96, 197, 291
Sukarno, President, 18, 26, 45, 247, 392
Sun, The (Australia), 521
Sydney Morning Herald, 258
Syed Sheikh Al-Hadi, 81
Syed Zahari, 163
Sweden, 315
Swedish Social Democratic Party, 319
Switzerland, 32, 386

Tamil Malar, 78
Tamil Muslim Union, 331
Tan Cheng Lock, Sir, 14
Tan Lark Sye, 110
Tan Siew Sin (later Tan Sri), 50, 177, 272, 288, 616
Telok Kurau School, 40
Thailand, 314
Thatcher, W.S., 42
Third China, The, 609, 616
Time Magazine, 15, 46
Times, The (London), 273, 287, 507
Tito, Marshal, 18, 156, 216
Toh Chin Chye, Dr: 28, 139, 142, 198, 267, 274, 275; letter from the Tunku, 286
Trudeau Pierre, 465, 470, 489
Tunku Abdul Rahman: 8, 20, 23, 27, 28, 42, 43, 68, 69, 77, 78, 83, 85, 87, 89, 102, 108, 137, 162, 163, 169, 175, 199, 202, 211, 212, 220, 231, 233, 239, 271, 273, 278, 282, 285, 304, 313, 339, 361, 508, 603, 609, 617; and formation of PAP, 13; and decision to separate Singapore from Malaysia, 279, 282

United Kingdom Manufacturers Association, 361
United Malays National Organization: 20,

27, 49, 67, 77, 79, 82, 83, 89, 108, 112, 133, 194, 199, 201, 208, 231, 238, 278, 280, 386, 609; support for PAP, 14; blamed by Lee, 237
United National Front, 16
United Nations: 159; Singapore, 116th member of, 8
United Peoples' Party, 26, 271
United States, 402, 407
University of British Columbia, 464
University of Hawaii, 587
University of Malaya Society, 97
University of Singapore Democratic Socialist Club, 459
Upsala University, 314
U Thant, 507
Utusan Melayu: 81, 82, 112, 210, 232, 240, 244, 258, 264, 271, 272, 276, 283, 286, 289; apologises to Lee, 386
Utusan Zaman, 268

Van, Molyvann, 411
Vasil, Dr R.K., 50, 83
Victoria University (Wellington), 248
Vietnam, 246, 248, 263, 306, 313, 316,

405, 478, 510, 550

Wallace, A.R., 88
Wang Gungwu, Professor, 617
Warsaw Pact, 309
Washington Post, 50, 510
Wee Chong Jin, 386
Whitehead, A.N., 558
Wilson, Harold, 10, 337, 340, 414, 418
Winstedt, Sir Richard, 67, 76
Wok, Inche Othman, 75
Wong Ah Fook, 73
Wong Pow Nee, 232
Woodhull, S., 125, 141, 144, 169
Workers' Party, 16
Wright, Richard, 595

Young, Gavin, 288
Young Mens' Christian Association, 59
Yusof bin Ishak, Inche, 112, 413, 436, 548, 590

Zuber Said, 94